Family and Succession Law in Nigeria

Family and Succession Law in Nigeria

Nwudego Nkemakonam Chinwuba

This book was originally published as a monograph in the International Encyclopaedia of Laws/Family and Succession Law.

Founding Editor: Roger Blanpain
General Editor: Frank Hendrickx
Volume Editor: Walter Pintens

Wolters Kluwer

Published by:
Kluwer Law International B.V.
PO Box 316
2400 AH Alphen aan den Rijn
The Netherlands
E-mail: international-sales@wolterskluwer.com
Website: lrus.wolterskluwer.com

Sold and distributed by:
Wolters Kluwer Legal & Regulatory U.S.
7201 McKinney Circle
Frederick, MD 21704
United States of America
E-mail: customer.service@wolterskluwer.com

ISBN 978-94-035-3960-7

e-Book: ISBN 978-94-035-3961-4
web-PDF: ISBN 978-94-035-3962-1

For my Mother
Unoma Diana Catherine CHINWUBA

The Author

Nwudego Nkemakonam Chinwuba is a Professor of Comparative Law in Family, Succession and Trusts. She has keen interest in Jurisprudence as Philosophy and legal Theory and has a Doctoral degree in Property Law. Family and Succession Law has been engaging and the author has combined a knowledge of all the subject areas of interest to her with the aim of providing comprehensive understanding of the subject while paying attention to achieving optimal readability.

Nwudego has enjoyed teaching the subject areas at both graduate and undergraduate level at the University of Lagos for over two decades. She also engages in the practice of the law in the area through offering of consultation service. She is a member of the Nigerian Bar Association, Nigerian Association of Law Teachers and a Solicitor and Advocate of the Supreme Court of Nigeria. She was an Executive of the Board of the Socio-Legal Scholars Association, United Kingdom and a Visiting Scholar to School of Law, University of Reading Berkshire, England between 2015 and 2016.

The Author

Table of Contents

Table of Contents

List of Abbreviations

AEA	Administration of Estate Act, 1992
AGJA	Acting Justice of Appeal of Western State (of Nigeria) Court of Appeal
ALL ER	All England Law Reports
All FWLR	All Federation Weekly Law Reports.
B, D, M, Etc. Act	Birth, Death & Marriage etc. (Compulsory Registration) Act, Cap B.9
CAP	Chapter in a Series of Laws of a Nation or State.
CLR	Commonwealth Law Reports (High Court of Australia Cases)
CRA	Child's Rights Act, 2003
CWLR	Commonwealth Law Reports
DLR	Dominion Law Reports
E.N.L.R	Eastern Nigeria Law Reports
ECSLR	Law Reports of East Central State
ER	English Reports
EWCA	England and Wales Court of Appeal
EWCH	England and Wales High Court
EWFC	England and Wales Family Court
FCT	Federal Capital Territory
FLR	Family Law Reports
FNLR	Federation of Nigeria Law Reports
FNR	Federation of Nigeria Reports
FSC	Selected Judgment of the Federal Supreme Court
JCA	Justice of the Court of Appeal
JSC	Justice of the Supreme Court
KB	Kings Bench
LFN	Laws of the Federation, 2004.
LPELR	Law Pavilion Electronic Law Reports
LSAEL	Lagos State Administration of Estate Law

List of Abbreviations

LUA	Land Use Act
MA	Marriage Act, Cap M6 (Laws of the Federation, 2004)
MCA	Matrimonial Causes Act, Cap M7 (Laws of the Federation, 2004)
MCR	Matrimonial Causes Rules Cap M7 (Laws of the Federation, 2004)
NA	No Action
NMLR	Nigerian Monthly Reports
NRNLR	Northern Region of Nigeria Law Reports
NSCQR	Nigerian Supreme Court Quarterly Reports
NWLR	Nigeria Weekly Law Reports
OJLS	Oxford Journal of Legal Studies
PLR	Pavilion Law Reports
Pt	Part
Q.L.R.N	Quarterly Law Report of Nigeria
QB	Queens Bench
SAN	Senior Advocate of Nigeria
SC	Supreme Court Cases
SCNLR	Supreme Court of Nigeria Law Reports
SCR	Canada Supreme Court Reports
TLR	Times Law Reports
UGSC	Ugandan Supreme Court
UILR	University of Ife Law Reports
UKHL	United Kingdom House of Lords
UKPC	The Privy Council of the United Kingdom
UKSC	United Kingdom Supreme Court
UKUT	United Kingdom Upper Tribunal
WACA	West African Court of Appeal
WLR	Weekly Law Report
WRN	Weekly Reports of Nigeria

Preface

Family and succession law in Nigeria is inspired by the country, Nigeria – a country that re-invents herself with geographically wide, good, and predictable climatic conditions, and well-endowed biotic and abiotic natural resources. She is a Federation of thirty-six States with a Federal Capital that is vested with the power of the States. The work provides a complete and updated account of the law, practice and socio-legal context of family and succession in Nigeria.

Family and succession law is pivotal in understanding a people and provides the most important lenses from which drivers of developmental changes can emerge.

A lawyer's question on family is always traced to orderliness in formation, record, and if need be, dissolution of marriage. At play in all family relations and the role of the State is the balance between State intervention and the prized contemporary values of liberty, individual autonomy, and limits of State intervention. The lawyer's question is a core function of statehood, critical and multidimensional – an accurate answer which provides a multidimensional solution to many issues of society. Is a society economically underdeveloped, disorderly, and only minimally productive? Efforts at a solution if addressed at a macro level may be unlikely to yield any fundamental shift, but if addressed from the base, the system of family and how it promotes individual optimism, then such efforts are an assured key to, at the minimum, a satisfying and flourishing society.

Sustainable development is a viable reason to re-order family life and succession to enhance synergy in these vital areas of human experiences and interaction. The twin subject areas of family and succession impact citizens in various ways: those who live within the shores of the country and others living abroad. The law impacts foreigners in the same way, those who interact with Nigerians locally and globally as well as Nigerian citizens who may have acquired new citizenship. Nigeria is a conservative society, and this is expressed principally in complex plurality of laws. The basis for the plurality of laws can be condensed into a struggle for identity which finds vent in the pull of rigid customs, modern law, religion, and tribal allegiances in different directions.

There is continuing frustration from the entanglement of Nigerian customary laws with modern law and, specifically, legislative interventions in personal laws. Customs usually become rigid and Nigeria as an example shows that this becomes more so with any extrinsic interruption and influences. This situation affects legal framework and structure particularly in questions regarding formation, dissolution, and annulment of marriages. The judiciary is not removed from the tension in the portfolio and plurality of laws. Thus, the relationship between the State legislative competence, its High Courts, Family and Probate Divisions, the Federal Legislative competence and the Federal High Courts remain murky, not to mention the Area and Customary courts or the Sharia Courts and the appellate system.

Nigeria is committed to an institutionalised register of vital civil status data. This is interwoven with the nation's interest in children, their right to life and survival. With respect to vital documentation on marriages and their dissolution, there is a continuing concern over who the Registrar is. Given that global mobility places Nigerians in many parts of the world and other nationals are also placed in Nigeria with attendant juridical questions on marital status, the answer to who the Registrar of marriages in Nigeria is an important one. So, also that of births and deaths.

In the area of succession, Nigerian jurisprudence is wholly inward bound aside from the implications of the Marriage Act, the norms of which originate in English customs and rules on the same subject. The place of gender relations cannot be overlooked in any question concerning the operation of family and succession law in Nigeria. As modernity and colonial structures introduced monogamy in Nigeria, it was welcomed by the elites and embraced as a social norm. The monogamous marriage regulated by the Marriage Act, however, excludes its succession model. Understanding succession in Nigeria is subject to three themes: the limitation on all forms of succession, by the preservation of customary inheritance patterns to the extent that they preserve primogeniture. Running parallel to customary limitation is Islamic law which is the principal religion for some states of the Federation. The third framework is testate or intestate succession in line with either a State law or the English Wills Act, 1837 and the amendment to it or the respective Administration of Estates Laws of the States.

The work adopts a comparative approach because the country's jurisprudence is integrated into and closely intertwined with Commonwealth jurisprudence. However, key differences between Nigerian, English, and other Commonwealth jurisdictions remain. In addition, case law involving citizens of the two countries or arising in the respective jurisdictions abound. This special developmental relationship between the two countries and conflict of law issues that have arisen because of migration, international marriages and inter-jurisdictional adjudications are ongoing: *Graham Wylie v. Hajara Wylie*; *GE v. KE & Anor*; *N v. D (Customary Marriage)*; *Mark v. Mark*; *Ohocuku v. Ohochuku; Anyaegbunam v. Anyaegbunam and James Egubson & Ors* v. *v. Joseph Ikechukwu; Kareem v. Secretary of State for Home Department; Agbaje v. Agbaje; Salubi v. Salubi* etc. The cases illuminate the understanding of family and succession law in Nigeria. *Graham Wylie v. Hajara Wylie* concerned a foreigner from the United Kingdom married to a Nigerian but whose petition for dissolution of the marriage was stuck out on domicile. *GE v. KE & Anor* involved persons living in the United Kingdom and centred on the determination of the content and implications of the customary law marriage of the people of South-Eastern Nigeria. *N v. D (Customary Marriage)* concerned declaration of marital status of a party alleging that a customary marriage had taken place. *Ohochukwu v. Ohocukwu* concerned the status of juxtaposed marriage rites and issues of conflict of laws regarding dissolution. *Agbaje v. Agbaje* concerned the extent to which a United Kingdom Court could intervene in the application for ancillary relief where a dissolution has taken place in another jurisdiction. *Mark v. Mark* is an influential case decided by the United Kingdom Supreme Court on a Nigerian marriage. *Anyaegbunam v. Anyaegbunam and James Egubson & Ors.* v. *Joseph Ikechukwu* are a typical feature of Nigerian marriages and the courts have taken the consistent position that a marriage in a church does not raise a presumption that marriage has taken place, let alone that it is monogamous.

Critical issues continue to emerge. Nigeria is a pro-life nation, with a Constitution guaranteeing life from foetal existence, but with attention to continuing challenge of the content and quality of life so guaranteed. The global distress occasioned by COVID-19 pandemic reinforces the expediency for global human co-operation. Family and succession law plays an important role in such co-operation.

I am grateful to the IEL – International Encyclopaedia of Laws team, and in particular, Professor Walter Pintens, Ms. Margot Leyson, for their encouragement and support, Ms. Kavya Shekar and the Production team for their professionalism and co-operation. I am grateful to my 'cheer-farers' daughter- Somtochukwu, son- Temitope, and grandson, Temilade Ebelechukwu; to my friends for their encouragement, Professor Chioma Agomo, Emeritus Professor Akintunde Obilade and Mr Adedoyin Olowe.

Deus Gratias.

Nwudego Nkemakonam Chinwuba
LL.B., LL.M., PhD, BL,
Solicitor & Advocate of the Supreme Court of Nigeria,
Professor of Comparative Law in Family, Succession & Trusts,
Faculty of Law,
University of Lagos, Lagos, Nigeria,
24 March 2020

General Introduction

1. Law is a developmental, experiential, and empirical subject optimised in the recognition that humankind is dynamic in form and space. Law and its usage are a continuing process of analysis, deductions, and application for the synergy of society. It springs from, is formulated, and applied in the light of, the experiences and changing circumstances of humankind with a view to achieving principled, uniform outcomes in any set of identifiable factual situations.

2. Family law fulfils the key attributes of law in this sense and therefore occupies a prime place in law subjects. The extent to which family law can provide harmonious strings for the private lives of citizens in a society impacts on each member and constituent families driving the synergy of the society in all spheres of engagement. The law on succession is imbued with similar attributes, raises similar concerns and aspires to similar objectives.

3. In Nigeria, the two subjects are knotted by religion, customs, colonial administration, and the tradition of stare decisis.

4. These knots were referred to by the Honourable Mr Justice Olabode Rhodes Vivour on 22 March 2021 on his valedictory as a justice of the Supreme Court of Nigeria.

5. The Supreme Court has held on several occasions that it is absolutely bound by the doctrine of Precedent or stare decisis. That in effect means: 'Stand by your decisions and the decisions of your predecessors, however wrong they are and whatever injustice they inflict.' There are some precedents that are clearly out of date and should no longer be followed. I am of the view that Precedents that no longer make sense anymore or are outdated should be laid to rest and never followed. On the need for reform of Limitation Laws I said that: 'There has been no reform of Limitation Laws in Nigeria. The general Limitation periods for some actions are too short. Judges should be conferred with discretion to extend Limitation periods when it is just and equitable to do so. Actions that readily come to mind are sexual abuse cases. The victims are usually too traumatized, under intolerable pressure, grief stricken and depressed for long periods. Consequently, when they eventually regain their composure, it is too late to file action in court, because of the short limitation periods provided by the law. This also applies to personal injury cases. Injuries that occur in a factory. The victim is usually a poor factory worker drawn into endless negotiation by a boss much aware of the Limitation period. Time to file action runs out, when the poor factory worker realizes he has been taken for a ride. He has a cause of action but sadly one that cannot be enforced. To my mind reforms are required with an urgency that makes delay an accessory.' We should reform our Limitation Laws as has been done in the United Kingdom (UK). 'INHERITANCE Numbers 27:7 reads: "The daughters of Zelophehad speak right. Thou shall surely give them a possession of an inheritance among their fathers brethren; and shalt cause the inheritance of their father to pass unto them." […]'

6. And Job 42:15 says that: 'And in all the land were no woman found so fair as the daughters of Job and their father gave them inheritance among their brethren.' The above informed my reasoning in *Ukeje v. Ukeje* (2014) 11NWLR (Pt.1418) p. 384. Where I held that a customary law which disentitles a female child from partaking in her deceased father's estate is in breach of section 42(1) and (2) of the Constitution, a fundamental rights provision guaranteed to every Nigerian. The said customary law is void as it conflicts with section 42(1) and (20) of the Constitution. Female children are entitled to an inheritance.

7. It is in this context that the law on family and succession in Nigeria is set down and analysed.

§1. Nigeria: Demographic Data

8. Nigeria is a country with an estimated population of over two hundred million people.[1] Nigeria, officially known as the Federal Republic of Nigeria is in West Africa – borders Niger Republic in the north, Chad in the northeast, Cameroon in the east, and Benin in the west. Nigeria is also estimated to be the most populous country in Africa with the most indigenous African race in the world. Nigeria belongs to the African Union and is a member of the Economic Community of West African States.[2] Nigeria is well endowed with biotic and abiotic natural resources. She is the eleventh member of the Organisation of Petroleum Exporting Countries (OPEC) and ranks eleventh in oil reserves in the world.[3] Aside from petroleum, Nigeria's other natural resources, include gold, natural gas, tin, iron ore, coal, limestone, niobium, lead, zinc, and arable land.

---

1. According to United Nations Data, estimated as 206,139,589 people at mid-year 2019, she ranks seventh, in the list of countries by population. Available at https://www.worldometers.info last accessed 16 Jan. 2020. Prior to the enactment of the Births, Deaths etc. (Compulsory Registration) Act, 1992 registration of birth in Nigeria was not compulsory, making accurate population data difficult.
2. The Community aims at ultimately becoming the sole Economic Community in the region for the purpose of economic integration and the realisation of the objectives of the African Economic Community by promoting co-operation and integration, for the establishment of an economic union in West Africa.
3. Nigeria Oil Reserves, Production and Consumption Statistics … available at: www.worldometers.info/oil/nigeria-oil (last accessed 17 Aug. 2020); Oil reserves in Nigeria – Wikipedia available at: en.wikipedia.org/wiki/Oil_reserves_in_Nigeria (last accessed 17 Aug. 2020); List of countries by proven oil reserves – available at: Wikipedia en.wikipedia.org/wiki/ (last accessed 17 Aug. 2020).

9. Nigeria is a member of the Commonwealth of Nations having gained her independence on 1 October 1960. James Wilson Robertson[4] was her last British Governor General[5] while Nnamdi Azikiwe was the first Nigerian Governor General.[6] The Nigerian currency is Naira.

10. The climate in Nigeria is tropical with remarkably splendid climatic conditions. Temperature is moderate. In the South, the weather and temperature are predictable. When it is sunny, and this is often, the sun beams with rays so beautifully and yet not scorching. It never beams so hot in the Southern parts and Middle Belts, at a maximum of 33°C. At other times, the sun's beams become just refreshingly soothing at less than 25°C because of the advent of the African monsoon – purifying cooling rains; nevertheless, the weather, remains very predictable. The sun rises beautifully and constantly with its golden hour between 6.26 am to 7 am. The sun sets in the same way, constantly and beautifully, at a same estimable time all year round, between 6.30 pm and 7 pm. Temperature peaks at an average of 25–33°C in the dry seasons but remains airy, with cooling breeze and stable atmospheric conditions. In the rainy season, the weather nestles somewhere between 20 and25°C, and in some places, lower. Overall, the rains pour in the rainy season, remaining cool and gentle while washing off some earth sands, a washing off, which proper care can avoid, properly laid drainages for instance, could be advantageous. This washing off is sometimes referred to as erosion. Nigeria has an abundance of sites of natural beauty.[7] Humidity is sometimes above 50% depending on the part of Nigeria. It is a large country.

11. The Middle Belt and South-Eastern states have some rocky, cold, and mountainous demography with greenery and vegetation in most areas making these parts of Nigeria a haven of atmospheric conditions, a delight for citizens, settlers, and tourists. Amazingly if one throws seeds in the gardens without efforts at digging, they sprout into full blossom. This is the intensity of fertile lands, at least, in the Southern and Middle Belt parts of Nigeria.

---

4. KT GCMG GCVO KBE KStJ.
5. Serving in Nigeria from 15 Jun. 1955 to 16 Nov. 1960. He served in a representative capacity for Queen Elizabeth as Head of State from 1 Oct. 1960 to 16 Nov. 1960. The Governor General wrote his memoirs on his nearly forty years in Africa. In the final chapter titled Reflections, he accounts the swift collapse and disintegration of his enterprise and that of his fellow British servants of the Empire, to construct viable States not only in the Sudan and Nigeria, but in all of Britain's former colonial African territories. Commenting on foreign concern about post-independence difficulties, he observed: 'Americans have asked me: "Why did you leave so soon, before the colonial territories were ready to rule themselves?"' And when I have answered, '"Partly, I am sure, because of your pressure on us to go," [they] have answered that they did not know then what they know now, and that we should have resisted their pressure'. J.W. Robertson, *Transition in Africa: From Direct Rule to Independence* 253 (Hurst 1974). Taken from https://en.wikipedia.org/wiki/James_Wilson_Robertson (last accessed 16 Sep. 2020).
6. Rt. Honourable Dr Nnamdi Benjamin Azikiwe considered Father of Nigerian Nationalism. The position was abolished after him.
7. Nduka Orjinmo & Fatima Muhammad, *Mpape Crushed Rock: Nigerians Flock to New Abuja beauty spot*, available at https://www.bbc.com/news/world-africa-53806880 (last retrieved 1 Sep. 2020).

12. The core Northern parts of Nigeria are dry in the day, sometimes very windy at nights and at other times, cold. The dry season in Nigeria is usually between November and March. The rainy seasons nestles between April to August and thereafter, windy until the harmattan advent seasons for Nigeria. December to January in most of the South are a pleasant time, teeming with cold harmattan winds and atmosphere of the advent of festivities.

13. Nigeria has considerable stability in politics and political structure. Equitable and effective governance is a different subject. There are also concerns of terrorism and sporadic attacks from herdsmen which mars free interstate travels now. Attack by herdsmen sometimes crosses over to highways in the South. The nature of crimes in the southern parts centres on the economic and/or primordial customary ritual order. Economic crimes are usually avoided by staying alert to any kind of fantabulous tales of fantabulous wealth. The majority of Nigerians are 'go-happy fellows' avoiding crimes – a positive aspect of patriarchy. Nigeria remains a viable country for tourism, get-up of business, going concerns and service ideas because of the make-up of her vast potentials in geographical spread, atmospheric conditions, and population. A considerable portion of the population has immense purchasing power for products and services.

14. A citizen of Nigeria is a person who is so by birth, registration, or naturalisation and by all other indices of section 28 of the Constitution of the Federal Republic of Nigeria.[8] At least six dominant tribes predated the amalgamation of the North and South of Nigeria. These are the tribes among other several minor groupings that form the independent State, known today as the Federal Republic of Nigeria. The major tribes are the Hausa, Benue and Tiv peoples, Fulani, Yoruba, and the Igbo. It is important to understand the diverse nature and culture of the people of Nigeria as these have permeated every aspect of modern Nigeria. The Yoruba are a homogenous tribe whose root is popularly traceable to Mecca and Medina in the Middle East. The documented history is traceable to the Oyo Empire with its capital in Ile-Ife. Ile-Ife is said to have flourished between the eleventh to fifteenth centuries and remains the principal religious centre of the Yoruba. The Hausas appear to be indigenous to the Northern Hemisphere but were conquered by the expedition and *jihad* of Uthman Dan Fodio, a Fulani. The Fulani are said to be companions and descendants of Uthman Dan Fodio. The Fulani are nomads and thrive in cattle rearing. They are also said to have migrated from Arabia. The Benue-Tivs are settled in the Middle Belt area of Nigeria which is also described politically as in the North of Nigeria. The Igbo have always been around the River Niger to the East of Nigeria. They are known to be republicans embracing governance by families and clans rather than broader centralised government. The Igbo people are best known for their segmentary lineage or cephalous way of life. Consequently, they operated and still do in substance, a kind of government without kings. The Igbo parlance, 'Igbo enwe eze' is a truism. Igbos share a common political system based on decentralisation of power and delegation of authority exercised by the holders of the staff of

8. Cap C23, Laws of the Federation, 2004. *See also* ss. 29 and 309 of the Constitution. *See* however, Special Immigrant Status Regulation, 2008 S. 1. 18 Of 2008.

authority, known as the *Ofo*. This distinctive political system makes them different from other parts of Nigeria who operate either religious or monarchical governments. This structure was reinforced and concretised by encounter with Christianity and colonialism. This outcome is so, because Christianity rather than upturn customs and cultures, aimed at assimilating them into the religion. The result of this is that the customs and traditions of the Igbos despite their near-total embrace of Christianity have remained and are now rigidified. Igbos are usually merchants known for commerce and entrepreneurship. The civil war in Nigeria between them and other indigenous nationalities in Nigeria also appears to have reinforced this lifestyle and style of governance to an insistence on self-governance as an indigenous people. Although this agitation may have been valid in the 1960s, it is doubtful whether this remains so, in contemporary times in the light of internal mobility and integration within and outside Nigeria. It may be that embrace of education, a more versatile means of livelihood, and balance between individualism and society may well be more progressive. This is more so since individualism as a core normative lifestyle for a society has failed consistently as a governance model creating some affluent individuals and larger aggrieved classes – typically a Hobbesian 'state of nature' – based on principles of self-preservation.

15. The Yoruba are more homogenous, maintain much of their customs and traditional religion. In this region, however it appears there is equal participation by the Yoruba in Islam and Christianity with the traditional religion always having an assured back seat almost. It is not unusual to see at intersections in major South West roads, acalabash of sacrifices for the consumption of diverse spirits and gods. The most known high priestess in Nigeria worshipped Orisha[9] and reclaimed the Osun grove making it a national monument and a world heritage site. An Austrian and Caucasian, Susanne Wenger, was the High priestess of Orisha until her death at 93, in Oshogbo, Osun State, Nigeria.[10]

16. In the North, Islam became the dominant religion with a few states as exceptions such as Kaduna State. Islam overshadowed the customs and cultural inclination of the indigenous people. Custom and culture in this part may be said to be the Islamic way of life. The Middle Belt appears to be predominantly Christian and as with the regions already noted, customs and culture remain alongside Christianity.

17. One thing appears to be common to the areas dominated by Christianity – retention of traditional customs and culture while the core north can now be said to be bound by the rules and practices of Islam. In Southern Nigeria, the customs of the people prevail invariably in all civil interactions and co-existence – from marriage to inheritance and devolution of property unless where such customs conflict with specific provisions of the Constitution.

9. Orisha denotes the many gods and goddesses of the Yoruba who may also be referred to as powerful but, mortal spirits.
10. Susanne Wenger: en.wikipedia.org/wiki/Susanne_Wenger; https://susannewengerfoundation.at/en/adunni-olorisha-last-interview; www.susannewenger-aot.org/susanne-house.

§2. Historical Background of Family and Succession Law

18. The word 'family' has gone through varying changes in content but perhaps not in meaning. In a more recent 'traditional' understanding in Western societies, it connotes a unit of human beings consisting of two parents: a husband, wife and their children living together as a unit. At some point this meant the basic unit in society traditionally consisting of two parents who are a man and woman reproducing and rearing their children. In many African societies, this last meaning remains the sense in which family is understood, except that the unit may also be formed with wives and concubines.[11] The people of the South East would customarily enquire of a patriarch about his 'home' which translates to wives, children, and concubines.[12] Not surprisingly, *James Egubson v. Ikechukwu*[13] is a Nigerian case where the constitution of a church provided for concubinage.

19. The earliest uses of *family* denoted 'a group of persons in the service of an individual', a sense that is now archaic.[14] Although this early meaning may seem far afield from the way *family* is used today, it is not surprising when it is considered that the word comes from the Latin *familia*, which meant 'household', a designation that included both servants and relatives.[15] Not surprisingly, the earliest families constituted some form of private government to which patriarchy, paternalism and patrilineal structures were well fitted extending to the Blackstonian unity of husband and wife. The unit implicated absolute powers in a hierarchical descending structure commencing from the father, mother, first son and others.[16] For instance, the Violence Against Persons (Prohibition) Act, 2015, a Federal Legislation, presumes women as minors, providing for the meaning of 'abandonment' by section 46. Abandonment of women and children and other persons under the Act, 'means, deliberately leaving women, children, and other persons under the perpetrator's care destitute and without any means of subsistence'. Other persons presumably refer to persons of inefficient mind.

20. While this form of family and marriage structure is still promoted as ideal in many African cultures, ethical and developmental concerns have begun to revise the option of marriage as intimate relationship between two parties with the focal point on the parties and children, as offspring of the intimacy.

---

11. E.N.U. Uzodike, *A Decade of the Matrimonial Causes Act, 1970*, 55 Nigerian Current L. Rev. 57 (1983).
12. *Kedu maka ezi na uno*?.
13. [1977] ALL NLR 194; [1976] 6 SC 1; [1977] LPELR-SC. 183/1975.
14. At https://www.merriam-webster.com/dictionary.
15. *Ibid.*
16. M.T. Reilly, *In Good Times and in Debt: The Evolution of Marital Agency and the Meaning of Marriage*, 87 Nebraska L. Rev. 373 (2008); Allison Anna Tait, *The Return of Coverture*, 114 Mich. L. Rev. 99 (2016); Hanoch Dagan, *Property's Structural Pluralism: On Autonomy, The Rule of Law, and the Role of Blackstonian Ownership*, 3 Brigham-Kanner Prop. RTS. Conf. J. (2014); *Tel Aviv University Law Faculty Papers.* Working Paper 181.

21. The idea of family as the main vehicle for sustaining humanity has continued to be of extreme importance to successive generations requiring a review of the term, its content, persuasions, and expressions. Not surprisingly, the formation of family primarily from marriage and its incidents create a status. This status whether it is drawn from the state, society or the individuals impacts the stability of society and therefore has always drawn the attention of the State. The prevailing type and nature of government do not affect this interest which law has in family. The impact of fundamental human rights majorly defined by dignity, liberty, privacy, and the rule of law on family is also underscored. It is therefore particularly important that the law regulating family is clear, certain, widely publicised, scrutinised from time to time, more so, when status affects property and the rights which relate to it. These rights do not only affect the parties to the marriage or family but may impact the third parties in diverse ways. Added to this is the increasing expansionist world view which promotes interactions between individuals of different countries, culture and religion who marry one another and found family. Nigeria recognises three types of marriages on which notions of family are based. These are: customary marriage,[17] Islamic marriage[18] and marriage under the Marriage Act.[19] Cohabitation is not recognised as a structure of family but creates a presumption of marriage and to the extent that children occupy a vital place in any of the structures, cohabitation cannot be dismissed.

22. The consequences of the different marriage structures have resulted in so much tension in the legal system with respect to family and succession. It is fashionable for persons who marry in Nigeria to juxtapose the statutory marriage on either the customary or Islamic variant with intricate and complex implications. Worthy of note is the interplay of gender power relations. A bride who wishes to have a statutory marriage seeks the security which a usual monogamous marriage offers, not just by excluding all others in sexual relations, but in property distribution in the event of intestacy or in fact, testacy. The bridegroom who concedes a statutory marriage has at the hierarchy of power relations, fathers who have gone before him. This power play resulted in the abrupt excision of a certain troublesome

17. This type of marriage is the indigenous form of marriage customary to all tribes in Nigeria.
18. This type of marriage is applicable to those who are faithful of the Islamic religion and who choose same as their personal law.
19. This is the marriage which is regulated under the Marriage Act in accordance with the provisions of the Constitution more fully described below. There are subsidiary rules and regulations under the Act, Marriage (Location of Marriages Offices) Directions L.N. 74 1971; Places for Celebration of Marriages (Delegation of Licensing Powers) Order L.N. 105 of 1967 pursuant to section 6 of the Act to be given effect by the Permanent Secretary Ministry of Internal Affairs (now Interior); Marriage Act (Delegation of Powers) Notice L.N. 44 Of 1973 pursuant to s. 3(1) of the Act interestingly provides for some functions for the State which the Federal Government now vehemently denies. 1. Delegation of powers to issue licenses under s. 13 of the Marriage Act (Cap M6.) The power conferred on the Minister to grant a license to marry by s. 13 of the Marriage Act is hereby delegated to and may be exercised by any of the following officers, that is to say: (a) the Permanent Secretary of the Federal Ministry of Internal Affairs; (b) the Permanent Secretary of any State Ministry which has been charged with the responsibility for marriage in the state concerned; or (L.N. 44 of 1973.); (c) any officer in any of the aforementioned ministries not below the rank of an Administrative Officer Class II, so however that nothing in this delegation shall prevent the exercise by the Minister himself of the power hereby delegated.

section of the Marriage Act, known as section 36 and the scuttling of the natural flow of the exercise of legislative competences of the Nation's Federal Legislature. This background is imperative to an understanding of all the principles and practice of law in relation to family and succession in modern Nigeria.

23. The importance of family and succession law in Nigeria is underscored by its place in all facets of the nation's policy outlook. A relevant directive principle of State policy is contained in section 15 of the Constitution which provides that:

(1) The motto of the Federal Republic of Nigeria shall be Unity and Faith, Peace and Progress.
(2) Accordingly, national integration shall be actively encouraged, while discrimination on the grounds of place of origin, sex, religion, status, ethnic or linguistic association or ties shall be prohibited.
(3) For the purpose of promoting national integration, it shall be the duty of the State to:
  (a) provide adequate facilities for and encourage free mobility of people, goods, and services throughout the Federation;
  (b) secure full residence rights for every citizen in all parts of the Federation;
  (c) encourage inter-marriage among persons from different places of origin, or of different religious, ethnic, or linguistic association or ties; and
  (d) promote or encourage the formation of associations that cut across ethnic, linguistic, religious and or other sectional barriers.
(4) The State shall foster a feeling of belonging and of involvement among various people of the Federation, to the end that loyalty to the nation shall override sectional loyalties.

24. Thus, the legal framework for family and succession law in Nigeria is underlined by pluralism and multiplicity of legal regimes which find vent in multiplicity of laws and processes depending on where one is in Nigeria. Other important factors are one's tribe, religion or customs and citizenship.[20] This in turn is expressed in the incidents, consequences of marriage and its dissolution. This complexity and intricacy extend to the composition and constitution of the family. Children and reproduction continue to form a key aspect of family law in Nigeria. As an example of the web-like nature of the subject and legal framework, the definition of who is a child is tasks even the mind of the most enlightened. Is the definition of a child to be taken from the Child's Rights Act,[21] where it is 18, the Marriage Act,[22] where it

---

20. A good general reading on this is I.O. Agbede *Legal Pluralism* (Shaneson C.I. Limited, Ibadan 1991). Some cases which have touched on the subject include *Ajibaye v. Ajibaye* [2007] All FWLR (part 359) 1321; *Olowu v. Olowu* [1985] LPELR 2604; [1985] 3 NWLR (part 13) 372; *Idehen v. Idehen* [1991] 6 NWLR (part 198) 382.
21. Number 6, 2003. Section 277 of the CRA defines a child as anyone under the age of 18. Section 21 also provides that no person under the age of eighteen can contract a valid marriage and any such purported marriage is null and void. This is in line with the Convention on the Rights of the Child which provides that a child for the purposes of the convention means any human being below the age of eighteen years.
22. Cap M6 Laws of the Federation, 2004. See for instance consent to marriage of minors, s. 21.

may be said to be 21, reinforced by Regulation 38(2)(b) of the Birth, Death etc. (Compulsory Registration) Act and Regulations, 1992,[23] the Matrimonial Causes Act,[24] where it may be anywhere between 16 to 21 years, the Matrimonial Causes Rules,[25] or the Constitution[26] which makes full age 'eighteen years' or any 'married woman'.[27] The extended family system reinforced by the absence of a viable social welfare system has had its own toll and works as an impediment on the best judicial and legislative efforts at providing order in the area of family life and succession.[28]

25. Family law and property rights are intertwined and correctly so. This is attributable to the nature of family and its incidents in law. In Nigeria, despite modernity and the embrace of some Western ideals, family property and primogeniture remain strong aspects of family law. Succession and intestate succession patterns as expressed in lineage are continuing intrinsic aspects of family law.[29] This work situates family and succession law in Nigeria in a contemporaneous and comparative setting. Thus, of high import are the norms regulating these subject areas in the indigenous setting prior to the colonisation of Nigeria by Great Britain and by the impact of global interaction, post-independence, and contemporary interactions which in themselves create a whole area of study. English law was introduced to many countries in Africa by a process of octroi and it remains influential in their affairs. As Pollock states many years before:

> Mention of our American learned friends and their ways of thinking reminds me that within the domains of the Common Law, and without any need of being handy with foreign tongues, there is a wide field for the expansion of our ideas and for the discipline of comparative study, a kind of study without which one may be a sound working lawyer for everyday work, but hardly an accomplished one. Too many of us, to their own loss and the disparagement of our lady the Common Law, pay no attention to the offshoots from her original stock that have been planted and taken root around the world.[30]

---

23. Cap B.9; S.1.6. Laws of the Federation 2004.
24. Cap M7, Laws of the Federation, 2004.
25. S.1.44 of 1983 made pursuant to ss 93 and 112 of the MCA, Cap M7, Laws of the Federation, 2004. Section 4 provides: 'infant' means a person who has not attained the age of 21 years; *see also* Order V, part, rule 5(1), etc. Order V, part 1, rule 5(1) a states that the rule applies to any child of the marriage living at the date of the petition who has not attained the age of 21 years. *See also* s. 72(3) on order for settlement of property not extending to children who have attained the age of 21.
26. Cap C23, Laws of the Federation of Nigeria, 2004.
27. Section 29(4) Constitution of the Federal Republic of Nigeria, Cap C23, Laws of the Federation of Nigeria, 2004.
28. Thus, both the Childs Rights Act and the Matrimonial Causes Act defines children of the marriage to include biological children or children who are so accepted by the parties to the marriage as their children. This is clearly distinct from adoption also recognised as children of the marriage. For Child's Rights Act *see* s. 277 and for the MCA, 2004 *see* s. 69.
29. Jelili Omotola, *Primogeniture and Illegitimacy in African Customary Law: The Battle for Survival of Culture*, 15(1) Ind. Int'l & Comp. L. Rev. 115 (2004); A.C. Diala, *Reform of the Customary Law of Inheritance in Nigeria: Lessons from South Africa*, African 14 Hum. Rts. L.J. 633–654 (2014).
30. Frederick Pollock, *The Lawyer as a Citizen of the World*, 37 L.Q. Rev. 41 (1932).

26. This set of circumstances implicate a subconscious societal resistance and tension which is mainly negative as it tends to have each legal framework static at a point and then pulling on the other for self-sustenance. This results in the impeding of the flourishing of the spirit of each legal framework which would otherwise have infused the legal regime with an intrinsic growth mechanism. Nevertheless, it must be borne in mind that Nigeria is a member of the Commonwealth of Nations and much of her contemporary laws are shaped by judicial nomenclature and their expressions in internal and external persuasions and dynamics. This is an overly complex and difficult legal environment to deal with, particularly when this is placed within the diversity of the country in language, culture, customs, and religion. The Marriage Act and Matrimonial Causes Act which are the principal statutory regulatory frameworks are drawn from a mixture of some originality and input from New Zealand, Australian and English framework on the subjects. The case law also draws from these jurisdictions. One common thread that continues to be a bond in Nigeria is that the English language is the uniform language of formal education throughout the country.

27. Another vital point to be borne in mind is that Nigeria was governed by the Military for decades in times past. Thus, sometimes the judgments of courts refer to legislative enactments in accordance with whether it came into force in a military or democratic era. Thus, with respect to the Federation, if the legislation came into force in the military era, it is a decree, rather than Act and with respect to a State of the Federation, it is an Edict in a military era and a law in a democratic dispensation.

28. It must be noted that the pronouncements of the judiciary in deploying a robust application of the non-discriminatory and deprivation provisions of the Constitution aims at reining in exclusions and aggrieved classes in the area of succession.[31] In the very recent case of *Delphine Zikere Okonkwo v. Amaka Ezeaku & Administrator-General/Public Trustee, Enugu State*, the Supreme Court reaffirmed this position although one would have thought that in subjecting an estate to equitable distribution among the children of an intestate, the Supreme Court would have followed its earlier decision in *Ukeje v. Ukeje*[32] rather than the principles of customary law. In *Delphine Zikere Okonkwo v. Amaka Ezeaku & Administrator-General/Public Trustee, Enugu State*,[33] the Supreme Court delivered a judgment regarding the estate of Late Mr John Chukwunweike Okonkwo (SAN).[34] The late Okonkwo was a lawyer with a distinguished career, resident in Enugu, South East

---

31. M. Htun & Weldon S., *State Power, Religion, and Women's Rights: A Comparative Analysis of Family Law*, 18(1) Ind. J. Global Legal Stud. 145 (2011); Emmanuel Durojaye, Woman, *But Not Human: Widowhood Practices and Human Rights Violations in Nigeria*, 27(2) Int'l J. L. Pol'y & the Fam. 176–196 (2013). Notable decisions in this area abound but two key ones by the Supreme Court are; *Ukeje v. Ukeje* [2014] 11 NWLR (part 1418) 384; 3 PLR/2014/150 SC; and *Salubi v. Nwariaku* [2003] 7 NWLR (part 819) 426. The non-discriminatory provision of the 1979 Constitution is contained in s. 39(2) and s. 42(2) 1999, Cap C23, Laws of the Federation, 2004.
32. [2014] 11 NWLR (Part. 1418) 384; [2014] LPELR – 22724 (SC) Electronic Law Reports.
33. [2020] 5 NWLR (Part 1718) 477–501.
34. An appellation of distinguished career in the legal profession in Nigeria.

of Nigeria. He had married a wife under the customs of the Igbos in 1976 with whom he had one daughter. He separated from her in 1988. Before contracting another marriage to another woman, Delphine, under the same native law and custom in 1992, he failed to divorce the first wife, formally. With Delphine, he had two children, a son and daughter. He did not marry any of the wives under the Act. He died intestate in 2005. Upon his death intestate, his estate was placed under the management of the Administrator General/Public Trustee. In a proceeding by the estranged wife to share in the estate of the intestate, the second wife disputed the claim. A certain affidavit deposed by the late Okonkwo acknowledged the second wife as his only legitimate wife. The Supreme Court considered that this was insufficient to disinherit the estranged wife as there was no formal return of the bride price or court dissolution of the earlier marriage and in the circumstances, nothing could expropriate the properties of the late Okonkwo to only the second wife and her children and the estranged wife was entitled to partake in the sharing of the estate of the intestate. In *Ukeje v. Ukeje*,[35] the patriarch, Lazarus Ogbonnaga Ukeje had died intestate in December 1961. He had real property in Lagos State although he was an Igbo from the South East of Nigeria. The appellants in the proceeding at the Supreme Court are his wife, Mrs. Lois Chituru Ukeje and son, Mr Enyinnaya Lazarus Ukeje, both of whom obtained Letters of Administration for and over the deceased's estate. The plaintiff, now respondent at the Supreme Court, is the daughter of the deceased. She had initiated the proceeding at the High Court for a declaration that she was the daughter of the deceased and therefore entitled to a share in the estate of her father. The trial judge found as a fact that the plaintiff, the daughter of the deceased, made the declaration as sought and that she was entitled to a share in the real property of the estate of the deceased. The judge had also declared the original Letters of Administration granted to the defendants to be null and void; ordered the defendants to prepare an inventory of the estate and/or render an account of all monies, transactions and/or properties which have come into their possession since the grant of the said Letters of Administration. The judge further granted an injunction restraining the defendants from further administering the estate of the deceased intestate and directed that the administration of the estate be turned over to the Administrator General until new Letters of Administration were issued. The defendants-appellants lodged an appeal, which the Court of Appeal Lagos (Division) dismissed as lacking in merit. At the Supreme Court, the appeal focused on the Igbo customary law which does not recognise inheritance by females. The court upheld the judgment of the trial court, holding that the Igbo customary law which does not recognise inheritance of a female from the estate of a father is void as conflicting with the fundamental right to freedom from discrimination set out in section 42(1)(a) and (2) of the 1999 Constitution. It held further that the circumstances of the birth of the child whether within or out of wedlock is irrelevant to the outcome.

35. [2014] 11 NWLR (Part 1418) 384; [2014] LPELR – 22724 (SC) Electronic Law Reports.

29. While English law and way of life may have impacted many, Nigerian indigenous societies have consciously resisted the dilution of patriarchy.[36] Thus, dispositions by wills, fecund disputes, and lengthy litigation, very few ventures into it.[37] In order to invalidate the Will of a deceased patriarch he would usually be alleged to have been unduly influenced or of unsound mind. As Adesanya notes, men of substantial estates now prefer to make gifts of their property in their lifetime to avoid this outcome.[38] The prudence and success of this approach is, of course, doubtful.

30. Continuing critical issues emerge as to what in fact should constitute a valid marriage within all the nagging concerns? What role should the State play in matrimonial disputes in terms of reconciliation, privacy, and individual autonomy? At play in all family relations and the State is the balance between State intervention and the prized contemporary values of liberty, individual autonomy and drawing the limits of State intervention.[39] Since the essential elements and incidents of marriage are, from a legalistic perspective, merely contractual should it not simply be a mere agreement between the parties to it? Other questions arise on ancillary matters to matrimony such as the best mechanism for property ownership in marriage and property rights, declarations, and adjustments on breakdown, as well as custody and the welfare of the child. Of immense importance are the impact of modernity and the attitude of Nigerian judiciary to children and children's welfare which has been astutely driven in the policy direction of the best interest of the child. Although there is no clear pattern to conclude that the strategy is removed from the customary brief of parental rights rather than responsibility.[40]

31. Some of the other issues are more broad-based and international in outlook. Under what circumstances should private international law and the conflicts arising therefrom be subsumed by an interest in the common good and humanity to accord recognition to marriages external to the jurisdiction? When, if at all, should one jurisdiction extend its concept and content of domicile to the status of marriage and breakdown of marital relationships conducted outside its jurisdiction? Within this

36. Ayodele Atsenuwa, *Constitutionalism and Legal Feminism: Stepping Stones or Impediments on the Long Road to Freedom for Nigerian Women?*, Maiden Professor Jadesola Akande Memorial Lectures 6–7 (Lagos, 2011 Nigerian Institute of Advanced Legal Studies)
37. Kole Abayomi, Wills: Law and Practice 9 (Mbeyi & Associates (Nig.) Ltd. 2004); B. Adesanya, *Marriage, Divorce and Succession: The Legal Aspects* (2009) a paper presented at a Seminar marking the 10th Anniversary of the Diocese of Lagos West (Anglican Communion) at the Archbishop Vinning Memorial Church Cathedral on the 12 Jun. 2009; O. Feyi-Sobanjo, *Overcoming Legal Challenges to Electronic Will Creation*, 1(8) ITECB 2 (2010).
38. Adesanya *ibid*, at 21, para. 9.07.
39. Some useful commentaries can be found in Carole Pateman, *The Shame of the Marriage Contract*, in *Women's Views of the Political World of Men* 67–97 (J.H. Stiehm ed., Transnational Publishers 1984); J.A. Rawls, *Theory of Justice* (Belknap Press 1971); J.A. Rawls, *Justice as Fairness*, in *A Restatement* (Erin Kelly ed., The Belknap Press of Harvard University Press 2001); Robert Nozick, *Anarchy, State and Utopia* (Blackwell Publishing 2006); Ronald Dworkin, *Sovereign Virtue – The Theory and Practice of Equality* (HUP 2001) Janet McLean, *Property as Power and Resistance*, in *Property and the Constitution* (Jean McLean ed., Hart Publishing 1999).
40. Nduka Orjinmo & Salihu Adamu, *Why Some Nigerian Families Lock Up Children and the Mentally Ill* available at: https://www.bbc.com/news/world-africa-53893271 (last accessed 4 Oct. 2020).

context, what are the rules to accommodate the child, define the applicable age and limit and contextualise wellness and paramount interest? In *Saheed Gbadebo Kareem v. Secretary of State for The Home Department*[41] the Upper Tribunal on Immigration strikingly noted the importance of evidence on relevant foreign law and its application in practice. The Tribunal noted:

> Whilst considering the issue of evidence of marriage, we remind ourselves that the proof of the law of another country is by evidence, including proof of private international law of that other country. Such evidence will not only have to identify relevant legal provisions in the other country but identify how they apply in practice. A lack of evidence of relevant foreign law will normally mean that the party with the burden of proving it will fail.[42]

32. The same questions apply to the laws on succession. As an example, despite the provision of the Matrimonial Causes Act which appears to make domicile in Nigeria uniform, and the principle that the personal law of a person governs the distribution of his or her estate on intestacy, in *Lawal Osula v. Lawal Osula*, the Supreme Court stated that the deceased who was originally from a different State of the Federation had acquired the domicile and personal law of the State where he lived a good part of his life and therefore fell to be governed by the latter State with respect to succession. Another difficulty arises with harmonising laws taken from other jurisdictions with conditions in Nigeria. Lagos State Law on administration of estates typifies one such anomaly.[43] On succession to real and personal estate on intestacy, the law provides by section 49(1)(3)(f) provides for *bona vacantia* in one breath and took it away in another by section 49(5) providing, that the default vested State interest be distributed in line with customs, among relations.[44]

33. The only perceivable scenario where *bona vacantia* can arise on intestacy will be where a foreigner naturalises as a Nigerian and has no relatives. It is thus ordinarily, difficult to conceive a case where the law envisages distribution of estate outside of customary law and second to whom such distributive regulation will apply.

34. These are but a few of the complexities which must be borne in mind in gleaning and understanding the law on family and succession in Nigeria.

§3. Sources of Family and Succession Law

35. At the apex of the sources of family and succession law in Nigeria is the Constitution. In the areas of family and succession law, it must be kept in mind that

41. [2014] UKUT 00024(IAC), para. 14.
42. *Ibid.*; *See* however, H.A. Olaniyan, *A Review of Judicial and Legislative Approach of Nigeria to Discretionary Jurisdiction Over Foreign Causes*, 3(12) Int'l J. Bus. & Soc. Sci. 204–218 (2012).
43. Administration of Estates Law, Ch. A3 Laws of Lagos State, 2004.
44. This is more fully discussed under Part IV on Succession.

aside from the constitutional provisions and interventions for customary and Islamic law norms, all the law whether in the context of the federal or the States are akin to one another and mainly in line with English, Australian and New Zealand laws on the same subjects before 1970. The Nigerian Constitution encourages and promotes founding of family and family life.[45] Interaction in this area of the law between Nigerians and foreigners abound. In *Marquis v. Marquis*[46] the Professor was married to an English lady, from whom he was separated. On return to Nigeria although separated but not divorced, he married a Nigerian woman under customary laws. Professor Olufemi Marquis died intestate on 6 May 1982. He had married the first plaintiff in 1960 at St. Mary's Catholic Church Sunderland, England. There were four children of the marriage. Professor Marquis subsequently married a Nigerian woman with whom he lived until his death, without dissolution of the first marriage, by whom he had three children. On his death the question of who was entitled to a grant of a Letter of Administration arose, and it was held that without doubt his first wife was so entitled, the court describing the wife under native law and customs as a mere mistress.

36. In *Salubi v. Nwariaku*[47] the wife who was of Irish descent accepted or condoned another relationship between her husband and a Nigerian woman along with her two children. In this case, the Supreme Court ruled for the first time that children born in or out of marriage were protected by section 42(2) of the Nigerian Constitution and entitled to share equally in the estates of their fathers. The subsection prohibits discrimination based on circumstances of birth or life.

37. In *Agbaje v. Akinnoye-Agbaje*[48] where the court applied Part III of the Matrimonial Family Proceedings Act, 1984 to resolve an inequity in the distribution of the property of a divorced Nigerian/British couple. In this case the couple had been married for thirty-eight years, lived, and had all five children in England. To dissolve the marriage, the husband turned to Nigerian Courts, a friendly patriarchal terrain, where the wife was awarded a mere life interest in a property in Lagos, Nigeria. The wife sought relief under Part III and got fuller and fairer relief. The Court noted that the purpose of the Act was, subject to the parties having substantial connections with England, to alleviate the adverse consequences of no or inadequate financial provision being made by a foreign court.

I. Constitution

38. At the apex of the legal system and legal structure of the country is a Constitution, which takes its commencement date as 5 May 1999. This was the date on which it was promulgated by the Military regime of the time as the Constitution of

45. Section 17(3)(h); *See also* Arts 18(1) and 27(1).
46. Unreported Suit Nos 1/685/84, 03/03/1986, High Court of Ibadan, Oyo State Nigeria.
47. [2003] 7 NWLR (part 819) 426.
48. [2010] UKSC 13.

the Federal Republic of Nigeria (Promulgation) Decree.[49] The Constitution formed part of the democratic dispensation when the country embraced the democratic form of governance soon after, on 29 May 1999. The Constitution has continued to suffer from a crisis of legitimacy.[50] The Constitution has since seen four alterations or amendments known as the Alteration Acts, 2010.[51] Of importance is Part III of the Constitution and in particular, section 315 which preserves existing laws in accordance with the legislative competences of the Federal and State legislative houses. Thus, all existing decrees as of 1999 became Acts of the National Assembly while Edicts of the States are laws and deemed enacted by the respective Houses of Assemblies of States.[52]

39. The Constitution creates a federation of thirty-six states[53] in addition to the Federal Capital Territory (FCT). There are three tiers of government, Federal, State and Local. The Constitution provides roles for each arm of government and the federating States. The First Schedule contains a list of the States of the Federation and the FCT. The FCT is treated as if it is a State and is mostly referred to as the FCT, Abuja although it has many adjourning towns which comprise the territory. The actual delineation of the FCT is to be found in First Schedule Part II of the Constitution of the Federal Republic of Nigeria.[54]

40. Aside from the laws and regulations guiding her governance within, Nigeria is also signatory to many regional and international instruments and treaties and a member of many such organisations. In international law nomenclature, Nigeria is a dualist state because treaties to which she is bound must also be subjected to internal validation by section 12 of the constitution of the country.[55] Some of these organisations to which Nigeria belongs and often become signatories to instruments and treaties emanating from them include the African Union, Economic Community of West Africa, and the United Nations.

---

49. Decree 24 of 1999 by the regime of General Abdulsalami Abubakar. For clamours on its inauthenticity and illegitimacy *see* for example, J.O. Ihonvbere, *How to Make an Undemocratic Constitution: The Nigerian Example*, 21(2) Third World Q. 343–366 (2000).
50. Democracy was usually commemorated on the 29th May until 6 Jun. 2018 when it was changed to 12th June. Democracy day marks the day the military handed over governance to an elected civilian government in 1999. It has marked the longest continuous civilian governance since Nigeria's independence in 1960 from British colonial rule.
51. Cap C23, Laws of the Federation of Nigeria, 2004.
52. Section 315(1) of the Constitution of Nigeria, Cap C23, Laws of the Federation of Nigeria, 2004.
53. Abia, Adamawa, Akwa Ibom, Anambra, Bauchi, Bayelsa, Benue, Borno, Cross River, Delta, Ebonyi, Edo, Ekiti, Enugu, Gombe, Imo, Jigawa, Kaduna, Kano, Katsina, Kebbi, Kogi, Kwara, Lagos, Nasarawa, Niger, Ogun, Ondo, Osun, Oyo, Plateau, Rivers, Sokoto, Taraba, Yobe and Zamfara.
54. Cap C23, Laws of the Federation, 2004.
55. *Ibid.*, 12. (1) No treaty between the Federation and any other country shall have the force of law to the extent to which any such treaty has been enacted into law by the National Assembly. (2) The National Assembly may make laws for the Federation or any part thereof with respect to matters not included in the he Exclusive Legislative List for the purpose of implementing a treaty. (3) A bill for an Act of the National Assembly passed pursuant to the provisions of subs. (2) of this section shall not be presented to the President for assent and shall not be enacted unless it is ratified by a majority of all the House of Assembly in the Federation.

41. Section 14 of the Constitution is significant as it presents an overview of the aspiration of the country as a nation:

1) The Federal Republic of Nigeria shall be a State based on the principles of democracy and social justice.
2) It is hereby, accordingly, declared that:
   a. sovereignty belongs to the people of Nigeria from whom government through this Constitution derives all its powers and authority;
   b. the security and welfare of the people shall be the primary purpose of government; and
   c. the participation by the people in their government shall be ensured in accordance with the provisions of this Constitution.
3) The composition of the Government of the Federation or any of its agencies and the conduct of its affairs shall be carried out in such a manner as to reflect the federal character of Nigeria and the need to promote national unity, and to command national loyalty, thereby ensuring that there shall be no predominance of persons from a few State or from a few ethnic or other sectional groups in that Government or in any of its agencies.
4) The composition of the Government of a State, a local government council, or any of the agencies of such Government or council, and the conduct of the affairs of the Government or council or such agencies shall be carried out in such manner as to recognise the diversity of the people within its area of authority and the need to promote a sense of belonging and loyalty among all the people of the Federation.

A. The Executive

42. Nigeria operates a presidential system of government, with an executive President and Vice at the Federal Level[56] and executive Governor and deputy Governor at the State level.[57] A Federal Minister whose office is akin to that of a Governor oversees the affairs of the FCT. The President is a Head of State, the Chief Executive of the Federation and Commander-in-Chief of the Armed Forces of the Federation. To be qualified for the position, a person must be a citizen of Nigeria by birth; have attained the age of 40 years; be a member of a political party and sponsored by that political party; and have been educated up to at least school certificate level or its equivalent.

43. By section 58(1) of the Constitution, the power of the Legislature to make laws is subject to assent by the executive, the President in the case of the Federation, and Governor, in the case of the States.[58] There are provisions, for instance, by

56. Chapter VI Part I, ss 130–144 of the Constitution covers issues of appointment, qualification, removal from office etc.
57. *Ibid.*, ss 176–190.
58. Section 100 of the Constitution of the Federation. Other procedures for assent and in relation to appropriation and taxation are provided in s. 59.

sections 58(5) and 100(5) providing for exceptions to or overreaching the mentioned assents and provisions for the full procedures for making laws by the legislature.

B. The Legislature

44. The country has a bicameral assembly known as a National Assembly for the Federation which consists of a Senate and a House of Representatives.[59] The Senate consists of three Senators from each State and one from the FCT, Abuja.[60] The House of Representatives ordinarily consists of 360 representing constituencies of nearly equal population as far as possible, provided that no constituency falls within more than one State.[61] There is a President and a Deputy President of the Senate, who are elected by members from among the members of the Senate; and a Speaker and a Deputy Speaker of the House of Representatives, who are elected by the members of the House from among themselves. The President or Deputy President of the Senate or the Speaker or Deputy Speaker of the House of Representatives is liable to vacate the office: where membership fails otherwise than by reason of a dissolution of the Senate or the House of Representatives; when the House first sits after any dissolution of that House; or removed from office by a resolution of the Senate or of that of the House of Representatives, as the case may be, by the votes of not less than two-thirds majority of the members of that House.[62]

45. Sections 58–62 of the Constitution contain the main modes of operation and conduct of activities of the National Assembly.

46. There is a House of Assembly for each of the State of the Federation.[63] Ordinarily, a House of Assembly of a State consists of three or four times the number of seats which that State has in the House of Representatives divided in a way to reflect, as far as possible nearly equal population. A House of Assembly of a State can only consist of a minimum of twenty-four and a maximum of forty members.[64] For operation, there is a Speaker and a Deputy Speaker of a House of Assembly who are elected by the members of the House from among themselves.[65]

47. Sections 100–102 of the Constitution contain the main modes of operation and conduct of activities of the State Houses of Assembly.

48. Section 4 of the Constitution contains the legislative powers of the Federation and its States. Part 1 of the Second Schedule of the Constitution contains the Exclusive Legislative List, which are functions within the exclusive competence of

59. Section 47 of the Constitution.
60. Section 48 of the Constitution.
61. Section 49 of the Constitution.
62. Section 50 of the Constitution.
63. Section 90 of the Constitution.
64. Section 91 of the Constitution.
65. Section 92 of the Constitution.

the Federal Legislature known as the National Assembly. The Federal Legislature shares a role with the State legislative assemblies of the federating states on the functions contained and listed in Part II of the Second Schedule known as the concurrent list. The respective legislatures are assigned functions to the extent prescribed in the second column opposite the listed items.[66] Section 4(7) of the Constitution defines the exact powers of State assemblies. Where a function or a matter is not indicated in either the exclusive or concurrent list, then it falls under the residual competence and a few Supreme Court cases have indicated that such subject matters are reserved for the State legislature.[67] In *Att. General of the Federation v. Attorney General of Lagos State*[68] the Supreme Court reiterated that all matters not mentioned in Second Schedule are reserved as legislative competences of States. It is not at all clear how this came to be as section 4(4)(b) of the Constitution also reserves the right of the national assembly to make laws on any other matter with respect to which it is empowered to make laws in accordance with the provisions of the constitution and on matters incidental or supplementary to those specifically listed in the exclusive and concurrent lists of the Second Schedule to the Constitution. In addition, it cannot be the case that where a novel matter requiring legislation arises, just because it is not listed on the exclusive or concurrent legislative competences, then only the States can legislate on same. The relevance of this note becomes more important on the discussion of succession under statutory marriage where the courts have used this argument to remove succession under statutory marriages from federal competence and vested the power effectively on the States.[69]

49. Formation of marriage, its dissolution, and the rights of children within that context other than marriages under Islamic law and customary law including matrimonial causes relating thereto fall under item 61 of the Exclusive Legislative List and are vested exclusively in the national assembly.[70]

50. When the same relations arise under customary law or Sharia they come under the residuary list. Questions of succession, whether testate or intestate, are also under the residuary list and therefore within the legislative competence of the States.

C. The Judiciary

51. The Constitution by section 6 vests judicial powers in the courts. The powers of the judiciary are contained in section 6 of the Constitution of the Federal Republic. The judiciary has an important role to play in Family law in Nigeria and

66. Section 4(4)(b) of the Constitution.
67. *Obusez v. Obusez* [2007] NGSC 21; [2007] 2 All N.L.R. 458.
68. S.C. 340/2010; [2013] LPELR – 2092 (SC).
69. *Salubi v. Nwariaku* [2003] 2 S.C. 161; [2003] 7 NWLR (Part 819) 426; [2003] LPELR-SC.120/1997; [2003] 20 WRN SC 53; *Obusez v. Obusez* [2007] NGSC 21; [2007] 2 All N.L.R. 458.
70. Item 61, Second Schedule, Part 1, the Constitution of the Federal Republic of Nigeria.

has been doing so.[71] The judiciary has always risen to the occasion on family matters and filled the gaps in twixt of customs, law, and modernity. It has done so mainly through the interpretation of the various fundamental human rights provisions contained in Chapter IV of the Nigerian Constitution.[72]

52. The Constitutional provisions for appointment of the Chief Justice of Nigeria and Justices of the Supreme Court, as well as rules guiding the composition and administration of justice are contained in sections 230–232. The maximum number of justices of the Supreme Court at any point in time is twenty-one. The same provisions for the State are contained in sections 270–274 except that terminologies defer and the head of the bench of a state is a Chief Judge while the other members of the bench are called judges.

53. Section 6(a) and (b) of the Constitution provide avenue for hearing and determination of all civil matters and obligations between individuals or individuals with government or authorities. Section 6(a) extends all inherent powers and sanctions of a court of law to the judicial arm of government. The Constitution categorises courts along the lines of the federation, States, local, district or area, Sharia or customary. Thus, there are Federal and State Courts. The Supreme Court is at the apex of the judicial structure. Section 22 of the Supreme Court Act[73] is an important provision which empowers the Court to sit as a Court of First Instance in certain cases. In family matters, the Supreme Court has mostly taken the position of respecting and not interfering with evidence and findings of facts of hierarchy of courts below.

54. The constitution names some superior courts of records. The superior courts of record in Nigeria are:[74]

(a) the Supreme Court of Nigeria;
(b) the Court of Appeal;

---

71. *Ukeje v. Ukeje* [2014] 11 NWLR (part 1418) 384; *Muojekwu v. Iwuchukwu* [2004] 18 NWLR (part 883) 196; [2004] 18 NSCQR 184; *Anekwe v. Nweke* [2014] 9 NWLR (part 1412) 393; *See also*, I.E. Sagay, *The Judiciary in a Modern Democracy*, in *Nigeria: Issues in the 1999 Constitution* 76–112 (I.A. Ayua, D.A. Guobadia & A.O. Adekunle eds, Nigerian Institute of Advanced Legal Studies 2000).
72. I.E. Sagay, *Legitimacy, Legitimation and Rights of Inheritance in Nigerian Contemporary Law*, 16, 17 & 18 JPPL 1 (1992 & 1993).
73. Cap 424, Laws of the Federation, 1990; Cap S.15, Laws of the Federation, 2004. Section 22 provides: the Supreme Court may, from time to time, make any order necessary for determining the real question in controversy in the appeal, and may amend any defect or error in the record of appeal, and may direct the court below to inquire into and certify its findings on any question which the Supreme Court thinks fit to determine before final judgment in the appeal and may make an interim order or grant any injunction which the court below is authorised to make or grant and may direct any necessary inquiries or accounts to be made or taken and generally shall have full jurisdiction over the whole proceedings as if the proceedings had been instituted and prosecuted in the Supreme Court as a Court of First Instance and may rehear the case in whole or in part or may remit it to the court below for the purpose of such rehearing or may give such other directions as to the manner in which the court below shall deal with the case in accordance with the powers of that court.
74. Section 6(5) of the Constitution.

(c) the Federal High Court;
(d) the High Court of the FCT, Abuja;
(e) a High Court of a State;
(f) the Sharia Court of Appeal of the FCT, Abuja;
(g) a Sharia Court of Appeal of a State;
(h) the Customary Court of Appeal of the FCT, Abuja;
(i) a Customary Court of Appeal of a State; and

such other courts as may be authorised by law to exercise jurisdiction on matters with respect to which a House of Assembly may make laws.[75]

55. Another superior court of record is the National Industrial Court. The other courts of record which are not superior exist for the States and of importance is the Magistrate Court of the States which is relevant with respect to matrimonial causes because it is empowered to enforce summarily, maintenance orders granted by a State High Court or High Court of the FCT, Abuja.[76]

56. Appeals lie from the Magistrate Courts to the High Courts. Appeals lie from the High Courts to the Courts of Appeal and to the Supreme Court. The Supreme Court is the highest National Court. The scope of appeal from the High Court is stated in section 241 of the Constitution:

(1) An appeal shall lie from decisions of the Federal High Court or a High Court to the Court of Appeal as of right in the following cases:
  (a) final decisions in any civil or criminal proceedings before the Federal High Court or a High Court or a High Court sitting at first instance;
  (b) where the ground of appeal involves questions of law alone, decisions in any civil or criminal proceedings;
  (c) decisions in any civil or criminal proceedings on questions as to the interpretation or application of this Constitution;
  (d) decisions in any civil or criminal proceedings on questions as to whether any of the provisions of Chapter IV of this Constitution has been is being or is likely to be, contravened in relation to any person;
  (e) decisions in any criminal proceedings in which the Federal High Court or a High Court has imposed a sentence of death;
  (f) decisions made or given by the Federal High Court or a High Court:
    (i) where the liberty of a person or the custody of an infant is concerned;
    (ii) where an injunction or the appointment of a receiver is granted or refused;
    (iii) in the case of a decision determining the case of a creditor or the liability of a contributory or other officer under any enactment relating to companies in respect of misfeasance or otherwise;

75. Section 5(5) a-k.
76. Following due procedures which is mainly registration of the judgment of the high court at the relevant Magisterial jurisdiction.

(iv) in the case of a Decree *nisi* in a matrimonial cause or a decision in an admiralty action determining liability; and
(v) in such other cases as may be prescribed by any law in force in Nigeria.

(2) Nothing in this section shall confer any of appeal:
(a) from a decision of the Federal High Court or any High Court granting unconditional leave to defend an action;
(b) from an order absolute for the dissolution or nullity of marriage in favour of any party who, having had time and opportunity to appeal from the Decree *nisi* on which the order was founded, has not appealed from that Decree *nisi*; and
(c) without the leave of the Federal High Court or a High Court or of Appeal, from a decision of the Federal High Court High Court made with the consent of the parties or as to costs only.

D. Sharia Court of Appeal

57. The scope of Appeal for the Sharia Court of Appeal is stated in section 262 of the Constitution:

(1) The Sharia Court of Appeal shall, in addition to such other jurisdiction as may be conferred upon it by an Act of the National Assembly, exercise such appellate and supervisory jurisdiction in civil proceedings involving questions of Islamic personal law.
(2) For the purpose of subsection (1) of this section, the Sharia Court of Appeal shall be competent to decide:
(a) any question of Islamic personal law regarding a marriage concluded in accordance with that law, including a question relating to the validity or dissolution of such a marriage or a question that depends on such a marriage and relating to family relationship or the guardianship of an infant;
(b) where all the parties to the proceeding are Muslims, any question of Islamic personal law regarding a marriage, including the validity or dissolution of that marriage, or regarding family relationship, a foundling, or the guardianship of an infant;
(c) any question of Islamic personal law regarding a wakf, gift, Will or succession where the endower, donor, testator, or deceased person is a Muslim;
(d) any question of Islamic personal law regarding an infant, prodigal or person of unsound mind who is a Muslim or the maintenance or the guardianship of a Muslim who is physically or mentally infirm or;
(e) where all the parties to the proceedings, being Muslims, have requested the court that hears the case in the first instance to determine that case in accordance with Islamic personal law, any other question.

E. Customary or Area Court

58. The customary and Area Courts are State Courts which aim at providing adjudicatory services at the grassroot. The customary courts are found mainly in the Southern States of Nigeria and the Area Courts in the States in Northern parts of Nigeria. The First Schedule to the Akwa Ibom State Customary Courts Laws, 2,000 as an example, provides for the jurisdiction of customary courts in civil causes and matters. By section 2(3)–(5) provides for unlimited jurisdictions:

> in causes and matters concerning the ownership, possession, occupation, or alienation of land …
> causes and matters relating to the succession of property and administration of estates under Customary Law
> … .and in matrimonial causes and matters between persons married under Customary Law or arising from or connected with Customary Unions and in suits relating to the custody of children under Customary Law.[77]

59. A typical example of jurisdiction for Area Courts is that of the FCT, Abuja Area Courts (Repeal and Enactment) Act, 2010. Section 10 of the Act,[78] provides that the court's jurisdiction is over Muslims or a person who voluntarily submits to the jurisdiction of the Area Court. It provides further that subject to the provisions of the Act and of any other written law, any person may institute and prosecute any cause or matter in an Area Court and such a person who institutes or prosecutes any cause or matter in an Area Court in line with the subsection of the Act shall in that cause or matter, be subject to the jurisdiction of that Area Court and of any other court exercising jurisdiction in that cause or matter.

60. The jurisdiction of the court over civil matters is set out in sections 13–16. Section 13 provides that an Area Court shall have jurisdiction and power to the extent set out in the warrant establishing it, and subject to the provisions of the Act and of the Civil Procedure Code, in all Civil Causes in which all the parties are subject to the jurisdiction of the Area Court. Section 15 provides that an Area Court shall, in civil cases and matters, administer Islamic law of the Maliki School of jurisprudence.[79] While section 16(1) provides that in any matter relating to the guardianship of children, the interest and welfare of the child shall be the first and paramount consideration. Section 16(2) further advances the interest of the child. Thus, whenever it appears to an Area Court that an order made by the court should, in the interest of a child, be reviewed, the court may of its own motion or upon the application of any interested person, vary or discharge the order.

---

77. Taken from J.I. Udosen, *The Judiciary and The Role of Customary Courts in Nigeria*, 5(6) Global J. Pol. & L. Res. 39 (2017). *See* for Kaduna State, p. 40.
78. Part III.
79. The Maliki Jurisprudence was founded by Malik ibn Anas in the eighth century. The Maliki school of jurisprudence relies on the Quran and hadiths as primary sources. Unlike other Islamic fiqhs, Maliki fiqh also considers the consensus of the people of Medina to be a valid source of Islamic law. Maliki – Wikipedia available at: en.wikipedia.org/wiki/Maliki last accessed 7 Aug. 2020.

F. Family Court

61. PART XIII of the Child's Rights Act establishes a Family Court. Section 149 provides that the Family Court shall be established for each State of the Federation and the FCT.[80] The principal function of the court is defined as the hearing and determining of matters relating to children.

62. Section 150 provides the structure of the Court which is at two levels: as a Division of the High Court at the High Court level and the Magistrate Court. Appeals lie from the family court at the magistrate level to family court at the High Court and from the High Court to the Court of Appeal.

63. Section 151 provides for the jurisdiction of the court, which is subjected to the provisions of the Act and other jurisdiction as may be conferred on it by any other law.

64. The Court has unlimited jurisdiction to hear and determine: 'any civil proceeding in which the existence or extent of a legal right, power, duty, liability, privilege, interest, obligation or claim in respect of a child is in issue; and any criminal proceeding involving or relating to any penalty, forfeiture, punishment or other liability in respect of an offence committed by a child, against a child or against the interest of a child'. Reference to civil or criminal proceedings includes a reference to a proceeding which originates in the Court and that which is brought by the Court at the High Court level to be dealt with by the Court in the exercise of its appellate or supervisory jurisdiction.

65. The Court is guided in any matter relating to, or affecting a child or a family, and at all stages of any proceedings before it, by the principle of conciliation of the parties involved or likely to be affected by the result of the proceedings. Its jurisdiction in this regard extends to any one of the parties named: 'the child', 'parents or guardian of the child', and any other person having parental or other responsibility for the child.

66. Section 162 specifies that no other Court shall exercise jurisdiction in any matter relating to children as stated; however, the jurisdiction of the normal criminal courts to try cases or offences by adult offenders in relation to the protection of the child or any other law is not affected.

67. Lagos State is the only State known to have complied with these provisions and established a Family Court.

80. 'Court' means the Family court established under s. 149 of this Act. All executive functions in relation to children are under the authority of the Federal Minister of the Federal Capital Territory by virtue of The Child's Right (Transfer of Certain Statutory Functions) Order S.I. No. 15 of 2005, a subsidiary legislation of the Constitution of the Federal Republic of Nigeria.

G. Local Government

68. Section 7 of the Constitution provides for local government as an arm of government and vests it with powers as well as functions. The functions of a local government are as conferred by section 7(5) and set out in the Fourth Schedule to the Constitution. The most important of these functions in relation to the subjects of family and succession are contained in the Fourth Schedule, item 1(i) 'registration of births, deaths and marriages'. There is also item 1(C) which covers establishment and maintenance of cemeteries, burial grounds, and homes for the destitute or infirm and item 2(C) for the provision and maintenance of health services.

H. Treaties

69. With respect to implementation of treaty which has affected family life as it relates to children, there is a complicated system of action between the Federal Legislature and the States.[81] Nigeria is signatory to many International Treaties. A few are:

Convention on the Right of the Child.[82]
African Charter on The Rights and Welfare of The Child.[83]
African Charter on Human and Peoples' Rights.[84]
Convention on the Elimination of All Forms of Discrimination against Women.[85]
International Covenant on Civil and Political Rights.[86]
Universal Declaration of Human Rights.[87]

I. Procedure for Adoption of Treaties

70. The procedure for adoption of treaties as national law is provided in the Constitution. Section 12 of the Constitution provides: (1) 'No treaty between the Federation and any other country shall have the force of law except to the extent to which any such treaty has been enacted into law by the National Assembly.' (2) 'The National Assembly may make laws for the Federation or any part thereof with respect to matters not included in the Exclusive Legislative List for the purpose of implementing a treaty.' (3) 'A bill for an Act of the National Assembly passed pursuant to the provisions of subsection (2) of this section shall not be presented to the

81. Section 12(1)–(3) of the Constitution.
82. 1990: Signature: 1990, Ratification/Accession: 1991.
83. 1990 OAU (later African Union in 2001).
84. Adopted 27 Jun. 1981, entered into force 21 Oct. 1986.
85. Signature: 1984, Ratification/Accession: 1985.
86. Adopted 1976: Signature: NA, Ratification/Accession: 1993.
87. Resolution 217 A (111) of 10 Dec. 1948.

President for assent and shall not be enacted unless it is ratified by a majority of all the House of Assembly in the Federation.'[88]

71. Thus, where the subject matter of the treaty is within the exclusive legislative competence of the National Assembly, that is, the subject matter is listed in the Exclusive Legislative List, the National Assembly can domesticate a ratified treaty as a matter of course in the usual course of its business within the Assembly. However, where the subject matter is one in which the States have concurrent competence or falls within residual matters, then the Constitution requires in line with section 12(3) that the Houses of Assembly in the Federation participate by ratifying the action of the National Assembly. There is no clear provision in the Constitution for the procedure for such ratification. It is not clear whether once a majority of the State Houses of Assembly participates, then it is taken that ratification has occurred automatically or further action needs to be taken in line with either the operational method of the National Assembly or the different Houses of Assembly.

72. The Child's Rights Act, 2003 (CRA) typifies the complex system of domestication of treaties as law in the country. Although Nigeria signed and adopted the Convention on the Right of the Child in 1991 (CRC) it could not be domesticated as law in Nigeria because of the complex system required by section 12. First, the specific subject of children, aside from references to fundamental human rights and education in the Constitution, is not listed either in the Exclusive Legislative or Concurrent List of competences of the National Assembly or that of the Houses of Assembly, leaving the matter as residual. Objections arose from some States based on some of the principles and articles of the CRC such as, the definition of who a child is and its relationship to marriage, culture, and religion. The necessary mandate to ratify the Convention could therefore not be obtained from all the 'House of Assembly' in the Federation. After years of complex negotiation and pressure from international organisations and News Media, a window was opened for a new National law for children, which aimed at incorporating the principles enshrined in the Convention on the Right of the Child and African Charter on the Rights and Welfare of the Child – resulting in enactment of the Child's Rights Act. The Act drew on these instruments to provide a comprehensive law for children with reciprocal rights, duties, and obligations, for children, parents, families and governmental authorities and powers for the Court. It was passed, assented to, and signed into a national law in 2003.

73. There remained objections even to the Child's Rights Act, for instance, on the legal effect of adoption which precluded marriage between adopted persons and other members of the family of the adopter. The CRA, just as the CRC, defines a child as a person under the age of 18 years. Some States also based their objection to the CRA on its conflict with the Children and Young Person's Act, a preferred legislation for the relevant States. The Children and Young Person's Act designates

---

88. Section 318 of the Constitution defines 'House of Assembly' – 'means the House of Assembly of a state'.

a child as an individual below the age of 14. [89] This law is no longer compiled as Laws of the Federation.[90] Some States, in the North and others, such as Lagos, however, retain its variant as Children and Young Persons Law.[91] It must be borne in mind that the provisions of the CRA by section 274 supersede all other laws on children in Nigeria. Lagos State, for instance, works within this objective of the CRA, being one of the twenty-five States that have enacted the CRA into law, as Child's Law, 2007 and established all facilitating institutions including a Family Court. Ultimately, the Child's Right Act being a legislation of the National Assembly applies as of course in the FCT, Abuja while States resorted to enacting the Act as State law or applying it by reference.

74. It remains unclear how residuary matters became exclusive to States; however, that is the position in practice, and Nigerian courts even at the apex level have made statements to that effect, at least with respect to certain subject matters.[92] As has been stated earlier, the provisions of section 12(3) of the Constitution require clarification because if the intendment of the subsection is to create a simple majority for the ratification of a treaty, where the subject matter of the treaty is not one on the exclusive legislative competence of the National Assembly and then the subject gains an automatic ratification, then the CRA would have met that criteria since at least twenty-five States of the thirty-six States now adopt the Child's Rights Act. This would then mean that the Convention on the Rights of the Child (CRC) now applies automatically to all States of the Federation. If automatic ratification is not the intendment, then the result is nearly the same, as it becomes easier for a Bill to be presented to the National Assembly for the domestication of the CRC. The highest majority required on resolutions by the Constitution is two-thirds making the result the same if a two-thirds majority as opposed to a simple majority is the intendment of the Constitution.

75. The States yet to enact the Child's Act into State law or adopt it by reference are Bauchi, Yobe, Kano, Sokoto, Adamawa, Borno, Zamfara, Gombe, Katsina, Kebbi, and Jigawa.[93]

J. The Foreign Judgment Reciprocal Act

76. The other Federal Legislation relevant to family and succession in Nigeria is the Foreign Judgment Reciprocal Act.[94] Overall this Act, makes judgment from a final court on monetary subject matter enforceable in Nigeria by registration if there

89. Last known compilation is, as Cap 32, Revised Laws of the Federation of Nigeria and Lagos, 1958.
90. *Ibid.*
91. Cap 1, Laws of Lagos State 1973.
92. S.C. 340/2010; [2013] LPELR – 2092 (SC).
93. Nike Adebowale 'UPDATED: 11 states in northern Nigeria yet to pass child rights law – UNICEF Official' Available at https://www.premiumtimesng.com/news/more-news/329511-12-states-in-northern-nigeria-yet-to-pass-child-rights-law-unicef-official.html of 11 May 2019 (last accessed 20 Oct. 2020).
94. Cap F35, 2004.

is reciprocity from the foreign country. Where there is no reciprocity, or the reciprocity and recognition is less favourable, the Act empowers the Minister of Justice by section 12 to deny such country access to registration and recognition. This order for non-access is also variable and modifiable.[95]

77. Section 2 of the Act provides that judgments given in the superior courts in Nigeria means judgments given in a High Court, Court of Appeal or the Supreme Court and includes, as the case may require given in any courts on appeals against any Judgments so given; and 'superior court in Nigeria means the High Court of a State or of the FCT, Abuja or the Federal High Court'.

K. Jurisprudence: (Case Law)

78. Nigeria was one of the many countries colonised by Great Britain.[96] It is thus not surprising that the coloniser affected the country with its laws and in many ways, culture. Nigeria continues to relate with the United Kingdom as a member of the Commonwealth. Generally, where there is no legislation or existing law on the subject, resort is made to pre-1900 laws of Her Majesty's Government, or the common laws of England and the rules of equity. A good example is the Married Women's Property Act, 1881; the Wills Act, 1837 and the Wills Amendment Act 1882. Other relevant English legislation which are still in use in Nigeria are the Statute of Frauds 1677, applicable by virtue of land-related transactions, estate contracts, land that is non-urban areas, secret trusts;[97] Infants Relief Act 1874 by which the age of majority is 21.

79. In addition, decisions from the United Kingdom Supreme Courts and High Courts of England and Wales are of persuasive authorities, so also are decisions from other Commonwealth Countries. In *Jadesimi v. Okotie-Eboh*[98] Uwais, J.S.C stated, 'It appears to me from the provision of section 45 of the interpretation Act Cap 89 of the laws of the Federation of Nigeria, 1958 that although Statutes of general application are applicable nevertheless their applicability is not without limitations.' The case raised and addressed some fundamental issues on marriage and succession framework in Nigeria. So much remains unanswered, nevertheless. The Matrimonial Causes Act, 1970 is taken from a mix of the Australian Act of 1959 and English Act of 1965. The Nigerian judiciary continues to draw on this authority particularly in private law. In *Williams v. Williams* Obaseki JSC noted:

> In stating the principles on which custody is to be decided, the learned editors of Rayden on Divorce ... made references to the provisions of Guardianship of Minors Act, 1971 and Guardianship Act 1973 both being English Statutes.

95. Section 12(3).
96. Now United Kingdom.
97. Nwudego Chinwuba, *Filling the Gaps Between Colonial Legal Heritage and Prevailing Local Customs in Family Relations: the Place of Secret Trust*, 24(1) African J. Int'l & Comp. L. 45–63 (2016).
98. [1996] 2 NWLR (part 429) 128–156.

The guiding principles enunciated in those Acts though not binding on this court, contain the kernel of the declarations in section 71 of our Matrimonial Causes Act, 1970 and I will adopt them as the necessary intendment of our law. [99]

80. This was the position taken by the Court of Appeal in the interpretation of the Matrimonial Causes Rules, 1983. In *Unegbu v. Unegbu*[100] the Court of Appeal was constrained to turn to the English Matrimonial Causes Rules, 1957. The court stated that the Rule as of 30 September 1960 continued to be in force by virtue of the various State High Court rules of Nigeria.[101] In *Okwueze v. Okwueze*[102] the Supreme Court noted that there was no clarity on the subject of age limit regarding custody and for guidance resorted to other legislation in the country, general law, customary law, academic literature, and the English Matrimonial Causes Act, 1973.

81. Agbaje v. Agbaje[103] involved the testing of Part III of the Matrimonial and Family Proceedings Act, 1984. The case is described as the first case under this part of the Act to have been heard by the Supreme Court. In addition to this, the case comes as a high authority having been a unanimous judgment of the United Kingdom Supreme Court. The case decided that despite a divorce proceeding having been conducted in another jurisdiction, an English Court where the necessary criteria exist could and should grant further relief. Such a criterion would include that there was appropriate connection between the United Kingdom with the parties or their property. *GE v. KE & Anor*[104] was another decision which connected England and Nigeria. *Kareem v. Secretary of State for Home Department*[105] is a tribunal decision which again concerned Nigerian customary marriages. Prior to this time there had been *Ohocuku v. Ohochuku.*[106] These issues are replicated in different countries of the world as Nigerians are great travellers and often settle in their host countries. The Matrimonial Proceedings (Polygamous Marriages Act, 1972) among other provisions, by section I(1) empowers the courts in England and Wales to make a declaration concerning the validity of a marriage notwithstanding that the marriage in question was entered into under a law which permits polygamy.[107] The Matrimonial Causes Act 1973[108] re-enacts the provision in section 47(1). Section 47(4) provides further that the section has effect whether either party to the marriage in question has for the time being any spouse additional to the other party. Although provisions may be made by rules of court: (a) for requiring notice of proceedings brought by

---

99. [1987] All N.L.R 253, 260.
100. [2004] 11 NWLR (part 884) 332.
101. Per Mohammed J. C. A. in *Unegbu v. Unegbu* [2004] 11 NWLR (part 884) 332, 354.
102. [1989] NWLR (part 109) 321 [1989] LPELR-SC. 202/1985.
103. [2010] UKSC 13.
104. [2014] EWHC 1938 (Fam).
105. [2014] UKUT 24 (IAC).
106. [1960] 1 ALL ER 253.
107. This particular section and s. 4 were repealed by the Matrimonial Causes Act, 1973, Cap C.18.
108. Cap 18, England and Wales.

virtue of this section to be served on any such other spouse; and (b) for conferring on any such other spouse the right to be heard in any such proceedings, in such cases as may be prescribed by the rules.

82. These scenarios thus necessitate a thorough consideration of customary marriages in Nigeria. It is difficult to achieve this without examining its twixt with statutory marriages. In a country where customs occupy a pride of place for perhaps, self-enlightened interests, there is no easy way to draw attention to the necessity of continuing evaluation of the customs to meet generational perceptions and contemporary human values.

83. To this end, quite aside from the laws and judicial decisions that have been noted above, the Nigerian Matrimonial Causes Act, 1970 and the MCA, 1973 bear close similarities in substance. A point of substantial departure is in the provision on guidelines for the exercise of discretion. Thus, although sections 72–75 of the Nigerian MCA confer wide discretionary powers on the Courts on the award of maintenance, adjustment of property rights and enforcement thereof, there is no wide guideline on how this discretion is to be exercised as is provided by section 25 of the MCA, 1973. In addition, because the English Law Reform Commission and the Judiciary are quick to respond to socio-legal circumstances, there are more legislation dealing with specific subject matters as they emerge, such as the Family Law Reform Act, 1987. To this the variations on Nigerian Law differ widely and will not be treated here. The other relevant legislation is the Matrimonial Proceedings and Property Act, 1970, which although, some provisions were repealed by the 1973 Act, remain relevant to Nigeria. The outcome of the decisions in *Pettit v. Pettit*[109] and *Gissing v. Gissing*[110] was captured in the Matrimonial Proceedings and Property Act, 1970, yet Nigeria appears to have applied those provisions intuitively through judicial actions. In this regard, it is to be borne in mind that the two cases were recognised in Nigeria as persuasive authorities and applied in some cases.[111] The import of this is that much of the law and developments in matrimonial causes in Nigeria is judiciary driven for which at any rate wide discretionary powers exist. Section 17 of the Married Women's Property Act, 1882 is treated as a declaratory right following the decision of the House of Lords in *Pettit v. Pettit.*[112] It is applied differently in Nigeria and has formed a basis for adjustment of property rights where customary marriage is involved and indeed statutory marriages.[113] The extent to which these powers come under judicial interrogation and intervention is another

109. [1970] AC 777; [1969] UKHL 5.
110. [1970] UKHL 3; [197] 3 WLR 255; [1971] AC 886; [1970] ALL ER 780.
111. *Egunjobi v. Egunjobi* [1976] WSCA 78; [1974] ECSLR 52.
112. [1970] AC 777; [1969] UKHL 5.
113. *Egunjobi v. Egunjobi* [1976] WSCA 78; [1974] ECSLR 52; *Oghoyone v. Oghoyone* [2010] 3 NWLR (part 1182) 564; [2010] LPELR – CA/L/26/2003; *Adaku v. Nwosu* [1992] 5 NWLR 273; *Oghoyene v. Oghoyene* [2010] 3 NWLR (part 1182) 564; *Toyin Arajulu v. Monday James* Unreported Suit No. 1/169/2015 Holden at Ibadan, Oyo State delivered 28 Feb. 2019. *See also* C.J. Efe, *The Need for the Statutory Introduction of the concept of 'Matrimonial Property' in Nigeria*, 63(1) J. African L. (2019); Michael Attah, *Divorcing Marriage from Marital Assets: Why Equity and Women Fail in Property Readjustment Actions in Nigeria*, 62(3) J. African L. 427–446 (2018).

matter. One thing is certain, the current legislation on matrimonial causes is more in tune with the customs of many parts of Nigeria. The process which makes divorce more complex and with intensive reconciliation provisions is more in line with the perceptions of marriage as an institution of perseverance and long suffering.

84. In the light of the nuances between Nigerian and English legal framework on matrimonial causes, references will be made to the MCA, 1973 and the rules thereto.

85. Section 258 of the Evidence Act[114] defines 'husband and wife' to mean: the wife and husband of a marriage validly contracted under the Marriage Act, or under Islamic law or a Customary law applicable in Nigeria, and includes any marriage recognised as valid under the Marriage Act.

86. These positions underlie the relationship of law and in particular the issues of family law with English jurisprudence and results in jurisdictional legal pluralism. Legal pluralism is very pronounced in family law in Nigeria and because of the activism of Nigeria in the Commonwealth, areas of conflict continue to emerge.[115] With legal pluralism also comes conflict of law issues. There is first the internal conflict of law and then international or external conflict of law issues.

§4. The Courts Administering Family and Succession Law

87. Family law follows the plural legal system in Nigeria. Thus, the administering Court depends on the classification of the marriage or personal law of the deceased in the case of Succession. Where the marriage is customary alone, then the relevant administering court with original jurisdiction is the customary court which may deal with issues regarding marriage and its dissolution. Succession with respect to customary laws is usually internal within families and if even brought before the regular court will be subjected to questions of validity from the areas. Appeals lie to the Customary Courts of Appeal. Where the marriage is statutory, then original jurisdiction lies with the State High Courts. Where the marriage is both customary and statutory there are different views as to the relevant Court to handle family issues. The better view is that the different marriages are treated differently. Some other view is that the parties should be considered to have abandoned the status of being married under customary law and yet others consider that marriage is a status and both marriages should be treated as conferring the status of being married on a couple who have conducted two separate marriages with one another.

88. Where the marriage is Islamic, then the primary courts are the Sharia Courts or Area Courts from which appeal lie to the Sharia Court of Appeal. Where the marriage is dual with both Islamic and statutory then the view with customs is applicable.

114. Cap E14, 2011 (not included in the complied Laws of the Federation, 2004).
115. *Agbaje v. Agbaje* [2010] UKSC 13; *see also* the Part III of Matrimonial Proceedings Act 1984.

89. All appeals on civil matters from either the customary Court of Appeal or the Sharia Court of Appeal by section 240 of the Constitution lie to the Federal Court of Appeal. The Section provides:

> Subject to the provisions of this Constitution, the Court of Appeal shall have jurisdiction to the exclusion of any other court of law in Nigeria, to hear and determine appeals from the Federal High Court, the High Court of the Federation Capital Territory, Abuja, High Court of a state, Sharia Court of Appeal of the Federal Capital Territory, Abuja, Sharia Court of Appeal of a state, Customary Court of Appeal of a state and from decisions of a court martial or other tribunals as may be prescribed by an Act of the National Assembly.

90. Succession has been said to be a subject matter belonging to the States. However, where the FCT is concerned, then succession matters will be subject to the Federal Administration of Estate Act. Under the present arrangement, the appropriate court will be the High Court of the FCT. Order 48 of the Court's Civil Procedure Rules provides for probate and administration while Order 49 provides non-contentious probate matters.[116] Rules 39 and 40 of Order 48 provide for the subject matters for foreigners who die in the FCT.[117]

§5. Customs

91. The Constitution and legislative framework of marriages allow for marriages under customary law and Islamic law but also allows the option to either celebrate marriages under the legislative framework alone or to superimpose the legislative one on either of the other two forms of marriages: customary or Islamic.

92. Prior to colonisation, many parts of Nigeria had only the customary legal regime and structure.[118] However, following the British colonisation of Nigeria, there are at least three broad legal frameworks in Nigeria, customary, Islamic, and legislative. This remains the case in many parts of Southern Nigeria, the Middle Belt, and some parts of the North East. The North West and North East and some parts of the South West had and still have the Islamic legal framework. Within the legal framework of customary law there is no homogeneity. The customs vary from place to place although the degree may be of higher or lesser degree between members of the same tribe who speak the same language. This is because of the formation, evolution and development of the country and the multiple cultural influences and expressions that have exacted on her.

---

116. High Court of the Federal Capital Territory, Abuja Civil Procedure Rules, 2004.
117. See further the judiciary and the list of superior courts of record in Nigeria, above, pp 21.
118. Great Britain means England and Wales. All laws from United Kingdom that were retained or being applied are those of England and Wales.

93. There are as many as 200 ethnic groups with varying languages and dialects, cultural extensions, or modifications in Nigeria. The laws, culture and customs that influence the present interaction on family, marriage and custom are dependent on tribal, geographical, historical-religious affiliation, colonial, migration and external influences. Section 21 of the Constitution, a fundamental and aspirational objective enjoins the state to protect, preserve and promote the Nigerian cultures which enhance human dignity and are consistent with the fundamental objectives and encourage development of technological and scientific studies which enhance cultural values.

94. The section notes and places emphasis on culture and not customs. Custom and culture are sometimes used interchangeably but this is not accurate usage. Culture is more complex than custom and includes but not limited to a people's historical and sociological evolution encompassing their knowledge, belief, art, morals, law, customs etc. It is often difficult to distinguish between Nigerian customary law and cultures. Both appear to be intertwined. A woman may not view some masquerades. This is the culture in relation to the outing of such masquerade and a woman viewing such a masquerade would be sanctioned. The sanction ranges from summary corporal punishment to sundry mystical, sometimes wholly superstitious 'occurrences' attributed to the 'offence'. This, in effect, invariably, transmutes a culture to custom and as such, a law: women and children must be indoors whenever a masquerade makes a performance.

95. Section 258 of the Evidence Act,[119] (EA), defines custom as a rule which, in a particular district, has, from long usage, obtained the force of law. Section 288 of the EA provides: Custom means a rule which, in a particular district has, from long usage obtained the force of law. By section 70, a list of specialised persons who can testify on the existence of custom is listed as: 'traditional rulers, chiefs or other persons having special knowledge of the customary law and custom'. Other references are any book or manuscript recognised as legal authority by people indigenous to the locality in which such laws or customs applies. Furthermore, section 73(2) provides that the expression, 'general custom or right' includes customs or rights common to any considerable class of persons.

96. There are other important provisions of the Evidence Act on customs starting from sections 16–19. Section 18(3) empowers the Court to declare as repugnant, customs which conflict with good conscience, equity, and natural justice – this is a principle recognised as the repugnancy doctrine in Nigerian jurisprudence. Section 19 provides for intensive enquiry and every fact is deemed to be relevant which tends to show how in particular instances a matter alleged to be a custom was understood and acted upon by persons then interested.

97. In *Godwin Ogolo & Ors. v. Joseph Ogolo & Ors*[120] the Supreme Court defined customary law:

---

119. 2011.
120. [2003] LPELR-2309 (SC); [2003] 18 NWLR (part 852) 494; [2003] 12 S.C (part I) 56.

> the organic or living law of the indigenous people of Nigeria regulating their lives and transactions. It is a mirror of the culture of the people. Under our law, customary law is a question of fact to be proved by evidence or judicial notice if it has been established as required by Sections 14(2) and 73 of the Evidence Act[121] ... Being a fact to be established by evidence, customary law must be specifically pleaded.[122]

98. In another Supreme Court decision, *Nwaigwe & Ors v. Okere & Anor,*[123] Niki Tobi JSC:

> And what is customary law? Customary law generally means relating to custom or usage of a given community. Customary law emerges from the traditional usage and practice of a people in a given community, which, by common adoption and acquiescence on their part, and by long and unvarying habit, has acquired, to some extent, element of compulsion, and force of law with reference to the community. And because of the element of compulsion which it has acquired over the years by constant, consistent and community usage, it attracts sanctions of different kinds and is enforceable. Putting it in a more simplistic form, the customs, rules, traditions, ethos arid cultures which govern the relationship of members of a community are generally regarded as customary law of the people.[124]

99. In *Lewis v. Bankole,*[125] Customary law was described as unwritten law recognised as law by the members of an ethnic group.[126]

100. The current Constitutional arrangement in Nigeria confers some powers on local governments to modify customs in written form. Customary law in Nigeria appears to have lost the internal elasticity that moderates law in the light of human experiences and changing circumstances submitting neither to social change nor written change. It lacks the internal mechanism for self-validity through transmutation of its existing expressions into renewed versions based on change and human evolution. Woefully, it also lacks a structured external mechanism for the same process of change since neither the national legislature nor the state legislature has the requisite structure to effect change. This leaves the regime at the mercy of the judiciary from whose prism the customs are assessed. In many cases, the composition

---

121. *Oyewunmi v. Ogunesan* [1990] 3 NWLR (part 137) 182, 207; *Taiwo v. Dosunmu* [1966] NMLR 67; *Otogbolu v. Okeluwa* [1981] 6–7 S.C. 99.
122. *Per* Edozie, J.S.C. at P. 16, paras A–C.
123. [2008] LPELR-2095(SC); [2008] 13 NWLR (part 1105) 445.
124. [2008] 13 NWLR (part 1105) 445, 481.
125. [1908] 1 NLR 81 at 100.
126. An exception to this is the publication by the Anambra State Ministry of Justice of a Manual of Customary Law for Use in Anambra and Imo states S.N. Chinwuba Obi, *Customary Law Manual: A Manual of Customary Laws Obtaining in Anambra and Imo States of Nigeria* (Government Printer 1977); This manual has no official legal status and is therefore not binding, however, it is meant to be persuasive authoritative, but displaceable by other evidence. *See also* Gaius Ezejiofor, *Sources of Nigerian Law*, in *Introduction to Nigerian Law* 42(C.O. Okonkwo ed., Sweet & Maxwell 1980).

and constitution of judges are from diverse customary, cultural and social background. In the end, the customs resist judicial pronouncements, even authority and its attempts of incursion into the status quo and *a fortiori*, change.

I. Customs and Application

101. The cultures in view were in many cases well engaged and ultimately conceived for the good of the society ranging from the need for primitive governance, war and defences, and security of citizens and their property. These basic needs produced and reinforced paternalism, patriarchy, and primogeniture. Autopsy was not in any way scientific but a traumatisation of a wife.[127] A woman as a wife must not succeed in or inherit landed property. She could only do so in trust and as a reward for bearing children and the descent is patrilineal. The circular motion for son preference and inheritance is the basis of the much-discussed, woman-to-woman marriages.[128] In *Muojekwu v. Ejikeme*,[129] expert evidence on the custom was given; 'I know the purpose of *Nrachi* ceremony in Nnewi. The ceremony is done to enable a daughter to conceive and birth children in her father's compound in order that the children if males will represent the father of the mother. Such children if males will inherit the mother's father's property.'[130]

102. Another witness stated:

> Nrachi ceremony is performed by a man who has no male child. He then chooses any of his daughters to stay in his family and produce children. He invites his extended family and presents one goat, eight kola nuts, and four gallons of palm wine to them and declares his intention to them. If the extended family accepts, then the goat is slaughtered and shared by the members. The daughter chosen can from then on start having issues for the father.[131]

---

127. Emmanuel Durojaye, *Woman, But Not Human: Widowhood Practices and Human Rights Violations in Nigeria*, 27(2) Int'l J. L. Pol'y & Fam. 176–196 (2013).
128. Jean Cadigan, *Woman-to-Woman Marriage: Practices and Benefits in Sub-Saharan Africa*, 29(1) J. Comp. Fam. Stud. 89 (1998). Jean gives a considerably full account of the nature, types and outcomes of the concept of woman-to-woman marriage in societies practising it, except for not identifying the principal motivating factors for the continuing practice of the custom in Nigeria where patriarchy and consequential son preference are the main propellers of the custom; Eunice Uzodike, *Nigeria: Defining the Ambit of Custom*, 29 Fam. L. 399, 401–402 (1990–1991); Clement Akpamgbo, *'Woman to Woman' Marriage and the Repugnancy Clause*, 14 Africa L. Stud. 87, 91 (1977); For an anthropological study of the subject see generally; I. Amadiume, *Male Daughters, Female Husbands: Gender and Sex in an African Society* (Zed Books 1998); *Re-inventing Africa: Matriarchy, Religion and Culture* (Zed Books 1998); for its practice in other parts of Africa, *see* Regine Oboler, *Is the Female Husband a Man? Woman/Woman Marriage Among the Nandi of Kenya*, 19(1) Ethnology 69–88 (1980); Beth Greene, *The Institution of Woman-Marriage in Africa: A Cross Cultural Analysis*, 37(4) Ethnology 395–412 (1998). Nwudego Chinwuba, *Daughter/Widow Retention in Nigeria: Survey and Analysis from Case Law*, 2(1) J. Comp. L. Africa 82–99 (2016).
129. [2000] 5 NWLR (part 657) 404,429.
130. *Ibid.*
131. *Okonkwo v. Okagbue* [1994] 9 NWLR (part 368) 301, 324.

103. Fabiyi, JCA who delivered the lead judgment noted: 'so with *Nrachi* ceremony performed on a daughter, she takes the position of a man in her father's house. Technically she becomes a 'man'. She must stay unmarried for the rest of her life to produce male children for her father'.[132]

104. In his judgment Niki Tobi, JCA stated: 'Let me now apply the provision of section 18(1) to the *Nrachi* ceremony of Nnewi. It is clear from the evidence of the witnesses that by the ceremony, a girl cannot marry. She stays in the father's house and performs only one natural function of a woman, and it is the function of procreation. Even here, the whole essence of the procreation, in the content or context of the *Nrachi* ceremony is to produce a male child; not a female child.'[133]

105. In the event which does happen, it may take several generations of performing the ceremonies for a woman in the lineage if, at all, to produce a male heir.[134]

106. Nigerian superior courts of record have consistently dismissed the custom as redolent of a different age even if as in one of the cases, *Okonkwo v. Okagbue*,[135] the Court noted, that the custom remains well, hale and hearty despite the pronouncements of the Courts.[136] It must be noted that the Violence against Persons (Prohibition) Act, 2015 defines, prohibits and penalises certain harmful traditional practices which are customs by sections 20 and 46. Section 46 defines harmful traditional practices to mean 'all behaviour, attitudes or practices which negatively affect the fundamental rights of women, girls, or any person and includes harmful widowhood practices, denial of inheritance or succession rights, female circumcision, mutilation or female circumcision, forced marriage and forced isolation from family and friends'.

II. Customs and Family Relations

107. Nigeria is a multi-cultural, ethnic, and religious country. It has a traditional and conservative outlook. When patriarchy and paternalism trump as they do in Nigeria, they not only affect family, politics, and economic indices but also, education, therefore, determining the pace of the law. Few, if any custom-as-law regimes conceptualise equality as a value.[137]

132. [2000] 5 NWLR (part 657) 404,422.
133. *Ibid.*, 404,431.
134. *Okonkwo v. Okagbue* [1994] 9 NWLR (part 368) 301.
135. [1994] 9 NWLR (part 368) 301, 324.
136. Other cases in this line of authority are: *Muojekwu v. Ejikeme* [2000] 5 NWLR 403; *Meribe v. Egwu* [1976] 3 S.C. 23; *Mojekwu v. Iwuchukwu* [2004] 11 NWLR (part 883) 196.
137. Ayodele Atsenuwa, *Can Two Walk Together, Except They Be Agreed?' Interrogating the Co-existence of Customary and Human Rights Law in Nigeria*, Being paper presented for the University of Lagos Law Faculty Seminar Series of Friday, 08/03/2013); Sope Williams, *Nigeria, Its Women and International Law: Beyond Rhetoric*, 4(2) Hum. Rts. L. Rev. 229 (2004).

108. In the foreword to the first edition of a text in family law in Nigeria, the then Chief Justice of Nigeria, T. O. Elias, noted that 'the extended family is a necessary compliment to the author's interesting study of a dynamic society such as ours which, despite its desire for economic and industrial change, is irrevocably committed at once to the ideal of remaining itself, and to the achievement of a measure of unity in diversity'.[138]

109. The author of the text, Nwogugu noted elsewhere:

> In any discussion of reform of family law, the question of the cultural background of the country will invariably arise. Nigeria has been a conservative society, clinging as much as possible to the past ... While it will be inappropriate, at this point, to argue that our values have been Europeanised, the truth remains that Nigeria is no longer an Island shorn of foreign influence. Consequently, conduct which in times past were regarded as unacceptable or even a taboo have today become the norm. Being part of the global village, Nigerians will increasingly seek to examine solutions to family problems adopted in other countries within and outside Africa. We can no longer be content to remain isolated in an era of increasing interrelation between Nigeria and the world.[139]

110. Majority of those who come under customary law also have their affairs governed by Christian precepts and way of life. The same is true of adherents of the Islamic faith, who may mix up this faith with either secularism, Christianity, or some customary precepts. Thus, most marriages in the areas where Christianity is prevalent will be a three-tier affair, comprised of customary, statutory, and Christian – usually in this order. That is, a customary marriage is first celebrated, followed by a statutory marriage in accordance with the Marriage Act and then a church worship and Banquet.[140] Nigerian law does not recognise marriage conducted in a place of worship unless the place of worship is recognised and licensed to celebrate marriages. Such license is issued by the Minister of Interior.[141]

111. In this light one can see the attachment to marriage but without the will to place it on the burner of modernity and changed and changing social circumstances. In any family structure, it becomes germane to revisit the context of formation, dissolution, and incidents thereof. For, after all, the law's interest in these relationships

---

138. E.I. Nwogugu, *Family Law in Nigeria* Xvi (Heinemann 1990); *See also* J.E. Omotola, *Primogeniture and Illegitimacy in African Customary Law: The Battle for Survival of Culture*, 15(1) Indiana Int'l & Comp. L, Rev. 115 (2004).
139. E.I. Nwogugu, '*What Next in Nigerian Family Law?*, [2006] 7 NIALS Founders' Day Lecture (Nigerian Institute of Advanced Legal Studies 2006) 7. This reiterates the concerns the Convention on Celebration and recognition of the Validity of Marriages 1978 addresses in what is described as 'an age of exponential growth of mobility.'
140. Marriage Act, Cap M6, Laws of the Federation, 2004.
141. Section 6 Marriage Act, Cap M6, Laws of the Federation, 2004.

must be well founded. What then is the relevance of law to nullity and its surrounding circumstances if the parties are free agents particularly in the light of fundamental human rights provisions? If there is a contract, then there is one. If there is none, then the parties remain free agents. How does the theme of voidable relate to notions of fundamental human rights and their regimes of privacy? In addition, how does the theme of restitution of conjugal rights relate with battery, domestic violence, and again fundamental human rights regime of liberty and freedom of association. Again, within the framework of marriage and family, how do children's rights play out if marriage is viewed from the prism of conjugal rights and procreation? If a child has inherent right to dignity and wellness once born should children be born at all cost or based on mutual love of parents and commitment to love them? Should spouses who are concerned with climate change and population be obliged to have children and if so, should the State regulate the number within its power to interrogate and regulate family relations?

112. Customs have robust rules relating to parenting, parenthood, and parental responsibilities according to the customs of the geographical groups in Nigeria. For instance, with respect to guardianships and fostering, the South West of Nigeria has structures for ensuring that children are socially cared for. This maybe attributable to the legendary monarchical governmental structure popular with this ethnic group. With the South East of Nigeria, where a robust republicanism has always been the case, what obtains is different in that self-actualisation is the underlying feature of parenthood, parenting and responsibility.

113. The status quo is thus difficult to change. In these circumstances where other areas of socio-economic interaction are difficult to change one can only imagine the case with family, its formation, constitution, dissolution, and definition. The result of these intrigues may preclude certain classes particularly less literate and rural women, as many are excluded as an aggrieved class and caught up on the negative side of developmental aspirations.

114. While the judiciary has been playing a significant role in advancing the interests of women in this class, a holistic legislative approach is to be preferred. A conscious approach must be embraced to bring about harmonisation and sustenance of the customary regime itself otherwise there is no doubt that it would wither altogether as time courses along.

III. Customs as Law

115. Customs once again play a very crucial role and needs to be kept in mind on any discussion on family and succession. Many customs have since transmuted into laws. Transformed to law, they are rigid keeping it on a continuing collision path with modernity and change. There is no single coherent or systematically developed body of jurisprudence that covers precisely what is or is not African customary law. Instead, one must examine evidence of a claimant's adherence to reasonably well-established norms of African culture and African traditions as the basis of considering whether there is evidence of African customary law.[142]

116. Thus, the party relying on the existence of any law under custom must prove it.[143] This is done usually by drawing on the knowledge of the custodians of customs from the villages such as village chiefs. There is an omnibus repugnancy clause by which a court, even when a custom is proved, may decline its application by invoking the repugnancy doctrine. This doctrine simply states that a custom that is repugnant to natural justice, equity and good conscience is unlawful.[144] Customs usually unwritten are sometimes restated. At least one such restatement exists for Anambra State.[145]

117. A custom may be judicially noticed when it has been adjudicated upon once by a superior court of record.[146] Where a custom cannot be established as one judicially noticed, it shall be proved as a fact and in any judicial proceeding where any custom is relied upon, it shall not be enforced as law if it is contrary to public policy, or is not in accordance with natural justice, equity and good conscience.[147] Section 19 is also very relevant as it provides that every fact is deemed to be relevant which tends to show how in particular instances a matter alleged to be a custom was understood and acted upon by persons then interested. In addition the expression 'general custom' or 'right' includes customs or rights common to any considerable class of persons.[148] Mwenda et al wrote of Zambia, a position reasonably applicable to most customs as law regime: 'while most common law jurisdictions in Africa have laws

142. Kenneth Mwenda, Florence Mumba & Judith Mvula-Mwenda, *Property-Grabbing under African Customary Law: Repugnant to Natural Justice, Equity, and Good Conscience, Yet a Troubling Reality*, 37 Geo Wash. Intl. Rev. 949, 950 (2005).
143. Section 16(1) of the Evidence Act, 2011.
144. It is also enacted as s. 18(3) Evidence Act, Cap E14, 2011.
145. S.N.C. Obi & C.D.C. Anyaegbunam, *The Customary Law Manual: A Manual of Customary Laws Obtaining in the Anambra and Imo States of Nigeria* (Government of Anambra State 1977).
146. Section 17 Evidence Act, cap. E14, 2011.
147. Section 18(1) and (3). See also statutes of general application – s. 19 of the Supreme Court Ordinance which was adopted by many other frameworks and is still applicable to customs states: Nothing in this ordinance shall deprive the Supreme Court of the right to observe and enforce the observance, or shall deprive any person of the benefit of any law or custom existing in the said colony and territories subject to its jurisdiction, such law or custom not being repugnant to natural justice, equity and good conscience, nor incompatible either directly or by necessary implication with any enactment of the Colonial Legislature, No. 4 of 1876. *See also* s. 14 of the Supreme Court Ordinance 1914 states that the Common law, the doctrine of equity, and the statute of general application which were in force in England at the date when the colony obtained a local legislature, that is to say, on 24 Jul. 1874, shall be in force within the jurisdiction of the court.
148. Section 73(2) *See also* ss 73(1) and 18(2).

to address the actions of individuals who embark on questionable customary practices that conflict with the country's legislative framework, the enforcement of such legislation is often weak due to various cultural, political, sociological, and economic factors'.[149]

118. The Constitution pays profoundly serious attention to customs. It provides for Customary Courts of Appeal for each State of the Federation and the FCT. By section 245:

> (1) An appeal shall lie from decisions of a customary Court of Appeal to the Court of Appeal as of right in any civil proceedings before the customary Court of Appeal with respect to any question of Customary law and such other matters as may be prescribed by an Act of the National Assembly.
> (2) Any right of appeal to the Court of Appeal from the decisions of a Customary Court of Appeal conferred by this section shall be:
> (a) exercisable at the instance of a party thereto or, with the leave of the Customary Court of Appeal or of the Court of Appeal, at the instance of any other person having an interest in the matter;
> (b) exercised in accordance with any Act of the National Assembly and rules of court for the time being in force regulating the powers, practice, and procedure of the Court of Appeal.

119. Significantly, by section 288(1) of the Constitution, it is provided that the President shall have regard to the need in respect of appointments to the offices of Justices of the Supreme Court and Justices of the Court of Appeal, to ensure that there are among the holders of such offices persons learned in Islamic personal law and persons learned in Customary law.

IV. The Toggle of Law and Customs

120. So many Nigerians admire and are proud of customs. One such customary notion is the relationship between science and custom in the perception of human, gorillas and chimpanzees, by which some customary norms perceive gorillas and chimpanzees as 'unfortunate human beings' choosing to remain in the wild, while science has gained a perspective that the duo of gorillas and chimpanzees are the closest to human species. Thus, the merits of customs are legendary.

121. However, custom, as the framework of norms and societal contracts over time, requires re-examination in the light of the nature of the human society and its propensity for change, adaptation, and growth. Absent, a continuing means of internal and external validity, the reduction of society into a state of nature is a certainty as those members of society who outgrow the customs and way of doing things will be unable to cope and would be forced out of the society overtime, leaving it to a

---

149. Kenneth Mwenda, Florence Mumba & Judith Mvula-Mwenda, *Property-Grabbing under African Customary Law: Repugnant to Natural Justice, Equity, and Good Conscience, yet a troubling Reality*, 37 Geo Wash. Intl. Rev. 949, 966 (2005).

base nature. The repugnancy doctrine has achieved minimal success in engaging customs, so has education also impacted minimally.

122. In *Okagbue v. Okonkwo*,[150] the Supreme Court took up one custom – the custom that a widow may continue to have children for and in the name of her deceased husband. The court stated that the custom was repugnant to natural justice, good conscience, and equity because it exposed womanhood to ridicule and promoted promiscuity. The custom has variants, and an examination shows that it served a purpose but in the light of modern understanding of marriage and medical advancement in reproductive health and rights is redolent of different age. In addition, the customs may not bear closer scrutiny under the modern rules of marriage, affinity, and consanguinity.

123. Nigeria has many tribes and a study of the socio-political evolution of the country will demonstrate a deep attachment to customs. That the people's law lies in their general consciousness is expressed by its expressions in the Nigerian experience. The received law and the people's law have been in constant toggle, with both resisting the other. This has ensured that tribal allegiance takes an upper stage in the affairs of the nation. This has most profound expression in personal lives where national legislation has ridiculously hard task taking root in the lives of the people. It is however evident that the customs must be tweaked, and from time to time, to bring it conformity with modernity and the ideal of human evolution in libertarian expressions.

124. Colonial heritage has had a dual impact on Nigeria. This implicates a toggle of civilisations. The ancient customs of the indigenous people of Nigeria are strong in content and logic. Their sustenance and continuing development require tweaking. First, because the customs are based on oral traditions and practices, their organising spirit is sometimes lost resulting in sheer rigidity. This rigidity is also a reflex from resistance to interference. It is thus intuitive and sometimes expressed fear of the Western culture and way of life subsuming the local customs and culture. An example is the bride price.[151] The practice of which remains but no one knows the true nature of the practice. An evaluation of the practice gives the impression that it represents an ancient sale transaction, particularly within a culture that has experiences in child marriage and slavery. However, viewed from a different lens, one may see a different image of a hold on the marriage that keeps track of the progression of the relationship. A libertarian relationship between customs and received law will allow for an evaluation of the custom in the prism of modernity to adapt it to modern thoughts but as *Mifumi (U) Ltd. & Others v. ATT. Gen. & Kenneth Kakuru*[152] demonstrates this is unlikely to be the case. The connectedness between

150. [1994] 9 NWLR (part 368) 301, 324.
151. See the research questions and responses from an administered questionnaire on the subject listed as appendices.
152. [2015] UGSC 13 (15 Aug. 2015); CONSTITUTIONAL PETITION NO. 12 OF 2007. *See also* J.D. Mujuzi, *Bride Wealth (Price) and Women's Marriage-Related Rights in Uganda: A Historical Constitutional Perspective and Current Developments*, 24(3) Int'l J. L. Pol'y & Fam. 414–430, 414 (2010).

dependent, independent post-independent and contemporary colonial legal heritage and customs thus create both local and international conflict. Another good example of this toggle is the operation and application of section 18 of the Wills Act, 1837 within the context of the Nigerian Interpretation Act on pre-1900 Laws of England. An attempt to resolve this conflict resulted in section 11 of the Lagos Wills Law.[153] Yet, this is no easy solution as this was possible for Lagos State to do because the matter fell into the residuary regime of State legislative competence.[154] This tension is unyielding regarding intestate succession and questions regarding celebration of marriages, particularly monogamous marriages.

125. Some may say that this tension is gender based and induced. However, some of the customs have characteristics of inherent rights for women particularly, women as daughters. Thus, customs of the South East of Nigeria demonstrate parallel governments of patriarchy and matriarchy expressed in well informed and advanced structured system.[155] It is typically with respect to women as wives and succession patterns that the conflict between customs and Western models is amplified. Thus, while women adopt the Western monogamy, the men oblige until questions of succession arise. The cases of *Salubi v. Nwariaku*[156] and *Ukeje v. Ukeje*[157] are clear epitomes of the latter position. Other cases that demonstrate internal conflicts in cases of succession include, *Idehen v. Idehen*[158] *Oke v. Oke*;[159] *Ajibaye v. Ajibaye.*[160] It is to be noted that gender discrimination and disinheritance of females as wives or daughters obtains differently in the South Western states of Nigeria from other States of the country. In the South West, daughters are entitled to an equal share of a deceased father's estate. Indeed, a first daughter has a prior right of choice to a brother where the father dies intestate but not wives.[161] In the rest of the country, customarily, the limitation is total, and females cannot inherit property whether as wives or daughter neither can they purchase landed property.

---

153. See the amendment to the 1837 provision by the Law of Property Act, 1925, Cap 20, s. 177(1) A will expressed to be made in contemplation of a marriage shall, notwithstanding anything in section eighteen of the Wills Act, 1837, or any other statutory provision or rule of law to the contrary, not be revoked by the solemnisation of the marriage contemplated and (2) This section only applies to wills made after the commencement of this Act. The section is now repealed by Administration of Justice Act, 1982 (c. 53, SIF 122:3), s. 75(1), Sch. 9 Pt. I available at: https://www.legislation.gov.uk/id/ukpga/1982/53.
154. By residuary competence is meant the engagement of s. 4(7) of the Constitution on the Legislative competence of the State.
155. Nwudego Chinwuba, *Daughter/Widow Retention in Nigeria: Survey and Analysis from Case Law*, 2(1) J. Comp. L. in Africa 82–99 (2016); Jean Cadigan, *Woman-to-Woman Marriage: Practices and Benefits in Sub-Saharan Africa*, 29(1) J. Comp. Fam. Stud. 89 (1998).
156. [2003] 7 NWLR (part 819) 426.
157. [2014] 11 NWLR (part 1418) 384; (2014) LPELR – 22724 (SC) Electronic Law Reports.
158. [1991] 6 NWLR (part 198) 416.
159. [1974] 3 SC 1.
160. [2007] All FWLR (part 359) 1321.
161. *Salami v. Salami* [1957] Western Region of Nigeria Law Report 10; *Sule v. Ajisegiri* [1937] 13 NLR 146; *Ricardo v. Abai* [1926] 7 NLR 58.

V. Primogeniture and Patriarchy

126. Primogeniture and Patriarchy are twin concepts which hold sway in Nigerian family and succession law. In *Oduche v. Oduche*[162] the Court of Appeal pronounced that Nigeria is a patrilineal society.

127. Patriarchy is a system or its variant whereby the father or eldest male is head of the family and descent is reckoned through the male line or a system of society or government in which men hold the power and women are largely excluded from it. Primogeniture is also an offshoot of patriarchy and is the right of succession belonging to the firstborn son, especially the rule by which the whole real estate of an intestate passes to the eldest son or sons and such variants of the practice. Institutionalised patriarchy and primogeniture, while having some positive native data registry, are retrograde in foisting son preference with its deleterious impact on women and children well-being, quite aside from its propensity in fuelling inefficient land use and institutionalising family ostracism and persecution.

128. Patriarchy is still a way of life in Northern as well as Southern Nigeria. Primogeniture, monogamy, and patriarchy, however, find rigid expressions in family and private property. This is because monogamy envisages equality and 'one at a time intimacy' and therefore, succession to private property is always closed. Patriarchy on the other hand being authoritarian in nature cannot be sustained in a monogamous culture. Patriarchy's main attribute is inequality of the sexes, male superiority, and the subjugation of women.[163] Patriarchy would find better expressions in cultures that practice polygyny.

129. In many parts of Europe and North America, 'family laws were historically patriarchal … . Liberalisation came only in the last third of the twentieth century'.[164] Thus, it was logical as Baroness Hale notes in *Ghaidan v. Godin-Mendoza* that 'a woman might automatically be paid three quarters of what a man was paid for doing exactly the same job'.[165]

130. Marriage in some other jurisdictions such as United Kingdom, has, at least in theory, developed from legally condoned patriarchy to a 'partnership of equals'.[166]

---

162. [2005] LPELR-5976.
163. M. Htun & Weldon S., *State Power, Religion, and Women's Rights: A Comparative Analysis of Family Law*, 18(1) Indiana J. Global Legal Stud. 145 (2011); Emmanuel Durojaye, *Woman, But Not Human: Widowhood Practices and Human Rights Violations in Nigeria*, 27(2) Int'l J. L. Pol'y & Fam. 176–196 (2013).
164. Htun & Weldon, *ibid.*, at 145,146; S. Harris-Short & Miles J., Family Law 58 (Oxford University Press 2nd ed. 2011).
165. [2004] 2 AC 557, 604.
166. Sonia Harris-Short & Miles Joanna, Family Law 58 (Oxford University Press 2nd ed. 2011).

131. One research finding on patriarchy found that Nigeria along with Israel and a few other countries have legal frameworks that perpetuate patriarchy.[167] According to this study 'these restrictions are: "consequential for more than women's autonomy and dignity, as they have broader implications. Societies that subordinate women are more likely to be authoritarian, and their populations poor, uneducated, unhealthy, and demographically imbalanced, with high rates of population growth"'.[168] This is an economically sound reasoning as primogeniture and patriarchal institutions inhibit alienation of land and its use – key attributes of economic development.[169]

132. The twin concepts of patriarchy and primogeniture, in addition to paternalism, may not be without their advantages. In societies with less than developed social welfare scheme or vital data statistics register, the concepts may provide the only viable option in modern calculus on the subjects, aiding in identity tracing and security. Some important literature considers the practices as an aspect of culture which must be preserved.[170] The law in Nigeria as the section on succession, which is examined below indicates, preserves primogeniture.

133. The Supreme Court in *Oduche v. Oduche* reaffirmed that Nigeria is a patrilineal society. This reaffirmation is important and buttresses the fact of the society being patriarchal as well.

134. Family is particularly important in Nigeria and so, the ancestry. Ancestry is prized and is traced through primogeniture and its ancillary, paternalism. Family is especially important in Nigeria and in the present times is reliant on primogeniture and patriarchy for sustainability. However, a well-ordered civil data registration system may be a viable alternative to the positive aspects of primogeniture, particularly if it is accepted that democracy is a veritable modern system of governance that advances the realisation of the potentials of the human being in the human family. The deleterious impact of primogeniture and patriarchy on developmental indices and society, however, far outweighs any perceived advantages.

135. The underlying driver of patriarchy, primogeniture and paternalism is an exaggerated sense of entitlement. This is expressed in their arrogation of authority by fiat, rather than merit to one segment of society, thereby, driving uncompromising inequality and tension in society. Modern society thrives in equality as a means of driving the most important and potent attributes of the human race – reason and liberty, that is, liberty based on reason. Reason assures society of the capacity of

---

167. M. Htun & Weldon S., *State Power, Religion, and Women's Rights: A Comparative Analysis of Family Law*, 18(1) Indiana J. Global Legal Stud. 145,158 (2011).
168. Htun & Weldon, *ibid.*, at 146.
169. Susan Rose-Ackerman, *Inalienability and the Theory of Property Rights*, 85 Columb. L. Rev. 931 (1985); R.A. Epstein, *Why Restrain Alienation*, 85 Columb. L. Rev. 970 (1985); Andreas Wacke, *Freedom of Contract and Restraint of Trade Clauses in Roman and Modern Law*, 11 Law & Hist. Rev. 1 (1993).
170. J.E. Omotola, *Primogeniture and Illegitimacy in African Customary Law: The Battle for Survival of Culture*, 15(1) Indiana Int'l & Comp. L. Rev. 115 (2004).

constituent members to embrace analytical reasoning and dialogue in conflict resolution. Reason aims at improving the human condition in a viable, sustainable manner. It is from this framework that a workable democracy emerges. Democracy is a replacement for patriarchy, as it viably and sustainably operates in institutionalised power distribution unlike patriarchy. A pure democracy may still drive patriarchy, but it would be in an informed free choice and *a fortiori*, sustainable framework.

136. Patriarchy and primogeniture limit development despite their apparent positive perspective of assuring undocumented lineage registry. The twin practice facilitates family ostracism, witch-hunting, and sundry easy forms of persecution, which in modern times, forestall global efforts at promoting self-actualisation, fundamental human rights and harnessing of the individual's potential for human capacity building and constructive contribution to society. In economic relations primogeniture and patriarchy forestall alienation of land, because of customs of burial of the remains of patriarchs in the patriarchal homes and last place of residence. Burial of human remains in the light of scientific evidence in an environment where many families are constituent private governments regarding provision of water and sanitary waste disposal leaves a lot to be desired in terms of not just health, but also aesthetics. Patriarchy and primogeniture also inhibit commodification of housing making it difficult to achieve efficiency in land use and housing for all. Patriarchy and primogeniture therefore, in modern human settings, have continuing deleterious impact on the overall developmental indices of a people. Policies aimed at stemming their impact and disadvantages are therefore important.

Part I. Persons

Chapter 1. The Status of a Person

§1. Definition of a Person

137. It is important to examine the different usages of the word 'person'. Its usage in ordinary language and other connotations do not always connote or convey the same meaning. In ordinary language, the words 'person' and 'human being' are used interchangeably. The question then is if they do connote or convey the same meaning, why are there different words for them?

138. In ordinary use, a 'person', an 'individual' are synonyms for a human being. Further specificities may arise as to: child, woman, female, male, man, sound, unsound,[171] 'lunar affected' or 'not lunar affected' or 'not so lunar affected'.[172] These are, just as, 'person' and 'individual', all descriptions of the human being. It is however of note that while 'person' or 'individual' more aptly refers to a state of capacity to act, the other descriptions qualify the state of being of the human person. This dichotomy does not occur in only English language. In Igbo language of the South East of Nigeria, for instance, quite aside from the distinction that exists in capacity and human hood, there are classifications of humans in accordance with the attributes of the person. There are also, in fact, classifications of animals in accordance with their attributes. Some human beings are described as being lower animals[173] while some animals are described as unfortunate human beings.[174] These descriptions of the human being are to be compared with that of the human of whom Rousseau wrote: 'savage man, destitute of every species of knowledge, experiences no passion but those of this last kind; his desires never extend beyond his physical wants, he knows no goods but food, a female, and rest; he fears no evil but pain, and hunger'.[175]

171. A.H. Westbrook, *Mental Health Legislation and Involuntary Commitment in Nigeria: A Call for Reform*, 10(2) Wash. U. Global Stud. 396–418 (2011); P.U. Ude, *Policy Analysis on Nigerian Lunacy Act (1958): The Need for a New Legislation*, 19(1) J. Psychiatry 1–6 (2015).
172. Daniel Nasaw, *How Offensive Is the Word 'lunatic'?* (BBC News Magazine) available at https://www.bbc.com/news/magazine-17997413 9.05.2012 (last accessed 29 Aug. 2020).
173. *Anumanu; onye futaluwa anumanu.*
174. *Ndu uwa gbulu.*
175. J.J. Rousseau, *Discourse on the Origin of Inequality* 11(Dover Publications, INC., 2004).

139. It is the duty of the State to create and sustain the enabling environment for individuals to develop fully. It is also the duty of the State to avoid environments of exclusions that reduce or inhibit the ability of human beings transmuting to the potentials that enable full participation in society. For, it is in the attainment and provision of the enabling environment for attainment of these attributes of being human, that the question, who is a person, becomes so much more compelling. Thus, the question translates to: is every human being a person and if so, as a human being is everyone entitled to participation in all the functions and potential attributes of a modern society? While every human being is entitled to inalienable rights, does every human being have the right to defend same and to what extent can every human being participate in a democratic society? The answers to these questions lie in the interplay of right and power in relation to others. Contemporary usage demands an examination of the nature and content of the person. Rawls emphasised a normative conception of the person as free and equal with the enablement to participate in the order of society:

> it is given by our moral and political thought and practice, and is studied by moral and political philosophy and by the philosophy of law. Since ancient Greece, both in philosophy and in law, the concept of the person has been that of someone who can take part in, or play a role in, social life, and hence who can exercise and respect its various rights and duties. In specifying the central organising idea of society as a fair system of cooperation, we use the companion idea of free and equal persons as those who can play the role of fully cooperating members. As suits a political conception of justice that views society as a fair system of cooperation, a citizen is someone who can be a free and equal participant over a complete life.[176]

140. Being a person implicates a democratic structure driven by the autonomy of the individual which aggregates into a system of governance. In Nigeria, 'person' is used interchangeably in all legislation and enactments including the Constitution and particularly in family and succession. Provisions on fundamental human rights are all recognised, conferred, and hinged on the 'person' although there is no definition of 'person' in the Constitution. In addition, there also appears to be no case law touching on the specific subject.[177] This appears indicative of the recognition of the idea that every human being is a person. Thus, in *Hassan v. EFCC*,[178] the Court of Appeal held that 'Fundamental rights have been defined as basic moral guarantees that people in all countries and culture allegedly have simply because

176. John Rawls, *Justice as Fairness – A Restatement* 24 (Erin Kelly ed., Belknap Press of Harvard University Press 2003) 24.
177. The Court addressed the question of lifting the veil and concluded that this could be done in the interest of social justice *International Offshore Construction Ltd. v. Shoreline Lifeboats Nigeria Ltd.* [2003] 16 NWLR (part 845) 157 CA.
178. [2013] LPELR-22595 (CA).

they are people … the human person possesses rights because of the very fact that it is a person, a whole, master of itself and of his acts … .'[179]

141. However, despite this tilt, the content and context of the law indicate that there is a dichotomy between person, personhood, and human hood. Thus, the Criminal Code provides a guidance on who a person is under Nigerian legal framework. Section 309 of the Criminal Code Act (a federal law) provides: a child becomes a person capable of being killed when it has completely proceeded in a living state from the body of its mother, whether it has breathed or not, and whether it has an independent circulation or not, and whether the navel-string is severed or not. This provision is replicated in section 307 of the Lagos Code. This provision indicates that human life commences at birth as provided in these sections.

142. A different position would appear from other provisions to be discussed below.

143. The question thus turns on who a person within Nigerian legal framework is and more broadly as universally understood. This question itself will turn on the objective of the law. Law focuses on a framework and structure. Framework addresses identification of the objects of the law while structure will address the subject matter of the law. In general, law strives at uniformity and this is not only just but is sensible as application and enforcement become easier. To this end, the objects of law are identified by the objective of the law. Thus, for general purposes of citizenship, the Constitution identifies its objects as persons, who are human beings. Not surprisingly, the Nigerian Constitution refers to persons and they are conferred with rights, duties, and obligations. This position would then appear to disadvantage the right to life adherents, but a look at the Criminal law framework demonstrates that this is far from the position.[180] This is because sections 228, 229, and 230 all replicated in the Lagos law prohibit abortion or an attempt to procure or facilitate abortion. There are also laws on criminal responsibility which turn on capacity, on childhood and mental handicap or inefficiency.[181] While the laws on the latter turn on personhood, the laws on anti-abortion raise the question whether they conflict with section 309 discussed above or protect the mother who a person is already. An overall view of the tenor of the law on crimes and family demonstrate that the law protects foetal rights. Thus, it can be concluded that Nigerian legal framework contemplates personhood from conception. That this is the position has no better evidence than section 17 of the Child's Rights Act. A child may bring an

179. Noted in *Megawatts Nigeria Limited v. The Registered Trustees of Gbagada Phase 2 Residents' Association & 3 Ors.*– Suit No: FHC/L/CS/982/2020 judgement delivered Friday, 25 Sep. 2020 at p. 10.
180. On this the discussion will be limited to the States in Nigeria which are not governed by Sharia law and/or the Penal Code. The discussion centres on the States that are governed by the Criminal Code. Crimes are under the Concurrent legislative competence of the States and the Federation. The Federation has the Criminal Code Act, Caps 77 and 38, Laws of the Federation, 1990 or 2004 respectively. Some States have enacted own Criminal Code such as Lagos, which has Criminal Code Law, Cap 17, Laws of Lagos State.
181. *See* s. 187 of the Companies and Allied Matters Act, 2020.

action for damages against a person for harm or injury caused to the child wilfully, recklessly, negligently or through neglect before, during or after the birth of that child (presumably through a next friend). Furthermore, where the father or mother of an unborn child dies intestate, the unborn child is entitled, if he was conceived during the lifetime of his father, to be considered in the distribution of the estate of the deceased father or mother.

144. Since Nigeria is a pluralistic society with plural legal systems, one must also ask what the tenor of these questions is under customary and Islamic law. Under customary law, while it appears that the understanding is that all human beings are persons, the operation of the customary law also leads to questions of first, what are the attributes to determine whether a person is a human being? In the light of this question and various actions of customs, including the place of women, caste system, human sacrifices it would be accurate to state that customary law distinguishes between human beings and persons. Capacity is very evident under customary law. The objection to customary law's perception of personhood is that it is based on the Hobbesian concept of the natural man where might is right and capacity is related back to survival. Hobbes for instance wrote:

> But for such as have strong bodies, the case is otherwise: they are to be forced to work; and to avoid the excuse of not finding employment, there ought to be such lawes, as may encourage all manner of arts; as Navigation, Agriculture, Fishing, and all manner of Manifacture that requires labour. The multitude of poor, and yet strong people still encreasing, they are to be transplanted into Countries not sufficiently inhabited: where nevertheless, they are not to exterminate those they find there; but constrain them to inhabit closer together, and not range a great deal of ground, to snatch what they find; but to court each little Plot with art and labour, to give them their sustenance in due season. And when all the world is overcharged with Inhabitants, then the last remedy of all is Warre; which provided for every man, by victory or death.[182]

145. It is to be noted that the Sharia law is an intrinsic aspect of the Constitution for the purposes of determination of personal rights between parties. However, some States of Northern Nigeria have extended Sharia law to criminal and other matters between Muslims. Section 232 of the Penal Code for Northern Nigeria provides that abortion can only be carried out for the safety of the life of the mother. However, sections 233–236 are in like terms as the Criminal Code Act and protects the foetus as well as the fully developed child at all stages of pregnancy and birth.[183] Ultimately the legal classification of person and personhood for all purposes is somewhat misleading. The meaning of person and personhood needs continual assessment as a state realisable from different angles and times, according to human

182. T. Hobbes, *Leviathan* Ch. XXIV 387 (Penguin Books 1985).
183. Penal Code (Northern States) Federal Provisions Act, Cap 345, Laws of the Federation, 1990; Cap P3, Laws of the Federation 2004.

experiences and changing circumstances. The appropriate minimum age for marriage in the twentieth century may not be appropriate for the humans of the twenty-first century. The physiology of humans may remain almost constant, but not so, the emotional and psychological states. Thus, while some thoughts would be satisfied with the impact of physical and psychological conditions as a measure of person and personhood, outward actions may in fact be a better determinant of the measure of capacity for marriage and other social interactions. The age, for instance, and qualification for political involvement including the capacity to vote may be better determined by factual human political experiences. Most cultures in Nigeria, for instance, recognise the ownership of property or the building of a house as an effective measure of emergence of personhood. Not surprisingly, some systems of governance find this robust definition of the emergence of personhood in the equilibrium of electoral colleges, and yet others find it in headship that springs from parliamentarianism.

146. A further reflection on personhood makes it clear that the business of the law with capacity is germane and legal engagement with the term must be taken more seriously. Take the definition of a child which can be minimally described as bemusing as a child remains the child of someone even at the age of 100 years, and unless the parent has departed, a parent would refer to a person of 100 years old as 'my child' and correctly so. To further compound the situation, a parent would always treat the person of 100 years as a child. It is, therefore, not quite clear why in English language and perhaps, in other languages, there is a race to define 'child' rather than personhood.

147. A general measure of person and personhood using age as the measure of capacity for marriage may be fallacious making it a counsel of prudence to leave windows for such eventuality.

I. Etymology and 'Person'

148. Etymologically, the word 'person' is said to be drawn from the word 'personare' which means mask. [184] In this sense it is said that the person is understood as the mask covering the face of an actor who recites verses of a scene in a play. People came to use 'person' to refer to the masked actor.[185]

149. In law, the term 'person' is contextual and content specific. Mchugh states:

> The difference between legal terms such as 'person' and 'human being' represents more than a question of standing or mere semantics. Within liberal democratic societies .... Such distinction may indicate substantive differences

184. Etymology is the study of the origin of words and the way in which their meanings have changed throughout history.
185. E.A.Q Adriano, *Natural Persons, Juridical Persons and Legal Personhood*, 8(1) Mexican L. Rev. 101, 104 (2015).

regarding fundamental concepts such as citizenship, membership in society, and the scope and essential nature of rights and liberties. In particular, judicial decisions regarding abortion have relied upon such distinctions in order to articulate some of the fundamental issues upon which such controversies are based.[186]

150. To this extent, Mchugh makes an important claim, a distinction between a human being and a person and human rights and civil right and concludes that there is a feminist critique to the dichotomy as 'the concepts are rooted in a male perspective that seek to protect "property" and individual autonomy against the desires and visions of those who would challenge the dominant social order'.[187]

151. This perspective continues to underlie debates on property and more so persons, particularly in family and succession law.[188] Exclusion and its power over others is a continuing theme in property law.[189] This theme also runs in family relations and the extent to which the law enables exclusion of others in family relations is the extent to which there must be a 'captain' in family relations. The focal point of concern is the continuing question of the effect of this imbalance of power relations on family life and specifically on women and children. In Nigeria, in *Oduche v. Oduche*,[190] the Court of Appeal unanimously held and pronounced that Nigeria is a patriarchal-patrilineal society and a child's name must flow from this structural framework. This patriarchal theme runs through family, property and succession law in Nigeria.[191] Primogeniture, that is, inheritance of family house by the eldest male child is an accepted custom in the whole of the South of Nigeria.[192] There are variations of the primogeniture rule that vests all property of the patriarch in the eldest son in some form of trusts for other children.[193] There is no known formal policy enquiry as at yet on the consequences and implications of sustaining the custom of primogeniture on economic and other areas of development such as the impact of inalienability of land, burial in homes and sundry deleterious implications of this seemingly perfect custom.

---

186. J.T. McHugh, *What Is the Difference Between a 'Person' and a 'Human Being Within the Law'*, 54(3) Special Issue on Pub. L. 445 (1992).
187. McHugh, *ibid.*, 445, 460–461.
188. More will be said of this on Status and property rights.
189. A.M. Honoré, *Ownership*, in *Oxford Essays in Jurisprudence* 107 (A.G. Guest ed., OUP 1961); M.J. Radin, *The Liberal Conception of Property: Cross Currents in the Jurisprudence of Takings*, 88 Colum. L. R 1666 (1988); A. Alexander Hill-Smith, *Rights of Parking and the Ouster Principle after* Batchelor v. Marlow, Conv 223 (2007).
190. [2005] LPELR-5976.
191. *Idehen v. Idehen* [1991] LPELR-SC.271/1989; [1991] 7 SC (part 111) 104 [1991] 6 NWLR (part 198) 382; *Oke v. Oke* [1974] 3 SC 1; [1974] 1 All N.L.R. (part 1) 443; *Olowu v. Olowu* [1985] 3 NWLR (part 13) 372; *Oyewale v. Oyewale* [1987] 2 NWLR (part 56) 238; *Oduche v. Oduche* [2005] LPELR-5976; For a research work and its deleterious impact in some specified countries *see*; M. Htun & Weldon S., *State Power, Religion, and Women's Rights: A Comparative Analysis of Family Law*, 18(1) Indiana J. Global Legal Stud. 146,158 (2011).
192. O.K. Edu, *A Review of Laws of Inheritance in the Southern States of Nigeria*, 24 J. Priv. & Prop. L. 100–120 (2004).
193. *Idehen v. Idehen* [1991] LPELR-SC.271/1989; *Olowu v. Olowu* [1985] LPELR 2604; [1985] 3 NWLR (part 13) 372.

II. Human and 'Person'

152. Rawls distinguishes a person from a human being and states:

> This conception of the person is not to be mistaken for the conception of a human being (a member of the species homo sapiens) as the latter might be specified in biology or psychology without the use of normative concepts of various kinds, including, for example, the concepts of the moral powers and of the moral and political virtues. Moreover, to characterise the person, we must add to these concepts those used to formulate the powers of reason, inference, and judgement. These are essential companion powers to the two moral powers and are required for their exercise and for the practice of the virtues.[194]

153. The Webster Dictionary indicates that the word 'human' was used for the first time in 1694.[195] Most dictionaries refer to and define 'person' rather than human being.[196] The Encyclopaedia Britannica offers a definition of 'human being':

> culture-bearing primate classified in the genus *Homo*, especially the species *H. sapiens*. **Homo sapiens**, (Latin: 'wise man') the species to which all modern human beings belong. *Homo sapiens* is one of several species grouped into the genus *Homo*, but it is the only one that is not extinct. Human beings are anatomically similar and related to the great apes but are distinguished by a more highly developed brain and a resultant capacity for articulate speech and abstract reasoning. In addition, human beings display a marked erectness of body carriage that frees the hands for use as manipulative members. Some of these characteristics, however, are not entirely unique to humans. The gap in cognition, as in anatomy, between humans and the great apes (orangutans, gorillas, chimpanzees, and bonobos) is much less than was once thought, as they have been shown to possess a variety of advanced cognitive abilities formerly believed to be restricted to humans.[197]

154. Being human has been an evolutionary condition and theme. It is the subject of both public and private law concern. In family and succession law being human raises the fundamental principle of domicile. Every human being has a domicile. This is what Rousseau explained when he noted that the human was distinguished in the earliest time from other lower animals in his ability to have an address.[198] In the South East of Nigeria, among the Igbos, this is replicated in the salute to a man who builds a house as having achieved a feat which the elephant could not. For Rousseau, 'But savage man living among other animals without any

194. John Rawls, *supra* n. 176.
195. At https://www.merriam-webster.com/dictionary/human%20being.
196. At https://www.google.com/search?q=human+beings+meaning&oq=human+being&aqs=chrome.2.69i57j46j0j46j0l4.11124j0j7&sourceid=chrome&ie=UTF-8#; https://www.merriam-webster.com/dictionary/human%20being.
197. At https://www.google.com/search?q=human+beings+meaning&oq=human+being&aqs=chrome.2.69i57j46j0j46j0l4.11124j0j7&sourceid=chrome&ie=UTF-8#.
198. J.J. Rousseau, *Discourse on the Origin of Inequality* 4, 5 & 11 (Dover 2004).

society or fixed habitation and finding himself early under a necessity of measuring his strength with theirs, soon makes a comparison between both, and finding that he surpasses them more in address, than they surpass him in strength, he learns not to be any longer in dread of them.'[199]

155. *Udny v. Udny*[200] is a classical judgment of the House of Lords. It was referred to in the Nigerian case of *Graham Wylie v. Hajara Wylie & Anor*[201] and with approval by the United Kingdom Supreme Court in *Mark v. Mark*[202] a case that concerned a Nigerian couple. In *Mark v. Mark*, Lord Hope of Craighead stated:

> Translated into language with which we are familiar today, the point that Lord Westbury was making was that cases where a question of public law is in issue must be distinguished from cases where the issue is one of private law. Public law issues raise questions which concern what Lord Westbury described as the person's political status. The criteria by which status for the purpose of these questions is to be judged may differ from country to country, according to the rules that it lays down as to who may lawfully enter or lawfully remain there. Private law issues, on the other hand, are referred to the law of the person's domicile. The criteria for the determination of a person's domicile are governed by a single principle which ought to be capable of being applied universally. The importance of this distinction has not always been recognised.[203]

156. In the domain of public law, in contemporary times, being human implicates a universal guarantee of some minimum attributes promoted as inalienable rights and championed by United Nations,[204] regional and local instruments. The core of these rights enhances or aspires to enhance individuality and the maximum realisation of potential of the human being. There is more, the rights contemplate compassion as a basic tenet of being human.[205] Tamblyn wrote in connection with compassion as a basic tenant of being human:

> The duty to help others is founded on a duty of compassion. Asking where the duty of compassion comes from, the response is '[t]he source of compassion is life. We esteem life. I do not mean merely that we each separately esteem our own individual lives, or even that we esteem all life. Rather, we esteem life itself. We can test this claim simply by asking ourselves whether we think life itself is a good thing. And how could we otherwise, given that we are all instances of life? Indeed, at a most fundamental level, there is nothing, but life.

---

199. *Ibid.*, 5.
200. [1869] LR 1 HL 441; [1867] SLR 3-109.
201. Suit No. FCT/HC/PET/206/17.
202. [2005] UKHL 42; [2005] 3 WLR 111; [2006] 1 AC 98.
203. [2005] UKHL 42 para. 5.
204. Universal Declaration of Human Rights to which Nigeria is a signatory and ratified 1993, Ratification and Enforcement Act, 1983; International Covenant on Civil and Political Rights 29 Jul. 1993; Convention on the Rights of the Child, 19th April, 1991.
205. Nathan Tamblyn, *The Duty to Help the World's Poor*, 23(3) King's L. J. 312, 324 (2012). *See also* Nwudego Chinwuba, *Development in Nigeria and the Imperative of redefining customs in Law*, 4 Uniuyo J. Com. & Prop. L. 142–163 (2020).

Also, we esteem life for its own sake, and not merely because it is the opportunity for activity. We can test this claim too, in the same way. When questioned about our reasons for saving a life, we do not say "I wanted him to be able to do things in the future." Instead, we say simply "I wanted to save his life," content that, that is a sufficient explanation'.

157. The human accomplishment of establishing minimal standards of rights for the human being in the domain of public law also contemplates the enhancement of the human mind and the provision of an environment conducive for the development of the mind. This goal is a collective one in the interest of all aimed at promoting civilised norms of societal living and cohesion. The promotion of family life does not detract from this core impetus. Some of these inalienable rights which advance family life are right to life, liberty, and security of person;[206] right to found a family according to local laws and local circumstances;[207] freedom of thoughts;[208] expression;[209] association;[210] etc. These rights are indicative of the human standing in her evolution as distinct from other closer and further species. The rights allow for the robust development of human being. Law has played a crucial role in advancing these themes. Law has played a role in advancing the rights of a wife, the autonomy of a wife for independent actions and building up of a wife's own identity. Law has also advanced the interests of children by defining the age of adulthood. In Nigeria, the rights of children extend to foetal rights. Thus, with the compulsory registration of births law, both live birth and stillbirth must be registered and a register for that purpose must be kept.[211] What it means to be human thus continues to engage society.

158. The scourge of the COVID-19 pandemic reinforces the need to ruminate over the place of compassion and other core rights of being human in relation to actors, non-actor and recipients of actions.[212] The pandemic noted, to have originated in Wuhan, China.[213] The COVID-19 virus, which caused the pandemic has been termed 'Chinese virus' by Donald Trump, the President of the United States of America. The President has consistently claimed that the government and peoples of China had ample time and opportunity to have contained the virus within China

206. Article 3.
207. Article 16.
208. Article 18.
209. Article 19.
210. Article 20.
211. Section 7 of the BDM Act, 1992, Cap B9, Laws of the Federation, 2004.
212. A pandemic disease is one that has spread over a large area, and is prevalent throughout an entire country, continent, or the whole world. When used by the World Health Organisation (WHO) a pandemic means a worldwide spread of a new disease. On March 11, the WHO officially declared the COVID-19 outbreak a pandemic due to the global spread and severity of the disease. The COVID-19 is so named because of the corona looking virus which began to spread amongst and between humans in 2019.
213. Explainer: What we know about the origins of the coronavirus pandemic available at: www.reuters.com/article/explainer-what-we-know-a... (last accessed 15 Aug. 2020).

and that China either failed or recklessly allowed the virus to escape with the resultant escape causing a pandemic.[214] The pandemic assailed critical aspects of the core indices of human capacity, including but not limited to human accomplishments of 'society', emotional well-being, health, education, etc. The economic impact, devastating loss of lives in droves and other consequences have been unquantifiable. These are all protectable rights envisaged in the portfolios of rights aimed at advancing human experiences and growth on earth.[215]

159. The preamble to the International Convention on Economic, Social and Cultural Rights.[216] captures the subject:

> recognition of the inherent dignity and of the equal and inalienable rights of all members of the human family is the foundation of freedom, justice, and peace in the world. And recognizing that these rights derive from the inherent dignity of the human person, the ideal of free human beings enjoying freedom from fear and want can only be achieved if conditions are created whereby everyone may enjoy his economic, social and cultural rights, as well as his civil and political rights, by promoting universal respect for, and observance of, human rights and freedoms, and realizing that the individual, having duties to other individuals and to the community to which he belongs, is under a responsibility to strive for the promotion and observance of the rights recognized in the present Covenant.

160. The evolutionary strides of law underscore the intuitive notions of being human. In *Re Shaw's Wills Trust*[217] the wife of George Bernard Shaw left money for what was described as a sort of finishing school for the Irish people, where 'self-control, oratory, department and the arts of personal contract' were to be taught. At that point in legal history, this was a novel kind of claim to qualify for charitable purposes under advancement of education. Varsey J concluded that the gift was charitable, stating that education included the promotion and encouragement of those arts and graces of life which are, after all, perhaps the finest and best part of

---

214. At https://donald+trump+claims+china+should+have+contained+covid+19+in+china+but+failed+to+do+so.#; https://www.google.com/search?client=firefox-b-d&q= available at: www.bbc.com/news/world-us-canada-52294623; Trump says China could have stopped COVID-19 and suggests … available at www.theguardian.com/world/apr/# (last accessed 15 Aug. 2020).
215. *See* the International Covenant on Economic, Social and Cultural Rights: Adopted and opened for signature, ratification and accession by General Assembly resolution 2200A (XXI) of 16 Dec. 1966 entry into force 3 Jan. 1976, in accordance with Art. 27.
216. Adopted and opened for signature, ratification and accession by General Assembly resolution 2200A (XXI) of 16 Dec. 1966 entry into force 3 Jan. 1976. Status of Nigeria – Signature: NA, Ratification/Accession: 1993. *See also* International Covenant on Civil and Political Rights :1976 Signature: NA, Ratification/Accession: 1993; First Optional Protocol to the International Covenant on Civil and Political Rights :1976; Status of Nigeria – Signature: NA, Ratification/Accession: NA; Second Optional Protocol to the International Covenant on Civil and Political Rights, aiming at the abolition of the death penalty :1991: Status of Nigeria – Signature: NA, Ratification/Accession: NA.
217. [1952] ALL E. R. 49.

the human character. Referring to *Re Price*:[218] Varsey J. noted that 'a body of persons established for the purpose of raising the artistic taste of the country and established by an appropriate document which confines them to that purpose, is established for educational purposes, because the education of artistic taste is one of the most important things in the development of a civilized human being.'[219]

161. In *Re Wedgwood*[220] with respect to trusts for the prevention of cruelty to animals, the court stated: 'A gift for the benefit and protection of animals tends to promote and encourage kindness towards them, to discourage cruelty, and to ameliorate the condition of the brute creation, and thus to stimulate humane and generous sentiments in man towards lower animals, and by these means promote feelings of humanity and morality generally, repress brutality, and thus elevate the human race.'[221]

III. Religion and 'Person'

162. In religion the human frame is the mask from which the actual being, 'person' acts. In religion, it has long been the case that the human frame is categorised as a mask. Religion views the human frame as a vessel just as the mask, which encapsulates the soul – the principal actor. Various religions express this idea. Buddhism, for instance, considers that the human being is but, only an expression of divinity through various reincarnating pathways, of which the human form is one. Buddhism is a religion and a philosophy that teaches three noble paths: purity, wisdom, and compassion, of which compassion is the greatest.[222] It also teaches four noble truths: the un-satisfactoriness of the human condition; 'the origin' or 'arising' which means the thirst or craving for inner truths; the cessation of grasping and attachments; and 'the way'. 'The way' is defined as a state of middle way expressed in balance, good sense and no extremes.[223] For the Buddhist, being human is a privileged state as one could also reincarnate as a beast or some other form of creation dependent on one's present expressions of thoughts and actions.[224] In the Southern parts of Nigeria, the belief in reincarnation and the human form as different stages of activities on earth is prevalent. Aside from reincarnation, there is the prevalent idea that life on earth is but an act of previously determined purposes and activities. As is relatively acknowledged, African names bear the marks of circumstances and or aspirations of parents in relation to the birth of a person. Babies are named based

218. [1943] C. 422, Cohen, J.
219. [1952] Ch. 163, 171; [1952] 1 All ER 49.
220. [1915] Ch. 113.
221. [1915] Ch. 113, 122.
222. Rob Nairn, *Tranquil Mind – An Introduction to Buddhism & Meditation* 20 (Kairon Press CC 2004).
223. Rob Nairn, *ibid.,* 31–45.
224. Reincarnation writes Nairn, largely traces the changes within the mind due to karmic forces (Karmic force is defined as the law of cause and effect). These changes produce states which are experienced as solid with different realms producing different manifestations in accordance with thoughts and actions in present incarnation or existence. Rob Nairn, *Tranquil Mind – An Introduction to Buddhism & Meditation* 56–57 (Kairon Press CC 2004).

on these circumstances and facts surrounding a birth. Many names remarkably indicate the return of a departed relation. Some of these names for the South West (the Yoruba) are 'Babade', translated to *a father has returned*; 'Iyabode', *a mother has returned*, equivalent names in the South East are respectively, 'Nnamadi' or 'Nnedi'. For the South East, it would not matter whether the name commemorates such a return, rites are performed to determine the question and the outcome noted all through the life of an individual.[225] Thus, the human frame is but an expression of an inner identity in the customs of the people of the South of Nigeria.

163. Christianity[226] considers the human frame in not-too-distant terms from Buddhism. The critical difference between the two religions on a person lies in the relationship of the person to the other. There are other critical differences in attitude towards the origin of the two religions and the question of reincarnation.[227] Christian theology considers the human frame a mask, the temple of the living God in whom one lives and has his being.[228] In Christianity the human being is a state of transformation in which it is the God in the human frame that lives devoid of the incidents of the thoughts and actions of the world – the 'world' signifying the continuing thoughts and actions of human beings who are not transformed through the renewal of their minds that inform right actions towards others.[229] For these religions, a human being is so in time and space and the human is only a form of being, as human.

164. Buddhism teaches the imperative on the human to embrace discipline for the detachment of the 'self' (outer human frame) in order to unmask, and thereby reveal the enlightened inner person while Christianity's distinctive theological basis is not just the unmasking of the inner being, but the active mandate of unmasking for the purpose of extending the personhood to many others. There might ultimately be no intuitive conflict between the two religions with respect to life in the 'hereafter' but in relation to life on earth, Christianity becomes the face of a conducive global environment for inalienable human dignity and self-actualisation.

---

225. For the people of South East of Nigeria one returns in human form seven times seeking perfection. The procedure for the identification of the reincarnated soul is intense involving rites and rituals by specialised persons and witnessed by family and friends. It has to be noted that these rites and some other customs relating to reincarnation found also in marriage rites do not necessary interfere with the fact that being a Christian is a custom with the people of the South East of Nigeria. In marriage rites, there would be a ceremony in honour of the reincarnated soul.
226. Christianity is the religion derived from Jesus Christ based on the Bible as sacred scripture and professed around the world by different denominations.
227. Some Christian denominations claim that the question put to Jesus, what then? Are you Elijah? Etc. The Holy Bible: The Book of John Ch. 1 verses 21–30 also varied in Matthew 11:14, which Jesus did not refute indicates that Christianity and Judaism do not contest the concept of reincarnation. Other denominations dismiss any notions of reincarnation asserting the scripture: 'It is appointed unto man once to die, then judgement.' The Holy Bible: The Book of Hebrews Chapter 9 verse 27.
228. The Holy Bible: First Corinthians Ch. 6 verse 19; Acts of the Apostles Ch. 17 verse 28. While some schools of thought consider reincarnation a feature of Christianity, some do not.
229. The Holy Bible: Epistle of the Apostle Paul to the Romans: Ch. 12 verse 2.

IV. Philosophy and 'Person'

165. There are two main schools of thoughts, one that agrees with religion that the human being is dual and the other that sees the human being as complete in being, that is with no intrinsic personality. The main objective of philosophical thinking has been the quest of gaining understanding and placing the human being and society in idea and reality in the best possible functional position. Who then should a person be?

166. The ideal human being is, has been the preoccupation of the philosopher. The first school draws inspiration from an outer world by which the inner person is closely related to an extrinsic ideal. To this view, perfection of the present can only be through a recognition of an all good extrinsic other. On the view of those who see the human as complete in being, perfection lies in making the best of what can be seen and felt. This dichotomy may be no more than a naturalistic and positivist bent in jurisprudence. It could also be more when driven in the purview of theology.

167. However, what it does speak to is the dichotomy between the perceptions of the human and the person. *Ubuntu* represents the African notions of philosophy. The African perceives all persons as humans. This is the starting point of African philosophical notions. These notions are typified by the perspectives on life by which every life is given a right of birth. In this perspective, a woman is of premium value. She is the vessel of life – a life-giver for the male and for the sustenance of descent and genealogy. *Ubuntu*'s philosophical connotations are: I am, because you are. In fact, the word *ubuntu* is part of the Zulu phrase 'Umuntu ngumuntu ngabantu', which literally means that a person is a person through other people. With origins in South Africa, it is an expression of all of Africa's notions of the human essence. It could also be variously defined as 'humanity'; 'I am because we are,' or 'humanity towards others,' but is often used in a more philosophical sense to mean 'the belief in a universal bond of sharing that connects all humanity.' *Ubuntu* is again reflected in Article 28 of the African Charter on Human and Peoples' Rights, which provides: 'every individual shall have the duty to respect and consider his fellow beings without discrimination and to maintain relations aimed at promoting, safeguarding and reinforcing mutual respect and tolerance'. The practice remains elusive to the African peoples and nations because the reverse could also easily, in fact, be the case, in a literal sense, that all humans do not have the capacity to be persons, and then, in an intuitive, extremely vile sense.

168. All thoughts can further be categorised as to whether they are deductive or inductive, or what the philosopher would classify as denoting essence and existence.

169. One school of thought thus considers that the human must be viewed from the inward and the essence. Descartes writes, 'I think, therefore I am'.[230] Another school considers that the human is all about 'the existence' and all issues of essence are either worthless or ought to be left to theology. For instance, Hart thought that in Jurisprudence, as in all philosophy, it is a mistake to think that particulars can be classified under general terms only based on their possession of specified common features.[231] Therefore general classifications, Hart thought, should be avoided. In this sense things should be treated as 'is'.

170. Plato, who is known by only one name and cited as one of the founders of Western religion and spirituality, first expressed the view of the perfect and imperfect man which is the concept of the duality of man, that is, man as the manifestation of the perfect idea. Aristotelian thoughts focus on the *'universals'*.[232] Aristotle, cited as the most famous student of Plato, on the other hand, had a shift in position. For Aristotle, if there was one ideal man and one imperfect copy then, in so far as they do not share identical characteristics, there would have to be a third man of whom they were both imperfect copies, and so *ad ifinitum*. And since men are animals, there would have to be some further 'idea' of which both the idea of man and the idea of dog were but imperfect copies. In the end the only real thing is the one you can see and feel.[233]

171. The human being, for Hegel is a rational being, a free agent whose essence can only reveal his externalities. Hegel wrote that:

> the free will … is the idealism which does not take things as they are to be absolute, while realism pronounces them to be absolute … .Even an animal has gone beyond this realist philosophy since it devours things and so proves that they are not absolutely self–sufficient … … … existence as determinate being is in essence being for another so that one aspect of property is that it is an existent as an external thing, and in this respect, property exists for other external things and is connected with their necessity and contingency. It is in the final analysis an existent as an embodiment of the will so that the 'other' for which it exists can only be the will of another person.[234]

---

230. Rene Descartes, *Philosophical Works of* Ed., by (E.S. Haldane & G.R.T. Ross, Two Vols, Cambridge University Press 1931).
231. Hart, *Definition and Theory in Jurisprudence*, 70 L.Q.R. 35 (1954).
232. Plato, *The Republic* Vol. X, 323 (Wordsworth Classics 1997); Aristotle, *Metaphysics* Book 1: Chapters 6 & 9 (Pomona Press 2008).
233. *See* Aristotle, *Metaphysics* Book I: Chapters 6 & 9 for criticism of Plato's Theory of Ideas and the rest of the book for Aristotle's theory of the Universals. Although Aquinas and centuries later, Suarez, thought that the right of property was not an aspect of natural law but a matter of social utility and convenience. Aquinas is seen as a disciple of Aristotle who influenced him greatly in his early days, but is seen more as a Platonian with his total allegiance to Augustinian philosophy; *see also* D.E. Allan, *Security: Some Mysteries, Myths, & Monstrosities*, 15(3/4) Monash U. L. Rev. 337 (1989).
234. G.W.F. Hegel, *Encyclopaedia Britannica, Inc.* 31.

172. This relation of 'will to will' for Hegel is the proper ground in which freedom is existent.[235] Kant like, Plato saw all that is real as emanating from a conceptualist rather than material origins. His views, which perpetuate the individualistic and exclusive notions of the human, are that human beings are a rational, dependent on reason and thus the enabling environment to reason and provide reason is the essence of society.[236] A pure analysis of the Spinozistic and Hegelian thoughts is that the life of man is a continual interaction of existence and essence.

173. For the first school, the intuitive and practical outcome of their view is like *Ubuntu*. One notices immediately that the first school has a view much like religion on the overall nature and evolution of the human. Relying on this view as the organising spirit of a society poses a problem for governance. This is because, the intuitive and practical process for understanding and recognising the indices of the view is an enterprise which only a few can aspire to or realise. The second view can be dismissed as its practical outcome is hedonism and history has been unable to sustain or validate this view as progressive for any society. This is not surprising as man is a dual being, that this is so, is not really one that should be a subject of debate.

174. The essence of a human is immensely affected by his existence and the extent to which his existence is satisfactory to the same extent or higher degree is his essence propelled to greater heights for a more functional and efficient existence that encompasses one, fellow human and environment. An understanding of the duality of the human is important in philosophy as it leads to balanced actions not only in relation to religion but also to interpersonal relationships in society. In this sphere the need for one to contribute positively to the environment for its very sake and then invariably for own good and that of others flows naturally through each one, one's works and society.

175. A whittling of the expression of the inner person, therefore, is a significant discount from the overall significance of life. A balance, therefore, must be the middle course. The middle course provides room for society to be organised around precepts and institutions that advance the view that the human being is a person to the extent that Ubuntu is not only a philosophical slogan but a real course of action. In this sense, the Western idea of libertarianism in reason and the Ubuntu meet at a confluence from which the organising spirit of society is law, law according to the experiences of goodness from the past brought into the present and projected into the future. In Western societies, the progress of society is predicated on law but driven by philosophy or economics.

---

235. G.W.F. Hegel, *Philosophy of Right* 31 (T.M. Knox trans, Clarendon Press 1942); *see also*, C.J. Berry, *Property and Possession: Two Replies to Locke – Hume and Hegel*, XII, Ch. IV, 89 (*Property* Nomos 1980); J.C. Carter, *The Ideal and the Actual in the Law*, 24 Am. L. Rev. 752, 770–771 (1890).

236. Victor Cathrein, *Property* Vol. XII, 5 (Catholic Encyclopaedia, 1911).

176. When Laws of society follow the middle course, an advancement is made because all of the inner essence of the human finds perfect expression. Laws should therefore aim at addressing immediate social issues in a way that accounts for the past, the present and the future. This is a systematic way that relates to the consciousness of the people determined from the culture and contemporary needs in a comparative framework obtaining in a global setting. A society cannot live in its own measurement and estimation of standards of life, totally oblivious of strides within and in other parts of the world. If this obtains, the legal framework is a failed regime from its start. Such a legal framework and *a fortiori* structure is an enterprise in self-deceit.

177. The duality of man is not a misconception as some branches of modern legal and philosophical thoughts claim. When reality is the finite and not the idea, the way is usually unclear, despite the best of intentions.[237] 'Without the world', says Hegel, 'God is not God'.[238] Rephrasing in own voice, Cohen states: 'God comes to be perfect, and therefore paradoxically – since God is perfect, since it is his nature to be perfect – He comes to be, only by manifesting Himself in the world. The Hegelian sentence "Without the world God is not God" identifies not a deficiency in God but a deficiency or incompleteness in a *conception* of God which neglects the Spinozistic truth that He is all reality.'[239] In this sense, the conceptions of philosophy and religion are not far from the other.

V. Law and 'Person'

178. A person and what this means could also be a subject of property and the law on property. The polemics of the relationship between being human and personhood permeates the depth of private property. There are always issues as to what can form the subject of acquisition and property. Thus, from Hobbes' occupational theory of acquisition of property[240] to Locke's labour theory of property and to Rousseau's[241]distinctive feature of the origin of inequality and the address of the

237. Aristotle, *Metaphysics* Book 1: Chapters 6 & 9 (Pomona Press 2008); Thomas Hobbes *Leviathan* Ch. XXIV, 294 (Penguin Books 1985); for thoughts on Hobbes, *see*, B.B. Lopata, *Property Theory in Hobbes*, 1 (ii) Political Theory 203 (1973); A.E. Taylor, *The Ethical Doctrine of Hobbes*, 13 Philosophy 407 (1938); Thomas Nagel, *Hobbes Concept of Obligation*, LXVIII Philosophical Rev. 68 (1959); Kelsen, *Pure Theory of Law*, 34 Tul. L. Rev. 269 (1959–1960); J. Bentham, *Of Laws in General* Appendix BI (H. L. A. Hart ed., OLG 1970); Robert Nozick, *Anarchy, State and Utopia* 174 (Blackwell Publishing 2006).

238. G.W.F. Hegel, *Lectures on the Philosophy of Religion* Vol. 1, 200(Trans. E.B. Speirs & J. Burdon Sanderson (eds) Routledge & Kegan Paul 1892) ; G.A. Cohen, *If You're an Egalitarian How Come You're So Rich* 83 (Harvard University Press 2000).

239. Cohen, *ibid*, 84.

240. John Locke, *Two Treatises of Government* Ch. V p. 285 (P. Laslett Cambridge University Press 2d ed. 1967, printed 2008); W.H. Hamilton, *Property – According to Locke*, 41 Yale L. J. 864 (1931); Jeremy Waldron, *Property Law*, in *A Companion to Philosophy of Law and Legal Theory* 3 (D. Paterson ed., Blackwell Publishers 1996); Jeremy Waldron, *The Right to Private Property* 31 (Clarendon Press 1988); L.C. Becker, *Property Rights: Philosophic Foundation* (Routledge & Kegan Paul 1977); Virginia Held, *Locke on Nozick* 169 (Social Research 1986).

241. J.J. Rousseau, *Discourse on the Origin of Inequality* 4, 8–11, 27 (Dover 2004).

human, personhood underlies the discourse on property.[242] It is obvious that in property parlance, the distinction has played a crucial role in enabling the owning and possession of other humans as slaves and captives. Indeed, it has enabled more sacrilegious propensities such as the ritual sacrificing of others, in particular women and children. In family relations, the absolute power of the father in a family presented a property-owning situation which could not arise where all humans were regarded as persons.

179. Personhood continues to be a topic of international debate and has been questioned critically during the abolition of slavery. In social and theological context, the debates on abortion and foetal rights and/or reproductive rights continue to rage. In the old case of *Hegarty v. Shine*[243] it was held that consent to sex implicates consent to the consequences and therefore, non-disclosure of sexual health did not vitiate consent. It must be noted, though, that the judges in the case appeared to have taken an exemplary position since sex outside of marriage was frowned at. While the decision in the case may no longer speak to modern understanding of sexual relations it does speak to the question of foetal rights in that with sexual relationship one should expect to conceive a foetus. This remains the approach in Nigeria with respect to foetal rights.

180. Other fields querying the meaning of personhood are animal rights activism, ontology, ethical theory, and in debates about corporate personhood.[2]

181. Processes through which personhood is recognised socially and legally vary cross-culturally, demonstrating that notions of personhood are not universal. Personhood is closely tied with capacity evinced in the legal and political concepts of citizenship, equality, liberty, and responsibility. According to one view, in law, only a natural person or legal personality has rights, protections, privileges, responsibilities, and legal liability. Another view is that the questions surrounding personhood exist because of misunderstanding due to semantics and that personhood precedes the semantics of law as law only accords recognition of person to an already existing status.[244] A closer scrutiny indicates that the subject is not an idle one. Adriano reviews theories of persons and personhood in commercial law and concludes that the whole concept of person and personhood exists because the rights and obligations which are aimed to be enforced and asserted already exists and only receive recognition juridically. In this sense, there is no difference between the natural and artificial persons especially as a human person who may be incapacitated acts in the same way a corporation would act, that is through agencies.[245] Thus, 'juridical persons are not created by law but recognized as legal entities with already

242. J.J. Rousseau, *ibid.*, at 5.
243. [1878] 4 L. R (Ireland) 288.
244. E.A.Q. Adriano, *Natural Persons, Juridical Persons and Legal Personhood*, 8(1) Mexican L. Rev. 101, 104 (2015).
245. *Ibid.*

existing rights and obligations. This recognition forms the basis of their legal personhood'.[246] Hence, not only humans have legal personhood, corporations of diverse classifications are also endowed with legal personhood. Section 18(1) of the Interpretation Act defines 'person' to include any body of persons corporate or unincorporated.

182. In *Anozia v. Att-Gen of Lagos State*,[247] the Court of Appeal stated that the term 'natural person indisputably denotes a human being. Contrariwise, the term "juristic person" is an entity, an artificial person, that is duly accorded recognition by aw as having the rights and duties of a human being'.

183. *Megawatts Nigeria Limited v. The Registered Trustees of Gbagada Phase* 2 *Residents' Association & 3 Ors.*[248] came before the Honourable Justice I. N. Oweibo of the Federal High Court in Lagos and judgment was delivered on Friday, 25 September 2020. The Claimants, a private limited liability company in Nigeria carrying on the business of infrastructure solution provider with speciality in mechanical, electrical, and piping engineering services, sought a declaration that the continuous interference of the Respondent (Association) with its operations, employees, contractors, and agents is illegal, oppressive, and unconstitutional. It claimed that the said activities of the respondent association and its trustees/agents were a violation of its fundamental rights as enshrined in sections 40 and 41 of the Constitution of the Federal Republic of Nigeria, 1999 (as amended). The claimant had, in January 2016, moved its head office into a private estate in Lagos, known as Gbagada Phase 2, with address as No. 7, Lanre Awolokun Street, Lagos.

184. The Respondents are the managers of the estate and their trustees, managing the estate as a Community Development Association under a Board of Trustees.

185. Before the hearing commenced, the Respondents raised a preliminary objection on jurisdiction of the court to entertain questions from an artificial person on fundamental human rights. The applicant responded to the preliminary objection in a written reply on point of law by which it contended, relying on statutory and judicial authorities, that fundamental human rights as contained in Chapter IV of the Constitution is not limited to natural persons but also to artificial persons once duly constituted.

186. The Court held that it had the jurisdiction to proceed with the case. It reasoned that by section 46(1) of the Constitution, any person who alleges that any of the provisions of the Chapter IV on fundamental human rights 'has been, is being, or is likely to be contravened in any State in relation to him may apply to a High court in that State for redress'. It held that based on all existing authorities on the subject and the Companies and Allied Matters Act, a limited liability company in Nigeria is a juristic person with rights and duties. Focusing its decision on rights, it

246. Adriano, *ibid.*, at 112.
247. [2011] 4 WRN 150, 182.
248. SUIT NO: FHC/L/CS/982/2020 judgement delivered Friday, 25 Sep. 2020.

held that while the rights of an artificial juristic person may not fully equate with that of natural persons, they do entitle the juristic person to enforce some of the fundamental human rights such as right of property, freedom of association, fair hearing[249] etc. The Federal High Court noted that the Supreme Court had also held that a juristic person may suffer harm as where its officers and directors are unduly arrested and detained which results in loss of reputation and financial loss.[250] Based on this analysis, the Court declared that the Constitution guaranteed freedom of association to all persons and the respondents could not coarse the claimants to become a member of their association despite its residency in the estate.

187. In reaching this conclusion, the court examined the notions of persons in Nigeria and noted that it is trite that where a company, or other body of persons, is registered under the Companies and Allied Matters Act, it is vested with the status of a legal entity and is regarded as a person. Relying on *Kasandubu v. Ultimate Petroleum Ltd.*,[251] it restated that a person means both artificial and natural persons, including sole or public bodies, corporate or incorporate.

188. Prest v. Petrodel Resources Limited[252] forms a curious case for matrimonial causes although the thrust of the case was corporate personality. The case reviewed the nature of ancillary relief and the extent of the Court's power in exercising discretion, but in this case the thrust of the litigation was whether the personhood of relevant companies was the same as that of the husband. The Supreme Court's answer was negative. It emphasised the deleterious legal impact of exercising the extensive scope of the court's discretion in tampering with or disregarding the personhood of corporations without compelling reasons.

189. The court while reviewing the question of person and personality restated a key feature of corporate personhood as legal personhood – a question which is rooted in law and not economics.[253] As Lord Sumption stated:[254] 'The separate personality and property of a company is sometimes described as a fiction, and in a sense it is. But the fiction is the whole foundation of English company and insolvency law. ... "we are concerned not with economics but with law. The distinction between the two is, in law, fundamental."'[255]

190. To this extent, in law, the person of a corporation once recognised is distinct from any other person,[256] including subsidiaries,[257] shareholders and has rights and liabilities of its own. A sole owner and controller of such a company did not

249. *Okechukwu v. EFCC* [2015] 18 NWLR (part 1490) 1, 24–25.
250. *First Bank of Nigeria Plc. v. A.G. Federation* [2018] 7 NWLR (part 1617) 121, 155.
251. [2008]7 NWLR (part 1086) 274.
252. [2013] UKSC 34.
253. Robert Goff LJ. in *Bank of Tokyo Ltd. v. Karoon (Note)* [1987] AC 45,64 restated with approval by Lord Sumption in *Prest v. Petrodel Resources Limited* [2013] UKSC 34, para. 8, p. 5.
254. [2013] UKSC 34 para. 8, p. 5.
255. *Bank of Tokyo Ltd v. Karoon* (Note) [1987] AC 45, 64.
256. *Salomon v. A. Salomon & Co. Ltd.* [1897] AC 22.
257. *Lonrho Ltd. v. Shell Petroleum Co. Ltd.* [1980] 1 WLR 627.

even have an insurable interest in the property of the company, although economically he would suffer from the destruction of such property.[258]

191. The search for right prisms of interaction and inter-relations is projected into the content of 'personhood'. Who can act? What are the indices for acting and the implications of the action in relation to oneself and to others? This translates to what are the expectations from a human being in society. Society commenced from individuality to family and then expectations of constituent members in family and society. This is the place of government and the family itself has, in the face of modern governments transmuted into private governments. The legal question of personhood centres on the attribute of extending one's self beyond one and the extent to which such capacity to extend matters to others and the society in time. This is the subject of personhood in law. To be human is a different subject for a human is so in being.

192. Law exists to define order in society and since humans are the main actors in society, definitions matter as they precede principles upon which society and order are constructed and structured. Law proceeds on experience. Experience underlies human affairs. Experience in turn demonstrates that there must be a difference between capacity, responsibility, and existence. The significant distillable difference between humans and other beings is development from one stage of being to another. This is the thrust of the discourse on human, person, and personhood. From a juristic perspective, the starting point of legal distinction of person from human being is relative to capacity.

193. In the eyes of law, it is clear that the person and personhood differ from 'human being'. This difference can be said to lie in capacity – capacity to account and be held accountable which in legal terms translates to the capacity to exercise rights and hold obligations. That personhood and childhood or coverture related to capacity to act is indicated by the legislative interest in it or the extension of one's self in thoughts and actions. A person is the state of being able to act. For instance, with respect to foetal rights, one would ask how there could be rights for foetus but the answer lies in the same way law creates a next of friend, guardian ad litem or agencies. The State steps into these shoes. This does not detract from the fact, that personhood is dependent on capacity whereas, being human is a state. All human beings have rights but not all have the power to act although all are duty bearers, some are not. A pro-abortion society would then have stricter interpretations of who a person is or what the content of personhood entails. An anti-abortion society such as Nigeria would have a looser conception of who a person is and the content of personhood. Typically, abortion in Nigeria can only be carried out on medical grounds to save the life of the mother. An example is section 203 of the Lagos State Criminal Code Law which provides 'a medical doctor is not criminally responsible for performing in good faith, with reasonable care and skill a surgical operation on

258. *Macaura v. Northern Assurance Co. Ltd.* [1925] AC 619.

any person for his benefit, or on an unborn child for the preservation of the mother's life and physical health, if the performance of the operation is reasonable, having regard to circumstances of the case'.[259]

194. Capacity is the confluence of humanness and personhood. The common features of personhood are the capacity to act and be acted upon and these turn on the ability to account and be held accountable according to and by law. The second turns on capacity to act. Within the capacity to act are two legal components, right, and power – the power to choose.

§2. Capacity

195. Capacity is a fundamental subject in human experience. Human experience demonstrates that society is only workable with capable human beings. In this sense, the order of human life experience, shows an intelligent structure from birth cum infancy to death. Capacity entails the sustenance of society, in contribution to the continual running of society. How capacity is defined and the approach of state policy to it are therefore subjects of immense importance in global sustenance of human life.

196. The capacity of a person is always relative and contextual. Capacity can mean the potential or suitability for holding, storing, or accommodating persons or things; an individual's mental or physical ability; or the faculty or potential for treating, experiencing, or appreciating.[260]

197. Legal capacity is defined as when a person has reached the age of 18.[261] Legal capacity is comprised of an individual's mental or physical ability to do things and or understand actions taken. Capacity to marry under the Marriage Act is at the age of 21.[262] The capacity to execute Will is controlled by adulthood and infancy. The mental capacity of individuals also plays a role in both family and succession law. Section 3(1)(d)(iii) of the Matrimonial Causes Act makes the mental capacity of a person relevant to the validity of a marriage. It provides that a marriage is void if a party is mentally incapable of understanding the nature of the marriage contract.

198. Section 5(2) of the MCA in relation to a voidable marriage restates this position: 'For the purposes of this section, "mental defective" means a person who, owing to an arrested or incomplete development of mind, whether arising from inherent causes or induced by disease or injury, requires oversight, care or control for his own protection or for the protection of others and is, by reason of that fact, unfitted for the responsibilities of marriage.'

259. Cap 17, 2011.
260. At https://www.merriam-webster.com/dictionary/capacity.
261. At https://dictionary.cambridge.org/dictionary/english/legal-capacity.
262. Section 18 of the MCA.

199. The United Nations Convention on the Right of the Child makes capacity for independent action or adulthood, the age of 18. This is also the position in the Nigerian Child's Right Act, 2003. However, the continuing existence of colonial laws mixed with contemporary enactments, customary law and Islamic law has resulted in various regimes of capacity in Nigeria's legal regime including family and succession law. The Marriage Act makes the age of adulthood 21. The age for valid contract is 21 but equally, the Companies and Allied Matters Act makes a valid age 18 years.[263] In other laws including those for crimes, 12 years may trigger certain penalties. Valid age ranges from anywhere between 14 and 18 for various actions. Customary law and Islamic law use different yardsticks ranging from mental capacity to biological factors.[264]

200. The Matrimonial Causes Rules by Order IX, Part 2, rule 6 defines an infant as a person under the age of 14 years. Thus, incest is committed with persons who are infants under the age of 14. Section 29 of the Constitution, for instance, defines capacity in terms of renunciation of Nigerian citizenship for the purposes of capacity as 'full age' and for this purpose, full age is 18 years or any woman who is married, who shall be deemed to be of full age.[265]

201. Capacity is a positive rule dependent on the specific law, the specific jurisdiction and one may add, the specific standard and person. It is in capacity and how it is defined that the prism of personhood is triggered and expressed in various forms – human rights, or Ubuntu; or human powers and duties; and however else it may be expressed and termed.

§3. Absentees

202. Some Laws in Nigeria specifically provide for missing persons or persons who may be absent for a prolonged period. This is quite aside from the provisions in the same respect for the administration of estate of a departed person. This is discussed under the laws of succession. The Evidence Act, 2011, Matrimonial Causes Act and Rules and Criminal Code Act all have specific provisions relating to absentees and missing persons. In addition, the Law of Trust has the missing persons rule in administration of the terms of a private trust.

263. Section 20(1). Citation – section 870.
264. *See* for further reading: M.A. AjaNwachukwu, *A Legal Analysis of the Nebulous Concept of Childhood in Nigeria*, 7 Beijing L. Rev. 122–126 (2016).
265. Section 29(4) of the Constitution of the Federal Republic of Nigeria, Cap C23, Laws of the Federation, 2004. Other rules with respect to infants are: infants may institute proceedings through next of friend who shall be appointed by the guardian ad litem of the infant. It is also provided that where an infant is a co-respondent or party named, such an infant may intervene in person or by a solicitor.

203. Section 15(2)(h) and section 16(2) of the MCA provide for presumption of death and absentees. Thus, by the first, the absence is a fact for irretrievable breakdown of marriage if the other party to the marriage has been absent from the petitioner for such time and in such circumstances as to provide reasonable grounds for presuming that he or she is dead. Section 16(2) is a provision on proof. Thus, where a petition is based on the fact mentioned in section 15(2)(h)of the Act:

(a) proof that, for a period of seven years immediately preceding the date of the petition, the other party to the marriage was continually absent from the petitioner and that the petitioner has no reason to believe that the other party was alive at any time within that period, is sufficient to establish the fact in question, unless it is shown that the other party to the marriage was alive at a time within that period; and
(b) a decree made pursuant to the petition shall be in the form of a decree of dissolution of marriage by reason of presumption of death.

204. The Evidence Act provides that the burden is on the person making the assertion to prove the absence for the period. Section 370 of the Criminal Code Act also exempts marriages conducted because of the absence as in the Matrimonial Causes Act, for seven years from falling into bigamous marriages.

205. Trust is another subject providing for absentees. Where there is a private trust and by virtue of what is sometimes referred to as 'the Benjamin order' a distribution can be made that excludes the absentee. This rule is drawn from the case of Re: Benjamin.[266] The court has a power to authorise distribution of the whole of the assets of an estate, although not all the beneficiaries or creditors have made themselves known to be able to receive their share. A typical situation being where the whereabouts or continued existence of a certain beneficiary is not known. This presumption is rebuttable on proof and the person may go against beneficiaries or the trust property. In *Re Green's Will Trusts*,[267] the testatrix left her property to her son, providing that it should go to charity if he did not claim it by 2020. The son had disappeared on a bombing raid in 1943, and all but his mother were satisfied that he was dead. A 'Benjamin' order was made, allowing distribution to the charity, the court being satisfied that this was overall, not contrary to the intention of the testatrix.[268]

266. [1902] 1 Ch. 723.
267. [1985] 3 ALL E. R. 455.
268. *See* generally J.I. Martin, *Hanbury & Martin's Modern Equity* 587–588 (Sweet & Maxwell 19th ed. 2012) para. 18-027.

Chapter 2. Registration of Civil Status

§1. Civil Status

206. Civil status is also termed marital status and is a term used in Forms requiring vital records to indicate and ascertain whether a person is married or single. In the simplest contexts, no further distinction is made. A status of married means that a person was married in a manner legally recognised by their jurisdiction. In many jurisdictions, the specific status might include information on whether one is: single; married; civil partner; divorced; co-habitant; judicially separated; separated; former civil partner; widowed; surviving civil partner or Unknown.

207. It is important to note from the outset that the process of and registration of vital records in Nigeria is considerably obsolete and obscure. A few things are responsible for this situation. They include the impact of illiteracy, polygyny, and a general apathy on the side of government.

208. That noted, the legal framework for civil status or vital data registration in Nigeria is centralised. The structure is drawn from the Constitution,[269] established by an Act[270] and subsidiary legislation[271] made pursuant to section 153 of the Constitution. The legislative competence on it springs from items 8 and 9 of the exclusive legislative powers of the Federal Legislature as enshrined in the Second Schedule, Part 1 of the Constitution as well as the Concurrent Legislative List of the Constitution. Item 8 of the Exclusive Legislative List provides for Census, including the establishment and maintenance of machinery for universal and continuous registration of births and deaths throughout Nigeria. Item 9 is on citizenship, naturalisation, and aliens. Some other items on the federal legislative competence relevant to registration of civil status are items 67 and 68. Item 67 is: 'Any other matter with respect to which the National Assembly has power to make laws in accordance with the provisions of this Constitution.' Item 68 is: 'Any matter incidental or supplementary to any matter mentioned elsewhere in this list.'[272] Section 318 of the Constitution defines 'Concurrent Legislative List' to mean the list of matters set out in the first column in Part 11 of Second Schedule to the constitution with respect to which the National Assembly and a House of Assembly may make laws to the extent prescribed, respectively, opposite thereto in the second column thereof. By item 23 of this list, the National Assembly may make laws for the Federation or any part thereof with respect to statistics so far as the subject matter relates to – any matter upon which the National Assembly has power to make

269. Section 153; Third Schedule, Part I of the Constitution – Clause 24.
270. Births, Death, ETC. (Compulsory Registration) Act, Cap B9 Laws of the Federation, 2004; (B,D, Etc. Act, 2004).
271. Births, Death, Marriages, Etc., (Registration) Regulations; (B,D, M, Etc. Regulations, 2004). [S.I. 6 of 1996.] Laws of the Federation, 2004.
272. *Att. Gen. of Ondo State* v. *Att. Gen. of the Federation & Ors.* [2002] JELR 56203 (SC).

laws; and the organisation of coordinated scheme of statistics for the Federation or any part thereof on any matter whether it has power to make laws with respect thereto.

209. The National Population Commission is established pursuant to section 153, under the Third Schedule, Part I of the Constitution. Clause 24 of the Third Schedule provides powers of the Commission:

(a) undertake periodical enumeration of population through sample surveys, censuses or otherwise;
(b) establish and maintain a machinery for continuous and universal registration of births and deaths throughout the Federation;
(c) advise the President on population matters;
(d) publish and provide information and data on population for the purpose of facilitating economic and development planning.

210. The Constitution also confers on the local government the function of establishment and maintenance of cemeteries, burial grounds as well as registration of all births, deaths, and marriages.[273] Section 7 of the Constitution provides that local government council's scope of operation is based on: (i) the common interest of the community in the area; (ii) traditional association of the community and (iii) administrative convenience.

211. There are 774 local government areas in Nigeria. Each has a Council with a Chairman.

212. The country has a Marriage Act which provides for marriage districts. The authority to designate such districts is the Permanent Secretary, at the Federal Ministry of Interior. Pursuant to section 3 of the Marriage Act, 1970, the Marriage (Designation of Districts) Order, the country has 143 Marriage Districts spread across Nigeria from the North to the South. However, the exact number today, if there are changes, is uncertain.

213. A major source of concern about registration of civil status in Nigeria is who the Registrar of marriages is. The claims on this are between the National Population Commission, Local Government Councils and Marriage Registry. There appear to be no quarrels on registration of births. In practice both local governments and the National Population Commission conduct registration of births. It is not clear at all if deaths are registered in Nigeria, unless and perhaps, where they occur in the hospitals. Two factors are responsible for irregular registration of deaths – customary and Islamic law. Under both regimes, there are peculiar rules for ascertaining deaths and burials.

---

273. Fourth Schedule Function 1 (c) and (i) of the Constitution of the Federal Republic of Nigeria. Cap C23, Laws of the Federation, 2004.

214. The question, who the registrar of marriages is and whether there is a conflict between the provisions of the Constitution on registrations is answered by the purposes of registration. The purpose of centralised registration is a record of civil status. It goes to continuing identification and ascertainment of civil status of an individual, not only with regards to marital status but also births and deaths. The purpose of a marriage registration is to have a recorded document of the completion of the marital act for public records.

215. Civil status is the registration of vital statistics by the government of a country. The most common way of achieving this is through civil registration, and more specifically, the registration of such vital biological data as births and deaths. Births would include live births and stillbirths. The United Nations contemplates civil registration to include live births, deaths, foetal deaths, marriages and divorces.[274] It defines civil registration as: 'the continuous, permanent, compulsory and universal recording of the occurrence and characteristics of vital events pertaining to the population as provided through decree or regulation in accordance with the legal requirements of a country'.[275] The ultimate goal of the United Nations is for civil registration to encompass annulments, judicial separations, adoptions, legitimations and recognitions of marriages.[276] Civil registration is carried out primarily for the purpose of establishing the legal documents required by law. These records are also the main source of vital statistics. Complete coverage, accuracy and timeliness of civil registration are essential to ensure the quality of vital statistics. There is also a framework within which civil registration exists – that framework should cover all vital events occurring in all geographic areas and all population groups in the national area.[277]

216. With respect to family and succession law, civil status is more commonly used to refer to the marital status of a person. In more modern usage, this will cover modern understanding of marriage. In Nigeria it refers only to marriage between a man and a woman or women. Nigeria prohibits same-sex marriages.[278] Polyandry is recognised in some customs in Nigeria. These variations in accepted marital forms are not uncommon. In *Saheed Gbadebo Kareem v. Secretary of State for The Home Department*[279] a case which concerned a Nigerian man claiming spousal relationship with a European Union member person, the tribunal noted:

---

274. Handbook on Civil Registration and Vital Statistics … https://www.unhcr.org/registration-guidance/chapter1/introduction-to-the-guidance-on-registration/ – UNSD available at unstats.un.org/files/Handbooks/crvs/crvs-mgt-E (last accessed 18 Aug. 2020).
275. At http://unstats.un.org/UNSD/demographic/sources/civilreg/default.htm *Unstats.un.org*. Accessed 18 Aug. 2020. *See also* Handbook on Civil Registration and Vital Statistics Systems Computerisation, United Nations New York, 1998.
276. The Hague Convention on Celebration and Recognition of the Validity of Marriages or Hague Marriage Convention is a multilateral treaty developed by The Hague Conference on Private International Law that provides for the recognition of marriages. signed: 1978: Entry into force: 1 May 1991. Nigeria is not a signatory to this Convention.
277. *Ibid.*
278. Same Sex Marriage (Prohibition) Act 2013.
279. (Immigration and Asylum Chamber) [2014] UKUT 00024(IAC).

The Member States do not share a common definition of spouse, each state defining marital relationships for itself. For example, in several Member States a person cannot be a spouse if of the same sex as the partner whilst the laws of other Member States describe such a person as a spouse. Similarly, whilst many Member States refuse to describe any person in a polygamous relationship as a spouse other than the person first married, the laws of other Member States may recognise all partners as spouses in certain circumstances. In terms of EU law, the law of marriage can be said to be within the competence of the Member States.[280]

217. By Article 16(2) of the Convention on the Elimination of all Forms of Discrimination Against Women[281] (CEDAW), State parties are required to avoid child marriages, specify a minimum age for marriage and make the registration of marriages in an official registry compulsory. Nigeria is a signatory to this Convention.[282]

218. In 1992, Nigeria's Federal government passed the Births, Death, ETC. (Compulsory Registration) Decree No. 69 which repealed the Births and Deaths (Compulsory Registration) Act, 1990.[283] This was under a Military government and by the provisions of section 315 of the Nigerian Democratic Constitution of 1999, the decree transmuted into an Act of the National Assembly. The Act is now known and cited as the Births, Death, ETC. (Compulsory Registration) Act, Cap B9 Laws of the Federation, 2004 (B, D, Etc. Act, 2004).[284]

219. The Birth, Deaths, Etc. (Compulsory Registration) Act is the enabling law for registration of Civil Status. The Act contains eight chapters. It has one schedule of repeals and definitions. Section 49 of the Act provides for subsidiary legislation which has been made for the regulation of administration of the provisions of the Act. The regulations are contained in the Births, Death, Marriages, Etc., (**Registration**) Regulations (B, D, M Etc. Regulation, 1996).[285]

---

280. *Saheed Gbadebo Kareem v. Secretary of State for The Home Department* [2014] UKUT 00024(IAC), para. 7.
281. Adopted 1979: Effective: 3 Sep. 1981: Signature: 2000, Ratification/Accession: 2004. It is to be noted that CEDAW due to constitutional constraints is yet to become fully enforceable although its contents are persuasive and Courts have referred to its content in some land mark decisions such as *Muojekwu v. Muojekwu* [1997] 7 NWLR (part 512) 283. Section 12 of the Constitution of the Federal Republic of Nigeria specifically requires legislative domestication through the National Assembly of international conventions before they can be legally enforced as a consequence, until an enabling legislation to domesticate the Convention is passed it remains persuasive.
282. Opened for signature on March 1, 1980 and entered into force on 3 Sep. 1981. Adopted on 18 Dec. 1979 by the United Nations General Assembly. Nigeria ratified it in 1985 without reservation, signed the Optional Protocol in 2000.
283. Cap 36 Laws of the Federation, 1990.
284. Section 318 of the Constitution defines an Act or act of the National Assembly as meaning any law made by the National Assembly and includes any law which takes effect under the provisions of the Constitution as an act of the National Assembly. *See also* s. 52 of Births, Death, ETC. (Compulsory Registration) Act and 51 of Births, Death, ETC. (Regulations) [S.1.6 of 1996]. When the enactment relates to a State of Nigeria it is known as a Law.
285. [S.I. 6 of 1996.] Laws of the Federation, 2004.

220. The Births, Death, ETC. (Compulsory Registration) Act is national in its application, that is, central. Item 61 of the Constitution confers legislative competence on the Federal Legislature, for formation, annulment, and dissolution of marriages, and it expressly excludes customary and Islamic law marriages, which are also recognised marriages in Nigeria. Significantly, though, vital civil data – a national responsibility encompasses marriages and their dissolution. The marriages covered are the statutory and customary law marriages. Registration of Islamic marriages, *Nikãh*, is implied since Area Courts are designed for Muslims. There is provision for registration of the *talak* – dissolution of Islamic marriage. Vital data documentation also extends to the use of the same data recorded and collated for births, deaths and marriages as statistical data for policy formulation surrounding the health of citizens and non-citizens in Nigeria.[286]

221. Section 51 of the Regulation defines the 'Commission' as the National Population Commission established under section 1 of the National Population Commission Act.[287] The Commission is a body corporate. It has a Chairman who is appointed by the President. It was established in 1988 with the statutory powers to collect, analyse and disseminate demographic data in the country. It is also mandated to undertake demographic sample surveys, compile, collate and publish migration and civil registration statistics as well as monitor the country's population policy.[288]

222. The Regulations confers on the National Population Commission authority to make regulations for the purposes of the Act and for the due administration thereof and without prejudice to the generality of the other provisions of the Act. Such regulations as the Commission may make are on the register of births, stillbirths, deaths, marriages, divorces, and other records required to be maintained under the Act.

223. The legislative intent and objective of the Birth, Deaths, Etc. (Compulsory Registration) Act is the provision of accurate and efficient civil status data – recording, collation, custody, and retrieval for local and international purposes. Thus, the operational agency, the National Population Commission, is the only authority to issue certified true copies of the content of the register of status of births, marriages, and deaths. The CRA requires all births, fostering and adoption to be registered with the National Population Commission. Thus, section 5(2) requires that the birth of every child must be registered in accordance with the provisions of the Birth, Death, etc. (Compulsory Registration) Act. Sections 112 and 142 create a foster and adopted children's register which are to be domiciled with the chief Registrar of the National Population Commission in accordance with the same Act. The Act by section 277 defines: 'Register of Birth' means the Register of Birth kept by the Commission.

---

286. Section 26 of the B, D, Etc., Act.
287. Cap 270 Laws of the Federation, 1990; N67, Laws of the Federation, 2004.
288. At www.Nigeriacrvs.gov.ng/.

224. Thus, the scope of civil status and vital data documentation in Nigeria encompass:

(i) The right of a human being to identity is captured by registration and documentation of all human births and death. The registration targets identification, documentation and maintenance of records and registry. The scope of registration extends to particulars of stillbirths[289] and the burial of such remains.[290] It also covers the particulars of foundlings.[291]
(ii) Marriages, their registration and dissolution.[292] Provisions cover the registrar,[293] registry, maintenance of records and registry.
(iii) Vital data documentation for the purposes of health policy directives[294] in line with the provisions of the African Charter on Human and Peoples' Rights.[295]

225. Lacklustre compliance with registration of births, marriages and death in Nigeria is aside from challenges identified above, traceable to the changes of governments and attendant lack of continuity in strategic policy directions, sensitisation, and awareness. Another important factor of lacklustre compliance is confusion on who the Registrar of marriages is. Other factors include multiplicity of governmental agencies on the subject, multiplicity of marriage laws, lack of political will on enforcement of the laws, etc. The provisions of the Act clearly indicate an appreciation of a background of low citizen's sophistication in matters of these kinds. Thus, the Second Schedule by item 'n' makes provision for dissemination of information on the Act.

226. It must be stated straight away that the Act provides a veritable tool and structure for registration of civil status were it to be properly implemented. The Chief Registrar is at the Centre and is the most important, although not, the highest placed functionary in the structural hierarchy of registration of civil status in Nigeria.

I. Structure of Birth, Deaths, Etc. (Compulsory Registration) Act

227. At the apex of the structure of the Act is the Registrar General. Section 2(1) of the Act provides for the Appointment of a Registrar-General by the Commission. Section 2(2) significantly provides that 'the Registrar-General may issue such general directions regarding registration of births and deaths as may be necessary for the efficient implementation of the Act and shall take steps to co-ordinate and unify the activities of all registration officials involved in the implementation of this Act'.

289. Sections 9 and 13.
290. For which a certificate of burial is required by s. 32.
291. Section 7.
292. Section 34.
293. Section 7.
294. Section 26.
295. Commonly referred to as the Banjul Charter: Adopted 27 Jun. 1981, OAU Doc. CAB/LEG/67/3 rev. 5, 21 I.L.M. 58 (1982), entered into force 21 Oct. 1986.

228. Section 3 of the Birth, Death, etc. (Compulsory Registration) Act provides for the appointment of the Chief Registrar for each State of the Federation and the FCT, Abuja. The Chief Registrar is subject to the Registrar-General and responsible for overseeing the activities relating to the registration of births and deaths within the State or the FCT, Abuja to which he is appointed. The Chief Registrar is vested with the power within the State to issue all information with regards to civil Status. It is to be noted that the vital data of marriages and health are omitted in this section. However, Regulation 6 specifies the duties of the Chief registrar to include these data.

229. Section 4 provides for the appointment of the Deputy Chief Registrar. Section 4(1) states: 'There shall be appointed for each Local Government Area within a State or each Area Council in the Federal Capital Territory, Abuja, a Deputy Chief Registrar.' Section 4(2) further provides: 'The Deputy Chief Registrar shall be subject to the general direction of the Registrar-General and the Chief Registrar and be responsible for the implementation of this Act within the Local Government Area or Area Council to which he is appointed.'

230. Section 5 provides for appointments outside the existing structure of the National Population Commission and states: 'The Commission may appoint for the purposes of this Act such other number of registrars of different grades as the Commission may consider necessary for the enforcement of the provisions of this Act.' However, Regulation 1(5) directs that the Commission may appoint such other officers for the Regulation Centres from the Local Government office or the Area Council office of the Commission to be known as Registrars.

231. The Registrar is the head of the registration centre. Section 6 of the Act specifies the requirements for registration centres. The Commission may establish such registration centres as may be necessary, specifying in each case, the catchment area, of such centres; appoint registrars in each of the registration centres; and notwithstanding these may appoint in the case of a prescribed institution, any officer or other employee thereof as institutional registrar for the purposes of this part of the Act. Regulation 6 streamlines the duties of the registrar:

232. A registrar shall:

(a) register in the proper register the event that should be registered under these Regulations;
(b) keep himself informed of all births, deaths, marriages, and divorces, as the case may be, occurring in his area of jurisdiction;
(c) perform such other duties as may be assigned to him from time to time, by the deputy Chief Registrar; and
(d) perform the other duties assigned to him under these Regulations.

233. Thus, the B, D, ETC. Act contemplates registration at a central Registry which is coordinated by the Deputy Registrar from the local government or area council level to the Chief Registrar of the State or the FCT. The hierarchy of authorities and efforts at secured documentation are clearly provided in the Act. The Regulations specify the responsibilities of all the other officers.

234. Regulation 1 specifies the **occupiers of the vital offices** required for the implementation of the Act reinforcing the fact that the Registrar of civil status is the National Population Commission.

235. Regulation 1(1) specifies the Registrar-General as the Chairman of the Commission: 'Without prejudice to the provisions of the Births, Deaths, Etc. (Compulsory Registration) Act (in these Regulations referred to as "the Act") the Chairman of the Commission shall also be known and referred to as the Registrar-General.'

236. Regulation 1(2) specifies the Deputy Registrar-General as the Director, Vital Registration Department of the Commission: 'The Director, Vital Registration Department of the Commission shall, for the purposes of these Regulations, also be known and referred to as the Deputy Registrar-General.'

237. Regulation 1(3) specifies the Chief Registrar as the Director of the Commission in each State of the Federation and of the FCT, Abuja. 'The Director of the Commission in each State of the Federation and of the Federal Capital Territory, Abuja shall be known as the Chief Registrar.' Regulation 1(4) is noteworthy as it specifies who the Deputy Chief Registrar is, as the Comptroller of the Local Government office of the **Commission** in the Local Government Areas of each State of the Federation and of the Area Councils of the FCT, Abuja.

238. The most important functions are reserved for the Chief Registrar of the State or the FCT. They are listed in Regulation 4:

(a) oversee the activities relating to the registration of births and deaths within the State or the FCT, Abuja, to which he is appointed;
(b) takes charge of the registration office of the Commission within the State or the FCT, Abuja;
(c) files all registrable certificates and documents in the appropriate register;
(d) compiles and makes monthly returns on all registrable certificates and documents to the Registrar-General;
(e) issues certified copies of any certificate or document registered upon payment of the appropriate fees;
(f) orders the binding, properly classified, of all certificate documents registered within a particular year;
(g) sends to the Registrar-General monthly, for filing, a copy of all entries made during the preceding month;
(h) indexes the information to facilitate search and identification;
(i) administers oaths for purposes of registration;
(j) accepts all registrable documents and judicial decrees and orders affecting the civil status of persons;

(k) transcribes and enter, file keep and preserve in a secure place all books required by law to be preserved;
(l) transcribes and enters immediately upon receipt all registrable documents and judicial decrees affecting the status of persons in the appropriate registers;
(m) receive applications for the issuance of a marriage licence and after determining that the requirements and supporting certificates and publication thereof for the prescribed period have been complied with, issue the licence upon payment of the fee specified in the Second Schedule to these Regulations;
(n) liaise with the Registrar-General in conducting public enlightenment for vital registration and assist in the preparation of demographic and other statistics for the Local Governments;
(o) file, keep and preserve records as required by the National Archives Act;
(p) submit status reports on the condition of the registered documents filed in the registry whenever there are changes of the previous status of files;
(q) re-construct destroyed or damaged registry records in compliance with procedures as may be specified by the Registrar-General, from time to time;
(r) make available at all times the required registration forms; and
(s) carry out such duties as are required, from time to time, by the Registrar-General or the Commission.

239. The regulation also has two schedules, the First Schedule is on the standard forms and format with which all registrations should comply. The Second Schedule is on fees. It is compulsory to comply with all the registration requirements. Failure to comply with registration is an offence for which the penalties are provided for in Part VIII of the Act, sections 46–48. The offences range from failure of the Registrar to carry out the stated functions of registration, parents or concerned persons failing to provide information, or put persons forward for any of the heads of registration. The time allowed for registration is sixty days, for registration of birth, marriage, or report of death. There are no fees required for registration of birth where it is done within the time specified. A birth certificate is issued for registration of birth. The process of registration covers procedures from the local registration point and then to the central office in the FCT.

240. The structure established by the B, D, Etc. Act, and B, D, M, Etc., Regulations, from down to the apex is: Registrar, Deputy Registrar, Chief Registrar, Deputy Registrar General and Registrar General. The operational offices are the customary or Area Court registry, the registration centres as catchment or other designated small group areas, the office of the Comptroller of the National Population Commission in each local government, the office of the Chief Registrar of the National Population Commission in the State Capital or the FCT, and the head office of the National Population Commission in Abuja, the capital of the Federation.

II. Vital Data for Health Purposes

241. As is usual with civil registration status, another principal objective is to use the data to drive other aspects of the socio-economic spectrum of the society.

Health is an important aspect of family life and development. Thus, another key governmental agency connected with the application of the B, D, Etc., Act is the Ministry of Health at Federal and State levels. Section 26(2) of the Act makes it mandatory for every Ministry of Health to procure, analyse and forward to the Chief Registrar in each State or to the Registrar-General in the case of the Federal Ministry of Health, such vital and health statistics on births and deaths as may be required.

242. In line with this connectivity, Article 26 of the **B, D, Etc., Act** provides that the Department in Health Ministries shall be responsible for statistics. Thus:

(1) The department responsible for statistics within the Federal Ministry of Health and the Ministry of Health in each State of the Federation and the FCT, Abuja, shall be responsible for the collection of vital statistics comprising:
  (a) the recording of births of Nigerians and non-Nigerians;
  (b) the recording of deaths of Nigerians and non-Nigerians;
  (c) the recording of stillbirths.

243. The African Charter on Human and Peoples' Rights makes provisions towards the health of individuals. Article 16(1) and (2) of the Charter provide: 'Every individual shall have the right to enjoy the best attainable state of physical and mental health' and 'States parties to the present Charter shall take the necessary measures to protect the health of their people and to ensure that they receive medical attention when they are sick.'

III. Registration of Marriages

244. Registration of marriages in Nigeria contemplates two parallel hierarchies. The marriage framework under the Marriage Act provides certificates and a line of registration that advances to the National Population Commission. The other hierarchy is the marriages under customs or Islamic law. These two marriages do not provide certificates and the closest legal path to authentication is the area or customary court where the marriages were conducted. The marriages are registrable either at the registry of the customary or Area Court where the marriage took place by virtue of the Births, Deaths (Compulsory Registration) Act. This first registration is for the purposes of proof of marriage. This tier is essentially for issuing of certificate after celebration of the marriage in the registry,[296] place of worship,[297] under the directives of the Minister of Internal Affairs[298] or the office of a Nigerian diplomatic or consular officer of the rank of Secretary or above where the marriage is between a Nigerian citizen and citizen of a foreign country.[299] The registration contemplated at these points involves the parties to the marriage.

296. Section 27 of the Marriage Act.
297. Section 25 of the Marriage Act.
298. Sections 13 and 29 of the Marriage Act.
299. Section 54; 49–53.

245. The second point is with the Registry of the National Population Commission specifically designated for the establishment and protection of status of marriage which encompasses dissolution. Registration of marriages as a civil status goes to perfection of a legal relation. It does not go to proof of marriage alone. Proof of marriage is, in fact, a matter between the parties to the marriage and is relevant for matters such as proof of name, children of the marriage, matrimonial causes, etc. The production of a certificate of marriage simpliciter is not proof of marriage. Conversely, non-production of a certificate is not sufficient in itself to deny the existence of a marriage. This is the main reason that there are viable presumptions of marriage quite aside from the production of a certificate.

246. In Nigeria, cohabitation between a man and woman raises a rebuttable presumption of marriage under Islamic or customary law.[300] In *N v. D* (Customary Marriage),[301] the Family Division of the High Court of England and Wales held concerning a Nigerian customary marriage that Nigerian law provides for a presumption of a valid marriage arising from cohabitation but chose not to call up presumptions since there was ample evidence of marriage, albeit on evidence other than certification. The court granted the wife's application for declarations of marital status under section 55(1)(a) of the Family Law Act, 1986.

247. Nigerian academics and writers have made consistent calls on the Federal government to provide a holistic resolution of concerns over who the Registrar of marriages is in Nigeria. One commentator wrote:

> One Constitutional problem that arises since the enactment of the 1979 Constitution and the extant 1999 Constitution is that there seems to be an imperfect devolution of powers with respect to marriage(s) among the tiers of government. The Exclusive list grants the Federal Government powers over 'formation, annulment and dissolution' of a statutory marriage. It can be assumed that this necessarily includes the registration of such marriages and issuance of the certificate. However, such an assumption is challenged by a provision of the fourth schedule, which vests in the local government councils, the power to register marriages. This ambiguity has created many controversies in recent times. The local government councils have established marriage registries, appointed marriage registrars, and issued marriage certificates for statutory marriages. Recently those issues have been litigated in several cases such as *Haastrup v. Eti-Osa Local Government*'[302] *Egor Local Govt., Edo State & Ors. v. Hon Minister of Interior*[303] amongst others.[304]

300. Section 166 of the Evidence Act, 2011.
301. [2015] EWFC 28.
302. FHC/L/870/2002 of 08/12/2004.
303. FHC/1/CS/1760/16 of 30/04/2018.
304. Abubakri Yekini, *Proof of Nigerian Marriages in Foreign Courts: Any Lessons from Kareem v. Secretary of State for Home Department?*, in *Reflections on Dynamics of the Law: Essays in Honour of O.A. Adigun Fagbohun* 460, 471 (Funminiyi Adeleke ed., Faculty of Law 2019).

248. Elsewhere, the Federal Government warned that Marriage Registries were the sole authorities to register and conduct statutory marriages:

> The Association of Local Governments Marriage Registrars of Nigeria has insisted that local government areas in the country have the exclusive power to register marriages, contrary to the claim of the Federal Government. The Ministry of Interior and local government councils in Nigeria had been on a war path for a while now over disagreement on the body responsible for the registration of statutory marriages in Nigeria. The Association of Local Governments Marriage Registrars of Nigeria, in a statement signed by its President, Sokeye Deji and Secretary, Chinda Joy Ruhuoma on Thursday, was reacting to publications in some national dailies by the Ministry of Interior which were warning Nigerians not to register their statutory marriages in the Local Government, stressing that the third tie of government lacked the constitutional power to do so.[305]

249. The question of who the registrar of marriages is in Nigeria is answered by reference to laws, their applications, and purposes. Law also seeks to provide order in social relations by providing authentication and proof of those relations. To fulfil the purpose of registration of marriages, the Constitution provides a clear guide. The Marriage Register Book for marriages under the Marriage Act is the appropriate guide and for a full civil status, the Register of the National Population Commission. Marriages must be registered at these two offices for purposes of proof and authentication. Regarding customary and Islamic marriages, the proper route of registration is from the area of customary courts to the National Population Commission. It is not enough for the local government to arrogate to itself, the registration and celebration of marriages; it must first be ascertained the purpose of the function vested on local governments by the Constitution and second whether having arrogated the function of registration of marriages to itself, it is in fact positioned to handle the claims it is making. As has been noted even with the customary marriages:

> The overall picture of efforts to register customary law marriages is unsatisfactory:
>
> > First, there is no systematic and compulsory system of registration in some parts of the country.
> >
> > Second, even in those areas where the Local Government authorities are empowered to make by-laws on registration of marriages, the exercise of that power is optional. The result is that a large number of Local Governments have not yet made any by-law in this respect.

---

305. Joshua Odeyemi, *Nigeria: Local Govts Have Exclusive Right to Register Marriages, Registrars Insist*, available at https://www.google.com/urlallafrica.com; https://allafrica.com/stories/201912060088.html; also available at: https://dailytrust.com/local-govts-have-exclusive-right-to-register-marriages-registrars-insist (last accessed 26 Aug. 2020).

Third, where by-laws for registration are in force, the resulting record may be of doubtful validity because the Registrar can only record such particulars of the marriage as are supplied to him. He does not record facts which are either within his personal knowledge or certified as true in a certificate.[306]

250. It must be added that nowhere has the local governments been authorised to issue certified true copies of marriage certificates. The proper role of the local government on the constitutional function conferred on it in this regard will be discussed below.

IV. Local Government and Registration of Vital Data

251. *Egor Local Government of Edo State & 2 Other Local Governments v. The Honourable Minister of Interior & 2 Ors.*[307] is a judgment that was well publicised. It was heard by a Federal High Court sitting in Lagos. The case was on the lawful authority to register marriages in Nigeria. The Court's judgment was that since a Court of the same hierarchy had adjudicated on the matter, the parties ought to have filed an appeal to a higher Court. In the earlier case which the court referred to, *Haastrup & Anor. v. Eti Osa Local Govt. & 2 Ors.*,[308] it was held that the local government councils in Nigeria are vested with the sole power to register marriages. Following that judgment, there is now uncertainty as to whether the local governments or the Marriage Registries are the proper authorities to register marriages. Prior to the decision, the Marriage Registry in the different marriage districts in the country celebrated marriages and issued certificates. Celebrating couples signed a Marriage Register Book. Subsequent cases since then have centred on certificates and the form it should take, with a Lagos High Court confirming that it should be in Form E as provided by the Marriage Act and that the variant previously issued by Local Government Councils was invalid. Married persons were directed to have the certificates of marriages by Local Government Councils reissued.

252. The judgment in *Haastrup & Anor. v. Eti Osa Local Govt. & 2 Ors.*[309] was based on the function assigned to the local governments by the Constitution. However, one would have expected that since monogamous marriage and its formation is in the exclusive legislative competence of the Federal Legislature, and a body, the National Population Commission is established under the Constitution, for the same purpose with an enabling Act reinforced by another Act with the same specific and

306. Accessed: https://www.wikiprocedure.com/index.php/Nigeria_-_Register_Customary_Marriage (9 Sep. 2020).
307. FHC/1/CS/1760/16 of 30/04/2018.
308. FHC/L/870/2002 of 08/12/2004.
309. *Ibid.*

ancillary purposes of registration of births, deaths and marriages, the National Population Commission should have been a party to the proceedings. The National Population Commission was not party to the litigation and the Court was not referred to the enabling legislation of the governmental agency or that on births, death, and marriages. In its judgment, the court did not also refer to the stated relevant legislation or office or did the court invite the counsels to address it on them.

253. The judgment, however, forms the law on the subject now in Nigeria. How this impacts third parties – internationally and locally is now a policy question for the government of Nigeria. The judgments in *Egor* and *Haastrup* clearly created more problems than solutions as the cases and agitations that followed the judgments demonstrate. The Local Government Councils are a grassroot linkage in the governance structure in Nigeria as elsewhere. Indeed, item 'n' of the Second Schedule of the B, D, Etc., Act makes provision for dissemination of information on the Act and the relationship between the administration of the Act and the local government. It states that 'the Chief Registrar of each State of the Federation and of the Federal Capital Territory, Abuja shall liaise with the Registrar-General in conducting public enlightenment for vital registration and assist in the preparation of demographic and other statistics for the Local Governments. As has been stated above, the Comptroller of the Commission is specifically empowered to oversee the operations of the commission at each local government area'.

254. Local Government Councils have been celebrating marriages. Where a local government celebrates marriages not being a body known or authorised for such functions, it should also comply with section 30 of the Marriage Act by ensuring that Form F is completed and forwarded to the registrar of marriages in a marriage district, who must then make necessary returns to the Chief Registrar of the National Population Commission. This becomes difficult since Marriage districts are far fewer than local government councils. Second as has also been earlier noted, marriage in Nigeria under the lawful framework of the Marriage Act is conducted, by the registrars of marriages or Ministers of places of worship, under license from the Minister of Interior, or in an office in a Diplomatic mission. This is a well-structured framework.

255. It remains unclear how the Local Government Councils in Nigeria came to celebrate Marriages rather than register them as indicated in the Constitution. Section 6 of the MA which provides for places for celebration of marriages does not include Local Governments. The Places for Celebration of Marriages (Delegation of Licensing Powers) Order,[310] made pursuant to section 6 which delegates the power for designation of places for celebration of marriages to the Permanent Secretary at the Federal Ministry of Internal Affairs (now Interior), does not include the Local Government Chairman nor the Local Government Council. The Supreme Court in *James Egubson v. Joseph Ikechukwu*[311] held that a monogamous marriage

310. L.N. 105 of 1967 retained as a subsidiary legislation to the Marriage Act, Cap M6, Laws of the Federation, 2004.
311. [1977] ALL NLR 194; [1976] 6 SC 1; [1977] LPELR-SC. 183/1975.

must be conducted in the specified places designated for marriages under the Act. Thus, a marriage which was conducted in a place of worship which had not applied to be granted a license was held not to qualify to celebrate monogamous marriages. Furthermore, the Local Government (Basic Constitutional and Transitional Provisions) Act[312] does not mention marriage at all. Local Government Councils have been in existence even as at the time of enactment of all the relevant laws: the MA, MCA, and BDM etc.

256. The Local Government (Basic Constitutional and Transitional Provisions) Act,[313] however, and the Constitution[314] confer powers on the local government as its own legislature and with powers to make by-laws. It is not clear whether these empower the local government to make laws at own whims and caprices, including celebration of marriage or perhaps, the function of registration of births, deaths, and marriages encompasses celebration of marriages. As has also been noted earlier, most of the councils have not enacted any by-laws.

257. The function of registration of births, deaths and marriages conferred on local governments is fundamentally for purposes of identification, questions regarding jurisdiction and domicile, and not for purposes of civil status (it is also for the same reason that the other register for grassroots marriages is the customary or Area Court where the marriage took place). This is more clearly reflected in the Matrimonial Causes Rules. That the purpose of the constitutional provision is merely for grassroots identification and governance and therefore an archive is demonstrated by the Constitutional operational coverage for local governments – locality[315] and items 4, 6 and 23 of the Concurrent Legislative List in the Constitution of the Federation.

258. Thus, for instance, the BDM etc., (Registration) Regulations, 2004 provides by section 38, that 'the registrar shall not issue his certificate as required under paragraph 1 of the regulation until he has been satisfied by affidavit: (a) that one of the parties has been resident within the district for at least fifteen years preceding the issue of the certificate'.[316] The requirement for Certificate of Notice under the

312. Number 7 1997, (included as Laws of the Federation, 2004, but without a Cap).
313. Section 1(5) of the LOCAL GOVERNMENT (BASIC CONSTITUTIONAL AND TRANSITIONAL PROVISIONS) Act provides that the legislative powers of a Local Government shall be vested in the Local Government Council and s. 1(6) provides that a Local Government Council shall have power to make by-laws on matters conferred on it by the Act or by an Edict or a Law. Section 28 of the same Act provides that the Local Government Council or Area Council is the legislature of the Local Government Area or Area Council, as the case may be and accordingly, the legislative powers of a Local Government or Area Council shall be exercised by the Local Government Council or Area Council.
314. Section 7(5) of the Constitution the legislative powers of a Local Government shall be vested in the Local Government Council.
315. *See* above – introduction to Registration of Civil Status.
316. Regulation 38– issuance of registrar's certificate.

Marriage Act is fifteen days.[317] It is again to be noted that the reference is to a district and not local government, but the subsection demonstrates the significance of identification by some locality in Nigeria.

259. It must be quickly stated that the fifteen-year requirement is not an accidental provision. This is the same period that a person who wishes to naturalise as a Nigerian citizen must have resided in Nigeria. Thus, section 27(2)(i) of the Constitution provides among other requirements that an applicant for naturalisation must have: '(i) resided in Nigeria for a continuous period of fifteen years'.

260. A proper evaluation of the constitutional provision on the functions of local government shows that they exclude a vital civil status data, 'marital status', in other words, the functions do not encompass a judicial resolution of any form of matrimonial cause and cannot therefore form a registry or register for the purposes of civil status which aims at establishing the civil status of an individual. Whereas, Part V, sections 30–34 of the Act, provides for registration of all customary marriages and if dissolved, registration to be done within sixty days specifically noting in section 30, 'notwithstanding anything contained in any other enactment'. Registration of *talak* – divorce of Muslims marriages is also covered. Regulations 34–41 of the subsidiary legislation – the B, D, M, Etc., Regulations provide for registration of statutory marriages, the notices, issuance of certificates, registration of marriage certificates and registration of dissolutions of marriages conducted under the Marriage Act.

261. In *Indyka v. Indyka*,[318] the court was asked whether, and if so when, it should recognise a decree of divorce granted in a foreign jurisdiction, the Court of Appeal held that:

> It is, [] a well-established principle of public policy applied by English Courts that so far as it applies within their part to ensure, the status of a person as married or single should be the same in every country which he visits, that is, that there should not be 'limping marriages'; and if marriages are to be dissoluble at all, this involves deciding what courts we should recognize as having jurisdiction to dissolve them, and it follows, therefore, that to the extent that the inhibition is removed by the extension of the jurisdiction of the English Courts themselves to decree of dissolution of marriages, the public policy requires English Courts to recognize the effectiveness of decrees of dissolution of marriages pronounced by courts in exercising their jurisdiction in circumstances which mutatis mutandis would entitle an English Court to exercise its extended jurisdiction to dissolve a marriage … For let us not pretend that the common law is changeless. If it were, it would have long ago been replaced by statutory codes. It is the function of the Courts to mould the Common law and to adapt it to the changing society for which it provides the rules of each man's duty to his neighbour, and that is what the Courts have been doing since 1953 in this

317. Section 11(1)(a) of the Marriage Act.
318. [1966] C.A. 3 ALL ER 583.

important field of Common Law … I think that in this present case we have the liberty, unfettered by any precedent to choose between the narrower basis of recognition of foreign decrees of dissolution which lately is adopted and the under basis which I have stated above. The latter seems to me to accord better with the public policy of avoiding limping marriages and with what the common man would think was common sense?[319]

262. Thus, it can be stated categorically that the Constitution could not have devolved a function on local governments beyond its ordinary scope of operation. It cannot but, be, conceded that Local Government Councils do not have the structure or machinery to meet the modern needs of registration of marriages and other civil status for local, *a fortiori*, international purposes. The local governments do not have the effective machinery to provide the hierarchical structure and roles envisaged for an intricate civil status data collation, maintenance, and retrieval for a country with a high population and geographical spread as Nigeria. There is also no known legislative provision for local governments to issue certified true copies of the content of registration made at local government offices. There are also no provisions for searches to be conducted at the Local Government Councils. The only logical deduction from the function conferred on the local government is repository for the functions stated above, and no more.

263. This is deducible from the language of the function, the content of the function, the operational scope of local governments and references made to the function by other legislation such as the BDM Act, the Matrimonial Causes Rules, and overall references with regards to grassroot identity. It is even more noteworthy that whereas there are supervisory structures for the Marriage Act and the Births, Deaths, Etc., Act, this is non-existent for the claims being made by the Local Government Councils. This explains why questions regarding the Council on the issues of registration of marriages are only adjudicated in a Court. Finally, the Child's Rights Act was enacted well into the democratic dispensation but nevertheless, by its section 277, defines the 'Register of Birth' to mean the Register of Birth kept by the Commission. If the MA were to be drawn up after 1992 (the year of enactment of the Births, Deaths Act), it would make the same reference with respect to marriages under the Act.

§2. The Registrar

I. Under the Marriage Act

264. The only duly authorised body to issue certificates of marriage in Nigeria is the registrar of the Marriage Registry. There are, however, references to the issuing of certificates in the B, D, Etc., Act. It is also claimed that the local governments issue certificates.

---

319. *Indyka v. Indyka* was cited with approval in *Agbaje v. Agbaje* [2010] UKSC 13; [2010] 1 AC 628; [2010] 2 WLR 709.

265. The provisions authorising the issue of certificate by the marriage registrar are contained in sections 24–30 of the Marriage Act. Section 24 provides that the Booklet for Certificates in Form E should be delivered by the Principal Registrar to the registrar of marriages who is to secure the same. The other sections make careful provisions for the process of signing, custody of duplicates, filings and returns. The office of the Principal Registrar having been revoked the responsibility now lies with the Chief Registrar of the National Population Commission. It must be stated that Nigeria has a well ordered and structured framework for a duly authenticated monogamous Marriage Registry. The hierarchy is evidently structured to ensure veracity.

266. A Lagos High Court in 2017 delivered a judgment in *Olumide Babalola v. Ikeja Local Government and Anor*[320] declaring the marriage certificates issued by local governments illegal and unconstitutional while restraining them from further issuance of 'Local Government Unified Marriage Certificate' to Nigerians.[321] The High Court followed the Supreme Court's decision in *Anyaegbunam v. Anyaegbunam*,[322] a case which is more fully discussed below.

267. The Claimant in the case applied for a declaration that the local government does not have the power to issue modified/customised marriage certificates different from the one provided for in Form E under section 24 of the Marriage Act and a declaration that the Registered Trustees of Association of Local Governments in Nigeria (ALGON) Unified Marriage Certificate is unconstitutional, null and void. The Court affirmed the position with regards to the form of the marriage certificates and declared that marriages that were already conducted in respect of which, certificates issued do not conform with Form E are valid in Law for all intents and purposes. It, however, ordered that the 'invalid certificates' be withdrawn and certificates in Form E issued to all couples affected. The High Court further declared in line with *Egor* and Harrison that registration of marriages is to be done by Local Government councils.[323]

268. Thus, certificates to monogamous marriages at this time in Nigeria are issued from the Federal Marriage Registries and Local Government Councils.

269. However, according to the lawful framework in accordance with available legislation on the subject, the first point of documentation is with the registrar at the

---

320. Suit NO. LD/1343GCM/16.
321. Peters Ifeoma, *Local Govt. 'Unified Marriage Certificate is Unconstitutional', – Justice Harrison*, available at dnllegalandstyle.com/Court room news (last accessed 27 Aug. 2020).
322. 1973 3 ECSLR 243.
323. Tokunbo Orimobi, *Ikoyi Marriage Registry – Government, Public Sector – Nigeria*, available at https://www.google.com/search?client=firefox-b-d&q=Tokunbo+Orimobi%2C+%E2%80%98 Ikoyi+Marriage+Registry+%E2%80%93++-+Government%2C+Public+Sector+%E2%80%93 +Nigeria#
(last accessed 26 Aug. 2020); Unini Chioma 'Class Action: Lagos State Orders Local Governments To Comply With Court Orders In The Marriage Certificates available at thenigerialawyer.com/ class-action-lagos-state-orders-loc...02.07.2017 (last accessed, 27 Aug. 2020).

Marriage Registry in the designated district. This registration happens as, of course, since the Notice and Certificate of Notice would have been issued at this point. Section 4(2) of the Marriage Act provides for the appointment of a fit and proper person to be the registrar of marriages for each marriage district, and a deputy registrar of marriages, who shall act in the absence or during the illness or incapacity of the registrar. Other relevant sections of the Act are sections 9, 10, 11, 25 and 26.

270. Section 9 provides that every registrar shall supply forms of notice gratuitously to any persons applying for the same. Section 10 requires that upon receipt of such notice the registrar shall cause the same to be entered in a book to be called the **Marriage Notice Book**, which may be inspected during office hours without fee. The registrar shall also publish such notice by causing a copy of the same to be affixed on the outer door of that office, and to be kept exposed there until a certificate is issued or until three months shall have elapsed. Section 11 provides that: '(1) The registrar, at any time after the expiration of twenty-one days and before the expiration of three months from the date of the notice, upon payment of the prescribed fee, shall thereupon issue a certificate to the applicants as in Form C in the First Schedule.'

271. All such certificates shall not be issued until the registrar has been satisfied by affidavit: (a) that one of the parties has been resident within the district in which the marriage is intended to be celebrated at least fifteen days preceding the granting of the certificate; (b) that each of the parties to the intended marriage (not being a widower or widow) is 21 years old, or that if either of the parties is under that age, the consent has been obtained in writing and is annexed to such affidavit; (c) that there is no impediment of kindred or affinity, or any other lawful hindrance to the marriage; (d) that neither of the parties to the intended marriage is married by customary law to any person other than the person with whom such marriage is proposed to be contracted.[324]

272. Section 25 provides that immediately after the celebration of any marriage by a minister, the officiating minister shall fill up in duplicate a marriage certificate with the particulars required as in the said Form E, and state and enter in the counterfoil of Form E, the number of the certificate, the date of the marriage, names of the parties, and names of the witnesses.

273. Section 26 provides for officiating Minister to transmit certificates to the registrar of marriages for the district for filing. Thus, the certificate must be signed in duplicate by the officiating minister, the parties, and by two or more witnesses to the marriage. The minister must also sign the counterfoil. The Minister shall then separate the duplicate certificate, deliver one certificate to the parties, and within seven days thereafter transmit the other to the registrar of marriages for the district in which the marriage has taken place, and the registrar shall file the same.

324. Section 11 of the MA.

274. The registrar must follow a solemn form in conducting a marriage. [325] The form encompasses a strict formality and ambience that accords with the moment in procedure and celebration of a monogamous marriage complying with affirmations from the parties and the role of witnesses. The registrar shall at the completion of the celebration, fill up, and with the parties and witnesses sign, the certificate of the marriage in duplicate. The registrar shall then fill up and sign the counterfoil as in the case of a marriage by a minister, and deliver one certificate to the parties, then file the other.[326] Section 32 provides that the certificate of the marriage celebrated and its certified true form shall be admissible in a Court or before persons whom it may concern as conclusive evidence of the marriage particulars it specifies:

> every certificate of marriage which shall have been filed in the office of the registrar of any district, or a copy thereof, purporting to be signed and certified as a true copy by the registrar of such district for the time being, and every entry in a marriage register book, or copy thereof certified as aforesaid, shall be admissible as evidence of the marriage to which it relates, in any court of justice or before any person having by law or consent of parties authority to hear, receive, and examine evidence.[327]

II. Under Customary and Islamic Marriages

275. There are no official marriage certificates for customary and Islamic marriages. The steps leading up to customary marriage are marked by public ceremonies and this, to some extent, provide evidence of the marriage, and the value of such evidence becomes severely diminished because it places reliance on the memory of persons who witnessed or participated in the ceremonies. With the passage of time such memory becomes dim and unreliable. In addition, the details and rites of customary marriages vary from one locality to another although in substance they may all be similar.

276. In modern times, celebrants keep an electronic recording and photographs of the event as evidence of the celebration. This is usually helpful but could also prove unreliable. At other times, a customary court or an Area Court may issue an Order of the Court as evidence of the marriage. The positive aspect of this is that the Order will be dependent on usual Court procedures backed up by witnessing on oath and attestation.

277. In view of these peculiarities, a Court order and Court registration are preferred first step to verifying customary and Islamic marriages. Section 30(1) of the B, D, Etc., Act makes it mandatory for the registration of customary marriages and their dissolution to be done within sixty days.

---

325. Section 27 of the MA.
326. Section 28 of the MA.
327. Section 32 of the MA.

278. Section 30 clearly provides:

(1) Notwithstanding anything contained in any enactment, every customary marriage contracted in or dissolved in Nigeria shall immediately after the commencement of this Act, be registered within sixty days in the area court or customary court where the marriage was contracted or dissolved.
(2) Every court registrar shall keep a marriage registrar and such books as may be prescribed by the Registrar – General and as soon as practicable after the end of each month deliver to the Chief Registrar such returns and in such form as the Registrar – General may require.

279. With respect to customary law and Islamic marriages, *Saheed Gbadebo Kareem v. Secretary of State for The Home Department*,[328] provides a good basis for appraising the issues of the Register and Registration on the two types of marriages. For the purposes of this analysis these two marriages are deemed on the same structure.

III. *Saheed Kareem v. Secretary of State for The Home Department*

280. The Upper Tribunal that heard the application on a purported Nigerian customary marriage stated:

> From this we infer that usually a marriage certificate issued by a competent authority will be sufficient evidence that a marriage has been contracted. Of course, a document which merely calls itself a marriage certificate does not have any legal status. A certificate will only have legal status if it is issued by an authority with legal power to create or confirm the facts it attests, that is, by an authority that has such competence. Where a marriage document has no legal status or where such status is unclear, other evidence may be used to establish that a marriage has been contracted. However, once again we find that these principles do not help us determine whether a person is a spouse because it will depend on identifying the authority with legal power to create or confirm that a marriage has been contracted.[329]

281. The applicant, a Nigerian citizen stated that he is married to a Dutch citizen who works and resides in the United Kingdom. Although the Secretary of State accepted that the person the applicant describes as his wife was a qualified person for the purposes of the Immigration (European Economic Area) Regulations 2006, the Secretary of State did not accept that the applicant is married under Nigerian customary law as claimed.

282. The applicant stated further that he married his wife on 26 November 2011 and that the ceremony in accordance with customary law was conducted by proxy

328. (Immigration and Asylum Chamber) [2014] UKUT 00024(IAC).
329. [2014] UKUT 00024(IAC), para. 13.

in his father's home in Mushin, Lagos State, Nigeria. The marriage was subsequently registered by the local customary court, which issued a marriage certificate. In support of his claim, the applicant produced an affidavit from his father, a court order, the marriage certificate and statements from the appellant and others.

283. The Secretary of State provided in evidence the Nigerian Births, Deaths, Etc. (compulsory Registration) Act, 1992 and two letters from the British High Commission, Abuja. The 'letters' from the British High Commission, Abuja stated how Nigerian law might be interpreted and applied, although this was not done from the point of view of a person with legal expertise. The Secretary of State's reason for disputing that the appellant was married in essence was that she does not believe that the evidence produced is sufficient to establish that the applicant is married according to Nigerian law.

284. The letters confirmed that proxy marriages, including those where neither the bride nor groom are present, are common and are recognised according to Nigerian customary law because such marriages are not merely the union of the couple but also the families. Second, that where legal requirements prescribe a marriage certificate to be presented, then only a certificate issued under the Marriage Act will be acceptable. Hence, most couples conduct 'registry weddings' in addition to their customary marriage.

285. The Tribunal noted further that:

(i) A Nigerian citizen can marry a foreigner by proxy under customary law in a ceremony that is held in Nigeria.
(ii) The validity of a customary marriage in Nigeria does not depend on it being registered within sixty days.
(iii) No certificates are issued in respect of customary marriages by any recognised official body and no official records are kept.

286. Some comments are necessary on these assertions. On issue (i), the submission of the High Commission is accurate. Proxy marriages are now considerably commonplace in Nigeria not because of the nature of the marriage, but the fact of international mobility and migration, and the inconvenience of long trips, aggravated by the hazards often experienced by parties travelling for customary marriage celebrations within Nigeria. The second reason many young people avoid the events leaving the outlandishness of the occasions to parents is because the society remains superstitious and parents who are cosmopolitan would rather travel to the villages for such rites and leave their children out of the trips, 'lest the great witches, wizards and demons' cast freaky spells. The witches and wizards could also operate in a more 'devastating frenzy by swapping destinies' – the destines of brilliant young men and women who have made residence in Europe and America. Not surprisingly, regarding travelling to villages for customary marriages, young people can be said to have as top priority, in their 'wish baskets' return of Mary Slessor.[330] Thus, it can be said that proxy for customary marriage has come to stay in many respects.[331]

287. On issue (ii), the High Commission is not so accurate as section 30(1) of the Act makes it mandatory for the registration of customary marriages and their dissolution to be done within sixty days.

288. On issue (iii), although there are no certificates issued in respect of customary marriages or Islamic marriages, there are, however, a court order could be applied for and issued as explained earlier on. In addition, two hierarchies of the process of registration reasonably authenticate a customary marriage in addition to physical examination of documented record of the event. This was properly articulated in *N v. D* (Customary Marriage).[332] The first is for the parties to celebrate the marriage complying with customary law precepts. The celebrants or the husband must then proceed to the Area Court's registry where the marriage took place and register the marriage. The second hierarchy of registration is for a registrar to liaise with the customary or Area Courts as the case may be, to ascertain the registrations done within a period, take the records and make returns to the Deputy Chief Registrar.

289. The Deputy Chief Registrar is the Comptroller of the National Population Commission at the Local Government of the Area Court or area council where the marriage took place. The Deputy Chief Registrar then makes further returns to the Chief Registrar of the State who issues all Certified True Copies of Registration of marriages to applicants. Today, this may take no more than a month and many government agencies in Nigeria pass information electronically on completion of processes to individuals. This is the position with the General Registrars' office in England and Wales. Copies of certificates are ordered online at a fee.

290. The Registrar of the customary or Area Court is also mandated as soon as is practicable to make returns of the registrations to the Chief Registrar of the National Population Commission in the State where the marriage took place. This provides a two-throng apparatus to ensure compliance between the Area Courts and the National Population Commission and that records are accurately kept. It is in fact all so simple, except for the dabbling of the Local Government Councils into the system.

330. Mary Mitchell Slessor (2 December 1848–13 January 1915) was a Scottish Presbyterian missionary to Nigeria. Once in Nigeria, Slessor learned Efik, one of the numerous local languages, then began teaching. Because of her understanding of the native language and her bold personality Slessor gained the trust and acceptance of the locals and was able to spread Christianity while promoting women's rights and protecting native children. She is most famous for having stopped the common practice of infanticide of twins in Okoyong, an area of Cross River State, Nigeria.

331. Research findings on the overall subject is placed in the Appendix.

332. [2015] EWFC 28.

291. The Tribunal in the *Kareem* also considered the provisions of B, D, M Etc., Act, 1992 which was presented in evidence by the Secretary of State for The Home Department. The Secretary disputed the perspectives from the High Commissioner's letters. The Tribunal noted:

> The details required for *registration* are the names of the bride and groom, their marital status, their occupations, their ages, their States of origin, the address of their usual place of residence, their nationalities, the name of the persons who consented to the marriage and the respective relationship of those persons to the bride and groom. The *certificate* should include most of these details together with the registration number, the date of marriage, the date of registration and the signature of the court registrar.
> We recognise that these provisions appear to give a different picture to that provided by the High Commission about whether a customary marriage could be registered and whether certificates could be issued. We do not know the reason for this difference. It may be something as simple as the relevant legislation never having been brought into force. This reflects the difficulties that arise in the absence of independent and reliable evidence regarding how the laws of a country are applied. We are unable to resolve this conflict … .[333]

292. First, it is noteworthy that the tribunal referred to a subsidiary legislation which is, the Regulations made pursuant to section 49 of the B, D, Etc., Act. Thus, the details referred to are in the Regulations.

293. Second, the Tribunal noted that the discrepancies between the information at the disposal of the High Commission and the provisions of the legislation may be attributable to 'something as simple as the relevant legislation never having been brought into force'. The legislation is very much in force so also are the major offices. There is a dearth of information about the Act, its objectives and operation. This limitation was fully appreciated in the Act.

294. In paragraph 42 of the Tribunal's finding, it stated that: 'In addition to these points, we are aware that the same Nigerian laws make provision about who can be a registrar. We have no evidence that the person who signed the certificate or the court order was a registrar. The court order, for instance, is silent on whether the marriage has been registered according to Nigerian law.'

295. This is the vital point. An order or certification does not amount to registration as required by law. A legal instrument must meet perfection indices to be so recognised and hence serve as notice to the whole world as evidence of what it represents. Any order from the customary or Area Court is required to be registered with the office of the National Population Commission. The key to ascertaining a valid, existing marriage is due registration with the Chief Registrar of the National Population Commission. Aside from the certified True Copies of entries made in the

333. [2014] UKUT 00024(IAC), paras 39 & 40.

Registers of the Deputy Chief Registrar, the register and the returns kept at the office of the Chief Registrar, section 41 of the Act provides for search of entries kept by Registrar General:

(1) A person shall be entitled at all reasonable hours upon payment of the prescribed fee to inspect any entry in any register and to obtain a certified copy of an entry.
(2) A certified copy of an entry in a register shall be receivable in evidence in all courts in Nigeria.

296. Second, the celebration of marriage is quite distinct from the function of its registration. A marriage may have been valid at a certain point in time but may no longer be in existence. Thus the B, D, Etc., Act provides for a register of marriage and divorce just as the Ghanaian framework.[334] The neighbouring country, Ghana, has the Ghanaian Marriage and Divorce (Registration) Law 1985. Again, this is all so simple, registration as a matter of civil status is a national matter. The Tribunal in *Awuku v. Secretary of State for the Home Department*[335] had no difficulty recognising a customary marriage that was registered under Ghanaian law. Ghana is a country with some diversity as Nigeria, although nowhere close with respect to population and geographical spread.

297. Awuku v. Secretary of State for the Home Department[336] requires a mention as it is a case that touched on *Kareem*. In *Awuku* the question was whether the law to govern the right of the appellant spouse was that of Germany or the United Kingdom. The qualifying national was resident in the United Kingdom. At the hearing by the First-tier Tribunal Judge, the marriage was proved to have been registered by the appropriate authority in accordance with the Ghanaian Marriage and Divorce (Registration) Law 1985. Permission to appeal to the Upper Tribunal in *Awuku* was granted on the basis that the judge had erred in failing to have regard to the decision in *Kareem* which required her to consider whether the marriage was recognised in the EEA national's home State, in this case Germany. The question on appeal to the Court of Appeal was the conclusion of the Upper Tribunal in *Kareem*: 'In such an appeal, the starting point will be to decide whether a marriage was contracted between the appellant and the qualified person according to the national law of the EEA country of the qualified person's nationality.'[337] The Court of Appeal rejected this position stating that this was tantamount to rewriting the laws on recognition of marriage in England and Wales and in private international law by which the rule is *lex loci celebrationis*.[338]

---

334. Section 31.
335. [2016] EWCA Civ 1303.
336. [2016] EWCA Civ 1303.
337. Paragraph 68(e).
338. Latin for 'the law of the land ***lex loci*** where the marriage was celebrated'. The Hague Convention on Celebration and Recognition of the Validity of Marriages or Hague Marriage Convention is a multilateral treaty developed by The Hague Conference on Private International Law that provides for the recognition of marriages. signed: 1978: Entry into force: 1 May 1991. Nigeria is not a signatory to this Convention.

298. It must be noted that in *Kareem* the Tribunal accepted the position that the *lex loci celebrationis*[339] of the marriage was applicable and that the recognition of such marriage was dependent on proof in the absence of appropriate recognisable legal documentation of the marriage. The court accepted that if the appellant is not married according to the laws of the country in which the marriage is said to have taken place, then he is not married according to the laws of England Wales. The problem arose with the other conclusion on the relationship of the EU national to the marriage and it is this aspect that was overruled by the Court of Appeal of England and Wales on the ground that it was contrary to the rules of private international law which makes the *lex loci celebrationis* the basis of recognition of marriages. This is also the situation in Nigeria. Sections 6(2) and 81 of the Matrimonial Causes Act enact the principles of *lex loci celebrationis*.

299. A Nigerian author commenting on *Kazeem* stated that: 'the English courts were misled to arriving at a conclusion that customary marriages are registrable in Nigeria under this Act. (Births, Deaths (Compulsory Registration), Act)'. The author further stated:

> They might have relied on the work of Professor Nwogugu who opined that the Act instituted a national registration system for customary marriages.[340] The Act predated the 1999 Constitution. Today, it is only a federal enactment whose provisions apply only in the Federal Capital Territory. By the provisions of the Fourth Schedule to the Constitution, only the Local Government Councils have the competence to register all marriages.[341]

300. Two assertions have been made by the author; that the B, D, Etc., Act applies only in the FCT. The basis of the assertion is unclear and is inaccurate. The position of the leading Family Law author, Nwogugu is clearly accurate. The second assertion is that the local governments have the sole competence to register marriages. If the author based this assertion on the authority of the cases of *Egor* and *Haastrup*, then that would be following judicial precedence set by the High Courts in the two cases, but the author based the assertion on the Constitution. The Constitution provides: '(1) The main functions of a local government council are as follows: (i) registration of all births, deaths and marriages.' The statement (provision) does not exclude other bodies from registering all births, deaths and marriages. That the word 'all' is used can also only be contextual in view of the legislative competences of the national assembly already explained and the overall tenor of the local government's operational coverage.

---

339. *Ibid.*
340. Abubakri Yekini above, nn. 304, 460, 475; citing E.I. Nwogugu, *Family Law in Nigeria* 76 (HEBN Publishers Plc. 2014).
341. *Ibid.*

IV. Marriage Registry and Registration of Vital Data

301. Section 86 of the Matrimonial Causes Act is on evidence and proof of marriage. It provides that in proceedings under the Act, the court may receive as evidence of the facts stated in it a document purporting to be either the original or a certified copy of any certificate, entry or record of a birth, death or marriage alleged to have taken place, whether in Nigeria or elsewhere.

302. This provision contemplates multi registrations and documentations. The drafters of the Act also clearly contemplated a civil registration system. It therefore identifies 'certificate, entry, or record'. It is also to be noted that the word used is 'or' and therefore disjunctive. It has earlier been noted that the Act itself makes no provision for a register of matrimonial causes. The author might then argue that the MCA was enacted before the Constitution but this is also unhelpful as the Constitution has had four alterations since enactment and has not touched the Act or the subject of marriages or its registration or births and deaths.

303. It is clear from the provisions of sections 11(1)(a) and 30 of the Marriage Act; Order V of the Matrimonial Causes Rules, and section 7(5) of the Constitution of the Federal Republic of Nigeria that marriages conducted in line with the provisions of the Marriage Act must be certificated at the relevant Marriage District Registry and registered in the Marriage Register Book. It is the duty of the registrar to then transmit the records to the National Population Commission which has the responsibility for the repository of civil status at all points in time from birth to death.

304. It is important to note the effect of the role of the Principal Registrar under the Marriage Act and its revocation by the B, D, Etc., Act. Section 5 of the Marriage Act provides that every registrar shall have an office at such place as the Minister shall direct. The office of the Principal Registrar shall be at such place as the Minister shall direct. This directive is evidently so ambulatory and irregular to be worth any attention as it would mean that no one knows at any point in time where the office of a Principal Registrar is or may spring up. Thus, by the Births Deaths Act, the office is abolished. The Order authorising the office and its functions is also revoked. The Act also places all functions of the Principal Registrar by section 34 of the Act and Regulation 50, in the office of the Chief Registrar of the National Population Commission. Section 34 of the BD Etc., Act thus provides for: 'Application of certain provisions of the Marriage Act': 'Any provision under the Marriage Act relating to the forwarding by the registrar of marriages to the principal registrar of a certified copy of all entries made by him during the preceding months in the marriage register of his area shall have effect and be construed as if references to the principal registrar were reference to the Chief Registrar under this Act'.

305. Regulation 50 is on revocation: 'Revocation of L.N. 72 of 1971 – The Marriage (Appointment of Principal Registrar, Registrars, etc.) Notice 1971 is hereby revoked'.

306. The erstwhile functions of the Principal Registrar under the Marriage Act are stated in sections 24, 30 and 31 of the Marriage Act. Section 24 is procedural and is on delivery and accountability for marriage certificates, forms etc. Section 30(3) requires the registrar to make returns to the Principal Registrar of duly issued certified true copies of certificates within ten days after the last day of each month.[342] Section 31 provides for rectification of clerical errors under the authority of the Principal Registrar. These roles are now for the office of the Chief Registrar of the National Population Commission under the B, D, Etc. Act.

307. With respect to the place of the Marriage Registry in the tier, while the Marriage Act provides for certification, filing and a 'marriage register book',[343] the Matrimonial Causes Act does not provide a register or registry. It only provides for decrees which should be a public document in the registry of the High Court granting the dissolution as to the decree made. Section 89 of the MCA also provides for the decree to be registrable in other courts but fails to mention a Register or registry for the decrees. Whereas, the B, D, Etc., Act, by Regulation 4(l) directs the Chief Registrar to transcribe and enter immediately upon receipt all registrable documents and 'judicial decrees' affecting the status of persons in the appropriate registers. The Act serves the purpose of legal perfection of civil status data.

308. Thus, the Marriage Registry is also ill-equipped for the function of a vital Civil Data Registry particularly with reference to requisite checks and balances. While a registrar of marriages can issue certified true copies of the marriage certificate and content of the marriage register book, it does not have information on actual marital status of the parties. Moreover, the revocation of the supervisory office of the Principal Registrar and its replacement with the Chief Registrar of the National Population Commission makes it questionable whether the registrar of marriages under the Act can now issue a valid certificate of the content of the Marriage Register Book. A task of a simple search, absent the national structure, will necessitate that an interested person travels to remote areas and any one of several impediments makes such an adventure as hazardous as incomprehensible. It is thus inconceivable that a country's marriage status or its vital civil status register is drawn solely from every nook and cranny of the country without a centralised oversight body.

§3. Registers and Certificates

I. Registers

309. The Register of Marriage as registration in Nigeria is triangular in structure. The triangular structure must be understood within the unique Nigerian experience in family and succession law. Thus, at the base of the triangle are registers of

342. It is to be noted that the office of the Principal Register is revoked, and the appropriate records is to be sent to the Chief Registrar of the National Population Commission in the relevant State.
343. Whatever this means. Section 32 of the Marriage Act.

the different marriages. On one side is the register for marriages conducted under the Marriage Act and on the other side of the base of the triangle are two registers: customary and Islamic law marriage registers. All the registers then converge at the National Population Commission through the relevant routes provided by the Births, Deaths (Compulsory Registration) Act.

II. Marriage Register Book

310. The first tier is the Marriage Register Book at the Marriage Registry in a designated marriage district.[344] The record to be filed is in **Form F** completed before a registrar of marriages at the Marriage Registry**.** This Book has a record of all marriages celebrated before a registrar at a Federal Marriage Registry in a Marriage District. The other places where records exist are at the point of celebrations, that is, recognised place of worship[345] or under license by the Minister of Interior to be celebrated at his pleasure,[346] or a diplomatic consular office.[347] The records of marriages in all the named places are required to be transmitted to the Marriage Registry. The registrar at the Marriage Registry is then to transmit records to the National Population Commission (the Principal Registrars' office having been revoked by the B, D, Etc., Act). Section 30 of the Marriage Act is on registry and evidence. It provides:

> (1) Every registrar shall forthwith register in a book to be kept in his office for such purpose, and to be called the Marriage Register Book, every certificate of marriage which shall be filed in his office according to the Form F in the First Schedule; and every such entry shall be made in the order of date from the beginning to the end of the book, and every entry so made shall be dated on the day on which it is so entered, and shall be signed by the registrar, and such book shall be indexed in such manner as is best suited for easy reference thereto.
> (2) The registrar shall at all reasonable times allow searches to be made in the marriage register book and shall give certified copies therefrom upon payment of the prescribed fee.
> (3) Within ten days after the last day of each month, every registrar shall send to the Principal Registrar a certified copy of all entries made by him during the preceding month in the marriage register book of his district, and the Principal Registrar shall file the same in his office.

311. The Births, Deaths Act revokes the office of the Principal Registrar which is replaced by filing with the Chief Registrar of the National Population Commission.

---

344. Section 30 of Marriage Act, Cap M6, Laws of the Federation, 2004.
345. Sections 6, 21–26.
346. Sections 13 and 29, Marriage Act, Cap M6, Laws of the Federation, 2004.
347. Marriage Act, Cap M6, Laws of the Federation, 2004.

312. The first step register for customary and Islamic marriages is at the registry of the customary or Area Court where the couples are resident, most presumably, the husband.

313. The second and apex hierarchy in the triangle is the superstructure – the National Population Commission.

314. Register at the Office of the Deputy Registrar – *the National Population Commission.*

315. Part III, Regulation 7 of the B, D, Etc., (Compulsory Registration) Regulations provides for the following registers.

316. It requires the Deputy Chief Registrar to maintain, keep and preserve in a secure place in his office, the following registers into which shall be properly entered the events specified in these regulations, that is:

(a) the Register of Births;
(b) the Register of Foundlings;[348]
(c) the Register of Stillbirths;
(d) the Adopted Children's Register;
(e) the Register of Deaths;
(f) Register of Statutory Marriages;
(g) Register of Customary Marriages;
(h) the Register of Divorces (Statutory);
(i) the Register of Divorces (Customary);
(j) such other Registers as may be specified, from time to time by the Registrar-General or the Commission.

317. The CRA, by section 142(1) requires the Chief Registrar to maintain an E51 – Adopted Children's Register. This is provided for in section 29 of the Births Death Act.

318. The Deputy Chief Registrar is subject to the general direction of the Registrar General and the Chief Registrar. Searches cannot be conducted at this office and certified copies are not issued from it. The same Register is available at the office of the Registrar General where searches can be conducted and certified copies issued at a fee.[349] The Register here is based on returns from the office of the Chief Registrar.

---

348. Regulation 51, the interprets: 'foundling' means:

(a) a deserted or abandoned child whose parents, guardian or relatives are not known; or
(b) a child committed to an orphanage or charitable or similar institution with unknown facts of birth or parentage.

349. Section 41 of the B, D, etc. Act.

319. The Regulations provide for the Chief Registrar to maintain the same Register based on returns from the Deputy Chief Registrar in his Office and to facilitate issuing of certified true copies of certificates and entries in Registers at a fee.[350]

320. The Register of the National Population Commission is structured after the General Register Office of England[351] and Wales.[352] This is where the similarity ends.

321. In England and Wales, while the office of the General Register superintends the functions of registrars and registry in collaboration with local authorities, which entails the hiring and payment of registrars by the local authorities, but local authorities cannot terminate the appointment of the registrars without the office of the General Register and the Registrar General. Thus:

> Registrars and superintendent registrars are appointed and paid by the local authority. The hours of attendance of registrars in their offices and outstations are also fixed by the local authority. The General Register Office assesses the amount of work to be performed in each district and sub district and this helps to determine the salary payable by the local authority to the officers But, although the officers are appointed locally they hold office during the pleasure of the Registrar General, which means that they cannot be dismissed by the local authority.[353]

322. In Nigeria, the National Population Commission is fully staffed and equipped for the purpose of its establishment. It is part of the Ministry of Interior. The hierarchy of filing and reporting in Nigeria is well structured between the Marriage Registry, the Area Courts and registrars of the National Population Commission. In fact, the Nigerian position totally excludes the role of local authorities as is practised in England by providing for a Deputy Chief Registrar who is known as a Comptroller of the Commission who seats in each Local Government Council and responsible for the implementation of the Act within the Local Government Area or Area Council to which he is appointed.[354]

III. General National Register

323. The Register of Marriages in Nigeria is with the National Population Commission. The register can be accessed from two points – one at the office of the

350. Regulation 4(2) of the B, D, M, (Compulsory Registration) Regulations.
351. At https://www.gov.uk/general-register-office.
352. *See also* that of Ireland – https://www.gov.ie/en/campaigns/af7893-general-register-office/; and that of Scotland.
353. Technical Papers Vital Registration and Marriage in England and Wales (International Institute for Vital Registration and Statistics 9650 Rockville Pike Bethesda, Maryland 20014 USA) available at: https://unstats.un.org/unsd/vitalstatkb/KnowledgebaseArticle50299.aspx last accessed 9 Sep. 2020.
354. Section 4(2) of the B, D, etc., Act.

Chief Registrar of the National Population Commission in the capital of each State of the Federation and the other at the office of the Registrar General of the Commission at the FCT.

324. The certified true copies of the content of the Register and searches are done with the Chief Registrar of the National Population Commission of each State or at the office of the Registrar General at the FCT.

325. A nation requires a general national register. The utility of this for all-round developmental indices does not require elaboration. The attempt to displace this segment of national institutionalisation by any reference to the function of a local government council is without basis. A function is but one of several routes to realise an objective. As a route, the local government is an easement.[355] The national objective is to have a civil status registry in a country surrounded by unbounded borders – a country with peoples of several tribes and different tongues.

326. Suppose that the Constitution was drafted by those who had no knowledge of the existence of the Births, Deaths, Etc., Act, they could not have been oblivious of thc Marriage Act, which is well publicised in public domain and within the legislative competence of the National Assembly. Thus, if the intendment was to establish a sole structure, then, rather than revoke the Marriage Act in a small part – 'the Appointment of Principal Registrars Notice',[356] the whole Act would have been repealed and all registrations would then devolve on local governments. Moreover, the role of the National Population Commission is also constitutionally enshrined. The Local Governments Council predictably appears to be emulating the roles of local governments in other jurisdictions such as America. Whereas this is not the case with Nigeria. The Nigerian system bears a closer resemblance to the British system. Second, should the present state of confusion continue, there is no supervision for local government records. This is very unsatisfactory.

327. As has been stated above, the structure of local government under the Nigerian Constitution does not equip it to be a register of any type but a simple repository of information. The legal and administrative framework and structure between the National Population Commission and the Marriage Registries are lawful and provide requisite solemn legal and conducive environment for monogamous marriages. The same qualities exist to the extent that is possible between the Commission and the framework for customary and Islamic marriages.

328. The legislative objective of the B, D. Etc., Act is to harmonise registration of vital civil status data in the Country, not limited to births and deaths. The BDM Etc., Act and the National Population Commission Act were enacted to provide vital data statistics in accordance with international obligations and are equipped to fulfil that role. The B, D., Etc., Act aims at resolving the problem of inauthenticity,

---

355. An easement is a nonpossessory right to use and/or enter onto the real property of another without possessing it.
356. Notice L.N. 72 of 1971.

achieving proper identification of potential spouses, registering their marriage and where there is a concluded matrimonial cause such as dissolution, register same.

329. The Act makes it easy for international and indeed, local trust to spring up for civil status data. It provides qualitative institutional and physical infrastructural capacity. The registry it provides for is more fit for the overall purpose of civil status data registration. Its procedure for registration, retrieval of record and searches for confirmation of vital data is effective. Most importantly, the Act and the procedure properly implemented would have removed a chaotic situation that has made certainty of civil status data – an intrinsic aspect of policy planning, social improvement and economic development elude previous generations and paved the way for better assurances.

330. The Ministry of Interior and Attorney General of the Federation have a role to play by re-presenting and reinvigorating the Act and its administrative authority as the viable and reinforced system of civil status registration in Nigeria through appropriate sensitisation channels as is duly provided in the B, D, Etc., Act and Regulations.

IV. Certificates

FEDERAL REPUBLIC OF NIGERIA
NATIONAL POPULATION COMMISSION
BIRTHS, DEATHS, ETC. (COMPULSORY REGULATION) ACT
(Cap B9 L.F.N.)
[Form M.3 (Regulation 38(1)).]

Registrar's certificate

I, ... Registrar of Marriages in the.................................
district of Nigeria, do hereby certify that on the............ day of... 20 …
notice was entered in the Marriage Notice Book of this District, of the marriage intended between the parties named described, such notice being delivered under the hand of … … … … … … … … … … … … … … … ..
one of the parties, that is-
Name
Condition
Occupation, rank or profession
Age
Consent
Dwelling … … … … … … … … … ….
Length of residence … … … … … … … ….
Notice entered...20.....................
Certificate...20....................
Was entered against the issue of this certificate on the........ day of........... 20............
Been cancelled … … … … … … … ....
WITNESS MY HAND this.... day of............ 20.............

....
Registrar of Marriage
....
District

Certificate of Notice under section 11 of the Marriage Act.

FORM C

Section 11

Registrar's Certificate

I, … … … … … … … … …, registrar of marriages in the … … … … … … … … ..district of Nigeria, do hereby certify that on the … … … … … day of … … … … … . notice was duly entered in the marriage notice book of this district, of the marriage intended between the parties herein named and described, such notice one of the parties, that is to say.

Name	Condition	Occupation, rank or profession	Age	Consent	Dwelling	Length of residence
A. B. C. D.	Bachelor Spinster	Boatman (as case may be) (as case may be)	19 (as case may be) 16 (as case may be)	E. F. the Father (as the case may be) G. H. the mother (as the case may be)		

Date of notice entered … … … … … … … … … … … … … … … … … 20 … … … …
Date of certificate given … … … … … … … … … … … … … … … … 19 … … … …
No caveat has been entered against the issue of this certificate; or
A caveat was entered against the issue of this certificate on the … … … … … … …
Day of … … … … … … … 20 … … …, but it has been cancelled … … .
Witness my hand this … … … … … day of … … … .20 … … … … … .
… … … … … … … … … … … … … … ..
A.B., Registrar of Marriages,

District.
Note – This certificate will be void unless the marriage is solemnised on or before the … … … … … day of … … … … … .19 … … … …
(A. B.)

Certificate of Statutory Marriage given by virtue of sections 24 and 25 of the Marriage Act.

FORM E[357]

Sections 24 and 25
Marriages celebrated in the … … … … at … … … … in Nigeria
Certificate of Marriage

No. Date 20 …	No.	When married	Names & surname	Full age of minor	Condition	Rank or Profession	Residence at time of marriage	Father's name and surname	Occupation, rank or profession of father
Name of husband.									
Name of Wife.									
Witnesses.									

Married at … … … … .by (or before) me, A. B., minister (or registrar as the case may be).
This marriage was celebrated between A. B., C. D. In the presence of us E. F., G. H.
… … … … … … … … … … … … … … .
… … … … … … … … … … … … … … ..
Witnesses.

357. Marriage Certificates under a Nigerian statutory marriage is to comply with this Form. Peters Ifeoma, *Local Govt. 'Unified Marriage Certificate is Unconstitutional', – Justice Harrison*, available at dnllegalandstyle.com/Court room news (last retrieved 27 Aug. 2020).

MARRIAGE ACT

Marriage Register Book in compliance with section 30(1).

FORM F

When married	Names and surnames	Whether full age or minor	Condition	Occupation	Residence	Father's name and occupation

Entered this … … … … … … ..day of … … … … … … … … … ....20 … … …, at the **District Registry** of Marriages at … . Registrar.

FEDERAL REPUBLIC OF NIGERIA

NATIONAL POPULATION COMMISSION

BIRTHS, DEATHS, ETC. (COMPULSORY REGULATION) ACT (Cap B9 L.F.N.)

[Form CM.I (Regulation 42(3)).]

Customary Marriage Register [358]

District.. LGA...
Town/village... State..
Regn. no.
Date of entry
Date of marriage
Names and surname
Age
Condition
Occupation
Residential address
Father's name and occupation
Signature of Court Registrar
***It is from this registration that a certified True Copy is issued by the Chief Registrar as evidence of the marriage. Below is the Form of the Certified True Copy of Registration.

358. A similar abstract for divorces is available as: [Form CMD.I (Regulation 43(2)).] Register of Divorces (customary).

FEDERAL REPUBLIC OF NIGERIA

NATIONAL POPULATION COMMISSION

BIRTHS, DEATHS, ETC. (COMPULSORY REGULATION) ACT

(Cap B9 L.F.N.)

[Form CC.1 (Regulation 47).]

Certificate of correctness of copy of entry in a register

I,..Registrar of.. for...district/registration area in the...
Local Government Area of ....State, do hereby certify that this is a true copy of
*Entry .... /Registration No. .... in the register..
WITNESS MY HAND this................................. day of.............................. 20 … … … … ....

… … … … … … … … … … … … … …
Signature of registrar

The forms to be used in line with B, D, (Etc.,) Act are required to be in the following format.

Forms of Notice and Certificate under the B, D, Etc., Act
Form of Notice under the B, D, Etc. Act.
FEDERAL REPUBLIC OF NIGERIA
NATIONAL POPULATION COMMISSION
BIRTHS, DEATHS, ETC. (COMPULSORY REGULATION) ACT
(Cap B9 L.F.N.)

[Form M.I (Regulation 35(2)).]

Notice of marriage

Registrar of Marriage for the … … … … … … … … … … … … … … … … … … district of Nigeria hereby give notice that a marriage is intended to be had within three months from the date hereof on me, the undersigned, and the other party herein named.
Name
Condition
Occupation, rank or profession
Age
Dwelling or place of abode
Consent if any, and by whom given
WITNESS my hand this... day of... 20...
....

Signature
....
Name
… … … … … … … … … … … … ….
Address

The Deputy Registrar is required to make a return based on information provided by the Registrar from the Area Court in the following Format to the Chief Registrar.

FEDERAL REPUBLIC OF NIGERIA
NATIONAL POPULATION COMMISSION
BIRTHS, DEATHS, ETC. (COMPULSORY REGULATION) ACT
(Cap B9 L.F.N.)
[Form CFR.2 (Regulation 48(1)).]
Returns by Deputy Chief Registrars
To the Chief Registrar State Local Government
Area Type of
register Number of entries for
the period Remarks,
if any
I, Deputy Chief Registrar of
Local Government Area of
State, do hereby furnish the above return and certify that the *attached are certified true copies of the entries of **births/stillbirths/adoptions/deaths/marriages/divorces which occurred in the local government area during the period from to
Witness my hand this day of 20
Signature of Deputy Chief Registrar
Attach the relevant certified true copies
****

Chapter 3. Personality Rights

331. Personality rights can be categorised from two perspectives. The first is defining personality based on human experience and then identifying the rights attributable thereto. The other is a definition based on modern usage of the term 'personality rights'.

332. Personality rights from the first perspective connote the combination of characteristics or qualities that form an individual's distinctive character. More specifically, scientists use more extensive definitions of personality such as in terms of the stable, organised collection of psychological traits and mechanisms in the human being that influences his or her interactions with and modifications to the psychological, social and physical environment surrounding them.[359] In this sense, personality rights refer to human rights and their enforceability.

333. Human rights are inalienable and human beings are entitled to them by virtue of their humanity. The United Nations recognise some of these rights and Nigeria has become signatory to all varying degrees.[360] Violations of human rights occur within a state principally in relations between a government and its own citizens. Second, it is essential and axiomatic that states remain primarily responsible in international law for enforcing the protection of human rights within their jurisdictions. In Nigeria, the jurisdiction to hear and determine allegations of human rights violation is conferred on the High Court by section 46(1) of the 1999 Constitution. The section states that '[a]ny person who alleges that any of the provisions of this chapter has been, is being or likely to be contravened in any state in relation to him may apply to a High Court in that state for redress.' By subsection 2, a High Court is vested with original jurisdiction to hear and determine any application made to it. The High Court may make such orders, issue such writs and give such directions as

359. R.R. Larsen & D.M. Buss, *Personality Psychology: Domains of Knowledge About Human Nature* (6th ed. 2018), https://www.google.com/search?client=firefox-b-d&q=Personality# (last accessed 10 Aug. 2020).

360. Convention on the Elimination of All Forms of Discrimination against Women (CEDAW) Signature:1984, Ratification/Accession:1985; Convention against Torture and Other Cruel, Inhuman or Degrading Treatment or Punishment:1987 Signature:1988, Ratification/Accession:2001;Optional Protocol to the Convention against Torture and Other Cruel, Inhuman or Degrading Treatment or Punishment:2006: Signature: NA, Ratification/Accession:2009; Convention on the Rights of Persons with Disabilities:2008; Signature:2007, Ratification/Accession:2010;Optional Protocol to the Convention on the Rights of Persons with Disabilities :2008: Signature:2007, Ratification/Accession:2010 Signature:2007, Ratification/Accession:2010.
International Convention for the Protection of all Persons from Enforced Disappearance:2010 Signature: NA, Ratification/Accession:2009; Convention on the Rights of the Child:1990: Signature:1990, Ratification/Accession:1991;Optional Protocol to the Convention on the Rights of the Child on the sale of children, child prostitution and child pornography:2002 Signature:2000, Ratification/Accession:2010;Optional Protocol to the Convention on the Rights of the Child on the involvement of children in armed conflict:2002: Signature:2000, Ratification/Accession:2012; Convention against Torture and Other Cruel, Inhuman or Degrading Treatment or Punishment:1987; Signature:1988, Ratification/Accession:2001;Optional Protocol to the Convention against Torture and Other Cruel, Inhuman or Degrading Treatment or Punishment:2006: Signature: NA, Ratification/Accession:2009.

it may consider appropriate for the purpose of enforcing or securing enforcement of any right to which the applicant may be entitled. The Constitution of Nigeria provides not only access to court but also outlines the procedure for the enforcement of the guaranteed rights. The procedure for the commencement and determination of such cases is contained in the Fundamental Rights (Enforcement Procedure) Rules, 2009 made by the Chief Justice of Nigeria pursuant to the authority conferred on him by section 46(3) of the 1999 Constitution.[361]

334. Personality rights based on modern usage is essentially the right to sue and be sued, that is, to be buoyed with capacity. Within this sense is the specific sense in which the right could be one of publicity, and sometimes referred to as personality rights. It is the right of an individual to control the commercial use of one's identity, such as name, image, likeness, or other unequivocal identifiers.[362] Personality rights in this latter sense are protected mostly by tort law such as defamation, passing off, injurious falsehood and Intellectual property law which covers copyright laws.

361. *See* for instance J.A. Dada, *Judicial Remedies for Human Rights Violations in Nigeria: A Critical Appraisal*, 10(1) J. L. Pol'y & Global. 1–18 (2013) also available at www.iiste.org (last accessed 10 Aug. 2010).

362. At www.en.wikipedia.org/wiki/Personality_rights (last accessed 10 Aug. 2020).

Chapter 4. Names

§1. Composition of a Name

335. A name in Nigeria is given at birth by parents, grandparents, friends and family. A person's first name may be anywhere between one and twenty. Many parents who are Christians will proceed to churches for baptism or dedication of the child. It is usual to then give a notable Christian name. The same goes for Muslims. The first name requires compulsory registration under the Birth, Death Registration Act as has been fully discussed under Registration of Status. The Child's Rights Act requires registration of birth in compliance with the provisions of the B, D, Etc., Act. Thus, it provides by section 5 that: 'every child has a right to a name and, accordingly, shall be given a name on his birth or on such other date as is dictated by the culture of his parents or guardian. The birth of every child shall be registered in accordance with the provisions of the Birth, Death, etc. (Compulsory Registration) Act, 1992'.

336. The surnames are patrilineal usually.[363] There are different monarchs as there are tribes in Nigeria and addressed as His Royal Highness (usually Patrilineal descent). There are princes and princesses. There are also Chiefs and High Chiefs. Most middle-class persons in Nigeria are simply Mr., or Mrs., or Ms. In the Northern States, men may be called 'Mallam'. In the South East, 'Mazi' and 'Ogbuevfi' have been popularised as an indigenous identification prefix for men, married women as Lolo and single women as 'Ada'. In the South East, everyone, true to the republican spirit gives him or herself a pseudonym as an inspirational and/or aspirational title. Sometimes, people's real names are subsumed by these titles in their lifetime. An example for a male is: *Akaepuchionwa* which translates to 'the moon cannot be covered by human hands'. An example for a female is, *Ojiugo* which translates to 'a golden kola nut'. The people of the South West are known for monarchies and the institutions springing therefrom. Titles with the people of South West include, Oba. This means a King; 'Otunba', etc., Wives of *Obas* are known as *Olori* and this translates variously to Queen, Princess, 'Head wife' etc.

§2. Surname

337. A surname is known to be second or third names. In Nigeria surnames are usually patrilineal and may be the name of the oldest ancestor in a lineage. At some other times, the surname is that of the immediate patriarch. The idea of having a surname although now usual may not always have been so.

363. *See* subhead – surnames below.

338. A woman usually bears the name of her, that of a husband although in the South West, the wives sometimes bear a variation of compound surnames that includes their maiden surname.[364] Where a child is born to a mother, the maiden name of the mother is the surname.[365]

339. Thus, a family or surname:

> is typically a part of a person's personal name which, according to law or custom, is passed or given to children from one or both of their parents' family names. The use of family names is common in most cultures around the world, with each culture having its own rules as to how these names are formed, passed and used. However, the style of having both a family name (surname) and a given name (forename) is far from universal. In many cultures, it is common for people to have one name or mononym, with some cultures not using family names. In most Slavic countries, as well as other countries including Greece, Lithuania and Latvia, for example, there are different family name forms for male and female members of the family. Issues of family name arise especially on the passing of a name to a new-born child, on the adoption of a common family name on marriage, on renouncing of a family name and on changing of a family name. Surname laws vary around the world.[366]

340. Plato, Aristotle are examples of names not known with surnames.

I. Acquisition of the Surname

341. There are circumstances when a person may acquire a surname such as upon remarriage, adoption. These are recognised in Nigeria.

342. For remarriage, the formal process is to conduct a formal process of change of surname following registration of the divorce and existing marriage. In adoption, the adoption proceedings would formalise the new name.

II. Change of the Surname

343. There appears to be no known enabling law for change of surname, but the practice is prevalent and involves a simple process. It would also appear that only citizens of Nigeria can change their names in Nigeria. A surname can be changed for various reasons provided that due process is followed. The main requirements are an affidavit or what is sometimes referred to as deed poll. This is an oath sworn to indicate the circumstances informing the need to change the name. This must be done in the Registry of a High Court before a commissioner of oaths. Subsequently

---

364. *Oduche v. Oduche* [2005] LPELR-5976.
365. *Ben Enwonu v. Spira* [1965] All N.L.R 657; *Muojekwu* v. *Ejikeme* [2000] 5 NWLR (part 657) 404.
366. At https://en.wikipedia.org/wiki/Surname.

an advert in a widely circulating newspaper is required. This is at a minimal cost. The affidavit, an excerpt of the newspaper publication, two passport photographs as a recent identification of the applicant in addition to an application letter addressed to the Director are taken to the Department of Publication, Civil Registry, Federal Ministry of Information and Culture where the name change is noted and gazetted.

344. While names may be changed for various purposes, they cannot be changed if any of the following reasons form the basis for the application or is found to be so:

To escape debt liability or hide from criminal liability.
To commit a crime, one is being alleged to have committed a crime.
To mislead, which usually involves taking the name of a famous person.
name that would intimidate, offend, be considered obscene or is a racial slur.

345. The Federal Ministries of Foreign Affairs and Interior may also effect name change in International Passports. In this case, below are some of the requirements which should accompany an application and to be submitted to: 'the Director, Department of Publication, Civil Registry, Federal Ministry of Information and Culture'. The requirements are:

For Married Persons:
Application Letter.
Copy of Marriage Certificate or Declaration of Marriage.
Affidavit from a Magistrate or High Court of Change of Name deposed to by Applicant.
Copy of Newspaper Publication of Change of Name (twenty-one days after publication).
Statutory evidence of change of name (if resident outside Nigeria in lieu of iii and iv).
Passport Booklet and Copy of Data Page of Passport.
Acknowledgement Slip & Evidence of Payment.

For Divorced Persons:
Application Letter
Decree Nisi and Decree Absolute or Declaration of Divorce
Evidence of Maiden Name
In case of Re-marriage, Certificate of Marriage with Current Spouse
Affidavit from a Magistrate or High Court of Change of Name deposed to by Applicant.
Copy of Newspaper Publication of Change of Name (twenty-one days after publication).
Statutory evidence of change of name (if resident outside Nigeria in lieu of v and vi).
Passport Booklet and Copy of Data Page of passport.
Acknowledgement Slip & Evidence of Payment.

For Widows:

Application Letter.
Certificate of Death of spouse from National Population Commission (NPC).
Evidence of Maiden Name.
In case of Re-marriage, Certificate of Marriage with Current Spouse.
Affidavit from a Magistrate or High Court of Change of Name deposed to by Applicant.
Copy of Newspaper Publication of Change of Name (twenty-one days after publication).
Statutory evidence of change of name (if resident outside Nigeria in lieu of v and vi).
Passport Booklet and Copy of Data Page of passport.
Acknowledgement Slip & Evidence of Payment.

§3. First Name/Name at Birth

346. The first name is given at birth. The official body for registration of births and citizenship is the National Population Commission. The local government where the child is born also registers the birth at a first-tier level in line with its functions under the Constitution of Nigeria.

347. The enabling law for registration of births is the BDM, etc. Act, 2004.[367] Part II, sections 7–16 of the Act provide for registration of births. The births covered include live,[368] born within or out of wedlock,[369] still born[370] or foundlings.[371] Parts VI to VIII make it compulsory for births and Names to be registered. Section 11 of the Act provides for rectification of registration and register for change of name or where no name was available and becomes so. The registration is to be done within sixty days of birth.[372] Regulation 7 provides for the Register.

367. Number 69, Cap B.9, Laws of the Federation of Nigeria, 2004 with subsidiary regulations contained in Births, Death, marriage, etc. Regulations S.1.6. 1996, in Laws of the Federation of Nigeria, 2004.
368. 'birth' includes a live birth and a stillbirth – s. 50 of the Act.
369. Section 13 of the Act.
370. Section 13. Section 50 of the Act defines 'stillborn child' means a child who had issued forth from its mother after twenty-eight weeks of pregnancy and which did not at any time after being completely expelled from its mother breathe or show any other sign of life and the expression 'stillbirth' shall be construed accordingly.
371. Section 51 of the Regulation defines 'foundling' mean to mean:
   (a) a deserted or abandoned child whose parents, guardian or relatives are not known; or
   (b) a child committed to an orphanage or charitable or similar institution with unknown facts of birth or parentage.
372. Section 10. Section 10(2) provides that births may be registered out of time but within twelve months. Unfortunately, the second Schedule to the Regulation provides that sixty days is out of time and makes thirty days the period of in-time registration.

348. Where a person finds a baby, the informant is discharged by having a certificate issued in his or her name after proper enquiries by the Registrar.[373] There is also a Register for foundlings[374] The Regulation provides for specific forms for registration. Thus, **Form B.1** below is regulation for information required for registration of birth while **Form B.2** is the Form the Certificate of Registration should take. It is to be noted that **Regulation 11(2)** requires that any similar Form may be used. Section 12 provides for registration of births of children born by parents who are unmarried. The persons to give information to the registrar for births are father and mother where they are married and where they are not; however, the primary person is the mother. Where these do not provide requisite information, any person conducting a baptism, an *imam* or naming ceremony is required to send a name or the *Wosikat*[375] within forty-eight hours of the event.[376] By section 16, the registrar may summon a person in writing who ought to register a birth to do so and the person must do so within forty-eight hours of receiving the summon.

349. A certificate of Birth is to be issued for live Births bearing the names of parents or parent or finder of a foundling as the case may be. Regulation 16 of the Regulations provide for Form B2 for Certificates where births are registered by parents or persons indicated as primary custodians while Certificate in Form B5 is for secondary custodians. Adopted children are required to be registered by Regulation 21 upon receipt of a direction from a court of competent jurisdiction. Regulation 20 provides for babies who are born on board a ship or aircraft. Regulation 22 provides that the record of birth of a person shall be kept secret except in the following instances:

(a) the person himself or any person authorised by him; or;
(b) the spouse, parent, child or guardian or institution legally in charge of the person, if he is a minor.
(c) a court or public officer, when necessary in the judicial, administrative, or other official proceedings, to determine the child's parents or other circumstances surrounding his birth;
(d) in case of the person's death, the next of kin or personal representative.

350. The Schedule of fees is contained in Second Schedule of the Regulations but are no longer valid having undergone changes and may now vary from State to state. A child registered within time, by the provisions of the Schedule, thirty days, the Act, sixty days will avoid payment for certificate of birth.

373. Sections 8(d) and 15 of the Act.
374. Regulation 12(1) d.
375. This word was misspelt, and the word meant is *Wosilat* which in itself may be symbolic for whatever virtues one aspires for. It may have Arabic origins or may be more in use by those who relate with Arabic.
376. Sections 13 and 14.

I. Registers and Certificates

351. There are two official registrars of births in Nigeria, the Local Government Council and the National Population Commission. The position of the Local Government Council is the same as with marriage registration. The local government is a registrar for repository purposes. The official issuer of certificates, certifier of the certificates and where search can be conducted is the National Population Commission.

352. The Register of Birth is provided for in Regulation 7 of the B,D, Etc. Regulations. It is kept at the office of the Deputy Chief Registrar who is the Comptroller of the National Population Commission in each Local Government. The certified true copies of the content of the Register and searches are done with the Chief Registrar of the National Population Commission of each State or at the office of the Registrar General at the FCT.

353. The official particulars required are contained in Regulation 12 and are:

> **for the Child:** Name; Date of Birth; Date of registration; Place of occurrence of birth; place of registration;
> **for the mother:** Name, maiden and marital; age; occupation; level of education; Marital status; place of usual residence;
> **for the father:** Name; address and usual place of residence; nationality; and level of education.

354. It is to be noted that the nationality of the mother is not provided as relevant.

§4. Forms

[Form B.1 (Regulation 11(2)).]
Information required for registration of birth
Registration Centre Birth Register Volume
Town/Village Entry Number
LGA Date of Registration
State
FOR OFFICIAL USE ONLY
Particulars of child
Name of child (surname first)
Date of birth
(3) Sex: male/female
(a) Place of occurrence hospital/maternity home/at home/traditional doctor's place
(b) Village/town (in registration area)
Type of birth: single/multiple (6) Birth order
Particulars of mother
Name in full (surname first)

Address of usual place of residence
Age at birth of child
Marital status: single/married/separated/divorce/widowed
Nationality Nigerian/non-Nigerian
If Nigerian, (a) State of origin (b) Ethnic origin
(a) Literate/illiterate (b) If literate, level of education
Occupation
Particulars of father
Name in full (surname first)
Address of usual place of residence
Age years Nationality Nigerian/non-Nigerian
If Nigerian, (a) State of origin (b) Ethnic origin
(a) Literate/illiterate (b) If literate, level of education
Particulars of informant
Relationship to child
Full name (surname first)
Address of usual place of residence
Signature or left thumb mark of informant Signature of registrar

[Form B.2 (Regulation 16).] – Certificate of Birth (for primary custodians)

FEDERAL REPUBLIC OF NIGERIA
NATIONAL POPULATION COMMISSION
BIRTHS, DEATHS, ETC. (COMPULSORY REGULATION) ACT
(Cap B9)
Registration centre Certificate number:
Town/village Volume Year Entry no.
LGA State
This is to certify that the birth, details of which are recorded herein, has been registered on … [day month year]
at this registration centre.
1. Full name:
(Surname first) (in block letters)
2. Sex:
3. Date of birth:
4. Place of birth: Town/village
5. Full name of father:
(Surname first) (in block letters)
6. Full name of mother:
(Surname first) (in block letters)
7. Place of issue:
8. Name of registrar:
Date … … … … … Signature of Registrar … … … … … .

[Form B.5 (Regulation 16). Certificate of registration of birth (for babies found)]

FEDERAL REPUBLIC OF
NIGERIA NATIONAL POPULATION COMMISSION BIRTHS, DEATHS, ETC. (COMPULSORY REGULATION) ACT (Cap B9 L.F.N.)
Regn. No … … … ..

Mr

… …

Registrar of Births and Deaths at registration area of … … … ..
Local Government Area of … … … ..State,
Do hereby certify that I have this day registered the birth of … … … … … … .
born on the … ..
child of … … … … … … … … … … … … … … … .
And … … … … … … … … … … … … … … … … … … …
(formerly … … … … … … … … … … … .)
Insert the names of the parents and the maiden name of the mother
Witness my hand this day … …. Of … .20/ **Signature of Registrar**

Chapter 5. Nationality

§1. Nationality

355. The subjects of citizenship, naturalisation and aliens are in item 9 of the exclusive legislative competence of the National Assembly. All matters related to these heads are therefore matters on which only the Federal Legislature can make laws on. The Constitutional provisions are contained principally in Chapter III, sections 25–32 of the Constitution. The relevant court for issues relating to these heads is the Federal High Court.

356. The Federal High Court is guided in the administration of justice by Federal High Court Civil Procedure Rules S.1.3., 2009. Items of original jurisdiction of the Court are contained in Part II, section 7 of the Federal High Court Act.[377] Item (h) of section 7 is on diplomatic, consular and trade representation which may be an indication that when it comes to probate matters in relation to foreigners who died in Nigeria, the court may be the appropriate court to refer to. In addition, item (i) is on citizenship, naturalisation and aliens, deportation of persons who are not citizens of Nigeria, extradition, immigration into and emigration from Nigeria, passports and visas. These provisions for original jurisdiction indicate that the proper court for these matters ought to be the Federal High Court and not State High Court.[378]

357. There are two major ways by which a person becomes a citizen of Nigeria – by birth, registration and naturalisation.[379]

I. By Birth

358. A person is a citizen of Nigeria in three ways:

(i) Every person born in Nigeria before the date of independence of 1 October 1960 either of whose parents or grandparents is of a community indigenous to Nigeria.
(ii) A person born in Nigeria after the date (presumably this includes on) either of whose parents or grandparents is a citizen of Nigeria.
(iii) For those born outside of Nigeria, one parent must be a Nigerian.

---

377. Cap 134 L.F.N. 1990 Act; Cap F12 L.F.N. 2004. A relevant subsidiary legislation is Federal High Court (Civil Procedure Rules) S.I. 8 2000.
378. See information on probate matters below as provided by the Lagos State High Court of Lagos State (Civil Procedure Rules) 2004.
379. The general provisions on citizenship by birth, registration and naturalisation are contained in Chapter III and in particular ss 25, 26, 27, 28, 29, 31 and 309 of the Constitution of the Federal Republic of Nigeria, Cap C23, Laws of the Federation, 2004.

359. Point (iii) is notable as it contemplates gender equality and must be distinguished from section 26(2). This provision must be read in conjunction with section 26(2) which contemplates grandparents.

II. Citizenship by Registration

360. This applies to persons who wish to register as citizens of Nigeria and is at the pleasure of the President of the country. The applicant must be of full age and capacity, good character and must have demonstrated an intention to be domiciled in Nigeria. The applicant is required to take the oath of allegiance in the form prescribed in Seventh Schedule of the Constitution. Drawing from section 29(4)(a), full age and capacity for the purposes of acquired citizenship must be taken to mean 18 years or by description, as in section 29(4)(b), a woman who is married. The section applies to two categories of persons:

(i) A woman who is or has been married to a citizen of Nigeria.
(ii) Every person of full age and capacity born outside Nigeria any of whose grandparents is a citizen of Nigeria.

361. Thus, while section 25 makes it as of right to be a citizen if born outside of Nigeria to at least a parent who is Nigerian, this section provides for people whose relationship to Nigeria is through grandparents.

III. Citizenship by Naturalisation

362. A person can become a Nigerian citizen by naturalisation. Section 27 provides for citizenship by naturalisation.

363. Subject to the provisions of section 28 of this Constitution, any person who is qualified in accordance with the provisions of this section may apply to the President for the same of a certificate of naturalisation.

364. (2) No person shall be qualified to apply for the grant of a certificate or naturalisation, unless he satisfies the President that:

(a) he is a person of full age and capacity;
(b) he is a person of good character;
(c) he has shown a clear intention of his desire to be domiciled in Nigeria;
(d) he is, in the opinion of the Governor of the State where he is or he proposes to be resident, acceptable to the local community in which he is to live permanently, and has been assimilated into the way of life of Nigerians in that part of the Federation;
(e) he is a person who has made or is capable of making useful contribution to the advancement; progress and well-being of Nigeria;

(f) he has taken the Oath of Allegiance prescribed in the Seventh Schedule to this Constitution; and
(g) he has, immediately preceding the date of his application, either:
    (i) resided in Nigeria for a continuous period of fifteen years; or
    (ii) resided in Nigeria continuously for a period of twelve months, and during the period of twenty years immediately preceding that period of twelve months has resided in Nigeria for periods amounting in the aggregate to not less than fifteen years.

§2. Special Immigrant Status

365. The Special immigrant status is a privileged status under the Special Immigrant Status Regulation, 2008 granted by the President of the Federation, pursuant to section 32 of the Constitution. It is granted to spouses of Nigerians who do not wish to become citizens of Nigeria. Such a spouse must have been in a continuous marriage and residence in Nigeria for at least a period of five years and may apply for indefinite residence permit which can be granted if it is proved satisfactorily that the spouse is of good character. Fees are applicable. The application is made to the Minister of Interior. The status aims at facilitating and enhancing the stay of the spouse in Nigeria.

366. By section 7, special immigrant status may be granted to the following persons: (a) a foreigner married to a Nigerian with a child or children who have been in Nigeria for a period of five years or more and wishes to remain in Nigeria with his or her Nigerian family; and (b) a foreign woman married to a Nigerian who does not want to or cannot be registered as a Nigerian citizen.

367. The special immigrant status exempts the holders from holding an elective political office or a position sensitive to Nigeria's security except with special clearance by the President. Another exception is where the holder renounces his or her citizenship to acquire the citizenship of Nigeria. The status is forfeited if the spouse leaves Nigeria and remains outside Nigeria with the intention of abandoning the country as his or her permanent residence, or commits a criminal offence such as felony, sabotage or espionage or some other offence which in the opinion of the President is inimical to the interest of Nigeria. The status will also be forfeited if the marriage to the Nigerian is annulled or dissolved. This provision reinforces the relevance of civil status register.

Chapter 6. Domicile and Residence

368. Domicile relates to the legal and juridical efforts to connect a person with a particular society for the purposes of identifying an applicable personal law. This is so far as an attempt can be made in defining the word and its content. It is different from residence although the two terms can be intricately intertwined as the cases of *Omotunde v. Omotunde*[380] and *Bhojwani v. Bhojwani*,[381] which are discussed more fully below, indicate.

369. There are thirty-six states in Nigeria with a Federal Capital that operates and is administered as a State. Domicile for purposes of citizenship and nationality is single in Nigeria. Any Nigerian citizen can live and administer his or her affairs in any State of the Federation as if an indigene for purposes of public law, commerce, and family under a Federal structure.

370. It must, however, be noted that the country also operates a notional State of origin feature, by which personal law can be related back to customs and national dues, affirmative action such as scholarships can be related back to a person's origin by ancestry or State. Nigeria also has a land use policy by which land is vested in the Governor of each State in trust for citizens.[382] Underlying the policy is a regulatory and monitoring idea to ensure a more effective land use and allocation.

371. The legal implication though is that all actions in relation to land are treated by the principle of *lex loci rei sitae* (*lex situs*). This means that the law of the place where the property is situated regulates transfer, devolution and inheritance, presumably. It has to be presumably because inheritance in Nigeria is usually by primogeniture which overreaches the basic principle *lex situs*. Where the land is in the FCT, then the Minister of the FCT enables laws for that purpose.[383] Furthermore, lands or property owned by the Federal government in different States is regulated by the President, federal Minister of Lands and Housing and in some cases the specific Minister of the ministry under which the land is held and generally, at the pleasure of the President.[384]

372. In legal terms, no one can be without a domicile as *Mark v. Mark*[385] demonstrates. A person gains a domicile at birth. In Nigeria, it is by the father's domicile and where this is impracticable by the mothers'. The Nigerian wife continues to

380. [2001] 9 NWLR (part 718) 252; [2000] LPELR 10194.
381. [1996] 6 NWLR (part 457) 661.
382. Land Use Act, Cap 202 Laws of the Federation, 1990; Cap L5, Laws of the Federation, 2004.
383. *See* Federal Capital Territory Chance of Land Use and Residential Density Regulations, S.1. 19 of 2008.
384. Section 51, Land Use Act.
385. [2005] UKHL 42; [2005] 3 WLR 111; [2006] 1 AC 98.

depend on her husband's domicile.[386] A person can remain domiciled in a jurisdiction even after he has left it if he has maintained sufficient links with that jurisdiction or has not displayed an intention to leave the domicile permanently.

373. Domicile could also be of choice or one may arise by abandonment of a person's domicile of choice and active demonstration of choosing a new domicile.[387] This is no more than an intention to be in a particular jurisdiction and to be there usually, lawfully. Asylum seekers and refugees are usually deemed not to have abandoned their domicile of origin, but one wonders where the divide should actually lie in these cases. Their domicile of origin is said to be in abeyance. The question of domicile is, in many cases, more concerned with the ability of a State and individuals to take responsibility and be held accountable. Thus, in the case of asylum seekers to what State should their allegiance be and who takes responsibility for them.

374. Abandonment could apply to domicile of choice or domicile of dependence. For domicile of choice, a person abandons a domicile of choice by ceasing to reside there and by ceasing to intend to reside there permanently or indefinitely, and not otherwise.[388] The burden of proving a changed domicile lies on the party who asserts the change.[389]

375. *Mark v. Mark*[390] is a case on the question of domicile which involved two Nigerian couple who lived in the United Kingdom. The husband had married the wife under a polygynous union and the wife was about the third of five wives. Their stay in the United Kingdom was informed by a complex set of circumstances. They had four children, all of whom were citizens of the United Kingdom. The husband had been a General in the Nigerian army, a Governor of a State in Nigeria and subsequently President of the Senate, the Upper House of the Nation's Assembly from 2007 to 2015.

376. On 17 July 2000, at the invitation of the husband's solicitors, the wife issued a petition for the dissolution of their marriage. At some point during the proceedings of dissolution, the husband objected to the jurisdiction of the English court and stated that he had commenced proceedings in Nigeria, which is not unusual. Nigerian husbands would rather have matrimonial causes adjudicated before Nigerian courts.[391] The husband's counsels, on his behalf, based their objection on the

---

386. *Ugo v. Ugo* [2008] 5 NWLR (part 1079) 1; 3 PLR/2017/328 SC; *Omotunde v. Omotunde* [2001] 9 NWLR (part 718) 252.
387. *IRC v. Duchess of Portland* [1982] 1 ALL E.R. 784. *See also Lord Advocate v.* Jeffrey [1921] 1 AC 146. *Attorney General for Alberta v. Cook* [1926] A.C. 444.
388. Taken from Dicey & Morris, *The Conflict of Laws* (10th ed. Stevens & Sons Ltd. 1980). Rule 13(1). *See* however, *IRC v. Bullock*; *see* generally M.P. Thompson, *Domicile of Dependence. The Last Remnant of a Relic*, 32(1) 237–240 (1983).
389. *Bhojwani v. Bhojwani* [1996] 6 NWLR (part 457) 661; *Fonseca v. Passman* [1958] WRNLR 41.
390. [2005] UKHL 42; [2005] 3 WLR 111; [2006] 1 AC 98.
391. *Agbaje v. Agbaje* [2010] UKSC 13.

fact that the wife was remaining unlawfully in England and without requisite approval from immigration. The unlawful stay arose from a complex set of circumstances.

377. The question before the House of Lords was whether the wife could acquire a domicile of choice in the light of her unlawful stay under the United Kingdom Immigration laws. If she could then, the United Kingdom would have jurisdiction in the matter, but if her stay was such that she could not, then she had no requisite domicile to confer jurisdiction on the courts. The question thus turned on the implication of lawfulness of stay on domicile. In this case, a stay which was unlawful from the beginning and one which turned unlawful on account of circumstances. In a unanimous decision, delivered by Baroness Hale the House of Lords held that there was a distinction, for the purposes of determining domicile, between an entry which was from the start illegal, and one, which was originally lawful, prior to becoming unlawful, and with the concerned person still present in the jurisdiction. To the latter, it was held that it is a question of fact and not law, whether the requisite intention to make the jurisdiction a domicile of choice was satisfied or not. In the current case, the house of Lords held that the wife satisfied the requirement for acquiring domicile of choice although she had remained in the country without requisite immigration approval. It is to be noted that the wife was granted the relevant immigration approval by the time the proceedings commenced.

378. *Udny v. Udny*[392] is a leading case on domicile and has been referred to in Nigerian cases on domicile such as *Ugo v. Ugo.*[393] The question before the House of Lords was the domicile of the respondent's father at the time of the respondent's birth which was relevant for the determination of the rights of the respondent to inheritance. The father had been born in Scotland but left Scotland and took a lease of a house in London. He had a castle in Scotland but that was not habitable. He visited Scotland frequently but had no residence there. In 1844, to avoid his creditors, he sold the lease and his personal possessions and left London for France. He did not manifest an intention to have a permanent residence in France. In 1846, his first wife died. He then began dating another woman who bore him the respondent in London in 1853. He subsequently married her and returned to Scotland in the hope of legitimising the respondent, and perhaps, avoid his creditors as well as bar the entail on his estates.[394]

---

392. [1869] LR 1 HL 441; [1867] SLR 3-109; Cited in the following cases: *Morgan* (as Attorney of Sir Peter Shaffer) *v. Cilento, & Ors.* ([2004] EWHC 188; *Re Flynn* ([1968] 1 WLR 103; *Agulian & Another v. Cyganik* CA [2006] EWCA Civ 129; *Gaines-Cooper v. HM Revenue and Customs* [2007] EWHC 2617 (Ch)); [2005] 3 WLR 111; [2006] 1 AC 98.
393. [2008] 5 NWLR (part 1079) 1; 3 PLR/2017/328 SC.
394. An entail is a limitation of the inheritance of property to certain heirs over a number of generations. Barring of entail means the freeing of an estate from the limitations imposed by an entail and permitting its free disposition. This was anciently done by means of a fine or common recovery, but later by a deed in which the tenant and next heir join. It is also termed breaking of entail or disentailment.

379. It was held that the father by returning to Scotland in the circumstances which he did, had revived his domicile of origin and had lost his English domicile of choice. Referring to Scott in La Virginie with approval, the House quoted: 'It is always to be remembered that the native character easily reverts, and that it requires fewer circumstances to constitute domicile in the case of the native subject than to impress the national character of one who is originally of another country.'

380. The dicta of Lords Hatherley LC and Westbury remain relevant to the understanding of domicile.[395] Lord Hatherley LC had stated:

> 'A change of [a person's domicile of choice] can only be effected animo et facto -that is to say, by the choice of another domicile, evidenced by residence within the territorial limits to which the jurisdiction of the new domicile extends. He, in making this change, does an act, which is more nearly designated by the word "settling" than by any one word in our language. Thus we speak of a colonist settling in Canada or Australia, or of a Scotsman settling in England, and the word is frequently used as expressive of the act of change of domicile in the various judgments pronounced by our Courts.' And ... 'It seems reasonable to say that if the choice of a new abode and actual settlement there constitute a change of the original domicile, then the exact converse of such a procedure, viz., the intention to abandon the new domicile, and an actual abandonment of it, ought to be equally effective to destroy the new domicile. That which may be acquired may surely be abandoned, and though a man cannot, for civil reasons, be left without a domicile, no such difficulty arises if it be simply held that the original domicile revives.'

381. While Lord Westbury stated:

> The law of England, and of almost all civilized countries, ascribes to each individual at his birth two distinct legal states or conditions; one by virtue of which he becomes the subject of some particular country, binding him by the tie of natural allegiance, and which may be called his political status; another, by virtue of which he has ascribed to him the character of a citizen of some particular country, and as such is possessed of certain municipal rights, and subject to certain obligations, which latter character is the civil status or condition of the individual, and may be quite different from his political status. The political status may depend on different laws in different countries; whereas the civil status is governed universally by one single principle, namely, that of domicile, which is the criterion established by law for the purpose of determining civil status. For it is on this basis that the personal rights of the party, that is to say, the law which determines his majority or minority, his marriage, succession, testacy, or intestacy, must depend.' and 'Domicile of choice is a conclusion or inference which the law derives from the fact of a man fixing voluntarily his sole or chief residence in a particular place, with an intention of

395. *See* for continuing relevance: *Mark v. Mark* [2005] UKHL 42; [2005] 3 WLR 111; [2006] 1 AC 98.

continuing to reside there for an unlimited time. This is a description of the circumstances which create or constitute a domicile, and not a definition of the term. There must be a residence freely chosen, and not prescribed or dictated by any external necessity, such as the duties of office, the demands of creditors, or the relief from illness; and it must be residence fixed not for a limited period or particular purpose, but general and indefinite in its future contemplation. It is true that residence originally temporary, or intended for a limited period, may afterwards become general and unlimited, and in such a case so soon as the change of purpose, or animus manendi, can be inferred the fact of domicil is established' and 'Domicile of choice, as it is gained animo et facto, so it may be put an end to in the same manner.'

382. In *Ugo v. Ugo*[396] the question of domicile of the petitioner formed the foundation or pivot of adjudication of the appeal to the Supreme Court of Nigeria. The husband and wife are Nigerians of the South East extraction. They voluntarily renounced their Nigerian citizenship for American. They later got married under their new citizenship. Evidence showed that at the time of the proceedings, they were American citizens. In 2002, the husband applied for dissolution of the marriage in the State of New York asking for other ancillary reliefs such as distribution of the properties the parties held in joint ownership. The application for dissolution of the marriage was on grounds of abandonment. The Supreme Court of New York dismissed the application in its entirety on the ground that the petitioner had not made out a case of abandonment. An appeal was not made against the decision. The petitioner subsequently relocated to Nigeria. In Nigeria, he petitioned for dissolution of his marriage with his wife at the Area Court in Abuja, the FCT. The Divorce was granted but later overturned when it was made known to the Upper Area Court that the wife was an American citizen resident in America. The Petitioner then brought a petition on the fact of irretrievable breakdown of marriage by section 15(2) (c and e). These facts of irretrievable breakdown are: the petitioner found it intolerable as a result of the respondent's conduct to live with her and that the couple had lived apart for three years immediately preceding the petition. The petition included the details of the New York proceedings. The respondent was served by substitution. Her counsel raised a preliminary objection as to jurisdiction, which the court dismissed after hearing full arguments from both parties. The Supreme Court held that the Jurisdiction of a court to hear a divorce petition is governed by the domicile of the husband and that by operation of law, a married woman takes on the domicile of her husband. It considered that the parties having acquired American citizenship and having not abandoned same retained their domicile of choice. That domicile remained valid and subsisting, enduring until their Nigerian citizenship held in abeyance, and being domicile of origin is revived. The Court concluded that that the petitioner ought to have appealed the judgment of the Supreme Court of New York if what he was doing was not forum shopping. It therefore sustained the judgments of the lower courts that had dismissed the petition.

396. [2008] 5 NWLR (part 1079) 1; 3 PLR/2017/328 SC.

Chapter 7. Mentally Handicapped Persons

383. Mental handicap has been defined as a general or specific intellectual disability, resulting directly or indirectly from injury to the brain or from abnormal neurological development. Both terms 'mental handicap' and 'mentally handicapped' are considered to have inappropriate and negative connotations.[397] Terms such as (a person with a) learning disability or learning difficulties are used instead.[398]

384. Mental handicap is also associated with a host of mental health (inefficiency) which may arise due to stress, loneliness, depression, anxiety, relationship problems, death of a loved one, suicidal thoughts, grief, addiction, ADHD,[399] self-harm, various mood disorders, or other mental illnesses of varying degrees.[400] According to the World Health Organization (WHO), mental disorders comprise a broad range of problems with different symptoms. However, they are generally characterised by some combination of abnormal thoughts, emotions, behaviour and relationships with others. Examples are schizophrenia, depression, intellectual disabilities and disorders due to drug abuse. Most of these disorders can be successfully treated.[401]

385. The WHO further states that the well-being of an individual is encompassed in the realisation of their abilities –, coping with normal stresses of life, productive work, and contribution to their community. Cultural differences, subjective assessments, and competing professional theories all affect how one defines 'mental health'.[402] In January 2020, WHO published:

> A new WHO self-help approach for managing distress and coping with adversity has shown to be safe and effective in a trial involving South Sudanese women living in Uganda. The results of the study, published in The Lancet Global Health today, indicate that guided self-help could be a promising strategy to address the vast gap in mental health support in humanitarian response situations. WHO will make the self-help intervention available for widespread use once positive results have been seen in a second trial.[403]

397. Collins English Dictionary (HarperCollins Publishers) available at: https://www.collinsdictionary.com/dictionary/english/mental-handicap (last accessed 28 Aug. 2020).
398. *Ibid.*, Daniel Nasaw, *How Offensive Is the Word 'Lunatic'?* (BBC News Magazine) available at https://www.bbc.com/news/magazine-17997413 9.05.2012 (last accessed 29 Aug. 2020).
399. ADHD is a neurodevelopmental disorder characterised by inattention, or excessive activity and impulsivity, which are otherwise not appropriate for a person's age.
400. At https://en.wikipedia.org/wiki/Mental_health (last accessed 29 Aug. 2020).
401. At https://www.who.int/mental_health/management/en/ (last accessed 29 Aug. 2020).
402. *Ibid.*
403. *Ibid.*

386. Mental handicap is better termed an inefficiency of the mind. This term contemplates a restoration of the mind to its full capacity. The mind operating efficiently is expressed in, and to, varying degrees of subjective well-being, self-evaluation, self-acceptance, acceptance of circumstances beyond one's control, acceptance of the human variable of human limitation, perceived self-efficacy, autonomy, competence, inter-generational dependence, and self-actualization of one's intellectual and emotional potential, among others. Thus, a changed attitude, support of others whether in learning disability or mental inefficiency has significant impact on the outcome or regeneration of the mind lacking in optimal efficiency.

387. The State and society have a role to play. The State as agency of society must accept its role in human cohesion and provision of a balanced pendulum for an inclusive society of co-existence and mutual respect. Society has the role of extending itself in self, then, to one another and to the environment. Not surprisingly, the WHO states its approach and strategy: 'Good mental health is related to mental and psychological well-being. WHO's work to improve the mental health of individuals and society at large includes the promotion of mental well-being, the prevention of mental disorders, the protection of human rights and the care of people affected by mental disorders.'[404]

388. The difference between intellectual disability and mental illness is said to sometimes lie in its method of assessment. The first is assessed by a psychologist while mental illness needs to be diagnosed and prescribed for by a psychiatrist.

389. With respect to intellectual disability, in Nigeria, there are no specific laws, and the challenges presented by those who need help in this regard are tended to privately by their families. However, with respect to mental illness, there is more concern from the general public on the subject and governmental inaction has seen increased academic commentaries on the subject. The mental health law in Nigeria is still in the lunar-age marred by superstition. Mentally inefficient persons are in practice termed mad people, either locked up or left to roam the streets until perhaps, they perish.[405]

390. In family and succession law in Nigeria, all actions concerning the mentally handicapped when it arises are conducted by 'his or her committee'. The preferred route of family members for contesting the validity of a Will in Nigeria is usually through the unsoundness of mind of the testator at the time of writing the Will.

---

404. *Ibid.*
405. Nduka Orjinmo & Adamu Salihu, *Why Some Nigerian Families Lock Up Children and the Mentally Ill*, available at: https://www.bbc.com/news/world-africa-53893271 (last accessed 4 Oct. 2020).

391. The only known law in respect of mental ill health is the Lunacy Act 1958, a slight variation of the one of 1916.[406] This Act is not reproduced in any of the modern compilation of the Law of the Federation. This position has been noted elsewhere:

> Currently, there is no composite Federal legislation regarding management of mental health in Nigeria. The Lunacy Act, 1916 as amended by the Lunacy Act 1959, which used to apply to managing mental health issues, and is as good as moribund because it was not included in the Laws of the Federation of Nigeria 2004. The law is largely a derivative of the common law and old legislation in the U.K. The equivalent Lunacy law of some of the federating states of Nigeria is not in any better position. The Mental Health Bill 2013 which would have significantly improved the situation is yet to be seriously considered and or passed into law by the National Assembly of Nigeria. Consequently, the existing mental health law in Nigeria remains largely custodial, fear mongering, and woefully compares with similar legislation in other parts of the world. In fact, as a colonial heritage, it can be considered a 'legal antique'.[407]

392. The Matrimonial Causes Act provides an insight in relation to capacity for marriage by section 5(2)(b). The subsection provides: 'Subject to this Act, a marriage that takes place after the commencement of this Act not being a marriage that is void, shall be voidable in the following cases but not otherwise, that is to say, where at the time of marriage- either party to the marriage is: (i) of unsound mind, or (ii) a mental defective, or (iii) subject to recurrent attacks of insanity or epilepsy.'

393. Lagos State Criminal Code Law also refers to 'unlawful release of mentally disordered persons'. It provides:

(1) Any person who:
- (a) unlawfully releases any person while being taken as a mentally disordered person to a hospital or any other place for the care of such persons or to a prison, or rescues any person during his confinement as a mentally disordered person in any such place;
- (b) being in charge of a person wilfully permits him to escape from custody while being taken as a mentally disordered person to a hospital or any other place;
- (c) being a superintendent of, or person employed in, any such place, wilfully permits a person confined there to escape; or
- (d) conceals any such person who has to his knowledge been rescued while being taken or confined, or has to his knowledge escaped from such confinement, commits a felony and is liable on conviction to imprisonment for three (3) years.

---

406. P.U. Ude, *Policy Analysis on Nigerian Lunacy Act (1958): The Need for a New Legislation*, 19(1) J. Psychiatry 1–6 (2015).

407. A.O.A. Yusuff, *The Rights of the Mentally Ill and the Nigerian Society: Enhancing Dignity in Mental Health through Legislation*, 52 J. L. Pol'y & Global. 172–184 (2016).

(2) The offender in subsection (1) of this section cannot be arrested without warrant.

394. Westbrook states that people who are mentally challenged in Nigeria are placed in prison custody.[408] At other times these individuals are chained in church premises or sundry witch-doctor's shrines and 'habitat'. It is not unusual to see these chained individuals led by a seemingly 'not-lunar affected' individual through the streets or market places soliciting alms. Such is the state of mental handicap in Nigeria, with the result that most families hide their own in chains in their private houses. The superstition surrounding 'lunacy' also advances this strategy of hiding persons with inefficient mind function as the thinking is that once the mentally inefficient person escapes and visits a marketplace, there would be no prospects of recovery. The other superstition which appears to have some universal superstitious support is that the persons are affected by the positioning of, or the mental inefficiency is determined by, or resembling the positioning of the moon, hence the descriptive term of the mental condition as lunacy.

395. According to Suleiman, who is of the Department of Pathology, Ahmadu Bello University Teaching Hospital, Zaria, Kaduna State, Nigeria:

> In Nigeria, an estimated 20%–30% of our population are believed to suffer from mental disorders. This is a very significant number considering Nigeria has an estimated population of over 200 million. Unfortunately, the attention given to mental health disorders in Nigeria is at best, fleeting; the level of awareness of the Nigerian public on mental health issues is also understandably poor, and the misconceptions regarding mental health have continued to flourish.[409]

396. It is regrettable that some laws about mentally handicapped persons more frequently refer to such persons as being of unsound mind. Another uniform position is the grouping with infants. Thus, quite aside from the Evidence Act, the Nigerian Companies and Allied Matters Act, 2020[410] consistently refers to infants as persons under 18 years and mentally handicapped persons as of unsound mind and so found, by a court of competent jurisdiction. Section 212 of the Companies and Allied Matters Act provides 'A person is not qualified for appointment as a trustee of a debenture trust deed if he is … (b) Less than eighteen years of age; (c) of unsound mind and has been so found by a court in Nigeria.'[411] The same wordings appear with respect to disqualification for appointment of receivers or managers of any property or undertaking of any company.[412]

408. A.H. Westbrook, *Mental Health Legislation and Involuntary Commitment in Nigeria: A Call for Reform*, 10(2) Wash. U. Global Stud. 396–418 (2011).
409. D.E. Suleiman, *Mental Health Disorders in Nigeria: A Highly Neglected Disease*, 10(2) J, Annals of Nigerian Med. 47 (2016).
410. Now repealed 'Companies and Allied Matters Act, Cap C20, Laws of the Federation, 2004'.
411. Section 212(1) (b) & (c) of the Companies and Allied Matters Act, 2020.
412. Section 550 of the Companies and Allied Matters Act, 2020.

397. Section 550 of the Act provides: (1) the following persons shall not be appointed or act as receivers or managers of any property or undertaking of any company: (a) an infant, (b) any person found by a competent court to be of unsound mind. However, some are more human dignity compliant. Thus the Administration of Estates Act employed the term, 'mental incapacity'[413] while the Evidence Act referred to 'mental condition'.[414]

398. The Matrimonial Causes Rules is replete with the description of the mentally handicapped, regrettably, as of unsound mind.[415] By Order VI, Part 3, rule 12, such an individual is described as a 'committee' and a committee is stated to mean 'a committee of the person'. The mentally handicapped person can sue in four ways: a committee may be willing to sue on behalf of the mentally handicapped person; the Attorney General may authorise someone to sue on behalf of the person; or a guardian – ad litem may be appointed to act for the person; or a public trustee or corporation sole may also act on the person's behalf.

399. Suleiman notes again:

> The 2006 WHO-AIMS report on mental health system in Nigeria made some telling revelations. It reports that 'there is considerable neglect of mental health issues in the country. The existing Mental Health Policy document in Nigeria was formulated in 1991. Since its formulation, no revision has taken place and no formal assessment of how much it has been implemented has been conducted … … No desk exists in the ministries at any level for mental health issues and only four per cent of government expenditures on health is earmarked for mental health.' It also unearthed other issues related to mental health. These include unavailability of essential medicines at health centres, unavailability of physicians to run primary health care centres and the lack or restrictions to the prescription of psychotropic medications. It also identified that there are only a few non-governmental organizations involved in individual assistance activities such as counselling, housing, or support groups. It concluded that 'in general terms, several countries in Africa are better resourced in regard to mental health personnel. Countries such as South Africa, Egypt, and Kenya have more psychiatrists per 100,000 persons and also have higher proportions of psychiatric beds. Also, many countries in Africa also give better official attention to mental health issues'.[416]

400. The note represents the summary of the lot of mentally inefficient persons in Nigeria.

---

413. Sections 19(3); 33(3) 40(1).
414. Section 83(1)(b); 172(2); 258(d)(d)b.
415. Order VI, part 3, rule 12 in the Matrimonial Causes Rules etc.
416. D.E. Suleiman, *Mental Health Disorders in Nigeria: A Highly Neglected Disease*, 10(2) J. Annals of Nigerian Med. 47 (2016).

Part II. Family Law

Chapter 1. Marriage

401. A lawyer's question regarding marriage runs through many branches of law, from jurisprudence, family, to constitutional etc.

402. The basic question is the content of formalities for marriage. Human experiences and circumstances have continued to play key roles in determining contemporary formalities for marriage – as a sustainable institution in which the State and international community have definite interests. Formalities in contemporary terms which concern the State and global community comprise of the capacity and capability to marry. The first entails age and consent. The second entails understanding of the obligations and rights involved in marriage. These dovetail to the outcome of marriage which is formation of family. The societal interest in marriage is to ensure that the formalities and particularly, the criteria of capacity and capability are met because, if they are not met, the burdens of failure to meet up with the obligations and rights in marriage inevitably fall on the society. Thus, a marriage must be a forum for the key objectives of realising a sustainable vibrant society in which contemporary human rights and standards exist for the flourishing of each human person – male or female.

§1. Family

403. The lawyer's question on family is always traced to orderliness, in formation, record, and if need be, dissolution. At play in all family relations and the role of the State is the balance between State intervention and the prized contemporary values of liberty, individual autonomy, and limits of State intervention. The lawyer's question is a core function of statehood, critical and multidimensional – an accurate answer to which, provides a multidimensional solution to many issues of society. Is a society economically underdeveloped, disorderly, and only minimally productive? Efforts at solution if, addressed at a macro level may be unlikely to yield any fundamental shift, but if addressed from the base – the system of family and how this promotes individual optimism, then such efforts are an assured key to, at the minimum – a satisfying and flourishing society.

404. Family law is a toggle between the limits of society and the elasticity of law and religion in every society. In modern times, economics has been added to this toggle.[417] The economy of family is intricately interwoven with the development of society. The relationship between shelter, being sheltered, home owning and rental laws affect family life in very important respects. The policy directions of government in these matters also impact the role of religion, law and economics in family life and wellbeing. A typical example is how these subject areas impact population, family planning and mortality.

405. How the government and the governed relate in the context of family is thus a key factor in the way a society fare.

406. In Nigeria, as in many African countries, this is even more so, because of the seeming inseparability of religion from custom, societal interaction, law, economic indices, politics, or governance. This has broadly affected the socio-historical and political life of the people of Nigeria. To draw a line between religion, political government, political economy, social interaction, history and indeed family has proved totally impossible. This is in spite of the Constitutional provision that the country is a secular State.[418]

407. Provisions of the Matrimonial Causes Act continually separate laws under the Act and the customary and Sharia regimes. Thus, on the one hand, there is a marriage structure that advances nuclear family relations. Nigerians who fall into this category are often content to have anywhere between two children and three, and they are often cosmopolitan – educated, the quality of life and content of population within the family are crucial to the economy of the family. With customary law and Islamic law marriages, the tide is different. Among those whose marriages are regulated by customary laws, the number of children and wives are dependent on the capacity of the man and the women.

408. The interposition of colonialism and now modernity on Nigerian society has had an interesting impact. Some would suggest an irresolvable conflict. This may not be without basis, as is, borne out by several sections of the Marriage Act. Some will suggest an overshadowing of customs and culture by modernity as is borne out by divorce laws, repugnancy doctrine and the membership of the country in regional and global organisations.

---

417. The use of economics here covers all micro and macroeconomics indices as they affect family and the finance available to each unit of family to achieve a reasonable level of material wellbeing. Economics may be defined or said to encompass an understanding of the forces that determine prices, of goods and services and also resources used to produce them at a microeconomics level. It deals with the behaviour of individual entities such as consumers, business firms, traders, and farmers. The other major branch of economics is macroeconomics, which focuses attention on aggregates such as the level of income in the whole economy, the volume of total employment, the flow of total investment, and so forth and what public policies might help a country achieve higher employment or greater price stability. See for a fuller understanding, Mark Blaug 'Economics' available at https://www.britannica.com/topic/economics (last accessed 30 Aug. 2020).

418. Section 10 of the Constitution. This provision is perhaps only declaratory considering that all it implicates is that the federation or a state shall not declare a religion as a religion for the State although it may in practice adopt one. The Federal government participates fully in religious activities so, Nigeria can be said to be a non-declaratory religious state and no more.

409. Others will suggest the resilience of customs and culture borne out by the continued commitment and interests of almost the generality of the populace in the prevalent customs and culture and particularly in relation to marriage and family. Neither the acceptance of Christianity or Islam or indeed modernity has resulted in any serious shift in the lives of the people from their attachment to customs and culture. One reason for this status may be the patriarchal interests and nature of the society and the acquiescence of women of the older generations in the incidents, implications, and consequences of patriarchy.

410. Marriage in Nigeria quite aside from the impact of plural legal regime is complex because of the system of family and rigid filial structure. For instance, consent is a key feature of marriage in Nigeria but the consent required is not just between the parties but also that of parents of both the groom and bride as well as theoretically, the extended family who must be part of the marriage celebration rites. Bride price is another key feature of customary marriages in Nigeria which many people now find incompatible with modern understanding of human relations and classification of legal rights.[419] The content and context of bride price in customary marriage rites and contemporary legal discourse continue to draw attention locally and internationally.[420] Bride price functions as the evidence of a continuing legal relationship between the bride, groom and their families and therefore as an element for the validity of marriage under customary marriage norms.

411. Dissolution of marriage is a problem creating many conflicts of laws issues. In *Ohochuku v. Ohochuku*[421] Wrangham J. stated that it is established by authority that an English Court did not have jurisdiction to dissolve a polygamous union although such unions had recognition for some limited purposes. His Lordship then proceeded to dissolve the marriage conducted in England and declined jurisdiction over the customary marriage which was conducted in Nigeria.

412. Some commentaries were made on the case at the time. Webb thought that the Court in *Ohochuku* proceeded on the conscious or unconscious understanding that only one marriage existed and that was the monogamous union. His view was that the Court ought to have taken the view that marriage created a status and the status of marriage once removed makes the parties free as single persons.[422] Eekelaar commenting on *Ohochuku* had the same view of the approach of the Court but concluded that it was expedient that polygamous marriages ought to be given more recognition in view of the position of Britain in the Commonwealth.[423] Agbede, also commented on the decision in *Ohochuku*.[424] In his view, the case could not hold

---

419. See results of questionnaires administered in this respect as Appendices.
420. *Mifumi (U) Ltd. & Others v. Att. Gen. & Kenneth Kakuru* [2015] UGSC 13 (15 Aug. 2015); *See also* CONSTITUTIONAL PETITION NO. 12 OF 2007.
421. [1960] 1 ALL ER 253.
422. P.R.H Webb, *Ohochuku v. Ohochuku 'A variation of Thynne v. Thynne'*, 23(3) The Mod. L. Rev. 327–331 (1960).
423. John Eekelaar, *Family Law and Personal Life* (Oxford University Press 2006).
424. I.O. Agbede, *Recognition of Double Marriage in Nigerian Law*, 17(3) Int'l & Comp. L.Q 735–743 (1968).

water on the nature of the relationship created by double marriage, customary and statutory as is usually the case in Nigeria. For him, they both complemented each other and ought therefore to be treated as a status. This position was taken by the Nigerian Supreme Court in *Jadesimi v. Okotie-Eboh.* [425] The Nigerian Supreme Court in a unanimous judgment delivered by Uwais JSC stated:

> 'It is a matter of common knowledge that most people in Nigeria who contract marriages under the Marriage Act, undergo a form of customary marriage earlier as a matter of practice and adherence to the customs of their forefathers. Some refer to such practice as traditional engagement' while others simply refer to it as solemnisation of customary marriage. It is never intended by the practice that the marriage under the Marriage Act should nullify the customary marriage or engagement but rather that it would supplement the practice or custom. The parties are of course aware that by applying the Marriage to their relationship, their marriage would become monogamous. However, it is a matter of common knowledge that in spite of the punishment provided under section 47 of the Marriage Act against any of the parties entering another customary marriage, the male folk in particular observe the restriction more in breach than obedience with impunity.[426]

413. The ideas from the commentaries on *Ohochukwu* discountenance the nature of divorce under customary law which surprisingly, Wrangham J. appears to have contemplated. Customary marriages contemplate family involvement in stages prior to dissolution. It is only where the interventions fail to bring about reconciliation that either the husband's family demands for the return of the bride price or the wife initiates the return by inviting the groom's family to collect the bride price. There is no hard and fast rule about the venue of the collection of the bride price although it is usual for the groom to collect it from the home of the parents of the wife. When the divorce is hostile, the bride price can be returned through a due process at the area or customary court in the locality. Generally, the customary marriages do not contemplate divorce and the process makes it so difficult that obtaining a customary marriage divorce is akin to the proverbial Carmel passing through the eye of a needle. The needle is the bride price. In Uganda the place of bride price in modern understanding of law and human rights regime was litigated from the Constitutional Court to the Ugandan Supreme Court in *Mifumi (U) Ltd. & Others v. Att. Gen. & Kenneth Kakuru.*[427] The main appellant MIFUMI (U) Ltd. was a non-governmental organisation in eastern Uganda representing the interests of rural women.

414. Twelve other parties joined in the litigation. The petition was to the Constitutional Court challenging the constitutionality of the custom of paying bride price as a precondition to contracting a valid customary marriage under Articles 2(1)(2), 137(3) and 93(a) and (d) of the Constitution of Uganda and rule 3 of the Constitutional Court (Petitions and References) Rules (S.1. 91/2005) They also

425. [1996] 2 NWLR (part 429) 128.
426. [1996] 2 NWLR (part 429) 128, 147.
427. [2015] UGSC 13 (15 August 2015); *See also* CONSTITUTIONAL PETITION NO. 12 OF 2007.

challenged the constitutionality of demanding refund of bride price as an essential prerequisite for the valid dissolution of a customary marriage and prayed the court for some declarations in respect of the petitions. The petitions are summarised as:

(i) Demand for bride price by parents of the bride from prospective sons-in-law as a condition precedent to a valid customary marriage is contrary to Article 31(3) of the Constitution that provides that marriage shall be entered into with the free consent of the man and a woman intending to marry, because the demand for bride price makes the consent of the persons who intend to marry contingent upon the demands of a third party.
(ii) Payment of bride price by men leads them to treat their wives as mere possessions. This, they claimed, perpetuates inequality between men and women which is prohibited by Article 21(1), and (2) of the Constitution.
(iii) Demand for bride price by parents of the bride from prospective sons-in-law in as much as it portrays the woman as an article in a market for sale amounts to degrading treatment, prohibited by the Constitution of Uganda in Article 24, which guarantees that every person shall be treated with dignity.
(iv) Use of bride price leads to social ills such as fathers forcing daughters to get married simply to collect a bride price and young women being removed from schools and forced into early marriages. Uneducated women may even fetch a higher bride price, or dowry, due to the assumption that women in a school setting are less likely to be undefiled.
(v) Bride price can even lead to inhuman and degrading treatment of corpses. In her affidavit, Felicity Atuki Turner notes that she has come across several cases where a wife's corpse has been denied burial pending the refund of the applicable bride price to the husband.

415. The Constitutional Court, by a majority of four to one, dismissed the petition holding that the practice of payment of bride price was not so notorious that the Court could take judicial notice of it. It held further that the demand and payment of bride price as condition precedent to the validity of a customary marriage and the demand for a refund of bride price as a condition precedent to the dissolution of a customary marriage were not barred by the Constitution. Lastly, the Constitutional Court also held that it was not essential for the Court to declare that the practice of demand for a refund of bride price on dissolution of marriage was unconstitutional because the Constitution itself under Article 50 and other appropriate law could adequately take care of any grievances arising from the abuse of the bride price custom.

416. The Court reasoned that where bride price is reached in a voluntary manner between the parties that is, the prospective couple – that such an agreement will then make the bride price a voluntary matter and with respect to the bride price paid to the parents of the woman, this should be taken as an appreciation for their parenting the bride. It also reasoned that the petitioners had not established that payment of bride price was commonly practised in Uganda. The Court agreed with the respondents that the custom and practice of payment of bride price or dowry was more an exchange of gifts from the families of a prospective couple unless proved and that at any rate, couples had other options for forming a marriage. As in Nigeria, couples know of the option but invariably most women will not consider that they are properly married without the customary marriage, although its potential prospect as polygamous stirs everyone in the face.

417. On appeal to the Supreme Court, it was held that the majority Justices of the Constitutional Court erred in law and fact: (i) when they dismissed the petition against the payment of bride price and its refund at the contracting and dissolution of marriage, respectively, as conditions precedent to the contracting of a valid customary marriage and the dissolution of customary marriage among various tribes in Uganda, and (ii) in taking the position that bride price means the same thing for all the different cultures in Uganda and failed to find that bride price is commonly practised in Uganda by all cultures.

418. The Supreme Court held further that the majority of the Constitutional Court erred when it failed to take judicial notice of the custom and practice of paying bride price. It also erred in failing to find that the payment and refund of bride price did promote inequality in marriages and its consequential role in promoting domestic violence in customary marriages. The Supreme Court emphasised that the Constitutional court erred in not declaring the undesirable effects of bride price on the basis that these could be remedied by other laws and means, other than declarations. It therefore made the following declarations:

(i) The voluntary exchange of gifts at marriage or during marriage between the groom to be and his wife to be and/or her parents and relatives and vice versa is not unconstitutional.

(ii) The custom and practice of demand of bride price by a woman's parents or her relatives from her husband to be as a condition precedent to a valid customary marriage practised by several tribes in Uganda is inconsistent with Articles 2, 21(1) and 2, 31(1)(b); 31(3), 32(2), 33(1), and 33(4) of the Constitution.

(iii) The payment of bride price, as a condition precedent for the validity of a customary marriage is inconsistent with Articles 2, 21(1) and 2, 31(1)(b); 31(3), 32(2), 33(1), and 33(4) of the Constitution.

(iv) The custom and practice of demand for refund of bride price as a condition precedent to a valid dissolution of a customary marriage is inconsistent with Articles 2, 21(1) and 2, 31(1)(b); 31(3), 32(2), 33(1), and 33(4) of the Constitution.

(v) The payment of bride price as a condition precedent to a valid customary marriage and of its refund as a condition precedent to the dissolution of a customary marriage which has been demanded for by a woman's parents and/or relatives undermines the dignity & status of women and is therefore inconsistent with Articles 32(2), 33(1) and (4), and 21(1) and (2) of the Constitution.

419. The outcomes of this case should also be the case for Nigeria. Bride price as an element of the validity of customary marriage should be disregarded and registration of customary marriage as is provided in Nigeria, by the Death, Births, Marriages (Compulsory Registration) Act enforced.[428] As it may be futile to expect a full-blown consideration of the subject in Nigeria, the judiciary and academia can play a vital role in this respect by deemphasising the relevance of bride price as an element of a valid marriage in Nigeria as is presently the case.

420. With respect to statutory marriage, Nigeria adopts the English approach that marriage law should support, rather than undermine the stability of marriage. Thus, there is a two-year rule to the effect that except where divorce proceedings are based on the facts of wilful and persistent refusal to consummate; adultery; behaviour involving the commission of rape, sodomy, or bestiality, no proceedings for divorce may be instituted within two years of a marriage without leave of the Court.[429] As one leading Family Law text puts it 'the rationale of this rule is "not only to deter people from rushing into ill-advised marriages, but also to prevent them from rushing out of marriage as soon as they discover that their marriage was not what they expected"'.[430]

421. Closely related to family is succession. Succession technically refers to gifts and transfers of property and *personalty* made at death by a person through a Will or operation of law. Where a Will is used it is known as testate succession. A Will may contain provisions of trust. Technical aspects of trust such as death bed declarations in relation to land which ordinarily Will not be accepted as a valid Will is recognised as a valid means of transfer of property.[431] When there is no Will and no trust is created or established, the process of distribution and administration of the property and other obligations of a person who is dead is referred to as intestate succession. The distinction is important because of the legal framework engaged.

422. The law of a monogamous marriage determines and creates marital rights and obligations, and it relates to the law of succession only according to law or the Will of the deceased spouse. The law of marriage under customary norms has very little relationship with succession under customary norms except in so far as the marriage is a linkage to children. Succession under customary law deals mainly with the inheritance of a deceased's property, and to a measure, the discharge of some of his obligations. However, because of the rigid attachment to customs and the role which customary marriage plays in the life of a Nigerian, it is a thorny issue trying to separate succession from marriage.

423. Children and reproduction are the key aspects of marriage and succession in Nigeria. So much is this the case, that a family law commentator stated:

---

428. *See* Appendix for some research by questionnaire conducted on the subject.
429. Section 30(1) of the Matrimonial Causes Act, Cap M7, Laws of the Federation, 2004.
430. E.I. Nwogugu, *Family Law in Nigeria* 151 (HEBN Studies in Nigerian Law 1990).
431. *Sen v. Hedley* [1991] Ch. 425; [1991] EWCA Civ 13.

> It is necessary to point out here an omission in the Act which, if we go solely by our own culture and social behaviour ought not to be. This is the non-inclusion of failure by a wife to produce children or more importantly to produce a male heir, as a ground for divorce. The African concept of marriage differs considerably from that of the European. To the African male, marriage exists only for procreation. The idea is not really to choose a partner, a companion or someone to cherish. A woman would enjoy such a state of affairs after she has performed satisfactorily, her primary function of procreation. Failure to achieve this role results in the immediate relegation of the woman and a further search for a more productive female. This attitude is widely accepted and greeted with approval both from the illiterates and the educated peoples in our society.[432]

424. The author may have discountenanced the impact of this societal pressure on women's emotional wellbeing and reproductive health. Reproduction and fertility are already debilitating for women. To therefore, make inability to birth and ensure the survival of a male child a fact of irretrievable breakdown will aggravate the already precarious position of a woman in marriage to permanent mental and physical handicap. In the current times, to meet up with these societal demands, many women may have so many female children with no male or no surviving male and many do end up with Vesicovaginal fistula (VVF).[433] Vesicovaginal fistula, or VVF, is an abnormal fistulous tract extending between the bladder (*vesica*) and the vagina that allows the continuous involuntary discharge of urine into the vaginal vault. In addition to the medical sequela from these fistulas, they often have a profound effect on the patient's emotional well-being.[434] Others, reproduce male children with mental disabilities, whereupon the husbands abandon wife and children or send them out and engage with other women. At other times, women simply perish in the process of living the husband and children behind. The author also discountenances some other implication of the pressure on women – the general tenor of human evolution and growth, the quality of a population and *a fortiori* unmerited male heirship.

425. Rahmatian commenting on the position described it as 'rather astonishing'.[435] The position of the writer on Nigeria is clearly at variance with the position in a society as United Kingdom. In *Ghaidan v. Godin-Mendoza*, Baroness Hale notes:

> First, the capacity to bear or beget children has never been a pre-requisite of a valid marriage in English law. Henry VIII would not otherwise have had the problems he did. Even the capacity to consummate the marriage only matters if one of the parties thinks it matters: if they are both content the marriage is

432. E.N.U. *A Decade of the Matrimonial Causes Act, 1970*, Nigerian Current L. Rev. 55, 57 (1983).
433. At https://en.wikipedia.org/wiki/Vesicovaginal_fistula.
434. *Ibid.*
435. *See* Andreas Rahmatian, *Termination of Marriage in Nigerian Family Laws: The Need for Reform and the Relevance of the Tanzanian Experience*, 10 Int'l J. L. Pol'y & Fam. 281, 294 (1996).

valid. A marriage, let alone a relationship analogous to marriage, can exist without either the presence or the possibility of children from that relationship.[436]

§2. The Nature of Marriage

426. Marriage writes Aguda is the foundation of society. For, 'every religion, every people, every civilisation has realised that the institution of marriage is the very foundation of society'.[437]

427. Elsewhere, it has also been stated: 'The Law of England says that marriage is a contract resulting in a status ... The Catholic Church gives an answer differing only in one word; marriage is a contract resulting in a relationship ... Now, relationship differs from status in this: that it is a God-made thing, which man cannot alter.'[438] Interestingly, in *Ghaidan v. Godin-Mendoza* Lord Millet noted:

> there is, indeed, a paradox at the heart of modern society. For centuries the civil and canon law, the common law of Europe as it has been called, did not require any form of religious or secular ceremony to constitute a marriage. Persons who openly set up home together and lived together as man and wife were presumed to be married; marriage was by habit and repute. The combined effect of the Council of Trent and the Marriage Acts put an end to all that. But there is nothing new in treating men and women who lived together as husband and wife as if they were married; it is a reversion to an older tradition.[439]

428. In *FamDHC & E (an alleged Patient) v. Sheffield City Council & E & S.*,[440] Munby J., stated marriage creates a status from which certain legal rights and duties automatically stem. Marriage also carries with it not merely all those intensely human, personal and emotional advantages that are obviously so important for so many but also a wide range of legal, social and fiscal advantages, many of which, of course, inure not just for the benefit of the married couple themselves but also for the benefit of their children.[441]

429. Marriage has always been a connecting factor between different people from the earliest understanding of human relations. Laws interest in marriage is always aimed at orderliness and more often the protection of the interest of the parties as family, security of women and children. The business of modern law is in

---

436. *Ghaidan v. Godin-Mendoza* [2004] AC 557; [2004] UKHL 30 para. 141.
437. Akinola Aguda, *Select Law Lectures and Papers* 99, 120-121; 86 (Associated Publishers (Nigeria) Ltd. 1971); 86; B. Oyebanji, *Proposals for Reform of Marriage Law in Nigeria*, in *The Marriage Laws of Nigeria* 147 (T.A. Aguda ed., Being Papers Presented at a National Workshop – Nigerian Institute of Advanced Legal Studies 1981).
438. E. G. M., 1932, p. 294.
439. [2004] 2 AC 557, 591 para. 93.
440. [2004] EWCH 2808 (Fam).
441. [2004] EWCH 2808 (Fam), para. 143.

how to create a balance between the interests of the parties and the State. Some have referred to this interest as power relations and how it should be managed to assure societal cohesion.[442]

430. Traditionally, the legal interest created in family relations and means of protecting it is in many ways in the nature of property interests and relations. This had to be so because of the almost initial universal perspective on gender roles. Complete marriage rites thus entailed activities that served the legal function of notice by performance rites in open space and before witnesses. The same features were also attached to dissolution. Having a Register of Marriages is an elementary feature of most legal systems. In Nigeria, the Supreme Court has repeatedly held that in line with the provisions of section 36(1) and (3) of the Constitution, and relevant provisions of the Matrimonial Causes Act and rules thereon,[443] dissolution or annulment of a marriage must be in open court and under no circumstances should a petition in respect of either be heard or determined before a judge in chambers.[444] With regards to customary and Islamic marriages, dissolution for the former would normally involve inner family members and with the latter, two forms of dissolution apply which may be said to entail some element of modern public record content. With respect to nullity, the rules and implications under customary law are nearly the same in most parts of South East and the oil producing states usually referred to as South-South Nigeria. Where marriage should not have been embarked on for being void, then it never happened at all and any issues therefrom are legitimated as if born out of wedlock. When the marriage is voidable, some rituals may be prescribed and conducted to validate the marriage.

431. Customary law marriage is a potentially, if not factually, polygamous marriage. In the case of most African customary marriages as was observed correctly, in *GE v. KE & Anor.*,[445] the rites of marriage are unwritten. However, the content and context of African customary marriage which, usually, essentially take the same pattern are in depth and contain not only elements of the experiences of the people, but also, legal, religious and philosophical foundations. As a typical example, for the South East of Nigeria, each typical marriage rite, consists of social interaction, legalistic transactions, philosophical reminiscences of communality by which eating must be done together and taken from the same dishes; religious rites encompass breaking of kola nuts and eating of garden eggs and then, rites of reincarnation. Within the rites there are futuristic dynamics catering to the event of break up, maltreatment or cruelty to the bride and even death.

432. As time passes and circumstances change, internal objective and validity of the content and objectives of the rites of customary marriage are either rejected or lost. In consequence extant generation live in 'reminiscence of the customs' and

442. Mark Henaghan, *The Normal Order of Family Law*, 28(1) Oxford J. Legal Stud. 165 (2008); John Eekelaar, *Family Law and Personal Life* (Oxford University Press 2006).
443. Cap M7, Laws of the Federation, 2004.
444. N.N. Chinwuba, *Requirement of Publicity in Marriage Framework: When Should We Construct Bridges or Build Walls?*, 1(1) Ahmadu Bello U. J. Contemp. Issues in Sharia & Comp. L. 1 (2020).
445. [2014] EWHC 1938(Fam).

desirous of sustaining the customs are unable to offer necessary explanation or background to the rites. Thus, to the modern observer, the attachment to the customs becomes baseless and also even so to stakeholders as they have no actual records. As an example, it would have been unheard of at a time in the not-too-distant past, at least the period prior to 1990, for a customary marriage to be conducted without the actual physical presence of the parties, what is now accepted as proxy marriages. It must be borne in mind that an aspect of the custom, is that upon the conclusion of the celebration of the rites, the couple must prove the virginity of the bride by presenting a blood-stained white sheet to the family and participants. Nevertheless, as a result of modernity and grave experiences such as tragic accidents *en route* to ancestral homes, inter-tribal and racial marriages, whereby one party is either unable or unwilling to go through the ceremonies, proxy marriages are now conducted customarily. The proceedings are not recorded at least in the modern sense, with a view to preservation of records. In the modern times there might be video recording for entertainment purposes. Another example is the modern dust-to-dust rites performed in the observance of burial rites upon the demise of a Christian. In many customs in the South East, it is an abomination for a widow to perform a dust-to-dust rite on a husband. To the onlooker, the reason is based on disrespect of the departed gentleman. However, the internal objection to the rite is deep with sociological mysteries. The Nigerian Supreme Court has held in a long line of cases, that a widow is not entitled to share in the estate of her deceased husband under customary law, since she, as a wife, is part of that estate.[446] The sociological mystery then is, should the dust to dust rite be performed, would that not entail that the wife is separated from the departed husband and would be at liberty to reject any overtures of being inherited? Catholic Church and the Catholic women parishioners on the one side and the custodians of customs on the other side – the toggle of customs and modernity rages on. [447]

433. Marriage in Nigeria can only be between a man and a woman. The question of transsexuals has never arisen in Nigeria and therefore difficult to comment on. Same-sex marriage is prohibited in Nigeria.[448]The Same Sex Marriage (Prohibition) Act, 2013 prohibits marriage between people of same sex, and punishment is fourteen years of imprisonment. Any such marriage is void and punishment extends to those who participate or witness any such union. Civil unions are also not allowed between the same-sex persons. There is a custom of woman-to-woman

446. *Akinnubi v. Akinnubi* [1997] 2 NWLR (part 486) 144; *Nezianya v. Okagbue* [1963] 1 All NLR 352; cited with approval in *Nzekwu v. Nzekwu* [1989] 2 NWLR 373; *Chinweze v. Masi* [1989] 1 NWLR (part 97) 255; *see* however, *Asikia v. Atuanya* [2008] 17 NWLR (part 1117) 484–524. See other commentaries Kenneth Mwenda, Florence Mumba & Judith Mvula-Mwenda, *Property-Grabbing under African Customary Law: Repugnant to Natural Justice, Equity, and Good Conscience, Yet a Troubling Reality*, 37 Geo Wash. Intl. Rev. 949 (2005); Lynn Khadiagala, *Negotiating Law and Custom: Judicial Doctrine and Women's Property Rights in Uganda*, 46(1) J. Afr. L. 1–13, (2002).

447. Chuks Collins, *Author Faces Threats Over Book on 'Dust-to-Dust' Rites for Women*, available at https://guardian.ng/news/nigeria/national/author-faces-threats-over-book-on-dust-to-dust-rites-for-women/ (last accessed 31 Aug. 2020).

448. Same sex Marriage (Prohibition) Act 2013.

marriage which exists in some States of Nigeria – in all states in the East of Nigeria and Ekiti State of Nigeria.[449] However, the context of gender content is a metaphorical fictional.

§3. The Capacity to Marry

434. The capacity to marry usually relates to marriageable age and consent to the marriage. The parties must usually be mentally capable of understanding the nature of the marriage contract. Other indicators of capacity are that the parties must be free to marry one another and not obligated to some other person by another marriage. There must also be compliance with the degree and avoidance of prohibited degrees of consanguinity or affinity.

435. In Nigeria capacity to marry is dependent on the intended type of marriage.

I. Capacity to Enter a Monogamous Marriage

436. The minimum age for marriage in Nigeria under the Act is 21 years. Thus, a registrar shall not issue certificate to marry until he has been satisfied by affidavit that each of the parties to the intended marriage is 21 years old.[450] The Marriage Act and other legislation have several provisions which support this position. The other section in the Act which supports this position is section 18 and is captioned: 'consent to marriage of minors'. The section provides:

> if either party to an intended marriage, not being a widower or widow, is under twenty-one years of age, the written consent of the father, or if he be dead or of unsound mind or absent from Nigeria, of the mother, or if both be dead or of unsound mind or absent from Nigeria, of the guardian of such party, must be produced annexed to such affidavit as aforesaid before a license can be granted or a certificate issued.

437. The other relevant provision on age of maturity and marriage is section 29(4) of the Constitution although it relates to renunciation of citizenship. The section provides that 18 years is full age and a married woman is of full age. It is not clear whether the subsection aims at providing protection for women who are married but below the age of 18 years or it aims at recognising 18 years as the age of marriage.

438. The Child's Right Act, which is a National legislation, makes 18 the minimum age of marriage.[451] Any marriage of a child under the age of 18 years is void.

449. N.N. Chinwuba, *Daughter/Widow Retention in Nigeria: Survey and Analysis from Case Law*, 2(1) J. Comp. L. Afr. 82–99 (2016).
450. Section 11(1)(b) of the Act.
451. Section 21.

Section 22 of the CRA provides punishment for direct and indirect facilitation of such marriage. The provisions are however subject to the earlier discussion on the applicability of the Act itself. The Act is subject to assimilation as State law. So far, however, only twenty-four States and the FCT have accepted the application of the Act as law.

439. Technically as monogamous marriage comes under the Exclusive Legislative competence of the National Assembly and the MA and MCA are Federal laws, it implies that celebration of monogamous marriages under the MA requires a minimum age of 21 years. For other forms of marriages, if the States have assimilated the Child Rights Law, the requisite age of marriage is 18 years.

440. The registrar must also be satisfied that there are no impediments respecting kindred, affinity or any other lawful hindrance to celebrating the marriage.[452] The Matrimonial Causes Act is also applicable with regard to capacity. Section 3 of the MCA provides that marriages shall be void where either of the parties is not of marriageable age. In addition, to be valid, a. marriage must not be within certain degrees of bloodline and affinity. Thus, section 3(1)(b) provides that marriages will be void if the parties are within the prohibited degrees of consanguinity or subject to section 4 of the Act of affinity. The prohibited degrees of consanguinity and affinity are listed in the First Schedule. For the purpose of the law it is immaterial whether the relationship is of the whole or half blood, or whether it is traced through a person whose birth was not within wedlock.

441. However, for affinity, the law makes an exception. Such persons may apply in writing to a judge for permission to marry.[453] Such rules also exist with respect to customary law marriages.

442. Other instances where capacity to contract a marriage is lacking and any attempted marriage void are where either of the parties is, at the time of the marriage lawfully married to some other person[454]

443. A party who is married under customary law to a person other than the one he or she is contemplating to marry under the Act is also incapacitated to do so. Thus, section 11(d) of the Marriage Act provides: 'The Registrar may issue his Certificate in the prescribed Form C as in First Schedule to the Act, provided amongst other conditions: "that neither of the parties to the intended marriage is married by customary law to any person other than the person with whom such marriage is proposed to be contracted"'.

444. In *Agbeja v. Agbeja*, the evidence of the plaintiff, 'wife' was:

---

452. Section 11(1)(c) of the Act.
453. Section 4(1).
454. Section 3(1). In this connection the Marriage Act makes it an offence by ss 33, 35, 46, 47.

> the deceased went to England in 1951. I had just delivered. He left me living with his mother at Ilesha. He returned from England in 1952. … I continued to live with his mother. When I thought it was time for me to get pregnant I wrote to him saying I would like to come to him, or he should come to me. He did not reply. Later I heard that he had impregnated a woman in England. I asked him and he said it was true. Then I said I did not mind and that I could continue to live with his mother. He refused. He asked me to pack out from his mother's house. I refused and continued to live there. Then in 1954 I heard that he had married another woman. Then in 1955 I left for my father's house. Up to 1955 the marriage between myself and the deceased was never dissolved.[455]

445. The Court established that the 'deceased' met the defendant-appellant in England and married her under native law and custom there. He lived with her in England where she had a daughter, the second appellant. The deceased first proceeded to Lagos and was soon followed by the appellant and her daughter. In Lagos they consolidated their union by marrying under the MA and lived as a family from 1954 to 1974 until the death of the patriarch. In his lifetime, a daughter by another woman, the second respondent who had been unknown to the appellant was brought to live with them. The deceased told her that he had not married her mother but only acknowledged the plaintiff-respondent. The appellant raised the respondent.

446. The case was decided in 1982. The court held that the appellant, 'English wife' who married the deceased according to Nigerian customary law in England and later by the MA was a 'mere mistress' or concubine. Although some will take the position that this case was wrongly or unfairly decided in the light of its peculiar circumstances, yet the MA is clear and by sections 11(d) and 35, a marriage under customary law incapacitates a person from marrying under the MA unless such marriage has been duly dissolved according to native law and customs or by customary court.

447. A good case from the Commonwealth that analyses capacity is *FamDHC & E (an alleged Patient) v. Sheffield City Council & E & S.*[456] The case concerned a preliminary issue brought before the Family Division of the High Court of Justice of England and Wales, in its inherent jurisdiction. The trust of the litigation was the meaning and content of capacity, that is, whether the capacity to marry is 'person-specific' or general. The question came up in relation to a patient E, a lady, who was 21. 'E' had medical challenges that left her with the mental capacity of a 13 year old. 'E' was in a relationship with an older man, 'S', who had a criminal past which included violent sexual crimes. The matter was initiated by the Sheffield City Council, a local social services authority with responsibilities for E. As at the time of the proceedings, E had moved in with 'S' and the relationship had become abusive. The Sheffield City Council commenced the proceedings to stop her from associating

455. [1985] 3 NWLR (part 11) 11, 17.
456. [2004] EWCH 2808 (Fam).

with 'S' or marrying him. An *ex parte* order was made which in substance prohibited 'S' from marrying E without first obtaining the leave of court to do so. Questions were raised in many areas but of relevance is the content and scope of capacity, for a person to give a valid consent to marriage.

448. Mr Justice Munby delivering the preliminary judgment on the subject noted first that at the age of 18, every adult is presumed to have the capacity, and the burden to prove otherwise is on those who assert it. In the circumstances, since E, was above 18, the burden was on the Sheffield City council to prove that she did not have capacity to marry. The second point was that under English law, the general rule is that the test of capacity is the ability (whether one chooses to exercise it) to understand the nature and quality of the transaction. On the capacity to marry between E and S, Munby J, emphasised earlier authorities affirming that *Park v. Park* (*In the Estate of Park deceased*)[457] still expresses the accepted position on the subject. In *Park* Singleton LJ, stated:

> Was the deceased … capable of understanding the nature of the contract into which he was entering, or was his mental condition such that he was incapable of understanding it? To ascertain the nature of the contract of marriage a man must be mentally capable of appreciating that it involves the responsibilities normally attaching to marriage. Without that degree of mentality, it cannot be said that he understands the nature of the contract.

449. Munby J, further referred to *Re B* (*Consent to Treatment: Capacity*).[458] In that case, the court stated: 'It is most important that those considering the issue should not confuse the question of mental capacity with the nature of the decision made by the patient, however grave the consequences. The view of the patient may reflect a difference in values rather than an absence of competence and the assessment of capacity should be approached with this firmly in mind.'[459]

450. Munby J. concluded that the question to be asked is specific to the general state of affairs and not to persons. The contract of marriage, as he stated, is a simple one which any person of normal intelligence can readily comprehend. The question to be asked therefore, is always the simple one of whether a person understands the nature of the contract to marry.

II. Capacity to Marry under Customs and Islamic Law

451. Customary and Islamic marriages contemplate the age of puberty for both males and females. Other questions in relation to capacity are not well spelt out but may be implied from the formalities for the celebration of the marriage under the

457. [1953] 2 All ER 1411; [1954] P. 112.
458. [2002] EWHC 429 (Fam), [2002] 1 FLR 1090, para. 100.
459. [2002] 1 FLR 1090, para. 100.

two systems. Some of the major factors to be taken into consideration in determining the capacity to marry under Islamic law and some customs are: puberty, consent and prohibited affiliations in terms of consanguinity or affinity. In Islam, marriage is dependent on maturity and categorised as to men in *ihtilam*,[460] and females in *haidah*.[461]

452. Capacity of the parties to consent to marriage is, of course, connected with what the age of a child is in Nigeria. As has been noted above this does not appear to be clear. In addition to this, is that children's rights except in relation to discrimination or deprivation[462] come under residuary matters that are not specifically assigned for legislative purposes. In consequence of this and by reason of section 12 of the Constitution the National Assembly could only enact the Childs Right Act but has lacked the necessary majority to have the Act effected uniformly as a Federal law. This leaves the States the choice to elect to adopt the same as specific State law.[463] This Act is an implementation of the United Nations Convention on the Right of the Child to which Nigeria is a signatory, but some States in the Federation have up until now not adopted the Act as applicable to the states.

453. Since there is no age specification for marriage under customary and Islamic law, this has resulted in rampant girl-child marriages in Nigeria and in particular the North of Nigeria. The factors giving rise to conformity with this situation include poverty, low level of education, political ties, harmful traditional practices, and religion.

454. In 2013, United Nations International Children Emergency Fund (UNICEF) estimated that 44% of girls in Nigeria are married off before their 18th birthday and the country also records the 11th highest rate of child marriage. These figures undermine the essence and efficacy of the combined import of sections 21 and 22 of the Child's Right Act which prohibit child marriage. A girl given out in early marriage in most cases is deprived of the right to education and privileges of growing up in dignity.

455. Apart from the micro consequences of child marriage on fertility, health and wellbeing, this practice has a far-reaching macroeconomic and sustainability consequence on the society. One such negative outcome of child marriage is increased and uncontrolled births, with attendant continuing population explosion which undermines the government's ability to plan and mobilise resources for sustainable development.

---

460. Wet dream for male.
461. Menstruation for female; *see* further, M.A. Ambali, *The Practice of Muslim Family Law in Nigeria* 3 (Tamaza Publishing 2003).
462. Section 42(2) of the Constitution of the Federation.
463. Twenty-six States of the Federation mainly from Southern Nigeria and the Middle Belt have enacted State laws based on the Child's Right Act. These include Lagos and Anambra States.

§4. FORMALITIES

I. Formalities of Customary Marriage

456. Customary law marriage is a potentially polygamous marriage. Polygamy is a state of marriage to many spouses although it must be noted that this term may be gender sensitive. Thus sociologist will refer to the marriage of a man to more than one wife as polygyny. When the reverse is the case, and a woman is married to more than one man then it is polyandry. Thus, polygamy is a compound word for both scenarios.

457. The following are the essential elements of a valid customary marriage.

(i) parties must possess the capacity to marry;
(ii) the intending couple must consent to the marriage;
(iii) payment of bride price by the prospective husband to the parents or guardians of the wife;
(iv) there must be a ceremony of marriage and the formal handing over of the woman to the man's family, usually, the head of the family; and
(iv) there must be cohabitation following the marriage.

458. In many of the customary marriages, the acceptance of the bride is ceremonial, and the husband's party is required, following cohabitation with the bride to conclude the marriage rites by a ceremony which formally introduces the wife to his own family. This ceremony is termed *isenete ibve mia.*[464]

459. In *Nickaf v. Nickaf,*[465] Akpata J.C.A observed that the payment of bride price is an essential requirement of marriage under customary law of most communities in Nigeria.

460. The antiquity of customary law marriages is that the relation is between families as opposed to individuals. Thus, whether the families bring about the formation of the marriage or the requisite acceptance of marriage between the individuals or it is the other way around, that the prospective couple find and accept each other before presenting their desires to families, the position is the same, families are involved in real terms and not just procedurally. In *Okpanum v. Okpanum*[466] the High Court of East Central State of Nigeria held that to constitute a valid customary marriage, the consent of parents must be given and cannot be dispensed with. This was reiterated in *Osamwonyi v. Osamwonyi*[467] where the Supreme Court held that both the consent of the bride and her parents were prerequisite to a valid marriage under the customs of the *Binis* in present day Edo State of Nigeria.

---

464. Return of the calabashes from the bride's family.
465. Suit No. CA/1E/79/84. (Unreported) Court of Appeal, Kaduna; *see also* E.I. Nwogugu, *Family Law in Nigeria* 56–58 (Heinemann 1990).
466. [1972] 2 ECSLR 561.
467. [1973] NMLR 26.

461. When the formation scales past this stage then it goes into the next which is preparation for the rites. Solemnisation is an essential aspect of the formation of marriage. The activities and content of the solemnisation or celebration vary from tribe to tribe and even clans and community. It is generally uniform in terms of method and content of the basic rites.

462. In the South West of Nigeria, bride wealth would now normally be exchanged. The bride wealth would normally consist of baskets of fruits and vegetables of different kinds. Some families still expect to and do exchange bride price. The significance of bride price in specie, is low in this part of Nigeria. These fruits and vegetables are of different kinds and have different significance. Thus, a basket would often contain coconut. The coconut signifies that the marriage will be of immense mystery to third parties – the relationship and life of the couple will be closed to third parties. The question who a third party is of course a different one. The third party will certainly not include the husband's family and in further particular, his mother. The basket would normally also contain alligator pepper signifying a reproductive union or fertility. Bananas and oranges also project the same significance. A bottle of honey would also be a major component of the content of the basket. It signifies marital bliss. Salt is also usually a content of the basket and signifies marital stability and balance.

463. The people of the South East, Middle Belt and Southern Kaduna of Nigeria are mainly Christians and Catholics. A good case is that of *Nickaf v. Nickaf.*[468] In that case, the 'wife' had sued the husband for libel over a publication he had caused to be made in the Newspapers to the effect that she was not his wife. In evidence before the trial court, the wife and her father stated that the parties had agreed to marry each other, resulting in some form of betrothal. The husband claimed that there was no payment of bride price and therefore the marriage was a nullity. The wife's family on the other hand, claimed that their community in Kagoro in Southern Kaduna did not require bride price as an essential element for the formation of marriage and that the bride price was offered by the husband but waived by her father. According to the family, this was in the presence of family members, and that her father did accept the proposal of marriage and symbolically handed her over in marriage. Subsequently, the husband and the wife agreed that the wife would change her name from Miss Titi Usman to Mrs. Titi Nickaf. They both published this change of name in a newspaper. They then had three children between 1972 and 1979. In some letters exhibited in evidence, written by the husband to the wife between 1972 and 1981, he addressed her as 'Dear Wife' and called himself 'yours ever, husband' and 'Love Hussy'. They cohabited between 1977 and 1978. The wife was then known in her workplace, official and social circles as Mrs. Nickaf. In 1981, the husband then caused to be published in a newspaper, an announcement that he was not married to her. In the action for libel, the husband admitted the publication but pleaded justification. He contended that he was not validly married to the wife as he did not the pay bride price and that there could be no valid waiver of bride price under customary law. The trial court held that there was a marriage between

468. Suit No. CA/1E/79/84. (Unreported) Court of Appeal, Kaduna.

the parties and as such, the publication constituted a libel. On appeal, the Court of Appeal while acknowledging that bride price is an indispensable element of customary marriage in most parts of Nigeria, took the position that the evidence before the Court was not sufficient for it to determine whether bride price was indeed an element in the validity of customary marriage in Kagoro and if it was, whether parties to a potential marriage had the requisite right to waive it. The court noted that where native law and customs required an act for the validity of a legal relation, a waiver of it would render the relation void. The Court held that the appellant could not establish that there was no marriage between him and the respondent.

464. The relationship between the church and customs in the South East of Nigeria has seen some variations in the rite and content of the customary marriage rites. The bride wealth is aimed at catering to the pleasure of everyone in the community and, particularly, the male members. The bride price goes to the father and mother of the bride.

465. The process of customary marriage in the South East (Igbos) is intensive. It is also in stages. Where the couples are to be married by proxy then, the requirements are varied, but not processes. The process commences with the prospective groom and bride having gained acquaintance, the groom in company of a few members of his family requests for an introduction to the inner caucus of the family of the bride. This is usually called a 'knock on the door'. The prospective couple could also have been arranged to be so by their families although consent would usually be gained one way or the other. When the inner family receives the proposal for marriage, and it is favourable, it would then present the proposal for marriage to the larger family. This stage of the process applies to both the groom and the bride. This is then followed by presentation and exchange of requirements for the marriage which is heavily tilted in favour of the bride's family and then the rites of marriage and celebration. There are two most important aspects of these process, one is the bride price and the other is the handing over of the bride. The bride price sometimes involves negotiations between men of the two families delegated to carry out the function. In recent times due to abuse, there has been fundamental intervention aimed at reducing the bride price by legislation. It is to be noted that a bride price is different from a dowry. The indispensable content of the basket of the customary marriage ceremony of the South Easterners of Nigeria are kola nuts, garden eggs, yams, hens, goats, and the highlight – well-rounded, delicate tasting and naturally balanced palm-wine in several calabashes tapped from the evergreen Palm Trees of the East of the Niger. Usually, the ceremony is held outdoors and under canopies within the residence of the head of the family or father of the bride.

466. The process among the Igbos and the solemnisation rites have mystical perspectives. For instance, in place of the usual two goats required as part of bride wealth, where the marriage is by proxy and the full compliments of the groom's family will not attend the ceremony, the number of goats required would normally increase by two, and in this case, castrated goats.

467. Re-incarnation is recognised and accorded a place in the customs and culture of the Igbos and this plays out in marriage ceremonies as well. Thus, one of the crucial contents of the bride wealth is a *hen* which is meant to be slaughtered for the 'incarnated' individual. It is to be noted that the person present in existence is the 'reincarnate' of an incarnate. Christians now reject this perspective. Thus, where celebrants are Christians, the rite excludes aspects of the original content of marriage rites, so there will be no hen as part of the requirement – a loss to the men who would have enjoyed the slaughtered and barbecued or sautéed sauce, well spiced and may be taken as soup. It is worth mentioning, although not immediate aspect of the ceremonial rites, that a woman must not eat the gizzard of any fowl – this is especially reserved for the patriarch of each household. In modern times, however, the gizzards are so in stock in shops in their millions and it is now not clear why the gizzard in the cooking pot of the household is in any way, a reserve. This part of the custom, unusual and some others, exclusive to the Igbos of Nigeria form the cornerstone of the understanding of the Igbos to a Jewish ancestry.[469]

468. In the South East, generally, a woman cannot be married while pregnant and the ceremonial rites for a woman who has had children for a proposing husband prior to the marriage have some slight variations. It must be noted that marriage in the South East is made significantly simpler for persons of other tribes and foreigners. Thus, the number of participants from a husband's family can be reduced to as low as two or three and the numbers replaced with fictitious symbolisms such as numbers of castrated goats.

469. *N v. D* (Customary Marriage)[470] was so correctly decided. In that case an English Court found a Nigerian customary marriage proved on facts based on the ceremony and ruled that this gave rise to a valid marriage in English law. D, the man was a Yoruba from South West of Nigeria although his family resided mainly in Lagos. N, the woman was from the South East of Nigeria. D, and N – the mother of his four children, agreed that they had been in relationship between 2002 and 2011. In 2012, apparently after speaking with a solicitor, N contended that they had married in a customary ceremony in their native Nigeria in 2005 which D denied. D disputed this, saying that there had been a large family party which did not amount to a marriage ceremony. 'N' applied to the Family Court for a declaration of marital status under section 55(1)(a) of the Family Law Act 1986.

---

469. 'The strong analogy which … appears to prevail in the manners and customs of my countrymen and those of the Jews, before they reached the Land of Promise, and particularly the patriarchs while they were yet in that pastoral state which is described in Genesis—an analogy, which alone would induce me to think that the one people had sprung from the other' available at: https://en.wikipedia.org/wiki/Igbo_Jews (last accessed 1 Sep. 2020); *see also* Chika Oduah, *Nigeria's Igbo Jews: 'Lost tribe' of Israel?*, available at:https://edition.cnn.com/2013/02/01/world/africa/nigeria-jews-igbo/index.html (last accessed 1 Sep. 2020); Daniel Lis, *Jewish Identity among the IGBO of Nigeria: Israel's Lost Tribe and the Question of Belonging in the Jewish State* (Afric 1st ed. 2014); Melanie Lidman, *Messianic Jews to Nigerians: You're Not 'Real' Jews* – Religious group from Arizona claims DNA testing proves that Igbo tribe are not genetically Jewish, drawing ire – available at: https://www.timesofisrael.com/messianic-jews-to-nigerians-youre-not-real-jews/ (last accessed 1 Sep. 2020).

470. [2015] EWFC 28.

470. Mr Justice Peter Jackson heard oral evidence from D and N and eight witnesses (four family members on each side), read written evidence and studied over 100 photographs of the celebration. The court also had the benefit of expert evidence from a jointly instructed Professor of Nigerian law. The court found that, on the balance of probabilities, the celebration had amounted to a customary marriage and, since that is a valid form of a marriage in Nigeria, there was a valid marriage recognised under English law.

471. The court made some significant findings:

(1) My overall conclusion from this material is that it strongly and, I find, conclusively corroborates the evidence of N and her family. This was not just a party or an introduction. It was a formal and joyful celebration. Taken individually, the photographs contain details that are without exception highly suggestive of the form of customary marriage described by Professor Nsugbe and many of the photographs are inexplicable in any other way. Taken as a set, the collection is exactly what one would expect as the record of a wedding. The assiduous way in which different family groups are posed and photographed speaks of nothing less. The fact that the photographs found their way into the family home in two albums, one conspicuously labelled, speaks for itself.
(2) During the earlier litigation, N has shown that she can be untruthful, in contrast, D was a voluble and unconvincing witness, though not without charm.
(3) D and his witnesses had no answer to the evidence in the photographic record. L, the main photographer, could not point to a single detail that was inconsistent with a wedding. Like D, he contended that any appearance of a wedding was misleading because of the absence of **key family members on D's side**.
(4) D argues that he would never have agreed to get married in the absence of his brothers and his sister R. He also urges that it would have been disrespectful for him to marry without involving his aunts and uncles from Lagos; moreover, that he would have invited the prominent cousin to play the part of senior male figure, as he had done at the two other family weddings.
(5) When faced with the question *'[D] would never have agreed to marry without his brothers and sister being there, would he?'* N spontaneously replied: *'Well he would because he did.'* In a similarly artless vein, N's sister E replied to the suggestion that D did not know he was getting married: *'How can someone who is getting married not know he is getting married?'*.
(6) I am satisfied that a dowry was paid in this case. The large amount of beverages and food paid for by D amply qualify as such. That is why they were prominently on display and why they were photographed. I also accept on balance the evidence of N's mother, brother A and cousin J that the handing over of a symbolic sum of money (immediately returned with a symbolic banknote retained) did take place in the living room of Father B's house. This does not appear in any photograph, but I do not believe that these witnesses, reliable in other respects, have fabricated this account.
(7) D paid significant sums of money to N's family before and after the event. He explains this as being a contribution from him, as a big name. I think it is highly unlikely that N's family would have accepted money from D if this was

merely a party. On the other hand, it is entirely appropriate, and consistent with the December e-mails, that D should have paid so that the requirements of the dowry would be met.

472. I conclude that D and N took part in a customary marriage ceremony. They both fully understood the commitments that they and their families were making. Their ignorance of the position under English law cannot undo this. A valid English marriage is not affected by the ignorance of the parties about whether it will be recognised elsewhere, and the same must apply in reverse. The contrary has not been suggested during these proceedings.

473. The court also noted that Nigerian law provides for a presumption of a valid marriage arising from cohabitation but chose not to call up presumptions since there was ample evidence of marriage. The court granted the wife's application for declarations of marital status under section 55(1)(a) of the Family Law Act 1986 and ordered that D pay N's costs on an indemnity basis.

474. It is perfectly accurate to note that the family members of non-Igbos would not be required to compulsorily attend the ceremony of a customary marriage provided they meet all requirements. In addition, the journey is a long one and the governments (both Federal and State) have done little to make the routes pleasurable. The other impediment to a full representation when the groom is from the South West is the mutual tribal suspicion and distrust between people of the South West and South East.

475. The next stage in the process is handing over the bride. In *Omoga v. Badejo*,[471] the Court reiterated that there must be a handing over of the bride. This is usually to the eldest male member of the groom's family and not to the groom. Where the marriage was conducted by proxies, their photographs are displayed and members of the family, a man and a woman from either side represent the couple.

476. In *Osamwonyi v. Osamwonyi*[472] the Supreme Court held that payment of bride price without cohabitation between the parties after handing over rebutted any presumption of marriage having taken place. Cohabitation is a vital element in determining whether a customary marriage is in existence.[473] The Court may presume existence of certain facts. The final ceremony, no less as important, is the welcome party and formal presentation of the bride to the groom's family which takes place at the pleasure of the groom's family.

477. Mr Justice Peter Jackson's summary of the evidence provided in *N v. D* (Customary Marriage)[474] is a picturesque of the Igbo customary marriage ceremony:

---

471. [1985] NCNL 1075.
472. [1973] NMLR 26.
473. Section 166 of the Evidence Act, 2011.
474. [2015] EWFC 28.

(i) In two photographs the entrance to the compound can be seen in the background. These show the reverse of a large banner (another was on the main road) on which N and D's names are emblazoned and a drawing of a calabash prominently appears. There is other writing that cannot be made out from the photographs, but I accept the evidence of N and her witnesses that it includes reference in Igbo to *'Igbankwu'*, a 'wine-carrying' or wedding. Whether or not the Yoruba guests could read that, it is impossible to imagine them being at cross-purposes with everybody else who could.
(ii) D's sisters wearing coordinated outfits.
(iii) Money being showered on the couple.
(iv) A close-up of a large number of banknotes on the ground.
(v) D's brother-in-law L and N's father shaking hands in a friendly and demonstrative way.
(vi) N and D standing face-to-face and very close while she sips palm wine from a plastic beaker.
(vii) N holding a ceremonial calabash said to have contained the palm wine afterwards poured into the beaker.
(viii) D's mother joyously embracing N's brother A.
(ix) D signing an autograph.
(x) D's mother and N's father dancing together.
(xi) D's sister S holding one of the CDs while standing with D and N and N's parents. N herself is holding an object that may be one of the large sack of cups brought as souvenirs by D's mother.
(xii) The couple with a group of women, one of whom is holding one of the CDs.

478. The customary marriage in the South East of Nigeria as has been noted earlier is more intense. This is for two reasons; the South East is almost homogenously Christian, and the impact of Christianity has created a toggle between the two cultures resulting in the rigidity of both. Thus, while in the South West a customary marriage is usually inbuilt into a statutory marriage, in the South East, it is often the case that a customary marriage suffices or is followed by a Statutory, Christian and Church marriages at different times. The first would be customary, and when reproduction is assured, then statutory and finally or on the same day, the church wedding.

479. The customary marriage holds far more significance to the Igbos but again equally so, the Christian celebration. To have all three is a win-win situation for the average couple from the South East of Nigeria. As will be noted in subsequent discussions, Nigerian law does not recognise church or mere Christian marriage proceedings as legal.

II. The Bride Price

480. A bride price is not the same as a dowry. Dowry is an amount of property or money brought by a bride to her husband on their marriage. While a dowry is usually made to a husband, the bride price as the description indicates is strictly for the wife. No doubt some customs in other parts of Africa or Asia may have the two coincide or may have only dowry at play, the concept of bride price in Nigeria is from the groom's family to the wife's family.

481. A first look at bride price from modern legal and commercial prisms will dismiss it as mere consideration making the customary marriage appear as contract of sale. This is more so when one considers the position of the South West where many families now place more emphasis on the basket accompanied with a formal letter of proposition and the unique merits of the conclusion of the Supreme Court of Uganda in *Mifumi (U) Ltd. & Others v. ATT. Gen. & Kenneth Kakuru.*[475]

482. There is however another view from the prism of the role of the return of the bride price. The bride price has to be returned by the bride's family when the marriage fails.[476] The bride's family can trigger its return or the groom's parents can request for its reclaim, this return aspect appears to indicate the commitment of the bride's family to the welfare and wellbeing of the bride. The customs of the Igbos of the South East has very important twist different from the expert's evidence that was preferred in *GE v. KE.*[477]

483. Women and daughters have a prime place in the family. They are, in spite of deprivation from succession, protected and cared for. Thus, a daughter always has a place in the father's house whether in life or death. While alive, should her marriage fail, she is welcome back home and any occupant of the family home, by the rules of primogeniture, must provide a dwelling space for her until her demise. On her demise she must be accorded due and full final respects. Thus, upon death, she must be laid in state at the father's home, again, this is not dependent on who is in the occupation of the home. For this reason, the bride price serves as a continuing legal interest of her family in her, not necessary with the groom's family but in her. Indeed, contrary to the evidence preferred in *GE v. KE* long separation does not delegitimise the customary marriage of the south easterners of Nigeria. So long as the bride price is not returned and accepted, the marriage continues to exist with all rights and obligations from both parties. Indeed, should a wife, while separated conceives and births, illegitimacy cannot operate as the child remains legitimate progeny of the husband.

484. The uniqueness of the South West ceremony is that it has a modern twist of an engagement letter all in one package of the traditional ceremony. There is also a bride price which in the modern-urban context is paid and then returned simultaneously to the parents of the bride. The position of elites of the South West is that

---

475. [2015] UGSC 13 (15 Aug. 2015); CONSTITUTIONAL PETITION NO. 12 OF 2007. *See also* J.D. Mujuzi, *Bride Wealth (Price) and Women's Marriage-Related Rights in Uganda: A Historical Constitutional Perspective and Current Developments*, 24(3) Int'l J. L. Pol'y & Fam. 414–430, 414 (2010).

476. In *Ochei v. Ochei* [1973] East Central State of Nigeria law Report 623, evidence of return of bride price was used as a corroborating evidence by the court that the marriage had broken down irretrievably in a petition under the Matrimonial Causes Act.

477. [2013] EWHC 1938.

a marriage should not bear any resemblance to a commercial transaction. Nevertheless, the families remain inclined to performing the marriage rites and perform a ritual of accepting but returning it. The ritual is yet to be tested in court in line with the views of the Court of Appeal in *Nickaf v. Nickaf*[478] that parties may not waive aspects of customs.

III. Formalities of Islamic Marriage

485. Formation of a Muslim marriage is a well-settled process. Marriage when conducted under Islamic law must comply with rules governing the validity and celebration of a Muslim marriage. There is a relationship between the religion and the law and the two contemplate one another. The marriage may be potentially or actually polygamous in practice but normatively is always a polygyny. For a valid Islamic marriage there is an offer and acceptance which needs to be within a contractual session and as a rule, before two male witnesses. Other elements of the marriage are consent, capacity, parental consent and solemnisation. Consent and solemnisation are before a Muslim cleric and in the presence of at least two witnesses. The man must pay the prospective wife, her *sadak* or *mahr* – this is the bride price and ordinarily whatever it is in terms of value becomes the property of the wife.

486. There is a condition to polygamy in Muslim marriage. This is said to be the capacity of the husband to meet the requirements and conditions stipulated under Islamic law, which requires a man to marry more than four wives only, in so far, as he can ensure equality of actions and marital justice among the wives. Some scholars dispute this, asserting that a man can marry more than four wives. This additional only makes his status irregular, which can be regularised when and if one of the extant wives departs. The basis of polygyny in Islam was explained: 'Polygyny provides a solution to some of life's problems. When there is a shortage of men, for example after a devastating war, many women will be unable to find husbands. Most women in that situation, given the option, would rather be a co-wife than no wife. If one maintains a strict monogamy in such a situation, moral depravity is bound to result.'[479]

487. The idea of equality among wives has also been explained:

> Notice that the Qur'an permits but does not command a man to have four wives. Furthermore, the Qur'an stipulates that a man is responsible for the maintenance of his wife or wives. If a man has more than one wife, he has to provide separate living accommodation for each of his wives. Multiple marriages are a heavy responsibility on the male. It is not a pleasure trip as some

478. Suit No. CA/1E/79/84. (Unreported) Court of Appeal, Kaduna.

479. Available at: 'Why does the Qur'an allow Muslim men to have four wives? https://www.islamcan.com/common-questions-about-islam/why-does-quran-allow-muslim-men-to-have-four-wives.shtml (last accessed 4 Sep. 2020).

people may assume. Some even imagine all kinds of sexual exploits involving a man and his wives altogether. However, such activity is not permissible in Islam. A man must divide his time equally among his wives. He may, for example, spend one night with each wife on a rotating schedule. If a man cannot maintain justice in the treatment of his wives, the Qur'an stipulates that he is to have no more than one wife.[480]

488. According to this view, polygyny in Islam must be viewed in context: 'In seventh-century Arabia, when a man could have as many wives as he chose, to prescribe only four was a limitation, not a license to new oppression.'[481]

489. A Muslim man may marry a Christian female but he cannot marry a pagan. While a marriage may be valid when a male marries a female adherent of any religion, a female may only marry a Muslim man.[482]

490. Islamic marriages have resemblance with customary marriages in that both are reflective of some form of contractual relations, although the content of divorce distinguishes the nature of contract contemplated. It may be legally contended that while the Islamic marriage is a simple contractual relation, the customary marriage contemplates at least a hybrid if not a full-fledged proprietary relationship. Its practice is mainly among people of North Central and North Western Nigeria. Islam is said to be split equally with Christianity in the South West of Nigeria, whose people also conduct Islamic type marriages. However, in the South West, it is unusual to see men married to more than one wife whatever, their religious adherence.

491. Halima[483] posits that Islamic marriage is a complete way of life, which dictates how an adherent lives from birth to death. From this prism, a Muslim it is said, acts against the dictates of his religion if he or she conducts any other form of marriage besides Nikãh.[484] The same view is espoused by Ambali[485] who posits that the laws of marriage and succession constitute part of a Muslim's faith, which is not subject to variance by human whims and caprices; and therefore, on this view, any Muslim who marries under the Marriage Act in Nigeria rejects the injunctions of Allah regarding marriage and succession.

---

480. Above, note 479.
481. Karen Armstrong, *Muhammad: A Western Attempt to Understand Islam* 191 (Victor Gollancz Ltd. 1991); taken from: *see* note 399.
482. Nwogugu, (Heinemann) 60.
483. Halima Doma-Kutigi, *Certification of Islamic Marriages in Nigeria: Realities, Challenges, and Solutions*, 7 Electronic J. Islamic & Middle Eastern L. 22–36 (2019).
484. It has been held by the United Kingdom Court of Appeal that *Nikãh* marriages are legally 'non-marriages', meaning spouses have no redress to the courts for a division of matrimonial assets such as the family home and spouse's pension if a marriage breaks down. Appeal Court Rules Islamic marriages invalid in UK – BBC News available at: www.bbc.com/news/uk-england-london-51508974 (last accessed 24 Dec. 2020 at 12.58 am); Islamic faith marriages not valid in English law, appeal court available at www.theguardian.com/world/feb/islamic-faith-marriages-not-val (last accessed 24 Dec. 2020 at 12.58 am).
485. M.A. Ambali, *The Practice of Muslim Family Law in Nigeria* (Tamaza Publishing 2003).

492. According to adherents of the religion, the rules of Islamic law are substantially written and not subject to modification. The rules from this prism are contained in the Holy Book of the religion and Hadiths. There is also Islamic jurisprudence written by Islamic scholars. Since the Holy Book of the religion and Hadiths are written, they are considered the two major sources of Islamic law and regarded as binding ordinances. They are rigid, dogmatic and immutable. Their content is held as not subject to social change and thus, any law or rule, which contradicts the two rational bases of Islamic legislation, is regarded as null and void. From this sense, forcing oneself into monogamy when there are circumstances that require a man to take additional wives amounts to making something unlawful *(haram)* for himself which has been made lawful *(halal)* for him. Furthermore, from the perspectives of succession, the position is also relevant to whether Muslims should conduct any marriage other than one governed by the religion. A Muslim never dies intestate as the manner of distributing a Muslim deceased's property is evaluated to be clearly articulated by Islamic law; therefore, a Muslim who marries under the Marriage Act has subjugated the rules of succession in Islamic law to the rules of succession under common law, which is applied through the administration of estates laws of various states in Nigeria.

493. To facilitate the full recognition of Islamic marriage, the Nigerian Shari-ah Court of Appeal is empowered by the Nigerian Constitution to adjudicate any question of Islamic personal law regarding marriage or in relation to family relationships; any question of Islamic personal law regarding succession where the deceased person is a Muslim; and in the case where all parties to the proceeding are Muslims and request the court that hears the case in the first instance to determine that case in accordance with Islamic personal law.

IV. Registration of Muslim Marriages

494. Registration of the marriage is already discussed under Registration of Status. Religion is considered a way of life from birth to death and is therefore not in conflict with the provisions and intendment of the Births, Deaths (Compulsory Registration) Act. Imam-Tamim points out that there are no provisions in the Quran or Hadith/Sunnah relating to choice or mandating or prohibition of registration of marriage.[486] Thus, the argument to register a marriage finds its impetus in challenges of unregistered marriages and, as such the obligation to register marriage is important as it is for the benefit of (*maslahah*) and protection of the society at large. The emerging trend now indicates that Muslim couples are becoming more aware of the need to have marriages registered for the purpose of meeting those obligations for which a marriage certificate is issued.

---

486. Muhammed Kamaldeen, *A Doctrinal Review of Literature on Multi-tiered Marriage in Nigerian Family Law*, Being paper presented at the Postgraduate Colloquium on Innovation in Postgraduate Research (Organised by Goal Centre, Islamic Science University Malaysia, USIM) on 10 Jun. 2015.

V. Consent

495. Both the groom and the bride must consent to the marriage. Consent needs to be oral and written. A formal proposal of marriage (*ijab*) and acceptance of the proposal (*qabul*) are expressions of the requirement of consent. A first-time bride is usually represented in the contract negotiations by her *Wali* – a male guardian or father who looks out for her best interests. Even so, the bride must also express her willingness to enter into marriage. Consent cannot be obtained from those who are legally unable to give it – such as people who are incapacitated, minor children, or those who have physical or mental impairments that limit their capacity to understand and consent to a legal contract.

496. According to available literature within the Maliki law, a woman cannot give consent and therefore, this must be given by her father, guardian or nearest male relation. [487]

VI. *Mahr* or *Dower*

497. Another essential requirement of Islamic Marriages is the compulsory payment of the bride price called *mahr*. The word *mahr* is often translated as ‘dowry’ but is described as ‘bridal gift.’ There is, however, a difference. Dowry relates to the bridal wealth or money from the bride’s family or bride to her husband. A bride price is money or property paid by the groom or his family to the parents of a woman (but not to the woman herself) upon the marriage.

498. The *mahr* is, however, for the bride. The bride has a right to receive a gift from the groom, which remains her own property as security in the marriage. The gift is payable directly to the bride and remains her sole property, even if the marriage fails and ends in divorce. The *mahr* can consist of cash, jewellery, property, or any other asset. The payment or an agreed-upon payment schedule is required at the time of contract. The *mahr* may also be deferred until termination of the marriage through death or divorce. In such an instance, the unpaid *mahr* becomes a debt on the husband’s estate.

499. Since the *mahr* becomes a charge upon the husband’s estate, it may mean that what it is, must have been stipulated in the lifetime of the parties. It also means that the gift contemplated is not a gift as generally understood.

500. Some Muslim cultures require payment of dowry from the bride. The recent suicide of a Muslim married woman, Ayesha Arif Khan, concerning payment of dowry has raised questions on the continuing relevance of this practice just as the bride price.

---

487. *See* for instance, E.I. Nwogugu, *Family Law in Nigeria* 215 (HEBN Publishers Plc. 1990).

VII. Solemnisation: *Walimah*

501. Another significant requirement of Islamic law of marriage is solemnisation of the marriage. This practice comes after the payment of the bride price.[488] It validates the marriage and brings the families of the contracting parties into a joint agreement. Two adult witnesses or more from each side of the families are required to verify the marriage contract. These adults serve as life witnesses not only during the subsistence of the marriage, but also if it comes to an end.

502. On the day of the Nikãh, which is the main day of celebration, the intending couples and their families meet at the slated venue (usually the bride's house, mosque, or hall). Soon after this, the Nikãh is commenced. There are usually two guardians present at the celebration venue, representing the two parties. The *mahr* is first made and thereafter, the officiating *Imam* asks the bride's guardian *(waliy)* three times in the presence of everyone, whether the bride accepts the groom as her husband with the decided *mahr*. Should the bride accede, the same question is asked of the groom's guardian the same number of times, should he accede, the *fatiha* (the Nikãh prayer) is recited. This is followed by the recital of the *khutba*, a religious discourse. Thereupon, blessings are showered upon the bride and the groom for a prosperous married life. The marriage is then announced.[489]

VIII. Formalities for Monogamous Marriage under the Marriage Act

503. In Nigeria, monogamy is extremely important to the Christians of the South and Middle Belt. It may underlie status symbol – between the educated and uneducated or the elite and non-elite, the Christian and non-Christian who is married. Section 15 of the Constitution one of the directive Principles of State policy underlies the dual structure of marriage registration, and other objectives and scope of the B, D, Etc., Act. It also underlies the retention of a national marriage framework under the exclusive legislative competence of the Federal Legislature. Section 15(3) of the Constitution provides that for the purpose of promoting national integration, it shall be the duty of the State to:

(a) provide adequate facilities for and encourage free mobility of people, goods and services throughout the Federation;
(b) secure full residence rights for every citizen in all parts of the Federation;
(c) encourage inter-marriage among persons from different places of origin, or of different religious, ethnic or linguistic association or ties; and
(d) promote or encourage the formation of associations that cut across ethnic, linguistic, religious and or other sectional barriers.

488. It should, however, not be understood that without the full payment of the dowry or its postponement, the celebration of the marriage cannot take place.
489. Halima Doma-Kutigi, *Certification of Islamic Marriages in Nigeria: Realities, Challenges, and Solutions*, 7 Electronic J. Islamic & Middle Eastern L. 22–36 (2019).

504. Thus, the law on legal monogamous marriages is drawn from the Constitution and a few other legislations. These are: Interpretation Act,[490] Marriage Act,[491] Matrimonial Course Act[492] (MCA), with the Matrimonial Causes rule a, subsidiary legislation to the MCA. There are also some other related laws such as the Marriage Validation Act, Foreign Judgment Reciprocal Act, the Administration of Estates Act, etc. For instance, section 18 of the Interpretation Act provides: In an enactment the following expressions have the meanings hereby assigned to them respectively, that is to say, 'monogamous marriage' means 'a marriage which is recognised by the law of the place where it is contracted as a voluntary union of one man and one woman to the exclusion of all others during the continuance of the marriage'. These legislations and their source in the Constitution in a diverse and complex country as Nigeria may also be an inherent emblem of integration through marriage and an ultimate objective in unification.

505. The hierarchy of courts in Nigeria have thus consistently held that customary law rules on marriage or the norms are inapplicable to statutory marriages.[493]Marriage under the Marriage Act, as is typical of such legislation, at least, within the Commonwealth provides a monogamous framework for those who choose to be bound by its terms. The MA attempts a distinction of the legal relationship which is created under it with customary marriages. It is a statement and definition of monogamy not according to religion but law. This is significant because the Act is sometimes said to have religious undertone; canonical and introduced by British colonialism. Monogamy according to religion, though, is strikingly different from the variant at law or under the Act as the brief synopsis of its content below will demonstrate. This is so at least, in one respect – the parties in a religious monogamy are not equal partners and therefore age is not so relevant and consent of the parties may not be real.[494] Monogamy according to law is typically an equality relations and to ensure that this is so, there are rules on age of maturity and a clear objective of consent that is real.

506. Nevertheless, within Christian, Customary and Islamic marriages in Nigeria, a good number are monogamous in practice. This category as *James Egubson v. Ikechukwu* [495] depicts.

IX. The Marriage Act

507. The Marriage Act regulates celebration of marriages.[496] The age of marriage under the Act is 21 years by section 11(1)(b).

490. Cap 123, Laws of the Federation, 2004.
491. Cap M6.
492. Cap M7.
493. *Olabiwonnu v. Olabiwonnu* [2014] LPELR 36330 (CA).
494. *Cheni v. Cheni* [1963] 2 WLR 2; *Ali v. Ali* [1962] 2 WLR 620.
495. [1977] ALL NLR 194; [1976] 6 SC 1; [1977] LPELR-SC. 183/1975.
496. Referred to and cited as Cap M6 Laws of the Federation 2004. It is sequel to Marriage Act: Cap 18 of 1914; 18 of 1916. 23 of 192; 58 of 1933; of 1958; L.N. 131 of 1954 and 1 of 1955.

508. The Act consists of nine parts and two schedules. The First Schedule contains specimen forms relevant to the celebration of marriage under the Act. It also contains a list of registrars and deputy registrars. Section 3 of the Act provides for the country to be divided into marriage districts on the order of the President.[497] The districts are contained in the First Schedule. The Second Schedule contains list of different fees payable towards the marriage process.

509. There is also a list of subsidiary legislation consisting of:

(1) Places of celebration of Marriages (Delegation of Licensing Powers) Order.
(2) Marriage (Designation of Districts) Order.
(3) Marriage (Location of Marriage Officer) Directors.
(4) Marriage Act (Delegation of Powers) Notice.
(5) Marriage (Appointment of Principal Registrar, Registrars, Etc.) Notice L.N. 72 Of 1971.[498]

510. Part 1 of the Act consists of six sections, the title, interpretations, divisions – of Marriage districts, appointment of registrars, offices of registrars, the process for licensing a public place of worship as a place for celebration of marriages under the Act. Section 6 provides for licensing:

(1) The Minister may license any place of public worship to be a place for the celebration of marriages and may at any time cancel such licence; in either case he[499] shall give notice thereof in the Federal Gazette.
(2) Every place of public worship licensed as a place for the celebration of marriages under any enactment repealed by this Act shall be deemed to be licensed under this Act unless and until the Minister shall cancel the licence in respect thereof.

511. In line with this section, there is the subsidiary legislation of Places of celebration of Marriages (Delegation of Licensing Powers) Order. The order provides:

512. The function heretofore vested in the National Council of Ministers and now devolving on the Minister by operation of law in respect, *inter alia*, of the licensing of places of public worship for the celebration of marriages under section 6 of the Marriage Act shall be and is hereby delegated to the Permanent Secretary of the Federal Ministry of Internal Affairs with effect as hereinafter appears, so however that the Permanent Secretary aforesaid shall have regard and give effect to any

---

It repeals Marriage Ordinance Cap; 95 of 1908 edition of the Laws of Southern Nigeria; the Marriage Proclamation, Cap 47 of the 910 edition of the Laws of Northern Nigeria, The Foreign Marriage Ordinance, 1913, No. 6 of Southern Nigeria.

497. Where the President is required to take an action, it would usually be a delegation to the Minister of Interior.

498. This Legislation has been revoked by the B, D, etc., (Compulsory Registration) Act as discussed in the Part 1 Ch. 2.

499. The masculine gender is mostly the preferred use in all legislation in Nigeria, but in practice gender mainstreaming is gaining grounds.

directions, given generally or especially by the Minister; and notwithstanding the delegation aforesaid the Minister may, if he thinks fit, himself exercise the function.[500]

513. Part 2 is on the preliminary processes of celebration of a marriage. It consists of eleven sections; parties to a marriage must file notice of marriage in the marriage district where the marriage is to take place.[501] This is to be in line with **Form A** as specified in the First Schedule to the Act. Provisions for persons unable to write in English or an uneducated person who is unable to append a signature are contained in section 8. This provides: 'If the person giving such notice is unable to write or is insufficiently acquainted with the English language, or both, then it shall be sufficient if he places his mark or cross thereto in the presence of some literate person who shall attest the same as in **Form B** in the First Schedule.' Other provisions in this part are: the duty of the registrar to provide requisite forms; record of the notice; provisions for issue of Certificate of Notice. An important provision is time frame for issuing the Certificate of Notice which should be a minimum of twenty-one days from the date of filing the notice or a maximum of three months from that day.[502] There are conditions attached to the issuing of the Certificate of Notice which are contained in subsections 11(1) (a)–(d), and these include ascertainment of age of at least 21 years; residency in the district for at least fifteen days prior to filing; compliance with affinity and consanguinity and none of the parties married under customary law to a different person. The time frame for conducting the marriage after the Certificate of Notice has been issued. Thus, by section 12, 'if the marriage shall not take place within three months after the date of the notice, the notice and all proceedings consequent thereupon shall be void; and fresh notice shall be given before the parties can lawfully marry'. Other important aspects of Part 2 of the Act are; caveat; procedure for treating the caveat; removal of caveat; Discretion of a judge as to costs with respect to caveat.

514. Part 3 is on Consent. This consists of three sections; consent requirements for persons under 21 years of age; provision for the uneducated or those uneducated in English language; provision for persons eligible to give consent where there is no one in the position of a parent.

515. Part 4 covers the celebration. It consists of nine sections, the conduct of marriage celebration has to be open in licensed places of worship specifically between 8 o'clock and 6 o'clock. Such celebration should have at least two other witnesses aside from the officiating Minister. The officiating minister acts so in a fiduciary position and good faith is a matter of utmost importance. Any question as to the validity the marriage is to be subject to the good faith of the officiating Minister in addition to the verifiability of the certificate of the Registrar issued in line with part two. The part also provides a description of the appropriate location for

500. Places for Celebration of Marriages (Delegation of Licensing Powers) Order L.N. 105 Of 1967. The Ministry Interior Has Now Replaced the Ministry Internal Affairs.
501. Section 7.
502. Section 11(1).

celebration of marriage. The record of marriages is to be kept with registrars and – officiating Ministers. Following the celebration of marriage by a Minister of a recognised place of worship, the duty of such a Minister to duly sign the certificate which must record appropriate biological and other data of the spouses. The part also contains provisions on the form a conduct a marriage should take when conducted by a registrar of marriages at his office. It also covers the specific time frame which is between 10 o'clock and for o'clock and the celebration must be in the open. Other provisions are: the duty of registrar to issue and sign the Certificate of marriage with the parties. This part also covers circumstances when a Minister issues a certificate circumventing the consent provisions by section 13 and the procedure to be followed.

516. Part 5 of the Act is procedural. It contains provisions for the form of record for marriages to meet the criteria of a public record; rectification of register, evidencing of marriage and admissibility of record.

517. Part 6 is on when a marriage will be invalid as well as provisions for the effect of prior marriage under customary law to any other person other than the parties who have been issued Certificate of Notice, marriages conducted in unapproved locations; using of false names, conducting of marriage without requisite approval; validation of all marriages under the Act for all imposes; prohibition of subsequent marriage under customary and exclusion of customary law from the scope of the Act.

518. Part 7 is on fees to be paid for the processes covered by the Act. It includes waiver of fees on grounds of indigence, customary payment to an officiating Minister, etc.

519. Part 8 prescribes offences and penalties. It creates offences for bigamy which in this case extends to customary marriages to persons other than to whom certificate of notice have been issued, false declarations, false caveats, pretence with regards to provision of consent. Unlawful performance or witnessing of marriage, failure of duty, or failure to perform role with regard to proper recording of marriage; issuing and transmission of certificate or register, marrying of minors – in this case persons below 21 years without requisite consent.

520. Part 9 is on foreign marriages.[503] This part of the Act covers circumstances when marriage is between citizens and non-citizens and the process by which such marriages shall be valid. It extends to valid locations. Section 49 of the Act provides that a marriage between parties, one of whom is a citizen of Nigeria, if it is contracted in a country outside Nigeria before a marriage officer, is as valid in law as if it had been contracted in Nigeria before a registrar in the registrar's office, provided it is conducted in the office of such an officer in the open and at the appropriate times.[504] Every Nigerian diplomatic or consular officer of the rank of

503. The sections covered are 49–53.
504. *See* s. 52.

Secretary is a marriage officer in the country to which such an officer is accredited.[505] While the status of the marriage officer must be at least a secretary, it is subject to such necessary modifications to accommodate prevailing local circumstances.[506] The office used by a marriage officer for the performance of diplomatic or consular duties is regarded as the marriage officers office for the purposes of the Act.[507]

X. Notice under the Act

521. Writing is a very crucial element of a valid contemporary contract. When a contract is written, in a specified form and registered even where in some cases, consideration is absent, it is considered a perfect and valid contract. The key element of validity is registration which provides any third party with at least constructive notice. Thus, with marriages under the Act, rules on notice and registration appear in two stages. Section 9 provides that parties wishing to marry under the Act, must comply with notice procedures and the registrar of marriages must provide such persons with the relevant forms gratuitously. Section 10 creates a register of notice called the Marriage Notice Book open for inspection to the public and makes further provisions as to publication. Thus, the registrar is required to publish such notice by causing a copy of the same to be affixed on the outer door of his office and to be kept exposed there until he grants his certificate upon twenty-one days or before the expiration of three months, on payment of prescribed fees. Section 12 provides that where marriage does not take place within three months after the issue of the Certificate of Notice, a new process of notice must be initiated and certificate issued before the parties may marry. Section 13 provides for dispensing of notice in some circumstances and by implication that the marriage may take place in a place other than a place of worship or in the office of registrar of marriages. Thus, the Licence by the Minister contemplates the specification of the place where marriage is to be celebrated. Section 13 provides:

> The Minister upon proof being made to him by affidavit that there is no lawful impediment to the proposed marriage, and that the necessary consent, if any. to such marriage has been obtained, may, if he shall think fit, dispense with the giving of notice, and with the issue of the certificate of the registrar, and may grant his licence. which shall be according to **Form D in the First Schedule**, authorising the celebration of a marriage between the parties named in such licence by a registrar, or by a recognised minister of some religious denomination or body.

505. Section 50.
506. *See* ss 52 & 53.
507. Section 51.

522. While, on the other hand, by section 23, the Minister may specify a place: 'a minister shall not celebrate any marriage except in a building which has been duly licensed by the Minister, or in such place as the licence issued under section 13 of this Act, may direct'.

523. It is to be noted that it is the Minister and not the Governor who has the power to circumvent the usual procedure of giving of notice to the registrar as well as obtaining his certificate where such Minister confirms by affidavit that there is no lawful impediment to the proposed marriage. It is only when the Minister is assured of the good faith of the situation that he may grant his licence in accordance with Form D of the Act authorising the celebration of a marriage by a Registrar or a minister of licensed place of worship or celebrate the marriage in that official capacity.[508]

524. The second stage where notice plays a legal role is after the parties have married. The provisions for registration of certificates of marriage, their handling by registrars and officiating ministers are contained in sections 24, 25, 26 27 and 28. For marriages coming under section 13, with respect to which the Minister of Interior may grant a licence, section 29 provides that parties and registrars must comply strictly, with all the provisions of registration and notice excepting the preliminaries specified in section 13. The Register of Marriages conducted in licensed places of worship must be transmitted by the registrar to the Principal Registrar[509] of marriages. It is the duty of the registrar of marriages for each district to allow searches to be made of all registers of marriages. This search would be at all reasonable times which in Nigeria should be from the hours of 8 am to 4 pm or sixteen Hours. The registrar may also issue certified true copy of such marriage certificate. Thus, the certificate and the register are public documents.

525. Obiekwe v. Obiekwe[510] decided under the earlier Act makes compliance with the provisions of the Act mandatory. The Supreme Court as well as the Court of Appeal have restated that the provisions of the Marriage Act, Matrimonial Causes Act and the rules thereto must be fully complied with.[511]

XI. Consent

526. Consent is a requirement of a valid marriage under the Act. Where the requisite consent between the parties is absent or unreal the marriage will not be conducted by the registrar. Should the marriage take place, it is void. Section 3(d) of

508. Section 23 of the Act. The reference to Governor by Boparai is therefore erroneous as the Act as has been explained is a Federal Act. *See* Harinder Boparai, *The Customary and Statutory Law of Marriage in Nigeria*, 46 (H. 3) The Rabel J. Comp. & Int'l Priv. L. 530–557 (1982).

509. Now Chief Registrar of the National Population Commission of the Capital of the State where the Marriage took place.

510. [1963] 7 Eastern Nigeria Law Report 196.

511. *Odogwu v. Odogwu* [1992] 2 NWLR (part 215) 59; *Menakaya v. Menakaya* [2001] 16 NWLR (part 738) 203; *Eluwa v. Eluwa* [2013] LPELR – CA.

the Matrimonial Causes Act provides for consent for marriage to be real and not vitiated. Thus, consent may not be real where it was obtained by duress or fraud or a party is mistaken as to the identity or the nature of the ceremony performed, or a party is mentally incapable of understanding the nature of the marriage contract. When any of the parties to a marriage is under the age of 21 years, such a party is treated as a minor and consent for the marriage is required from some specific persons other than the parties. For such a consent to be valid, it must be written and attached to an affidavit stating the basis for the consent. This must then be produced to the registrar before a certificate for the marriage is issued. The consent must be from the father of the party who is under the age of 21 years. Where the father is dead, or has an illness of the mind, or not available such as where he is not in the country, then that of a mother is acceptable. Where any of the persons are unable to write and sign the documents related to the consent or is unable to communicate in English language, then a prepared document to which he is to place his mark and cross must be done in the presence of persons stated.[512] Where there are no parents or guardian, then the Governor, a judge of the High Court of the State or the FCT or any officer of or above the cadre of assistant secretary will have to provide consent.[513] It is also to be noted that even where the Minister is to bypass the giving of notice, the Minister must ensure that requisite consent has been duly obtained either between the parties or as stipulated by the Act.

527. Widows or widowers are exempt from the consent provisions.

XII. Other Relevant Provisions

528. The registrar must also be satisfied that one of the parties to the impending marriage has been resident within the district in which the marriage is intended to be celebrated at least fifteen days preceding the granting of the certificate.[514] This provision which goes to identification may now be meaningless in contemporary times in the country. In 1970, hotels and non-resident accommodations were few and far between but today these are located in every nook and cranny of the country. It is thus easy to stay in one of these accommodations for the stated number of days without any form of residency. The provision of fifteen years in the B, D, Etc. (Compulsory Registration) Act is more apt for the intended objective of proof of residence and or citizenship.

512. Section 19(1)(a)–(g).
513. Sections 18–20 of the MA contain the consent provisions. Sections 48 of the MA makes it an offence punishable by 2 years' imprisonment to marry anyone under the age of 21 without require consent.
514. Section 11(1)(a) of the Act.

XIII. Proof of Marriage

529. Proof of marriage is not a difficult task in Nigeria. There are many reasons for this position, which includes, but not limited to the framework of customary and Islamic law marriages which are not documented forms of marriage. Proof is thus necessary but not dependent on documentation. In this respect, the Evidence Act provides for cohabitation as raising a presumption of marriage.[515] The reason is that Nigeria is a conservative society, it is very unlikely that two persons, male and female outside affinity and consanguinity, who are cohabiting are not married. Not surprisingly, the burden is on the person who among the cohabitants is contending marriage to prove the non-existence of the marriage.

530. The distillable reasons for proof being loose are traceable to a few factors. A large number of the population is not exposed to the necessity of certification and registration of marriages. Another factor is that a sizable number of the populace is not literate. Furthermore, the laws on the subject are usually privileged in the sense that only the few who are connected with them, such as those in the legal profession and governmental agencies have knowledge of the practice of the laws and regulatory framework. In addition, registration became compulsory only from 1990, the year of the first enactment of a law on registration of births, deaths, and marriages. Finally, as a patriarchal society, it is in the enlightened self-interest of the patriarchs that the legal framework remains in a state of fluidity.

531. With monogamous marriages, the standard of proof is provided in section 82 of the matrimonial causes Act is loose and in favour of the respondent. It states:

(1) For the purposes of this Act, a matter of fact shall be taken to be proved if it is established to the reasonable satisfaction of the court.
(2) Where a provision of this Act requires the court to be satisfied of the existence of any ground or fact or as to any other matter, it shall be sufficient if the court is reasonably satisfied of the existence of that ground or fact, or as to that other matter.

532. Sections 33 and 34 of the Marriage Act make it clear that registration does not go to validity but perfection. Thus, the section states: 'All marriages celebrated under this Act shall be good and valid in law to all intents and purposes.' Section 33 of the Act provides for invalid marriages and a marriage will be invalid in the following circumstances:

(i) where either of the parties to a marriage, at the time of the celebration is married under customary law to any other person;
(ii) both parties knowingly and wilfully acquiesce in its celebration – in any place other than the office of a registrar of marriages or a licensed place of worship except under license issued by the Minister under section 13;
(iii) or under a false name or names;

515. Section 166, Evidence Act, 2011.

(iv) or without a registrar's Certificate of Notice or license issued under section 13;

(v) or celebrated by a person not being a recognised minister of some religious denomination or body or a registrar of marriages.

533. The section closes with: 'But no marriage shall, after celebration, be deemed invalid by reason that any provision of this Act other than the foregoing has not been complied with.'[516]

534. In *Obiekwe v. Obiekwe*[517] where the parties did not knowingly and wilfully acquiesce in the marriage in a Church without requisite licence, their marriage was not declared null and void.

535. However, *Christopher Anyaegbunam v. Catherine Anyaegbunam*[518] indicates that the absence of a marriage certificate may be prejudicial to a claim of marriage under the Act, although it may not be the only way of proving the existence of a marriage. The production of the Certificate of Marriage in required Form E pursuant to the provisions of sections 24 and 25 of the Marriage Act is crucial to a claim of marriage under the Act and the rights derivable from the marriage. Exceptions may arise where there is evidence to the satisfaction of the Court that although this is not in existence, a marriage did take place presumably under special licence as in section 13 of the Act. This presumption is subject to proof. Such proof must lead to the conclusion that a marriage did take place at a public forum or at least met the requirements of the Act as to notice, publicity, witnessing, attestation and registration.[519]

536. In an action to prove monogamous marriage under the Act, the court is not, however, bound by a marriage certificate. The court may receive as evidence of the facts stated in it, a document purporting to be either the original or a certified copy of any certificate, entry or record of a birth, death or marriage alleged to have taken place, whether in Nigeria or elsewhere.[520]

537. A marriage certificate in Nigeria goes to reinforcement of evidence and is not the proof of marriage. If there are other indices such as registration of which a litigant obtains the certified true copy, then the proof is consistent with the requirements of the law. A petitioner contesting a monogamous marriage in Nigeria should petition for jactitation of the marriage. Otherwise, he or she will be subjected to the strictest proof.

---

516. Section 33(3).

517. [1963] East Central State of Nigeria Law Report 196.

518. [1973] LPELR-SC. 18/1973; [1973] ANLR 320; [1973] 4 S.C. 84.

519. Relevant references made by the Supreme Court include *Piers v. Piers* [1849] 2 H.L. Cas. 331; *Obiekwe v. Obiekwe* [1963] 7 E.N.L.R. 196; *Akuwudike v. Akuwudike* [1963] 7 E.N.L.R. 5; *Ponticelli v. Ponticelli* [1958] 1 All E.R. 357,360; *Hill v. Hill* [1959] 1 All E.R. 281 P.C.

520. Section 86 of the MCA.

538. The Supreme Court examined the point of validity of a marriage under the Act in *Anyaegbunam v. Anyaegbunam.*[521] The petitioner (respondent at the Supreme Court) in a suit brought before the Enugu High Court,[522] had prayed that she should be judicially separated from the respondent-appellant. She also prayed the court to grant her custody of their two children, *alimony* pendente lite, and secure sums by way of maintenance for herself and the said children. Following the service of the amended petition on him, the respondent-'husband' entered appearance 'on protest.' In compliance with the provisions of rule 14(2) of the Matrimonial Causes Rules, 1957, the respondent moved the court on 11 January 1972 for Orders summarised as 'the marriage between him and the petitioner was a customary marriage followed by church marriage or church blessing; that the court having no jurisdiction to adjudicate on customary or church marriage cannot therefore properly entertain the petitioner's action for judicial separation'.

539. The trial court deciding that jurisdiction in a preliminary matter ordered a trial on it. At the hearing, the respondent was made to prove his claims that there was no statutory marriage between him and the petitioner.[523] On Counsel's re-examination of the petitioner, a certificate of marriage conducted by a Catholic Church and signed by a priest was produced, but the respondent denied knowledge of its existence. The trial court held that on the evidence of the documents tendered by the petitioner on examination and re-examination of the petitioner, and the oral evidence adduced, that although there was no registrar's certificate produced by either of the parties, that the marriage in the Catholic church did take place and that at all times, the parties had intended and did consider their marriage a monogamous one. The judge concluded after examining some cases:

> The petitioner believed that she underwent a monogamous marriage and in fact, so did the respondent. His conduct in writing to the wife that she must accept the status quo and that his children were not illegitimate belies his claims. It will be expected that if the respondent had entered into an understanding with the petitioner that their marriage was a polygamous one he should remind her of that understanding in one of his letters to the petitioner. The respondent failed to do so. On the evidence, I am of the opinion that respondent's evidence is nothing more than a cock and bull story. I disbelieve it.[524]

540. The court then ruled that it had jurisdiction to hear the case. It is from these set of circumstances that the appeal at the Supreme Court is based.

541. The Supreme Court found that in the absence of any rebutting evidence, it was difficult to see how the learned trial judge could have found as he did that 'the

---

521. [1973] LPELR-SC. 18/1973; [1973] ANLR 320; [1973] 4 S.C. 84.
522. In the then South East region of Nigeria.
523. It is to be noted that the Supreme court stated that this was a wrong order and that the petitioner who made the claim of being married to the respondent ought to have been made a plaintiff at the hearing.
524. [1973] LPELR-SC. 18/1973; [1973] ANLR 320; [1973] 4 S.C. 84.

petitioner believed that she underwent a monogamous marriage' or 'that the petitioner did not know at any time of the marriage that a Registrar's Certificate was necessary'. The Supreme Court noted that the only evidence before the trial court was that of the respondent-appellant and that even if he disbelieved the evidence as he was entitled to do and as he had done, there is still no relevant evidence on which he can base his belief that the ceremony the parties conducted was a monogamous marriage. The Supreme Court stated further:

> Therefore, by virtue of the above provisions of the Decree, the matrimonial causes in respect of which jurisdiction is conferred by section 2 thereof on the High Court of a State apply only to those arising out of a monogamous marriage. Since the petitioner/respondent has failed to testify and prove by evidence that she underwent a ceremony of marriage with the respondent/appellant at the Roman Catholic Church at Abatete[525] on 16th January, 1961, and that the said marriage is monogamous the learned trial judge, on that ground alone, should not have entertained the petition.[526]

542. In the event, the ruling of the trial court was set aside and the petition for judicial separation struck out.

543. This conclusion of the Supreme Court is relevant because the same view was expressed concerning a church ceremony for a marriage in *James Egubson v. Ikechukwu.*[527]

544. In sum, a church ceremony in Nigeria is not evidence of a monogamous marriage. That a church ceremony is a monogamous marriage is subjected to the strictest proof of which the best known is a certificate of marriage in Form E of the Act to be found in the First Schedule to the Marriage Act and registration both at the Marriage Registry with the registrar of Marriages in the Marriage Register Book and the Chief Registrar of the National Population Commission in each State of the Federation and the FCT.

545. With respect to customary or Islamic law marriages, within Nigeria, it is sufficient to prove celebration of the marriage and cohabitation.[528] The cases outside of Nigeria demonstrate correctly that proof consistent with jurisdictional requirements must be met. In this respect, persons need to register the marriages as already discussed above. In Nigeria, there are such rules with other jurisdictions. Thus, section 3(1)(c) of the Matrimonial Causes Act makes a marriage void, where it is not a valid marriage under the law of the place where the marriage takes place, by reason of a failure to comply with the requirements of the law of that place with respect to the form of solemnisation of marriages. Section 6(2) of the same Act is

525. A town in Anambra State, formerly part of the South East region of Nigeria.
526. [1973] LPELR-SC. 18/1973; [1973] ANLR 320; [1973] 4 S.C. 84.
527. [1977] ALL NLR 194; [1976] 6 SC 1; [1977] LPELR-SC. 183/1975.
528. Section 166 of the Evidence Act, 2011. The requirements of the validity of these forms of marriage are dealt with below.

also relevant and provides for the validity, of certain marriages conducted before the Act and marriages conducted outside Nigeria: 'A provision of this Act shall not affect the validity or invalidity of a marriage where it would not be in accordance with the rules of private international law to apply that provision in relation to that marriage.'

§5. EFFECTS OF MARRIAGE

546. The legal effects of marriage are expressed in changed rights and obligations between the spouses and with issues of the marriage. Spouses are entitled to conjugal rights and the laws in Nigeria continue to empower husbands despotically over wives and children. In Nigeria these are not strongly expressed as in many Western and other jurisdictions. Under customary and Islamic laws this is even more so. Under customary and Islamic law, fathers have sole rights and custody of children. The core rights and obligations are only reflected in property adjustments which find vent in dissolution and other matrimonial causes and succession. The state of legal effects of marriage in Nigeria is typified by the law on bigamy and its disuse as well as domestic violence.

I. Bigamy

547. The effect of plurality of legal frameworks for marriage has created a loophole which is continually exploited mainly by husbands. Although the legal framework in Nigeria has provided for bigamy since colonial dispensation, the only known Nigerian case on the subject involved an English couple.[529] Aguda notes the background to the problem:

> As Europeans commenced to settle here, relatively permanently, and in some appreciable numbers, it became necessary to introduce a system of marriage which would be more in line with their own personal law. And what was of equal importance, the new converts into Christian faith were forced to believe that unless they abandoned their customary system of marriage their souls would not be saved. In most cases those who had more than one wife were not allowed to take sacrament. Hence the first Marriage Ordinance was passed in 1863. This was replaced by the Marriage Ordinance 1884 … . It became necessary in 1914 to pass a Validation Ordinance which validated retrospectively certain marriages and extended the provisions of the Marriage Ordinance to some other parts of Nigeria. We need not go into details of these here. It is perhaps only pertinent to note that even today some Roman Catholic Churches still continue to perform marriage ceremonies without complying with the Marriage Act, the legal validity of which is very doubtful, except as taking effect as marriages under customary law.[530]

---

529. *R. v. Princewill* [1963] N.N.L.R. 54.

530. T.A. Aguda, *Select Law Lectures and Papers* 66–67 (Associated Publishers (Nigeria) Ltd. 1971).

548. Some provisions of the Marriage Act such as 11(1)(d), 33, 35, 39 and 47 aim at resolving the loophole – the fact that a marriage under the Marriage Act does not in practice, forestall subsequent marriages under customs, unless a man is persuaded not to embark on such a course of action.

549. Monogamy can hardly operate without its twain concept, bigamy. However, in Nigeria, bigamy is 'dead'.[531] Bigamy is in such state of disuse that the Nigerian Law Reform Commission notes: 'the Commission considers it a bad policy to leave on the statute book a serious crime which has existed for over sixty years, which is committed in large numbers each year by people in high places and low, and in respect of which there has never been a conviction. Such a law makes a mockery of the legal system and tends to create the impression that laws can be broken with impunity'.[532] The Marriage Act[533] and the Criminal Code Act provide for the offence of Bigamy. Section 370 of the Criminal Code Act provides 'Any person who, having a husband or wife living, marries in any case in which such marriage is void by reason of it taking place during the life of such husband or wife, is guilty of a felony, and is liable to imprisonment for seven years.'

550. In 2011, the Lagos State, by its Criminal Code Law finally removed bigamy from its own laws for falling into disuse.[534] The implication of this legislative action though remains to be seen and is not clear at all. It is not clear whether it means a legitimisation of a marriage under the Act and subsequent several marriages under customs since this remains an offence under Federal Laws which are constitutional. The only logical meaning to be attributed to this legislative action of Lagos Stated is perhaps, a simple weeding out of irrelevant information from its Laws.

551. Nwogugu asks:

> Should the offence of bigamy be retained in our law? A positive answer should be given because it reflects our constitutional and legal framework. Once a man is given the freedom to move from the monogamous to the polygamous union at will and irrespective of the feelings of his partner, we would have undermined our legal system. What is required is the cultivation of strict obedience to and enforcement of the law. There is a role for education and enlightenment of women as to their legal rights.[535]

552. Aguda[536] supports this view:

---

531. *Kuforiji & Anor. v. V.Y.B. (Nigeria Ltd.)* [1981] 6–7 SC 25.
532. Number 1 of December, 1980 at 15 (also repeated in Vol. 2 of 1980).
533. Section 39: 'Whoever, being unmarried, goes through the ceremony of marriage under this Act with a person whom he or she knows to be married to another person, shall be liable to imprisonment for five years.'
534. Cap 17, 2011.
535. Emmanuel Nwogugu, *What Next in Nigerian Family Law?*, [2006] 7 NIALS Founders' Day Lecture 20, 22 (Nigerian Institute of Advanced Legal Studies 2006).
536. Emmanuel Nwogugu and Akinola Aguda are men with distinguished career in the legal profession and academics in Nigeria. Indeed, all the comments on the subject are by men.

> The vast majority of Nigerian men may be, the percentage is over 95, practice polygamy in one form or the other. A number of these ostensibly practise monogamy but have one or two other 'wives'. Some of them who are cautious do not perform 'marriage ceremonies' with the other 'wives'. But some in fact do perform these ceremonies to which they in fact invite people who have to do with administration of justice including Police Officers, Doctors, Lawyers, Ministers of State and Religion, top civil servants, etc., who do attend such ceremonies with full knowledge of the correct situation. The fact is that, as I have said earlier, some of these people themselves have perhaps indulged in a similar breach of the law.[537]

553. In *Kuforiji & Anor. v. V.Y.B.*[538] the Supreme Court stated that bigamy was a dead letter law, even though 'in our Statute book'.[539] The same position was taken by Honourable Justice Ibidapo-Obe: '... even though nine persons out of ten in Nigeria are bigamists. This is bound to be so because, despite the strict provisions of the law, the society accepts plurality of wives. The doctrine of *desuetudo* will continue to keep the criminal law of bigamy and the provisions of sections 47 and 48 of the Marriage Act in our statute books as dead letters'.[540]

554. In *Okwueze v. Okwueze*[541] the petition was for custody of children of the marriage, but despite the express observation of the Supreme Court that the case before it involved bigamy, it proceeded to resolve the custody issue. In *Egbuson & Ors v. Joseph Ikechiuku*[542] the founder of a Christian Church subsequently married a total of six wives in disregard of the express wording of the constitution of the church providing for monogamy. The Supreme Court held that the marriages were in accord with the constitution of the church which had also sanctioned concubinage.[543] *Taiga v. Moses-Taiga*[544] and *Agbeja v. Agbeja*[545] presented similar facts. It is not to be supposed that the men are alone on this, for as Aguda mentions elsewhere; 'both men and women collude in the matter'.[546]

555. Similar issues arose in *Jadesimi v. Okotie-Eboh.*[547] The cases illustrate the frustration of the legislature and the judiciary with the situation. In all the cases,

537. T.A. Aguda, *Select Law Lectures and Papers* 86 (Associated Publishers (Nigeria) Ltd. 1971).
538. [1981] 6–7 SC 25.
539. [1981] 6–7 SC 25 – Obaseki, J.S.C.
540. K. Ibidapo-Obe, *The Judicial Approach to the Customary Law Marriages in Nigeria*, in *The Marriage Laws of Nigeria*, Being Papers Presented at a National Workshop 128, 132 (T. O. Aguda ed., Nigerian Institute of Advanced Legal Studies 1981).
541. [1989] 3 NWLR (Pt. 109) 321; [1989] LPER – SC. 202/1985.
542. [1977] LPELR – SC 183/1975; [1977] ALL N.L.R. 194; [1977] 6 S.C. 1.
543. This case is discussed fully below.
544. [2005] EWCA Civ 1013; [2012] 10 NWLR (part 1308) 219.
545. [1985] 3 NWLR (part 11) 11.
546. Akinola Aguda, *Select Law Lectures and Papers* 86, 99,120–121 (Associated Publishers (Nigeria) Ltd. 1971).
547. [1996] 2 NWLR (part 429) 128–156.

there was no indication that Part III or any of its sections such as 62 and 68 of the MCA on intervention by the Attorney General was put into motion either by the Court or the Attorney General.

556. When a man marries under the Act has, he elected monogamy? The factual situation demonstrates that the choice is only momentary. An example is where a man was married to a particular woman under customary law but is separated from her and the bride price yet to be refunded where this is the culture and proposes to another woman who insists on marriage under the Act. A notice is issued, and the marriage is conducted. The Marriage Act provides that such a marriage should not be conducted and therefore the marriage is void. The question is who institutes the proceedings since this is a criminal offence? The State does not take on the action for bigamous marriages clearly provided for both in the MA, the MCA and the Criminal Code. The second scenario is a man marries one woman under the Act, and subsequently marries as many as he desires under customary law. By the Act, all the subsequent marriages under customs are void but the marriages under customs are valid under that legal regime and indeed the regime does not recognise the marriage under the Act, as it does not contemplate a conflict of law situation. A third variant will be where a man is married to two or more women under customary law and he then chooses to marry one under the Marriage Act. The actual situation is that in each of the cases he remains married to the women under customary law. Are the children to then be described as born out of wedlock, particularly as the State does not institute an action in bigamy against the man. The law in Nigeria has since resolved the question of children in the children's favour. Thus, it has been suggested elsewhere that bigamy in Nigeria is best classified and treated as a civil wrong.[548]

557. In *Jadesimi v. Okotie-Eboh*,[549] the counsel to the second defendant argued that the second marriage which was under the Act although, involving the same parties, if taken to its logical conclusion would result in the children born before that marriage being classified as children born out of wedlock. However, the children were duly born within a marriage – the customary marriage. Thus, the direction taken by the Court of Appeal is that the parties had elected a new law and structure of marriage and in this case, as no third party was affected, the second marriage created a legal right between the parties.

558. At the Supreme Court, Justice Uwais who delivered the lead judgment stated that the import of section 47 of the Marriage Act is that it is lawful for parties married under customary law to contract a marriage under the Act and that it is an offence punishable by imprisonment for a person married under customary law to

548. Nwudego Chinwuba, *Human Identity: Child Rights and the Legal Framework for Marriage in Nigeria*, 51(4) Marriage & Fam. Rev. 305–336 (2015).
549. [1996] 2 NWLR (part 429) 128–156.

get married under the Act to a third party.[550] This judgment, appearing fair is simplistic. It is suggested that a principle-based approach would have yielded long-term benefits in this all-important area of marriage, family and succession law – long-term principle that categorises the different marriage regimes, therefore establishing a logic people can relate to rather than a fiat which people work to evade.

559. The question is whether in fact, the section simply makes it legitimate for the same parties who have been married under customary law to be able to conduct a marriage under the Marriage Act. Is it perhaps the case that the Marriage Act addresses the sequence of marriage for the two regimes? Thus, if the marriage under the Act happens first, then the parties are precluded from any other form of marriage howsoever. That this latter is the likely interpretation of this section is evinced in the character of the legal relations envisaged by the Act. In this sense, a second marriage after a marriage celebrated in compliance with the Act, whether with the same person or another simply whittles down the value of the marriage contemplated by the Act. That this is so is borne out first, by section 35 and then 46. Section 35 provides: any person who is married under this Act whose marriage is declared by the Act to be valid shall be incapable during the continuance of such marriage of contracting a valid marriage under customary law but, save as aforesaid, nothing in this Act, contained shall affect the validity of any marriage contracted under or in accordance with any customary law or in any manner apply to marriage so contracted.

560. The section appears to advance the ordering of or sequence of marriages and seeks to give people a choice to be either married under the Act or customs but not both.

561. The efforts may however have yielded extremely poor results. Section 46 provides: whoever contracts a marriage under provisions of this Act or any modification or re-enactment therefore being at the time married in accordance with customary law to any person other than the person with whom such marriage is contracted shall be liable to imprisonment for five years.

562. This section appears to confirm that the Act is interested in the ordering of marriage where two marriages are celebrated. This gives force to the fact that the intendment of the Act or at least the interpretation of the relevant sections as they appear is that a celebration of marriage should extinguish the rights and duties under customary law and subsume the customary marriage into a statutory one. This conclusion, however, is an impediment to and circumvention of contemporary legal theory and structure. The following conclusions can be drawn as far as the relationship between the Act and customary law marriage is concerned:

(1) Section 35 recognises the co-existence of the two regimes of marriage.
(2) Section 39 makes it an offence for one person who having married under the Act to engage in a different marriage with any or other persons.

---

550. *Ibid.*

(3) Section 46 addresses circumvention of the Act in order to take advantage of the polygamous character of customary marriage.
(4) Section 47 aims at consolidating the Act as a different regime and an alternative to customary marriage. It attempts to provide an option that discourages double celebrations of marriages.

563. Interpreting a similar but less strict version of the provisions in *Osamwonyi v. Osamwonyi*[551]the Supreme Court held that to invalidate a marriage celebrated under the Marriage Act, on the ground that, at the time of the aforesaid marriage, there was a subsisting marriage under native law and custom by one of the parties requires a strict proof of the existence of the customary marriage. The marriage under native law and custom must be proved with a high degree of certainty. In the circumstances of the case, the Court having affirmed the decision of the lower court that there was no proof of a subsisting customary marriage held that there was no ground to declare the marriage under the Act a nullity.

564. In *Jadesimi v. Okotie-Eboh*[552] the deceased who was a Minister of Finance in Nigeria was one of the fatal victims of the coup plot in Nigeria on 15 January 1966. While alive, he had married a Nigerian woman sometime in 1942 under customs. In 1961, the deceased celebrated another marriage with the same woman in accordance with the then statutory framework for marriage.[553] In 1947, the deceased had written a Will which was duly executed and deposited at the Probate Registry in Lagos, the only registry in existence at the time. No one had knowledge of the existence of the Will as at the time of the testator's death. In consequence, his widow who had two children applied for a Letter of Administration for his estate. There were also other children of the deceased by other mothers whom he was not recorded as having married. The Letter of Administration was issued in favour of the widow, her two children and another child. The estate was subsequently administered by agreement, in accordance with the Letter of Administration. Sometime in 1974, the existence of the Will of 1947 was discovered. The second defendant also raised a point that another Will written in 1964 was discovered in the Safe of the deceased testator. Five questions were raised at the High Court for consideration. Two are of continuing relevance and are:

(1) Whether the Will of 1947 was revoked by the later marriage of 1961 in the light of section 18 of the Wills Act, 1837?[554]
(2) Whether the customary laws of the Urhobos and/or the Itsekiris could operate to render the Will void?[555]

551. [1973] NMLR 26.
552. [1996] 2 NWLR (part 429) 128–156.
553. This is the marriage Act, Cap 115, Laws of the Federation of Nigeria, 1958; Except for, perhaps, expunction of s. 36 of the Act, the Marriage Act Cap M6 Laws of the Federation 2004 remains the same.
554. This is a statute of general application by virtue of s. 45 of the Interpretation Act, Cap 89 Laws of the Federation 1958 or Cap 192, 1990.
555. The Urhobos and Itsekiris are major tribes of the current Delta State of Nigeria. Delta State was formerly a part of the Mid-West region of Nigeria later split into current Edo and Delta States.

565. The trial court answered both questions in the negative validating the Will of 1947. The case went on appeal. At the Court of Appeal only the first question was considered. The court answered the question in the positive and set aside the judgment of the High Court.

566. The same question was the crux of the appeal to the Supreme Court. The first respondent who is the widow of the deceased was absent and unrepresented. The appellant's counsel argued that although the Wills Act was applicable in Nigeria as a Statute of general application, it was applicable only where local circumstances permitted and that section 18 thereof could not be applied in Nigeria. The counsel argued that in particular, the provisions of sections 11 and 47 of the Marriage Act operated to restate the ordinary interpretation and consequence of section 18 of the Wills Act. He further contended that since it is usual for persons who have married under the Marriage Act to have conducted another marriage under customary or Islamic law, the import of the judgment of the Court of Appeal is to delegitimise all the actions between the parties before the second marriage such as make the children 'illegitimate'. On the other hand, counsel to the second respondent argued that section 18 was applicable in Nigeria in spite of the extant peculiar circumstances of superimposing of one type of marriage on another. She disagreed with the counsel to the appellant that the monogamous marriage was a surplusage and argued that the marriages all had different consequences. In sum, she argued that the deceased testator having chosen to marry under the Act embraced the provisions of the Wills Act, 1837. Counsel to the third respondent held the same view with her. Delivering the lead judgment, Uwais J.S.C stated:

(1) Nigerian legal system is enabled to resort to laws as are existent in England on or before 1 January 1900.
(2) Section 18 of the Wills Act is to be applied in Nigeria subject to local circumstances.
(3) Sections 11 and 47 of the Marriage Act recognise customary marriage and its co-existence usually with marriage under the Act.

567. The Court noted the continuing disregard of the male folk for the legal implication of the Marriage Act and their penchant for disregarding the strict regime of monogamy which the Act establishes.

568. The other Justices buttressed the position of the Chief Justice. Onu, J.S.C reaffirmed that although the latter provision in section 47 is more of a window dressing in that it is observed more in breach than in conformity and obedience in Nigeria, its purport is clear and unambiguous. Ighu J.S.C thought that the effect of the provisions of the Marriage Act is that customary marriage where it is combined with a statutory one is converted to a monogamous one but in so far as section 18 of the Wills Act is concerned it must be applied in line with the Marriage Act, such that marriage to the same person under the two regimes cannot operate the same way it would in a society where only one framework of monogamous marriage is recognised. Wali J.S.C concurred with the judgment of the Uwais JSC but reaffirmed that the provisions of the Marriage Act in Nigeria were being observed more in form than in substance and Adio J.S.C concurred fully with the judgment of the Chief Justice. The Supreme Court unanimously allowed the appeal setting aside the judgment of the Court of Appeal and restoring the judgment of the High Court. It pronounced the validity of the last Will and testament dated 21 August 1947 and revoked the Letters of Administration.

569. The same problem arose with *Salubi v. Nwariaku*[556] almost on similar facts, but being more recent, the question of children having been resolved, the Supreme Court held unequivocally that children born in or out of wedlock in Nigeria are to be treated equally on questions of the intestacy of their parents, perhaps, specifically, fathers.

570. Another case typifying the toggle of customs and law is *James Egubson v. Joseph Ikechukwu.*[557] The facts leading to the claim in the case are that the defendant, who is also the sole founder of a Church, had, in disregard of the church constitution that mandated members to be the 'husband of only one wife', taken six wives. The Founder had been married to only one wife under customary law rites, although celebrated in the Church. The Founder had in fact, prior to becoming polygamous, encouraged the first Plaintiff who was married to two women to put away one of them and conduct a monogamous union with only one. The plaintiff and some other members are the plaintiffs contesting the headship of the church – the primary impetus for the litigation.

571. On the findings of the Court, the defendant started the church based on a vision he received while, previously a photographer and labourer in a farm in Sapele.[558] He had received visions on the central doctrines, creeds and teachings for the Church. These were written down at the time, and presented in evidence as the Immutable Rules and Conducts of St. Joseph Chosen Church of God. The immutable Rules and Conducts contained nine chapters. Central to the dispute is Chapter 7 with the sub-heading – 'Marriage'. Clause 7(a) indicated that 'marriage is a contract between one man and one woman'.

572. There was another document termed 'Rules and Regulations' – drawn up as a Constitution by the Solicitor of the Church on guidance and instructions from the defendant-founder. There were three other documents but only the Rules and Regulations was required for registration of the Church as a Land Perpetual Succession entity. The Rules and Regulations set out the aims and objects of the Church, the machinery for the management of its properties and the appointment of trustees. A certificate of Incorporation No. 717 of 1964 was granted to the Church. The defendant-founder was unanimously elected as the sole trustee of the Church for life. The Church flourished.

556. [2003] 7 NWLR (part 819) 426; [2003] 2 SC 161.
557. [1977] ALL NLR 194; [1976] 6 SC 1; [1977] LPELR-SC. 183/1975.
558. A town in the then Mid-West region of Nigeria and now part of Delta State.

573. In 1967 at the outbreak of civil war in Nigeria, the defendant moved from the Mid-West to, and remained in the Eastern parts of Nigeria, then known as Biafra. In Biafra, the defendant asserted that the elders in the church in Biafra, supported his taking additional wives, which he did. At the end of the civil war, the defendant returned to Sapele to continue with his vision and the Church founded but met stiff opposition which resulted in the litigation.

574. At the High Court, the plaintiffs had six heads of claims which turned on a determination of the marital status of the defendant and their implication on the cannons of the church. They sought the following:

(i) A declaration that the defendant had ceased to be a member of the Saint Joseph's Chosen of God.
(ii) An order for the removal of the defendant as a sole Trustee of Saint Joseph's Chosen Church of God.
(iii) An order for the plaintiffs to be appointed Trustees of the Church in the stead of the defendant.

575. There were three other claims on accounting from the defendant for the period he was sole trustee, up until his purported removal. The learned trial judge found no evidence of abuse of trust by the defendant. The Court thus declined the invitation to appoint the plaintiffs as new trustees, but ordered the defendant to provide the plaintiffs with an account. [559]

576. The appeal thus turned on issues 1, 2 and 3 on the marital status of the defendant. The Supreme Court stated that the doctrines of a church are not the business of a Court of law. A court will not concern itself with the soundness or unreasonableness of any religious doctrine, but is entitled to ascertain whether those doctrines as are agreed to, have been breached and the legal consequences of any such breach.[560] Sir Udo Udoma, J.S.C delivering the lead judgment stated:

> We think, however, that to determine the true position and authority of the defendant vis-à-vis the rest of the membership of the church and in relation to the power of the plaintiffs as regards ex-communication from the church, recourse must also be had to the Rules and Regulations which, as stated before, deal with the machinery for the governance of the church as an institution and the management of the property of the church subject to truth in terms of the Land (Perpetual Succession) Act.[561]

559. Claims three to six were independent of the first three and are: an order that the defendant renders an account as Sole Trustee of the Church up to the time of the proceedings and scope as determined by the Court; payment over to the said Church of all sums found due upon taking such account; delivery to the said Church of all properties and assets of the Church in possession of the defendant.
560. The case of *General Assembly of the Free Church of Scotland & Ors. v. Lord Overtoun* [1904] A.C. 515, 516 otherwise referred to as *Bannaytyne v. Overtoun.*
561. [1977] ALL NLR 194; [1976] 6 SC 1; [1977] LPELR-SC. 183/1975.

577. In consequence, the court took the position that the status of the defendant did not fall for determination under the general law but under the rules of the Church and those rules were contained, in two documents – the immutable Rules and Conducts; and the Rules and Regulations. The immutable Rules and Conducts were described by the court as the Memorandum of Association of the Church, or as the Court further put it 'the basis of the foundation of St. Joseph's Chosen Church of God'. The Rules and Regulations were described as the Articles of Association which dealt with the working of an institution and the management of the property of the church under the Land (Perpetual Succession) Act.

578. The Supreme Court reached the decision that the defendant had not breached the rules of the Church since the church could not be described in any way, as a Church observing the tenets of monogamy, noting that the church approved of 'concubinage' and polygamy under specified conditions. In addition, the Church having never applied for a licence as a place of worship for celebration of marriages under the Marriage Act, could not conduct monogamous marriages as recognised under the Act, therefore, the marriages it conducted fell to be recognised, only, as customary marriage – a potentially polygamous union.

579. An ongoing[562] example is that of the former Minister of Aviation and his 'wives'. The former Minister had separated from his wife, Precious – 'a beauty queen' with whom he had lived a life as celebrities. In a separation that is viral, Regina another wife, previously unknown, came forward to state that she was the legally married wife to the former Minister, their marriage having been conducted both in a customary form in Ghana and the Marriage Registry in Apapa, Lagos. Regina stated emphatically that she permitted the former Minister to marry Precious, because she was not always available and that the former Minister had introduced them and they had become well acquainted. The former Minister came forward to confirm this and established his continuing intimate relations with Regina, whom he claimed to love to no ends. To the question: 'It's a bit confusing now. Did he marry Precious while still married to you?' Regina responded:

> Very, very married. I talk to him every single day. We talk every single day, sometimes, we talk for hours or less. I used to live in Nigeria but a few years ago, I came to Ghana because I wanted my daughter to be in a particular school. So I came down to Ghana and we were going back to Nigeria at weekends and we got back before school every week. After a while, it became a little bit too stressful, so our visits reduced to like one weekend in a month, then one weekend every three months and all. With all the political activities in Nigeria and everything, it was also a better environment here in Ghana than in Nigeria. He paid a dowry on Precious, I think this year February. I felt it was the right thing to do because they have four children, and it is only right

562. Jayne Augoye, *INTERVIEW: Why I Allowed Fani-Kayode Marry Precious Despite Our Union-Regina Fani-Kayode*, 3 Oct. 2020, available at: https://www.premiumtimesng.com/entertainment/naija-fashion/418194-interview-why-i-allowed-fani-kayode-marry-precious-despite-our-union-regina-fani-kayode.html (last accessed 6 Oct. 2020).

> for him to do the right thing. I am still married to him, I am his legal wife and everything, but the circumstances demanded a little bit of you know, and because of the children.[563]

580. In any examination of the context of polygamy and monogamy it is to be noted that as the Supreme Court stated in *Jadesimi v. Okotie-Eboh*[564] the law on monogamy which is the Marriage Act is obeyed in breach. Men would always prefer the customary marriage and are not about to voluntarily, without some principled logic, accept a change from the *status quo*. This has resulted in the continuing co-existence of both frameworks of marriage in Nigeria. Many men do not consider the regime monogamy in Nigeria, a serious challenge to polygamy.

581. The legal theory of bigamy is thus somewhat complex in Nigeria. Where there are other wives, on any evaluation, there is at least, notice of equitable interests and no legal interests can arise. Any monogamous marriage thus placed on them is void *ab initio* and triggers the offence of bigamy in Lagos or anywhere else in Nigeria, despite the efforts of Lagos at abolishing bigamy. This is the only critical logical legal argument. Otherwise having been exposed to a customary marriage of which incidents are among others, its potentially polygamous nature, with more than one woman, either a new party or the extant parties can lay claim to any form of exclusivity. However, where a man goes on to marry a person, first, under customary law and then by the Act, the particular nature of the customary marriage which is subsumed in the legal nature of a monogamous marriage implies the extinguishing of the polygamous character of the customary marriage. Yet, something remains, this is the other distinguishing characteristic of the two marriages, the processes of dissolution. A dissolution of a monogamous marriage does not dissolve the polygamous marriage. If it does not, then in law the marriage continues to exist. It exists, however, only for the purpose of dissolution where the parties are in a continuing state of disagreement. The man and the woman having married under customs are now incapacitated to conduct any further marriage unless the marriage under the customs is dissolved. The argument that the matter falls for determination on the marital status of the parties and no more, so that upon the dissolution of the monogamous marriage the status ceases to exist is not sustainable.[565] This is because the incidents and consequences of a monogamous marriage and a polygamous one conducted in Nigeria are so distinct and compartmentalised that they are on parallel lines. Marriage under the Act confers on either spouse some quantum of rights both with regard to property and children. In Nigeria, the Matrimonial Causes Act continues to make a wife an agent of the husband for necessaries where she is deserted.[566] Also, a child born by a monogamous wife while married or within 280 days after dissolution of marriage, she remaining unmarried, is presumed the child

---

563. *Ibid.*
564. [1996] 2 NWLR (part 429) 128–156.
565. P.R.H. Webb, *Ohochuku v. Ohochuku 'A variation of Thynne v. Thynne'*, 23(3) The Mod. L. Rev. 327–331 (1960).
566. Section 42(3) of the MCA.

of the husband.[567] This is subject to section 84 of the MCA which provides for evidence of non-access: 'Notwithstanding any rule of law, in proceedings under this Act either party to a marriage may give evidence proving or tending to prove that the parties to the marriage did not have sexual relations with each other at any particular time, but shall not be compellable to give such evidence if it would show or tend to show that a child born to the wife during the marriage was illegitimate.'

582. A customary marriage, on the other hand, confers rights on husbands and not wives or children. The customary marriage focuses on a wife as a vessel of procreation. If the husband deserts her or she deserts her husband, presumption of paternity is activated and stands so activated unless bride price is returned. There is no question of evidence of access or non-access while married, children and their custody belong to husbands. A wife does not have the advantage of maintenance, adjustment of property rights or even declaration of any right whatsoever under customary law. Should she die while separated from the husband but not fully divorced, she has no rights of burial within the husband's family although, while alive she remains a subject for inheritance if she is so inclined and the husband's family consider her of 'merchantable quality'.[568] In many customs and culture a wife, is the autopsy of her husband.[569]

583. Where the case, is that a couple are married under both regimes of law, and the statuary marriage is dissolved, but not the customary marriage, the couple remain married and none of the parties can comply with the requirements of a subsequent monogamous marriage with any other party under the Marriage Act. The man may marry another wife under customary law but the wife cannot, except she belongs to the few tribes in Nigeria that practice polyandry. Thus, to say that the status of marriage is dissolved does very little to advance the position of the woman in the scenarios, particularly in a society such as Nigeria, where adultery has many non-verifiable and, or, superstitious consequences for women.

584. The other scenario is that the parties conduct the monogamous marriage first. In this case, nothing needs to be done as the monogamous marriage creates a legal right that stands unaffected by a subsequent customary marriage, where the parties are the same persons. As long as a customary marriage is unregistered it can only take effect as an equitable right. The Marriage Act by its provisions aims at this last scenario by placing importance on the sequence of the type of marriage but its impact has yielded no known results. The customary marriage is usually conducted first.

---

567. Section 165 of the Evidence Act, 2011.
568. This is almost a general practice in all areas of indigenous Nigerian population. *See Akinubi v. Akinubi* [1987] 2 NWLR (part 486) 144.
569. Emmanuel Durojaye, *Woman, But Not Human: Widowhood Practices and Human Rights Violations in Nigeria*, 27(2) Int'l J. L. Pol'y & Fam. 176–196 (2013).

585. Should a legislation clearly specify that the intent of the parties is to determine the matter where the parties as, is usually the case, first form a customary marriage and then one under the Act, and that the subsequent marriage subsumes the customary marriage, then a principled pattern would have been established. The intent of the parties should thus be the key to unravelling the nature of the legal relations created just as the Supreme Court reasoned in *James Egubson v. Joseph Ikechukwu.*[570] It would follow that, questions, forms and possibly administration of oaths would be initiated for the celebration rites of the subsequent marriage under the Act. This is likely to engage the conscience of the parties which in the long run may affect the processes of the customary tenure. The peculiar circumstances of Nigeria are unlikely to allow for a judicial review of customs as was done in Uganda.

586. The complexities of the letters of the law as they stand are unworkable and only lay down a different law in practice. The consequences of this state of affairs are multifarious and one area is the interest of the State in population. Population control and family planning are gaining ascendency in global family policies, in Nigeria they remain an autonomous private realm and women in Southern Nigeria are increasingly choosing small families. Any positive impact of this choice, however, remains to be seen in the face of unchecked bigamy and impact of patriarchy.

587. More than the impact of bigamy on population and the synergy of family life, is its overall impact on societal cohesion and advancement of human evolution. The idea of bigamy and the impact of its unenforceability in Nigeria are devastating. Its unenforceability detracts from the finer essence and aspiration of persons and permeates the society in circular motions undermining human ideals of trust and honesty. It advances and undermines emotional health and stability for adults and children, reinforcing the baser human propensities and thereby, forestalling constructive deployment of the mind for so many.

II. Domestic Violence

588. Domestic violence is not any single behaviour but rather a pattern of many physical, sexual, and/or psychological behaviours perpetrated by a current or former intimate partner or children. It is gender-neutral although, mostly perpetrated against women. The Violence Against Persons (Prohibition) Act, 2015, a Federal Legislation, defines domestic Violence. It means by section 46 of the Act 'any act perpetrated on any person in a domestic relationship where such act causes harm or may cause imminent harm to the safety, health or wellbeing of any person'. This includes spousal battery and violence in private sphere. Domestic violence is also known as domestic abuse, spousal abuse, battering, family violence, dating abuse, and intimate partner violence (IPV). It covers a pattern of behaviour which involves the abuse by one partner against another in an intimate relationship such as marriage, cohabitation, dating or within the family. Domestic violence can take many

570. [1977] ALL NLR 194; [1976] 6 SC 1; [1977] LPELR-SC. 183/1975.

forms, including physical aggression or assault (hitting, kicking, biting, shoving, restraining, slapping, throwing objects, battery), or threats thereof; sexual abuse; emotional abuse; controlling or domineering; intimidation; stalking; passive/covert abuse and economic deprivation.

589. The Lagos State Protection against Domestic Violence Law, 2007 by section 18 interprets domestic violence as: any acts of physical abuse; sexual abuse and exploitation but not limited to rape, incest and sexual assault; sexual starvation; emotional, verbal and psychological abuse; economic abuse and exploitation; denial of basic education; intimidation; harassment; stalking; hazardous attack including acid bath with offensive or poisonous substance; damage to property; entry into the complainant's residence without consent where the parties do not share the same residence; or any other controlling or abusive behaviour towards a complainant, where such conduct harms or may cause imminent harm to the safety, health or well-being of the complainant; and deprivation.

590. The family unit is structured and promoted by society to provide order, security, stability, and happiness, in short – a haven for its members, yet there is an increasing rate of reported and unreported cases of domestic violence and in the worst-case scenarios – death of the victim within the family unit. The spate having become worrisome in the country, there has been legislation from the Federal to the state Levels to address the issue. The following are identifiable reasons for domestic violence in Nigeria, use of drugs or alcohol (a drunk or a person who is high can hardly control himself at the slightest perceived provocation by the wife), infertility, couple's age difference, witnessing or being a victim of domestic violence as a child, unemployment, particularly of the male partner.

591. Section 295 of the Criminal Code empowers parents to chastise children. Section 55(1)(a) and (d) of the Penal Code of Northern Nigeria provide that an assault by parent or guardian for the purpose of correcting his child or ward or by a man on a woman is not an offence if they are married, if native law or custom recognises such 'correction' as lawful, if there is no grievous hurt.

592. Section 6 of the Criminal Code exposes women to further abuses by effectually legalising forced sexual intercourse. It provides that 'unlawful carnal knowledge means carnal connection which takes place otherwise than between husband and wife'. The Violence against Persons (Prohibition) Act, 2015 a Federal Legislation, provides for the offence of rape but the provision does not cover married persons. The Act, however, goes to some considerable distance to ameliorate the impact of the powers in a husband in the provisions of the Criminal Code and Penal Code. It thus provides for offences for domestic violence, economic abuse and forced financial dependence. It also defines harmful traditional practices and spouse and spousal battery providing duties and penalties. The Act by section 45 repeals and supersedes related provisions in both the Criminal Code and Penal Code. This leaves the question of scope and application to the court.

593. The effects of domestic violence can be devastating and long lasting especially on children and adolescents. Children are often principal victims of domestic violence. Witnessing abuse and living in an environment where someone else, usually a caregiver is a victim of abuse, can be psychologically devastating for a child. There are reports that children who are hit by parents have higher rates of depression than those whose parents disciplined in other ways and are more likely to think about suicides. Some researchers have also found that children whose mothers were abused by their partners have intelligence quotients (IQs) lower than usual. Violence is a threat to adolescents' well-being. Research demonstrates that the adolescent may become socialised in violent behaviour. He or she may become confused and angry. A child who has undergone or witnessed violence may become withdrawn, anxious, or depressed on one hand; on the other hand, the child may become aggressive and exert control over younger siblings or other people's children. They may become aggressive, becoming troublesome at home and at school. They may also become withdrawn, isolating themselves from others and may underachieve in academics and may develop low self-esteem, finding it difficult to trust others. The anger and stress experienced by victims may lead to depression and other emotional disorders sometimes leading to suicide. Victims may also exhibit harmful health behaviour like excessive smoking, alcohol abuse, use of drugs and engaging in risky sexual activity.

§6. Void and Voidable Marriage

594. The MCA makes detailed provisions for when a marriage may be void or voidable and are contained in sections 3 and 5.

595. A void marriage is one which in legal prisms never took place and therefore, is non-existent.

596. A voidable marriage is one which on the petition of one of the spouses may lose its validity on the order of the Court. A void marriage may be so, because the parties lack the capacity to marry or formalities for a recognised marriage were not met either within Nigeria, or the jurisdiction where the marriage took place. Another important basis for a marriage to be void is failure to comply with prohibited degrees of consanguinity or affinity. A void marriage lacks external validity but may well be imbued with internal validity. A voidable marriage on the other hand assumes external validity but lacks an internal validity. The question which family law must resolve is the boundaries of the State in making rules on this aspect of family, especially in the light of modern exigencies on human rights and the impact of these rules on societal cohesion and children's wellbeing.

597. Any person can petition the Court to declare that a marriage is void. Where, however, the formalities were met, but some circumstances exist which are recognised by law as impeding the justification for the marriage, the marriage is voidable and in the case of statutory marriages in Nigeria, may be avoided by a petition from one of the spouses. The proceedings and provisions of the law for both in Nigeria are termed 'nullity'. Sections 34–38 provide for nullity proceedings. Section 34 provides that subject to the provisions of the Act, a petition for nullity of marriage may be based on the ground that the marriage is void, or on the ground that the marriage is voidable at the suit of the petitioner.

598. A proceeding for nullity is one seeking the aid of the court to establish that a marriage could not have taken place because of certain conditions discovered or highlighted after the apparent celebration of a marriage. In *Anyaegbunam v. Anyaegbunam*[571] the Supreme Court stated that 'in petitions for nullity, the law is that the ceremony of marriage must be strictly proved'.[572] The claim may arise from a defective formation proceeding of the 'marriage' such as not complying with the formalities of a marriage according to law. The claim may also arise from the express declaration by statute that a marriage under certain conditions is a nullity. A good example of the first will be not meeting up with the age of capacity. A typical example of the latter is provided in section 3(1)(c) of the MCA: 'the marriage is not a valid marriage under the law of the place where the marriage takes place, by reason of a failure to comply with the requirements of the law of that place with respect to the form of solemnisation of marriages'.

599. The word, 'nullity' and its meaning is said to originate dating back to 1560–1570, from the Medieval Latin word *nūllitās*; *nullitalis*; or *nullus* and meant 'not any', and then French as *nullité*, before it was used by the Anglo French at about 1580 AD, to mean 'a state of nothingness'; etc. The process bringing about nullity in matrimonial causes is known as 'annulment' and the order annulling a purported marriage is known as a decree of nullity. Annulling a marriage is favoured by Catholicism over dissolution of marriage and within Catholic etymology, the annulment of marriage is called 'declaration of nullity' and pre-secularism, was conducted by the Ecclesiastical courts.

600. Technically, if a marriage never took place, then it is thought that there may be no need to obtain a decree of annulment, and one may simply act as though the marriage never took place. At other times, declaration of nullity of marriage as opposed to a decree of nullity is said to apply to marriages which are void as void marriages are considered as never having taken place. Thus, the courts only declare formally that which is the state of affairs as is sometimes done with respect to jactitation of marriage in certain jurisdictions. On the other hand, Annulment applies to a marriage that is valid until otherwise ordered by decree to be null and void, with consequences.

601. The Marriage Act provides circumstances when a marriage celebrated can be invalid. The MCA provides for the circumstances and procedure for inviting the court to establish that the marriage is in fact, legally null and void. The proceeding for nullity is instituted by petition.[573] Where both a petition for a decree of nullity

571. [1973] LPELR-SC. 18/1973; [1973] ALL NLR 320; [1973] 4 S.C. 84.
572. [1973] LPELR-SC. 18/1973, 15.
573. Section 54(1).

and a petition for a decree of dissolution of the purported marriage are before a court, the court is bound to hear and determine a petition for nullity first.[574]

602. The outcomes of nullity but not status, in the MCA, are the same as dissolution of marriage. This extends to adjustment of property rights. Thus, 'marriage' is defined as including a purported marriage that is void but does not include one entered into according to Muslim rites or customary law' … ."[575] The conflict between void and voidable marriages runs through the MCA. Section 2(2) (b) and (c) make separate provisions for proceedings in respect of the two; (b) 'nullity of a voidable marriage'; or and (c) 'nullity of a void marriage'. Section 34 titled: 'Ground for decree of nullity of marriage' provides for a petition for nullity based on the ground that the marriage is void, or on the ground that the marriage is voidable at the suit of the petitioner. The Act does not provide for relief for void marriages although it recognises a proceeding for it and enforcement of maintenance from such a proceeding. Thus, by section 56 titled: 'Decree nisi in first instance'; the Act provides for a decree for voidable marriage but not for void marriage. Again, on the effect, section 38 provides for the children where the marriage is voidable but not where it is void. Subsection (1) provides that, 'a decree of nullity under this Act of a voidable marriage shall annul the marriage from and including the date on which the decree becomes absolute'; and (2) 'Without prejudice to the operation of subsection (1) of this section in other respects, a decree of nullity under this Act of a voidable marriage shall not render illegitimate a child of the parties born since, or legitimated during, the marriage'.

603. The conclusion to be drawn is that in Nigeria, if one considers that a marriage is void, it is better to petition for a decree in line with the Act and rules. To buttress this position, is the rule with respect to third part intervention. Order XXII, Part 1(1)(b) provides for a decree of nullity of void marriage. The provisions for third-party intervention are contained in sections 64 and 65. Section 64 is on intervention by the Attorney General of the Federation or by delegation – the Attorney General of the State and section 65 is by interested persons with leave of court. Furthermore, the rule provides for class representation. Thus, where persons included in a class of persons are affected by proceedings to which the Part applies, a court may, if it is satisfied that it is expedient, either by reason of the difficulty in ascertaining the persons who are included in that class of persons or for the purpose of saving expense, may by order, appoint a person or persons included in that class of persons to represent all the persons included in that class of persons.[576]

604. A petition for a decree of declaration of nullity of marriage by person or persons who are not parties to the marriage or proceedings for a declaration or order of nullity is to be made in Form 61.[577]

---

574. Section 29 of the Act.
575. Section 69 of the MCA.
576. Order XXII, part 3, rule 5(3).
577. Order XXII, part 3, rule 4(a).

I. The Provisions and Case Law on Nullity

605. Sections 3–6(a) provide for the validity, invalidity of marriage and avoidance of marriage within Nigeria while section 6(2) provides for the same position under private international law. The circumstances covered are, aside from requirement of general compliance with the requirement of law for the celebration of marriage;[578] that either of the parties is lawfully married to someone else at the time of the purported marriage. It would not matter what type of marriage was in existence once it is with someone else other than the parties.[579] In *Oghoyone v. Oghoyone*,[580] the Court restated this position in affirming the judgment of the lower court that the marriage between the parties is void.[581] In that case, the appellant had married Wilhemina Agatha Huyssodin, a Dutch national in 1990. While that marriage was subsisting, he married the respondent on 9 April 1994 at the Lagos City Hall. It was in the light of this circumstance, that the respondent at the Court of Appeal had commenced a proceeding at the High Court of Lagos State, in the Ikeja Division for a declaration that the marriage between her and the appellant is null and void. The trial court declared the marriage void. The appeal was on distribution of property between the parties on account of the provisions of 72(1) and (2) the application in respect of which, Rhodes Vivour JCA who delivered the judgment of the Court Appeal stated, applied to the parties because section 69 of the MCA retains a void marriage as a marriage for the purposes of adjustment of property rights between the parties.

606. Another invalid marriage is where the parties are within prohibited degrees of consanguinity.[582] It is immaterial whether the relationship is of the whole blood or half blood, or whether it is traced through, or to any person who has been born out of wedlock.[583] Another basis of invalidity is that the consent of either of the parties is not real either because: (i) it was obtained by duress or fraud; (ii) a party is mistaken as to the identity of the other party; (iii) of the nature of the ceremony performed and (iv) the party is mentally incapable of understanding the nature of the marriage contract.[584] The final basis of invalidity is that either of the parties is not of marriageable age.[585]

607. Section 6(2) is important and excludes the operations of the Act by the principles of *lex loci celebrationis*. It provides that 'a provision of this Act shall not affect the validity or invalidity of a marriage where it would not be in accordance with the rules of private international law to apply that provision in relation to that marriage'.

---

578. Section 3(1)(c) of the MCA.
579. Section 3(1)(a) of the MCA.
580. [2010] 3 NWLR (part 1182) 564.
581. [2010] 3 NWLR (part 1182) 564, 583.
582. Section 3(1)(b) of the MCA. The degrees of consanguinity is contained in the first schedule to the MCA.
583. Consanguinity is relation by blood line but affinity is relationship by marriage.
584. Section 3(1)(d) of the MCA.
585. Section 3(1)(e) of the MCA.

608. A petition for a decree of nullity where the marriage is voidable is based on the provisions of section 5 of the MCA. The Act by section 5 provides that where the purported marriage is not one that is void by virtue of section 3, then it is voidable where consummation of the marriage is impossible on account of the incapacity of one of the parties to do so. [586] This is quite different from the ground of dissolution on wilful and persistent refusal to consummate the marriage. A purported marriage could also be voidable if either of the parties has an illness of the mind in the form of unsoundness, defectiveness due to arrested or incomplete development of the mind, or recurrent attacks of 'insanity' or epilepsy.[587] Other basis of nullity proceeding for a voidable marriage is where one of the parties has a venerable disease in a communicable form.[588] It is to be noted that section 5(c) and (d) are grounds of nullity under the MCA, 1973.[589]

609. The Court has wide discretion on whether to order a decree of nullity on a voidable as opposed to void marriages. Section 36 makes nullity by the petitioner based on a voidable marriage as provided in section 5(1)(a) that is incapacity to consummate the marriage, dependent on knowledge, and condonation. First, by section 35, the party suffering the incapacity cannot bring the petition. The court must then enquire as to whether the incapacity is a continuing condition as at the commencement of the proceedings and whether the petitioner did not know of the condition as at the time of the marriage. It must also be that the incapacity is not curable;[590] the respondent refuses to submit to such medical examination as the court considers necessary for the purpose of determining whether the incapacity is curable and fails to submit to proper treatment for the purpose of curing the incapacity. Other factors to be considered by the Court in ordering a decree of nullity of a voidable marriage where the petition is on incapacity to consummate include, the conduct of the petitioner since the marriage, delay, and other reasons which in the view of the Court and in the circumstances of the case, would make it harsh and oppressive to the respondent, or contrary to the public interest to order a decree of nullity. The Act does not define public policy. However, a cue may be taken from the Constitution where the Constitution provides for derogation from some fundamental human rights in the interest of defence, public safety, public order, public morality, or public health.

610. Where the other basis of voidable marriage in section 5(1)(b), (c) or (d), that is illness of the mind or communicable deceases or the wife is pregnant by another man is engaged, then the conditions for nullity are contained in section 37. The petition must be filed not later than twelve months after the date of the marriage, the petitioner must have been ignorant of the facts constituting the ground as

586. Section 5(1)(a).
587. Section 5(2).
588. Section 5(1)(c).
589. section 12 (e) & (f).
590. *See also* s. 5(1)(a).

at the time of the marriage and marital intercourse has not taken place with the consent of the petitioner since the petitioner discovered the existence of the facts constituting the grounds.

611. Section 35 of the Act defines those who may institute proceedings by exclusion. A decree of nullity of marriage shall not be made on the petition of the party suffering from the incapacity to consummate the marriage unless that party was not aware of the existence of the incapacity at the time of the marriage. A decree can also not be ordered on the petition of the party suffering from the disability of the disease or of the wife, where she is pregnant by some other man.[591]

612. The provisions which may not bear scrutiny in contemporary times clearly demonstrate that the matrimonial causes as recognised in Nigeria by the Act are clearly invasive and thus a matrimonial offences regime. It may be that the provisions for void and voidable marriages as enacted in the MCA would find better vent if they are also enacted in the MA.

II. Comparison with Nullity under the English MCA, 1973

613. Nullity provisions under MCA, 1973 are contained in sections 11–16 of that Act. While the MCA provides that the action must be instituted within twelve months,[592] the MCA, 1973 provides that action can be commenced within three years.[593] Section 15 of the MCA, 1973 provides that the periods for the validity and effectiveness of Decree *nisi* and absolute should also apply to nullity.

614. Just as a decree of nullity in Nigeria by section 38 is not retroactive in its operation, so it is with the English provisions by section 16. Interestingly, both sections refer to voidable marriage and not void marriages. Section 16 of the MCA, 1973 provides that a decree of nullity granted after 31 July 1971 in respect of a voidable marriage shall operate to annul the marriage only as respects any time after the decree has been made absolute, and the marriage shall, notwithstanding the decree, be treated as if it had existed up to that time. The MCA is distinct by the provision of section 69 which defines marriage to include one that is void or voidable evidently, for the purposes of ancillary orders.

615. Section 11 of the MCA, 1973 captures two grounds on which a marriage is void under the Act, that is to say, existing lawful marriage[594] while the other case is by deduction,[595] in that the Nigerian Interpretation Act states that marriage is between a man and woman and the Same Sex (Marriage Prohibition) Act, 2013 prohibits same-sex marriages and makes such marriage punishable by imprisonment for

591. Section 5(1)(d).
592. Section 37(b) of the MCA.
593. Section 13(2); except where the petitioner is relying on incapacity or wilful refusal to consummate the marriage.
594. Section 11(b) MCA, 1973.
595. Section 11(c) MCA, 1973.

fourteen years. The age of marriage is 16 under the MCA, 1973[596] while MCA only refers to 'marriageable age'. The age of marriage in Nigeria is 21 under the Marriage Act but eighteen under the Child's Rights Act. Another important basis of nullity in the MCA 1973 which is not contemplated by the MCA is section 11(d). The section provides that in the case of a polygamous marriage entered outside England and Wales, that either party was at the time of the marriage domiciled in England and Wales.

616. However, as has been noted above, the section on void marriages is distinct from the provisions of nullity under the MCA. Section 12(b) of the MCA, 1973 which provides for nullity on ground of being voidable where the marriage has not been consummated owing to the wilful refusal of the respondent to consummate it, is a fact of irretrievable breakdown in the MCA, except that the Nigerian provision in section 15(2)(a) contemplates a continuing and persistent situation.[597] The Nigerian Act contemplates that the petitioner has been making overtures and efforts aimed at consummation until the filing of the petition while the English position appears to contemplate technical, once and for all refusal to consummate. For the English position, refusal to consummate may be due to religious reasons or forced marriages.[598]

III. Nullity under Customary Law Marriages

617. The concept of nullity can be said to be alien under customary since enquiries are an intrinsic aspect of the procedure of the marriage. However, where it exists, it would have the high sounding description of abomination or taboo. In both cases, cleansing rituals will be conducted to either validate the marriage by cleansing or void it altogether. There might also be instances of ostracism where some persons may have been declared outcasts. This position is now unlawful throughout Nigeria. The only contemplatable circumstances in modern times which may necessitate nullity of marriage will be breach of rules of customary consanguinity

IV. Nullity for Islamic Marriages

618. Capacity to contract is a condition precedent to a marriage under Islamic law. The effect of incapacity to contract renders such a marriage void. A valid Islamic marriage must meet the requisite legal capacity to do so.

619. One notices that *talaq* is the ending of the marital relationship by the instigation of the husband, involving specific, well-known phrases and procedure.

---

596. Section 11(a)(ii).
597. Section 15(2)(a).
598. *Singh v. Singh* [1971] 2 WLR 963; *Jodla v. Jodla* [1960] 1 WLR 236; *Kaur v. Singh* [1972] 1 WLR 105; *A v. J (Nullity Proceedings)* [1989] 1 F.L.R. 110.

620. A woman goes about separating from her husband by a different route, and this is by what is known in contemporary English language as nullify. Termed *Faskh*, it is annulment of the marriage contract and dissolution of the marital bond completely, as if it never happened, and this can only be done by means of the verdict of a *Qaadi* (religious judge) or a sharia ruling.[599] To annul a marriage, the wife must provide four independent witnesses acceptable to the *Qaadi*, who has the discretion to declare the evidence unacceptable.[600] In certain circumstances, an unrelated Muslim can petition a *Qaadi* to void the marriage of a Muslim couple who may not want the marriage to end.

621. The grounds for *Faskh* are irregular marriage; forbidden marriage; a marriage was contracted by non-Muslim husband who adopted Islam after marriage; the husband or wife became an apostate after marriage; or a husband is unable to consummate the marriage. For the Sunni Maliki school of jurisprudence, the wife or the husband may seek annulment of the marriage on grounds of cruelty, disease, life-threatening ailment and desertion.[601]

599. Available at: https://islamqa.info/en/answers/133859/the-difference-between-khul-talaaq-and-faskh-ways-of-en (last accessed 30 Sep. 2020).
600. Available at: https://en.wikipedia.org/wiki/Annulment (last accessed 30 Sep. 2020).
601. In these cases, the wife is required to provide two male witnesses or one male and two female witnesses or in some cases four witnesses. *See* https://en.wikipedia.org/wiki/Annulment (last accessed 30 Sep. 2020).

Chapter 2. Divorce

§1. Divorce

622. Divorce in monogamous marriages in Nigeria is still aptly embedded in the term 'dissolution of marriage' which implies a process. There is a compound ground for divorce which is 'irretrievable breakdown of marriage'. However, since there are routes embedded in one another through which such a divorce can take place, the divorce is still a matrimonial offence regime cloaked in matrimonial causes. This section discusses divorce and ancillary matters to it. The other matrimonial causes still in Nigerian law are, judicial separation, restitution of conjugal rights and jactitation of marriage. These will be discussed as well.

623. There are different routes to divorce under customary and Islamic marriages. Divorce under these systems will be dealt with after divorce under monogamous marriages.

624. Matrimonial Causes refers to the meaning as provided by section 114(1) of the Matrimonial Causes Act (MCA).[602] The law on matrimonial causes springs from item 61 of the Exclusive Legislative competence of the National Assembly as listed in the Constitution, 'the formation, annulment and dissolution of marriages other than marriages under Islamic law and Customary law, including matrimonial causes relating thereto'. The court hearing a matrimonial cause must take evidence to determine the cause. Wide powers are, however, conferred on the courts both at first instance and appellate levels. Section 82 provides for the nature of proof and treatment of evidence. On the very important provision of section 82(1) of the MCA, on evidence and standard of proof regarding matrimonial causes the Court of Appeal interpreted it in *Omotunde v. Omotunde*.[603] Thus, this part of the discourse is on matrimonial causes in respect of monogamous marriages formed under the Marriage Act.

I. Sources of Law

625. Prior to the enactment of the Matrimonial Causes Act,[604] causes arising from matrimony were adjudicated based on common law rules, case law and some pre- and post-1900 legislation and rules of England. Subsequently, there was the Marriage Ordinance, 1958.

626. Today the law on monogamous matrimonial causes is drawn mainly from Nigerian case law, the Marriage Act; Matrimonial Causes Act; the Interpretation

602. Cap M7, Laws of the Federation, 2004.
603. [2001] 9 NWLR (part 718) 252.
604. Cap M7, Laws of the Federation, 2004.

Act;[605] the Married Women's Property Act, 1881 (England);[606] the Maintenance Orders Act[607] and the Constitution of the Federal Republic of Nigeria.

627. The Court vested with original jurisdiction is the High Court. There are thirty-six States in addition to the FCT. Each State and the FCT has a High Court, while the Magistrate Court has secondary jurisdiction with respect to enforcement of Maintenance Orders.[608] Appeals lie as of right to the Court of Appeal which are Federal Courts and then to the Supreme Court.[609] Appeals can be granted with leave of Court[610] either from the court where the original jurisdiction laid or the court to which the appeal is sought on any order made ex parte; relating only to costs; made with the consent of the parties. Another instance is where a party to a proceeding for dissolution or nullity of marriage has wasted time, having had time and opportunity to appeal from any Decree *Nisi* which was subsequently made absolute and by the MCA, by effluxion of time.[611]

628. With respect to enforcement of maintenance Orders at the Magistrate Court, appeal lies from the court to the High Court on any action. This is without prejudice to any right of appeal that may have arisen based on the judgment issuing the maintenance order.[612]

629. Cases from the Commonwealth are of persuasive authority; referred to quite often and are legal authorities to the present day. The Matrimonial Causes Act is notable for vesting wide powers in the High Court. These powers extend not only, to the matrimonial causes but also to ancillary reliefs. Section 9 provides for the transfer of cases from one High Court to another in the interest of justice and provides for exercise of discretionary powers by the Court.

630. In *Eluwa v. Eluwa*[613] the Court of Appeal stated that in Nigeria, matrimonial proceedings are regulated by the Matrimonial Causes Act, 2004 and the rules thereto referred to as the Matrimonial Cause Rules, 2004. The latter has a commencement date of 1 October 1983 although both are subsequently treated as one piece of legislation and compiled as one body of law in the Laws of the Federation, 2004. Section 112(1) of the MCA provides for the Matrimonial Causes Rules which once it took effect ousted the application of the rules of Court for the time being in

605. Cap 192 LFN 1990; Cap I23 L.F.N. 2004.
606. This Act is applicable as a Statute of general application in all States of the Federation except the South West States, where it is re-enacted as State laws with little or no variation. In the core North, Islamic law applies to those who are Muslims and hold out Sharia law as their personal law. Non-northerners who live in the North would still have the Act as applicable law to their affairs.
607. Cap 215 L.F.N. 1990; Cap M1 L.F.N. 2004. An Act to Facilitate the Enforcement in Nigeria of Maintenance Orders made in England or Ireland and vice versa.
608. Sections 91 and 92 of the MCA.
609. Section 76 MCA.
610. Section 77 MCA.
611. Section 58 MCA.
612. Section 78 MCA.
613. [2013] LPELR –CA/C/180/2012.

force, in England by virtue of Order 1, rule 2 of the Rules. [614] Order 1, rule 2 on cessation of English Rules states: 'The rules of court for the time being in force in the High Court of Justice in England providing for the practice and procedure of that court in respect of divorce and matrimonial causes, shall cease to apply in Nigeria when these Rules come into force.' In *Unegbu v. Unegbu*[615] the Court of Appeal in dealing with a specific order discussed below which had no hitherto been pronounced compared the Nigerian rules with the English rules distinguishing them. The Court noted that although, the rules were not to be complied with blindly,[616] 'Rules of court, particularly in divorce proceedings which are highly technical in nature, are meant to be obeyed.'[617]

631. Section 114 of the MCA defines 'matrimonial cause' to mean:

(a) proceedings for a decree of dissolution of marriage; nullity of marriage; judicial separation; restitution of conjugal rights; or jactitation of marriage;
(b) proceedings for a declaration of the validity of the dissolution or annulment of a marriage by decree or otherwise or of a decree of judicial separation, or for a declaration of the continued operation of a decree of judicial separation, or for an order discharging a decree of judicial separation;
(c) proceedings with respect to the maintenance of a party to the proceedings, settlements, damages in respect of adultery, the custody or guardianship of infant children of the marriage or the maintenance, welfare, advancement or education of children of the marriage, being proceedings in relation to concurrent, pending or completed proceedings of a kind referred to in paragraph (a) or (b) of this subsection, including proceedings of such a kind pending at, or completed before, the commencement of this Act;
(d) any other proceedings (including proceedings with respect to the enforcement of a decree, the service of process or costs) in relation to concurrent, pending or completed proceedings of a kind referred to in paragraph (a), (b) or (c) of this subsection, including proceedings of such a kind pending at, or completed before, the commencement of this Act; or
(e) proceedings seeking leave to institute proceedings for a decree of dissolution of marriage or of judicial separation, or proceedings in relation to proceedings seeking such leave.

632. There are three primary concerns that must be first resolved before any matrimonial cause can be determined. These are jurisdiction, domicile, and appropriate court of the proceeding. When the cause is filed, then the court must ascertain the nature of the cause to determine the appropriate forum within the court for the proceedings, that is whether in open court or the judge's chamber. Where the cause is on dissolution of marriage or nullity of a purported marriage, the law is that it

614. *See also* s. 93 of the MCA providing for wider powers of enforcement of Decrees made under the Act.
615. [2004] II NWLR, (part 884) 332, 359.
616. [2004] II NWLR, (part 884) 332, 362 – Pats-Acholonu, JCA.
617. [2004] II NWLR, (part 884) 332, 359 – Mohammed, JCA.

must be heard in open court. As the Supreme Court stated in *Oviasu v. Oviasu*[618] hearing a matrimonial cause in open Court advances notions of justice, the solemnity and formalism which openness confers on the outcome of cases and more so matrimonial causes. However, where other causes are involved, the court is vested with a discretionary power on the application of the parties to hear and determine the proceedings either wholly or in part, in chambers. This power extends to the hearing of custody applications.

633. Although many decisions on the pre-1970 Act and Rules exist, the same cannot be said of the post-1970 Act and the 1983 Rules thereon. The main reason for this is the nature of matrimonial causes, the resolve to pursue the case and financial status of the parties. Many of the post-1970 cases end up at the high court where they stay unreported. The MCA provides for *forma pauperis* only with respect to remission of court fees but does not provide for services of counsel.[619] Unlike in the United Kingdom, legal aid is not readily available or immensely helpful. Quite aside from accessibility, section 9 of the Legal Aid Act[620] defines a person entitled to legal aid as someone whose income does not exceed Five Thousand Naira[621] per annum or persons granted such treatment by the President of the country. Thus, only the considerably rich who are resolute can keep pace with the time and financial outlay to litigate matrimonial causes up to the Court of Appeal and Supreme Court, for, usually, it is cases litigated up to this hierarchy of courts that they get reported.

634. In *Unegbu v. Unegbu*,[622] earlier Superior courts decisions were not available on the main subject matters – domicile and verification. The subject matter of the litigation was whether verification of the facts on a Petition was to be on the same continuous page as in the English Matrimonial Causes rule 1957.[623] The Court of Appeal had to draw insight from relevant English authorities and interpretation of a similar provision. In *Omotunde v. Omotunde*,[624] the subject was the interpretation to be given to domicile as provided in section 2(3) of the MCA. Adekeye, JCA stated: 'in section 2(3) the word domicile used gives the connotation of residence. Little wonder the learned trial Judge in his ruling … concluded (using it as residence)'.[625] This was clearly because the High Court did not have access to any earlier judgment on the subject.

618. [1973] ALL N.L.R 730.
619. Section 112(1)(g). *Forma pauperis* is a Latin term allowing a poor person to bring suit without liability for the costs of the suit.
620. Cap L9, Laws of the Federation, 2004.
621. NGN 5,000 (Naira is the Nigerian Currency and has been exchanged since 2015 at between NGN 350 to NGN 400 for USD 1).
622. [2004] 11 NWLR (part 884) 332.
623. S.1. No. 619 (L.4) incorporating the Matrimonial Causes (Amendment) Rules, 1957, S.1. No. 176 (L.2.); *see* further O.M. Stone, *Matrimonial Causes Rules*, 20(4) Mod. L. Rev. 415–417 (1957).
624. [2001] 9 NWLR (part 718) 252.
625. [2001] 9 NWLR (part 718) 252, 280.

II. Background of English Matrimonial Causes

635. The history and laws on dissolution of marriage in England have witnessed progressive stages of development.

636. The earliest stage was at 'no access to divorce' (since marriage was perceived as a sacrament); to a complex process of annulment or private bill which in turn led to an Act of Parliament, and to no fault divorce in the 1996 Act.[626] The earliest form of divorce was often at great costs in time and money. The Matrimonial Causes Act, 1857 removed litigation from Ecclesiastical Courts to Civil Courts. This advanced a model of marriage based on contract rather than sacrament. At this stage, the rights projected for dissolution of marriage were highly tilted in favour of a husband with limited or no rights to wives. The Matrimonial Causes Act, 1923 provided for adultery as sole ground of divorce for either a wife or a husband. Just like in Nigerian customary marriages and indeed marriage under the Act, adultery appeared tolerable for a man, and a wife, was required prior to the 1923 Act, to prove additional fault to adultery. The 1923 Act was further simplified by the 1937 Act. The Divorce Reform Act, 1969 was a major legislative intervention as it introduced the concept of irretrievable breakdown. Ultimately the impetus for irretrievable breakdown of the marriage as the best ground for divorce was propelled in England by the work of the Commission[627] and the Archbishop of Canterbury.[628]

637. A consideration of both works resulted in the formulation of the fundamental presumption that the aims of a good divorce law, was to buttress, rather than undermine, the stability of marriage, and when, regrettably, a marriage has irretrievably broken down, to enable the empty legal shell to be destroyed with the maximum fairness and the minimum bitterness, distress, and humiliation. In England, the consequence of the deliberations was the passing of Divorce Reform Act, 1969. The 1969 Act is significant because it abolished the old grounds of divorce replacing it with irretrievable breakdown of the marriage, but which could be established only on proof of five facts. Thus, section 1 of the Act provides: after the commencement of the Act, the sole ground on which a petition for divorce may be presented to Court by either party to a marriage shall be that the marriage has broken down irretrievably.

638. Criticisms of the Act and the sole ground of breakdown formed a series of objections; one being that the facts are the trigger for divorce rather than the irretrievable breakdown. Thus, a fact must be such that demonstrates the breakdown, and not the other way round. For, if, the breakdown is the main point then the petitioner should be given the discretion to provide the nature. An account of breakdown in this sense will certainly wear out everyone and result in a simple no-fault divorce.

---

626. Family Law Act, 1996 Cap 27.
627. Cmnd 9678 and Cmnd 3123 – Reform of the Grounds of Divorce. The Field of Choice.
628. Putting Asunder formed the report of a group appointed by the Archbishop of Canterbury in January 1964 to review the state of the law on divorce.

639. The 1970 Matrimonial Proceedings and Property Act was enacted in response to the call for legislative intervention in *Pettit v. Pettit*[629] and *Gissing v. Gissing*.[630] This was followed by the 1973 Matrimonial Causes Act. The main intervention provisions of the 1973 Act are sections 24 and 25 which respectively provides for adjustment of property rights in terms very close to section 72 of the Nigerian Act more fully discussed below. Section 25 sets out guidelines which a court should follow to do so, and was considered in more contemporary detail in *Prest v. Petrodel Resources Limited.*[631]

640. The 1973 Act repealed some major Acts such as the 1969 Act and the Matrimonial Proceedings (Polygamous Marriages) Act 1972. The 1973 Act was followed by a significant Act, the 1984, Matrimonial and Family Proceedings Act, 1984 under which the Nigerian family dispute of *Agbaje v. Agbaje*[632] was decided. This was followed by the Family Law Reform Act, 1987 and the Family Law Act, 1996. The 1996 Act contains the general principles underlying divorce law. Seen as facilitating divorce too easily, the 1996 Act appears to be in suspense with the 1973 Act remaining the main active Matrimonial Causes Act.

641. Prior to this progression, that the petitioning spouse, should be granted divorce only if the other spouse had done some matrimonial wrong was force of law. The matrimonial wrong must thus be intended. In *Gollins v. Gollins*,[633] the House of Lords found that when the petitioner husband persisted in a certain way of behaving which brought on both physical and emotional ill health on the respondent wife; that it cannot be stated in defence that his behaviour was not intended to bring on this adverse state of affairs. Thus, the absence of intention could therefore provide no defence to the petition for the dissolution of the marriage. As the House observed, it is fair that allowances are made, particularly when a condition is brought on by misfortune, but no one would now maintain that cruelty cannot be proved against such a person if his acts are sufficiently grave and really imperils the other spouse.[634]

642. It must be noted that while the 1969 Act whittled the old bars to divorce such as collusion section 17(1), section 8(1) abolished failure to comply with a decree of restitution of conjugal rights as a ground for divorce or judicial separation. Section 20 of the Matrimonial Proceedings and Property Act, 1970 now provides that no person shall after the commencement of this Act be entitled to petition the High Court or any county court for restitution of conjugal rights.

629. [1970] AC 777; [1969] UKHL 5.
630. [1970] UKHL 3; [1971] AC 886.
631. [2013] UKSC 34.
632. [2010] UKSC 13; [2010] 1 AC 628; [2010] 2 WLR 709.
633. [1964] AC 644.
634. Lord Reid in *Gollins v. Gollins* [1964] AC 644, 698.

III. Comparable Notes with Nigeria

643. Living in different households as proof of living apart perhaps demonstrates the problem with juxtaposition of laws based on acculturation. In England, it is argued that living apart is a difficult basis for proving separation for the purposes of divorce since the lower income cadre may not be in a financial position to afford different homes, in Nigeria perhaps this is the easiest aspect to accomplish. Another criticism of the basis for divorce from the English position which is the same with the Nigerian position is stated by Lowe:

> a fundamental objective of the current law is to minimize the bitterness, distress and humiliation experienced by the parties in obtaining their divorce from the system, particularly the behaviour fact, which encourages each to make allegation against the other and to portray the other in as bad a light as possible to support the petition. This provokes resentment, hostility and distress in the other spouse at a time when the couple are experiencing severe distress and unhappiness in coming to terms with the ending of their marriage. Their emotional misery is simply compounded by the legal process.[635]

644. While research shows that ground 2 on behaviour of the respondent forms the main basis for divorce in England, this is fact 3 in the Nigerian Act (section 15(2)(c)), the no-fault fact in the Nigerian Act is section 15(2)(f) and is the most used fact.[636] This is 'that the parties to the marriage have lived apart for a continuous period of at least three years immediately preceding the presentation of the petition'.

645. There are a few cases on fact 3, section 15(2)(c), of the Nigerian Act – on behaviour and the response of the other party. This seems to work on the occasional instances where the petitioner is the husband. As a result of the fluidity of Nigerian marriage framework in which adultery by a man is tolerated, husbands rarely institute petitions and when they do so, they are more likely to proceed on the fact of 'behaviour'. They are less likely to muster the patience required for the three-year wait preceding the petition. It would appear that in Nigeria, these rare cases support the position of Lowe on the washing of dirty linen and bad behaviour, would range from accusation of wickedness to witchcraft and adultery.[637]

635. Nigel Lowe, *Grounds for Divorce and Maintenance Between Former Spouses/England and Wales*, available at ceflonline.net/wp-content/uploads/England-Divorce (Last accessed 27 Feb. 2020).
636. *Okafor v. Okafor* [1976] 6 High Court of Lagos State Law Reports 1727; *Omotunde v. Omotunde* [2001] 9 NWLR (part 718) 252.
637. Nigel Lowe, *Grounds for Divorce and Maintenance Between Former Spouses/England and Wales*; *Ayangbayi v. Ayangbayi* [1979] 10–12 CCHSCJ 1; *Ibeabuchi v. Ibeabuchi* [2016] LPELR 41268 (CA); *Omotunde v. Omotunde* [2001] 9 NWLR (part 718) 252.

IV. Jurisdiction of Courts

646. Jurisdiction can be defined as the power or authority vested in a court to adjudicate on matters and enforce the outcome of its adjudication. Section 6 of the Constitution vests all judicial powers in the judiciary with all inherent powers and sanctions of a court of law. The Constitution vests power on the National Assembly to enact laws on all matters related to the formation, annulment and dissolution of marriage other than those under Islamic or Customary law. The MCA is an offshoot of this power.

647. The judicial powers vested in the Courts cover all inherent legal and equitable jurisdictions. By section 109 of the Matrimonial Causes Act, jurisdiction conferred on the High Court in matrimonial causes encompasses grant of decrees, declarations, award of damages and grant of an injunction. Injunction could be by interlocutory order or otherwise (including an injunction in aid of the enforcement of a decree), in any case in which it appears to the court to be just or convenient to do so and either unconditionally or upon such terms and conditions as the court thinks just.

648. Jurisdiction is concerned with three spheres; a delineated legal geographical space, subject matter and the individual. The first two ambits are somewhat always straight forward. In Nigeria, jurisdiction in matrimonial causes with respect to geographic space is one. The subject matter is explicitly defined by the Constitution and related legislation. It is with the last that legal theory as well as, case law has some difficulties – jurisdiction with respect to the individual, referred to as domicile.

649. The MCA vests the power to conduct matrimonial cause proceedings in the High Court of each State of the Federation and of the FCT. Curiously the Act confers jurisdiction in matrimonial matters on the High Courts of State rather than on Federal High Court, since matrimonial cause as has been noted earlier is within the exclusive legislative competence of the National Assembly. It has been argued that this is an accident of history. Other arguments include that to meet the demands of justice, it is in the public interest since the Federal High Court is in only twenty-four states of the Federation and were even fewer before now.

650. In the Supreme Court's decision of *Orker & Anor. v. Iyortyom & Ors.*[638] Okoro J.S.C. reinforced the authority of the Constitution and stated: 'It is now well settled that jurisdiction is the life wire of a Court as no Court can entertain a matter where it lacks the jurisdiction. It is also well settled that the jurisdiction of Courts in this Country is derived from the Constitution and statutes.'[639] This position was reiterated in *Inakoju, Ibadan South East & 17 Ors v. Adeleke, Dauda & Ladoja*[640]

638. [2014] 14 NWLR (Part 1428) 575, 611 B-D.
639. Referred to and espoused in the case of *Ogbuji & Others v. Amadi* [2014] LPER-34282 CA.
640. [2007] S.C. 272/2006; [2007] 2 M.J.S.C. 1.

and *Att-Gen Anambra State v. Okeke.*[641] In *Osibamowo v. Osibamowo*[642] it was decided that jurisdiction is of utmost importance and that once a proceeding raises a question on jurisdiction, the question must first be resolved before any further action can be entertained on the matter.[643] In *Omotunde v. Omotunde*[644] the Court of Appeal held that before a court finally determines a case pending before it, it has the jurisdiction to determine questions of jurisdiction, but once that is determined and the court declines jurisdiction, it is functions officio – such a decision can only be referred to an appellate court. It took the position that the right to review the earlier High Court's decision no longer inhered in a High Court of equivalent jurisdiction, and therefore could not spring from it. The question of jurisdiction extends to cases heard and determined by the Sharia Courts. Thus, in *Alhaji Ibrahim Ahmad Goronyo v. Aljahi Isa Mai Alewa Goronyo*,[645] Tanko Muhammed JCA, stated: 'The lower court thus lacked jurisdiction to entertain the appeal. It has been repeatedly held by the Supreme Court and this Court that any proceeding however well conducted, if conducted without jurisdiction is a nullity.'

651. Nigeria operates an adversarial system of justice delivery. Pleadings are its life wire. Jurisdiction is the authority by which a Court must decide matters brought before it for litigation or to take cognisance of issues presented before it in a formal way for its decision.[646]

652. Jurisdiction covers the question whether marriage exists at all[647] or it is voidable[648] to dissolution of the marriage[649] and ancillary reliefs[650] such as the grant of maintenance allowance pending dissolution of the marriage,[651] custody of the children as well as the general making of orders for separation.[652]

653. The court's jurisdiction also covers variation or modification of orders made as to maintenance, custody or settlement and in particular the court can, in relation to orders made in relation to maintenance, custody and adjustment of property, discharge the order if the party in whose favour it was made marries again or if there is any other just cause for so doing.[653] The court must, however, do so within

641. [2007] 12 NWLR (part 782) 575; The Constitution provides for the composition and appointments of the judicial officers of Courts from ss 230–296.
642. [1991]3 NWLR (part 177) 85.
643. [1991] 3 NWLR (part 177) 85, 275.
644. [2001] 9 NWLR (part 718) 252.
645. [1999] LCN/0514(CA).
646. *Sayton v. IMB Ltd.* [2002] 5 NWLR (part 760) 397, 410.
647. Section 3.
648. Section 5.
649. Section 15(2).
650. Sections 69–75.
651. *Ibid.*
652. *Ibid.*
653. Section 73(1)(j)(i). *see also* ss 70, 71 and 72 of the Matrimonial Causes Act, Cap M7.

its purview as a court of justice, exercising the discretion judiciously such as that the court might have been misled or the circumstances of the parties have so changed to warrant the variation.[654]

654. Jurisdiction for matrimonial causes is a two-part question – subject matter and personal. The Court must first ensure that the subject matter falls within its jurisdiction – original or appellate as is provided in section 1 and section 2(1) and (2) of the MCA. Section 2(2) and (3) provide for personal jurisdiction of the Court over the petitioner. Only a person domiciled in Nigeria can institute an action for matrimonial cause.

655. Once a High Court ascertains jurisdiction or the Supreme Court which is extremely rare, exercises its powers under section 22 of the Supreme Court Act as a Court of First Instance and orders maintenance, then a court of summary jurisdiction, which is stated to be a Magistrate Court can enforce it.[655]

656. It is to be noted that once maintenance is ordered by the High Court then jurisdiction, enforcement and rules relating thereto are equally conferred on Magistrate or District Courts for enforcement of the order in a summary manner.[656] Section 91 provides for the process of enforcement of such summary jurisdiction. Thus, the order for maintenance must be registered at the court of summary jurisdiction which may then enforce as though it is an order for maintenance of a deserted wife made by the court of summary jurisdiction. The enforcement must comply with the form as presented in the Third Schedule to the Act. In this case, a Court of summary jurisdiction in Nigeria is any Magistrate Court. However, the powers conferred on the Magistrate Court for this purpose does not extend to hearing or determining matrimonial causes.[657]

V. Domicile

657. The basis of personal jurisdiction in matrimonial causes is domicile. Domicile is the other half of the determination of jurisdiction and its determination is a key factor on the question whether or not a Court has the requisite jurisdiction to adjudicate a case.

658. This is reaffirmed by several cases including *Omotunde v. Omotunde.*[658] Section 2(2) and (3) provide for capacity to institute proceedings for matrimonial

654. Section 73(2) and (3).
655. Section 2(1)(b) of the Act.
656. Section 2(1)(b). *See* ss 91(1) & (2) 92 emphasised by s. 93. *See* further s. 114(2) which states 'a reference in this Act to a court having jurisdiction under this Act or exercising jurisdiction under this Act shall be deemed not to include a reference to a court having jurisdiction under this Act or exercising jurisdiction under this Act by virtue only of section 91 or 92 of this Act or the Third Schedule to this Act'.
657. Section 114(2).
658. [2001] 9 NWLR (part 718) 252.

causes. Anyone domiciled in any State of the Federation and in the FCT Abuja can institute matrimonial proceeding in the High Court of the State or any other High Court or the High Court of the FCT. It is important to note that that once domicile in any State in Nigeria is established, the petition can be brought before any State High Court whether or not the parties reside in that particular State or not.[659] Since the Court has wide discretionary powers on matrimonial causes, if the provision is being abused or put to fraudulent purposes, a court can deny jurisdiction and transfer the case.

659. The MCA by section 2(2) provides that proceedings for a decree for any named matrimonial cause; dissolution of marriage; nullity of marriage; judicial separation; restitution of conjugal rights; or jactitation of marriage may be instituted under the Act only by a person domiciled in Nigeria.[660] The facts upon which the court will make the findings about being domiciled in Nigeria are required to be stated in the petition by Order 5, Part 1, rule 3(C). The rule states that the petition must indicate the domicile or residence of the petitioner in Nigeria. As a result, sometimes residence, as was done at the High Court in *Omotunde* is treated as domicile which has been declared by the Court of Appeal as wrong.[661]

660. In a petition for dissolution of marriage or nullity of purported marriage, if the domicile of the petitioner is not established, the court will lack jurisdiction to pronounce upon the validity or otherwise of the marriage. The proceeding for matrimonial causes may be instituted only by persons who are domiciled in Nigeria.

661. The compulsory data to be completed by a petitioner in Form 6, must include particulars of the domicile of the petitioner. In *Graham Wylie v. Hajara Wylie & Anor*,[662] the petitioner, Graham Wylie of United Kingdom and specifically Northern Ireland, married to a Nigerian woman was denied a hearing of the petition as the respondent wife pleaded with the court that he was not domiciled in Nigeria for the purposes of section 2(2) and (3) of the MCA. The Court ruled that the essence of Order V, rule 3(ii and iii) was to facilitate the Court's ascertainment that indeed a petitioner was domiciled in Nigeria to engage the jurisdiction of the court. The relevant rules are:

> that the petition shall state that the Petitioner is, within the meaning of the Act, domiciled or resident, as the case may be, in Nigeria and; the facts but not the evidence by which the facts are to be proved upon which the Court shall be asked to find that the Petitioner is within the meaning of the Act, domiciled or resident, as the case may be, in Nigeria shall be stated in the petition in as concise a form as the nature of the case allows.

---

659. Section 3(3).
660. Section 7 provides for the domicile requirements of a deserted wife which is discussed below.
661. *Omotunde v. Omotunde* [2001] 9 NWLR (part 718) 252, 278.
662. Suit No. FCT/HC/PET/206/17.

662. As the Court found, the petitioner who was living in Nigeria between 2004 and 2010 had returned to the United Kingdom and settled back there. The Court held that the particulars stated showed the Petitioner's address to be in Northern Ireland and therefore, there is no way he could be said to be domiciled in Nigeria and the petition was therefore struck out for lack of jurisdiction. It is thought that the strict application of the rules would work hardship against foreign petitioners where the wives choose to obstruct a petition. It is to be preferred if the rule and the law were to take account of circumstances such as this to provide qualifications where a petitioner is a foreigner whose domicile of origin is revived on account of unforeseen circumstances as in the present case where the petitioner left Nigeria because he had lost his job. In the circumstances of the case even where the petitioner is willing to institute an action in the United Kingdom, it is very unlikely the courts there will assume jurisdiction and should they be willing, the respondent in Nigeria most likely would be unwilling to participate for various reasons. This has the propensity to frustrate the whole idea of not foisting unwilling spouses on each other.

663. The burden to prove changed or substituted domicile is on the party who asserts it. Domiciles are of three different types, origin, choice and dependency. The domicile in operation is a question of fact to be proved by evidence. A domicile of origin is presumed as the fact of the domicile of a person. Any change by choice must be proved by the party asserting it.

664. Domicile is a person's place of habitual residence. Perhaps adding habitual may be a preferred usage for the purposes of legal residence. It can also be described as a person's fixed, permanent and principal home for legal purposes.[663]

665. A person can have only one domicile at a time[664] unmarried children's domicile goes with that of their parents. In Nigeria, usually their fathers, failing that, then their mother's. Thus, domicile can be of origin acquired by birth. A married woman's domicile is dictated by her husband's domicile in Nigeria.

666. Common law jurisdictions and this applies to Nigeria, will only recognise a divorce proceedings if at least one of the parties to the petition was domiciled in the jurisdiction conducting the divorce.[665] In England, in January 1974 the well-established rule that the domicile of a wife was the same as that of her husband and changed according to any change in his domicile was eradicated from the law by the Domicile and Matrimonial Proceedings Act, 1973.[666] Lord Denning had described it as 'the last barbarous relic of a wife's servitude'.[667]

---

663. Merriam Webster [1829] – last visited 30 Nov. 2019 at https://www.merriam-webster.com.
664. *Omotunde v. Omotunde* [2001] 9 NWLR (part 718) 252.
665. *Agbaje v. Agbaje* (Nigeria); *see also Agbaje v. Agbaje* (UK) [2010] UKSC 13.
666. Section 1.
667. *Gray v. Formosa* [1963] pp. 259, 267. *See* further M.P. Thompson, *Domicile of Dependence: The Last Remnant of a Relic* 32(1) Int'l & Comp. L.Q. 237–240 (1983).

667. This rule remains in Nigeria and was again applied in *Omotunde v. Omotunde*[668] and *Ugo v. Ugo.*[669] It is not clear how it is so, considering that section 2(2) of the MCA merely states: 'Proceedings for a decree … may be instituted under this Act only by a person domiciled in Nigeria.' While section 2(3) states: 'For the avoidance of doubt it is hereby declared that a person domiciled in any State of the Federation is domiciled in Nigeria for the purposes of this Act and may institute proceedings under this Act in the High Court of any State whether or not he is domiciled in that particular State.' The use of the masculine gender in section 2(3) cannot be the basis of retention of the rule as the use of masculine gender for laws in Nigeria is a rule rather than an exception. In fact, section 15(1) specifically provides that either party to the marriage may present a petition for the dissolution of a marriage. The MCA therefore does not provide for dependent domicile.

668. Where the parties then divorce, children acquire the domicile of the party who has custody or with whom he or she lives usually. Where time is allowed or shared between parents then unmarried children acquire the domicile of the father. With regard to the latter position, there is no clear authority in Nigeria.

669. Where the marriage is void, a new domicile does not emerge for the woman or children. With voidable marriage it may be different. Upon death or divorce in Nigeria, a changed domicile arises only by choice and action.[670]

670. A petition by order V, Part 1 rule 1(3)(c) and (d) must not only indicate the particulars relating to the domicile or residence of the petitioner in Nigeria, but also, particulars of the cohabitation of the parties to the marriage.

671. It is important to note the provision of section 7(1) and (b) of the MCA on a deserted wife's deemed domicile which a wife can acquire if she was domiciled in Nigeria immediately before her marriage or immediately before the desertion or has been resident in Nigeria at the date of instituting the proceedings and has been so resident for three years prior to that time. The deserted wife's domicile by sections 7 and 81(3) has two arms, one is where the deserted wife was domiciled in Nigeria immediately before her marriage or the desertion. Thus, a deserted wife who is domicile din Nigeria either before her marriage or before her desertion is domiciled in Nigeria. The other is where the wife is resident, in Nigeria at the date of the proceedings and has so been for three years before that date. In any of the stated scenarios, the wife is taken to be domiciled in Nigeria. Section 81(3) provides for the deserted wife where the proceeding for a dissolution of marriage was conducted in a foreign country. Thus, it may be that the proceeding was instituted at the instance of a deserted wife and it resulted either in annulment or dissolution, the wife will be deemed to have been domiciled in that country at the date of the institution of the proceeding, in so far as she was so domiciled either immediately before her marriage or immediatcly after the desertion in that foreign country. The position

668. [2000] LPELR 10194; [2000] 9 NWLR (part 718) 252.
669. [2008] 5 NWLR (part1079) 1; 3 PLR/2017/328 SC.
670. *Unegbu v. Unegbu* [2004] 11 NWLR (part 884) 332.

will be the same if instead of the date of the proceeding and desertion the deserted wife had been resident in that foreign country for three years preceding the date of institution of the proceeding.[671]

672. An important judicial decision on domicile is *Omotunde v. Omotunde.*[672] The case demonstrates that Nigerian matrimonial causes may not be too far placed from an inquisitorial approach. The case first came before a High Court which struck it out for the absence of jurisdiction. The case was then re-listed before another High Court which declined to entertain it and then to the Court of Appeal.

673. At the Court of first instance, it was held that there was an absence of personal jurisdiction over the petitioner, who the court decided was not domiciled in Nigeria:

> In addition, Section 2(3) of the Act spells out which person can be said to be domiciled in Nigeria. Such a person must be domiciled in any State of the Federation i.e., in any of the current thirty-six States and the Federal Capital that make up Nigeria. Section 2(3) of the Matrimonial Causes Act does not say that a person that is domiciled outside Nigeria should be taken as domiciled in Nigeria and any contrary view to this must be wrong. In the case of the petitioner who has been consistently domiciled in the United States of America since 1993 up to the time he filed his petition on the 21st day of April, 1998, it cannot be said of him as of 21/4/98 when he was filing his petition through his learned Counsel he was domiciled in Nigeria. The petitioner having failed to comply with the condition precedent set in Section 2 of the MCA Cap 220 of 1990 is roundly incompetent to request this court to order a Decree nisi dissolving the marriage between him and the respondent.[673]

674. The pleadings at the Court of Appeal in the light of the above background, were very complicated ranging from what courts could or could not do, to the principal subject of matrimonial cause. Aside from the question of domicile, the case touches on what a court is competent to do, if, in a petition for matrimonial causes, it finds it does not have jurisdiction and also touches on evidence and proof. The principal matrimonial cause for adjudication is section 15(2)(f).[674] The parties admitted that they had lived apart for three years. However, determining the cause engaged the question whether the petitioner who is habitually resident in the United

671. This goes to recognition of proceedings resulting in decrees of annulment and dissolution of marriage made by a foreign country. *See* s. 81(2) of the Matrimonial Causes Act, Cap M7.
The Act commenced on the 17 Mar. 1970.
Section 81(9) defines foreign country to mean a country or part of a country, outside Nigeria.
672. [2001] 9 NWLR (part 718) 252.
673. *Ibid.*, 252, 280.
674. That the parties to the marriage have lived apart for a continuous period of a least three years immediately preceding the presentation of the petition.

States of America met with the requisites of domicile to present his petition in Nigeria. Furthermore, also relevant to the cause, were section 82 of the Matrimonial Causes Act[675] and Order VII, rule 1(d) of the rules thereon. Order VII, rule 1 states:

(1) The respondent or a co-respondent in proceedings instituted by petition, or a person named in a petition, may, by filing an answer:
  (a) deny a fact alleged in the petition;
  (b) state that he does not know and cannot admit the truth of a fact alleged in the petition;
  (c) allege a fact; or
  (d) admit the truth of a fact, being a fact material to proceedings, instituted by the petition, to which he is a party or in which he is entitled to intervene under subsection.

675. The specific questions of appeal were: whether a Court which finds that it has no jurisdiction, can without, a hearing of the case strikes it out, particularly where in the instant case, an application for the case to be struck out was not before the court? Whether a petition for a matrimonial cause can be determined based on an admission by any or both of the parties; in default and without proof?

676. The counsel for the appellant argued that based on jurisdiction, competence and duty, a trial court can set aside the decision of another High Court which, without jurisdiction struck out a case before it. He noted that neither party to the proceedings had applied for the case to be struck out. In addition, that a court could set aside a judgment or order granted under certain circumstances, one of which, will be an order obtained but which amounts to a nullity. The Counsel, however, argued that the court acted in error, since the petitioner was in fact domiciled in Nigeria based on the marriage certificate and place of marriage in Ekiti, Nigeria. On the implication of Order VII, rule 1(d), the petitioner argued that it is not necessary to prove an admission – as in Law what is admitted needed no further proof,[676]and that dissolution of marriage should be a painless exercise.[677]

677. On the other hand, the counsel to the respondent answered that the Supreme Court had decided in several decisions that where in the course of proceedings, there has been a fundamental defect, which affects the jurisdiction and competence of the court, the proceedings and orders, are a nullity. Given such a scenario, the court that made such order can invoke its inherent power to set same aside. However, where the case is that the court is competent, and the proceedings and order are a result of an exercise of the judge's judicial discretion, the decision is only appealable. On the

675. Section 82 is on standard of proof and provides: (1) For the purposes of this Act, a matter of fact shall be taken to be proved if it is established to the reasonable satisfaction of the court, (2) Where a provision of this Act requires the court to be satisfied of the existence of any ground or fact or as to any other matter, it shall be sufficient if the court is reasonably satisfied of the existence of that ground or fact, or as to that other matter.

676. *Ramalu v. Umunna* [1977] 5 NWLR (part 505) 321, 326.

677. *Greenfell v. Greenfell* [1978] 1 ALL NLR 561, 566; *Lasebikan v. Lasebikan* Unreported Hoy 136D'/82 of Oyo State, Nigeria delivered 07/04/83.

implication of admission of fact by a party, the respondent objected to the position of the appellant, first, on the ground that the application was oral but should be in writing and supported by affidavit evidence. Second, that although both parties admitted that they had lived apart for three years, this was not enough for a Court to consider an order for a dissolution of marriage. Proof through evidence, as far as the respondent was concerned, remained indispensable.[678]

678. The court commenced its adjudication with the question whether the court of first listing had jurisdiction to strike out the case. It answered that question in the negative. It held that the proceedings of the Court below were a nullity as the court did not have jurisdiction to strike out the case when the parties did not apply for such a relief. The Court of Appeal further stated that parties are bound by the reliefs sought from the court and the court does not have jurisdiction to grant what was not claimed. The order of striking out could not be regarded as consequential since the order applied for is a Decree *Nisi*. If a Decree *nisi* could not be ordered, then an appropriate consequential order is to overrule the application and direct parties to proceed to trial.

679. Second, the Court of Appeal held that a court does not make declarations as of right either on admissions or in default of pleadings but by proof and evidence. It referred to section 44(3) of the Matrimonial Causes Act, which states 'the court shall not grant a decree of dissolution of marriage without receiving evidence by the petitioner in support of the petition'. Third, where a jurisdictional issue being so pivotal is raised *suo motu* by the court the parties must be accorded the opportunity to respond to it.[679] Thus, as the respondent who raised the issue of domicile was not given the opportunity to address the court on it, the decision of the court amounted to a breach of fair hearing and any order based on this procedure, was a nullity.

680. On domicile, the court held that the facts upon which the Court will make its findings are required to be stated in the petition in compliance with Order 5, Part 1, rule 3. The court in determining domicile takes certain guidelines into consideration:

(i) All the facts and circumstances available to it, for the determination of domicile.
(ii) The burden of proof for a changed domicile lies on the person asserting it.
(iii) The intention to have a new domicile must be proved with perfect clearness.

681. Referring to section 2(2) of the Matrimonial Causes Act, and Order V, Part 1, rules 3(2) and (3),[680] the Court stated that section 2(3) of the MCA used the word domicile as if, it referred to residence and that such an interpretation, might have

678. *Bello v. Eweka* [1981] 1 SC 101.
679. [2001] 9 NWLR (part 718) 252, 277.
680. Rule 3(2) 'The petition shall state that the petitioner is within the meaning of the Act, domiciled or resident, as the case may be in Nigeria. Rule 3(3); the facts, but not the evidence by which the facts

informed the reasoning and decision of the High Court to strike out the case because the petitioner's habitual residence in the United States where he worked as a medical practitioner disqualified him of a Nigerian domicile. On the evidence, between 1988 and 1993, the petitioner returned to Nigeria for only ten days and also on 21 April 1998 at the time of the petition. Aside from these two occasions, he had not been in Nigeria from 1988 to 1998.

682. The Court concluded that the respondent had not proved that the petitioner had changed, abandoned or lost his domicile of origin, which is Nigeria, because he resides in the United States of America.

683. On the interpretation of reasonable satisfaction of the Court as standard of proof of evidence, provided by section 82 of the MCA, the Court stated that 'it must depend on the exercise of judicial powers and discretion of an individual judge. It however entails adducing all available evidence in support of an assertion before the Court'.[681] On the application of section 15(2)(f) the Court held that the fact of irretrievable breakdown as contained in the section, has the factor of the absence of fault, so that once the number of years of living apart has been met, there is no discretion for a court to exercise. It is mandatory to grant a decree. The Court, however, denied that it had the jurisdiction to grant the decree and ordered that the case be returned for enlisting before the High Court and assigned to another judge of the judicial division for trial.

684. Another important decision on domicile is *Sunil Kishinchand Bhojwani v. Nitu Sunil Bhojwani*[682] in which three important questions were addressed. These were domicile, jurisdiction of Nigerian courts in a matrimonial cause where another Country has assumed jurisdiction, and the registration of a foreign judgment from such a cause.

685. The petitioner was born in Singapore in 1965 while the respondent was born in Nigeria in 1963. The petitioner since 1979 had been a Company Director of the Family Business in Nigeria – directing its operations. The parties had married in England but were resident in Nigeria until 1993. In 1993 due to the political crisis then pervading the country, the respondent, and the children of the marriage, moved residence to Singapore and subsequently, to England. The petitioner (appellant at the Supreme Court), had filed for divorce in Nigeria, to which the respondent objected on the ground that both parties were not domiciled in Nigeria. The High Court ruled that it had the requisite jurisdiction to hear and determine the matter. The respondent appealed and the Court of Appeal on an examination of a complex set of documents and circumstances, overturned the decision of the High Court. The appellant again, appealed to the Supreme Court on this denial of his relationship to

are to be proved, upon which the court shall be asked to find that the petitioner is, within the meaning of the Act domiciled or resident, as the case may be, in Nigeria shall be stated in the petition as concise a form as the nature of the case allows.'

681. [2001] 9 NWLR (part 718) 252, 284.
682. [1996] 6 NWLR (part 457) 661.

Nigeria. In the meantime, the respondent who was still resident in England, petitioned for a divorce in England, to which the petitioner who was preoccupied with the litigation in Nigeria, paid little attention. The English Courts heard the petition and a Decree *Nisi* for a dissolution of the marriage was granted. The attempt to register the judgment in Nigeria was, however, being resisted by the appellant although this was not before the Supreme Court. The Supreme Court ruled that since there was a subsisting decision on the matrimonial cause by an English Court, the option open to the appellant was not with it or any other court in Nigeria, but an appeal of the subsisting decision in England. It held that delving into the subject matter of domicile was, in the circumstances, nothing but 'flogging a dead horse'. Belgore JSC who delivered the lead judgment stated: 'Our Courts are to determine issues that are live. To now delve into the issue of domicile and the consequent jurisdiction of Nigerian Courts will merely be academic.'[683] The Court further ruled that although the appellant was resisting the registration of the judgment of the English Court pursuant to Foreign Judgements (Reciprocal Enforcement) Act (Cap 112 Laws of Federation of Nigeria 1990), the subject not being before it, it could not adjudicate on it. It noted *obiter*, that the Court of Appeal in overturning the decision of the High Court had failed to pay adequate scrutiny to the evidence which showed that it was the political crisis in Nigeria in 1993 that removed the respondent from Nigeria.

686. There are five principal matrimonial causes to which there are related ancillary causes discussed below.

§2. GROUNDS FOR DISSOLUTION OF MARRIAGE

687. Section 15 of the MCA is the principal provision for dissolution of marriage and is titled, 'Grounds for dissolution of marriage'. By subsection (1) 'a petition under the Act by a party to a marriage for a decree of dissolution of the marriage may be presented to the court by either party to the marriage upon the ground that the marriage has broken down irretrievably' and (2) 'The court hearing a petition for a decree of dissolution of a marriage shall hold the marriage to have broken down irretrievably if, but only if, the petitioner satisfies the court of one or more of the following facts … .' The facts are discussed below.

688. The theoretical sole ground for dissolution of marriage in Nigeria is irretrievable breakdown of the marriage. Dissolution of marriage in Nigeria, is more akin to the law of the English Divorce Reform Act, 1969, but not quite like the English MCA, 1973. While in theory all the Acts appear to make irretrievable breakdown the sole ground of dissolution of marriage, the role of proof and the burden of proof creates some practical differences. For instance, in the first two that is, the DRA 1969 and the Nigerian Act, the Court commences with a presumption that the marriage has broken down irretrievably otherwise the petitioner will not be in

683. *Bhojwani v. Bhojwani* [1996] 6 NWLR (part 457) 661, 666.

court.[684] The presumption is then rebutted if the petitioner cannot prove any of the facts in the UK 1969 Act, section 2(1) and in Nigeria, section 15(2). In the MCA 1973, the Court is invited to enquire into the facts first and then unless it is satisfied on all the evidence that the marriage has not broken down, irretrievably, it shall … grant a decree of divorce.[685] Thus, for the MCA 1973 the facts determine the breakdown of the marriage. What the MCA 1973 actually does is to give both parties a chance to address their marriage both internally and extrinsically. The Nigerian Act and the 1969 United Kingdom Act place all the burden of proof on the petitioner. The burden is a hard one and totally unsuitable for a matrimonial enquiry. This is despite the consensual fact of dissolution for the United Kingdom, two years and Nigeria, three years. The MCA, 1973 is thus an improved regime of matrimonial cause disputation.

689. Although the MCA contains only one ground for the dissolution of marriage – irretrievable breakdown, judicial pronouncements and overall examination of the Act reveal that this is far from the position. The position is in fact the other way round as the petitioner must pass through the proverbial Carmel's eye to satisfy the Court, through one of the stated grounds that the marriage has in fact broken down because of the fact on which the petition or cross-petition is based. In many sections of the Act and rules that the intendment is to find a fault, slips from the wordings. For instance, courts have stated a few times that fault needs to be found in order for the court to trigger certain provisions of the Act such as bars to the petition and maintenance and its quantum. Commencing from the title of the dissolution provision, section 15 is titled in the plural, rather than singular as 'grounds'. Another section is 55, which provides that 'save where other provision in that behalf is made by the Act, the court upon being satisfied of the existence of **any ground** in respect of which relief is sought shall make the appropriate decree'. No reference is made to irretrievable breakdown rather the reference is to the grounds. Section 53(1) also states that a 'decree may be made or refused under this part of this Act by reason of facts and circumstances not-withstanding that those facts and circumstances, or some of them, took place before the commencement of this Act or outside Nigeria'. Another clue is from the Rules by which Order V, Part 1, rule 1(3)(g) provides: 'the fact but not the evidence by which the facts are to be proved, relied on as constituting the ground or each ground specified in the petition, stating, if more than one ground is so specified, the facts relating to each ground, as far as practicable, separately'. The bars to a petition also make it clear that the legal framework is more inclined to keeping spouses together despite the prevailing circumstances between the spouses. Aside from this, there is also the provision on maintenance and adjustment of property rights which empower the court to keep the parties together even when a petition has been heard and the parties cannot be reconciled.[686]

684. DRA, s. 1; MCA, s. 15(1).
685. Section 1(4).
686. Section 75(1) & (2).

690. When these provisions are placed side by side with the pronouncements and language of the courts as earlier demonstrated Nigerian law is a matrimonial offence regime in practice and indeed, in letters.

691. When a petition is filed it is mandatory for the judge to attempt a reconciliation of the parties.

I. Conciliator/Reconciliation

692. It is mandatory for a High Court before which a petition is filed to engage the parties in conciliation and reconciliation either the judge, alone, with the parties or with their counsels. The Court may also engage a marriage person with experience or training in marriage conciliation to make these efforts.

693. Conciliation aims at placating parties and stopping the anger between the parties. Reconciliation is the restoration of friendly relations between the parties. Conciliation has legal utility as it aids the court in arriving at more efficient outcomes. The Matrimonial Causes Act makes reconciliation a duty for the matrimonial causes process. Section 11(c) and section 14 provide for a marriage conciliator but generally reconciliation is used in the Act.

694. As a conservative society, reconciliation of couples is perceived as a duty in all marriages. On occasions this approach has gone awry with the parties harming each other. All the hierarchy of courts work through reconciling the parties. In almost all of the cases reaching the Supreme Court, the courts would make no orders as to cost and state emphatically that this was to aid the spirit of reconciliation. Indeed, the Court of Appeal has held in *Ahmad Moktar Jabre v. Mrs Dorra Jabre* that the matrimonial cause for the decree of restitution of conjugal rights, as far as Nigerian jurisprudence is concerned, is aimed at reconciling the parties.[687] A Certificate is required by Order II, rule 3, to be filed attesting that efforts had been made at reconciling the parties as part of the petition.

695. The MCA provides details and guidance for a formal process and scheme for reconciliation.[688] A judge who has acted as a conciliator for the parties must recluse himself from the proceeding unless the parties request him to continue with the proceedings.[689] Where a marriage conciliator acts as such, then he must be bound to secrecy in a formal way by oath.[690] A conciliator so engaged shall enter, make or subscribe to secrecy by affidavit, an oath or affirmation of secrecy as is prescribed in the Second schedule to the Act. Information or interaction received at the

687. [1999] 3 *NWLR* (Pt. 596) 606 at 617; [1999] LPELR. 8133; [1999] LCN/0622 (CA). Section 47 of the MCA provides for the ground for the decree of restitution of conjugal rights.
688. Sections 11–14 of the Matrimonial Causes Act, Cap M7, 2004. Additional provisions are contained in ss 17 and 30(4).
689. Section 12.
690. Section 14.

stage of conciliation or in the course of reconciliation shall not form part of the proceedings and is inadmissible as evidence in any Court for whatever reasons or purposes. The form of Oath or Affirmation by the marriage conciliator is to be found in the Second Schedule. It bounds the conciliator not to disclose information received in that capacity except in so far as it facilitates the proper discharge of the function of a marriage conciliator.

II. The Legal Framework

696. The provisions for reconciliation and the role of the court are contained in sections 11–14 MCA and Order II of the Rules. Section 11 enjoins a court to facilitate reconciliation where there is an inclination that from the conduct of the parties and the proceedings these could be possible but not where the proceedings are of such a nature that it would not be appropriate to do so. Where the case is inappropriate, there will still be required, a Certificate to that effect as filed as part of the petition indicating that the proceedings was of such a nature that reconciliation could not be broached.

697. The court is empowered to adjourn proceedings for the purpose of facilitating reconciliation. Where after fourteen days, the parties wish or one of them wishes the proceedings to continue then the court is to resume hearing. The case may also be transferred to another judge as may be appropriate.

698. Section 12 is important as resumption of hearing and the exercise of discretion to transfer to another judge applies when it is the judge before whom the petition is filed, that has acted as a conciliator. Where a judge has acted as conciliator under section 11(1)(b) of the Act, but the attempt to effect a reconciliation has failed, the judge shall not, except at the request of the parties to the proceedings, continue to hear the proceedings, or determine the proceedings and in the absence of such a request the proceedings shall be dealt with another judge. Thus, the judge must at the minimum alert the parties as to their rights and enquire of the parties whether they would wish the case to proceed before the court or another court.

699. Where a Decree *nisi* has been ordered, it may be rescinded by the Court where the parties are subsequently reconciled.[691] Further provisions relating to the place and function of reconciliation in the proceedings for a matrimonial cause and in particular, dissolution of marriage are contained in sections 17 and 30(4) of the Act.

700. Order II, rule 2 requires that a petition under section 15(2)(a–g) presented by a solicitor must also have a Certificate, entered or written in the petition or document and signed personally by the Solicitor. This certificate has a format in accordance with **Form 3**, or **Form 3A** (whichever is appropriate) and has to be entered

691. Section 60 of the MCA.

or written rather than attached. This presumably aims at 'the continuity of the documents' rather than as an attachment. Thus, the certificate ought to follow the approach approved by the Court regarding Verification and form a continuous part of the petition. **Form 3** obliges the legal practitioner or his associate when participating in a matrimonial cause to sign and attest to personal knowledge that efforts at reconciliation have taken place, while **Form 3A** envisages impersonal and indirect involvement such as where one of the parties is out of the State or jurisdiction where the petition is being heard. In such a case the legal practitioner representing the party within the State or jurisdiction must get a legal practitioner who is outside the jurisdiction of the hearing and where one of the parties is, to conduct the requirement of conciliation and the former must attest to it as in **Form 3A**. **Evidence and Proof**.

701. The court hearing a matrimonial cause must take evidence to determine the cause. Wide powers are, however, conferred on the courts both at first instance and appellate levels. Section 82 of the MCA provides for the standard, nature of proof and treatment of evidence. The section provides:

(1) For the purposes of this Act, a matter of fact shall be taken to be proved if it is established to the reasonable satisfaction of the court.
(2) Where a provision of this Act requires the court to be satisfied of the existence of any ground or fact or as to any other matter, it shall be sufficient if the court is reasonably satisfied of the existence of that ground or fact, or as to that other matter.

702. In *Oviasu v. Oviasu,*[692] the Supreme Court stated that the section is clear enough and can be adequately catered to utilising construction under known and settled principles or canons of construction. In *Omotunde v. Omotunde*[693] the Court of Appeal stated that 'what is reasonable satisfaction of the court is difficult to define. There is no kind of blanket descriptions for same either, but it must depend on the exercise of judicial powers and discretion of the individual judge. It however entails adducing all available evidence in support of an assertion before the court'.[694]

703. In *Oviasu v. Oviasu,*[695] the Supreme Court also rejected the position that the burden of proof for adultery in England is the same as in England, asserting that in Nigeria it is a mere balance of probabilities.

704. The statement underlies family law in Nigeria. Yet certainty in this all-important area of the law must not be left at an aspirational level but must be a policy position. Exercise of discretion in law has long been viewed from the prism

692. [1973] 11 SC 315.
693. [2001] 9 NWLR (part 718) 252.
694. *Ibid.*, 252, 284.
695. [1973] 11 SC 315.

of law and fact. The assessment of the facts before the Court is guided not by the whims and caprices of the judge but by law.

705. Where a discretionary power is vested in Courts on the questions of facts, there must be guidelines on how those facts are to be evaluated, to determine how to apply the law. Thus, the conduct of the parties, rules of evidence, etc. That the discretionary powers vested in the courts are as to facts and not law have been reiterated in *Eluwa v. Eluwa.*[696] At the High Court evaluation of facts is a critical aspect of justice delivery where the parties, witnesses and documents are physically examined and evaluated. Their assessment is taken to be most persuasive and, on this account, the higher courts have consistently stated that interfering with the decision reached by the High Court is mostly on point of law. Thus, a matter of fact shall be taken to be proof if it is established to the reasonable satisfaction of the Court.[697]

706. Wide discretion also exists on ordering of maintenance and custody despite failure of principal relief heard and determined on merit.[698] Section 10 of the MCA enjoins all courts having jurisdiction under the Act severally, to act in aid of, and be auxiliary to one another in all matters under the Act. While sections 25 as 57, allows the Court a discretion not to make a decree absolute until satisfied with the arrangements in the first case for the respondent and in the second for the children of the marriage yet to attain the age of 16 years. Section 105 confers on the court discretionary powers in the nature of a garnishee or *Mareva* order to facilitate execution of court orders and avoid the frustration of its orders where one party attempts to deal with a property in order to avoid the judgment of the Court.

III. Burden of Proof

707. A petitioner must prove the case for the matrimonial cause. A judgment in default is unknown in matrimonial causes. Admission by the parties makes the task of taking and proving evidence easier but does not obviate the duty of proof.[699] Thus, in *Omotunde v. Omotunde*,[700] Adekeye, JCA stated:

> As regards the admission on the face of the pleadings of the parties. An admission pursuant to section 19 of the Evidence Act[701] is a statement oral or documentary which suggests any inference as to any fact in issue or relevant fact, and which is made by any of the persons, and in the circumstances … It is trite also that averments contained in pleadings are no evidence – so that the court

696. [2013] LPELR – 22120 (CA).
697. Section 82.
698. Section 75(2).
699. *Omotunde v. Omotunde* [2001] 9 NWLR (part 718) 252, 276; *Ibeawuchi v. Ibeawuchi* [1974] UILR (part 1) 67; *Olowu v. Olowu* Suit No. AB/51/7/OF 10/04/1973.
700. [2001] 9 NWLR (part 718) 252.
701. Cap 117, Laws of the Federation, 1990 now s. 20, Evidence Act, 2011 which is yet to be a part of the collection of laws.

has to take evidence to support such averments in order to do substantial justice to the parties. By virtue of sections 135, 136 and 137 of the Evidence Act […] the onus placed upon the plaintiff is to establish his case by credible, satisfactory and convincing evidence based on the pleadings by preponderance of evidence of probability. Pleading is the life wire of the proceeding in our adversarial system of civil jurisprudence – the main function of which is to focus with much certainty as far as is possible on the various matters actually in dispute amongst the parties and those in which there is agreement between the parties by avoiding element of surprise being sprung on the opposite party. […] It is embodied in the Uniform High Court (Civil Procedure) Rules adopted by each State, that pleading shall contain only statement of material facts in a summary form on which parties rely for his claim and defence and not evidence by which they are to be proved.[702]

708. Section 44(3) of the MCA provides that the Court shall not grant a decree of dissolution of marriage without receiving evidence from the petitioner in support of the petition. The burden to prove in a matrimonial proceeding is on the petitioner.[703] The respondent also needs not defend the petition although service of the defendant must be effected and proved. If the respondent does answer the petition, there is a duty to cross-examine and the Courts have consistently held that failure to do so may prove perilous to the respondent's case.[704] In *Amadi v. Nwosu*[705] the Supreme Court stated: 'It is a settled principle of law, that where an adversary or a witness called by him testifies on a material fact in controversy in a case, the other party should, if he does not accept the witness's testimony as true, cross-examine him on that fact, or at least show that he does not accept the evidence as true,. Where, as in this case, he fails to do either, a Court can take his silence as an acceptance that the party does not dispute the facts.'[706]

709. It will be noted that the court states that the Nigerian system is 'adversarial system of civil jurisprudence' whereas in *Prest v. Petrodel Resources Limited,*[707] Lord Sumption states that the United Kingdom system is more of an inquisitorial than adversarial system. An inquisitorial system is a legal system in which the court, or a part of the court, is actively involved in investigating the facts of the case. This is distinct from an adversarial system, in which the role of the court is primarily that of an impartial referee between the prosecution and the defence.

---

702. [2001] 9 NWLR (part 718) 252, 276.
703. Sections 131, 132, 133, 134 and 136 of the Evidence Act, 2011 has been held to apply. *See* further, *Damulak v. Damulak* [2004] 8 NWLR (part 874) 151; *Nanna v. Nnanna* [2006] 3 NWLR (part 966) 1; *Ibrahim v. Ibrahim* [2007] 1 NWLR (part 1015) 383; *Mueller v. Mueller* [2006] 6 NWLR (part 977) 627.
704. *Uzokwe v. Uzokwe* [2016] LPELR 40945.
705. [1992] 5 NWLR (part 241) 273.
706. *Uzokwe v. Uzokwe* [2016] LPELR 40945 at p. 16.
707. [2013] UKSC 34.

710. In *Prest* the Court stated that it is not enough to suggest that where a party was unwilling to proffer evidence or indeed to appear in court for cross-examination as did happen in *Prest* the court is entitled to make wide presumptions, converting open-ended speculation into findings of fact.[708] While it is true that in ordinary civil cases, the concept of burden of proof, was a main factor which inhibits the drawing of adverse inferences from the absence of evidence or disclosure, this approach cannot be adopted and applied in the same way in relation to proceedings such as in *Prest*, for matrimonial causes is more of an inquisitorial than adversarial proceeding.

711. Adopting the view of Lord Lowry in *R. v. Inland Revenue Commissioners, Ex p. TC Coombs & Co.*,[709] with this slight modification, Lord Sumption stated:

> In our legal system generally, the silence of one party in the face of the other party's evidence may convert that evidence into proof in relation to matters which are, or are likely to be, within the knowledge of the silent party and about which that party could be expected to give evidence. Thus, depending on the circumstances, a prima facie case may become a strong or even an overwhelming case. But, if the silent party's failure to give evidence (or to give the necessary evidence) can be credibly explained, even if not entirely justified, the effect of his silence in favour of the other party may be either reduced or nullified.[710]

712. Although Nigerian civil system is adversarial, and the courts, in principle, have stated often that matrimonial causes is based on the same system, the practical approach of the courts and the provisions of the MCA are inspired by, and evince an inquisitorial system. This latter approach is to be preferred.

713. An adversarial system provides fair play in matrilinies but not in patrilinies. An inquisitorial system on matrimonial causes, gives women and children a fair space in a patrilineal culture.

IV. Petition for Dissolution of Marriage Within Two Years of Marriage

714. The MCA as with similar common-wealth provisions on the subject, forbids dissolution of marriage before the expiration of two years of its celebration.

715. However, in certain circumstances, the court can determine such petition and grant a decree of dissolution of marriage. Such a petition can only be entertained with leave of court.[711] The provision is circumscribed though, by section

708. [2013] UKSC 34, para. 44. *See* British Railways Board *v.* Herrington for the views of Lord Diplock which appeared to support the Nigerian position. [1972] AC, 877, 930–931.
709. [1991] 2 AC 283, 300.
710. [2013] UKSC 34, para. 44.
711. Section 30(1) of the MCA.

30(3) which provides the ground upon which the court will grant leave. The court is to grant leave before the expiration of two years only where, if it fails to do so, exceptional hardship will befall the applicant or petitioner. The other appropriate instance for that discretion is in cases involving exceptional depravity on the part of the other spouse.

716. There are factors the court must consider in reaching a decision whether to grant leave. Section 30(4) enjoins courts to pay regard to the interests of any children of the marriage and the probability of reconciliation between the parties within the two-year period. Section 30(5) and (6) provide for the exercise of court's discretion on events which may prove that a leave granted by the court was on misrepresentation or concealment of vital, or relevant facts or information. The court on realising this state of affairs may either adjourn proceedings or dismiss same. Section 30(8) makes provision for petition on facts that may have arisen within the two-year period even where leave was granted or not granted.

717. The provisions on limitation of time do not apply to petitions based on wilful refusal to consummate, adultery and respondent's bad or intolerable behaviour.

V. Irretrievable Breakdown

718. The MCA states that the ground for dissolution of marriage is irretrievable breakdown. Section 15(1) provides that a petition under the Act by a party to a marriage for a decree of dissolution of the marriage may be presented to the court by either party to the marriage upon the ground that the marriage has broken down irretrievably. The Act confers wide discretion on the court to assess whether or not the marriage has in fact, broken down. In real terms, the enquiry is as to whether one of the parties is at fault and blame to be apportioned accordingly. That this is the case is clear on closer examination of the provisions for reconciliation and penalties for third-party interference. The final arbiter in the question of whether or not the marriage has broken down is the judge. In the case of the English MCA, 1973, the latter position is the same – the judge is the final arbiter of whether or not the marriage has broken down irretrievably. However, there is a crucial difference in the approach of irretrievable breakdown. In the MCA, 1973, the parties are more in control of the relationship and unless the Court finds that the relationship has not broken down irretrievably, it is not to intervene. In this case, the court assesses when the State will support a matrimonial cause. It examines the content and relationship of the parties to it. There is only one no-fault fact in the Nigerian MCA, and that is section 15(2)(f).

719. Section 15(2) of the MCA provides that the court hearing a decree of dissolution of marriage shall hold the marriage to have broken down irretrievably if, but only if, the petitioner satisfies the court of one or more of the following facts:

(a) that the respondent has wilfully and persistently refused to consummate the marriage;

(b) that since the marriage the Respondent has committed adultery and the petitioner finds it intolerable to live with the respondent;
(c) that since the marriage the respondent has behaved in such a way that the petitioner cannot reasonably be expected to live with the respondent;
(d) that the respondent has deserted the petitioner for a continuous period of at least one year immediately preceding the presentation of the petition;
(e) that the parties to the marriage have lived apart for a continuous period of at least two years immediately preceding the presentation of the petition and the respondent does not object to a decree being granted;
(f) that the parties to the marriage have lived apart for a continuous period of at least three years immediately preceding the presentation of the petition;
(g) that the other party to the marriage has, for a period of not less than one year failed to comply with a decree or restitution of conjugal rights made under this Act;
(h) that the other party to the marriage has been absent from the petitioner for such time and in such circumstances as to provide reasonable grounds for presuming that he or she is dead.

720. It is to be noted that while the Nigerian Act has its wording in the positive, both the English DRA, 1969 and MCA, 1973 have their respective sections dealing with dissolution in the negative. Thus section 1(2) of the latter provides that the court hearing a petition for divorce shall not hold the marriage to have broken down irretrievably 'unless the petitioner satisfies the court of one or more of the following facts, that is to say … '. This is not much different from the earlier Act which by section 2(1) provides, following section 1, on irretrievable breakdown: 'The court hearing a petition for divorce shall not hold the marriage to have broken down irretrievably, unless the petitioner satisfies the court of one or more of the following facts … .'

721. While both jurisdictions could be said to still hold on to matrimonial offence regimes, one can say more so, surprisingly, is the English jurisdiction. To take an example, in *Okafor v. Okafor*,[712] although both the petition and cross-petition were not fully proved, the Court on the provisions of the Nigerian provision still granted a Decree *nisi* on the evaluation of the whole circumstances of the case.

722. The following are the facts which must be proved to sustain a claim of irretrievable breakdown of marriage. Issues related to the facts are discussed under each head.

VI. Wilful and Persistent Refusal to Consummate the Marriage: 15(2)(a)

723. The court must hold the marriage to have broken down irretrievably if the petitioner is able to satisfy it, that there is a case of wilful and persistent refusal to

712. [1976] 6 High Court of Lagos State Law Reports 1727.

consummate the marriage. Legal consummation means full intercourse – it must be ordinary and complete. It would, however, not matter whether there is satisfaction as it is not the quality of sexual intercourse but the action of intercourse that matters. Wilful refusal to consummate may be established where a party ought to facilitate a ceremony for consummation and fails to do so. Wilful refusal implies subjective and objective positions. There must be no just cause for the refusal. Thus, the subjective position must implicate that the party refusing is not neglecting to consummate but is intent on not consummating.

724. The wilful and persistent refusal must be on-going as at the time of filing of the petition. Thus, section 21 provides: 'The court shall not find that a respondent has wilfully and persistently refused to consummate the marriage unless the court is satisfied that, as at the commencement of the hearing of the petition, the marriage had not been consummated.' This is a ground of nullity for English MCR, 1973. The relevant section 12(b) states that the marriage shall be voidable only, if the marriage has not been consummated owing to the wilful refusal of the respondent to consummate it.[713] That the marriage is only voidable is also to be preferred.

725. The bond between the couple must be shown to have broken down.[714] The marriage between the parties must be shown to have broken down.[715] These were the decisions taken in *Ochei v. Ochei*;[716] *Oghenevbede v. Oghenevbede.*[717] In *Okafor v. Okafor*[718] the Court noted that the parties had met the facts listed for irretrievable breakdown of marriage and granted a Decree *Nisi* subject to the provisions for decree absolute which is based on effluxion of time.

726. The restriction not to petition for a divorce in the first two years of marriage does not apply to this head of fact of irretrievable breakdown. Thus, section 30 provides that proceedings for a decree of dissolution of marriage shall not be instituted within two years after the date of the marriage except by the leave of the court but not with respect to wilful and persistent refusal,[719] adultery and intolerability by the petitioner,[720] and behaviour based on stated instances under section 16(1), or to the institution of proceedings for a decree of dissolution of marriage by way of cross-proceedings.

713. The guidelines for granting a decree of nullity are contained in s. 13 of the Act and includes the acquiescence of the petitioner.
714. *Ladipo v. Ladipo* [1980] FNLR 179.
715. *Ibid.*
716. [1973] East Central State of Nigeria Law Report 623.
717. [1971] 3(1) University of Ife Law Report 104.
718. [1976] 6 High Court of Lagos State Law Reports 1727.
719. Section 15(2)(a).
720. Section 15(2)(b).

VII. Respondent's Adultery and Its Intolerability by the Petitioner: 15(2)(b)

727. Adultery has been defined as consensual intercourse between two persons of opposite sexes, at least one of whom is married to a person other than the one with whom the intercourse is had, and since the celebration of the marriage. Thus, to establish adultery, there must be sexual intercourse, the sexual intercourse must be voluntary and at least one of the parties must be married. Adultery requires physical evidence of sexual intercourse between the parties that are alleged to be in the adulterous relationship.

728. In *Ochei v. Ochei*[721] the Court stated that adultery is difficult to prove and that there are two aspects to its proof. First, is the proof of cohabitation for the purpose of the adulterous act with a specific individual and then, the opportunity for the act. There might be a general cohabitation or tendency to adultery which does not attach to any particular individual but when a particular person is cited it is necessary to ensure that such act did take place with the party and the standard of proof for the act with a particular individual is very high. The evidence should go farther and show general cohabitation with that particular individual or else prove strong inclination of that individual and the petitioner to commit adultery and opportunity for them to commit the alleged adultery. The Court concluded:

> When these are established the Court may then as a matter of inference, find that the petitioner has committed adultery with the party cited. The evidence against the party cited in this case definitely fell below the standard required in these type of cases. No doubt considerable suspicion may attach to the party cited but that is not proof of his adultery with the petitioner. On the issue of adultery I have to observe that it may be desirable but that it is not even necessary to give the name of or prove the person with whom the alleged adultery was committed.[722]

729. On the evidence, the court held that while there was a general cohabitation between the petitioner with some person or persons there was no proof that it was with the person cited. It is to be noted that in the judgment it was stated that the standard of proof for adultery in a matrimonial proceeding is as strict as in a criminal case. The petitioner is therefore put to the strictest proof of not only the adultery, but of the person cited. The onus to prove adultery lies on the party who alleges it.

730. Proof of adultery is not enough. The petitioner must prove that he or she has found it intolerable to continue living with the respondent following the adultery.[723] This was reiterated in *Ochei v. Ochei.*[724] The courts have taken judicial

721. [1973] East Central State of Nigeria law Report 623.
722. *Ochei v. Ochei* [1973] East Central State of Nigeria law Report 623, 628; *Ibeabuchi v. Ibeabuchi* [2016] LPELR 41268. *Per* Abiru, J.C.A. (P. 32, Paras. C-E).
723. This is subject to s. 28 on the petitioner's adultery and or condoning of same by the respondent. The provisions are usually referred to as discretionary bars to dissolution of marriage.

notice of the fact that Nigerian wives would normally tolerate adultery on the part of husbands.[725] Under customary law marriage norms, adultery *simplicita* is sufficient ground for a man to divorce his wife but not vice versa.

731. The template of the Nigerian provision on adultery and damages must be analysed from the patriarchal socio-legal context where usually, adultery is a sin of the wife – the alleged adultery is by the wife with another male. This is why the fact of the adultery is not the issue but its intolerability. It is a husband who is likely to be intolerant towards adultery and therefore, the focal point of the action is irretrievable breakdown, a petition to which the wife is unlikely to respond.

732. In English law adultery became a ground for providing evidence of the irretrievable breakdown of marriage starting from the DRA, 1969 but successful litigation may make the petitioner to receive damages which was not punitive or exemplary. In the MCA, 1973 it became one of the facts for proving irretrievable breakdown without payment of damages but with the 1996 Act all references to adultery were removed.

VIII. Standard of Proof for Adultery

733. The standard of proof necessary to establish adultery is as provided in section 82 of the MCA. According to the Court in *Ahmad Moktar Jabre v. Mrs Dorra Jabre*,[726] 'the standard of proof required in ... Section 82(1) of the Matrimonial Causes Act 1970 ... is proof upon the establishment of the fact to the reasonable satisfaction of the court'. This excludes a prima facie proof and requires reasonable satisfaction upon evidence adduced in court. Section 134 of the Evidence Act provides for preponderance of probabilities.

734. The discretion vested in the Court is wide. However, the proof of adultery is a question of fact not law. The standard is one on which the Courts differ slightly but there is one common ground, the proof is high, certainly above ordinary civil standard of proof. This standard is reasonable and objective. It is aimed at ensuring that the person alleged to be the adulterer is indeed, one. This is more so when the courts note that adultery is common particularly with the male folk and the provision itself adds the caveat that the petitioner must not only prove the adultery but must find the adultery so intolerable to make living with the respondent intolerable. In *Ochei v. Ochei*[727] for instance, the Court noted that the petitioner in spite of the allegation of the adultery was willing to have his wife back and that it was the wife –respondent that was obdurate. In *Oviasu v. Oviasu*[728] and *Oke v. Oke*[729] the Court

724. [1973] East Central State of Nigeria Law Reports 623; *see also Angelina Ijenwa Okafor v. Samuel Nduka Okafor* [1970] Suit No. 0/6D/71 (Unreported).
725. Karibi-Whyte in *Adaku Amadi v. Nwosu* [1992] 5 NWLR 273.
726. [1999] LCN/0622 (CA).
727. [1973] East Central State of Nigeria law Report 623.
728. [1973] ALL N.L.R 730.
729. [1972] 2 University of Ibadan Law Report 124.

held that the standard of proof was one of balance of probability but in *Opajobi v. Opajobi*[730] it was held that the standard of proof for adultery was a high one and beyond reasonable doubt almost as high as is applicable in criminal cases.[731] In *Oviasu v. Oviasu.*[732] the appeal was based on the decision of the Benin High Court in which the appellant-petitioner brought a petition for the dissolution of her marriage to the respondent on three grounds namely:

(i) Adultery by the first respondent and co-respondent and other women.
(ii) Cruelty.
(iii) Desertion.

735. The learned judge in his judgment dissolved the marriage on the ground of desertion by the petitioner rather than from an answer from the respondent. The main issues that arose in the course of proceedings are that:

(1) Counsels to both parties did not know of the existence of the MCA-then MCD 1970, and were given leave by the Court to reformulate the petition, file supplemental petition and answer, inserting the ground that the marriage had broken down irretrievably.
(2) In the course of proceedings, the Counsel to the petitioner pointed out that the case was heard in chambers at the High Court and that neither party had requested or applied for this.
(3) The trial judge noted that the standard for proof of adultery in Nigeria and England is different.

736. At the Supreme Court, citing *Bastable v. Bastable*,[733] it was held that in England proof of adultery was a criminal standard whereas in Nigeria, it is the civil standard of preponderance of evidence. The Supreme Court in addition, rejected reference to the rule of English decisions as authorities in construing provisions of the Nigerian law dealing with standard proof.

737. In a more recent case, the Court of Appeal in *Ibeabuchi v. Ibeabuchi*[734] set out some conditions.[735] As the court noted, it is axiomatic that adultery is essentially an act which can rarely be proved by direct evidence. It is matter of inference and circumstances. Certain conditions are contemplated for adultery to be inferred:

(i) Evidence of disposition and opportunity for sexual intercourse with a person other than the spouse.

730. [1980] Federation of Nigeria Law Report 217.
731. *See also Okala v. Okala* [1973] 3 East Central State Law Report 67.
732. [1973] ALL N.L.R 730.
733. [1968] 3 All E.R. 701.
734. [2016] LPELR 41268 (CA).
735. Habeeb Abiru JCA, [2016] LPELR 41268 (CA).

(ii) General cohabitation– where it is established that there is a state of general cohabitation between a man and a woman, adultery is presumed between them.
(iii) Confession and admission of adultery.
(iv) Entry in register of birth – entry of birth by the wife which omits the – name of the child's father or simply gives a name other than the husband amounts to an admission of adultery.
(v) Frequent visits to hotels.[736]

IX. Adultery and the Party Cited

738. The MCR defines a co-respondent to mean a party to proceedings who is specified in the petition instituting the proceedings, as a person with whom the respondent is alleged to have committed adultery. However, judicial pronouncement indicate that it is only when damage is sought from the other party to the adultery that the person is joined in the petition as a co-respondent otherwise, such a party is to be cited and no more.

739. As was indicated in *Ochei v. Ochei,*[737] the name of the alleged person with whom adultery was committed must be added to the Suit as 'A.B. cited'. Oputa J.,[738] stated that such a party is not usually referred to as a co-respondent … but as the party or the person cited.[739] There are good reasons for this approach. The first is that the primary interest of the law with matrimonial causes is the principal cause of action to which is added the interest of the law expressed in either preserving the marriage or formalising its irretrievable breakdown. To this extent, adultery in itself, in the Nigerian law is not a fact of irretrievable breakdown, it is the petitioner's intolerability of it that is. There are also secondary issues that impede adultery as a fact of breakdown when the bars are considered. If the third party is joined, another disadvantage is that it inhibits reconciliation of the parties which is prioritised by the Law. Thus, it can be deduced that the law does not contemplate the third party as a necessary actor in the proceeding to warrant being joined as a co-respondent as a matter of course. The focus is on the petitioner and the response to the action of the respondent. However, also relevant to the provisions on adultery, is the constitutional provision of fundamental human right to fair hearing.[740] Section 32(1) while providing that a person alleged to have committed adultery with a specified person shall be made a party to the proceeding subjects this mandate to the rules. The rules in turn by Order IX, rules 1 and 2 specify that persons are not party to the proceedings simply because they have been cited in the petition but because they affect or are affected by the proceedings. Thus, only persons who have committed

736. *Erhahon v. Erhahon* [1976] 6 NWLR (part. 510) 667; *Alabi v. Alabi* [2007] 9 NWLR (part 1039) 297; [2008] ALL FWLR (part 418) 245; [2007] LPELR 8203.
737. [1973] East Central State of Nigeria law Report 623.
738. Later Justice of the Supreme Court.
739. [1973] East Central State of Nigeria Law reports, 623, 625.
740. Section 36(1) of the Constitution of the Federal Republic of Nigeria, Cap C23.

rape or sodomy on or with a specified person are obliged by the rules to become parties to the proceedings and by way of intervention.[741] It is to be noted that section 32(1) and 32(3) of the MCA refer to cases where the alleged adulterer or adulteress is known and mentioned. Order IX, rule 3(1) deals with cases where the alleged adulterer or adulteress is not specified and requires that the court shall not set down the suit for trial unless it has made an order dispensing with the naming of the person. The petitioner can amend the petition if in the course of the proceedings, he or she ascertains the name of the person alleged to have committed the adultery.

740. A critical analysis of the provisions shows they cannot bear close scrutiny in the light of the Constitutional provisions to fair hearing. Section 32(3) while making provision for an appearance by the alleged third-party adulterer, hinges his or her dismissal from the proceedings on the close of the case for the party to the marriage not on the defence of the alleged adulterer or adulteress. This is all in a proceeding that requires a high standard of proof but fails to consider the position of the principal alleged third-party wrongdoer.

741. It is only when a petitioner contemplates damages from the adulterer or adulteress that the petitioner is required to note and specify such a claim as an ancillary relief.[742] Another time in which it may be desirable to join the person alleged to have committed the adultery with a spouse is where he or she is so connected with the parties in inextricable ways such as cohabiting with the respondent or has children for the respondent. While the law contemplates avoidance of multiplicity of action, it is also the case that failure to join the alleged adulterer or adulteress complicates the proceeding because of the constitutional requirement of fair hearing.

742. If one is cited as the cause of the breakdown of a marriage, surely a right inheres in the person to be heard. A balance must thus be made between the contemplation of the law and other rights. Where a person is cited as a person with whom a spouse committed adultery, it is not enough that the person is dismissed from the case as is provided by section 32(2) because the person may proceed to bring an action against the petitioner for defamation to which privilege may not succeed as a defence.

743. The rule and law thus require an amendment that accommodates the alleged person with whom adultery was committed, first as to notice and then joinder on his or her own initiative or at the intervention of the court. That the person with whom adultery was alleged to have been committed must be made a party to the proceeding, is therefore, not accurate.[743]

---

741. Section 32(2) and Order 9 rule 2.
742. Order 14 rule 4(3) indicates that where a claimant is, by his application for ancillary relief, seeking an award of damages under s. 31 of the Act, the application shall specify the amount of damages sought.
743. Emmanuel Nwogugu *Family Law* (HEBN Publishers Plc. 1990) 165.

X. Damages for Adultery

744. Damages are recoverable from the person with whom a spouse committed adultery in Nigeria. When a petitioner intends to recover damages from the person with whom the spouse has committed adultery, then the person who is alleged to have been the partner must be joined as co-respondent unless the petitioner intends to bring an independent action against such a person on determination of the petition. This will, however, amount to a waste of the court's time as the courts are mandated to as far as is practicable to dispose of all the matters in relation to one matrimonial cause at once.

745. The claimant either in a supplementary petition or answer or ancillary relief, must indicate the specific amount of damages contemplated in relation to award of damages for adultery.[744] Some factors taken into consideration in awarding damages are: 'the value of the adulterous spouse to the claimant/petitioner; injury to the claimant/petitioner's feelings; the co-respondent's means and conduct; the alleged adulterer's knowledge that the alleged adulterous spouse is married'. Section 30 covers the requirements for awarding damages on a claim of adultery.Thus, a party to a marriage, whether husband or wife, may in a petition for a decree of dissolution of the marriage alleging that the other party to the marriage has committed adultery with a person may claim damages from that person on the ground that the person has committed adultery with the other party to the marriage and, the court may award damages accordingly.[745] However, the MCA provides guidelines to consider before awarding such damage. First, the quantum of damage must be specified. Second, the court shall not award damages against a person where the adultery of the respondent with that person has been condoned, whether subsequently revived or not, or if a decree of dissolution of the marriage based on the fact of the adultery of the respondent with that person, or on facts including that fact, is not made.[746] Third, damages shall not be awarded in respect of an act of adultery committed more than three years before the date of the petition.[747] The court may direct in what manner the damages awarded shall be paid or applied and may, if it thinks fit, direct that they shall be settled for the benefit of the respondent or the children of the marriage.[748]

746. The basis for the proceedings and award of damages is as at common law and English jurisprudence and includes damage done to the petitioner's prestige, loss of consortium and socials, hurt to family feelings and feelings. The relief for the petitioner if proved in line with section 15(2)(b) is dissolution of the marriage and ancillary reliefs can follow. Condoning is a defence which in matrimonial proceedings works as an absolute bar.[749]

---

744. Order VIII, part 1, rule 14; Order XIV, part 1, rule 4(3) of the MCR.
745. Section 30(1).
746. Section 30(2).
747. Section 30(3).
748. Section 30(4).
749. *Alabi v. Alabi* [2007] 9 NWLR (part 1039) 297; [2008] ALL FWLR (part 418) 245; [2007] LPELR 8203.

747. In Nigeria, adultery does not have any impact on the maintenance claims.[750]

748. Section 31 covers the requirements for awarding damages on a claim of adultery. Thus a party to a marriage, whether husband or wife, may in a petition for a decree of dissolution of the marriage alleging that the other party to the marriage has committed adultery with a person may claim damages from that person on the ground that the person has committed adultery with the other party to the marriage and, the court may award damages accordingly.[751] However, the MCA provides guidelines to consider before awarding such damage. First, the quantum of damage must be specified. Second, the court shall not award damages against a person where the adultery of the respondent with that person has been condoned, whether subsequently revived or not, or if a decree of dissolution of the marriage based on the fact of the adultery of the respondent with that person, or on facts including that fact, is not made.[752] Third, damages shall not be awarded in respect of an act of adultery committed more than three years before the date of the petition.[753] The court may direct in what manner the damages awarded shall be paid or applied and may, if it thinks fit, direct that they shall be settled for the benefit of the respondent or the children of the marriage.[754]

749. There is a global trend to abolish damages for adultery. Adultery is considered a moral wrong in contemporary times. The South African Constitutional Court made incisive statements on why adultery should no longer be determined in monetary terms in dismissing a claim on damages for adultery in *DE v. RH.*[755] The act of adultery by a third party, was noted by the Court, as lacking wrongfulness for the purposes of a *delictual* claim making it unreasonable to attach *delictual*[756] liability to it. Public policy requires that husband and wife sustain their marriage through love and mutual commitment and at this day and age, it just seems mistaken to assess marital fidelity in terms of money.

750. Similar views were expressed in *Pritchard v. Pritchard.*[757] However, the position on payment of damages for adultery in English Law remains unclear. Some

750. Section 31(1) provides: A party to a marriage, whether husband or wife, may, in a petition for a decree of dissolution of the marriage alleging that the other party to the marriage has committed adultery with a person or including that allegation, claim damages from that person on the ground that that person has committed adultery with the other party to the marriage and, subject to this section, the court may award damages accordingly.
751. Section 31(1).
752. Section 31(2).
753. Section 31(3).
754. Section 31(4).
755. (CCT 182/14) [2015] ZACC 18; 2015 (5) SA 83 (CC); 2015 (9) BCLR 1003 (CC) (19 Jun. 2015).
756. This is essentially tort law as understood in English jurisprudence. South Africa and Sri Lanka refer to conducts of the nature of a civil wrong as delict and therefore, delictual. The word has origins in Latin *delictum*.
757. [1967] 3 ALL ER. 601.

authors note that damage for adultery is abolished.[758] A practical search confirms this and finds that the co-respondent may justifiably be required to pay for the cost of the proceedings. However, the law now specifically enacting the abolition does not appear clear.

751. The Law Reform (Miscellaneous Provisions) Act 1970[759] of the United Kingdom provides by section 4, that 'after this Act comes into force no person shall be entitled to petition any court for, or include in a petition a claim for, damages from any other person on the ground of adultery with the wife of the first-mentioned person'.[760] This section has since been repealed by the MCA, 1973, by section 54(1), Third Schedule. Again, section 5 of the Law Reform (Miscellaneous Provisions) Act provides on abolition of actions for enticement, seduction and harbouring of spouse or child in tort, but it is not clear whether it is still in operation. This is because there are no known current outstanding effects for the Law Reform (Miscellaneous Provisions) Act, 1970.[761]

752. However, section 49(1) of the MCA, 1973 retains the place of a co-respondent, making it mandatory that such a person be joined in a petition where adultery is the basis of the breakdown in a petition for dissolution of marriage or judicial separation. It provides: 'Where in a petition for divorce or judicial separation or in any other pleading praying for either form of relief, one party to a marriage alleges that the other has committed adultery, he or she shall make the person alleged to have committed adultery with the other party to the marriage, a party to the proceedings unless excused by the court on special grounds from doing so'.

XI. Discretion Statement and the Petitioner's Adultery

753. Section 28 of the MCA contains the discretionary provisions on which the court may bar a petition for decree of dissolution of marriage. By section 40, these provisions also extend to judicial separation. Section 28(a) provides that the court may, at its discretion bar a decree of dissolution of marriage if since the marriage (a) the petitioner has committed adultery that has not been condoned by the respondent or, having been so condoned, has been revived. Situations where the adultery has not been condoned would engage cases where the respondent did not know of the adultery but the petitioner chooses to bring it before the court. The cases reveal that courts are happy to have the petitioner admit and indicate the adultery rather, than put the court through the process of discovering it.

758. Sue Jenkinson, *The Co-Respondent's Role in Divorce Reform after 1923*, in *Fifty Years in Family Law: Essays for Stephen Cretney* 201–215 (Rebecca Probert & Chris Barton eds, Intersentia, 2012) fn. 88; *see also* Sun Weifei, *Damages for Adultery and Interference with Marriage Relation: From the Perspective of Anglo-American Law* 31–48 (Peking University School of Transnational Law 2016); *see* 35.
759. Chapter 33.
760. Sue Jenkins, *ibid.*, 215 fn. 88 – citing s. 4, which is in fact, abolished by the Matrimonial Causes Act, s. 54(1) Sch. 3.
761. Available at: https://www.legislation.gov.uk/ukpga/1970/33/section/5 (last accessed 5 Oct. 2020).

754. In a suit for divorce or judicial separation the petitioner's own adultery is a discretionary bar. The Petitioner may plead own adultery by providing a Discretion Statement and praying the court to exercise a discretion of dissolving the marriage in spite of the admission of adultery. Although the discretion statement has long been criticised in other jurisdictions. Discretion statement has been tagged a 'roguish thing' which can be abused and 'there is no longer a case for a discretion statement. Such a statement, if it ever did serve a useful purpose, does not do so now. It imposes a heavy and, quite often, an intolerable burden on a petitioner. It has already become a "roguish thing" and ought to be abolished before it can do further harm'.[762] In Nigeria, the discretion Statement remains relevant.

755. Its origin is founded in a consistent legislative concern for the integrity of marriage and reluctance to sever its tie.[763] In exercising the discretionary power vested in it, the courts have been concerned to balance the rights and interest of the person who may have been wronged in a matrimonial cause and also the interests of society and its public morality.

756. The Matrimonial Causes Rules makes extensive regulations and rules guiding the form and content of Discretion Statement. Order V, rule 13 provides that where a petitioner has committed adultery since the marriage but before the filing of his petition, his petition shall state that the court shall be asked to make the decree notwithstanding the facts and circumstances set out in his discretion statement.

757. The discretion Statement is required to be in the format provided in Form 30 of the Rules. The required content and other procedures are contained in ORDER XI, Part 5, rules 28–30; and Order V, Part 2, rule 13. discretion statement will be necessary if adultery is committed since the marriage before the filing of the petition or answer, or at the time when the petition or answer is filed; or after the filing of that petition or answer but before the trial of the proceedings as soon as practicable after committing the adultery.[764] The discretion statement should be filed where there is a petition either for dissolution of marriage or judicial separation under any of the heads listed in section 15(2) of the MCA as facts that may prove irretrievable breakdown. The same facts apply to judicial separation by section 39 of the MCA.

758. Order XI, Part 5, rule 29 provides for the form and content of discretion statement:

(1) A discretion statement, which shall be in accordance with Form 30, shall state particulars of the acts of adultery committed by the petitioner or respondent, as the case may be, since the marriage (other than acts stated

762. N.S. Tessy, *Is a Discretion Statement Necessary?*, 21 Mod. L. Rev. 48, 56 (1958). *See* for instance *Coleman v. Coleman* [1955] 1 WLR 1235. In this case, the Court placed weight on a previous adultery committed by the petitioner which was not indicated in the discretion statement. On appeal, this was overturned.
763. N.S. Tessy, *ibid*; *see also* Rupert Cross, *The Absolute Bars to Divorce*, 9 Mod. L. Rev. 75 (1946).
764. Order XI, part 5, rule 28.

in any other discretion statement filed by him for the purposes of the proceedings), the circumstances giving rise to the commission of the act of adultery and the grounds upon which the court shall be asked to make a decree of dissolution of marriage or of judicial separation notwithstanding the adultery.

(2) Where a petitioner or respondent alleges that an act of adultery set forth in his discretion statement has been condoned, he shall state in the discretion statement particulars of the facts that are alleged to constitute condonation of the adultery.

(3) Where, in a discretion statement filed by a petitioner or respondent, the petitioner or respondent states that he has committed adultery and that he and the person with whom he has committed adultery are living together as if they were husband and wife, it shall not be necessary for a further discretion statement to be filed setting forth particulars of any further acts of adultery committed by him with that person.

759. Other requirements are that the discretion statement has to be signed by the party; the matters set forth in it have been verified by the affidavit of the party written on it; and it is enclosed in a sealed envelope having written on it the words 'Discretion Statement', the number of the proceedings and a certificate— (i) if the party is represented by a legal practitioner, signed by the legal practitioner; or:

760. (ii) if the party is not so represented, signed by the party, certifying that the statement is duly signed and verified, and that it bears the date on which it was signed. Rule 30(1) provides for service on the other party where the content of the discretion statement is not adultery or other 'matrimonial offence' indicated in the pleadings. A notice of the discretion statement must be served on the other spouse. Failure to serve such notice may, however, be excused if the discretion statement does not prejudice the other spouse at the hearing.[765] Rule 31 further requires a petitioner where the petition does not contain the statement referred to in Order V, Part 2, rule 13, to serve a notice of his intention to ask the court to make the decree notwithstanding the facts and circumstances set out in the discretion statement. The service is to be effected if the respondent has an address for service for the purpose of the proceedings or if the petitioner is claiming custody of a child of the marriage who is in the care of the respondent; or some other interested party to the proceedings with an address.

761. The Nigerian case of *Enekebe v. Enekebe*[766] illustrates the attitude of the Court to discretion statements. In that case, the husband had petitioned for dissolution of his marriage with his wife, Christina. They had married in 1938 and lived in Kano, a city in the North of Nigeria. Christina left their home in 1942 and had not returned until the filing of the petition. In his petition, the husband alleged adultery, cruelty and persistent nagging. He also admitted to adultery and living in that

765. Order XI, part 5. *See also* rule 31; *See* further Order V, rule 13 where custody of child[ren] of the marriage is involved.

766. [1964] NGSC 56.

state with two other women with whom he has children. The trial judge found that adultery was not proved against Christina but that she had been cruel to her husband before leaving Kano. The judge dismissed the petition on the ground of the husband's delay in petitioning. The Federal Supreme Court stated on an appeal against the dismissal of his petition, by the husband, that while the husband's discretion statement of his adulterous relationship with two other women was commendable, the Court could not exercise a discretion in his favour to dissolve the marriage because of the long delay in petitioning. The court noted that its sympathies were with the petitioner on his desire to dissolve the marriage with Christina in order to formalise customary marriages with the other two women with whom he was living and with whom he had children, it was constrained to bar the petition because of the delay in bringing it. The Court noted and approved the line of reasoning affirmed in *Blunt v. Blunt*[767] *on conditions* which a court should take into consideration in exercising a discretion. These are:

- the position and interest of any children of the marriage;
- the interest of the party with whom the petitioner has been guilty of misconduct, with special regard to the prospect of their future marriage;
- the question whether, if the marriage is not dissolved, there is a prospect of reconciliation between husband and wife;
- the interest of the petitioner, and, in particular, the interest that the petitioner should be able to remarry and live respectably;
- the interest of the community at large which is to be judged by maintaining a true balance between respect for the binding sanctity of marriage and the social considerations which make it contrary to public policy to insist on the maintenance of a union which has utterly broken down.

XII. Behaviour of Which the Petitioner Cannot Be Reasonably Expected to Live with: 15(2)(c)

762. This is the third fact on which a petition for divorce can be based. In the MCA, the guidelines of behaviours which will qualify for a decree of dissolution of marriage are stated in section 16(1)(a)–(g).[768] Although behaviour is usually an

767. [1943] A.C. 517, 525.
768. This provisions are supplementary to s. 15: (1) Without prejudice to the generality of s. 15(2) of this Act, the court hearing a petition for a decree of dissolution of marriage shall hold that the petitioner has satisfied the court of the fact mentioned in the said s. 15(2)(c) of this Act if the petitioner satisfies the court that: (a) since the marriage, the respondent has committed rape, sodomy, or bestiality; or (b) since the marriage, the respondent has, for a period of not less than two years: (i) been a habitual drunkard; or (ii) habitually been intoxicated by reason of taking or using to excess any sedative, narcotic or stimulating drug or preparation, or has, for a part or parts of such a period, been a habitual drunkard and has, for the other part or parts of the period, habitually been so intoxicated; or (c) since the marriage, the respondent has within a period not exceeding five years: (i) suffered frequent convictions for crime in respect of which the respondent has been sentenced in the aggregate to imprisonment for not less than three years; and (ii) habitually left the petitioner without reasonable means of support; or (d) since the marriage, the respondent has been in prison for a period of not less than three years after conviction for an offence punishable by death or

omnibus fact in many jurisdictions in the common wealth, and particularly so in England and Wales, it is not a popular one in Nigeria. Families avoid placing stigma on any parent as this will likely run in the family, sometimes for generations. In addition, the burden to prove such intolerable behaviour is on the petitioner who must discharge same.

763. In *Uzokwe v. Uzokwe*[769] the Court of Appeal said that this issue is one of fact for the Court and the court has the responsibility to admit evidence, weigh same and reach conclusions on which the law must be applied. In achieving this role, a trial judge must have regard to, among other things; admissibility, relevance, credibility and conclusions to be drawn from the evidence. The court then has to weigh the evidence on probability and having been satisfied, only then can the judge apply the law to the facts. It shall be sufficient if the Court is reasonably satisfied of that ground or fact or as to other matter.[770] It would appear though, that most of the cases coming under this fact present cruelty, aggression, witchcraft and general misconduct as the content of the intolerable behaviour. On the part of the courts, it also appears that they do not revert to the guidelines in section 16(1)a–g.

764. In *Akinbuwa v. Akinbuwa*,[771] the behaviour centred on the respondents penchant for voodoo practice and incidentals. There was also allegation of aggressiveness or cruelty which the petitioner claimed, prevented his relations from visiting. This content is similar to those alleged in *Damulak v. Damulak*,[772] as also in *Uzokwe v. Uzokwe*.[773]

765. In *Uzokwe*, the Court of Appeal restated the petitioner's grouse:

> That brings me to other intolerable acts the petitioner alleged against the respondent. His evidence-in-chief reveal that the respondent has not been speaking to him for years. That she was uncontrollable. She would leave the

---

imprisonment for life or for a period of five years or more, and is still in prison at the date of the petition; or (e) since the marriage and within a period of one year immediately preceding the date of the petition, the respondent has been convicted of: (i) having attempted to murder or unlawfully to kill the petitioner; or (ii) having committed an offence involving the intentional infliction of grievous harm or grievous hurt on the petitioner or the intent to inflict grievous harm or grievous hurt on the petitioner; or (f) the respondent has habitually and wilfully failed, throughout the period of two years immediately preceding the date of the petition, to pay maintenance for the petitioner: (i) ordered to be paid under an order of, or an order registered in, a court in the Federation; or (ii) agreed to be paid under an agreement between the parties to the marriage providing for their separation; or (g) the respondent: (i) is, at the date of the petition, of unsound mind and unlikely to recover; and (ii) since the marriage and within the period of six years immediately preceding the date of the petition, has been confined for a period of, or for periods aggregating, not less than five years in an institution where persons may be confined for unsoundness of mind in accordance with law, or in more than one such institution.

769. [2016] LPELR-40945.
770. *Erhahon v. Erhahon* [1976] 6 NWLR (part 510) 667.
771. *Akinbuwa v. Akinbuwa* [1998] NWLR (part 559) 661, 671.
772. [2004] & NWLR (PI-874) 151.
773. [2016] LPELR-40945.

house at will and stayed as long as she wished. In 1999, she was to travel outside the country, but never told him until a day to her departure. She did not tell him where she was travelling to. Eventually she travelled and stayed for 3-months. She was travelling for conferences and coming back days after the conference had ended. Her behaviour kept his sisters and parents away from his house for over twenty years it was only his father who would come once in a while. She was weird and wherever she went people made nasty comments about her. She is aggressive. She indoctrinated the children of the marriage against him, the petitioner. She would not allow his mother cook in the kitchen and she engaged in verbal abuse against her. She called his mother all sorts of name: witch. She connived with the A.C. of Police in Aba, Mr Gwadebe and he was arrested in his hospital bed on 15/01/2003 and locked up in cell, in Umuabakwa and Umuahia for three days.[774]

766. This type of hyped up allegations would normally trail this head of fact. The Matrimonial Causes Rules, appears to contemplate this head as cruelty despite the admonition of the courts that cruelty is of the old regime of matrimonial offences.[775]

767. Thus, Order V, Part 2, rule 12(1) and (2) are very relevant and states:

(1) A petition for a decree of dissolution of marriage shall State the ground and the facts in support thereof on which the decree is sought.
(2) For the purpose of these Rules, a fact specified in a paragraph of section 15(2) of the Act and specified in the first column of the following table may be stated in a pleading or affidavit in the terms set out in the second column of that table opposite the paragraph:

Paragraph a	refusal to consummate
Paragraph b	adultery and intolerability
Paragraph c	Cruelty
Paragraph d	desertion for at least one year
Paragraph e	separation for at least two years

768. The application and provisions of guidance on behaviour with respect to matrimonial causes demonstrate the inherent problem with matrimonial causes in Nigeria. The provision on behaviour and reasonableness as provided in section 15(2)(C) and its ancillary 16(1)a–g are almost at the level of being hilarious. The

774. [2016] LPELR-40945, 14–15.
775. *Ochei v. Ochei* [1973] East Central State of Nigeria law Report 623.

ancillary provision contemplates a female driven divorce system, perhaps one where patriarchal structure is on the attack but in Nigeria it is a male weapon, thereby putting the ancillary provision in disuse.[776]

769. In *Ayangbayi v. Ayangbayi*,[777] the petitioner-husband sought the dissolution of the marriage with the respondent-wife on the sole ground that the marriage has broken down irretrievably – in that since the marriage the respondent has behaved in such a way that the petitioner cannot reasonably be expected to live with the respondent. There were ten children of the marriage.

770. The Court found as a fact that the respondent had conducted herself several times in such a manner that the petitioner cannot reasonably be expected to live with her or put up with her conduct. The judge described the respondent and her actions as 'wicked' and 'wickedness'.

771. The Court stated the test to be adopted under section 15(2)(C); the Court must find that the behaviour of the respondent was sufficiently grave to make it unreasonable for the petitioner to endure it and live with the respondent. The counsel to the respondent argued that the petitioner having lived with the respondent for as long as two decades cannot now be heard to claim that he could no longer live with her. The Court held in response that 'the fact that a person had endured a condition or situation even for twenty years or more, does not mean that he should continue to endure and live with it for the rest of his life even though the parties have married for better for worse'.[778]

772. In view of the circumstances the Court held that it was satisfied that the requirement of section 15(2)(c) of the MCA had been met and ordered a Decree *Nisi* on dissolution of the marriage. The Court also resolved the issue of the custody of children and awarded maintenance and support.

773. The respondent stated that she did not require to be maintained although the counsel made an oral application for settlement of property. To this, the Court held that such application must be contained in the petition and answer.[779]

XIII. Desertion: Section 15(2)(d)

774. Desertion is a subjective and objective state of affairs. It is the intended and actual bringing to an end of cohabitation with a spouse without just cause or consent of the other party. The respondent must have deserted the petitioner for a continuous period of at least one year immediately preceding the presentation of the petition.

---

776. Section 16(1) a–g of the MCA.
777. [1979] 10–12 CCHSCJ 1.
778. Page 6. *Pheasant v. Pheasant* [1972] 1 ALL ER 587; *Ash v. Ash* [1972] 1 ALL E.R. 583.
779. *Springette v. Defoe* [1992] FLR 388 (CA).

775. In *Oghenevbede v. Oghenevbede*,[780] the High Court provided a definition for desertion: 'desertion in law is the separation of one spouse from the other with an intention on the part of the deserting spouse of bringing cohabitation permanently to an end without reasonable cause and without the consent of the other spouse'.[781] Where reasonable cause exists for one of the parties to leave the matrimonial home then there is a case of constructive desertion.[782] Desertion is deemed to be continuous although the parties may have resumed cohabitation for a period or periods not exceeding six months but such period or periods of cohabitation will not be regarded as part of the period of desertion.

776. Where it is not the respondent that caused the desertion or deserted petitioner, the Courts will not grant a decree of dissolution.[783] A deserted party may also avail him or herself of the right to take a proceeding for the restitution of conjugal rights, where the conditions are met. This will obviously depend on the nature of desertion and may aid in proving desertion more easily.

777. There are two perspectives under the MCA, one party may abandon the other or one party may provide just cause for the other party to leave. By the MCA, in the second scenario, the party providing the just cause is the party deserting. Section 18 provides 'that a married person whose conduct constitutes just cause or excuse for the other party to the marriage to live separately or apart, shall be deemed to have wilfully deserted that other party without just cause or excuse, notwithstanding that, that person may not in fact have intended the conduct to occasion that other party to live separately or apart'.[784] By section 20, where a mental inefficiency results in insanity of the deserting party the desertion continues unless it is shown that the insanity is in fact the cause of the desertion. The section is titled, 'Desertion continuing after insanity'. It provides that where a party to a marriage has been wilfully deserted by the other party, the desertion shall not be deemed to have been terminated by reason only that the deserting party has become incapable of forming or having an intention to continue the desertion, if it appears to the Court that the desertion would probably have confirmed if the deserting party had at become so incapable. Section 2(4) of the English MCA, 1973 puts it in this terms: '… the court may treat a period of desertion as having continued at a time when the deserting party was incapable of continuing the necessary intention if the evidence before the court is such that, had that party not been so incapable, the court would have inferred that his desertion continued at that time'.[785]

778. The standard of proof is by a preponderance of probability and in this case, to the satisfaction of the Court. Corroboration of the evidence of desertion is desirable although not absolutely necessary but some judges insist on corroboration. In

780. [1971] 3(1) University of Ife Law Report 104.
781. *Ibid.*, 104, 106; the court cited *Hopes v. Hopes* [1949] 2 All ER 920; [1949] 227 CA; *Perry v. Perry* [1952] 1 ALL ER 1077.
782. *Ochei v. Ochei* [1973] East Central State of Nigeria law Report 623.
783. *Odili v. Odili* [1973] ECSNLR 82.
784. MCA, Cap M7.
785. Cap 18.

addition, where the case is undefended, independent evidence on the separation for one year is unnecessary where a corroborative evidence as to the circumstances and terms of the parting is made available to the court. In *Ogehenevebede v. Ogehenevebede*,[786] the petitioner sought for divorce on the ground that the respondent deserted him and that they had lived apart for a continuous period of at least three years immediately preceding the presentation of the petition. The petition was undefended but in the Form of Acknowledgment of service filed by the respondent, she indicated that she would not defend the action and that she would apply for the custody of the children although she failed to make the application to the court as indicated. The respondent had earlier filed a petition at the High Court for the dissolution of the marriage to which the petitioner in the present suit had answered, also praying for the dissolution of the marriage but the petition was struck out for want of prosecution. On the current petition, the facts before the court were desertion and living apart for three years preceding the petition. There were two children of the marriage. Both children were at the time of the petition living with the respondent. The evidence proffered by the petitioner showed that the respondent on the day mentioned in November, 1964 left him by packing out of the house while uttering the words 'that she was no longer interested in the marriage'. The petitioner pleaded that efforts by his church members and other well-wishers to prevail on the respondent to return to the matrimonial home yielded no positive results. The Court held that the evidence establishing the circumstances and conditions leading to the parting of the respondent from the matrimonial home must not only be sufficient but must be corroborated in some material particular by independent evidence other than that of the petitioner. Ovie-Whiskey J. stated:

> The evidence adduced by the petitioner in this case is very scanty and insufficient to prove desertion. There is no corroborative evidence as to the circumstances and terms of the parting from the matrimonial home by the respondent. I consider it necessary in order to prove desertion that the evidence establishing the circumstances and conditions leading to the parting of the respondent from the matrimonial home must not only be sufficient, but it should be corroborated in some material particular by independent evidence other than that of the petitioner. In this case, the petitioner's evidence as regards the circumstances in which the respondent left the matrimonial home is not only unsatisfactory, but also uncorroborated by any other evidence. In my judgment, the petitioner has failed to prove the matrimonial offence of desertion against the respondent.[787]

779. This passage of the judgment demonstrates the perception of Nigerian courts in spite of the no fault regime of the Matrimonial Causes Act which was duly noted by the judge when he categorically referred to the matrimonial no-fault regime earlier in his judgment that 'a court shall hold that the marriage has broken down irretrievably if, but only if, the petitioner satisfies the court of several facts set

786. [1971] University of Ife Law Report 104.
787. [1971] 3(1) University of Ife Law Report 104, 107.

out in section 15(2) of the Matrimonial Causes Decree, 1970'.[788] In addition, the court in this case as in some others, referred to the facts for ascertaining irretrievable breakdown as offences.[789] It is clear that the restatement of the section in these terms means that the application is seen from the perspective of fault. It is, however, difficult to see how the decision and the court's approach to desertion would fare in a real no-fault divorce regime and in view of human rights advancement such as the right to personal liberty,[790] movement[791] and association.[792] These rights are duly guaranteed by the Constitution and it remains to be seen how a court will balance a feature of their ouster by any form of agreement including marriage.

780. On the facts of the case, however, the parties having lived apart for six years, the Court held that the marriage had broken down irretrievably.

XIV. Living Apart for a Continuous Period of at Least Two Years: 15(2)(e)

781. Living apart under section 15(2)(e) is predicated on the couple having been living together in the same household. Thus, where they are not, even if they live in the same building but not the same household then such separate living does not qualify for a fact under irretrievable breakdown. As on desertion, resumption of cohabitation for a period of six months or less in the interval before the presentation of the petition does not counteract the deemed continuity of living apart. For the purposes of living apart no account is to be taken of any one period (not exceeding six months), or any two or more periods (not exceeding six months in all), during which the parties resumed living with each other, provided that no period during these times in which the parties lived with each other shall count as part of the period of the desertion or of the period for which the parties to the marriage lived apart.[793]

782. The important content and contemplation of the provision is that the dissolution is consensual not necessarily that the respondent is not represented or the suit is undefended. The Matrimonial Causes Rules enjoins the Court to ensure that the petition comes with facts and the respondent is heard. The respondent may demonstrate that there is no objection to the proceeding by filing an appearance. Thus, once there is evidence that the respondent was served, it would not be relevant to the proceeding that representation is not made in fact. There are some arguments that the respondent must indicate this by a positive action but this is not implicit from the subsection.[794] The subsection also addresses reconciliation based on the fact that dissolution and nullity of marriages are required to be in open court. Some respondents who do not desire publicity will opt for absence from the proceedings

788. *Ibid.*, 104, 106. The Decree referred to is now the Act.
789. *See also Ochei v. Ochei* [1973] East Central State of Nigeria law Report 623.
790. Section 35 of the Constitution, Cap C23, Laws of the Federation.
791. Section 41 of the Constitution, Cap C23, Laws of the Federation.
792. Section 40 of the Constitution, Cap C23, Laws of the Federation.
793. Section 17(2).
794. E.I. Nwogugu, *Family Law* 188–191 (HEBN Publishers Plc. 1990).

and decline entering any pleading. As an instance, if a party does not desire the matrimonial cause and has done everything to stop it and takes the position that the other party may have the day then, there is no reason in principle to require that the party does more than is in fact needed – enter an appearance. This head and the subsequent one is more in use in Nigeria when the petitioner is a wife. The reason is because men in Nigeria are unlikely to be disposed to waiting out the period and appears more inclined to come under intolerable behaviour or adultery.

XV. Three-Year Continuing Separation and Living Apart Preceding the Petition: 15(2)(f)

783. This separation is for a period of three years immediately preceding the presentation of the petition. The point of living in the same house hold applies in this fact as well. As the court noted in *Oghenevbede v. Oghenevbede*[795]for the purpose of section 15(2)(e) and (f), the parties to a marriage shall be treated as living apart unless they are living with each other in the same household. Once the period of living apart for three years is proved, dissolution of the marriage becomes nearly a right. In *Omotunde v. Omotunde*[796] the Court of Appeal held that on the facts before it, the applicable law is section 15(2)(f) of the Matrimonial Causes Act, whereby, 'a court hearing a petition for the dissolution of a marriage shall hold the marriage to have broken down irretrievably if the parties to the marriage lived apart for a continuous period of three years immediately preceding the presentation of the petition. The law is that the provision is mandatory and the court has no discretion to exercise'.[797]

784. In *Okafor v. Okafor*[798] the court stated that this ground did not necessitated further enquiries once it is proved that the parties had lived apart for three years. The difference between this head and the earlier one is that the other party need not consent or object to the dissolution of the marriage. In *Ochei v.* Ochei[799] living apart was for a continuing period of seven years which was well over three years, the court held that once a fact of living apart for three years is relied on and proved then the petitioner is entitled to dissolution of the marriage.

785. The line is very thin, although discernible. In the former, the other spouse has a chance to object and failure to, brings it in line with the present fact. The courts often refer to this as desertion or treat it as such. In *Omotunde v. Omotunde*,[800] the court held that section 15(2)(f) does not envisage any fault or intent but the factual situation of the parties having lived apart. It, however, stated that

795. [1971] 3(1) University of Ife Law Report 104.
796. [2001] 9 NWLR (part 718) 252.
797. [2001] 9 NWLR (part 718) 252, 284.
798. [1976] 6 High Court of Lagos State Law Reports 1727.
799. [1973] East Central State of Nigeria law Report 623.
800. [2001] 9 NWLR (part 718) 252.

despite the wording of the subsection, a discretion still inheres in a court. In consequence of its position, although, the three-year period had been met by the petitioner, the Court ordered relisting of the suit at the High Court and its assignment to another judge of Oyo State High Court, Ibadan Division for determination on merit.

786. Yet it must be asked whether where a couple as in the very case of *Omotunde v. Omotunde*[801] separated by agreement at the initial stage and one party is living apart on that understanding, should it remain a right of the petitioner to have an order of dissolution? One must come to the conclusion that this could not be the intent of the law. Consequently, the three-year period must be hinged on a clear action taken by one of the parties which is indicative that the marriage was on the brink of breaking down prior to the separate living. This is because, cases have demonstrated that sometimes the couple started to live apart because one of them, usually the male goes abroad either for further studies or for economic improvement and then re-appears with a litigation for dissolution of marriage or where the marriage is under customary law, simply abandons the other.[802]

XVI. Failing to Comply with Decree of Restitution of Conjugal Rights: 15(2)(g)

787. The section provides for dissolution of the marriage where after one year a respondent fails to comply with a decree for restitution of conjugal rights.[803] As has been highlighted earlier, in Nigeria the decree of restitution of conjugal rights more, fully discussed below, aims at reconciling the parties. Thus, by section 51 of the Act, enforcement of decree of restitution of conjugal rights shall not be by attachment.

XVII. Presumption of Death after Seven Years of Absence: 15(2)(h)

788. This provision is linked with section 16(2) based on which after seven years of desertion, or continuing absence, the court by ordering a decree of dissolution of marriage, can confirm a presumption by the petitioner that the other spouse is dead. Section 16(2) provides: where a petition is based on the fact mentioned in section 15(2)(h) of this Act:

(a) proof that, for a period of seven years immediately preceding the date of the petition, the other party to a marriage was continually absent from the petitioner and that the petitioner has no reason to believe that the other party was alive at any time within that period is sufficient to establish the fact in question unless it is shown that the other party to the marriage was alive at a time within the period; and

801. *Ibid.*
802. *Marian Olutunde Agbeja & Olufunke Agbeja v. Olusola Idowu Agbeja & Madam Kehinde Agbeja Komolafe* [1985] 3 NWLR (part 11) 11; E.I. Nwogugu, *supra.* n. 139, 7; T.A. Aguda, *supra.* n. 530.
803. The matrimonial cause for Decree of restitution of conjugal right is contained in ss 47–51.

(b) a decree made pursuant to the petition shall be in the form of a decree of dissolution of marriage by reason of presumption of death.

789. The petitioner must prove, that nothing has happened in the interval or interim to provide an indication that the other party may still be living.[804]

XVIII. Other Matrimonial Causes

A. *Judicial Separation*

790. Judicial separation, is a separation of married couple by due legal process although by law, they remain married. It has in the past, been referred to as 'separate maintenance' 'divorce a *mensa et thoro*',[805] or 'divorce from bed-and-board'.

791. The Supreme Court stated in *Anyaegbunam v. Anyaegbunam*[806] that a petition for judicial separation is based on a valid marriage. The basic effect of judicial separation is the formal withdrawal from cohabiting in the marriage. Judicial separation may be relevant where the parties are separating harmoniously and require formal financial settlements or custody of the children of the marriage. The parties remain married in other respects. They could also offer an alternative option in cases where there are strong moral objections, cultural reasons or religious beliefs for a party to the marriage not wanting to obtain a divorce.

792. A decree of judicial separation relieves parties of cohabiting with one another but not, other obligations; status and rights of the parties to the marriage. In judicial separation proceedings, the court does not have to consider whether the marriage has broken down irretrievably whereas it must do so when a petition for dissolution is presented.

793. There is only one stage to the decree of judicial separation, whereas in a dissolution, there is a two-stage process of Decree *nisi* followed by decree absolute.

794. The provisions on judicial separation are contained in sections 39–46 of the MCA. A petition may be brought under one or more of the facts for dissolution of marriage contained in sections 15(2) and 16(1). Section 41 specifies the effect of decree of judicial separation. A decree of judicial separation relieves the petitioner from the obligation to cohabit with the other party to the marriage but, it does not, in any other way, affect the marriage or the status, rights and obligations of the parties. So, for instance, joint powers of husband and wife are not affected. The section refers to or presumes the wife as a minor. The section provides that 'a wife, during

804. *Nwankpele v. Nwankpele* [1972] 2 CCJCJ 101.
805. Latin, for 'from table and bed', but more commonly translated as 'from bed and board'.
806. [1963] ALL NLR 320.

separation under a decree of judicial separation, is not prevented from joining in the exercise of any power given to herself and her husband jointly'.[807]

795. Failure by a husband to pay maintenance duly ordered by court will render him liable for necessaries supplied to his wife.[808] It is a statutory flavour to the common law doctrine of the duty of a husband to maintain his wife and children by enacting on his continuing liability for necessaries following a decree of judicial separation.

796. It would appear that it would not matter if the wife is ordinarily self-sufficient, for, once the decree of judicial separation has been granted and the maintenance ordered is not paid, then the husband is liable for all necessaries obtained by his wife. In *Eniola v. Eniola*,[809] Okuribido J. noted that the overriding duty of a husband is to maintain his wife and children.

797. The provision of section 42(3) on necessaries is otiose and has never been relevant to the Nigerian situation. It has been abolished in England by section 41 of the Matrimonial Proceedings Act, 1970. Section 41 of the Matrimonial Proceedings and Property Act, 1970 abolishes all rules of law or equity conferring on a wife authority as agent of necessity of her husband, to pledge his credit or to borrow money on his credit.[810]

798. Should one of the parties to a decree of judicial separation die, while a decree of judicial separation is in force, then the other survives the other as a joint tenant to any property.[811] This provision is also present by section 40 of the English of the Matrimonial Proceedings and Property Act.

799. A proceeding for decree of dissolution of marriage may be instituted while a decree for judicial separation is in force.[812] The fact by which a decree of judicial separation was ordered forms sufficient proof of that fact in a proceeding for dissolution of marriage brought on the same or substantially the same ground or facts.[813] This is, however, subject to the fact that a petitioner must provide facts and evidence in support of a petition for dissolution. In other words, if the petition for dissolution, is on facts outside of the facts used for the proof of evidence for judicial separation, the petitioner has the burden to prove the new facts, since the facts for judicial separation need not be irretrievable breakdown but may be one of the facts to prove the irretrievable breakdown.

807. Section 43.
808. Section 42(3).
809. [1979] 10–12 CCHCJ, 59.
810. In furtherance of the provision, s. 41(2) provides that s. 20(4) of the Matrimonial Causes Act, 1965 which is a direct equivalent of s. 42(3) the Nigerian MCA, ceases to have effect.
811. Section 42(2) of the MCA, Cap M7, 2004.
812. Section 44.
813. Section 44(2).

800. A key feature in the provision for judicial separation is in the question of intestacy. By section 42(2) of the MCA, where a party to a marriage dies intestate as to any property while a decree of judicial separation is in operation that property shall devolve as if that party had survived the other party to that marriage. The section titled the effect on rights to sue, devolution of property, etc. provides: (1) While a decree of judicial separation is in operation, either party to the marriage may bring proceedings in contract or in tort against the other party. (2) Where a party to a marriage dies intestate as to any property while a decree of judicial separation is in operation, that property shall devolve as if that party had survived the other party to the marriage. A clue as to the interpretation of the provision can be taken from the English provision which appears clearer. Section 18(2) of the MCA, 1973 provides that while a decree of judicial separation is in force and the separation is continuing then, either of the parties to the marriage dies intestate as respects all or any of his or her real or personal property, the property as respects which he or she died intestate shall devolve as if the other party to the marriage had then been dead.

801. Thus, judicial separation does not affect existing Wills. Where a decree of judicial separation has been granted and the parties remain separated, if either dies intestate, his or her property will devolve as if the other spouse was already dead, so the surviving spouse will not benefit.

802. A decree of judicial separation can be discharged by either of the parties but with the consent of both or at the instance of the court where the parties resume cohabitation.[814]

XIX. Restitution of Conjugal Rights

803. A decree of restitution of conjugal rights is brought against a husband or wife who is living away from a spouse without a justifiable lawful reason. The decree orders the party who is living away to return to the other party. A decree of restitution of conjugal rights implies that the guilty party is ordered to live with the aggrieved party. The decree can only be based on a valid marriage under the MA.

804. The provisions on restitution of conjugal rights are contained in sections 47–51 of the MCA. The decree of restitution of conjugal rights in Nigeria is regarded as a tool of reconciliation. Thus, the decree remains very relevant in Nigeria. In *Moktar Jabre v.* Mrs. *Dorra Jabre*[815] the Court of Appeal reiterated the position that the joint import of sections 47 and 51 of the MCA is to facilitate reconciliation between the parties. It held that there could be no question of maintenance before the disposal of a suit on restoration of conjugal rights. According to Oyeleye Omage, J.C.A. in *Ahmad Moktar Jabre v. Mrs Dorra* Jabre:[816]

---

814. Section 45 of the MCA.
815. [1999] 3 NWLR (part 596) 606 at 617; [1999] LPELR. 8133.
816. [1999] LCN/0622(CA).

> [maintenance] does not apply to a party who seeks relief for a restoration of conjugal right or specific performance as provided for in Section 47 of the Matrimonial Causes Act 1970. Section 47 is without doubt subscribed in the law for a reconciliation of the parties to the marriage, where they are estranged. The issue of an order for maintenance of the spouse at an interlocutory stage cannot be said to assist the intention of the law for a restoration of conjugal right as the application stood before the court. In fact, Section 51 of the said Act on the same issue provides as follows: A decree of restitution of conjugal rights shall not be enforceable by attachment. The section in my view seeks to avoid any action that may deter restoration of conjugal right. An order for maintenance before the hearing of evidence will not encourage amity between the parties.

805. Section 47 provides that a petition under the Act by a party to a marriage for a decree of restitution of conjugal rights may be based on the ground that the parties to the marriage, whether or not they have at any time cohabited, are not cohabiting and that without just cause, the party against whom the decree is sought refuses to cohabit with, and render conjugal rights to, the petitioner. While section 49 provides that the court can only make such a decree, where it is satisfied that the petitioner is sincere and truly wishes to render conjugal rights to the respondent. Furthermore, that efforts in the form of a written request in a conciliatory manner has been made towards getting the respondent to restore conjugal rights. This latter may be waived where the Courts ascertains that special circumstances exist that may validate such waiver.

806. Section 50 places a duty on a husband who petitions for the decree to provide a home where the parties would actually cohabit and to notify the other spouse. Section 51 is particularly of importance as it limits the enforcement of the order by denying attachment.

807. In *Adaku v. Nwosu*,[817] Karibi-Whyte stated that Nigerian women condone adultery, from their husbands so often and the result is that it is not so unusual that a man may desert a wife and his family from time to time. Thus, while it may be the case that the decree of restitution of conjugal rights has outlived its usefulness in England and other European nations, this is not the case with Nigeria. Canvasing for its abolition in Nigeria is misplaced. The decree continues to be a relevant tool by which the court can compel husbands in a patrilineal society such as Nigeria to become more alive to their responsibility. It may also assist the court more easily to ascertain that a husband or wife has indeed deserted the other. It provides a veritable ground for which husbands can be made within law to live up to maintaining their families. Where the decree is granted it is to be in accordance with Form 39 of the MCR.

---

817. [1992] 5 NWLR 273.

XX. Arguments for Retention or Abolition of the Decree of Restitution of Conjugal Rights

808. There are campaigns for its abolition in Nigeria.[818] There were also campaigns for its abolition in English law. It was subsequently abolished by section 20 of the Matrimonial Proceedings and Property Act, 1970 which provides: "No person shall after the commencement of this Act be entitled to petition the High Court or any country court for restitution of conjugal rights..

809. Prior to its abolition in English Law, the English Law Commission[819] called for memoranda and evaluated the place of the decree of restitution of conjugal rights in modern times. This was also the case with Republic of Ireland[820]

810. The English Law Commission proposed abolition based on the outcome of the memorandum received and concluded: that 'The comments we have received in reply to our working paper have shown an overwhelming support for the abolition of the remedy of restitution of conjugal rights. We recommend, therefore, that the remedy should be abolished.'[821] The same result was reached by the Republic of Ireland which resulted in provisions in Family Law Act, 1995.

811. The arguments for retention were that it aided in saving of marriages and afforded provision of financial relief that might not be available otherwise. It also aided clarity of the circumstances of the separation as well as provided emotional relief that the action of the responding party is not based on desertion or its equivalent.

812. The arguments for abolition covered grounds that were more persuasive. These were:

- there were other means available to save a marriage other than through the proceeding of restitution of conjugal rights;
- there are other effective means for providing financial relief;
- while the proceeding may show a case of desertion, there are also other effective means of showing same;
- restitution proceedings may have no response from the other spouse and sometimes reconciliation can occur even in proceedings for dissolution of marriage;
- a court order directing adult parties to live together does not aid reconciliation and may cause one person to become a nuisance to the other;
- the mere fact that the remedy of restitution of conjugal rights is so rarely used of itself, indicates that the remedy is not an effective one.

---

818. Chimezie Onuzulike, *Otiosity of Proceedings and Decrees for Restitution of Conjugal Rights*, available at ledapnigeria.org/otiosity-of-proceedings-and-decrees-for-restitution-of ... (last accessed 7 Mar. 2020).
819. 1969, Law Comm, No. 23.
820. Family Law Act, 1995. This followed the recommendation of the Law Reform Commission LRC 6 – 1983 on report on restitution of conjugal rights and Jactitation of marriage and related matters.
821. 1969, Law Comm, No. 23.

813. Failure to comply with a decree of restitution of conjugal rights is a fact of irretrievable breakdown for dissolution of marriage conducted under the Marriage Act in Nigeria.[822] An agreement for separation, is not a defence to proceedings of restitution of conjugal rights.[823]

XXI. Jactitation of Marriage

814. Jactitation Means A Boastful Declaration Or Display. The Etymology Of The Word Is Probably From Latin or French.[824] In its Latin form, *jactatio*, it is used to refer to some medical condition in acute illness that makes a person restless leading to tossing of the head and body. The word soon became part of legal proceedings in matrimonial causes. Legal proceedings for jactitation of marriage were recorded as having been brought before the Ecclesiastical Courts in England in 1685.[825] It continued as a cause in matrimonial proceedings in English and Irish laws as where one person falsely asserts that he or she is married to another. The wronged party could obtain an order restraining further repetitions of the falsehood. Jactitation of marriage is a continuing feature of Nigerian matrimonial causes. It is, however, rare in Nigeria as it was in the English and Irish jurisdictions.

815. In the English case of *Lord Hawke v. Corri*,[826] the Court articulated the purpose of jactitation of marriage as being for the protection of persons against the extreme inconvenience of unjust claims and pretensions to a marriage which has no existence whatever. In *Thompson v. Rourke*[827] the English Court of Appeal stated that the action is very rare and the form of defamation and almost of a criminal nature. It also laid down that the court will not make a decree in a jactitation suit in favour of a petitioner who has at any time acquiesced in the assertion of the respondent that they were actually married. The only known Nigerian case on the subject is *Ayeni v. Owolabi*[828] case on the subject referred to both cases.

816. There are two possible scenarios of jactitation, a non-existent marriage or a failed marriage. It is only the person to whom the boasting specifically pertains to, that can file a petition. Thus, a spouse of the prospective petitioner cannot petition.

817. Section 52 of the MCA provides that where a respondent has falsely boasted and persistently asserted that a marriage has taken place, between the respondent and the petitioner, a decree of jactitation of marriage may be issued. This provision stands alone in the Act and does not appear to have any other specific relief other than the decree. Ordinarily, relief should be in the form of an injunction and damages. These are provided in the MCA as general reliefs at the discretion of

822. Section 15(2)(g); *see also* s. 102(1) & (2) of the MCA.
823. Section 48.
824. Available at: https://www.merriam-webster.com/dictionary/jactation (last accessed 2 Oct. 2000).
825. Available at: https://en.wikipedia.org/wiki/Jactitation (last accessed 2 Oct. 2000).
826. [1820] 2 Hagg. Cons. 280; 161 English Reports 743.
827. [1893] Prob. 70.
828. [1980] 2 Q. L. R. N 241.

the court. However, where a petitioner seeks damages, the quantum must be specified. Section 52 further states that the making of the decree shall be at the discretion of the Court, notwithstanding anything contained in the Act.

818. There are rules which dictate the required content of a petition for jactitation of marriage.[829] The petition for jactitation of marriage is required to be in Form 60. Form 60 requires a petition to provide the dates, times and places at which the respondent is alleged to have boasted about the marriage with the petitioner. The petition must specifically indicate that there is no marriage between the parties and that the petitioner has not acquiesced in the alleged boastings and assertions. The petition must also indicate the dates on which, and the times and places at which the respondent is alleged to have boasted and asserted that a marriage had taken place between the petitioner and the respondent and the particulars of those boastings and assertions.

819. Possible defences available to a respondent include the truth of the existence of a marriage, denial or repudiation of the allegation of boasting or estoppel based on acquiescence.

820. The English Family Law Act, 1986, abolished jactitation as a matrimonial cause.[830] Republic of Ireland also abolished it and rather empowered the Circuit Family Court to make a declaration on the status of marriages.[831] England also has a similar claim for declaration of status.

§3. Procedure and Formalities for Matrimonial Causes

821. Nigerian Courts take procedure for instituting an action in matrimonial causes very seriously. Adherence to procedure as required by the MCA and rules is critical to the outcome of a proceeding in matrimonial causes. Although, the Rules provide for discretionary powers of the court to waive or not waive compliance with the rules, the courts have demonstrated continual disinclination to waive the rules, rather insisting that the rules are as important as the Act and are an intrinsic part of the Act- both must be complied with. In *Eluwa v. Eluwa* the Court of Appeal stated:

> these Rules, and all rules of court, which impose a legal duty, obligations and therefore a burden on a party or officials to take steps aimed at the orderly and expeditions determination of an appeal in and by the court are meant to be and must be obeyed and complied with by them. It is not for any party or official of courts to take the Rules of a court for granted even if they were in discretionary terms, let alone in mandatory tenor and expect that courts would as a matter of course, condone the attitude for no tenable reason. All rules of courts

829. Order XXII, part 2, rule 3.
830. Section 61 of the Family Law Act, 1986.
831. Family Law Act, 1995. This followed the recommendation of the Law Reform Commission LRC 6 – 1983 on report on restitution of conjugal rights and Jactitation of marriage and related matters.

are not made and meant to be ignored, disregarded or for fun and left to the whims of parties or officials of court but are bound to be obeyed and complied with The failure or neglect in the case was however waived as the Court of Appeal thought it did not go to the root of the question of jurisdiction of the court and the respondent did not suggest that it prejudiced the case.[832]

822. In the instant case the petitioner pleaded 15(2)(c) and (e) which though poorly presented in a language the High Court thought was incoherent, the Court of Appeal affirmed the judgment of the High Court on dissolution based on the grounds indicated, and in particular 15(2)(c).[833]

823. It must be noted that the incoherence concerned language as opposed to failure to comply with forms and procedure.

824. An action for matrimonial causes may be for a decree or declaration. A decree may be made in respect of all five main matrimonial causes. The other causes are ancillary and are based on resolution of the main causes. A proceeding for a matrimonial cause on dissolution of marriage or nullity of purported marriage must be instituted by petition. Thus, section 54(1) of the Matrimonial Causes Act provides that: subject to the provisions on a proceeding for judicial separation, a matrimonial cause of [of dissolution or nullity] shall be instituted by petition. Other causes may in addition, to being brought formally, before the court, be made orally in the course of the proceedings on the principal petitions.[834]

825. The Court is empowered and enjoined to hear and determine all proceedings included in one petition as far as this is practicable.[835] This provision enables the court to dispose of all the proceedings at one point.

826. An application for judicial separation can be instituted alongside a petition for dissolution of marriage or nullity or by an independent petition. A proceeding for Restitution of conjugal rights and Jactitation of marriage are also to be instituted by petition. With respect to hearing the proceedings on judicial separation, restitution of conjugal rights and jactitation of marriage, the court may choose to separate these and hear the proceeding in chambers or where it was hearing it in chambers choose to continue in open court.[836]

---

832. [2013] LPELR – CA/C/180/2012; *per* Mohammed Garba, J.C.A.
833. Thus the court noted that both parties had prayed for the dissolution thereby leaving no doubt whatsoever that the marriage between them has in fact and indeed broken down irretrievably and they both simply want an official judicial pronouncement putting an end to it. The Court further affirmed the award of maintenance to the respondent based on all available verifiable means of the petitioner at NGN 250,000 per month.
834. Section 11 of the MCA.
835. Section 54(4) of the MCA, 2004, Cap M7.
836. Section 9 of the MCA; Order 9, rules 1–3 of the Rules.

827. A respondent may in an answer to a petition, seek any decree or declaration that the respondent could have sought in a petition. Where there is a petition and cross-petition, the courts have held that both must be heard and determined separately.

I. Form of Petition

828. A petition for dissolution of marriage, nullity or judicial separation is required to be filed, in a specified format. This is, as in Form 6.[837] Petition for a decree for restitution of conjugal rights should be in Form 7. A petition for jactitation of marriage should be in accordance with Form 60.[838] The detail content of the Forms appears in the Rules as an appendix.

829. Section 30(1) provides that proceedings for a decree of dissolution of marriage shall not be instituted within two years after the date of the marriage except by leave of the court. Where this is the case, that is, an application is being proposed before the expiration of two years of the marriage then, the application could be made ex parte.[839] The same process applies to a decree of judicial separation.[840] The petitions must state the ground and facts supporting the petition. The petition should also have the marriage certificate attached to it.[841] Where the marriage certificate is not in English language, then it must be translated and the contents verified by the translator in an affidavit. The affidavit must indicate that the translator confirms that he has the competence to do the translation.[842] This applies to both petition and application for leave to petition.[843]

830. Order IV is the specific order on applications for leave of court to institute proceedings for dissolution of marriage and judicial separation before the expiration of two years.[844] There seems to be some variance between Order IV and V, though. Order IV, rule 3 states that Marriage certificate is to be filed with application for leave: (1) at the time when an application under section 30 or 40 of the Act for leave to institute proceedings is filed, the applicant shall, unless he is unable to do so, also file a marriage certificate in respect of the marriage to which the application relates. While Order V, Part 6, rule 27(2) states: this rule shall not apply in relation to a petition instituting proceedings in pursuance of leave granted under section 30 of the Act.

---

837. Order V, parts 2 and 3.
838. Order XXII, part 2, rule 2.
839. *See* ss 30, 40 and 54(3) of the MCA. *See also* Order III, part 1 and Order IV of the Matrimonial Causes Rules.
840. Order V, part 4. Part 5 contains the rules for petition of restitution of conjugal rights.
841. Order V, part 6, rule 27(1)(d).
842. Order V, part 6, rules 27(3) and (4).
843. Order IV, rules 3(1); (2); (3) and (4).
844. *See* however, Order V, part 6, rule 27(1)(2).

831. The only logical conclusion will be that in applications for leave to institute proceedings when the marriage has not been up to two years, filing of petition along with the marriage certificate may not be mandatory. The reason for this is, however, not clear.

832. A petition in addition to complying with forms of petition under Order V, rule 3 of the MCR, 1983, on bio data and other details of the parties to the marriage, must state the specific ground/fact; or grounds/facts; relied upon for matrimonial relief.[845] Arrangements and provisions for children are required to be stated on the petition where children of the marriage are living at the date of the petition.[846]

II. Verification of the Petition

833. A very vital aspect of a matrimonial cause proceeding on dissolution of marriage is verification. Dissolution of marriage in Nigeria can only be obtained by a petition to the High Court. A petition must be in in a prescribed form not only in format but also, in content.[847] All information stated on the Petition must be verified. Verification means that the information on the Petition and the affidavit verifying same must be a continuous document.

834. Order V, Part 1, rule 10(1) provides that a petitioner shall, by an affidavit written on his petition and sworn to before his petition is filed, verify the facts stated in his petition of which he has personal knowledge, and depose as to his belief in the truth of every other fact stated in his petition.

835. The Court of Appeal has stated categorically that a petition must be verified by a petitioner and this means that the petition must be contained in a continuing document.

836. *Unegbu v. Unegbu* [848] addressed the important question of verification. In it, the Court acknowledged that a comparative approach was desirable in reaching its conclusions since, the Matrimonial Causes Act drew generally from the New Zealand Act, 1928; Australian Act of 1959 and the English Act of 1965 and that the Matrimonial Causes Rules 1983 also drew from the Matrimonial Causes Rules of England, 1957.[849] Thus, the Court in considering the import of Order V, rule 10(1) of the MCR, 1983, drew its analysis from rules 6(1) and 3 of the English MCR, 1957, and cases decided on the rule, but only on a persuasive basis.

845. *Eluwa v. Eluwa* [2013] LPELR – CA/C/180/2012.
846. Order V, part 1, rule 14.
847. Order V, Matrimonial Causes Rule, 1983, Laws of the Federation, 2004.
848. [2004] II NWLR, (part 884) 332, 336.
849. *Unegbu v. Unegbu* [2004] II NWLR (part 884) 332, 336.

837. The petitioner had filed for dissolution of marriage at the High Court of Enugu, in Enugu State Nigeria. The petition, had an Affidavit with the title and Suit Number of the petition not as continuation of the Petition, but as an attachment. There was also attached, a Notice of Petition of the same date and the Marriage Certificate. The appellant as respondent at the High Court filed a motion on notice seeking for an order of the trial court to strike out the petition as being incompetent since it did not comply with Order V, rule 10(1) of the Matrimonial Causes Rules. The rule provides: (1) A petitioner shall, by an affidavit written on his petition and sworn to, before his petition is filed:

(a) verify the facts stated in his petition of which he has personal knowledge; and
(b) depose as to his belief in the truth of every other fact stated in his petition.

838. The High Court dismissed the motion stating that the irregularity was not of the measure to affect the validity of the petition.

839. The appeal on an interlocutory application is on this point. The principal question identified by the Court of Appeal for determination is: did the respondent comply with Order V, rule 10(1) of the Matrimonial Causes Rules by attaching to the petition the affidavit verifying the facts for the dissolution of marriage, rather than having the affidavit run as a continuous part of the petition?

840. The counsel for the appellant argued that on the existing authorities[850] compliance with the rule is mandatory. He contended that the word: 'on' should be given its ordinary meaning. The Counsel to the respondent relying on *Obadiaru v. Uyigue* objected first, to the rule being interpreted as the same with the English rule on the subject and second, that what is required is compliance with the rule in substance, and not form.[851]

841. Mohammed, JCA[852] delivering the lead judgment noted that thirteen years after the MCA 1970 came into existence, neither the Court of Appeal nor Supreme Court had pronounced specifically on Order V, Part 1, rule 10(1) of the MCR, leaving the Court constrained to draw guidance from the English MCR 1957 and cases thereon. According to the Court, the 1957 Act remain in force in Nigeria by virtue of the provisions of the various High Court Laws and such laws as were in substantial conformity with the law and practice of the High Court of Justice in England as at 30 September 1960.[853] This statement must be taken to be different from the Rules which by Order 1, rule 2 on: 'cesser of English Rules' states: 'The rules of

850. *Udo, Re* [1987] 4 NWLR (part 63) 120, 121; *Tukur v. Governor of Gongola State* [1988] 1 NWLR (part 68) 39, 42; *Maiwada v. F.B.N. Plc.* [1997] 4 NWLR (part 616) 606,611; *Ogbuka v. Ogbuka* [1972] 2 ECSLR (part 2) 558; *Abbah v. Abbah* [1973] 3 ECSLR 214, 216–27; *see* further, *Adibuah v. Adibuah* 1 ECSLR 127, 133–134 – where it was held that unless the verifying affidavit follows immediately at the end of the petition, the rule had not been complied with. The petition ws nullified.
851. [1986] 3 SC 39, 44.
852. Later Chief Justice of the Supreme Court.
853. [2004] 11 NWLR (part 884) 332, 354, para. 1.

court for the time being in force in the High Court of Justice in England providing for the practice and procedure of that court in respect of divorce and matrimonial causes, shall cease to apply in Nigeria when these Rules come into force.'

842. The relevant provision of the English MCR, was, however, distinguished from the Nigerian rule. The rules, 6(1) and (3) are:

> 6(1) every petition shall be supported by an affidavit by the petitioner verifying the facts of which he has personal knowledge and deposing as to his belief in the truth of the other facts.
> (3) The affidavit in support of the petition shall be contained in the same document as the petition and shall follow at the foot or end thereof.

843. The Court having examined the cases and the English position, held that there was a 'significant'[854] distinction between the English and Nigerian MCR in that the words 'every petition shall be supported by an affidavit' is no longer in the Nigerian rules. Consequently, that the Nigerian rule was distinguished in that it mandates the petitioner to have the affidavit 'on' the petition implicating an ordinary interpretation of the word, 'on'. The court stated further that all duties imposed on a petitioner by Order V, Part 1, rule 10(1) of the MCR were mandatory. These duties are:

(i) a petitioner shall write an affidavit on his petition;
(ii) the affidavit shall be sworn to before his petition is filed;
(iii) the petitioner shall verify the facts stated in his affidavit of which he has personal knowledge;
(iv) the petitioner shall depose as to his belief in the truth of every other fact stated in the petition.

844. The Court referred to *Oyedu v. Oyedu*[855] and *Grace C. Omodon v. J.C. Omodon*[856] both of which were decided, before the Matrimonial Causes Rule, 1983, and concluded that it is mandatory to have the affidavit of content appear on the same document as the petition.

845. The court also reviewed the unreported case of *Uyanwa v. Uyanwa*[857] where the verification required was contained in a separate document as in the present case and in which the Court held that the requirement of verification was not met and struck out the case.

846. It was therefore, held that for the present case, the respondent's affidavit is contained in a separate document separately headed and deposed to, which does not satisfy (i) above. According to the Court of Appeal, 'definitely for the purpose of

854. [2004] 11 NWLR (part 884) 332, 356.
855. [1972] 2 ECSLR 730.
856. [1966] NMLR 288.
857. Suit No. 0/6D/98 delivered by Iyizoba J. on 7 Jul. 1998.

the rule, the petition of the petitioner and his affidavit cannot be the same… because the rule requires the writing; of one; (The affidavit) on the other (the petition)'.[858] Thus, the affidavit as attached rather than sworn to as a continuous part of the petition, did not verify the records provided on the petition.

847. With respect to duty (ii), it determined that although, the affidavit was sworn to on the same day as the filing of the petition, the second requirement – 'the affidavit shall be sworn to before his petition is filed' was met with respect to timing.

848. On duty (iii), the Court found that aside from the bio-data section of the affidavit, the affidavit merely stated in paragraph (2) 'that paragraphs 1 – 9 of the petition are true to the best of my knowledge'. This was described as scanty and inadequate to verify the facts stated in the respondent's petition of which he has personal knowledge. The affidavit failed to disclose which of the facts stated in the petition were in fact derived from his own personal knowledge which is a distinct requirement of the MCR.

849. On duty (iv), it was held that the petitioner satisfied the duty of deposing to his belief in the truth of every other fact stated in his petition. The court concluded that the petition failed to meet the duties specified in (i) and (iii), although it satisfied the requirements of (ii) and (iv), therefore the appeal was allowed since the facts were not verified by a deposition on the petition, the petition did not comply with the Rules. Mohammed JCA concluding his lead judgment stated:

> Finally, I am of the firm view that the language of Order V Rule 10(1) of the [MCR, 1983] is mandatory and has not been complied with in the present case by the respondent in filing his petition at the court below. It is therefore true … that a petition such as is envisaged by the provisions of the MCR, 1983 had not been properly placed before the lower court which ought to have upheld the preliminary objection by striking out the petition.[859]

850. Aside from the lead judgment, Pats-Acholonu, JCA[860] provided a guidance on the proper format a verification should take in the following terms:

> I have carefully examined the import of this rule. Is the manner adopted by the petitioner respondent the correct proceeding, where the relevant content to wit, the verifying affidavit is completely not connected to the petition except by reference made to it? I think not. I have indeed endeavoured to be persuaded by the argument of the learned counsel for the respondent but much as I tried, I am not so persuaded. This is the usual case where I believe the tone of the wordings of the statute sends out a message that it should be done in that way.

858. [2004] 11 NWLR (part 884) 332, 357 – Mohammed, JCA.
859. [2004] 11 NWLR (part 884) 332, 363.
860. Later Justice of the Supreme Court.

> Besides there is a need to bring certainty to this aspect of the law on Matrimonial Causes so that in future counsel filing this sort of document should be careful enough to reflect the verifying affidavit 'on' the petition not outside the petition. What I am saying is that apart from the required heading 'In the matter of the petition (name of the petitioner) which in this case is Emmanuel Chike Unegbu[…],[861] the verifying affidavit should not bear, the heading of title "in the High Court of … " for that matter, because the verifying affidavit should and ought necessarily by the operation of the law be made to be part (wholly of entirely) of the petition.'.[862]

851. Olagunju JCA while expressing serious misgivings on how to achieve the feat required in the rules, thought that the draftsman of the rule must be blamed for its clumsiness particularly in the light of section 90(a) of the Evidence Act but agreed that in the circumstances prevailing in the case, the requirement of the rule was not met and the affidavit as attached, did not verify the facts on the petition.[863]

III. Fees and Relevance to Petition

852. Fees are a serious aspect of the application and filing of proceedings on matrimonial causes and may be a legal impediment to the proceedings, even if the petition happens to be filed. Section 112 of the MCA provides for fees to be paid in accordance with practice and procedure of courts in line with the provision made therein. The MCR subsequently provided for payable fees in Order XX while the schedule of fees payable is specified in the Second Schedule to the MCR. The Supreme Court has held that where the fees are paid but not reflected by the Court registrar, it cannot be taken against the party to which it concerns. *Ibeabuchi v. Ibeabuchi*[864] advances the position that petitions for dissolution of marriage or matrimonial causes in line with section 114(1) of the Act must be accompanied by payment of appropriate fees as regulated in Order 23 of the Matrimonial Causes Rules. The fees are subject to waiver processes at the discretion of the Court which may waive, postpone in whole, or in part for special reasons.

IV. Service of the Petition

853. Order VI of the Matrimonial Causes Rules provides for service of petition and the various ways in which this can be done lawfully. rule 1 states the General provisions relating to service of Documents while rule 7 states the process for substituted service. By rule 1, where service of a document is to be made on a respondent or a person, service may, be effected, either in or outside of Nigeria:

---

861. His Lordship referred to *Gapp v. Gapp & Leverson* [1859] 4 SW 2 T 2781; 164 ER 152; *Steed v. Steed* [1864] LR 1 PD 364.
862. [2004] 11 NWLR (part 884) 332,364.
863. *Ibid.*, 332,367.
864. [2016] LPELR-41268 (CA); CA/K/322/2012.

(a) by delivering the document to the person personally;
(b) by serving the document on the person by post;
(c) if the person has an address for service for the purpose of the proceedings, by delivering the document at that address or by posting the document (under prepaid postage) as a letter to the person, or his legal practitioner, as the case may be, at that address; or
(d) by delivering the document at, or by properly addressing and posting (under prepaid postage) the document as a letter to the person at, the last address of the person known to the person on whose behalf the document is being served.

854. Rule 7 provides for substituted service in accordance with the order of the Court and such service once done in line with the court's direction is deemed to be due service of the document on the person intended to be served. Section 7(1) thus states that where a court, upon application made ex parte by a party to the proceedings under the rules, is satisfied that it is not reasonably practicable for the party to effect service of a document in a manner specified in any of paragraphs (a) to (d) (above), the court may order that service of the document be effected in a manner specified in the order or that the giving of notice of the document and of its effect by advertisement or otherwise, as specified in the Order, be substituted for service of the document. Section 7(2) states that where an order has been made by the court authorising the giving of notice of a document by advertisement, the form of the advertisement shall be approved by a Registrar.

V. Determination of Petition Must Be in Open Court

855. Petitions must be heard in open court.[865] This has been strictly applied by the Supreme Court. However, it is uncertain, how this position can bear closer scrutiny in the light of normative elements of due process, human rights and the right to privacy, the aim of the law in preferring reconciliation of the parties and the larger social policy of order and peaceful co-existence.

856. Openness in marriage rites is clearly traceable to the perception of marriage as property relations. This is typified by the key essential elements of property relationship – proprietaries; certainty, use, registration and notice. In modern times and in line with modern legal conceptions, the time has come to revisit under what circumstances dissolution of marriage should remain a public affair, short of registration of the outcome of the proceedings. It is thought that only persons closely related to the proceedings should be part of it. In this respect, the approach of customary law is to be preferred. The MCA is replete with conciliatory provisions and the Courts have also stated specifically that the provisions on restitution of conjugal right are aimed at reconciling disputing couples.[866] It is difficult to see how open court hearing can facilitate the realisation of this objective.

865. This is discussed more fully below.
866. *Ahmad Moktar Jabre v. Mrs Dorra Jabre* [1999] LCN/0622 (CA); [*1999*] 3 *NWLR* (Pt. 596) 606 at 617; [1999] LPELR. 8133.

857. Two Supreme Court decisions illustrate the position of the law on proceedings for dissolution of marriage or nullity mandatorily being in open court, and not in the Chamber of the judge. The cases are *Oviasu v. Oviasu*[867] and *Menakaya v. Menakaya.*[868] In *Oviasu v. Oviasu*[869] the appeal was on the decision of the Benin High Court in Edo State of Nigeria, in which the appellant-petitioner petitioned for the dissolution of her marriage with the respondent on three grounds; adultery between the first respondent and co-respondent and other women; cruelty and desertion.

858. The learned judge of first instance dissolved the marriage on the ground of desertion by the petitioner rather than from the answer from the respondent. At the Supreme Court, the petitioner pleaded that the case was heard by the judge of first instance, in chambers and that neither party had requested or applied for the proceedings to be heard in Chambers.

859. The Supreme Court in a considered judgment held that the trial court was very biased against the petitioner and that the failure to hear the case in open Court was fatal to notions of justice, the solemnity and formalism which openness confers on the outcome of cases and more so matrimonial Causes. Based on this, the court held that a fundamental irregularity which touched the legality of the whole proceedings including the judgment and incidental orders had occurred. A trial *de novo*[870] was ordered.

860. In *Menakaya v. Menakaya*[871] the marriage between the petitioner-husband and the respondent was celebrated at the Marriage Registry, Barnet, London, England. There were three children of the marriage. The petition was for a dissolution of the marriage and custody of the three children. The dissolution was brought by the husband on the ground that the marriage had broken down irretrievably. The fact or evidence of the irretrievable breakdown was that the respondent had constructively deserted the petitioner for a period of four years and failed, despite all efforts and attempts at reconciliation, to communicate with him by any means. The petitioner, therefore, claimed that he could not reasonably be expected to live with the respondent again.

861. The respondent denied all the allegations in her answer to the petition and filed a cross-petition. In her cross-petition, while alleging facts which made her life unbearable with the petitioner did not deny or aver that the marriage had broken down irretrievably. Thus, there could not be a consensual dissolution of the marriage. The respondent rather, sought an order dismissing the petition; decree for

867. [1973] ALL N.L.R 730.
868. [2001] 16 NWLR [2001] LCN/2778 (SC), SC.169/96.
869. [1973] ALL N.L.R 730.
870. Starting from the beginning a new trial.
871. [2001] 16 NWLR [2001] LCN/2778 (SC), SC.169/96.

judicial separation on behaviour; custody of the children of the marriage with reasonable access to the petitioner; maintenance of the respondent and children; and payment of costs for the litigation.

862. The evidence before the court showed that earlier efforts had been made at negotiated settlement of maintenance and support to which the petitioner and respondent were not in total agreement. Counsels to both parties also reported to the court that efforts were being made towards reconciling the parties, but then, filed a joint application praying the Court to hear the petition in chambers.[872]

863. In response to this application, the Court considered sections 54; 103 and 114(1) of the MCA. It further considered Order I, rule 9, sub-rules (1) and (4) of the Matrimonial Causes Rules.

864. The learned trial judge thereafter, granted the application to hear the petition in chambers and did so. In chambers, each counsel described and expatiated on the extent of the proposals of their client. In his judgment Ononiba, J., the learned trial judge made the following statement: 'There is no agreement at all on the reimbursement of accommodation expenses ... but totally rejected by the petitioner. Having outlined the position of the parties, it is now my responsibility and, I should add, a painful duty to use judicial discretion to make awards or accept any of the proposals in the areas of disagreement.' The High Court ordered a Decree *Nisi* and other ancillary reliefs of maintenance, custody and visitation rights.

865. The parties were dissatisfied with the judgment and the respondent appealed. The Court of Appeal dismissed the appeal and affirmed the decision of the trial judge.[873]

866. Dissatisfied with the judgment at the Court of Appeal, the respondent appealed to the Supreme Court. The respondent's grounds of appeal at the Supreme Court were principally, whether the judgment of the lower court was null and void for having the proceedings conducted in the chamber of the judge. This is despite the fact that the parties had applied for this option. Other grounds were that the judgment delivered by the High Court was on a day that was within the vacation of the court. The Court of Appeal had stated that the parties having applied for the proceedings to be heard in chambers were estopped by this conduct from subsequently objecting to the proceedings which were so held. This introduction of estoppel by conduct also formed a ground of appeal to the Supreme Court. Other grounds of appeal included that the High Court dissolved the marriage on grounds not known to law; monetary awards not based on relevant facts and the appellate court failing to comply with the duty of an appellate Court in hearing an appeal.

872. Under Edict No. 16 of 1987 s. 43.
873. There was a dissent judgement, Ejiwunmi, JCA allowing the appeal and ordering a retrial of the petition *de novo* before another judge.

867. The counsel to the petitioner adopted the questions as formulated but then filed a cross-appeal.

868. The Supreme Court noted in its judgment that from the judgement of the High Court, it was clear that there was no consent between the parties on any of the issues raised and admonished the trial court for filling gaps for the parties even in the absence of any sworn affidavits from the parties. It further noted that the failure of the respondent at the High Court to cross-examine the petitioner was perilous to her case.

869. Mohammed J.S.C. who delivered the unanimous ruling of the court stated that 'The law is that it is mandatory that proceedings in respect of petition for dissolution of marriage shall be in public.'[874] Referring to *Oviasu v. Oviasu*[875] with approval, the Supreme Court declared that parties to the proceeding cannot by their action or inaction waive the operation of the law on the subject. It went further to state that estoppel and its doctrines applied with respect to personal rights and not to statutory requirements of a public nature. In consequence the court held that any decision made by a court, contrary to a mandatory statutory provision is a nullity. Furthermore, that there was no meeting of minds between the parties at the trial court, and the court therefore, did not have sufficient evidence on which it arrived at its decision. Ultimately, the Court concluded that conducting the proceedings in chambers made the whole process at the High Court and at the Court of Appeal void. The appeal was allowed, a retrial of the petition and cross-petition *de novo* was ordered before another judge of Anambra State. The cross-appeal before the Supreme Court was dismissed as it was based on a non-existent judgment. Ogundare JSC who agreed with the lead judgment, however, also considered the provisions of the Constitution on what amounted to fair hearing. His Lordship also referred to section 36(3) of the Nigerian Constitution which provides: 'The proceedings of a court or the proceedings of any tribunal relating to the matters mentioned in subsection (1) of this section (including the announcement of the decisions of the court or tribunal) shall be held in public.' Subsection (1) provides that 'in the determination of his civil rights and obligations, including any question or determination by or against any government or authority, a person shall be entitled to a fair hearing within a reasonable time by a court or other tribunal established by law and constituted in such manner as to secure its independence and impartiality'.

870. He added that the learned counsels to the parties agreed that there was no consent judgment and therefore the decisions of the High Court could not be taken as such but that what is self-evident from the judgment is that the proceedings leading to it were as a result, of 'discussions in chambers'. In his judgment he also examined and considered sections 54(4); 103(1) and Order 1, rule 9. His Lordship concluded that: 'the cumulative effect of all these provisions is that hearing of a petition is to be in open court.'[876]

874. [2001] 16 NWLR (part 738) 203, 236; [2001] LCN/2778 (SC).
875. [1973] ALL N.L.R 730.
876. [2001] 16 NWLR (part 738) 203, 248.

871. In consequence, his Lordship concluded that 'as the learned trial Judge sat in a place other than as authorized by the Constitution, the Act and the rules made thereunder, the proceedings leading to his judgement suffered from such a fundamental vice that vitiated the entire proceeding and rendered the judgement delivered null and void'.

872. Commenting on Order 1, rule 9(4) which Niki Tobi JCA had described as 'confused' his Lordship stated 'I pause here to comment briefly on the above observation. With profound respect to the learned Justice of the Court of Appeal, I do not share his view that Order 1 rule 9(4) is in any way confused. I have already set out the rule earlier in this judgement. It empowers the court to take certain proceedings referred to in paragraphs (c)–(e) of the definition of matrimonial cause in Section 114(1) of the Act in chambers or in open court. In respect of proceedings of the kind referred to in paragraphs (a) and (b), however, proceedings must be in open court. And where proceedings of the first kind are taken along with proceedings of the second kind such proceedings can only be in open court.'[877]

VI. Analysis of the Law

873. In *Menakaya v. Menakaya*[878] Niki Tobi JCA, at the Court of Appeal stated that, the subsection while poorly drafted, can only have one meaning ascribed to it since sub-rules (1)–(3) deal with hearing of judicial separation, restitution of conjugal rights and jactitation as discretionary matters within the power of the court to opt for a chamber or open court hearing.

874. Ogundare JSC's position that the subsection is so simple is and the meaning which his Lordship ascribed to it is not that easily distillable from the ordinary reading of the rules or indeed, the relevant provisions of the Act.

875. The main rule which Niki Tobi JCA referred to is Order, 1, rule 9 (4). The rule itself is titled 'Chambers' and the subsection provides: 'This rule shall not authorise a court sitting in chambers to hear proceedings that relate to proceedings for an act of a kind referred to in paragraph (a) of the definition of "matrimonial cause" where it is practicable for the court to hear those proceedings at the same time as the proceedings for such an act.' The paragraph (a) referred to in the rule is-'dissolution of marriage' and paragraph (b) is 'nullity'.

876. The other sub-rules (1)–(3) of the Order are:

(1) Proceedings of a kind referred to in paragraph (c), (d) or (e) of the definition of 'matrimonial cause' may be heard by a court sitting in chambers.
(2) A court sitting in open court may adjourn proceedings of a kind referred to in sub-rule (1) of this rule for consideration by the court sitting in chambers.

877. *Ibid.*, 203, 250.
878. [2001] 16 NWLR [2001] LCN/2778 (SC), SC 169/96.

(3) A court sitting in chambers may adjourn proceedings of a kind referred to in sub-rule (1) of this rule for consideration by the court sitting in open court.

877. These sub-rules (i.e., (1)–(3)) are plain and refer to judicial separation, restitution of conjugal rights and jactitation which clearly are authorised to be under the judge's discretion whether or not chamber proceedings are ideal. However, sub-rule 4 is so inelegantly drafted that its meaning is not clear and can only be implied by excluding what had been covered in sub-rules (1)–(3), and deducing that what was not covered must then fall outside the category of subjects under the discretion of the judge.

878. Again, it is true that section 36(3) of the Constitution provides for civil proceedings to be held in open Court, this is a requirement in reference to fair hearing – a fundamental human right. it is not at all clear that this pertains to matrimonial causes in respect of which there are specific legislation or that the provisions of the MCA or the rules thereon are in conflict with other tenors of fundamental human rights such as family and privacy provided for in section 37.[879] Second, it is only his Lordship, who, in fact, was concurring with a lead judgment that has taken a position of relating the proceedings for matrimonial causes back to the Constitutional tenor of open court proceedings, a prerequisite for the determination of civil rights between parties for the purposes of fair hearing. Third, his Lordship agrees that by Order 1, rule 9(4), proceedings in respect of other matrimonial causes other than dissolution of marriage and nullity can be taken in the chambers of the judge which evidently detracts from the same Constitutional provision in section 36(3).

879. While, a hard posture for open proceedings for matrimonial causes may be the case with other jurisdictions such as the English, the provisions of the MCA and the rules do not appear to altogether support the hard line position of the Nigerian judiciary on the space for proceedings on dissolution of marriage and nullity. When sections 103 and 104 are jointly examined, it would appear that the High Court in *Menakaya v. Menakaya*[880] was, in fact, correct in its approach. The best that can be said in support of the hard line of the Nigerian Supreme Court is that the interpretation of sections 103 and 104, could produce a result which makes it discretionary in fact, that proceedings for matrimonial causes can take place in the chambers of a judge or in open court but that the delivery of judgment must be in open Court. Unfortunately, the court did not consider section 104 of the Act. The combination of these provisions and Order XXIII, rule 1, appear to completely support the approach adopted by the High Court in *Menakaya v. Menakaya.*[881] Moreover, the requirement for publicity is easily met with a due process of registration of the outcome of the proceedings where there is a change of status.

879. The section provides: 'The privacy of citizens, their homes, correspondence, telephone conversations and telegraphic communications is hereby guaranteed and protected.'
880. [2001] 16 NWLR [2001] LCN/2778 (SC), SC 169/96.
881. *Ibid.*

VII. The Provisions and Rules

880. The first section dealing with the subject is section 54 of the MCA, titled 'Institution of proceedings'. It states:

> (1) Subject to the next succeeding subsection, a matrimonial cause of a kind referred to in paragraph (a) or (b) of the definition of 'matrimonial cause' in section 114 (1) of this Act shall be instituted by petition.
> (2) A respondent may, in the answer to the petition, seek any decree or declaration that the respondent could have sought in a petition.
> (3) Proceedings of a kind referred to in paragraph (c) of the definition of 'matrimonial cause' in section 114 (1) of this Act that are in relation to proceedings under this Act for a decree or declaration of a kind referred to in paragraph (a) or (b) of that definition:
> (a) may be instituted by the same petition as that by which the proceedings for that decree or declaration are instituted; and
> (b) except as permitted by the rules or by leave of the court, shall not be instituted in any other manner.
> (4) The court shall, so far as is practicable, hear and determine at the same time all proceedings instituted by the one petition.

881. The next succeeding section is 55, titled 'Duty of court'. It provides: 'Save where other provisions in that behalf are made by this Act, the court, upon being satisfied of the existence of any ground in respect of which relief is sought, shall make the appropriate decree.'

882. Then, there is section 103, titled 'Hearings to be in open court'. It provides:

> (1) Except to the extent to which rules of court make provision for proceedings or part of proceedings to be heard in chambers, the jurisdiction of a court under this Act shall, subject to the next succeeding subsection, be exercised in open court.
> (2) Where in proceedings under this Act the court is satisfied that there are special circumstances that make it desirable in the interests of the proper administration of justice that the proceedings or any part of the proceedings should not be heard in open court, the court may order that any persons not being parties to the proceedings or their legal advisers shall be excluded during the hearing of the proceedings or the part of the proceedings, as the case may be.

883. Surprisingly, section 104, titled 'Proceedings to be heard by judge alone' then provides: 'Proceedings at first instance constituting a matrimonial cause shall be heard and determined by a judge sitting alone as the court.' Section 11(1) further refers to 'the judge constituting the court' with respect to a duty to consider reconciling the parties to the marriage prior to and in the course of adjudication.

884. Order XXIII, rule 1, is titled ''Consent orders' and states:

> Nothing in these Rules shall be taken to prevent the court from making, with the consent of the parties to proceedings and in accordance with the practice of the court, an order (not including an order of a kind referred to in paragraph (a) or (b) of the said definition of 'matrimonial cause') determining the proceedings or relating to the proceedings. An order made under this sub rule may be varied on the application of a person who had not been served with the petition or application instituting the proceedings.

885. Finally, Order XXI, rule 2 is titled, 'Non-compliance with Rules not to render proceedings void' and states: 'Subject to these Rules, non-compliance with these Rules, or with a rule of practice and procedure of a court applicable under the Act to proceedings, shall not render proceedings void unless the court so directs, but the proceedings may be set aside, either wholly or in part as irregular, or may be amended or otherwise dealt with in such manner and upon such terms as the court thinks fit.'

886. It is to be noted that the Supreme Court has held that by Order I, rule 9(1), proceedings with respect to judicial separation; restitution of conjugal rights; or jactitation of marriage can be legitimately held in chambers unless they form part of a process of dissolution of marriage or nullity of marriage, in which case by Order 1, rule (9)(4) any of the causes engaged, must be heard together with the proceedings for dissolution in open Court. In addition, reconciliation overtures which is a mandatory pre-hearing procedure can be held in the Chambers of the court.[882]

VIII. Bars to a Decree of Dissolution of Marriage

887. Bars are provided by the MCA to stop a petitioner under certain circumstances, from obtaining a decree of dissolution of a marriage from a court. Bars to dissolution of marriage could be absolute or discretionary. There are three absolute bars to a petition for dissolution of marriage in Nigeria. The three absolute bars are commonly referred to as the three 'c's – Collusion, Condonation and Connivance. Discretionary bars are also three; petitioner's adultery, desertion and conduct which has been conducive to the commission of a matrimonial cause. The distinction between absolute and discretionary bars are implicit from the terms, the one is complete in itself. Thus an absolute bar, if, proved stops the petitioner from obtaining the dissolution of marriage petitioned for. For discretionary bars, the courts have a discretion to withhold or grant a decree of dissolution of the marriage in spite of proof of the action which would otherwise constitute a bar.

888. It is sometimes stated that the reason for a continuing fault finding regime in the Nigerian matrimonial causes framework, is to provide courts with the window to trigger the bars to dissolution of marriage. The MCR[883] specifies that a petitioner instituting proceedings for a decree of dissolution of marriage or of judicial

882. Section 11(1)(b) MCA.
883. Order V, part 1, rule 7.

separation upon a ground specified in any of paragraphs 15(2) (a)–(g), of the Act or section 39 of the Act, as the case may be, shall contain a statement that the petitioner has not connived at that ground; and a denial that he has condoned that ground, or a statement of all facts relevant to the question whether he has condoned that ground, including any facts relevant to the question whether that ground has been revived. Second such a petition instituting proceedings for a decree of dissolution of marriage or of judicial separation shall contain a statement that in bringing the proceedings, the petitioner has not been guilty of collusion with intent to cause a perversion of justice.

889. Sections 26 and 27 of the MCA contain the provisions on absolute bars. Section 26 provides that a decree of dissolution of marriage shall not be made if the petitioner has condoned or connived at the conduct constituting the facts on which the petition is based. It, however, provides exceptions for situations where a party to the marriage is confirmed to have an illness of the mind that is characterised as unsound, is unlikely to recover and has been confined in an institution established for such purpose, for a period anywhere between five and six years.[884] Section 27 makes it an absolute bar for a petitioner who, in bringing or litigating the proceedings of dissolution of marriage, has been guilty of collusion with intent to cause a perversion of justice.

890. The discretionary bars are provided in section 28 and arise where there has been adultery by the petitioner which has not been condoned by the respondent or one which was condoned and has been revived; the petitioner has wilfully deserted the respondent before the matters on which he relies in the petition or in the case of issues extending over a period of time, the petitioner had wilfully deserted the respondent before those times. The last discretionary bar is where the habits of the petitioner have, or the conduct of the petitioner has conduced or contributed to the existence of the matter relied upon by the petitioner. Section 105(4) further provides that a party or a person acting in collusion with a party may be ordered to pay the costs of any other party, or of a *bona-fide* purchaser or other persons interested, of and incidental to any such instrument or disposition and the setting aside or restraining of the instrument or disposition.

891. The law on bars draws from the English position. The Judicature Act, 1925, by section 178(2), provided the impetus for absolute bars. Section 178(2) of the Act provides that the court shall dismiss a petition for divorce if it is not satisfied as to the absence on the part of the petitioner of connivance at adultery, condonation of adultery or cruelty, or collusion with the respondent whatever be the ground of the petition. Section 178(1) required the courts to enquire into the existence of the matters raised by subsection 2. It equally influenced the development of discretionary bars and the attitude of the court to exercising the discretion vested in it, with respect to the conduct of the petitioner and in particular, the discretion statement. Other influences include the Matrimonial Causes Act, 1923, 1937 and 1967. It is

884. Section 16(1)(g) of the MCA.

worth noting that advancements have been made, but the English jurisdiction originally required that male adultery had to involve incest, bigamy or desertion to form a basis for dissolution of marriage.

892. The question of condonation and connivance often arise or arose with the matrimonial offence of adultery. It is only collusion that is distinct and leads to unsavoury social responsibility and therefore, perversion of justice. Thus, condonation and connivance are, or ought to be irrelevant where adultery is not treated as a matrimonial offence or an offence at all, bigamy being of a different character. In such regimes where adultery is more of a fad than a crime, therefore, adultery is of no consequence, and so also, should, the co-respondency regimes. [885] In Nigeria, however, the co-respondency regime is well and hearty but with a tilt to ensure the fidelity of the wife. Some other laws are also relevant to any examination of the bars. Section 82 of the Nigerian MCA only requires reasonable satisfaction of the Court to prove all matters. Moreover, section 83(2) while making a husband and wife competent witnesses excludes them from being compelled to disclose communication made in the course of the marriage. Section 186 of the Evidence Act, however, provides that unless a party has attempted disproving an adultery, no party, whether witnesses or party to the proceeding or not, is to be compelled to give evidence on adultery.

893. Absolute bars are said to be based essentially on matrimonial offence regime, but as has been highlighted above, the MCA cannot be said to be anywhere close to being free of a matrimonial offence regime. Indeed, some of the cases continue to treat the matrimonial causes explicitly in that sense. Overall, except for the three-year fact, Nigerian Courts continue to operate in practice if not principle, the matrimonial offence regime. Condonation is obviously a means by which the law is still saddled with the idea of reconciling a spouse to the other by holding a spouse to an earlier forgiveness of the wrong and reinstatement as spouse. Connivance implicates the participation of the other spouse in the wrong or at least the encouragement to do so while collusion is more self-explanatory.

894. It is clear that all the bars except for collusion, cannot bear close scrutiny in the light of fundamental human rights and contemporary realities of marriage, family order and the best interest of children.

IX. Decrees

895. The MCA vests wide discretionary powers in the court on the making of appropriate decrees. A decree is an order usually having the force of law.[886] In matrimonial causes a decree has the force of law. *Nisi* originates from the Latin word *nisi*, meaning 'unless'. A Decree *nisi* or in Latin 'rule *nisi*' is a court order that will

885. *See* for an interesting reading from the United Kingdom jurisdiction, Sue Jenkinson, *supra.* n. 758, 201–215.
886. At https://www.merriam-webster.com/dictionary/decree.

come into force at a future date unless a particular condition satisfactorily challenges its taking effect or is met. Unless the condition is met, the ruling becomes a decree absolute 'rule absolute' and is binding on the parties to the proceeding. These terms have become almost peculiar to matrimonial proceedings. A Decree *nisi* takes effect at a specified time unless previously modified or avoided by cause shown, further proceedings, or a condition fulfilled.[887] A Decree *nisi* can be avoided for instance, by the petitioner deciding to reconcile with the respondent or a party showing some other cause as to why the decree should not take effect. In any of the cases, the aid of the court will be required to lift or rescind the decree and dismiss the petition.

896. Some preliminary remarks must be made with respect to some provisions of the MCA on decrees. Section 16(2)(a) provides that a decree made when a person has been continually absent from the other spouse in line with fact section 15(h) shall be in the form of a decree of dissolution of marriage by reason of presumption of death.[888] Section 33 of the MCA provides for remarriage by a party. This can be legitimate once a decree of dissolution is made absolute. The decree is treated as though the marriage had been dissolved by death.

897. The determination of a matrimonial cause can result in a decree once the Court is satisfied of the existence of any ground in respect of which relief is sought.[889] Section 56 provides that for dissolution of marriage or nullity of voidable marriage, the decree must be *nisi* at first instance. The Decree *nisi* becomes absolute by effluxion of time subject to variations provided in section 57, or special circumstances which appeals may necessitate or the general discretion of the court. Section 58(1) and (b) govern the first two scenarios, that is where there are children of the marriage who are yet to be sixteen and those who have attained that age as at the date of the ordering of the Decree *nisi*. Where the children are in the first category, section 57 applies and the procedure of the decree becoming absolute is governed by section 58(1)(a). Where they are in the second category section 58(1)(b) applies. Section 58(1)(b) provides for where there are no children under the age of 16 as at the date of the order of the Decree *nisi*. In this case, the Decree *nisi* shall become absolute on the expiration of a period of three months from the making of the Decree *nisi*. The scenario covered by sections 57 and 58(1)(a) is discussed in the next section.

898. The Act makes additional provisions for varying the time when the Decree *nisi* becomes absolute with respect to appeals or prospects of appeal. The Court of first instance, whether or not it made the decree or a Court of Appeal, based on whether there is an application for, or prospect of appeal, can extend the expiration date when the Decree *nisi* ought to have become absolute by effluxion of time. Section 58(2) gives wide discretion to the Court to consider when the decree becomes absolute by having regard to the possibility of an appeal or further appeal, and based

887. At https://www.merriam-webster.com/dictionary/nisi.
888. Section 16(2)(b).
889. Section 55 of the MCA.

on that judgment, make an order extending the period at the expiration of which the Decree nisi will become absolute; or reducing the period for which the Decree *nisi* will become absolute. Once the appeal is determined or the reason for a fresh enquiry with the same or the Court is determined, then section 58(3) is engaged and twenty-eight days become the first option duration period for the decree becoming absolute.[890] Section 58(3) provides for where there is, in fact, an appeal and how the Decree *nisi* becomes absolute – at the expiration of a period of twenty-eight days from the day on which the appeal is determined or discontinued; or on the day on which, in the particular circumstances, the decree would have become absolute under subsection by general effluxion of time of three-months had the appeal not been instituted, whichever is the later.

899. The MCA defines an 'appeal', in relation to a Decree *nisi*, to mean – an appeal, application for leave to appeal or intervention, against or arising out of the Decree nisi; or an order under the last preceding section in relation to the proceedings in which the Decree *nisi* was made; or an application under section 60 or 61 for rescission of the decree or an appeal or application for leave to appeal arising out of such an application.[891]

900. The Court also has power to refuse to make a decree in the course of proceedings for a decree of dissolution of marriage, if on the application of respondent for maintenance, it is not reasonably satisfied that the petitioner will pay the maintenance or that there is an effective arrangement for maintenance to be made.[892]

901. Section 58(4) provides that a Decree *nisi* shall not become absolute where either of the parties to the marriage has died. This clearly impacts on property and devolution rights. The parties may also decide to reconcile their differences. The Court is thus obliged to make an order subject to such changed circumstances which must be brought to the attention of the Court.

902. The interval between the Decree *nisi* becoming absolute is different between Nigerian and English jurisdictions. The provisions of the MCA, 1973 on Decree *nisi* on provides that the Decree *nisi* has to be made absolute by the Court. Section 1(5) provides: 'Every decree of divorce shall in the first instance be a decree nisi and shall not be made absolute before the expiration of six months from its grant unless the High Court by general order from time to time fixes a shorter period, or unless in any particular case the court in which the proceedings are for the time being pending from time to time by special order fixes a shorter period than the period otherwise applicable for the time being by virtue of this subsection.'

903. In practice, the petitioner must apply for the decree to be made absolute. The English position which not only provides for a longer interval between the Decree *nisi* and absolute but also requires the continuing active intervention of the

890. Section 58(3)(a).
891. Section 58(5).
892. Section 25 of the MCA.

court is to be preferred. It provides better opportunity for conciliation allowing things to settle down one way or the other. It thus gives the Court more opportunity of actively intervening in any development regarding the marriage and the decree issued. Not surprisingly, Lord Sumption, had stated in *Prest v. Petrodel Resources Limited*[893] that the approach of the law in that jurisdiction is more inquisitorial than adversarial. In addition, the English position is more likely to limit foul play that may centre on property and financial interests as no award in respect of these can take effect until the decree of dissolution is made absolute.

X. Decree Absolute and Children

904. Decree *nisi* becomes absolute when there are children of the marriage only as contemplated by the law in sections 57 and 58(1)(a). In this case, there are two scenarios. There are children of the marriage who are below the age of 16 as at the date of the order of Decree *nisi*, or as at that date are sixteen, but special circumstances exist which require that section 57 applies. The contemplated special circumstances necessitate that the time the decree becomes absolute or the action of the court is subjected to the welfare of the children of marriage.

905. Section 57(1) provides that a Decree *nisi* cannot become absolute unless the Court by order, has declared:

a. That it is satisfied that proper arrangements in all the circumstances have been made for the welfare and, where appropriate, the advancement and education of those children or
b. That there are special circumstances that the decree nisi should become absolute notwithstanding that the Court is not satisfied that such arrangements have been made. The age component here is for children under the age of sixteen (16) at the date of the decree nisi.

906. Section 57(3) provides for exercise of discretion for the application of the section in relation to children who have attained the age of 16 years as at the date of the Decree *nisi*.

907. A decree absolute crystallises without further action on the part of the Court in Nigeria. Therefore, a court determining a matrimonial cause relating to dissolution of marriage, nullity or judicial separation is required to pay closer attention to children's welfare in the determination of such proceedings. The MCA provides for all affairs in relation to children to be properly addressed and settled before a Decree *nisi* or decrees in respect of other related causes is ordered. In addition, in determining an application for leave to institute proceedings before the expiration of two

893. [2013] UKSC 34.

years of the formation of the marriage, in relation to dissolution of marriage, nullity or judicial separation. the court must also pay close attention to the interest of any children of the marriage.[894]

908. The MCA interprets marriage.[895] In interpreting marriage, it defines 'children of the marriage'. Children of the marriage is defined by inclusion and therefore not closed:

(a) any child adopted since the marriage by the husband and wife or by either of them with the consent of the other;
(b) any child of the husband and wife born before the marriage, whether legitimated by the marriage or not; and
(c) any child of either the husband or wife (including an illegitimate[896] child of either of them and a child adopted by either of them) if, at the relevant time, the child was ordinarily a member of the household of the husband and wife, so however that a child of the husband and wife (including a child born before the marriage, whether legitimated by the marriage or not) who has been adopted by another person or other persons shall be deemed not to be a child of the marriage.

909. Where all necessary arrangements are made as at the date of the determination of the proceedings, then the normal period of three months apply but where the arrangements are made subsequent to that date, then thereafter, twenty-eight days from the making of such arrangements or the three-month period, whichever is later. Thus, section 58(1)(a) provides for instances where section 57 applies. The Decree *nisi* shall become absolute by force of the section at the expiration of a period of three months from the making of the decree; or a period of twenty-eight days from the making of an order under section 57(1) as above, with regard to the declaration of the Court, whichever is the later. The Section applies to only dissolution of marriage or nullity of voidable marriage.

XI. Comparable Notes with English Jurisdiction

910. Section 41 of the English MCA, 1973 has similar provisions for children but the section has some striking differences and extends the provisions to judicial separation. The section in spite of whatever, else may be said of the MCA, 1973 indicates that the Act contemplates in principle and practice, a 'no fault divorce'. The section also leads to the conclusion that policy makers envisage that person who applies for or petition for matrimonial causes must be certain that they wish to proceed with it. Regrettably, the section also leads to the conclusion that patriarchy is still very much at play even in England and therefore the masculine descriptive gender runs through the section. The Section unlike the Nigerian provisions which

894. Section 30(4) of the MCA.
895. Section 69 of the MCA.
896. *See* the position on the question of illegitimacy below.

defines children only in relation to marriage. While the English provisions attempts to capture all the minors that may have bonded with the family, the Nigerian provision confers discretion only with respect to age of the children of the marriage.

911. On the whole, section 41 is a progressive one. The section makes provisions for how the court should proceed with making a decree absolute or other orders when the welfare of minor children is involved. The section defines children commendably, with respect to family. This is important as it embraces modern notions of humanness and family. The section refers to 'a minor child of the family' and with respect to the other categories may then include one who is above sixteen, but perhaps, below eighteen as at the date of the order.

912. The section also defines welfare in relation to a child. This includes the custody and education of the child and financial provision for him but does not exclude other kinds of actions or inactions that may amount to welfare.[897]

913. Thus, 'children of the family' are: any minor child of the family who at the date of the order divorce, nullity of marriage or judicial separation is under the age of 16; receiving instruction at an educational establishment; undergoing training for a trade, profession or vocation – whether or not he is also in gainful employment. It also includes any other child of the family to whom the court exercises a discretion as falling in that category and by an order directs that the section shall apply. The court is to be guided in the exercise of discretion with this last category by reaching a conclusion that there are special circumstances which make it desirable in the interest of the child that the section should applied to the child or children.[898]

914. The Court cannot make a decree absolute or grant other orders without first enquiring as to arrangement for children of the family and making categorical declarations that it is satisfied one way or the other, on its findings on the arrangements for welfare of the children of the family. The Court must therefore, if this is its finding, before making any of the orders, declare that there are no children in respect of which the section applies.[899] It must, if it finds, that there are children to which the section applies, declare so, and provide the names of the children in the decree or order. The decree or order must also state the arrangements made for the welfare of every child, their adequacy or limitations or where it is impracticable for the party or parties to make any such arrangements, the court must also, so declare.

915. Thus, it must also make declarations in other categories and these are: that the children to whom the section applies are named in the order and that arrangements for the welfare of any such child named has been made and is satisfactory,[900] or that it is impracticable for the party or parties appearing before the court to make

897. Section 41(6).
898. Section 41(5).
899. Section 41(1)(a).
900. Section 41(1)(b)(i).

any such arrangements.[901] It could also be, but the court must also declare so, that there are circumstances making it desirable that the decree should be made absolute or should be granted, as the case may be, without delay, notwithstanding that there are or may be children of the family to whom the section applies and that the court is unable to make a declaration to their welfare.[902]

916. Where the situation is that it is desirable to make an order or grant a decree in spite of the a finding that there exist interests in the welfare of children which it cannot arrange, then the court shall not make an order declaring that it is satisfied, unless it has obtained a satisfactory undertaking from either or both of the parties to bring before the court within a specified time, the welfare arrangements for the children named in the order.[903]

917. If the court makes absolute a decree of divorce or nullity of marriage, or grants a decree of judicial separation, without having made an order under any of the required circumstances, the decree shall be void but, if such an order was made, no person shall be entitled to challenge the validity of the decree on the ground that the requisite conditions were not met.[904] Where based on any of the said conditions, however, the court refuses to make an order in any proceedings for divorce, nullity of marriage or judicial separation, it shall, on an application by either party to the proceedings, make an order declaring that it is not satisfied with all the circumstances mentioned above.[905] This last provision in section 41(3) is interesting. Thus, once the court has met the conditions it is required to extract from the findings, the exercise of the discretion is impeachable. Spouses who then approach the court for any of the stated matrimonial causes must be certain that they their marriage has indeed broken down irretrievably and must not waste the time of the court.

XII. Rescission of Decrees or Other Orders Following a Decree *Nisi*

918. The parties may become reconciled after a court has ordered a Decree *nisi*, the MCA makes provision for the rescinding of the order. This has to be on the application of the parties and before the decree becomes absolute.[906] The Decree *nisi* could also be rescinded on the ground of miscarriage of justice. Thus, an application of a party to the proceedings may be considered and the Decree nisi rescinded or the proceedings ordered for rehearing, if a court is satisfied that there has been a miscarriage of justice by reason of fraud, perjury, suppression of evidence or any other circumstances justifying such a conclusion.[907]

---

901. Section 41(1)(b)(ii).
902. Section 41(1)(c).
903. Section 41(2).
904. Section 41(3).
905. Section 41(4).
906. Section 60 of the MCA.
907. Section 61 of the MCA.

XIII. Registration of Decrees

919. Registration of decrees is the function of the registrar or other proper officer of the High Court. The Registrar or other proper officer of the court by which the Decree *nisi* was made is required to prepare and file a memorandum of the decree and of the date upon which it became absolute.[908] The section does not state who has the responsibility to follow up on the Decree *nisi*, since it takes effect by effluxion of time or in the time frame discussed above on the exercise of the court's discretion. Section 59(1) states: 'Where a decree nisi becomes absolute, the registrar or other proper officer of the court by which the decree was made shall prepare and file a memorandum of the fact and of the date upon which the decree became absolute.'

920. Section 59(2) provides for any person, upon application to the Registrar or other proper officer of the court, and payment of relevant fees, to be entitled to obtain a certificate evidencing the dissolution of the marriage. It further provides that such a certificate shall in all courts and for all purposes be evidence of the matters specified in the certificate. Order XXIII of the MCR defines 'registrar' to mean the Chief Registrar, Deputy Chief Registrar, or registrar of the court.

921. Section 89 of the MCA provides for enforcement of decrees by other High Courts within Nigeria and by subsection 1, facilitates the registration of decrees by a court in accordance with rules of court in another court with jurisdiction under the Act, which may be a High Court of another state, the FCT or the Magistrate Court in exercise of summary jurisdiction.

922. Regulation 41 of the B, D, M, Etc., (Registration) Regulations requires information on dissolution of marriage to be provided in a central manner. Thus, the registrar of the National Population Commission, an office that has been fully discussed in the section on registration of civil data is required to liaise with the High Court of the area on issues of dissolution of marriage. A specific Form or one similar to it is prescribed to be used in providing the requisite information.[909] The registrar for the area upon receipt of information and data specified in Regulation 41(1) is required to furnish certified copy of all entries made during the preceding month to the Chief Registrar of the National Population Commission in the structure already discussed in the section on registration of Civil data.

923. Section 41(1) provides the information which the registrar should receive from the High Court. The registrar for the area in which a statutory marriage has been dissolved by a court of competent jurisdiction shall, upon receipt of the notice of the dissolution by the Registrar of the High Court make in the Register of Divorces (Statutory) an entry stating the following:

(a) the full names of the husband;

---

908. Section 59(1).

909. This is Form MD.1 set out in the First Schedule to the Regulations.

(b) the full names of the wife;
(c) the date of marriage;
(d) the date of filing the action for dissolution of the marriage;
(e) the name of the party who filed the action;
(f) the court in which the action was filed;
(g) date of receipt of notice of dissolution;
(h) the decision of the court;
(i) the effective date of dissolution.

924. It is again clear that only a central registration system can satisfy the need of registration of civil status. The scheme of obtaining certificates of decrees of dissolution of marriage from the registrar of the High Court or any other officer is clearly unworkable. First of all, Nigerian Courts works administratively only through a registrar and so, who the other proper officer of the Court is, is not clear at all. Second, it is difficult to contemplate how one can know when, or where a dissolution of marriage has taken place, in order to apply for the requisite information about a decree bearing in mind, the complex geographical and court structure of Nigeria. Third, and most importantly, since the MCA makes effluxion of time the default way by which the Decree *nisi* of the Court becomes absolute, absent this, some wide exercise of discretion of the court, it is expected that only the parties who have been separated can return to the court to provide this information to the court. There is no mandatory provision placing this duty on the parties.

925. From the international perspective, Nigeria recognises dissolution of marriage by superior courts of other Nations in line with section 81 of the MCA. Registration of the Dissolution, Maintenance and related issues will be registrable in line with the reciprocity rules of the Foreign Judgment (Reciprocal Enforcement) Act,[910] and in line with relevant civil procedure rules. Others may be dealt with in line with reciprocal international relations or requirements as indicated by individual jurisdictions.

XIV. Enforcement of Orders

926. Section 88 provides for enforcement by attachment. An attachment is a legal process of seizing property for the purposes of satisfying a judgment. The type of properties that can be seized and manner of conducting the attachment are detailed in the Third Schedule to the MCA. Section 88(1) empowers the court to enforce by attachment or other process, an order made by it on payment of maintenance or costs or in respect of the custody of, or access, to children. Subsection 2 specifies conditions under which a person who has been taken into custody in this connection can be released. Such a release can only be by the order of the court. The court must be satisfied that the person has complied with the order in respect of which the attachment was made, before ordering a release. The court has a judicial

910. Cap F35, Laws of the Federation 2004.

discretion to order the person's release notwithstanding that he or she has not complied with the order of ancillary relief of custody etc. Subsection 3 provides that after six weeks of non-compliance with orders in connection with the subject matter in subsection 1, the person ordered shall be deemed to be an insolvent person and may be kept in custody for a period not exceeding six months. The court can exercise judicial discretion on the period of restraint.

XV. Dissolution of Customary Marriages

927. A customary marriage may be dissolved formally by a customary court in the area where the marriage was conducted or informally in a customary manner. The former is not popular and happens mainly in urban centres such as Lagos and Ibadan.

928. Customary dissolution is better known. The main component of dissolution of a customary marriage as has been discussed under bride price and is its return or refund. This entails a process of dissolution perfected by return of the bride price to the groom's family. The families of the spouses engage one another in a meeting on the issues necessitating the dissolution. Once the families meet minds on this, the bride price is refunded and the marriage is at an end. Parties are free to remarry, and by parties is meant, the wife as the man was free to marry as many wives as he chose all along.

929. The dissolution is usually fault based but ultimately the process involved demonstrates that the main ground on which customary marriage is dissolved is irretrievable breakdown. Irretrievable breakdown is established by the families sitting as arbiter over causes which range from usual matrimonial offences – adultery, behaviour extending to laziness, rudeness or disrespect to groom's family and witchcraft, etc.

930. In many cases, the parties simply separate, by for instance, the wife sent to the village or rural setting while the husband remains in the city. The separation, does not equate to dissolution. Dissolution only occurs with the bride price refunded. Sometimes, the divorce may be hostile in which case a customary court in the area where the marriage took place is approached and the bride price may be deposited at the court following a simple procedure. This may be the case where it is the groom's family requesting the bride price and the bride's family refuses to return it. In such a case, the only resolution will be the intervention of the court –a situation which is the combustion for polygyny *a fortiori*, bigamy as the husband usually, will be unwilling to approach the court.

931. Section 43 of the BDM etc. (Compulsory Registration) Act and Births Death and Regulation 42 of the Marriage etc. (Registration) Regulations,[911] require compulsory registration of the dissolution of a customary marriage within sixty

911. S.1.6. of 1996.

days. This is to be done in the Area Court or customary court where the marriage was contracted and a notice of dissolution entered in the Register of Divorces (Customary) with the information detailed in the rules and as in Form CMD.1.

XVI. Dissolution of Islamic Marriage

932. Marriage under Islamic law can be dissolved either non-judicially or judicially. A judicial dissolution is done in the Area Court where the marriage took place.

933. The non-judicial divorce appears more common and includes the rejection of the continuation of the contract of marriage with a wife by the *talak*. The *talak* itself is of two types, the 'revocable' and 'irrevocable'. In the former, the *talak* is uttered once or twice in the course of three circles of menstruation. Where the woman is past age of child bearing; three months. The marriage stands dissolved on the third count. Prior to that third count, a husband may be reconciled to his wife and the marriage is not dissolved. According to the tradition applicable in Nigeria, the Maliki School, all the *talak* require a three-month interregnum known as *Iddah* or *iddat* by which a three-month suspension of dissolution is triggered between the *talaks*. The interregnum may result in reconciliation, however, where it does not and the third talak is pronounced then dissolution crystallises.

934. The other type of *talak* is the uttering of the *talak* thrice at one sitting upon which the marriage stands immediately dissolved. In this case the *talak* when invoked can only be revoked where the woman actually celebrates another marriage with a different husband whereupon, she may qualify to be reconsidered to remarry the earlier divorce husband. The idea is said to be to teach the woman the virtue or lesson of gratitude for her erstwhile husband who she may have disdained or taken for granted. This type of *talak* is a modification through time and is rejected as legitimate by some other Islamic schools.

935. Marriage could also be dissolved non-judicially by agreement or consent through a bargain which involves the release of a wife in consideration for a monetary payment or return of the *mahr*. The *mahr* may be refunded by parents or guardian of the wife.

936. The grounds for divorce under this type of marriage as in customary law marriages are usually fault based. As in customary marriages, dissolution under Islamic marriage is to be registered under the B, D, Etc. (Compulsory Registration) Act.

§4. Effects

I. Custody of Children

937. The principal effect of divorce is a determination of the custody of children of the marriage.

938. When marriage is formed and continuing, custody of children under customary marriages, Islamic marriages or statutory marriages is with both parents.

939. Upon dissolution of marriage or separation, custody under customs and Islamic law are somewhat straightforward. It could be done by institutionalised judicial process under the various customary court or Area Court laws of the States or informally according to customs or Sharia law. However, under the MCA, it is an ancillary proceeding which is dependent on the determination of the principal proceedings. Custody could also be decided under the specific State Infants Laws where there is no statutory marriage, and customary or Islamic law is not applicable. This was the position asserted by the Supreme Court in *Okwueze* v. *Okwueze* [912] a case which is discussed more fully below.

II. Custody under the Matrimonial Causes Act

940. Under the MCA, custody is an ancillary proceeding to a principal relief of matrimonial cause. A custody proceeding in relation to decree of dissolution or nullity of marriage, judicial separation or restitution of conjugal rights is conducted according to the rules and the provisions of the MCA. The most important provisions are sections 63, 69 71 and 88 of the MCA. Section 63 enables the intervention of Attorney General in related matrimonial causes, where the custody or guardianship of children is involved. Section 69 provides the meaning of 'children of the marriage'. This has been discussed under 'Decree Absolute and Children'. Then there is section 71 which provides the law and guidance for the making of orders. Section 88 provides for enforcement by attachment.

941. In *Oduche v. Oduche*[913] the Court stated that section 71(1) of the Matrimonial Causes Act was the guiding compass for custody proceedings. The court must consider the following factors, age of the child[ren] education, welfare and general upbringing, the arrangements made for their accommodation, the conduct of the parties to the marriage. Indeed, of paramount importance at all times is the interests and welfare of the child[ren].

942. The court is empowered to adjourn proceedings and possibly require expert witnessing from a welfare officer on matters relevant to the proceedings.[914] Custody

912. [1989] NWLR (part 109) 321 [1989] LPELR-SC. 202/1985.
913. [2005] LPELR-5976, 1.
914. Section 71(2) of the MCA.

can be granted to a person other than a party to the marriage.[915] Section 71(4) provides for access to the child from either party to the marriage where the child is with one of them or where the court has granted custody of the child to another person.

943. Orders V and XVI of the rules are relevant to custody proceedings. The children for whom custody proceedings apply are clarified and it is required that specific information is provided in a petition or application. In general, the children covered are as stipulated by section 69 of the MCA but the rule puts parties to proof on claims made under that section. Order XIV stipulates the rules for custody proceedings. The relevant rules are 20 –24. A Form 46, is required to institute the proceedings. The Court may consider custody after the filing of the petition for matrimonial cause related to children, and before the answer is filed from a respondent;[916] after the commencement of the proceedings but before the determination.[917] The court may hear a custody application by leave of court during the proceedings, either in writing or orally[918] and may grant custody, in an ex parte application if, there is an urgent reason to do so.[919] There must be fourteen days' notice between the application and hearing of the case for custody where there is no urgency.[920]

944. Order XIV, Part 4, rule 20(1) states:

> Where proceedings for ancillary relief, being proceedings seeking an order with respect to the custody, guardianship, welfare, advancement or education of a child of a marriage pending the disposal of proceedings, are instituted by a petition or by an answer to a petition, the petitioner or respondent, as the case may be, may, at any time after the filing of the petition or answer, set the proceedings for ancillary relief down for hearing by filing a request in accordance with Form 46.

945. Section 97 of the Child's Rights Act provides that a Court hearing a matrimonial case in which a child may be involved may direct that proper proceedings be taken in the Family Court at the High Court level for making the child a ward of Court. The court has powers to raise the question of wardship even where there is no application before the Court.[921]

946. The case law on the subject typifies the problem with custody proceedings in Nigeria. Custody proceedings are more troublesome than the divorce proceedings and indeed ancillary relief such as maintenance and settlement. In this respect,

915. Section 71(3) of the MCA.
916. Rule 21(1).
917. Rule 22.
918. Rule 23(2).
919. Rule 23(1).
920. Rule 21(2).
921. Section 96(1) of the CRA.

the difficulties arise from the feuding parents, not the law. Nigerian courts have fashioned very peculiar, consistent and seemingly apparent successful approach to dealing with custody. Overall, the courts are very patient with child custody proceedings.

947. Legislation and the judiciary are in perfect consonance on the subject, and this is anchored on what is the best interest of the child. The Courts have consistently held in line with all the provisions of law, the Constitution, MCA, MCR and Child's Rights Act – that this is paramount. While custody proceedings in English jurisdiction appear to favour mothers as being better equipped to take custody of children of the marriage, in many cases, Nigerian courts resort to a gender based peculiar cultural ethos – that females are best raised by mothers and sons by fathers. Thus, in *Odusote* v. *Odusote*[922] the Court referring to *Tabansi v. Tabansi*[923] with approval reaffirmed that a female child of tender age is better in the custody of a mother.

III. Case Law Analysis on Custody

948. Williams v. Williams[924] was an appeal before the Supreme Court. A Decree *nisi* had been granted in respect of the divorce proceedings between the appellant and respondent.[925] The appellant who already had custody of two, of the three children of the marriage, applied for the custody of the third, a female who was in the actual custody of her mother, the respondent.

949. The trial court had granted custody of the child to the respondent on her application. The Court of Appeal reversed this decision and leave for an appeal was granted for the suit to proceed to the Supreme Court.

950. Five questions were formulated for determination.

(i) Did the learned trial judge correctly direct himself as to the law applicable to the matter?
(ii) Did he correctly identify all the facts and circumstances he had to take into account in reaching a decision?
(iii) Can it be affirmatively asserted that he gave improper weight to or ignored any of the relevant facts and circumstances?
(iv) Can it be affirmatively asserted that his decision is otherwise wrong?

---

922. [2012] 3 NWLR (part 1288) 478.
923. [2009] 12 NWLR (part 1155) 415, 432.
924. [1987] NWLR (part 54) 66; [1987] All N.L.R. 254; [1987] 4 SC 32.
925. In accordance to s. 56 of the MCA, a decree of dissolution of marriage or nullity of a voidable marriage under this Act shall, in the first instance be a decree nisi. Upon a decree nisi for the dissolution of marriage, the decree becomes absolute in two ways – by effluxion of time where the three months' statutory period applies or a period of twenty-eight days after appropriate arrangement for the care and welfare of the children of marriage who are under 16 years or in exceptional cases above that age applies. *See also* ss 57 and 58.

(v) If the answer to questions (i) and (ii) are in the affirmative and to questions (iii) and (iv) in the negative, was the majority decision of the Court of Appeal correct in law in re-opening the learned trial judge's decision in the exercise of his discretion and reversing his decision on the grounds upon which he did?

951. The Courts through the High Court agreed on the applicable law as section 71 of the MCA which it stated contains the guidelines the courts are to follow in proceedings for custody of children of a dissolved marriage.

952. The Supreme Court took the opportunity to restate the law in this area. It stated that an order for custody is not a penal order on either parent and should not be construed as one. Rather it should be seen as one of high responsibility by the court. The paramount welfare of the child must be the focal point of the proceeding for custody but that the conduct of the parties was also a factor. The court further noted that for a child of tender years, education abroad may give a distorted view of life, apart from robbing the child of knowledge of his own country of origin in which he will ultimately live and work.[926] As Obaseki J.S.C. stated: 'it appears to be the fashion among certain classes of people to regard provision of educational opportunities for children of tender years outside this country as the ultimate. Their judgment has not yet been called into question and until then, time will tell whether what has been done is in the best interest of the child'.[927]

953. The Supreme Court drew on the judgment of the English Court of Appeal in *Allen v. Allen*[928] to arrive at the following conclusions:

(i) Custody hearings must be devoid of blame of any of the parents.
(ii) The two parties must be heard orally and physically.[929]
(iii) Flowing from (ii) above the discretion of the court must be exercised based on the whole circumstances of the case and in particular, the conduct of the parties.
(iv) That adultery has been committed by the mother does not impede her chances of custody.
(v) That custody may be awarded to some other relation aside from the mother.
(vi) That infant children should rarely be taken away from their mothers.
(vii) That custody that would facilitate removal of a child from her environment, in this case, country of origin must be approached with extreme caution.
(viii) That joint custody divided into control and responsibility is as good as sole or joint custody without division of responsibility.

926. [1987] NWLR (part 54) 66; [1987] All N.L.R. 254; [1987] 4 SC 32.
927. [1987] LPELR-SC 117/1985, p. 6.
928. [1948] 2 All ER 413 and RE W (an infant) [1963]2 ALL ER 706. The Supreme Court arrived at a most unimpeachable humanistic and legal approached to the questions of custody.
929. The Supreme Court and harsh words for the lower Courts for arriving at any decision at all without hearing from the respondent at the hearing and at the Court of Appeal.

954. In the event the court unanimously decided that the appellant and respondent shall have joint custody of their daughter, the mother exercising care and control of the child while the respondent takes charge of the education of the child. There was no order as to costs.

955. In *Odogwu v. Odogwu*[930] the husband petitioned for dissolution of the marriage on the ground of its irretrievable breakdown based on adultery of the respondent. The question of custody arose on the Decree *nisi* ordered by the High Court. The High Court granted custody of the three children of the marriage to the husband – petitioner. At the time of the order, the children were in the actual custody of their mother, the respondent, at this stage of the proceedings. The order of the trial court was that the custody of the children be to their father the petitioner. The respondent did not comply with the order. She rather filed a notice of appeal against the decision and a stay of execution pending appeal. The latter was refused by the High Court and on the same day an application for stay of the same execution of judgment of the High Court was made to the Court of Appeal. The application was subsequently struck out for want of prosecution. In the meantime, the appellant-husband deposed to an affidavit that he came across the three children in a run-down taxi and has had to take them with him to his own residence. The respondent wife, however, re-applied to the Court of Appeal for stay of execution of the judgment of the High Court. The Court of Appeal heard the application and made four orders of which the fourth is the most relevant. In it, the Court ordered that if as alleged, the respondent has forcibly obtained custody of the children, he shall return the children to the applicant-wife within seven days from the date of order.

956. As the Supreme Court noted this order is significant. The significance lies in the disobedience of the order by the appellant-husband. The Supreme Court took serious swipe at the petitioner – appellant and ultimately by a majority decision insisted that the appellant must comply with the order of the Court Appeal. The dissent judgment of Olatawura J.S.C. is instructive on the arguments of counsels and the final decision of the Supreme Court on the subject. He expressed the view that the Court ought to determine the case on its merits while downplaying the disobedience of the court order by the appellant – father.[931]

957. In *Okwueze* v. *Okwueze* [932] the appellant, who is the wife in this proceeding, sought the ancillary relief of custody of their four children. The appellant and respondent were married under customary law. The report appeared to indicate that the respondent was also validly married under the Marriage Act to another person as at when he conducted a customary marriage with the appellant. Uwais J.S.C. who delivered the lead judgment stated:

> First of all, there are more to the case in the Customary Court than really meets the eye. The appellant in her evidence showed that the respondent was 'legally

930. [1992] 2 NWLR (part 22) 539 [1992] LCN/2179 (SC).
931. [1992] 2 NWLR (part 22) 539, p. 570.
932. [1989] NWLR (part 109) 321 [1989] LPELR-SC. 202/1985.

married' to his first wife before he married her according to native law and custom. The question that follows is do the words 'legally married' refer to a marriage under the Marriage Act ... This observation becomes necessary if in fact there was no valid marriage between the parties in this case, the question of determining the custody of the children cannot be said to have come under the jurisdiction of the Customary Court; but will be governed by the provision of Infant Law, Cap 49 Laws of Ondo State, 1978, in which case the jurisdiction of the Customary Court would have been ousted.

958. At the customary court, the appellant had applied for the dissolution of their fifteen-year marriage on the grounds of lack of love, ill treatment and rejection since two years. She also pleaded to refund forty Naira dowry to her husband. The husband's claim was for reconciliation failing which custody of the four children of the marriage. The husband's bid for reconciliation was rejected and the divorce was granted on the following terms:

> In this circumstance, therefore, we have no option but to grant that their marriage be dissolved. Judgment for plaintiff, Divorce granted. Plaintiff to pay N40.00 being dowry to defendant. Issues of the marriage 4: ... Plaintiff to release the immediate custody of all four children to the respondent husband.

959. The appellant was unsatisfied with this judgment and filed an appeal to the High Court.[933] The appellant also applied to the customary court for stay of execution of the order of custody of the children of the marriage pending the determination of her appeal by the High Court. The order of stay was duly granted by the customary court. The main grouse of the appellant's appeal at the High Court was the award of custody to the respondent-husband. At the High Court, Balogun J. held that the customary court did not avert its enquiry to the provision of section 23 of the Customary Courts Law Cap 33 of the Laws of Ondo State, 1980.

960. The High Court considered these provisions along with custody under statutory marriages and awarded custody of all four children to the appellant. It set aside the order made by the customary court. It also ordered that either of the parties was at liberty to apply for variation of the order on changed circumstances. The respondent appealed to the Court of Appeal which restored the order of the High Court. The appellant-wife then appealed the decision to the Supreme Court.

961. As had been pointed out the Supreme Court took the position following an analysis of section 35 of the Marriage Act[934] that the subsequent customary marriage between the parties was invalid. It therefore considered the matter based on status of the parties as unmarried parents of the children. It stated that the general position under customary law is that the father of a legitimate or legitimated child

933. Appeals from customary Courts lie to the High Court.
934. Cap M6.

has absolute right to custody of the child. The court noted that the appellant at the customary court did not raise the issue of custody, and this meant in this regard, no evidence was adduced or taken.

962. In the particular circumstance of the Yoruba[935] customary law on the subject, the court stated that certain features were discernible:

(i) The best interest of the child.
(ii) The age of the child. A child that had not been weaned would normally go with the mother.
(iii) A child that has attained the age of 5 will go with the parent best able to provide for the child.
(iv) The gender of the child – in this connection a Court would consider a mother in a better position to raise a daughter.
(v) The Court may exercise a discretion to order custody to a relative rather than parents.

963. The Supreme Court reaffirmed (iv), above,[936] and restated that the only proper manner in which the custody of a child under customary law can be determined is by specifically taking evidence to establish what is in the best interest and welfare of the child.

964. In the circumstances, the Supreme Court took the position that two of the children were above 18, one was four months away from eighteen and only the last child was just a little above thirteen. To the Court only the last of the children, a female could be in custody of either parents. The Court awarded custody of the last child to the appellant based on all the circumstances of the case and without order as to costs.

965. In *Eluwa v. Eluwa*[937] the second issue for the court to consider was custody of the children. The high court had found that the petitioner was relying on remarrying for the care of the children whereas the respondent had well-laid out arrangements for the continued care, education and maintenance of the children.

966. The Court of Appeal restated, affirming the position of the High Court that the welfare of the children was of paramount importance and a vital factor but that it is important to consider each case contextually. This would take account of the context of the proceedings and its background. The court drawing on a long line of cases,[938] distilled the following factors to be considered in awarding custody:

935. Yorubas are the people of South West Nigeria. If the couple had been married, the applicable customs would have been that of the man but as they were unmarried then, or the court had discountenanced the marriage, it had to be that of the woman. *See Ben Enwonwu v. Spiro* [1965] 2 All N.L.R. 233; *see also Muojekwu v. Ejikeme* [2000] 5 NWLR 403.

936. Eso J.S.C., p. 336; Uwais JSC also took the same position; at p. 335.

937. [2013] LPELR –CA/C/180/2012.

938. *Otiti v. Otiti* [1992] 7 NWLR (part 252) 187; *Nana v. Nana* [2006] 3 NWLR (part 966) 1; *Williams v. Williams* [1987] 2 NWLR (part 54) 66; *Odogwu* v. *Odogwu* [1992] 2 NWLR (part 225) 539;

(1) Degree of familiarity between the children and each of the parents respectively.
(2) Degree of affection between the child and each of the parents respectively.
(3) Income and provision in life of each of the parents.
(4) Arrangements made by the parties for the education of the child.
(5) Changed circumstances such as one of the parents now living as man and wife with a third party, who may not welcome the presence of the child.
(6) Young children should as far as practicable live and grow up together.
(7) The age of the parents and in this case, that one of the parents is still young and may wish to marry and the child may become an impediment.

967. The Court of Appeal stated quite clearly that these factors are only some, to be considered and so each case is to be decided on the peculiar facts and circumstances in the proceedings. It considered that the High Court had adopted the right approach in considering and evaluating the evidence before it in granting custody of the two children of the marriage to the respondent. **Comparable Notes with the MCA, 1973**

968. Section 42 of the MCA, 1973 is in similar terms with section 71 of the Nigerian MCA, except that custody can be granted before or on granting a decree or at any time thereafter and where any proceedings for divorce, nullity or judicial separation are dismissed after the beginning of the trial, either forthwith or within a reasonable period after the dismissal. Here the child should be under the age of 18. Thus the court may make such orders as it thinks fit for the custody and education of any child of the family who is under the age of 18.[939]

969. Section 42(2) of the MCA, 1973, makes it possible unlike section 71(3) of the Nigerian MCA, for the Court, where it cannot make an order granting custody of a child to the parties to the proceeding to direct that proper proceedings be taken for making the child a ward of court. The Nigerian provision rather gives the court wide powers but does not provide a process by which a person other than the parents of the child[ren] can be granted custody. The Child's Rights Act, however, makes those provisions and is discussed under custody proceedings.

IV. Custody under Customary Law Marriages

970. On informal dissolution of marriage under customary law marriages, fathers have absolute control of children unless he provides some privileges. However, some customary law spouses dissolve their marriages in the customary courts, in which case, the relevant laws will apply. For instance, section 23 of the Customary Courts Law Cap 33 of the Laws of Ondo State, 1980, provides: 'in any matter relating to the guardianship and custody of children the interest and welfare of the

---

Lafun v. Lafun [1997] NMLR, 401; *Alabi v. Alabi* [2007] 9 NWLR (part 1039) 297; [2008] ALL FWLR (part 418) 245; [2007] LPELR 8203; *Afanja v. Afanja* [1971] 1 UILR 105.

939. Section 42(1).

child shall be the first paramount consideration … wherever it shall appear to a customary court that an order made by such court, should in the interest of a child, be reviewed, the court may, of its own motion or upon the application of any of his relatives or guardian vary or discharge such order'.

V. Custody under Islamic Marriages

971. It would appear that under Islamic marriages, on dissolution, custody of children would be with mothers provided, she has the physical and mental capacity to care for the children. The other instance where a mother may lose custody is, if she remarries. A mother has custody of her female child until such a female child marries and for the male child until, he attains puberty. Where for some reason a mother, after dissolution of marriage, is incapable of having custody, then custody would be granted to any of her female relations in order of some specific priority.[940] The husband under Islamic marriages is required to maintain his children irrespective of who has custody of them.

940. Available at: https://www.naijalegaltalkng.com/dissolution-of-marriage-and-custody-of-children-under islamic-law (last accessed 9 Oct. 2020).

Chapter 3. Cohabitation Without Marriage

972. Cohabitation without marriage in Nigeria is discouraged. Not surprisingly, this attitude has been judicially noticed in *N v. D* (Customary Marriage),[941] it raises a rebuttable presumption of marriage.[942]

973. Cohabitation, however, with or without some form of 'irregular marriage' is very rampant in Nigeria. There is a compelling need for women to have children. Prior to colonisation and modern trends, polygyny was acceptable and provided the framework for many women to fulfil the need of having children under the umbrella of marriage. Times and circumstances have, however, changed. Religion plays a key role. For the Muslims, religion promotes and sustains polygamy but in the South and Middle Belt, many are Christians. The need of women to have children and monogamy has thus created a nebulous marriage system. Children are protected by the Constitution – a protection which may, not altogether be altruistic. Nevertheless, where cohabitation without marriage, results in children, the Constitution protects the children from all forms of discrimination and deprivation based on circumstances of birth.[943]

974. Nigerian society is, in many ways, hamstrung by customs, unyielding in modern society, to rationality. Another perspective is that a customs framework, to which is added religion are but, a play on power. Peters writes: 'Habits and traditional practices and norms die hard. Abolition of traditions, customs and cultural practices and accepted way of life of a people can only succeed where the mores and sensibilities of the group concerned are repulsive to such traditions, customs and culture. Otherwise any legislative intervention may be tantamount to effort in futility. This proposition applies with equal force to the practice of polygamy.'[944] It is correct that the sensibilities of the average Nigerian are not repulsed by such traditions, customs and culture. The difficulty lies though, with the dogmatism of the sensibilities based as they were, not on informed rationalisation.

975. The impact of polygamy[945] under customary norms and Islamic law in Nigeria, with their offshoots of patriliny, patriarchy and son preference has provided a huge avenue for a fluid and nebulous marriage system. The result is that a considerable number of women are in fact, single and may be cohabiting in different forms and stages with 'husbands', a situation which is extremely exploitative of women and children particularly in the absence of a formal law for declaration of status and filiation. Writing of the situation, Peters notes again, and very importantly:

941. [2015] EWFC 28.
942. Section 166 of the Evidence Act, 2011.
943. Section 42(2) of the 1999 Constitution.
944. Dele Peters, *Feminism and the Institution of Polygamy: A Forward-Looking Approach*, 4 & 5 Nigerian Current Legal Probs. 1, 24 (1996–1998).
945. In this section polygamy is used in place of polygyny for consistency.

cultural cum societal attitudes often seem to weigh heavily in the mind of Nigerian women in deciding whether or not to get married or remain single. For instance, in a survey by the writer in Mushin and Ikeja areas of Lagos, it was discovered that majority of women in polygamous union in the pool were in the union not so much for the essence of marriage but to avoid the alleged 'societal stigma' associated with single motherhood. But, ironically, these women are more or less de facto single –mothers. For instance, twenty –five out of forty of them said they were financially independent, expect little or no financial or material provisions from their husbands, and are only in the union for the sake of marital status. Seventeen of them were in their second marriage. But surprisingly more than 50% of twenty unmarried ladies in yet another pool would rather be in a polygamous union than be single mother.[946]

976. It is easy to deduce that poverty in the country has enormous fuel from this state of affairs as there is need for a legal framework for providing for women and children in these circumstances. In addition, the population continues to rise with no attendant policy direction on how to stem the tide. Women in all the forms and stages of the arrangements have son preference. Needless to add, the preference for sons results in many female children, fewer sons, and repeat of the circle with its deleterious expressions in economic, political, and social terms.[947] In the absence of a formal social welfare scheme, women rely on children in the present and for the future, as social security reinforcing a state of desperation. As an example, it is not uncommon to see children of school age not in school, but in some form of income earning endeavours. At the moment the country is in a state of siege by youths making demands on the government – demands which, without addressing the background problems, are an exercise in futility.[948]

977. Drawing from Peters once again:

> Modern feminism on the one hand is a foreign value while polygamy on the other hand is a native and indigenous culture which though old is not archaic. Advocates of the former find the latter 'another example of male dominance over women'. An Africanist is therefore justified to castigate such a foreign

946. Dele Peter, *supra.* n. 944, 25.
947. N.N. Chinwuba, *Human Rights and Child's Wellbeing as Impetus for Sustainable Development in Nigeria: Why Accountability in Adult Relationships is Crucial*, Madonna U. L.J., 62–81 (2013–2014).
948. Shola Lawal & Adenike Olanrewaju, *Nigerians Demand End to Police Squad Known for Brutalising the Young,* available at: https://www.nytimes.com/2020/10/12/world/africa/nigeria-protests-police-sars.html of Oct. 12, 2020 (last accessed 16 Oct. 2020); 'SARS: Presidential panel on police reforms okay 5-point demand of End Sars Nigerian protesters' available at: https://www.bbc.com/pidgin/tori-54528118 of 13 Oct. 2020 (last accessed 16 Oct. 2020).

> culture as an intruder set to 'destroy the traditional fabric of Nigeria's well nurtured and properly articulated and accepted polygamous institution of marriage'. Can we therefore find a common ground for the operation of both value systems in which rights accruable to one will be recognised without an impingement by the other?[949]

978. Monogamy as a foreign value has now acculturised in Southern Nigeria in particular, as monogamy plus+ or monogamy++ as the case may be.[950] In the North, the dividend is no less palatable as the practice of young men who may be formally married to several women now witnesses a situation of vast number of children and the failing reproductive health of young women who bear the children.

979. The interpretation of section 42(2) of the Constitution on non-discrimination and deprivation based on circumstances of birth needs to be interpreted broadly and expanded to cover the right of women and children to be maintained in spite of an absence of a formal marriage. The labour of women who usually have custody of children in these arrangements as well as monetary expenditure, the education and upkeep of children ought to be provided for in a formal manner. This will not only satisfy the economic needs presented, it will also provide an effective mechanism that checks the trend. It is a forward-looking approach for a better ordered and progressive society that advances key indices of modernity which most Nigerians welcome. The indigenous customs of many Nigerian societies required men to maintain their concubines and children. The common ground, which Peters identifies is at best, only wishful. There is no better evidence of this than his conclusion:

> We do not call for an outright prohibition through legislative intervention for reasons hitherto stated. Our position, however, is that the institution has outlived its usefulness, if any, and that its practice constitutes an infringement of the fundamental human rights of women (and children too) who are the usual victims of this custom. We believe that with the proffered approach coupled with increased level of awareness among the Nigerian women population, polygamy as an institution, may soon be an institution of the past in Nigeria.[951]

980. It is conceded that legislation on the practice of polygamy as bigamy, will yield very little practical results. To Peters' credit, he identifies the problems in an impartial way but the author's proposition for their resolution leaves gaps. The major gap is the human need for biological origin – the sustained interest in the role of fathers in the lives of children and children's sustained interest in that relationship. This is what is most often exploited by some men.

---

949. Dele Peters, *supra.* n. 944, 20.
950. Monogamy+ will be a monogamous marriage by a man and one wife under customary law. Monogamy++ will be an additional female with child[ren] but no type of marriage and yet monogamy+++ which will be an additional relationship that produces a child but ends quickly.
951. Dele Peter, *supra.* n. 944, 26–27.

981. A practical constructive outcome presumably may only be found in holding men accountable to selves, women, children and society.

982. The CRA has a related provision, although with very minute utility or impact. Section 68 of the Act provides that where the father and mother of a child were not married to each other at the time of the birth of the child, the Family Court established under section 153 of the Act may, on the application of the father, order that he shall have parental responsibility for the child, or on the application of the mother, order that she shall have parental responsibility for the child or the father and mother may by agreement have joint parental responsibility for the child. The Court may also make orders on residency of the child. The Act, a domestication of the Child's Rights Convention is not uniformly accepted in the country because of the inability to sign it into a Federal Law. It, however, remains the benchmark for child's rights in the country. Some twenty-one States accept it and have enacted it into Law, but only Lagos State has a Family Court.

983. Where cohabiting persons separate, issues of property may be resolved in a declaratory manner or through the legal vehicle of trust. The latter was adopted in *Oghoyene v. Oghoyene.*[952]

---

952. [2010] 3 NWLR (part 1182) 564; [2010] LPELR – CA/L/26/2003.

Chapter 4. Filiation

§1. Filiation

984. Every child is required to have a name by two important legislation – the Child's Rights Act[953] and the Birth, Death, Etc., Act.[954]

985. Filiation is the process of determining kinship relation or family ancestry. The relation is by blood and relative to societies and so, also is the process. Some societies are patriarchal while others are matrilineal. In Nigeria, the relationship is patrilineal and filial relationship is traced through a paternal lineage and not maternal.[955] The term 'patrilineal' is thus used in delineating the ancestry. On the other hand, a matrilineal society, is a group adhering to a kinship system in which ancestral descent is traced through maternal rather than paternal lines. In a matrilineal society, surnames are derived through matrilineal ancestry. Property, such as land, is handed down from mother to daughter.[956]

986. The neighbouring country to Nigeria, Ghana, has a large segment of her society that is matrilineal – the Asante, or Ashanti. The Asante is one of the few matrilineal societies in West Africa. The Minangkabau of Sumatra, Indonesia, is the world's largest matrilineal society. In Minangkabau society, the man traditionally marries into his wife's household, and the woman inherits the ancestral home.[957] In matrilineal systems, men marry into the families of the wives the reverse is the case with patrilineal societies where men seek wives and bring them into their own families.[958] Furthermore, husbands and wives post-marital residence arrangements are likely to live in separate households, maintaining relationships with own families. This is unlike in patrilineal culture where wives are wholly bound to their husband's family and may remain a guest both in husband's family and own kinship family. Some research point out that the pattern of post marriage residence in matrilineal systems leads to less co-operation between spouses, although children and mothers fare better than they would in patrilineal societies.[959] In matrilineal societies, the economy is controlled by women while the men control religious and political activities. The most important offshoots of the different systems of descent are in name, marriage and custody.

987. Although there is no formal structure or process for determining filiation in Nigeria, paternalism and primogeniture provide an informal structure.

---

953. Section 5(1) of the CRA.
954. Section 7 of the B,D, etc., Act and Regulation 9.
955. *Oduche v. Oduche* [2005] LPELR-5976.
956. It must be noted that matriarchy and patriarchy are systems different from patriliny and matriliny. Matriarchy is a system of governance where women play dominant role just as in patriarchy.
957. Available at: https://www.britannica.com/topic/matrilineal-society (last accessed 9 Oct. 2020).
958. P.R. MacDougall, *The Right of Women to Name Their Children* 3 L. & Ineq. 91 (1985).
959. Sara Lowes, *Matrilineal Kinship and Spousal Cooperation: Evidence from the Matrilineal Belt*, available at: https://scholar.harvard.edu/files/slowes/files/lowes_matrilineal.pdf (last accessed 10 Oct. 2020).

I. Children Born in Wedlock

988. Children are born in marriage in Nigeria according to the strata of marriages already fully discussed above. Under customary and Islamic marriages, filiation is traced to fathers who have absolute authority over and custody of all children.

989. When marriage is under the Act, filiation is also presumptively traceable to fathers but with respect to custody in matrimonial causes, the courts have interpreted the provisions of the MCA liberally.[960] There are no special provisions for formal determination of filiation or Orders. Courts have stated that presumption of paternity in marriage is a valuable doctrine deserving of protection.[961]

990. Section 69 of the MCA provides a definition of 'children of the marriage'[962] to include, 'biological and adoptive children'. Biological children are those born by the spouses within the marriage or by either of them before the marriage. For the latter, the effect of the marriage on the status is irrelevant. Children covered, also include those accepted by the spouses into the marriage as theirs if, at the relevant time, the child was ordinarily a member of the household of the husband and wife, so long as such a child has not been adopted by any other person.

991. Thus, in general marriage under the MA secures the filiation of children as defined in section 69. Proof of adultery does not automatically displace the presumption so engaged.

992. The other relevant provision is section 84 which provides for evidence of non-access in certain circumstances and excludes such evidence where it has the likelihood to make a child, one, not born of the parties to the marriage. Section 165 of the Evidence Act[963] provides effectively for presumption of paternity in respect of a child born to married persons.

993. It provides that where a child was born during the continuance of a marriage or 280 days after the dissolution of the marriage, the mother remaining unmarried, then the Court is entitled to presume paternity.

994. Where marriage is under the Act and there is an allegation of adultery, to determine the status of a child, barring the application of presumptions, the guiding credibility test for dispute as to pregnancy or paternity of a child are stated in *Megawalu v. Megawalu*[964] and restated in *Ibeabuchi v. Ibeabuchi.*[965] In *Ibeabuchi v. Ibeabuchi*[966] the Court of Appeal stated that these are:

960. Custody proceedings is discussed below.
961. *Oduche v. Oduche* [2005] LPELR-5976, 1.
962. Section 69 (a, b, c,).
963. Evidence Act, 2011.
964. [1994] 7 NWLR (part 359) 718.
965. [2016] LPELR 41268 (CA) CA/K/322/2012.
966. *Ibid.*

(i) The opportunity of access for sexual intercourse between the husband and the wife at the material time.
(ii) The opportunity of access for sexual intercourse between the wife and the third person.
(iii) The physical condition of the husband at the material time.
(iv) The time of birth and time of the sexual acts by each contestant.
(v) Sometimes, blood tests of the parties, to confirm blood groups ... , etc.

995. Thus, the presumption provided by marriage on the filial status of a child is rebuttable, but as the Court of Appeal stated in their unanimous judgment in *Oduche v. Oduche*[967] the evidence required to displace such presumption must be very strong, clear and compelling to demonstrate that there was no sexual relationship and there could not have been such opportunity, between a man and his wife. Section 165 of the Evidence Act, 2011 is a replication of section 148 of the previous Evidence Act,[968] on which the Court adjudicated the pleadings of the parties in *Oduche v. Oduche.*[969]

996. *Oduche v. Oduche*[970] is a case on the extent to which the law and the Court in Nigeria connect sanctity of marriage and presumption of paternity. The parties were married on 8 September 1984. As at the time of the petition for dissolution of the marriage, they had three children, two males and one female. The oldest was 14 years old. The case determined the context of a name in Nigeria, custody and conditions under which an appellate court will overturn the verdict of a trial court. The wife in this case was involved in an adulterous relationship and had changed the names of the children of the marriage twice to names other than that of the husband.

997. The court connected sanctity of marriage with presumption of paternity and held that it is presumed that a couple are parents of the children of the marriage. It further held that the fact that the wife in this case, was living in a notorious adultery, was not sufficient in itself, to rebut the presumption. In addition, that the failure of the husband to submit to medical examination, did not affect the presumption. Following *Elumeze v. Elumeze*;[971] *Egwuwoke* v. *Egwunwoke Nwadike & Ors.*[972] and *Watson v. Watson*,[973] Rhodes Vivour JCA who delivered the lead judgment stated 'the principle underlying the rule is obvious. It is most undesirable to enquire into the paternity of a child where parents have access to each other. The presumption of legitimacy under Section 148 of the Evidence Act is a rebuttable presumption of Law which can only be displaced by showing that the parties to the marriage had

967. [2005] LPELR-5976, 1.
968. Laws of the Federation, Cap 112, 1990; Cap E14 2004.
969. [2005] LPELR-5976, 1.
970. [2005] LPELR-5976.
971. [1969] All N.L.R. 301.
972. [1966] All N.L.R. 301.
973. [1933] 2 All E.R. 1013.

no access to each other. Evidence must be strong, that is to say, it must be proved that access was impossible on account of illness, impotence'.[974]

998. On the wife changing the family name of the children to other names, the court stated categorically 'This is a patrilineal and not a matrilineal society, and some features of family life are elemental. Children take their father's name and not their mother's name.'[975] On overturning the verdict of a trial court, it reiterated that an appellate court will scarcely exercise a discretionary power differently from a trial court as the trial court is best positioned to exercise such discretion having conducted the trial and observed the parties and witnesses. Thus an appellate court, will not interfere if the discretion has been judicially exercised but where it was exercised arbitrarily, or tainted with some illegality or irregularity, the court will have a duty to intervene, and may reverse or modify the exercise of discretion by a trial court.

II. Children Born Out of Wedlock

999. There are four main ways in which children may be born out of wedlock in Nigeria. A child could be born to unmarried parents, or married parents through adulterous relationship or to parents who are separated. The fourth way is through the age long custom of widow-daughter retention.[976]

1000. In Nigeria, as in most patrilineal societies, when a child is born to an unmarried mother, the child's descent is traced to the mother's father. The mother provides a surname for the child. This position has been restated in two cases *Ben Enwonwu v. Spira*[977] and *Mojekwu v. Ejikeme.*[978] In the latter case, the Court of Appeal stated categorically that a child must have an identity and be assimilated into a family.[979]

1001. Nevertheless, different geographical groups have customs for assuring assimilation of children into families. This may be through presumptions of paternity or its variants. There are no uniform customs on this. In the South West of Nigeria, paternal acknowledgement is prevalent.[980] In the South Eastern States, by virtue of a well-established paternalistic republican form of customary governance, inclusiveness underlies human identity and *a fortiori*, there is a well-developed system of assimilation of children into families.

974. [2005] LPELR-5976, 1, 4.
975. *Oduche v. Oduche* [2005] LPELR-5976, 1, 8.
976. Nwudego Chinwuba, *Daughter/Widow Retention in Nigeria: Survey and Analysis from Case Law,* 2(1) J. Comp. L. Afr. 82–99 (2016).
977. [1965] ALL NLR 657.
978. [2000] 5 NWLR (part 657) 403.
979. This system of descent is distinct from matriliny.
980. Alfred Kasunmu, *The Principle of Acknowledgement or Recognition of Paternity Under Customary Law in Nigeria*, 13(3) ICLQ 1093–1103 (1964); *Romaine v. Romaine* [1992] 4 NWLR (part 238) 600; *Alake v. Pratt* [1955] WACA 20; *Cole* v. *Akinyele* [1960] SCNLR 192.

1002. In the South eastern States, where a woman is unmarried, the position is that every child is assimilated into the maternal family.[981] The father of a child borne by an unmarried woman has no related status under the customary law of the people of the South East. Furthermore, a pregnant woman cannot be given in marriage. She must first be delivered of the baby who is assimilated into her family before a marriage can be conducted between her and such a putative father. Suppose that the father does in fact, subsequent to a pregnancy, marries the woman, he remains without a related status to the child. Some rites may be performed to allow him custody of the child but the child does not bear his name. The Courts have in general denied recognition of these customs discountenancing them under the repugnancy doctrine.[982]

1003. In the South West, paternal acknowledgment is prevalent. In the latter case, an unmarried father may, through the observation and performance of certain rites and meeting up with certain conditions, be given paternal rights but usually, not custody.[983]

1004. In the South eastern parts, there is customary presumption of paternity once a woman is married although, she may have committed adultery or may be separated from the husband. Any child born in the course of the marriage is presumed a child of the marriage no matter how open a case of adultery might appear or how long a separation between the spouses has been. This presumption continues to run unless there is a formal dissolution of the marriage, concluded by return of the bride price. Children born after the demise of a husband under the age old customs of daughter-widow retention are assimilated as biological children of the deceased.[984]

1005. In the South West, there appears to be no custom of presumption of paternity whether the woman is married or unmarried. Children can only be assimilated into filiation by a father's positive action.

1006. Edet v. Essien,[985] is a case that emanated from parties of the Efik tribe in the South Eastern part of Nigeria.[986] The wife, of the defendant Inyang, had been betrothed to the plaintiff by the customary payment of bride price, before she attained adulthood. Inyang later married the defendant with the consent of her parents, also paid the customary bride price and concluded the ceremony by cohabiting with her. They had two children. However, the bride price that the plaintiff had paid for the earlier betrothal of Inyang was not returned to him. The plaintiff sued the defendant for the custody of the two children of the marriage on the ground that in the absence of the return of the bride price, Inyang remained his bride. The court

981. *Muojekwu* v. *Ejikeme* [2000] 5 NWLR (part 657) 404; *Ben Enwonwu v. Spira* [1965] All N.L.R 657.
982. *Okonkwo v. Okagbue* [1994] 9 NWLR (part 368) 301.
983. Alfred Kasunmu, *supra.* n. 980.
984. *Okonkwo v. Okagbue* [1994] 9 NWLR (part 368) 301.
985. [1932] 11 N.L.R 47.
986. This area is now grouped as the South-South.

declined to uphold and apply the custom on the ground that it was repugnant to natural justice, equity and good conscience. The court allowed the paternity of the two children to remain with the defendant who was their biological father.

1007. However, the case ought to have been decided on legal principles – resort to repugnancy doctrine was unnecessary. This is because, the custom as law was valid. Until return of bride price, a previous marriage remains in place. In *Edet*, first of all, cohabitation with a bride is an intrinsic element of the ceremony of customary marriage. In that part of the country, the ceremony is complete only with cohabitation, concluded by a formal introduction of the bride to the groom's family. Since there was no cohabitation between the parties, the second ceremony overreached the first in legal theory and this should have been sufficient to determine the dispute between the parties.

1008. Mariyama v. Sadiku Ejo[987] involved a separation from the husband and consequent pregnancy. In this case, the customary presumption of paternity was upheld.

1009. DNA[988] tests can be ordered to determine paternity. It can be said to have been accepted in Nigerian legal system by implication of the guidelines (v) set in by the Court of Appeal in *Ibeabuchi v. Ibeabuchi*[989] listed below[990] and the decision in *Adeyemi v. Abayomi.*[991]

1010. In *Adeyemi v. Abayomi*[992] the High Court in Lagos was faced with determining a complex case of paternity. Faced with this daunting task, the Honourable Judge, Phillips A. A. declared:

> I could not lay my hands on any law promulgated in Nigeria on this issue, so pursuant to sections 10, 13, 16 and 17 of the High Court Law, Cap 60 Laws of Lagos State 1994, my only recourse is to the Law in England. The power of the court to order blood tests is governed by sections 20 and 21 the Family Law Reform Act, 1969 of England … It is therefore time for our legislative houses to start considering the promulgation of similar legislation here in Nigeria. The 1969 law in England has already been amended to include what they call scientific tests and since therefore we have started to experience paternity disputes in this country it is imperative that the proper statutes are put in place to assist the populace, the Lawyers, the Doctors, the Forensic Scientists and of course the Judges that will have to adjudicate on such matters. This is an

987. [1962] NRNLR 81.
988. Deoxyribonucleic acid, (DNA) is a genetic material unique to each individual. A self-replicating material that is present in nearly all living organisms as the main constituent of chromosomes. It is the carrier of genetic information-specific sequence of bases which constitutes the genetic information.
989. [2016] LPELR 41268 (CA) CA/K/322/2012.
990. (Under children born in wedlock).
991. [2002] FWLR (part 332) 136.
992. *Ibid.*

opportune time to do so now that we are enjoying a democratic dispensation. A Government for the people is in place and we are no longer suffering under the yoke of dictatorship.[993]

1011. The plaintiffs, husband and wife at the High Court, claimed among other reliefs a declaration of the parentage of a baby girl who was born on 17 December 1994 at the Oluwaseyifunmi Clinic, in Lagos State. The clinic is owned and run by the 2nd defendant. The 2nd plaintiff, the wife, who was pregnant with a twin, had registered for ante-natal processes at the Clinic of the 4th defendant. The 4th defendant transferred her to the 1st defendant's Clinic. On 16 December 1994, the 2nd plaintiff was delivered of the first of a set of twin, who according to the administrators of the clinic, was still. The second of the twin was delivered live, on 17 December.

1012. The midwife – 2nd defendant, claimed the child required medical attention and purportedly took the child to the Lagos University Teaching Hospital (LUTH), at Idi-Araba, Lagos State. She returned to the plaintiffs, without the child, claiming the child had died. She also failed to deliver-up the remains of the child to the plaintiffs. The plaintiffs accepted their tragedy, leaked their wounds and carried on.

1013. Then, sometime in 1995, the plaintiffs watched on the National television, the Nigerian Television Authority, the 1st defendant conducting a celebration of having had a miraculous birth of a baby girl at the age of 65 years. The plaintiffs suspicion was aroused, as they recalled that the same woman had been in the premises of the Oluwaseyifunmi Clinic at the time the 2nd plaintiff was delivered of her 'children'. Further investigations began to yield surprising results and the matter was reported to the Nigerian police. The police arrested the 1st and 2nd defendants, that is the 65-year-old celebrant and the midwife. Serological tests were carried out on the two contesting 'mothers'. In the meantime, a 3rd claimant for the child appeared who is the 3rd defendant. She was joined as a defendant to the proceeding, having made a claim for the parentage of the same child, been delivered of a baby in the same clinic, about the same time, and under similar, seemingly tragic circumstances.

1014. The 3rd defendant subsequently counterclaimed against the plaintiffs that she was the rightful mother of the disputed child.

1015. The police decided to conduct a DNA test on all contesting parents. Blood samples were taken and sent to the Cell Mark Diagnostics in Britain. The test was returned with the 3rd defendant as the mother of the disputed child. Dissatisfied with this outcome, the plaintiffs instituted the proceedings claiming *inter alia*, that the test carried out by the Police was not error-proof and not in conformity with laid

993. [2002] FWLR (part 332) 136, 169–170, paras H–A; & 171, E–F.

down procedure for the conduct of DNA testing in Britain which ought to have been directed by a court and not the police. Their claim denied any power in the Nigerian Police to determine filiation.

1016. It was a difficult decision in all the circumstances, the Court had no precedent to rely on. The police gave evidence that it was a novel case. The Court commended the police for the actions taken by them and at great cost. It noted that although, in England and Wales only a court could order a DNA test, the police had no choice in the face of three contending mothers to do what was reasonable in the circumstances. An expert witness gave evidence that as at the time of the proceeding between 1995 and 2012, there were no laboratories in Nigeria to conduct DNA tests and this was the basis for referring the test to one in Britain. In delivering the judgment after seven years of going back and forth the judge apologised, stating:

> The subject matter of this suit is a female child who is now an infant. At the time this suit was instituted in 1995, she was however a baby of just a few months old. It has taken us all just over 7 years to reach the end of this matter in the High Court and for this delay, I apologise. The wheels of justice grind very slowly in this country of ours and it is about time something concrete is done by all of us that serve at the Temple of Justice to ensure that matters filed in court are dealt with speedily, especially matters such as this one, where the life and the stability of a new born child are at stake. Without the necessary sanctions in our Rules of Court there is precious little a Judge can do, to ensure that there are no unnecessary delays occasioned by the absence of counsel and unwarranted requests for adjournments, without being accused of sacrificing justice and the right to be heard, at the altar of haste. Once again therefore, I apologise for the delay in coming to the end of this matter and hope that the affected families involved will be able to put the trauma this matter has caused them behind them and be able to move on from here.[994]

1017. The case determined that the police having taken the most appropriate action in the circumstances, the results of the DNA are adopted and the child, that of the 3rd defendant. The plaintiffs were awarded damages in the sum of five Million Naira although, the court did so with regrets, noting that nothing could assuage the anguish of the parents-plaintiffs. The 2nd defendant was taken to the cleaners for her inhuman actions and ordered that she deliver up the remains of the child of the plaintiffs whom she claimed had died in the Lagos University Teaching Hospital. She was also ordered to pay twenty-five thousand Naira as costs to the plaintiffs and the 3rd defendant. The 2nd defendant was also facing criminal charges.

994. [2002] FWLR (part 332) 136, 142, paras D, E, F, G.

1018. In a related case which was conducted both in Nigeria and United Kingdom, involving Nigerians, *Moses-Taiga v. Taiga,*[995] despite the protests of the counsel to the defendant-respondent, the English Court of Appeal ordered a DNA test to ascertain paternity and awarded maintenance for children prior to determination of the civil status of the parties.

1019. The other core area where the circumstances of birth are brought to play is with respect to inheritance in succession. In a line of cases commencing with *Marquis v. Marquis,*[996] Nigerian Courts began to deal with the question of intestate inheritance when children are born out of wedlock.

1020. In Kehinde Da Costa & Other *v.* Juliana Fasehun & Others, Oladipo Williams J. stated:

> If section 39(2) of the Constitution[997] is made applicable to the accepted facts in this case, it would follow that all laws which are based on sound social norms and public policy in order that they should regulate the actions of persons who have voluntarily submitted themselves to be bound by those laws either because of conscience, belief, religion or accepted practice, have been swept away by the present Constitution. If that was so, as claimed by the plaintiffs in this case, it would mean that a person who by his actions during his life time has agreed to recognise, accept and practice monogamy would after his death intestate, create a situation which would compel those responsible for the administration of good government and justice to allow his property to become a booty for all and sundry. In my view that cannot be the intention behind the present Constitution. If I were to interpret Section 39(2) of the Constitution as urged by learned Counsel for the plaintiffs, I would have subscribed to an absurd and chaotic situation.[998]

1021. However, the tide turned for children starting from *Olulode v. Oviosu*[999] when in a High Court decision, Onalaja J. took the position that the Constitution should be interpreted in a liberal and elastic manner, and that the pith and substance of the provision on non-deprivation of children is the abolition of the status of legitimacy and illegitimacy and to treat every child equally. This was followed by Sagay who stated in reference to the judgment in *Kehinde Da Costa & Other v. Juliana Fasehun & Others*[1000] '... in the first place the reference to the natural but illegitimate children of the deceased as "all and sundry" who are out for a booty is both

995. [2005] EWCA Civ 1013; [2012] 10 NWLR (part 1308) 219.
996. Unreported, Suit No. 1/685/84, delivered 3 Mar. 1986, High Court of Ibadan, Nigeria.
997. This section is replicated as s. 42(2) in the existing Constitution.
998. Unreported, High Court of Lagos, Suit No. M/150 80 delivered 22 May 1981; *see also* I.E. Sagay, *supra.* n. 72, 1, 16.
999. Unreported, High Court of Lagos State, Ikeja Judicial Division, Suit No. M/133/81 delivered 27 Jan. 1981.
1000. Unreported, High Court of Lagos, Suit No. M/150 80 delivered 22 May 1981.

unfortunate and grossly incorrect. Where a man has children outside his marriage, **whom he acknowledges,** under no circumstances can such children be regarded as "all and sundry"'.[1001]

1022. Two distinctive authorities from the apex court put paid to the polemics. These are *Ukeje v. Ukeje*[1002] and *Salubi v. Nwariaku.*[1003] In the former, it was held that a daughter who was born out of wedlock was entitled to inheritance of her father's real property. The second case held that children who were born out of wedlock were entitled to participate in the distribution of their father's estate. In the latter case, although, the father of the children had acknowledged them in his lifetime, and were both accepted by his wife, who was originally Irish, the decision was reached based on the provisions of the Constitution. The Court reached this decision by interpreting and applying section 42(2) of the Constitution on non-discrimination or deprivation based on circumstances of birth or sex etc. Thus, despite definitions such as appears in the Lagos State Wills Laws, which defines child as including legitimated children, adopted children or children acknowledged by a father,[1004] the Supreme Court has repeatedly applied equality to distribution of the estate of fathers whether acknowledged or not, in so far as the evidence imputes paternity to a father.

1023. As was noted earlier, Nigeria is a pro-life nation, but the fallout of gender-related preferences and sundry practices as paternal acknowledgement, leave in their trail many orphanages, orphanages better known and more commonly referred to as 'motherless babies homes'. Underlying the description is the need to return to the drawing table on the content and quality of life not only for children, but for all, and address the socio-legal context that leaves children belonging to mothers when they are homeless and orphans.

III. Currency of the Distinction

1024. The first point to be made is that legitimacy and legitimation in Nigeria are now subjected to section 42(2) of the Constitution which provide for non-discrimination and non-deprivation from circumstances of birth.[1005] This provision

1001. Space will not allow mention of all the numerous cases in this area of the law because it is the norm rather than the exception that Nigerian men have one wife and several children from several women in their life time whom they leave to their fate to struggle and war over what he leaves behind after his demise. However see a few in Uzodike, *Nigeria: Defining the Ambit of Custom*, 13 ULJFL 399, 403 (1989); R.A. Onuoha, *Discriminatory Property Inheritance Under Customary Law in Nigeria: The Need for Reform*, in *Law and Real Property Rights in Nigeria* – Essays 230, 244 (I.O. Smith ed. in Memory of Professor J.A. Omotola Faculty of Law, University of Lagos 2008); N.N. Chinwuba Cohabitation: Human Dignity and One Aspect of Gender Insensitivity 14(4) The Int'l J. Hum. Rts. 624–634 (2010).
1002. [2014] 11 NWLR (part 1418) 384.
1003. [2003] 7 NWLR (part 819) 426.
1004. Section 26 Lagos State Administration of Estates Law.
1005. I.E. Sagay, *supra.* n. 72, 1.

is a fundamental human right which is justiciable.[1006] Second, the account of 'children of the marriage' provided in section 69(b), to wit: 'any child of the husband and wife born before the marriage, whether legitimated by the marriage or not' makes it clear that the filial status of a child is not subjected to notions of illegitimacy but is of utmost importance and protected. In the Supreme Court decision in *Salubi v. Nwariaku*,[1007] Ayoola JSC, stated: '... It suffices to hold that the court below was right in holding that the trial court had jurisdiction to entertain the claim before it and that **the two issues born out of wedlock** are entitled to equal shares with **the two other issues of the marriage** of the deceased and the widow.'[1008] Kalgo J.S.C. agreeing, stated: The Court of Appeal also found that the **two children born out of wedlock are entitled to share in the estate of their late father in conformity with the provisions of section 39 of the 1979 Constitution, I entirely agree with these findings.**[1009] Other justices of the Supreme Court who agreed with the unanimous ruling are: Kutugi, Idris JSC (presiding), Mohammed, Uthman JSC and Uwaifo, Samson J.S.C.

1025. This decision was followed by another Supreme Court decision in *Ukeje v. Ukeje*.[1010]

1026. The Births, Deaths Act and the Births, Deaths, Marriages (Registration) Regulation carefully provides for children born out of wedlock – carefully adopting terms that are in conformity with modern human rights framework.

1027. Section 12 of the B, D, Etc., Act provides:

> Notwithstanding anything in the foregoing provisions of this Act, in the case of a child born out of wedlock, no person acting as father of the child shall be required to give information concerning the birth of the child and the registrar shall not enter in the register the name of any person as the father of the child except:
>
> (a) at the joint request of the mother and the person acknowledging himself to be the father of the child and in which case that person shall sign the register together with the mother; or
> (b) at the request of the mother on production of:

1006. *Ukeje v. Ukeje* [2014] 11 NWLR (Pt. 1418) 384; 3PLR/2014/150 SC [2014] LPELR – 22724 (SC) Electronic Law Reports; *Salubi v. Nwariaku* [2003] 7 NWLR (part 819) 426. For a fuller view on thoughts on this in Nigeria, *see* Nwudego Chinwuba, *Interaction of Customs and Colonial Heritage: Their Impact on Marriage and Children in Nigeria*, 110(1) von Anthropos 1–20 (2016); Nwudego Chinwuba, *Human Identity: Child Rights and the Legal Framework for Marriage in Nigeria*, 51(4) Marriage & Fam. Rev. 305–336 (2015).

1007. [2003] 7 NWLR (part 819) 426.

1008. *Ibid.*, 426, 456.

1009. *Ibid.*, 426,458–459. Section 42(2) of the 1999 Constitution is the exact replication of s. 39(2) of the 1979 Constitution.

1010. [2014] 11 NWLR (part 1418) 384; 3 PLR/2014/150 SC. Both cases are discussed more fully below, under intestate succession.

(i) a declaration in the prescribed form made by the mother stating that the said person is the father of the child; or
(ii) a statutory declaration made by that person acknowledging himself to be the father of the child.

1028. Section 14 of the B, D, M Etc., Regulation provides:

Nothing in these Regulations shall be construed as requiring:

(a) the father of a child born out of wedlock to give information concerning the birth of the child; or;
(b) the registrar to enter the name of any person as the father of the child except in the circumstances specified in section 12(a) and (b) of the Act.

1029. There are snippets of dated laws on the subject which ought not to be of much concern. Thus, the High Court of the FCT, Abuja Civil Procedure Rules, 2004 provide an example of requirement for legitimation proceedings in Nigeria. Where a petition is presented, it must be by a person of full age and capacity, if an infant or person who is mentally handicapped, the petition should be by a next friend. To this petition, must be a respondent. The respondent is the Attorney General of the Federation or any person who may be affected by the legitimation of the petitioner. The Court is also empowered to direct a person or persons not made respondent in the Petition to be made respondents. Thus, rule 1 of Order 50 provides:

(1) A petition shall be headed 'In the matter of the Legitimacy Act', and 'In the matter of – (the person to be declared legitimate)', in the prescribed form, with variations as circumstances may require and shall state among other matters:
  (a) the place and date of the marriage concerned;
  (b) the status and residence of each parent and the occupation and domicile of the father of the person whose legitimacy the Court is asked to declare:
    (i) at the date of his birth; and
    (ii) at the date of the marriage.
  (c) whether there are other living issues of the parents of such person and the respective names and dates of birth of all such issues;
  (d) a person (if any) affected by the legitimacy and the known value of any property involved;
  (e) whether any previous proceedings under the Legitimacy Act, regarding the paternity of the person or the validity of the marriage leading to his legitimacy have been taken in any court; and
  (f) that there is no collusion.

1030. Rule 1 of Order 50 refers to a Legitimacy Act which is not in the compilation of the Laws of the Federation, 2004.

1031. Parental responsibility has been an aspiration of current human rights regime. To responsibility should also be a correlate function, which in the case of family, is the duty of children to their families and societies. The duty of children requires emphasis as much as the responsibility of parents. Neither assimilation nor presumption advances or promotes an objective of the duty incumbent on a child, to be assured the conditions of development to contribute to the good of society, and this ought to be as important as parental responsibility.[1011]

1032. Viewed from this prism, assimilation and presumptions are now unsuitable for the progress of human evolution. Both advance dishonesty in adult relations at the expense of children. The better system is one that has a clear process for declaration of status and filiation orders with all modern systems of proof which should advance an internal validity of the societal expectation of every human being. The Births, Deaths Act, can be extended by the National Assembly to establish a Filiation process that determines ancestry while the Courts can, based on the process make necessary orders.

1011. *See* s. 24 of the Constitution of the Federation and s. 19 of the Child's Rights Act, 2003.

Chapter 5. Adoption

§1. Adoption

1033. In *Prince Aka O. Ibiam v. Mrs. Obiageli Akanu Ibiam & Anor,*[1012] the Court defined an adoption as the creation of a parent-child relationship by judicial order between two parties who usually are unrelated. This relationship, it stated is brought about only after a determination that the child is an orphan or has been abandoned, or that the parents' parental rights have been terminated by Court order.

1034. Adoption has been gaining acceptance in Nigeria. Uzodike asserts that adoption, has changed 'from finding children for childless couples to securing suitable homes for unfortunate children and protecting their interests'.[1013] However, the prevailing impact of patriarchy, marriage and socio-economic circumstances in Nigeria, makes children necessary and undermines the assertion that adoption has become a regime for finding homes for unfortunate children. It remains a regime for fulfilling adult need for children.

1035. Odetoyinbo's narrative captures the currency of the relationship between adults and children in Nigeria:

> I have felt suicidal, … when I decided I wanted a baby, I was almost 35. While I was married for six years, I didn't have a child. And here I was 10 years after I had gotten married, the hope of getting a child was looking bleak because there was no husband and then age was also a factor. I told my mother about my intention and my mother answered *olorun a se oko fun e* (God would make you a husband). And I told her, 'I did not tell you that I needed a husband, I said I wanted a baby'. My mother is a Christian who thinks that it is ungodly. To cut the long story short, I had a baby in 2006. My mother loves my child; she is the strongest supporter. I just needed a reason to wake up in the morning. I wanted someone to love because, let's face it, I am a human being. When I was married the labels I had were barren, childless, HIV Positive, so I got all those labels and I was thinking, 'what exactly am I living for?' To me, it was like I had failed on all fronts. So, one thing I genuinely desired was to have a child.[1014]

1036. Egbemode echoes this position. In her view, when women find their 'biological clock fast ticking', and are moving in circles with suitors, they should procreate leaving incidental and ancillary matters to providence.[1015] It is from this prism that adoption must be viewed.

1012. [2017] LPELR-42028(CA).
1013. Eunice Uzodike, *Trends of Human Rights Campaign in Family Law* 23 (University of Lagos Inaugural Lecture Series 2011).
1014. Morolake Odetoyinbo, *Why I Must Marry Again, Encounter, Saturday Sun* Ng. 33, 44 (23 June 2012).
1015. Funke Egbemode, *Every Woman's Desperate Zone*, *Sunday Sun* Ng. 72 (Sun Publishing Limited, Vol. 6, No. 501) 25 November 2012).

1037. In addition, the legal effect of adoption is couched normatively to advance and protect the interest of the adopter. However, in formulating and advancing policies for adoption, it is important to bear in mind the lessons of history:

> The child is not the mere creature of the State. In the current climate, these words have particular potency for parents facing the permanent and irrevocable termination of their very parenthood. The lessons of history tell us two things. First, the special position of the birth parents has always been recognised and protected in English law of adoption. Second, responsibility for ensuring the legitimate rights and interests of the birth parents are properly weighed in the decision-making process is rightly entrusted to the independent authoritative adjudication of the courts. Our trust in the courts fulfilling this function may have been shaken in recent times. However, as the political momentum gathers towards further reform of adoption, now more than ever, it is vital that we do not lose sight of these two most fundamental principles.[1016]

I. The Law on Adoption

1038. The law on adoption in Nigeria is State-based although largely drawn from the Child's Right Act, 2003.[1017] The CRA by section 146 recognises an Adoption Order made under any law in force in any part of Nigeria, or the law of any other country other than Nigeria. Such an adoption order has the like validity and effect as if the adoption has been effected as an Adoption Order under the Child's Rights Act. Section 274(1) of the Child's Rights Act provides that the provisions of the Act supersedes the provisions of all enactments relating to children with respect to matters it deals with and adoption is one of those matters. PART XII of the Child's Right Act (CRA), covers adoption.

1039. The most visible State Adoption Law is that of Lagos State, the Child's Right Law, 2007. Lagos State has, in compliance with the provisions of the Childs Right Act, established a Family Court.

II. Services and Facilities

1040. The State Governments are required, for the purpose of adoption, and in the case of the Federal Government, within the FCT, to establish and maintain within the State and Abuja specific services with appropriate facilities. The services are designed to meet the needs of, a child who has been or may be adopted; parents and guardians of such a child and persons who have adopted or who may adopt a

1016. Sonia Harris-Short, *Holding On to the Past? Adoption, Birth Parents and the Law in the Twenty-First Century*, in *Fifty Years in Family Law Essays for Stephen Cretney* 147, 160 (Rebecca Probert & Chris Barton eds, Intersentia 2012).
1017. Number 6, 2003.

child. Other services stipulated to be maintained include, arrangements for assessing a child and prospective adopters, placing the child for adoption and, counselling for persons where they have problems relating to adoption. The nature of the problem contemplated is not stated.[1018]

1041. They are also required to provide facilities or ensure that such facilities are provided by adoption services approved by appropriate authority. The facilities required to be maintained include – temporary board and lodging for a child where such is required according to the circumstances surrounding the child. This, should extend to the child's mother in exceptional circumstances.

1042. There are no known adoption services in the country which is a huge gap leaving room for malfeasance. Thus, many seeming adoptions in Nigeria are private arrangements.

III. Jurisdiction of Court

1043. The Family Court has the sole jurisdiction to deal with applications for adoption order. It does this in line with the rules of the Court. PART XIII of the Child's Rights Act establishes a Family Court. Section 149 of that part, provides that the Family Court shall be established for each State of the Federation and the FCT. The Court has a two-level structure – a Division of the High Court and the Magistrate Court. The principal function of the court is defined as the hearing and determination of matters relating to children. Lagos State has a Family Court and the FCT has a Family Court as a division of the Magistrate Court. Rules for enforcement of the provisions of the CRA are passed into law by the Chief Judge of the State or that of the FCT.

1044. The Chief Justice of Nigeria is empowered to make rules for the Family Court.[1019] However, since the Act is in effect operative only as a guiding law, the function which was meant for the Chief Justice of Nigeria devolved on the Chief Judge of each State and the FCT.

1045. The rules are to regulate the general practice and procedure of the Court on adoption and also with regard to:[1020]

(i) application for adoption orders being heard and determined otherwise than in open court;
(ii) admission of documentary evidence of consent required in compliance with section 132 of the Act;
(iii) admission and evaluation of Report of a Child Development Officer.

1018. Section 25 of the CRA.
1019. Section 136 of the CRA.
1020. Section 137 of the CRA.

1046. Where a Magistrate Court, in its family jurisdiction determines an application for adoption order, by postponing it and making an interim order, an appeal from such exercise of jurisdiction lies to the High Court. Where the High Court exercises original or appellate jurisdiction appeal lies with the Court of Appeal.[1021] The proceedings on appeal in respect of an application for adoption order are to be conducted in chambers.[1022]

1047. The Court shall, in reaching a decision relating to the adoption of a child, have regard to all the circumstances. It should have first consideration for the needs of the child, such as requisite facilities to safeguard and promote the welfare and best interest of the child throughout childhood. To achieve this, it must ascertain, as far as is practicable, 'the wishes and feelings of the child regarding the decision', giving due consideration to those wishes and feelings, in the light of the age and understanding of the child.[1023] The religious upbringing of the child is considered important and the court must as far as, is practicable take account of the wishes, if any, of the parents or guardian of the child in this regard.

1048. There is an omnibus clause requiring that the Court must be satisfied based on report of the appropriate investigating officers that the adopter or adopters are suitable to adopt the child for whom adoption is sought.[1024]

IV. Procedure

1049. The Court is empowered to specify the nature of the form to be used for Application. The Form must have attached to it:

(i) for married persons, marriage certificate or a sworn declaration of marriage;
(ii) birth certificate or sworn declaration of age of each applicant;
(iii) two passport photographs of each applicant;
(iv) a medical certificate of the fitness of the applicant from a Government hospital; and
(v) such other documents, requirements and information as the Court may require for the purposes of the adoption.

1050. When the application is received, the court orders an investigation which is conducted by any of the persons listed – a child development officer; supervision officer; or such other persons as the Court may determine.[1025] The investigation facilitates the Court's assessment of the suitability of the applicant[s] as an adopter[s] and of the child to be adopted. The functions of the investigators include the assessment of third-party relationship with the child, that is, whether a person who

1021. Section 138 of the CRA.
1022. Section 138(1)(c) of the CRA.
1023. Section 126.
1024. Section 129 of the CRA.
1025. Section 126(2).

is not a parent or relative of the child has any right or obligation towards the child and if it is necessary to obtain the consent of the person in compliance with the consent provisions of the Act.[1026]

1051. There are other requirements with regard to capacity in granting an adoption order some of which are in the alternatives.[1027] The applicant, or in the case of a joint application, both, or, at least, one of them and the child should be resident in the same State. The applicant has been resident or, in the case of a joint application, both of them have been resident in the State in which the application is made for a period of at least five years. The applicant is a citizen or, in the case of a joint application, both applicants are citizens of Nigeria. The child has been in the care of the applicant for a period of at least three consecutive months immediately preceding the date on which the order is made; and the applicant has, at least twelve months before the making of the order, informed the social welfare officer of his intention to adopt the child. Where an application is by a married couple, who are a parent and step parent of the child, and the Court considers that the application is one better determined under Part VIII of the Act, that is, that it could be effectively disposed of under a custody proceeding, then it must dismiss the application for adoption.

1052. Section 143 prohibits all forms of payment by the adopter or any other persons, except with the sanction of the Court. There is a sanction for failure to comply, either by imprisonment or a fine or both.

1053. The Act also prohibits sub-adoption. Section 144(1) prohibits taking the child outside the State where the adoption order was made for purposes of sub-adoption to a different party. It also applies to taking the child out of the country. The sanction could be fine, imprisonment or both. This does not mean there can be no interstate adoption. Rather, the provision portends some form of protection through movement, in view of the fact that the country is very big and complex making it easy for the sub-adoptee to disappear with the adopted child. The Act aim is to forestall child trafficking. A Minister may, however, intervene to authorise such sub-adoption. Section 145 empowers the Minister to grant a licence, subject to all the necessary consents, for a child to be transferred to a person, subject to such conditions and restrictions as may be appropriate. Section 277 defines 'Minister' to mean the Minister charged with responsibility for matters relating to children and 'Ministry' to be construed accordingly. The Ministry of Youth, Social welfare, and Culture and such sundry authorities in Nigeria handle issues related to adoption at Federal or State level.

1026. Section 132 (3). The Act specifies that this particular function is to be carried out by a 'Child Development officer and not the other persons listed'.
1027. Section 131 of the CRA.

V. Capacity to Adopt

1054. There are specific conditions to be met when persons desire to adopt. A single person wishing to adopt must be above the age of 35 years. The Act requires adopted children to conform with the gender of the adopter where the applicant is single.

1055. Married persons desiring to adopt should each, have attained the age of 25 years or have an order authorising them to jointly adopt a child. Married persons could also adopt a child if either has obtained the consent of the other spouse to adopt unless in line with section 132 of the Act, the Court considers that the consent is being unreasonably withheld or it falls under any other exercisable discretion of the court listed in that section. Where a married person is the sole applicant for an adoption order, the court may, if it thinks fit, refuse to make the order if the consent of the spouse of the applicant to the making of the order is not first obtained.[1028]

1056. How the provisions with respect to a prospective single person adopter are to be harmonised with section 131(1) is unclear. The subsection stipulates that 'An adoption order shall not be made in respect of a child unless the applicant or, in the case of a joint application, one of them, is not less than twenty-five years old and is, at least, twenty-one years older than the child.'. One interpretation is that the latter provision is in the alternative. Thus, a single applicant may either be 35 years old or be at least 21 years older than the child and in the case of married persons, one of them must be at least 21 years older than the child to be adopted. It would appear though that the joint reading of sections 129 and 131(1) would mean that the age required for adoption is anywhere between 21 years, one minute or hour and 35 years for single persons and 25 years for married persons. The Act does not stipulate a minimum age for the child to be adopted. It does define a child as a person under 18 years.[1029]

VI. The Child

1057. The child to be adopted could be given up freely by the parent[s]. There is no age requirement. Where children are abandoned, the general position is that they should be taken to some official authority such as the police. It is from such an authority that the processes for adoption commence.

1058. A child may be adopted notwithstanding that the child is under a corrective order.[1030] In such circumstance, if the Court is satisfied that the adoption would be for the welfare and best interest of the child, it may suspend the corrective order

1028. Section 132(1) of the CRA.
1029. Section 277 of the CRA.
1030. Section 139(1).

and direct that the child be under the care of the applicant for a period of at least three consecutive months immediately preceding the prospective date of determining the adoption order.

1059. Similarly, a child may be adopted although there is a maintenance order for the child. A successful adoption order, however, overreaches the maintenance order. It does not matter whether the maintenance order is under the Act or any other law.[1031]

1060. Section 157 protects the identity of the child. Thus, unless by special permission under the Act, it is prohibited to have published, the name, address, school, photograph, or anything likely to lead to the identification of a child who is being considered for adoption. The permission presumably will be by the court or the Minister. There is sanction for failure to comply with the provision which could be a fine of Fifty Thousand Naira or imprisonment for a term of five years or to both such fine and imprisonment.

VII. Consent

1061. Consent is necessary with respect to an adoption or interim order for adoption. The consent of the parents of the child or, where there is no surviving parent, the guardian of the child is a condition for considering an application and granting an adoption or interim order.

1062. An investigation officer may also ascertain as earlier stated, that a person other than the parents or guardian has relative rights or obligations towards the child, in which case the consent of such a person is required. The Court may forego the requirement of consent where a child is neglected or persistently abused or ill-treated, and there are compelling reasons in the interest of the child why the adoption order should be made in spite of a requisite consent.[1032]

1063. The Law stipulates that the consent must be real and not vitiated. Thus, a court making an adoption order must ensure that every person who has given a consent understands the nature and effect of the adoption order for which the application relates. Counselling service by relevant adoption service is therefore compulsory. The applicant must also not have received or agreed to received, and no person has made, given or agreed to make or give to the applicant any payment or other reward in consideration of the adoption other than what the Court may approve.[1033]

1031. Section 140.
1032. Section 128.
1033. Section 133 of the CRA.

1064. In giving a consent, knowledge of the identity of the applicant for the adoption order is not necessary. The Court may dispense with consent if it is satisfied that the person, to give it cannot be found or is incapable of giving his consent or is withholding his consent unreasonably. Furthermore, while an application for an adoption order is pending in any Court, a person who has given his consent to an adoption order cannot withdraw the child from the care and possession of the applicant without the leave of the Court. To grant leave for withdrawal, the Court must consider, the welfare of the child.

VIII. The Adoption Order

1065. After the Court ascertains that all conditions have been met, then it may make the Adoption Order as sought. The Adoption Order is in the form specified in the Fifth Schedule to the Act. The Court has wide discretionary powers in making adoption orders. It may impose such terms and conditions as it considers fit, and may require the adopter, by bond or otherwise, to make provisions for the child.[1034]

1066. The court may make the order interim, as the circumstances dictate. It may postpone the determination of the application and make an interim order giving the custody of the child to the applicant for a period not exceeding two years on such terms and conditions as it thinks fit. The terms and conditions attached to the order cover provision for the maintenance, education and supervision for the welfare of the child. The order may also require the relationship subjected to the supervision of a Development Officer. The Development Officer is drawn from the Ministry subject to the appointment of the Minister.

1067. An adoption order extinguishes all legal rights, duties, obligations and privileges of the biological parents or any earlier adoptive parents. These are all rights, duties, obligations and liabilities, including any other order under the personal law applicable to the parents of the child or any other person, regarding the future custody, maintenance, supervision and education of the child. The rights extinguished extend to, religion of the child; appointment of a guardian for the child; giving of consent or notice of dissent to marriage.[1035]

1068. The child stands to the adopter as if, a biological child with all rights of parenting.

1069. Section 69 of the MCA defines children of the marriage as including any child adopted since the marriage by the husband and wife or by either of them with the consent of the other. Section 114 of the MCA states that adopted in relation to a child, means adopted under the law of any place (whether in or out of Nigeria) relating to adoption of children.

1034. Section 134 of the CRA.
1035. Section 141(1)(a).

1070. The Matrimonial Rules also are relevant. Order V, Part 1, rule 5 stipulates that in a petition for dissolution or nullity proceedings certain particulars of children must be indicated. Rule 5(1)(c) requires the indication of particulars of any adopted child of the parties to the marriage.[1036] The particulars to be stated in a petition are the date on or about which consent to the adoption of the child was given or the child was placed in the care of another person or persons with a view to adoption.[1037]

IX. The Register

1071. Sections 142 of the Child's Rights Act, and 29(1) of the Births, Deaths, Etc., (Compulsory Registration) Act complement the other on registration and provision of register for adopted children.

1072. Section 142 of the CRA, covers the field and provides that the Chief Registrar of the National Population Commission is to maintain a Register to be called and known as the E51 Adopted Children Register. Entries to be made in the register are those specified by an adoption order. Second, an adoption order is required to contain a direction to the Chief Registrar and the National Population Commission to make an entry as stated. If the determination of an application for an adoption, shows that the date of the birth of the child whose particulars are to be entered in a register are identical to, a child, to whom any entry in the Register of Births kept by the Commission relates, the adoption order must indicate a further direction to the Chief Registrar to cause the earlier birth entry in the Register of Births to be marked – 'Adopted' and to include in the entry relating to the adoption of the child in the Adopted Children Register the day of the child's birth. In the case of a previously adopted child, being adopted again, the order shall direct the Chief Registrar and the Commission to cause the previous entry in the Adopted Children Register in respect of that child to be marked Re-adopted.[1038]

1073. A certified copy of an entry in the Adopted Children Register can be obtained. Without an order of the Court, no person can conduct a search on any Register or books or any index on an adopted child. A stamped or sealed certified copy of an entry by the Chief Registrar's office is proof of the adoption. Where the copy of the entry includes the date of the birth of the child to whom it relates, it shall be proof also of the date without any further evidence as though the same were also a certified copy of an entry in the Register of Births. The Chief Registrar has a responsibility to keep an index of the Adopted Children Register which must be kept in the Registry. The Chief Registrar is also required to keep such other registers and books and make such entries therein as may be necessary to record, in connection with an entry in the Register of Births which has been marked Adopted.

1036. Order V, part 1, rule 5(1)(c)(d).
1037. Order 5, rule (2)(b).
1038. Section 142(4).

1074. On the revocation of an adoption order, the Court must communicate this status to the Chief Registrar. The entry in the Adopted Children Register relating to the adopted child and the marking with the word Adopted or Re-adopted of any entry relating to the child in the Register of Births must then be marked cancelled. A copy of an extract of an entry in any register that is cancelled shall be deemed to be an accurate copy of both the marking and the cancellation.[1039]

X. Case Law

1075. As has been noted above, an adoption order must be made by a court of competent jurisdiction, the Family Court, but in States without family courts, the regular courts, usually a High Court.

1076. In *Prince Aka O. Ibiam v. Mrs. Obiageli Akanu Ibiam & Anor,*[1040] the principal question the learned trial judge had to determine was whether the appellant is the only male child of late Dr Francis Akanu Ibiam, the patriarch who died intestate in 1995. It decided that the respondent was an adopted male child. At the Court of Appeal, it was held that without the production of an adoption order by a competent court of record, the appeal succeeded.

1077. At the High Court, the respondent had distilled the following issues for determination:

(1) Whether under Native Law and Customs or Statute Law, the late Ezeogo Dr Akanu Ibiam adopted the 1st defendant-respondent.
(2) Whether in the circumstances of this case, there has been substantial compliance with the Adoption Law (Cap 6), Laws of Eastern Nigeria, 1956, by the plaintiff's father when he applied for the adoption of the 1st defendant and carried out his obligations under the law?

1078. He claimed the following declarations:

(a) that he is a son of late Dr Akanu Ibiam by legal adoption;
(b) that his adoption was in accordance with customary adoption and the custom and tradition of Unwana.

1079. He further claimed an order of perpetual injunction restraining the appellant, his servants, agents or privies from compelling the 1st defendant to change his family name from Akanu Ibiam or ejecting him from the family house of late Dr Akanu Ibiam.

1039. Section 142(10).
1040. [2017] LPELR-42028(CA).

1080. It was not disputed that the appellant was the only biological child. It was also not in dispute that the late Akanu Ibiam had two daughters, who are married and live with their respective husbands. The appellant, however, disputed the claim by the first respondent that he is an adopted son of the patriarch. The respondent had the onus of pleading and proving he is an adopted son of the patriarch. The appeal was commenced by the appellant on a Notice of Appeal in the lower Court on 19 September 2005 against the decision in favour of the respondent by Hon. Justice B.C. Nosike of the Enugu State High Court. The learned trial judge held that the respondent was an adopted child of the patriarch. In arriving at that judgment, the court stated:

> With reference to Exhibits D, E and I, the Books concerned the family of Ezeogo Akanu Ibiam, his wife, and blood children. There is no evidence that the authors were aware of the fact that Ezeogo Akanu Ibiam, had fostered or adopted child. The books did not advert to that aspect of the philanthropy of Ezogo Akanu Ibiam. They are therefore irrelevant for that purposes … It is therefore hereby ordered that the 1st defendant having been adjudged an adopted son of Ezeogo Akanu Ibiam should be involved in the application for letters of Administration of the Estate of Ezeogo Akanu Ibiam. The caveat entered by the 1st defendant has been overtaken by this judgment.

1081. Analysing sections 3–7 and 14 and 15 of the Adoption Law (Cap 7),[1041] the Court of Appeal, held that the Adoption Law is couched in such a manner as to cover adoption under native Law and custom and an adoption order was required to prove adoption in both legal regimes.

1041. Revised Laws of Enugu State of Nigeria, 2004 Vol. 1.

Chapter 6. Parental Authority

§1. Parental Authority

1082. Three main compartmentalisations can be drawn from the term, parents; parenthood, parenting, and parental responsibility. Parenthood is that unique status of being parents – originally only attributable to biological, filial relationship to two persons, a father and a mother of a child. The status now extends legally, to adopted children. Parenting on the other hand is the discharge in love of the duties and rights and the decision of impacting apparently and proactively the experiences of individual parents or the aggregate of these duties, rights and experiences in raising a child for the good of the parents, the child and with the ultimate objective of contribution of goodness to society. Parental responsibility is the demand and requirement of parenting from individuals whether or not they are so inclined to discharging them. The Constitution and the CRA and in other cases, the Children and Young Persons Law, provide what laws are there for regulatory parental responsibility.

I. The Law

1083. Section 328 of the Constitution defines 'child' in a broad manner to include 'a step-child, a lawfully adopted child, a child born out of wedlock and any child to whom any individual stands in place of a parent'.

1084. The Child's Rights Act refers to 'parental responsibility' rather than authority. Section 277 provides the meaning:

(a) all the rights duties, powers, responsibilities and authority which by law a parent of a child has in relation to the child and his property; and
(b) the rights, powers and duties which a guardian of the estate of the child appointed, before the commencement of this Act to act generally would have had in relation to the child and his property, and includes, in particular, the right of the guardian to recover or receive in his own name or the benefit of the child, property of whatever description and wherever situated which the child is entitled to receive or recover.

1085. Article 19 to which Uzodike refers provides that: 'States Parties shall take all appropriate legislative, administrative, social and educational measures to protect the child from all forms of physical or mental violence, injury or abuse, neglect or negligent treatment, maltreatment or exploitation, including sexual abuse, while in the care of parent(s), legal guardian(s) or any other person who has the care of the child.'

1086. These steps have been taken in Nigeria and enacted as Part II of the Child's Rights Act and in particular sections 11 and 13. Consequently, by section 14 of the Act, every child has a right to parental care and, protection. A child can only be separated from parents without the child's consent only in the child's best interest for the purpose of education and welfare or in exercise of a judicial determination in accordance with the provisions of the Act. In addition, every child has the right to maintenance by his parents or guardians in accordance with the extent of their means, and the child has the right, in appropriate circumstances, to enforce this right in the family court.

II. Authority

1087. In Nigeria, the torch light for raising a child is the legendary line: 'spare the rod and spoil the child'. Thus, an influential commentator opines that 'while it is important to protect and safeguard the human rights of children to freedom from degrading and humiliating treatment and to have respect for their physical integrity, it should not be done to their own detriment. The interest of children will be decimated by prohibition and criminalisation of corporal punishment and such a step must be discouraged in our society'.[1042]

1088. In *Ekeogu v. Aliri*[1043] the plaintiff, aged eleven brought the action through her next friend, her mother. The 1st defendant was a teacher who had exerted corporal punishment by flogging, on the plaintiff. She was one of several students who were flogged. The flogging resulted in the permanent damage to the plaintiff's left eye resulting in blindness. The defendant claimed as at the time the action was brought that it had become statute barred, being a public servant protected by section 2 of the Public Officers Protection Law, Cap 106, Laws of Eastern Nigeria, 1963 as applicable to Imo State. The section makes actions against public officers' statute barred unless brought within three months of the cause of action.

1089. On the said date, there was an incident of theft in a nearby Palm Produce depot. The thief was caught and was being beaten up by an irate mob. The 1st defendant according to evidence, desiring to demonstrate to the class pupils the possible effect of theft, instructed his class pupils, including the plaintiff to witness the mob action. The plaintiff together with other pupils in the class obliged and went to the said depot. Soon after, the bell rang for resumption of classes and all the pupils, including the plaintiff began to run back towards the class. Suddenly, the 1st defendant picked a cane and began to flog the pupils as they ran into the classroom. As the plaintiff attempted to run into the classroom the 1st defendant aimed at her face and discharged his cane right across the face of the plaintiff. The cane landed on the plaintiff's left eye and the plaintiff cried out in pain and anguish. The plaintiff lost balance and collapsed on the floor. The 1st defendant ignored the cries of the plaintiff and continued to flog the other pupils.

1042. E.N. Uzodike, *Trends of Human Rights Campaign in Family Law*, University of Lagos, Nigeria Inaugural Lecture Series, 2011, 35 (University of Lagos Press 2011).

1043. [1991] LPELR-SC.10/1990; [1991] 3 NWLR (part 179) 258; [1991] 3 SCNJ 45; [1991] 3 S.C 58.

1090. In the light of the sequence of actions and inaction of the plaintiff, the High Court judge stated that he was not protected by the Law. Pursuant to Order 29, rule 3, of the High Court rules, the court ordered that the applicant, John Ekeogu file his Statement of Defence to the action within twenty-one days from the ruling. The 1st defendant (now appellant) dissatisfied with the ruling of the High Court appealed to the Court of Appeal, Port Harcourt Judicial Division. The Court of Appeal, on hearing argument from counsel, dismissed the appellant's appeal, holding that the act complained of, was not done by the appellant in the execution of a public duty. Kolawole, JCA., who delivered the lead judgment put it as follows:

> If the averments contained in paragraphs 6, 7 and 8 of the Statement of Claim are admitted by the appellant, the action of the appellant is beastly and without jurisdiction. What wrong did the respondent commit to necessitate such a brutal action on the part of the appellant which caused the loss of the left eye of an eleven-year-old pupil? If, as a result of the flogging of the respondent, death were to result, could it be said that the appellant was acting in pursuance of public duty? I do not think so. Could the appellant take cover under Section 2(11) of the Public Officers Protection Law? That will defeat the purpose of the legislation. The Public Officers Protection Law is not a licence for the commission of criminal acts under which a public officer will then seek sanctuary without answering the very grave allegations levelled against him which he is assumed to have admitted as true at the stage of the demurrer. In my view the appellant must offer an answer as to why he did what he was alleged to have done, an act which patently he did not do in pursuance of any official duty.

1091. Aggrieved by the decision of the Court of Appeal, the appellant has further appealed to this court on only one ground of appeal.

1092. At the Supreme Court, it was held that the only issue to be decided was whether the action was statute barred or not. The Supreme Court took the position that it was statute barred and that the teacher was acting within the course of his duties as a teacher in the school.

1093. In my view, the lead justice of the Supreme Court stated: the words used in this legislation are plain and unambiguous and should be given their ordinary and natural meaning. A careful reading of the section shows that its provision applies to an action brought against a public officer for any act done either – (i) in pursuance or intended execution of any Law of public duty or authority, or (ii) in respect of any alleged neglect of default in the execution of Law, duty or authority.

1094. According to Uzodike, 'it is the writer's view that the legislature should not meddle with reasonable family autonomy all in the name of children's human rights to bodily integrity. The removal of all parental immunity for hitting children as required by art. 19 of the CRC has a great potential to harm stable family life and privacy'.[1044]

1095. In Nigeria, it can be said that parental authority over children is nearly absolute.

1044. E.N. Uzodike *supra.* n. 1042, 34–35.

Chapter 7. Guardianship

§1. Guardianship

1096. A guardian of a child in Nigeria is a person appointed as a guardian in accordance with the provisions of section 85 of the Child's Rights Act.[1045] Consent is relevant to the determination of whether a guardianship relationship exists between a person and a child. The section thus requires that a person appointed as a guardian must have consented to the appointment. Children is defined as biological, adopted, fostered, and those under guardianship and wardship.[1046]

1097. By section 274 of the Child's Rights Act, the Act supersedes all enactments relating to children, and their care to the extent of any inconsistency.[1047] The Act aims at consolidating child centred legislation, incorporating the principles and rights of the child as encapsulated in the Convention on the Rights of the Child and African Charter on the Rights and Welfare of the Child into a National law.

1098. The provisions on guardianship are contained in Part IX of the Child's Rights Act. Order IX, Part II of the Matrimonial Causes Rules, indicates the rules to guide the decision on representation, by a guardian *ad litem* where an infant is a respondent in a matrimonial cause, is a party named or cited.

1099. There are three identifiable ways from the provisions of the Act by which guardianship arise. They are parental guardianship (in the sense in which guardianship is related to parental responsibility and custody), care guardianship (in the sense of care equated with parenting and its responsibility) and representative guardianship (capacity to act as a next friend or guardian *ad litem*).

I. Parental Guardianship

1100. A guardian in this sense, has parental responsibility for the child.[1048] Section 83(1) provides that the parents of a biological child are the guardians of the child and, in the event of the death of a parent, the surviving parent becomes the guardian of the child. A surviving parent who has guardianship of a child may, in contemplation of death, by deed, appoint a guardian for the child. This applies to married or unmarried persons. An appointment made by a will which is not signed by the testator, shall have effect only if it is signed at the direction of the testator. A guardian has all such powers over the estate, as the case may be, of a child as a guardian appointed by will or otherwise by virtue of the rules of common law, equity, or appropriate personal law.[1049]

1045. Other than a guardian of the estate of a child, s. 277 of the CRA.
1046. Section 277 of the CRA.
1047. One such law is the Children and Young Persons Act Cap 31 with variations of State laws.
1048. Section 82(2) of the CRA; *see also* ss 89 and 90 of the Act.
1049. Section 87 of the CRA.

1101. It is inappropriate in a strict legal sense to refer to the parent of a child as his/her guardian. This is because parenthood has intrinsic duty of guardianship and restating it may whittle down this natural role. Equating guardianship with parenthood is a faulty premise that tends to undermine the duties and responsibilities attached to parenthood with its intrinsic role of parenting. The parent is the lawful and biological father or mother of a child and natural rights and duties attach to the status. This meaning while legally extending to adoption should clearly preclude the role of parenting as guardianship.

1102. Guardianship is an imposed status which is subject to voluntary acceptance. Section 85 of the Child Rights Act, 2003 makes this explicit. Guardianship is a fall back social or individualistic construct to engage the primary objective of the parent. To equate parenthood therefore with guardianship is to relieve that status of the natural duties and responsibilities inherent in the status. This position is reinforced by the provisions of section 17 which vests a right to sue for damages against injuries received while in the womb. Section 17(2) and (3) confer right to inheritance even when unborn but born and surviving either parent.

II. Care Guardianship

1103. The parents may be unfit to be guardians of a child jointly or severally, in which case, if an application is made by a member of the family or an appropriate authority, the court may appoint a person to be a joint guardian with the parent or parents of the child. Where a guardian is appointed to act jointly with a parent or parents of a child and the appointed guardian considers the parents unfit to have the custody of the child, the guardian may apply to the Court, which may make an order that the guardian becomes the sole guardian of the child. The order may cover the custody and right of access of the parents to the child, having regard to the welfare of the child and may also extend to payment towards the maintenance of the child by a parent or the parents.

III. Guardian *ad litem*

1104. Where a person is appointed as guardian *ad litem* the guardianship is only for specific purposes involving a representation of the child and his or her interest in certain proceedings. It does not entail parental responsibility for the child. [1050]

1105. The Court in determining whether it is necessary to appoint a guardian *ad litem* is required to do so, in accordance with the Rules of Court and safeguard the interests of the child. In addition, the Court, is empowered, notwithstanding any enactment or rules of law to the contrary, to take account of any statement contained in a report made by a guardian *ad litem* for the purpose of determining proceedings related to a child involved in an application. Any evidence given in respect

1050. Section 82 of the CRA.

of the matters referred to in the report, in so far as the statement or evidence is, in the opinion of the Court relevant to the question which the Court is considering is admissible in evidence.

1106. The Minister may by regulations provide for the establishment of panels of persons from which guardians *ad litem* appointed by the court may be selected.[1051] The regulations may, in particular, make provisions – as to the constitution, administration and procedures of the panels; require two or more specified Local Governments to make arrangements for the joint management of a panel; for the defrayment by the State Government of expenses incurred by members of panels; for the payment by the State Government of fees and allowances to members of panels. The regulations may also extend to the qualifications for membership of a panel; the training to be given to members of the panels; the co-operation required of specified Local Governments in the provision of panels in specified areas; and for monitoring the work of guardians *ad litem.*

1107. The Rules of Court are also required to apply to provisions on assistance which the court may require of a *guardian ad litem.* They also extend to the special care expected of the *guardian ad litem* where an order of a specified kind has been made in the proceedings in question, or application for variation or discharge of the order is to be made. The *guardian ad litem* is also expected to participate and contribute usefully to proceedings of a review.

1108. Where the child concerned in a proceeding does not have a guardian *ad litem* appointed on his or her behalf, and is not represented by a legal practitioner, the Court may appoint a legal practitioner to represent the child. The conditions to be met for the Court to appoint a legal practitioner are that no guardian *ad litem* has been appointed for the child; the child has sufficient understanding to instruct a legal practitioner and wishes to do so; it appears to the Court that it would be in the best interest of the child for him to be represented by a legal practitioner: A legal practitioner so appointed is required to represent the child in accordance with the Rules of Court.

IV. Rights of a Guardian *ad litem*

1109. Where a person has been appointed as a guardian *ad litem*, he is entitled at all reasonable times to examine and take a copy of any record by the State Government or an appropriate authority compiled in connection with the making, or proposed making, by any person of any application under the Act with respect to the child concerned. The guardian *ad litem* also has rights, to other records so far as those records relate to that child and is in the custody of the State Government or an appropriate authority and was compiled in connection with any function referred to the social service committee. Where a guardian *ad litem* takes a copy of a record

1051. Section 90(1) of the CRA.

which he is entitled to examine as stated, then notwithstanding anything to the contrary in any enactment or rules, the copy is admissible as evidence of any matter referred to in any report which he makes to the Court in the proceedings in question or evidence which he gives in those proceedings.[1052]

V. Other Relevant Matters

1110. Where two or more persons act as joint guardians of a child and they are unable to agree on any question affecting the welfare of the child, any of them may apply to the Court for its direction, and the court may make an order regarding the question in dispute. Where the Family Court is yet to be established in accordance with the Act, the jurisdiction of a court to appoint or move guardians by virtue of the High Court Laws or any other written law, remains relevant.[1053]

1111. The Act preserves orders made by any court, relating to the guardianship or custody of a child before the commencement of the Act until other provisions are made under and by virtue of the Act. The order must, however, not be inconsistent with the Act.[1054]

VI. Termination of Guardianship

1112. The appointment of a guardian may be brought to an end at any time by an order of the Court on the application of a natural parent or any person who has parental responsibility for the child. It may also be brought to an end, with leave of the Court on the application of the child concerned, on the application of an appropriate authority or in any family proceedings, if the Court considers that it should be brought to an end notwithstanding that no application, has been made.

§2. Wardship

1113. The provisions on wardship are contained in Part X of the Act. An application for wardship is required to be made in compliance with the rules contained in Third Schedule to the Act.[1055]

1114. The Family Court has jurisdiction in all matters pertaining to wardship.[1056] An application for wardship can be made by a private person, an authority

1052. Section 91(1) of the CRA.
1053. Section 92(2) of the CRA.
1054. Section 92(1) of the CRA.
1055. Section 99 of the CRA.
1056. Sections 93 and 94 of the CRA.

or raised by the Court in a proceeding before it. The application in line with the Third Schedule of the Act is by originating summons in which the applicant must state the relationship with the ward.

1115. It is only by an order of the court that a child becomes a ward of court. The court after consideration of the application may order wardship to either of the parents of the ward or an independent person. It may, in considering an application or adjudication before it, raise the question of fitness of parents. Where it therefore, appears to the Court that there are exceptional circumstances making it impracticable or undesirable for a ward of court to be, or to continue to be under the care of either of his parents or any other person, the Court may, if it thinks fit, make an order committing the care of the ward to an appropriate authority.[1057] In some similar assessment of circumstances by the court, it may also order the removal of the child from such earlier authority and place the child under the supervision of an independent person or another authority. It may, with regard to such period as the court thinks fit, order that the ward be under the supervision of a child development officer or other appropriate authority. Such authority may be the police.

1116. The court in making an order, has powers to order upkeep and maintenance of the child which could be payable by one parent to another or from both to whoever, the court has given care of the child.[1058] The court is required to be guided by what is reasonable having regard to the means of the person or persons making the payment. Such an order will cover payment of the period of the order. The order, however, may direct that the payment continues until the ward of court attains the age of majority and such order may provide that any sum which is payable, having regard to the age of the child be paid directly to the ward.

1117. Furthermore, where the ward of court is living with his parents or lives with them at any time during the period covered by the order, there shall be no order for maintenance and no liability towards same shall arise. If the ward of court resides with parents for a period of three months after an order has been made, the order shall cease to have effect. The Court has wide powers in this respect, and may from time to time, by an order, vary or discharge any previous order.

1118. The court may make the order to cover a specific period subject to expiration after the period. It may, also order the end of the wardship on an application from an applicant, an appropriate authority or it may do so even, without an application. Upon the order being made, the child who is for the time being a ward of court ceases to be a ward of court.

1119. A Court hearing a matrimonial case in which a child may be involved may direct that proper proceedings be taken in the Court at the High Court level for making the child a ward of Court.[1059]

1057. Section 96(1) of the CRA.
1058. Section 95 of the CRA.
1059. Section 97 of the CRA.

Chapter 8. Kinship and Relations of Affinity

§1. Kinship and Relationships of Affinity

1120. A marriage in Nigeria conducted under the Marriage Act is void if the parties are within the prohibited degrees of consanguinity or, of affinity by section 4 of the MCA.[1060] Section 11(1)(C) and 2 of the Marriage Act provide that the Registrar of Marriages, before issuing a Certificate of Compliance with Notice must obtain an affidavit from the parties proposing to be married that they do not fall within the prohibited degrees of consanguinity or affinity – subject to exceptions on affinity. Failure to comply with this may result in imprisonment for two years. Where the parties are married without compliance the marriage is void by section 3(1)(b) of the Matrimonial Causes Act.

1121. Consanguinity is relationship by blood traced to a common ancestry. Affinity is a relationship by marriage. Persons who have a consanguineous relationship are altogether prohibited from becoming married to one another under the Marriage Act. The First Schedule to the MCA providing the list of consanguineous relationships specifically states that it is immaterial whether the relationship is of the whole blood or half blood, or whether it is traced through, or to any person whose parents were or are not married to each other.

1122. In certain customs and under Islamic marriages, the prohibition is not as total as in a marriage conducted following the Act. In some customs in Nigeria some degrees of cousins including second and perhaps, first can marry legitimately. Some of those customs are of the Kogi people of Nigeria. In other customs, the marriage is conducted after certain customary expiation and ablutions.

1123. The provisions of the Child's Rights Act on the legal effect of an adoption order are to make adopted children related by blood. There are prohibitions clearly stipulated by section 147(1) of the Child's Rights Act. Marriage is prohibited between an adopter of a child and the adopted child and also prohibited between a natural child of the adopter and the adopted child. Any such marriage is null and void. There is also a sanction of imprisonment for a term not exceeding fourteen years if a person is convicted on this account. Although section 141 of the Child's Rights Act is on devolution of property which takes effect following an adoption, it would appear to also have connections with consanguinity. Section 141(4)(b) provides that a person related to the adopted child in any degree shall, unless the contrary intention appears, must be construed as a reference to the person who would be related to him in that degree if he were the natural child of the adopter and were not the child of any other person.

1060. Section 3(1)(b) of the Matrimonial Causes Act.

1124. Where the relationship is one of affinity, there could be waivers to permit the parties marry under the Act. To have the waiver, an application is made to a judge of the High Court for waivers.[1061]

1125. The First Schedule to the MCA contains the list of prohibited degrees of consanguinity and affinity made pursuant to section 3 of the MCA and is provided below.

1126. Consanguinity Affinity Marriage of a man is prohibited if the woman is, or has been his:

Ancestor	Wife's mother
Descendant	Wife's grandmother
Sister	Wife's daughter
Father's sister	Wife's son's daughter
Mother's sister	Wife's daughter's daughter
Brother's daughter	Father's wife
Sister's daughter	Grandfather's wife
	Son's wife
	Son's wife
	Daughter's son's wife

1127. Marriage of a woman is prohibited if the man is, or has been, her:

Ancestress	Husband's father
Descendant	Husband's grandfather
Brother	Husband's son
Father's brother	Husband's son's son
Mother's brother	Husband's daughter's son
Brother's son	Mother's husband
Sister's son	Grandmother's husband
	Daughter's husband
	Son's daughter's husband
	Daughter's husband

1061. Section 4 of the MCA.

Part III. Matrimonial Property Law

Chapter 1. Rights and Obligations of Spouses

§1. General Principles

1128. The rights and obligations of spouses depend on the nature of marriage entered by the parties. Generally, under customary and Islamic marriages, rights and obligations are simplistic, in the sense that the framework appears simple but their interplay and consequences on societal synergy and cohesion are complex, and therefore, must continue to receive rationale evaluation.

1129. Marriage under the Marriage Act is the main framework that confers rights and obligations on parties to a marriage. However, the framework is again largely influenced by the peculiar customs, culture, and way of life of the people. Thus, although most of the provisions of the Matrimonial Causes Act are based, as has been noted earlier, on the laws of member nations of the Commonwealth, the provisions on spousal rights and obligations underwent an 'eagle eye' to reflect the peculiar customs, culture, and way of life of the Nigerian.

§2. The Household Expenses

1130. Nigeria, being a patriarchal society, the general position is that the household expenses are provided by husbands or fathers. In practice, though, women take responsibility for household expenses covering feeding and clothing of the children and themselves. As has been made clear by the cases already analysed, these are not considered in the questions of redistribution of property or adjustment of property rights on breakdown of marriage.

§3. The Matrimonial Home

1131. In general, there is no matrimonial home regime in Nigeria. Parties specify their interest in the property by their contributions thereon. Since, the country is a patriarchal society, husbands are more likely to have purchased, inherited, or built any home in which spouses reside.

§4. Transactions Between Spouses

1132. Nigeria recognises transactions between spouses in so far, as the transactions are well documented and receipted.

Chapter 2. The Marriage Settlement

1133. In Nigeria Marriage settlement is recognised under all the marriage regimes, subject to the general patriarchal structure of the society already fully highlighted and analysed.

Chapter 3. The Legal Matrimonial Regime

1134. The Matrimonial Causes Act defines the rights and obligations accruable from the marital relationship. Part IV of the MCA and sections 69–75 cover Maintenance, Settlement, Property variation and related provisions while sections 88–94 are on enforcement of order in relation to these proceedings. The provisions relate mainly to the process and outcomes of judicial separation, dissolution of marriage, nullity, and custody proceedings. The Act specifies its scope on Maintenance, Settlement, Property variation by section 69 and application mainly in sections 70–73. Section 69 provides an interpretation of 'the marriage' that is covered and 'who' comprise the children of the marriage. Thus, marriage for this part includes a purported marriage that is void but does not include one entered according to Muslim or customary rites. The principal provision for maintenance is section 70. Section 71 is on custody and maintenance of children; section 72 is on settlement of property and 73 is on guidelines and power of the court.

1135. Other related provisions on maintenance are, sections 16(1)(f), 23 and 42(2). Section 16(1)(f) is a fact for establishing irretrievable breakdown based on the respondent's behaviour and the petitioner's intolerability of it. This is where the respondent has habitually and wilfully failed, throughout the period of two years immediately preceding the date of the petition, to pay maintenance ordered to be paid to the petitioner by agreement or on a decree of judicial separation. Section 23 provides a restriction where the court is not satisfied that reasonable attempts have been made by the petitioner to enforce the order or agreement under which maintenance was ordered or agreed to be paid. Another related provision on maintenance is section 42(2) which makes a husband who is ordered to pay maintenance to his wife, and who fails to do so, liable for necessaries supplied for the wife's use. This provision, which is clearly anachronistic, could never have been applied or had any practical effect in Nigeria.

§1. Maintenance

1136. Maintenance in ordinary usage is the act of maintaining or the state of being maintained.[1062] It is also variously used as the process of preserving a condition or situation or the state of being preserved. Its meaning in matrimonial property is not far removed.

1137. Under customary marriages, the question of maintenance of a wife when a marriage is dissolution does not arise. *Adaku Amadi v. Nwosu*[1063] a Supreme Court decision settles the point.

1138. Maintenance following a dissolution of marriage under Islamic law involves a complex set of circumstances. The period of interregnum known as

1062. At https://www.merriam-webster.com/dictionary/maintenance.
1063. [1992] 5 NWLR 273.

Iddah or *iddat* requires that maintenance of the wife as an obligatory role of the husband, continues. *Iddah* or *iddat* is known as a waiting period prelude to a full dissolution. Subsequent to the dissolution of the marriage, maintenance ceases and in fact, the wife is required to refund the dowry. It must be borne in mind that the structure of societies and their legal regimes under customs and Islam are patriarchal in theory and practice, therefore, children are the sole responsibility of a husband as an extension of 'self-caring for and taking custody of children are thus a more important fallout of estrangement of spouses.

1139. The Matrimonial Causes Act, theoretically, aims at a different regime from customary and Islamic marriages. As far as the provisions of the Act and their application in case law reveal, the regime of maintenance provided by the Matrimonial Causes Act is only one step from the other regimes, in that the wife's good behaviour is an important factor on which the question of being maintained turns. Thus, 'where the applicant for maintenance is the party at fault, the size of maintenance and whether it would be awarded at all depends on the gravity of the party's misconduct'.[1064] The Act itself as has been noted earlier contemplates maintenance for only the wife. Bad behaviour, then means, majorly that there are no children of the marriage.[1065] In *Kpilah v. Ngwu*,[1066] the Court of Appeal, reviewing the basis and guidelines for award of maintenance noted that the court must give weight 'to all other relevant circumstances to allow the court to give consideration to peculiar culture and way of life'. Thus, in *Sotomi v. Sotomi*,[1067] although the decree of divorce was granted against the wife for behaviour, intolerable to the husband-petitioner, he was nevertheless enjoined to maintain the wife and children.

1140. Under the Matrimonial Causes Act, maintenance is an ancillary relief to a principal relief. Section 75(4) of the MCA defines principal relief as relief of a kind referred to in section 114(1) on paragraph (a) or (b), which defines 'matrimonial cause'. The paragraphs cover dissolution of marriage, judicial separation, nullity, restitution of conjugal rights and jactitation of marriage. It is unclear how maintenance can apply to jactitation of marriage. It could, however, apply to restitution of conjugal rights since Nigerian jurisdiction treats this cause as a driver of reconciliation.

1141. A husband or wife may apply for maintenance – in practice only wives do.[1068] The maintenance may be for oneself and for children of the marriage. Section 70 subsection (4) requires the court not to make an order for maintenance of

1064. The Court of Appeal in *Kpilah v. Ngwu* [2018] LPELR – 45395 (CA)., 23 affirming the case *Ajayi-Ajagbe v. Ajayi-Ajagbe* [1978] CCHCJ 193.
1065. E.N. Uzodike, *supra.,* n. 11.
1066. [2018] LPELR – 45395 (CA)., 24.
1067. [1976] 2 FNR 104.
1068. That this is the contemplation of the Act is also evident in the provision of s. 1(3)(a)(i) which provides for orders with respect to the maintenance of wives or children or the custody of or access to children. Emphasised in *Okafor v. Okafor* [1976] 6 High Court of Lagos State Law Reports 1727, 1734.

children of the marriage who have attained the age of 21 years unless there are special circumstances to justify maintenance for the benefit of a child who has attained that age. An application for matrimonial ancillary relief must follow the technical details, form, and terminology of the Act.[1069] In *Olu-Ibukun v. Olu-Ibukun*,[1070] the Supreme Court stated that the term 'alimony' has no place in Nigerian laws. In *Onyia v. Onyia*[1071] the Court of Appeal also rejected the use of alimony as anachronistic and inappropriate.

1142. A party applying for maintenance may do so before or after the determination of a petition for dissolution of marriage or nullity proceedings. An application for maintenance after the determination of the petition may be made, but with the leave of court. The court has wide discretionary powers to award maintenance taking into consideration the usual factors for exercising such discretion, ensuring that discretion is exercised judiciously and not arbitrarily.[1072] The court's discretion extends to award of maintenance pending the determination of the proceedings. The guideline is provided in section 70, subsection (2). The subsection is also subject to the rules of court. The court may therefore, in proceedings for an order for the maintenance of a party to a marriage, or of children of the marriage, pending the disposal of proceedings, make such order as it thinks proper, having regard to the means, earning capacity, age, children and conduct of the parties to the marriage and all other relevant circumstances. In applying for maintenance, the application must state and provide evidence of means. Where the spouse on whom the duty to maintain lies, earns a salary, evidence of the salary and properties owned by the spouse. Earnings have been held to include potential earnings.[1073] The salary of the spouse can be attached for purposes of maintenance. The age of the spouse and number of years the parties have been married are also key relevant factors. An elderly applicant would be considered to have invested all useful work years in the marriage and therefore be awarded a more generous maintenance. The same factors are considered in the award of maintenance where the application is considered after the determination of the principal relief.

1143. Maintenance can cover lump sum or any periodic payments in line with section 73(1)(b). Deeds may be executed in respect of same, and trustees, appointment, or removal of etc., to assure that the order of the court is carried out.[1074] Maintenance when made after the determination of the principal relief is made to commence in arrears from the date on which the originating summons was issued. When maintenance is made pending the determination o of the proceedings, the

1069. *Olu–Ibukun v. Olu-Ibukun* [1974] 4 E.C.S.L.R 704.
1070. [1974] 4 E.C.S.L.R 704.
1071. [1985] Monthly Court Reports (part 11) 15.
1072. *Olabisi Akinboni v. Bolajoko Akinboni* [2002] 5 NWLR (part 761) 564; *Erhahon v. Erhahon* [1997] 6 NWLR (part 510) 667, 683.
1073. *Kpilah v. Ngwu* [2018] LPELR – 45395 (CA).
1074. Section 73(1)(d).

court is restricted to ordering provisions that allow the spouse and children to sustain their standard of living prior to the petition. However, maintenance after the determination of the proceedings is aimed at permanence and therefore, property may be brought into play.

1144. The courts pay attention to conduct of the parties to the petition which is a crucial factor to be considered in the question of award of maintenance. [1075] Sections 70(1) and (2) require the court to take the conduct of the parties and other relevant factors into account. The court may award maintenance as exemplary in spite of the earning capacity of a party. This leaves room for the personal perceptions of individual judges to play out. Thus, that the wife deserted the husband and rejected overtures at reconciliation worked against award of maintenance.[1076]

1145. It is to be noted, however, that this does not have to be so, as the Act provides by section 70 subsection (3), that the court may make an order for the maintenance of a party notwithstanding that a decree is, or has been made against that party in the proceedings to which the proceedings with respect to maintenance are related. Furthermore, the rules specifically provide that the fact that adultery is proved against a party should not bar such a party from being maintained. It is expected that conduct and all other circumstances must be considered in the light of the subsection.

1146. A court is empowered to discharge an order for maintenance if the party in whose favour it was made marries again or if there is any other just cause for so doing.[1077]

I. Assessment of Maintenance

1147. The assessment of maintenance is a crucial aspect of the law on the subject. Maintenance is not assessed based on assets such as the house of the respondent but on earnings. In the early cases the position of the Supreme Court was that maintenance is not geared towards property adjustment or redistribution but strictly to assure the wife the standard of living she was used to, in the case of maintenance pending the determination of the proceedings, and for maintenance after the determination of the proceedings, according to the overall assessment of the court based on the criteria stated in sections 70(1) and 73 of the MCA. This was the approach taken in cases such as *Olu-Ibukun v. Olu-Ibukun*[1078] and *Negbenebor v. Negbenebor.*[1079] Thus, in awarding maintenance, these early Supreme Court cases made a distinction between capital assets and recurring income. Recurring income was preferred for purposes of awarding maintenance and capital assets were totally

1075. *Ibeabuchi v. Ibeabuchi* [2016] LPELR 41268 (CA).
1076. *Onyia v. Onyia* [1985] Monthly Court Reports (part 11) 15.
1077. Section 73(1)(f) of the MCA.
1078. [1974] 4 E.C.S.L.R 704.
1079. [1971] 1 All N.L.R. 210.

excluded. Second, flowing from *Okafor* where parties have separate earnings, there would be no difficulties with declaring their individual rights. In *Negbenebor v. Negbenebor*[1080] the applicant prayed the court for reliefs bordering on maintenance for herself and three infant children.[1081] The crucial findings by the Supreme Court are that in the computation of and assessment of maintenance what needs to be taken into account is the income and not property or assets. According to Justice Sowemimo J.S.C: 'indeed it is clear to us that the learned trial judge was in error in the manner in which he treated the matter of the house as part of the assets as distinct from respondent's income which is the basis on which assessment of maintenance is made'. More recent cases have followed these Supreme Court cases, affirming their currency.[1082] In *Kpilah v. Ngwu*,[1083] the Court of Appeal, stated that 'in arriving at a determination the court must take note that "the apex Court held that, the husband's income was his salary and distinct from his assets"'.[1084]

1148. There are views to the effect that property such as house and savings ought to form part of computation in an order for maintenance. According to this view, the word 'means' should be interpreted and applied in a broad context.[1085]

1149. Two pivotal approaches are discernible from case law on the Court's exercise of power to order maintenance. One is in awarding maintenance pending determination of the principal matrimonial cause and the other is on determination of the suit. In the former case, the courts adopt the approach of minimal intervention until the suit is heard and determined and in the second case, the courts aim at resolving the financial provisions for the other spouse and children permanently. The first position may be attributable to the interpretation the courts have given to section 75 subsection (1) of the MCA, which requires that the court shall not make an order for maintenance where the petition for the principal relief has been dismissed. Although, it may exercise a discretion where it is satisfied that the proceedings for the principal relief were instituted in good faith, but was dismissed, and there is no reasonable likelihood of the parties becoming reconciled.[1086]

1150. In *Olu-Ibukun v. Olu-Ibukun*[1087] the main relief was a petition for the dissolution of the marriage between the petitioner and her husband, the respondent. In answering the petition, the respondent admitted that the marriage had broken down irretrievably but on facts other than those stated by the petitioner. The question

---

1080. [1971] All N.L.R. 210.
1081. The case came under the Matrimonial Causes Act, 1950, s. 23(1) and could therefore only be a guide for current action under the Matrimonial Causes Act 1970 (2004).
1082. *Kpilah v. Ngwu* [2018] LPELR – 45395 (CA).
1083. [2018] LPELR – 45395 (CA)., 24.
1084. These are the cases of *Negbenebor v. Negbenebor* [1971] 1 All NLR 210 and *Olu-Ibukun v. Olu-Ibukun* [1974] 1 All NLR (part 1) 513.
1085. E.N. Uzodike, *Maintenance – Sixteen Years After the Matrimonial Causes Act*, 8 & 9 J. Priv. & Prop. L. (1987 & 1988) 21; referring to *Olu-Ibukun v. Olu Ibukun* [1974] All N.L.R (part 1) 513 & *Negbenebor v. Negbenebor* [1971] All NLR 210.
1086. Section 75(2)(b)(ii).
1087. [1974] LPELR – SC. 200/2973 [1974] All N.L.R. 463; [1974] 2 S.C. 35; [1974] 4 E.C.S.L.R 704.

before the court was application made for maintenance of the wife pending the disposition of the petition. On affidavit evidence and following the English rules on alimony *pendete lite* the trial court made some orders. The respondent appealed. On appeal, the Supreme Court reiterated that the MCA provides for the process of maintaining a wife pending the disposal of the suit by section 70(2) and the provision is in *pari materia* with section 84 of the MCA, 1959 of Australia.

1151. However, since at that time the Matrimonial Causes Rules had not been made, it resorted to the Australian Matrimonial Causes Rules. By section 204(6) and 210 of the Australian rules the court's enquiry should not only be limited to matters of conduct in the proceedings for principal relief (unless this is admitted), they should also extend to the various circumstances under which orders for maintenance in pending proceedings can be obtained. These include the peculiar circumstances of the parties with regard to the station in life and the financial position of each of the parties.[1088]

1152. The Supreme Court, adopting the approach of the Australian Court in *Wills v. Wills*,[1089] stated that an order of maintenance pending determination of a petition must not be structured for a wife to share the husband's fortune, but only to ensure that the wife lives approximately in the position to which she has been accustomed to until the determination of the petition. It emphasised that matrimonial causes must be instituted only according to the provisions of the Act and the rules thereon and that the Act had adequate provisions for maintenance pending the resolution of the petition.

1153. In the circumstances, the appeal was allowed, the judgment of the lower court set aside and the petition sent back to the Lagos High Court for re-hearing before another judge who was enjoined to hear the main petition expeditiously.

1154. The second distillable approach is from *Okafor v. Okafor*[1090] where the court made a fundamental statement that underlies the policy direction of the law and any evaluation of the policy direction in this area. According to the court, 'The sort of claim which the Respondent appeared to have laid out on the Petitioner's earnings to my mind, was a negation of the new social development and series of law reforms which entitle a married woman to own property separate from her husbands'.'. Thus, where the parties demonstrate that they have different earnings or have prepared for separate financial arrangements the court will enforce such arrangements. The courts in Nigeria are not known to interfere with property rights otherwise.[1091] Although the court did not refer to section 17 of the Married Women's Property Act, 1881, it affirmed the right of a woman who married under the

1088. *Jeffery v. Jeffery* [1941] 72 C.L.R. 570.
1089. [1961] 2 ELR 136.
1090. [1976] 6 High Court of Lagos State Law Reports 1727.
1091. The provisions of the MCA in this respect and case law are discussed below under property adjustments and variations.

Act, to own property independently from her husband.[1092] In that case, the parties married in 1965 in a London Marriage Registry and cohabited for five years at an address in London. They had their only child within this time. The respondent subsequently moved out of the matrimonial home alleging that the petitioner-wife had rejected his authority to control the earnings of the petitioner or to have a joint bank account. The petition was brought by the wife on the ground that the marriage had broken down irretrievably since the parties had lived apart for three years. The Court underscored the right of the wife to manage her own resources and granted a Decree nisi as well as custody. There was no application for maintenance. In *Ayangbayi v. Ayangbayi*,[1093] the respondent stated that she was self-sufficient and did not need to be maintained.

II. Comparable Notes with the MCA, 1973

1155. The MCA, 1973 has more elaborate provisions on the subject which support equitable matrimonial property regime.

1156. The extent to which the MCA, 1973 is at variance with the Nigerian regime has been of much debate as many would like to see the Nigerian regime adopt a more pragmatic property distribution model between spouses. The question left unanswered though is whether these provisions have proved satisfactory in the United Kingdom and second, whether the same provisions will work well for the Nigerian environment seeing that historical and social circumstances differ. Sections 23–25 of the MCA, 1973 govern financial provisions in connection with divorce proceedings etc.

1157. Section 23 is on payment of lump sums while section 24 is on adjustment and transfer of property. Section 25 is on the considerations to take into account by a court exercising its powers under the financial provision s orders. Section 25 subsection (1) appears to be in the same light as section 70 of the MCA. That appears to be the end of the similarities. The MCA, 1973 contemplates an equitable redistribution of property within certain guidelines. The Nigerian MCA only contemplates maintenance of the wife and children. In reality the Nigerian MCA as has been pointed out above, does not contemplate a husband being maintained. Section 72 of the MCA which is discussed below, contemplates the exercise of discretion on property only for the purposes of maintenance. In comparing the two jurisdictions, this perspective must be borne in mind.

1158. Section 25 of the MCA, 1973 provides: 'It shall be the duty of the Court in deciding whether to exercise its powers under section 23(1)(a)(b) or (c) or 24 above in relation to a party to the marriage and, if so, in what manner, to have regard to all the circumstances of the case including the following matters, that is to say:

1092. It must be noted that under customary law, a wife did not have this advantage as she herself remains, by the continuing logic of the law and courts, capable of being inherited.
1093. [1979] 10–12 CCHCJ (Lagos) 1.

(a) The income, earning capacity, property and other financial resources which each of the parties to the marriage has or is likely to have in the foreseeable future.
(b) The financial needs, obligations and responsibilities which each of the parties to the marriage has or is likely to have in the foreseeable future.
(c) The standard of living enjoyed by the family before the breakdown of the marriage.
(d) The age of each party to the marriage and the duration of the marriage.
(e) Any physical or mental disability of either of the parties to the marriage.
(f) The contributions made by each of the parties to the welfare of the family, including any contribution made by looking after the home or caring for the family.
(g) In the case of proceedings for divorce or nullity of marriage, the value to either of the parties to the marriage of any benefit (e.g., a pension) which, by reason of the dissolution or annulment of marriage, that party will lose the chance of acquiring'.

1159. In the light of these guidelines, to exercise those powers as to place the parties, so far as it is practicable and having regard to their conduct, just to do so, in the financial position in which they would have been if the marriage had not broken down and each had properly discharged his or her financial obligations and responsibilities towards the other.

1160. Prest v. Petrodel Resources Limited[1094] is a case that examined the import of the power conferred on the courts by the MCA, 1973 to do justice between the parties, although the thrust of the case was corporate personality. The case reviewed the nature of ancillary relief and how far a court can go in awarding and enforcing ancillary relief. The United Kingdom Supreme Court considered the implication and application of section 24 of the Matrimonial Causes Act, 1973 and the impact of sections 25 and 37 on the powers conferred on the court in section 24. The Supreme Court stated that the powers conferred by section 24 are not unlimited but that import of section 25 is a power in the court to consider property interests whether in possession or reversion or the interests in a company and its shares in assessing the income of a spouse. In analysing that interest, the court must be guided by the presumption that the financial affairs of a family are more likely to be in the hands and control of the husband, who invariably is more likely to be unwilling to cooperate on such enterprise, as did happen in the present case. Thus, the court noted that it is not enough to find that a party was unwilling to proffer evidence or indeed appear in court for cross-examination as did happen in *Prest* and then, for the court to make wide presumptions. According to Lord Sumption who delivered the lead of a unanimous judgment, a court cannot on account that a party did not avail himself for cross-examination convert open-ended speculation into findings of fact.[1095]

1094. [2013] UKSC 34.
1095. [2013] UKSC 34, para. 44. *See* British Railways Board *v.* Herrington for the views of Lord Diplock which appeared to support the Nigerian position. [1972] AC, 877, 930–931.

1161. The case concerned proceedings for ancillary relief following a dissolution of the marriage between the parties. The parties to the marriage who were also the principal parties in the proceedings are Michael and Yasmin Prest. They were married in England. At the time of the proceedings, both had dual nationality, Nigerian and British. Michael was born in Nigeria and Yasmin in England. The matrimonial home was in England and a second home in Nevis, although, the husband is a business man whom the judge found to have been resident in Monaco from about 2001 to the date of the proceeding. Yasmin petitioned for divorce in 2008 and a Decree *nisi* was granted in the same year. She subsequently applied for ancillary reliefs joining seven companies. The petition was determined in her favour with the High Court ordering that properties in varying legal ownership of the seven companies be transferred to her. In dealing with the question of the application for ancillary relief, the High Court referred to Part II, sections 23, 24 and 25 of the English Matrimonial Causes Act, 1973.[1096] The properties of the companies were shown to be beneficially in the ownership of Michael although controlled by intermediate entities. The evidence showed that at all times, Michael dealt in the properties of the company beneficially. It was also found as a fact, that all the companies did not have real or functional directors – some were relatives, nominal secretary and even cleaners. The court held that there was a wide discretion available to the court with respect to cases of this type which extended to overreaching corporate personality through application of section 24. It, however, chose not to enforce the order of the court through a general route of piecing the corporate veil of the stated companies, since it concluded that the authorities showed that unless there was an abuse for a purpose that in some relevant respect is improper, the separate legal personality of the company could not be disregarded. In this case, there was no relevant impropriety. The judge ordered that Michael procure the transfer of the matrimonial home to Yasmin and pay additional lump sum of GBP 17.5 million and periodic payments at the rate of 2% of the sum while it remained outstanding, together with GBP 24,000 per annum and the school fees for each of their four children. In addition, he awarded costs in favour of the wife, with a payment of GBP 600,000 on account.

1162. As of the date of the judgment, the matrimonial home had been transferred to the wife but only subject to a pre-existing charge in favour of BNP Paribas to secure a debt of undisclosed amount. Ten per cent of the money ordered to be paid as cost had also been made on condition to satisfy a requirement for appeal.

1163. The respective companies appealed the decision on the ground that there was no jurisdiction to order their property to be conveyed to the wife, Yasmin, in satisfaction of the husband's judgment debt.

1096. Section 23 provides for periodical and lump sum payments to a spouse or for the benefit of children of the marriage. Under s. 24(1)(a), the court may order that 'a party to the marriage shall transfer to the other party … such property as may be so specified, being property to which the first-mentioned party is entitled, either in possession or Page 2 reversion'. Section 25 provides for a few matters to which the court must in particular have regard in making such orders, including, at s. 25(2)(a), the 'income, earning capacity, property and other financial resources which each of the parties to the marriage has or is likely to have in the foreseeable future'.

1164. At the Court of Appeal, the jurisdiction to do so under section 24 was denied and disapproved in the majority position. At the Supreme Court it was noted that apart from paying school fees of the children, the husband had not complied with any other part of the judgment and showed no intention of doing so if he could possibly avoid it. Indeed, the Court noted further that the husband had done all he could to frustrate the wife's claim on him. Michael had also sought declarations in proceedings holding in Nigeria that the companies were incorporated and held in trust for his siblings.

1165. The Supreme Court considered that an examination of the true import of section 24 of the MCA, 1973 was important, since 'for some years it has been the practice of the Family Division to treat the assets of the companies substantially owned by one party to the marriage as available for distribution under section 24 of the Matrimonial Causes Act, provided that the remaining assets of the company are sufficient to satisfy its creditors'.[1097] It then stated that there are three possible legal bases on which the assets of the companies might be available to satisfy the judgment of a court – a court may under exceptional circumstances be entitled to disregard the corporate veil in order to give teeth to its judgment; the same power may exist under section 24 of the MCA, 1973; or the companies might in the particular circumstances of the case be regarded as a trustee of the properties for the husband but not because he is a sole controller or shareholder.

1166. On the first possibility, the court found that the law correctly takes the position of assuming that all persons, natural or artificial are honest in their dealings on questions concerning their rights and obligations. Thus, any evidence of dishonesty to take advantage of a corporate personality will form a basis for lifting the corporate veil. To reach this conclusion, there must be proof of such dishonesty and this will amount to fraud which must be pleaded and proved.[1098] In the circumstances of the particular case, it was found that the structure of the companies as the husband arranged it, preceded the case. The properties were thus duly vested in the companies and not the husband making lifting of the veil inappropriate to resolve the judgment debt. On the second possibility, the court held that section 24 was clear in meaning and its interpretation recognised. This interpretation is that the property contemplated in the provision is one which the party has legal or equitable interest in possession or reversion.[1099]

1167. On the third, the Supreme Court stated the well-known implications of a trust relationship, ultimately holding that in view of the circumstances surrounding the purchase of the properties, and the provisions of purchase money, the husband

1097. [2013] UKSC 34, para. 7.

1098. *Mueller v. Mueller* [2005] LPELR-12687 (CA); *Lazarus Estates Ltd. v. Beasley* [1956] 1 QB 702, 712.

1099. The court noted the effect and impact of s. 25(2)(a) which requires the court to have regard to factors such as income and earning capacity and noted that this is not opposition to s. 24 in so far as the income is independent of the company's assets no matter the access which a party has to that asset.

held a resulting trust in the properties of the company and the properties were thus liable to be transferred to the wife for the enforcement of the payment of the lump sum and the order of the Family Court.

§2. Property Rights: Adjustments or Settlement?

1168. In *Ayangbayi v. Ayangbayi*[1100] the High Court stated that the court's discretion to order settlement of property can only be exercised if it is contained in the petition or answer to the petition. This is, however, not borne out by the MCA or the rules. Thus, ancillary reliefs whether with respect to maintenance or settlement of property may be instituted in the petition, answer or by application of the court and even an application without leave of the Court. In the latter case where the application is in relation to an order made on the items listed in para-C of section 114, the definition section and paragraph for maintenance and settlement.[1101]

1169. There is no matrimonial property regime in Nigeria whether under customary, Islamic or marriage under the Act. Under the MCA, by Order IXV, Part 1, rule 4(g) one of the particulars required for maintenance which a claimant must indicate is: 'the ownership of the home in which the claimant is residing and the terms and conditions upon which the claimant is occupying or otherwise residing in that home'. In this sense the culture of incidents of marriage found expression in the Act despite being modelled on the Australian and English perspectives. Under the MCA, section 72 is the nearest provision for any variation in property rights and it is by way of settlement. That the section refers to a settlement *stricto sensu* is well reflected in trust implications and abundance of trust language and terms. The general position for property rights and their declaration is proof of contribution to any property claimed.[1102] As would normally, be the case, the wives who find themselves in such circumstances are unable to prove any real contributions.

1170. Adaku Amadi v. Nwosu[1103] illustrates the currency of the no-matrimonial property regime in Nigeria. The appellant Adaku Amadi was the wife of the vendor of the property in dispute, who had sold what she assumed as a matrimonial home to a third-party purchaser, the respondent. The dispute arose because the wife asserted a right to the property as a matrimonial home, and therefore joint ownership with her husband. At the High Court it was found in evidence that the land, was her husband's share from a family land which was partitioned for individual use. The appellant's husband then built on the land, with the wife claiming she had made some contributions towards the construction, by paying for the sand used and labour employed. However, the evidence before the trial court, which was accepted at the Supreme Court, is that the appellant's husband, PW1 solely financed the

1100. [1979] 10–12 CCHSCJ 1, 8.
1101. *See* further and generally, Order XIV; and Order XIV, part 1, rules 1–6.
1102. *Olabiwonnu v. Olabiwonnu* [2014] LPELR-36330; *Essien v. Essien* [2009] 9 NWLR (part 1146) 306; *Nanna v. Nanna* [2006] 3 NWLR (part 966) 1.
1103. [1992] 5 NWLR 273.

building of the house on the disputed piece of property. Evidence showed that as at the time of the proceeding, the appellant-wife and the children of the marriage continued to live in the house although her husband had since moved residence, having used the proceeds of sale to build a new house. The husband claimed he had requested his wife and children to move into the new house, but they declined to do so. At the trial court, it was stated that the property was not jointly owned.

1171. The husband testified on behalf of the respondent-purchaser and the appellant-wife did not cross-examine him. Now on appeal, the Supreme Court restated the position that any fact not pleaded must be discountenanced in judgment. Second, that failure to cross-examine a witness was tantamount to acceptance of the evidence proffered.

1172. The Supreme Court affirmed the judgment of the trial court that the property was not jointly owned and marriage does not change or affect the right of the husband to the property, a right which entitled him to sell without reference to the wife. The Supreme Court also held that section 17 of the Married Women's Property Act, 1882 is inapplicable since the marriage between the appellant and vendor-husband was a customary one.

§3. Settlement of Property under the MCA

1173. The power of a court to touch on property interest is derived in section 72 of the MCA. The section is titled: 'Power of court in proceedings with respect to settlement of property'. Although, there are references in case law to section 17 of the Married Women's Property Act, 1882,[1104] (MWPA) the Act is not appropriate to a proceeding under the MCA but to declaration of rights of the spouses as to their respective interests in any property in dispute. The MWPA is a statute of general application by virtue of received English Law and its application in Nigeria is discussed below.

1174. The MCA contemplates maintenance provisions for the wife and 'children of the marriage'. Thus, section 72 aims at satisfying maintenance orders and not distribution or adjustment of property interests. Section 72(1) of the MCA empowers the court to order the parties to the marriage, or either of them, to make for the benefit of all or any of the parties to, and the children of, the marriage, such a settlement of property to which the parties are, or either of them is, entitled (whether in possession or reversion) as the court considers just and equitable in the circumstances of the case. The power of the court in this regard extends to property covered by ante-nuptial and post-nuptial settlements on the parties to the marriage or either of them, or the children of the marriage.[1105] By section 72(2) therefore, the court may, make such order as the court considers just and equitable for the benefit

1104. A Statute of general application in Nigeria.
1105. Section 72(2).

of all or any of the parties to, and the children of the marriage, of the whole or part of property dealt with by ante-nuptial or post-nuptial settlements.

1175. Section 72(3) limits the benefiting children by age. Thus only children who are below the age of 21 years, can benefit, unless the court is of opinion that there are special circumstances that justify the making of such an order for a child of the marriage above that age. By 73(1)(d) the court is empowered to order that any necessary deed or instrument be executed, and that the documents of title be produced or such other things be done as are necessary to enable an order to be carried out effectively or to provide security for the due performance of an order. Section 73(1)(e) empowers the court to appoint or remove trustees.

1176. To give effect to the action of a Court in relation to property adjustments and rights re-ordering, section 74(1) of the MCA provides enforcement empowers and the court can take necessary actions to give effect to its order regarding a property through transfer processes and procedures that covers incidental expenditures. The subsection titled: 'Execution of deeds, etc., by order of court' provides that where a person who is directed by an order under the Act to execute a deed or instrument, refuses or neglects to do so, the court may appoint an officer of the court or other person to execute the deed or instrument in his name and to do all acts and things necessary to give validity and operation to the deed or instrument.

1177. Section 75 provides that all orders on maintenance, custody and property settlement must be premised on the determination and grant of a principal relief. It provides conditions where exceptions can be made. The first exception is that where the principal relief fails, there can be no order of settlement. Second, to exercise the power conferred by the section the court must have first heard the proceedings for the order at the same time as, or immediately after the proceedings for the principal relief. The other relevant provision is section 75(2)(ii) which directs the court not to make an order for maintenance that engages section 72 of the Act, in its exercise of discretion in cases where a petition for the principal relief has been heard and dismissed and the court has determined that there is no reasonable likelihood of the parties becoming reconciled.

I. Analysis of the Provisions

1178. As has been noted above, the applicant for maintenance is required to clearly indicate a relationship to any property listed on the petition or application for settlement. The use of the world 'settlement' in section 72 indicates a trust and more particularly a trust for sale of such property which may extend to any ante-nuptial or post-nuptial property.

1179. Settlement has different meanings. It could be structured, a provision for future periodic payments, instead of a onetime cash payment. In law, however, *settlement* relates to trust and property structure. This refers to a relationship evidenced by deed (also called a trust instrument) whereby real estate, land, or other property is given by a settlor in trust so that the beneficiary only has the limited right to the property (e.g., during their life), but usually has no right to transfer the land to another or leave it in their own Will. Instead the property devolves as directed by the settlement. That, this latter is the settlement referred to, is made clear by the title of section 72 which is: 'Power of court in proceedings with respect to settlement of property'. Furthermore, that a trust relationship is intended is reinforced by reference to appointment and removal of trustees in section 73(1)(e).

1180. The Nigerian jurisdiction on trust follows the English Trust and the classical authority is *Cook v. Fountain.*[1106] Since the trust concept cannot be called into operation easily, nor does a court impose on itself, the duty to create or perfect an imperfect gift as a trust, it is clear that the MCA contemplates a serious assessment of the circumstances that will shift the provision on maintenance from recurring income to property adjustment.[1107] The section aims at maintaining the party and children of the marriage and not to create a matrimonial property regime for the purposes of redistribution of property. This is more so as section 73(1)(j)(i) confers power on the court to discharge the order if the party in whose favour it was made marries again or if there is any other just cause for so doing. The Supreme Court of Nigeria has demonstrated very serious reluctance in deploying these provisions as a window for even settlement, making redistribution of property unthinkable. *Agbaje v. Agbaje*[1108] and *Egunjobi v. Egunjobi*[1109] are the nearest to settlement of property in Nigerian case law. In the former, the Court awarded the wife a life interest in a property and in the latter an equitable interest.

II. Comparable Notes: The MCA, 1973

1181. On a cursory perusal, section 24 of the English MCA, 1973 contains provisions on property rights adjustment almost in the same terms as the Nigerian provisions.[1110] There is, however, a distinctive difference, by the use of the word 'transfer' of property in the MCA, 1973 with resultant outcome in cases such as *Prest*[1111] and *Agbaje v. Agbaje.*[1112] Furthermore, while the English MCA, 1973 confers express power on the court to take account of contribution of the parties to the welfare of the family and other household activities during the marriage, in adjusting property rights, the Nigerian law and case law only do so by implied judicial discretion.[1113]

1106. [1676] 36 ER 984; Lord Nottingham warned that careless declaration of trust will presume people out of their properties. This remains the position with English Trust.
1107. *Milroy v. Lord* [1862] EWHC J78, [1862] 4 De GF & J 264, All ER 783, [1862] LT 178; *Re Rose* [1952] EWCA Civ 4, [1952] TR 175.
1108. [2010] UKSC 13; [2010] 1 AC 6281; [2010] 2 WLR 709.
1109. [1976] WSCA 78; [1974] ECSLR 52.
1110. *See* s. 72, Cap M7, 2004.
1111. [2013] UKSC 34.
1112. [2010] UKSC 13.
1113. Section 25(1)(f) of the MCA, 1973.

1182. Again, while Nigeria caps age limit for consideration of its provisions at 21 years,[1114] the MCA, 1973 puts the age limit at 18 years.[1115] Again although section 30 of the MCA, 1973 is in similar terms as section 74(1) of the MCA, 1970, the former by section 30(a) refers clearly to a conveyancing counsel, an indication of the requirement of expertise in transfer of property and property law, the latter refers to an officer of the court or other person, an indication that transfer is not intended.[1116]

1183. The MCA provides that an order for settlement of property cannot be made where the petition for the principal relief has been dismissed.[1117] Settlement of property and declaration of entitlements can thus be made in the course of granting the Decree *nisi* particularly as it becomes absolute by effluxion of time whereas the English position contemplates a return to the Court for a Decree *nisi* to be made absolute.[1118] Thus, the MCA, 1973 by section 23(5) provides that such orders can only take effect after a decree for dissolution of marriage or nullity has become absolute. This would also be the case, technically with judicial separation. This omission in the Nigerian MCA is also a pointer to the fact that no adjustment of property rights is contemplated in the provisions.

III. The Impact of *Agbaje v. Akinnoye–Agbaje*

1184. In *Agbaje v. Akinnoye–Agbaje*[1119] the appellant and the respondent, both Nigerians, met and married in England. They subsequently acquired the citizenship of the United Kingdom in 1972 but were nevertheless majorly resident in Nigeria. In 1975 the appellant bought property in England called 'Lytton Road' where their children stayed with a nanny. There was one other property in England and another in Nigeria. They had five children who were all born in England and, all but, one was educated there. They were married for 38 years and all their children had become adults and independent of their parents. The spouses separated in 1999 at which point the respondent came to live in Lytton Road where she was living until the hearing of the appeal.

1185. It is to be noted that the respondent-petitioner had, before the application under Part III, petitioned for divorce in Nigeria against the appellant-respondent,

1114. Section 72(3).
1115. Section 29.
1116. Section 74(1).
1117. Section 75(1).
1118. Section 1(5) of the English Act provides that every decree shall in the first instance be a decree nisi and shall not be mad absolute before the expiration of six months from its grant unless the High Court by general order from time to time fixes a shorter period, or unless in any particular case the court in which the proceedings are for the time being pending from time to time by special order fixes a shorter period than the period otherwise applicable for the time being by virtue of this subsection.
1119. [2010] UKSC 13 [2010] 1 AC 628; [2010] 1 FLR 1813; [210] 2 ALL ER 877.

and the divorce was decreed. The respondent was awarded a life interest in a property in Lagos which on conversion from local Nigerian currency amounted to a capital value of about GBP 86,000 and a lump sum payment of GBP 21,000 for the appellant-respondent. Not satisfied with this judgment, the wife sought a remedy in England. Against these set of circumstances, the respondent sought relief under Part III of the Matrimonial and Family Proceedings Act 1984.

1186. The High Court granted her the leave to do so as required under Part III. Under this part, the Act provides the qualification and requirement for applying for financial relief after a divorce or annulment is granted by foreign court.[1120] Section 13 of the Act provides for how an order for financial relief should be made – the applicant must have the leave of the court to do so in accordance with rules of court and the court shall not grant leave unless it considers that there is substantial ground for the making of an application for such an order.

1187. Furthermore, the court may grant leave under the section notwithstanding that an order has been made by a court in a country outside England and Wales which required the other party to the marriage to make any payment or transfer any property to the applicant or a child of the family. The leave where it is granted may be subject to such conditions as the court thinks fit.

1188. The appeal had raised for the first time, at an appellate level, the proper approach to the operation and application of Part III of the 1984 Act. The High Court ordered that the Respondent received a lump sum equal to 65% of the sale proceeds of Lytton Road (equivalent to about GBP 275,000) on condition that she relinquished her life interest in the Lagos property. The award represented 39% of the total assets.

1189. The Court of Appeal set aside the judgment of the High Court on the reasoning that the High Court failed to take proper account of the connection of the parties and their marriage to England. At the Supreme Court, the main issue for determination is the proper approach to adopt in applying Part III.

1190. In delivering the judgment of the Supreme Court, Lord Collins noted that Part III of the Matrimonial and Family Proceedings Act, 1984 was enacted to give the English Court the power to grant financial relief after marriage had been dissolved (or annulled) in a foreign country.

1191. The court provided the background to the Act through a line of cases, involving citizens from Hungary to Pakistan and Poland and through the Law Commission and consequent enactment of the Act. Referring to *Indyka v. Indyka*,[1121] the Supreme Court underscored the basis of the enactment of the Act. Prior to the Act it was difficult to intervene in remedying injustice where a dissolution of a marriage had already been decreed by another jurisdiction, as the parties would then have

1120. Section 12(1) and (2).
1121. [1966] C.A. 3 ALL ER 583.

been relieved of the status of 'married'.[1122] There were also academic calls as well as pressure on Parliament for intervention. This resulted in the matter being referred to the Law Commission. The work of the Commission culminated in the recommendation to allow financial provision to be ordered after a foreign divorce not only, in cases where no financial provision had been made, or could have been made, in the country where the divorce was granted but also, where the provision was inadequate. The Law Commission for England and Wales also recommended a filter mechanism requiring leave of the Court to make an application to the English Court.

1192. This background produced Part III of the 1984 Act for England and Wales[1123] and as it turned out, the Nigerian couple were the first to test the waters.

1193. The jurisdictional requirement for the intervention of the Court is contained in section 15 of the Act and will apply if either of the parties on the date of the application for financial provision or on the date when the divorce in the foreign country took effect, was domiciled in England and Wales. It would also apply where there is proof of habitual residence of either of the parties for one year ending on the date of the application for the foreign divorce or a beneficial interest by either or both, at the date of the application, in a dwelling-house in England and Wales which was at some time during the marriage used as a matrimonial home.

1194. It is always incumbent on the court to consider and establish whether England and Wales are an appropriate venue for application.[1124] There are other issues to be considered in arriving at a decision to make an order one way or the other. These include:

- the connection of both parties to England and Wales;
- the connection of both parties to the country granting or that granted the divorce or annulment or judicial separation;
- connection with any other country or jurisdiction;
- consideration of received or potential receipt of relief for applicant or child of the family from such jurisdiction;
- availability in England and Wales of any property in respect of which an order could be made;
- enforceability and the length of time within which the application is brought from the time since the date of divorce, annulment, or judicial separation.[1125]

1195. Section 17 authorises, on substantive hearing, financial provision orders and property adjustment orders in line with sections 23 and 24 of the MCA, 1973.

1122. *Torok v. Torok* [1973] 1 WLR 1066; *Quazi v. Quazi* [980] AC 744.
1123. Part IV for Scotland to which his Lordship noted has significant difference from Part III. The Law for Northern Ireland is equivalent to Part III.
1124. Section 16(1) and (2).
1125. Other issues addressed by s. 16 are contained in (3) and (4) in relation to other related laws applicable to maintenance regulation in England and Wales.

Section 2 of the Act makes special and perhaps restrictive dealing in a house which was a matrimonial home in England and Wales.[1126]

1196. Lord Collins further stated that section 18(2) of the Act is in the same terms as section 25(1) of the MCA, 1973 which stipulates matters that should be considered by the Court exercising its powers and specifically, that attention must be paid to 'all the circumstances of the case'. There are other familiar listed factors to be considered in the exercise of the statutory discretion, designed to achieve a fair outcome.[1127] In all the circumstances the Supreme Court ultimately restored the judgment of the High Court.

IV. Nigerian Case Law Analysis on Property Adjustment

1197. Despite some runaway High Court decisions to the contrary, the Supreme Court of Nigeria has consistently decided that rights of property of married persons is based on entitlement and therefore declaration of rights.[1128] The route to this position is peculiarly Nigerian and not based on the views expressed by the House of Lords on section 17 of the Married Women's Property Act, 1882, which is discussed below. The Court of Appeal has one decision standing on property adjustments and distribution but since it appeared to have proceeded on the peculiar circumstances of the case which turned on contract, trusts and nullity of the marriage, this cannot be taken to have laid down any precedent on settlement of property or division of property on dissolution of marriage.

1198. Two clear relatively recent cases have applied trusts to property rights between separating spouses – *Toyin Arajulu v. James Monday*[1129] and *Oghoyone v. Oghoyone.*[1130]

1199. Toyin Arajulu v. James Monday[1131] concerns dispute between a couple whose marriage under customary law had broken down over a few properties in Ibadan, Oyo State of Nigeria. The parties had been married under customary marriage in 1997. There are four children of the marriage. At the instance of the defendant-husband, the marriage was dissolved in 2014 by an order of a Grade 'C' customary court in Ibadan, Oyo State. The claimant subsequently filed the present suit as the defendant-husband sought to have her vacate of one of the properties. She also disputed the husband's claim to sole ownership of a second property. Her claim was that she contributed to the purchase of the properties, contributed as a

1126. *See* s. (2)(1)(a-8); (3)(a & 8).
1127. Sections 18(1)–(3); 25(2)(a)–(h) and 25(1)&(2) of MCA, 1973. Relevant and related cases are *White v. White* [2001] 1 AC 596; *McFarlane v. McFarlane* [2006] UKHL 24, [2006] 2 ACA 618.
1128. Michael Attah, *Divorcing Marriage from Marital Assets: Why Equity and Women Fail in Property Readjustment Actions in Nigeria*, 62(3) J. Afr. L. 427–446 (2018).
1129. [2019] Unreported Suit No. 1/169/2015 of the High Court of Oyo State Holden at Ibadan.
1130. [2010] 3 NWLR (part 1182) 564.
1131. [2019] Unreported Suit No. 1/169/2015 of the High Court of Oyo State Holden at Ibadan.

wife and mother, providing supervisory services in the business of the defendant. The husband denied that the claimant made any financial contributions to the properties.

1200. The Chief Judge who adjudicated the matter gave judgment in favour of the claimant. He ordered that the completed three-bedroom flat be retained by the claimant for the beneficial use of the children and herself. The use for her was subject to remarriage. The Chief Judge also declared a trust for sale of the proceeds for the uncompleted building. This was to be divided equally between the parties.[1132]

1201. In arriving at this decision, the learned Chief Judge relied on what was seen as the wide discretion conferred by section 17 of the Married Women Property Law of Oyo State, Cap 83 Laws of Oyo State to determine issues of ownership of property as it thinks fit when in dispute.[1133] The court also noted that section 20 of the same law limited the principles of the law to marriages celebrated under the Marriage Act. This, the judge thought, however, must be considered in the light of the recognition of customary law marriages by the same law which is revalidated by the recognition accorded to the status by section 35 of the Marriage Act.[1134] The Court, relying on *Hine v. Hine*,[1135] stated: 'the determination to me transcends strictly legal rights on property ownership but involves simply what is fair, just and equitable in the circumstances of this case'.

1202. The case which would appear fair to the hegemony of married women would collapse in the light of property law, public interest in policy directions in marriage and *stare decisis*. In the first place the Supreme Court has severally determined the position of a wife under customary law. To apply the provisions of the Marriage Act to a marriage celebrated under customary law is to infuse additional confusion into an already confused legal framework. While the Marriage Act makes references to customary marriage, it does so to clarify the relationship between the two regimes. The Matrimonial Causes Act repeatedly explicitly excludes customary law and Islamic law marriages from its provisions.[1136] Section 17 of the Married Women Property Law of Oyo State is in tandem with section 17 of the MWPA and clearly is declaratory provision not a distributary provision.

1203. In *Oghoyone v. Oghoyone*,[1137] the petitioner-respondent's case was for nullity of the marriage between the appellant and herself. She alleged that the appellant was in a subsisting marriage with another woman, when he (the appellant) married her, and that the marriage with her was therefore void. She sought a declaration to this effect. She sought other reliefs on ownership of property acquired during the

1132. Page 29 of the judgement.
1133. The provisions are in the same terms as s. 17 of the Married Women's Property Act, 1882.
1134. The court's decision the discountenanced the decision of the Supreme Court in *Amadi v. Nwosu* [1992] 5 NWLR 273 which may not have been cited to it.
1135. [1962] 1 WLR 1124, 1128.
1136. Section 69. Furthermore, the Constitution which enables the Acts also excludes both forms of marriages – item 61, Second Schedule, of the Constitution.
1137. [2010] 3 NWLR (part 1182) 564.

relationship between the parties. The parties had signed a document as a memorandum of understanding for the sharing of the joint business interests and properties, in the event, which did happen of the marriage breaking down.

1204. The appellant also cross-petitioned for a decree of nullity of the marriage and other reliefs with respect to property in respect of which he claimed exclusive ownership. At the trial, the court declared the marriage void. It further declared that the property in which the parties had lived in the course of the purported marriage was jointly owned and ordered its sale. The proceeds of sale were then to be divided in two equal parts between the parties while, the other property in dispute was in the exclusive ownership of the appellant. The appellant was dissatisfied with the decision of the court with respect to the joint ownership and appealed.

1205. The respondent dissatisfied with the declaration of exclusive ownership also cross-appealed.

1206. Some of the issues for determination at the Court of Appeal were the nature of a void marriage and whether section 17 of the Married Women's Property Act, 1882, a Statute of General application in Nigeria could validly be applied with respect to a dispute of property rights between parties to a void marriage. Furthermore, that since the parties had signed a memorandum of understanding on the rights to property, they were bound by the document in line with section 132(1) of the Evidence Act and therefore, further evidence cannot be led, orally to contradict, alter, add to, or vary it. There was also the additional issue of whether a memorandum of understanding which did not exhaustively list all the properties disputed meant the exclusion of the properties not listed. Rhodes-Vivour J.C.A. delivering the lead judgment to which the other Justices concurred, referred to sections 69 and 72(1) and (2) of the Matrimonial Causes Act,[1138] to show that a void marriage is one without legal consequences but that section 72(1) and (2) gave wide discretions to the Court to do justice between the parties. In his judgment, in interpreting and applying this section, reference must be made to section 69 of the Act which provides that marriage includes a purported marriage that is void.

1207. The court further referred to section 17 of the MWPA. It affirmed that a written documentation duly signed by parties guides distribution of property and rights between them provided there is no mistake but in the case under consideration, the property in issue was not listed on the document signed as a memorandum of understanding between the parties.

1208. On this note, the Court of Appeal affirmed the reasoning of the High Court and held that the MWPA applied. However, it also noted that if, on the other hand, the fact that the marriage is void means no property rights accrued, then the parties were simply living together as friends or in a similar manner. It would then fall on a court to resolve any property interests between the parties in the ordinary manner

1138. Cap M7, 2004.

of contractual relationship.[1139] The judge did find as a matter of fact, that while the appellant provided the funds for the purchase of the land, the respondent contributed funds towards the building in respect of which she provided receipts. The Court of Appeal holding that the case was correctly decided, at trial stated:

> I am satisfied that the order of the learned trial judge on … was fair, just, and equitable. It would be unconscionable for any party to claim exclusive ownership. Bearing in mind the changing social and economic realities, a Judge is to ascertain the parties' shared intentions actual, inferred with respect to the property in the light of their conduct. In that light, I am satisfied that when the going was good the parties made contributions to ensure that they had good living accommodation. When the going turns bad it is only right and equitable that each side recoups its contribution and calls it a day.[1140]

1209. It can be said that by this judgment, the Court of Appeal effectively introduced the trust relationship into de facto relationships in Nigerian jurisprudence.[1141] It appears to have correctly followed the developments and the law on distribution of property in these circumstances through the vehicle of the trust in circumstances where persons are unmarried and if the provisions of section 69(1) which makes a void marriage also subject to the settlement and variation provision of section 72, were applied, the judgment would also be correctly decided.

1210. In *Ibeabuchi v. Ibeabuchi*[1142] the appellant (husband) filed the petition for a decree of dissolution of marriage on the ground that the marriage with his wife had broken down irretrievably. He pleaded the facts of the respondent having wilfully and persistently refusing to consummate the marriage and behaving in a manner that the petitioner could not reasonably be expected to live with her. The appellant sought in addition to the relief of a decree of dissolution of the marriage, exemplary and aggravated damages for adultery by a named third party. In answer, the respondent sought an order dismissing the petition and cross-petitioned seeking the same reliefs on the same ground but on the fact of the appellant's cruelty, adultery, and desertion and in addition, an order for the payment of lump sum amount to her and an order against a named co-respondent to pay specified sum to the respondent.[1143] There was only one child of the marriage.

1211. The trial judge dismissed the petition and granted the reliefs sought by the respondent. It is in respect of this judgment that the petitioner appeals. From the appeal, four grouses against the order of the trial court were:

1139. Page 584 para. 1.
1140. [2010] 3 NWLR (part 1182) 564, 584.
1141. *Mitchell v. Mitchell – Marr v. Collie* [2017] UKPC 17; *Stack v. Dowden* [2007] UKHL 17; *Carlton v. Goodman* [2002] EWCA GV 545; *Westdeutsche Landesbank v. Islington LBC.* [1996] AC 669; [1996] 2 W.L.R. 802.
1142. [2016] LPELR-41268 (CA); CA/K/322/2012.
1143. Note that the Matrimonial Causes Rules defines a co-respondent as a party to proceedings who is specified in the petition instituting the proceedings as a person with whom the respondent is alleged to have committed adultery.

(i) Whether it was just and fair to have awarded one house to the respondent as well as monetary damages.
(ii) Whether a paternity test ought not to have been ordered in order to determine the paternity of the only child of the marriage being contested.
(iii) Whether the trial court validly assumed jurisdiction to entertain the respondent's cross-petition.
(iv) Whether an advertisement was necessary to prove the adultery of the respondent in marrying another man during the subsistence of the marriage with the appellant since a certificate to that effect has been tendered in exhibit.

1212. The petitioner-appellant's counsel argued along property rights-based entitlements, relying on the Supreme Court's decision in *Adaku Amadi v. Nwosu.*[1144] In this case, however, the Court of Appeal took the position that the question depends partly on the timing of purchase of the property and the nature of contributions made. According to the Court of Appeal, the most firmly established guidelines that courts are enjoined to take into consideration in determining a question of settlement[1145] of property is whether or not the property in question or some other property was acquired by the parties or by one of the parties during the course of the marriage, and if so, what was the contribution of each party to the cost of acquisition.[1146] The court relying on *Rimmer v. Rimmer*[1147] with approval[1148] took the position that it is correct that the contribution of a party does not necessarily have to be in the nature of a cash outlay for the purchase or development of the property. It can be by way of moral and/or financial contribution to the business of a husband by a wife where the property is purchased from the profits of the business.[1149] It is, however, essential that the property should have been purchased in the course of the marriage or where the property was purchased before the marriage, that the payment for the property was completed after and in the course of the marriage as in the case of a property purchased on mortgage.

1213. The court reversed the decision of the High Court to the extent that it had declared the respondent- wife entitled to the only house in dispute and denied that the property was a matrimonial property. The Court of Appeal appeared to present the position that if the property had been bought in the course of the marriage then contributions which were made towards maintaining the property by the wife might have counted for something.

1144. [1992] 6 SCNJ 59.
1145. It is to be noted that settlement as used here is not in the strict sense of a trust and real estate but in adjustment of property rights between married persons or annulled marriages.
1146. [2016] LPELR-41268 (CA) *per* Habeeb Abiru JCA.
1147. [1952] 2 ALL ER 863; [1953] 1 QB 63.
1148. Other cases citied with approval as established guidelines are: *Coker v. Coker* [1964] LR 188. *Egunjobi v. Egunjobi* [1976] WSCA 78; [1974] ECSLR 52. *Aderounmu v. Aderounmu* [2003] 2 NWLR (part 803) 1; *Mueller v. Mueller* [2006] 6 NWLR (part 997) 627; *Oghoyone v. Oghoyone* [2010] 3 NWLR (part 1182) 564; [2010] LPELR – CA/L/26/2003.
1149. *Sanders v. Sanders* [1967] 116 CLR 366; *Watchell v. Watchell* [1973] ALL ER 829; *H v. H* (*Financial Provisions Marriage*) 1975 1 ALL ER 367; *Kaffi v. Kaffi* [1986] 3 NWLR (part 27) 173.

1214. In *Egunjobi v. Egunjobi,*[1150] to which the Court of Appeal also referred in *Ibeabuchi v. Ibeabuchi,*[1151] a house was in dispute between the appellant and his wife the respondent. The High Court had awarded the respondent one-third of the interest in the property. The respondent had presented receipts of her contribution to the property. The appellant opposed the grant of the interest while the respondent cross-appealed that she ought to have been granted a half interest. Relying on the dicta of Viscount Dilhorne, Lord Diplock and Lord Reid in *Gissing v. Gissing* the Court of Appeal held that a trust arose the moment the respondent began contributing to the building of the property. According to Akinkugbe J.A. in the lead judgment of the Western State Court of Appeal, 'the appellant who was aware of the fact that the respondent was making her contribution, by operation of law, became from the time the contributions were made, trustee for the respondent'.[1152] The Court referred to *Pettit v. Pettit*[1153] and *In Re Rogers' Question*[1154] with approval and took the position that in the absence of express agreement the court would refer to the inferred common intentions of the parties. On this, the court stated that the contribution of the respondent is 1:2 of the appellant's proved financial outlay and that is one-third of the proved total cost of the building. It held further affirming the decision of the lower Court that the respondent was entitled to one-third of the property thereby dismissing the appeal and cross-appeal. Again, trust law appeared to have been used here to dispose of the matter.

1215. Fakayode, **AG.J.A**, in a dissent judgment took the position that the only identifiable quantifiable contribution of the respondent should be refunded to her. This judgment could of course not bear scrutiny as the judgment was in effect to pay to the respondent the exact amount proved as contribution without even considering interest, or the appreciation of the property and incidental contributions of the respondent in a matrimonial project.

1216. In *Oghoyene v. Oghoyene*[1155] the Court of Appeal clearly appeared to have toed a different line by opting for the concept of trust in adjusting the right in property to the property that was not included in the ante-nuptial. The Court of Appeal went so far to take this position stating that even if the party's marriage was a nullity then the property between them will be shared in a just manner. The Court did not indicate what trust it applied but presumably it was resorting to constructive trust as the evidence available to the Court did not indicate the known circumstances under which an express or resulting trusting could apply.[1156]

1150. [1976] 2 FNLR 79.
1151. [2016] LPELR-41268 (CA); CA/K/322/2012.
1152. [1976] 2 FNLR 79, 83.
1153. [1970] AC 777; [1969] UKHL 5.
1154. [1984] 1 ALL ER 328.
1155. [2010] 3 NWLR (part 1182) 564; [2010] LPELR – CA/L/26/2003.
1156. Resulting trusts are said to arise in certain specific instances of presumption in favour of a purchaser; presumption of advancement and presumption where the property is purchased in the name of one person for several. There is also the presumption, now of family home when held in joint names. Hanbury & Martin, *Modern Equity* 10–33 (Jill Martin ed., Sweet and Maxwell 19th ed. 2012).

1217. In *Ibeabuchi v. Ibeabuchi*[1157] the approach of recognising contribution in value in other indirect enterprises is novel although not based on any clear approach, or authority with the result that it is likely to be struck down should the opportunity present itself at the Supreme Court. The Court of Appeal referred to *Egunjobi* but in *Egunjobi*, the respondent provided receipts and proved the contribution made. It would then not have mattered whether the property was bought within marriage or out of it as *Oghoyene* demonstrates.

1218. In *Toyin Arajulu v. Monday James* the High Court referred to *Hine v. Hine* one of the cases coming under Lord Denning's new model constructive trust but arrived at its decision principally by the Oyo state's equivalent of section 17 of the Married Women's Property Act, 1882. This decision is to say the least curious, having been decided long after the Supreme Court's decision in *Adaku v. Nwosu*[1158] where the Supreme Court had clearly excluded the application of section 17 of Customary Law Marriages.[1159] Whether the exclusion by the Nigerian Supreme Court is justified or not, one would have thought that it is an existing law coming from the apex court and should have been followed. It would appear that *Toyin Arajulu v. James Monday*[1160] failed to take account of this Supreme Court's decision or can the case be said to be on all fours with *Oghoyene v. Oghoyene*[1161] with which it appears to have arrived at conclusions based on imputed trust. Section 17 of the Married Women's Property Act, 1882 (MWPA) is a well-noted provision in Nigerian Family law. However, as the House of Lords noted, in *Pettit v. Pettit*,[1162] section 17 of the MWPA was meant to address a socio-property context – to wit facilitate a married woman's right to own property. Thus, if section 17 of the Married Women's Property Right Act, 1882 were to be properly applied as a declaratory provision, the right of the wife under a customary marriage would stand, as the apex court has consistently stated, as a right to own only those properties which she personally acquired in line with the Constitutional provisions on right to own property and to non-discrimination.[1163] The provisions for settlement or variation of property right can therefore apply only to marriage conducted in accordance and compliance with the provisions of the MA as provided in the Matrimonial Causes Act.

1219. A long line of authorities, principally, Supreme Court, have noted that under customary marriage a woman has no rights to the property of her husband whether *inter vivos* or on devolution.[1164] Under customary law, a wife until *Anekwe*

1157. [2016] LPELR-41268 (CA); CA/K/322/2012.
1158. [1992] 5 NWLR 273.
1159. *Adaku Amadi v. Nwosu* [1992] 5 NWLR 273; *per* Karibi-Whyte.
1160. (Unreported Suit No. 1/169/2015 of Oyo State) delivered 2018.
1161. [1992] 5 NWLR 273.
1162. [1970] AC 777; [1969] UKHL 5.
1163. *Ukeje v. Ukeje* [2014] 11 NWLR (part 1418) 384; [2014] LPELR – 22724 (SC) Electronic Law Reports. and *Anekwe v. Nweke* [2014] 9 NWLR (part 1412) 393; [2017] LPELR-42103 (SC) may apply by analogy but certainly *Oghonoye v. Oghonoye* [2010] 3 NWLR (part 1182) 564; [2010] LPELR – CA/L/26/2003.
1164. *Nezianya v. Okagbue* [1963] 1 All NLR 352.

v. Nweke[1165] can only have a hybrid of life interest in a matrimonial property subject to good behaviour. Although in arriving at the decision that a woman had more than a life interest in the matrimonial home the apex court referred to *Nezianya v. Okagbue*[1166]with approval signifying that it was only improving the status of a wife by one step; to wit she could not be ousted from the property in her lifetime. One would notice that this was the conclusion in *Agbaje* in Nigeria.

1220. It needs to be noted that the danger in dealing with property between separated couples is well demonstrated by the cases considered and while doing justice, the court must bear in mind the legal rights of all parties within the contextual historical, social, and economic policy direction and implications in a country like Nigeria. It is important to view property rights and redistribution between spouses from a very holistic and careful prism. With Nigeria a more restrained approach is to be preferred based on a careful utilisation and application of section 72 of the MCA, until such a time a new legislation backed approach is adopted. To follow English jurisprudence on this subject, particularly case law, may not prove a counsel of prudence.[1167] The cases decided mainly at the English Court of Appeal with Lord denning as Master of the Rolls, have all been turbulent and only began to show policy stability with legislative intervention such as the MCA, 1973 and some conclusive pronouncements by the House of Lords.

1221. There is thus with respect to matrimonial causes in Nigeria, no policy-based approach on maintenance or property distribution.

V. Comparable Notes on Section 17 of the MWPA

1222. There are three major ways in which married couples can have property adjustment in England. Where the parties desire to divorce, orders can be made under the MCA, 1973 for variation or distribution of property. Property, includes houses, land, vehicles etc. Where the couple or the court considers that a clean break is most appropriate, the adjustment and distribution of property will be conducted to support this new status. However, where the issues concern entitlement and declarations or mere separation, parties may move from the stream of Trust of Land and Appointment of Trustees Act, 1996 and section 17 of the Married Women's Property Act, 1882. In these cases, the shares in which the beneficial interest in the property is held will be of relevance and the court has no power to alter those shares.

1165. [2014] 9 NWLR (part 1412) 393.
1166. [1963] 1 All NLR 352.
1167. *Hine v. Hine* [1962] 1 WLR 1124; *Eve v. Eve* [1975] 1 WLR 1338, [1975] 3 All ER 768, [1975] EWCA Civ 3; *Cooke v. Head* [1972] 2 All ER 38, [1972] 1 WLR 518; *Bernard v. Joseph* [1982] 2 WLR 1052; and then, *Gissing v. Gissing* [1970] 3 WLR 255, [1971] AC 886, [1970] 2 All ER 780, [1970] UKHL 3; *Pettit v. Pettit* [1969] 2 WLR 966, [1969] 2 All ER 385, [1970] AC 777, [1969] UKHL 5; *Hammond v. Mitchell* [1992] 2 All ER 109, [1991] 1 WLR 1127; and more recently, *Stack v. Dowden* [2007] 2 WLR 831, [2007] UKHL 17, [2007] 2 All ER 929, [2007] AC 432.

1223. The provisions for dissolution also apply to nullity and care for children including settlement of property on a child.

1224. In *Pettit v. Pettit,*[1168] the House of Lords roundly and unequivocally denied that section 17 of the MWPA was a property adjustment provision but rather a declaratory provision aimed at a formal declaration of the existing property rights between the spouses. The House reasoned that the provision in question was enacted at a time when patriarchy was very much on the prowl in England and Wales, and there was no way in which an enactment would have been passed that was aimed at redistributing the property rights of husbands. If there was need to change the Law, the House of Lords stated that it had to be through parliamentary action and not a judicial route. Indeed the Matrimonial Proceedings and Property Act[1169] and the Matrimonial Causes Act, 1973 followed. Section 24 of the latter allows the courts within the parameters set in section 25 and recently reappraised in *Prest* to adjust and vary property rights between husband and wife and children of the family. Section 39 of the Matrimonial Proceedings and Property Act reaffirms the position of the House of Lords that section 17 is a declaratory provision and is a power of declaration in the courts with respect to disputes between husband and wife on property. Section 37 addresses the concerns which *Pettit v. Pettit*[1170] and *Gissing v. Gissing*[1171] raised. The section provides:

1225. It is hereby declared that where a husband or wife contributes in money or money's worth to improvement of real or personal property in which or in the proceeds of sale of which either or both of them has or have a beneficial interest, the husband or wife so contributing shall, if the contribution is of a substantial nature and subject to any agreement between them to the contrary express or implied, be treated as having then acquired by virtue of his or her contribution a share or an enlarged share, as the case may be, in that beneficial interest of such an extent as may have been then agreed or, in default of such agreement, as may seem in all the circumstances just to any court before which the question of the existence or extent of the beneficial interest of the husband or wife arises (whether in proceedings between them or in any other proceedings).

1226. This provision is practical and differs from the Nigerian position as explained in *Adaku v. Nwosu*[1172] and *Ibeabuchi v. Ibeabuchi.*[1173] In both case, the first at the Supreme Court and the second at the Court of Appeal, the decisions clearly excluded properties purchased prior to marriage from any form of variation or adjustment of rights which in from all perspectives is retrograde.

1168. [1970] AC 777; [1969] UKHL 5.
1169. Cap 45 an act on provisions with respect to ancillary and other relief in matrimonial causes and to certain other matrimonial proceedings. The Matrimonial Causes Act, 1973, Cap 18 repealed the whole of Part 1 of this Act as well as ss 34, 35, 40, 41 and 42 and s. 43(2) and (4) the words from the beginning to 'of this Act'.
1170. [1970] AC 777; [1969] UKHL 5.
1171. [1971] AC 886.
1172. [1992] 5 NWLR 273.
1173. [2016] LPELR 41268 (CA) CA/K/322/2012.

1227. As Lord Reid noted in *Pettit v. Pettit*:[1174]

> for the last twenty years the law regarding what are sometimes called family assets has been in an unsatisfactory state. There have been many cases showing acute differences of opinion in the Court of Appeal. Various questions have arisen generally after the break-up of a marriage. Sometimes both spouses have contributed in money to the purchase of a house: sometimes the contributions of one spouse has been otherwise than in money, sometimes one spouse owned the house and the other spent money or did work in improving it; and there have been a variety of other circumstances. It might be possible – to decide this case on somewhat narrow grounds without examining the wider questions, but I do not think that would be satisfactory.[1175]

1228. In *Pettit v. Pettit*[1176] the appellant and respondent married in 1952.

1229. Both lived in the house the appellant inherited for nine years. The husband-respondent claimed to have carried out a number of improvements for which he claimed GBP 800. The house was sold in 1961. The appellant used the proceeds to acquire another property and a surplus remained. With the consent of the appellant, the respondent used the surplus to purchase a car.

1230. The spouses lived in the new house for four years. Thereafter, the appellant filed for and obtained a divorce from the husband on the ground of cruelty. The respondent claimed that on the new house, he had done some improvements, performed works and supplied materials to the tune of GBP 723. He sought a declaration that he was beneficially entitled in the proceeds of sale of the house in the sum of GBP 1,000 and an order that the Appellant pay this sum to him. An order was made that the Appellant pay to him the sum of GBP 300. In dismissing the appeal, the Court of Appeal held that they were bound by the decision in *Appleton v. Appleton.*[1177] Lord Denning's approach in *Appleton v. Appleton*[1178] which the Court of Appeal felt bound to follow was what is reasonable and fair in the circumstances as they have developed seeing that they are circumstances which no one contemplated before.

1231. The Appellant had legal aid for the proceeding and Lord Reid expressed the view that this enabled the argument to range widely and it was at least desirable, if not necessary, to deal with and settle the various issues which were raised.

1232. According to Lord Reid, it is recognised that Courts have the power to modify or adjust common law to existing circumstances but in doing so, it is important to bear in mind two spheres of actions: these are recognition of a difference

1174. [1969] 2 WLR 966.
1175. [1970] AC 777; [1969] UKHLS; HL/Po/Ju/4/3/1187, p. 1, para. 2.
1176. [1970] AC 777; [1969] UKHLS.
1177. [1965] 1 W.L.R. 25.
1178. *Ibid.*

between cases dealing with 'lawyers law' and cases 'dealing with matters which directly affect the lives and interests of large sections of the community and which raise issues which are the subject of public controversy and on which laymen as well as lawyers are able to decide'. On such matters as the latter, it is not for the court to proceed on their view of public policy for that would be to encroach in the province of parliament'.

1233. Lord Diplock focused on the position between the parties at the relevant time of the transaction. The House of Lords opted for the option of Parliamentary intervention but gave teeth to the law as it is. It stated that section 17 of the Married Women's Property Act was a procedural law which gave power to the Court to determine and declare existing property rights to identifiable properties of the parties in an expedited fashion which is why jurisdiction to do so was simplified and laid in the County Courts. The Court was in other words, restating the simple property law position that the Courts as Lord Nottingham noted in *Cook v. Fountain*[1179] could not presume anyone into or out of a property through the route of the trust:

> There is one good, general, and infallible rule that goes to both these kinds of trusts; it is such a general rule as never deceives; a general rule to which there is no exception, and that is this; the law never implies, the Court never presumes a trust, but in case of absolute necessity. The reason of this rule is sacred; for if the Chancery do once take liberty to construe a trust by implication of law, or to presume a trust, unnecessarily, a way is opened to the *Lord Chancellor* to construe or presume any man in England out of his estate. [1180]

VI. Relevance of Trust Law

1234. In *Springette v. Defoe*[1181] Steyn LJ noted 'trust law does not allow property rights to be affected by telepathy'.[1182] Where property is purchased in joint names of a couple without any declarations as to quantum of ownership, the presumption where the evidence supports it will be quantum in line with contributions as made to the property.

1235. The Court must according to Lord Diplock, in *Pettit* do its utmost best to distil the common intention of the parties both as to title and quantum. Having established title then quantum, if this cannot be factually distilled then the enquiry must turn on equality is equity.

1236. The common intention which is supported by Lord Diplock's analysis is 'inference' as opposed to imputation. The position of Lord Diplock gained grounds

1179. [1676] 3 Swan, 585.
1180. [1672] 3 Swanst, 585; 36 ER 984.
1181. [1992] FLR 388, 394.
1182. *Ibid.*

with cases such as *Lloyds Bank v. Mitchell*;[1183] *Lloyds Bank Plc. v. Rosset.*[1184] While the common intention was accepted at the Court of Appeal it was rejected at the House of Lords although the House was willing to apply trust by operation of law or a proprietary estoppel. *Stack v. Dowden* varied the positions and indicated that a conveyance into joint names showed both a legal and beneficial joint tenancy, unless and until the contrary is proved.

1237. The burden will be on the person seeking to show that the parties did intend their beneficial interests to be different from their legal interests, to prove this and show in what way. It did not matter that the parties contributed equally. In *Jones v. Kernott*,[1185] the United Kingdom Supreme Court stated that conduct in relation to the property must be looked at broadly to take into account the common intention of the parties which is deducible objectively from their conduct. The Supreme Court further restated the principle to apply is a presumption of joint tenancy and not resulting trust unless rebutted, whenever a married or unmarried couple engage in the purchase of mortgage of a house or flat in joint names for joint occupation.[1186] **Enforcement**

1238. Sections 88–94 of the MCA are provisions for enforcement of the orders on ancillary reliefs. Sections 88 and 89 confer wide discretionary powers on the court to enforce maintenance by attachment. Section 90 of the MCA facilitates recovery of moneys as judgment debt. Subsection 2 of section 90 facilitates a charge on the estate of the party even upon his or her death. This has to be by leave of the court and may be from the court which issued the decree or in which it is registered. Section 91 provides for summary enforcement of orders for maintenance.

1239. Thus, where a court has made an order for payment of maintenance, the order may be registered in accordance with rules of court in a court of summary jurisdiction of a State of the Federation, and an order so registered may, subject to rules of court, be enforced in the same manner as if it were an order for maintenance of a deserted wife made by the court of summary jurisdiction.

1240. Section 92 provides for enforcement of maintenance orders by attachment or earnings An order under the Act for the payment of maintenance may be enforced in accordance with the Third Schedule to the Act which specifies various ways in which the order for maintenance may be met. Section 93 provides for enforcement by other means other than those specified in the provisions of the Act.

1241. Where a party deals with a property to avoid the judgment of the court or its orders, section 105 provides wide discretionary powers to order execution or a

1183. [1992] 2 All ER 109. [1991] 1 WLR 1127.
1184. [1990] UKHL 14.
1185. [2011] UKSC 53; UKSC [2010] [2011] Fam Law 133.
1186. [2011] UKSC 53; UKSC [2010] [2011] Fam Law 133. *See also Abbott v. Abbott* [2007] UKPC 53; [2007] 2 All ER 432; *Stack v. Dowden* [2007] 2 WLR 831. [2007] UKHL 17; [2007] AC 432 para. 69. *See* however, *Oxley v. Hiscock* [2005] EWCA G V 546; [2004] 2 FLR 669; [2005] Fam 211.

charge over such property involved in the dealing, however, taking into consideration the interest of bona fide purchasers for value without notice. The nature of the dealing could be in the form of a sale or gift.[1187]

1187. Section 105(5).

Part IV. Succession Law

1242. In Nigeria, aside from those matters of succession governed by customary laws or Islamic law, the Probate registry deals with succession. Customary courts have probate divisions especially in the South West of Nigeria. The word 'succession' under Islamic inheritance is used as *Mirath*, another usage is *Al-faraid*. The law on succession is mainly religiously framed.

1243. The Probate Registry properly so-called is a department of the State High Court and is under the direct headship of the Chief Judge of the State who must approve a grant of probate or issue of a Letter of Administration. There is a grant of probate when a Will is executed by the Testator, while a Letter of Administration is issued when the testator dies intestate, or testate but without appointment of executors.

1244. Practice and procedure concerning Probate and administration of probate are basically uniform in Nigeria, at least in the States which do not practice Sharia law as personal law. The practice of Islam must be noted as different in the core Northern States of Nigeria and the South. The South West of Nigeria has a split population of Christians and Muslims but are also homogenously adherents of the Yoruba native law and customs. Thus, the inheritance pattern according to Yoruba customary laws appears to be the preferred method among people of the South West. The Eastern parts of Nigeria are predominantly Christians but again also generally subject to the Igbo native law and customs, which again appears a preferred method of inheritance. The people of the Middle Belt are in many ways, as the people of the South East. The principal legislation governing succession are the Administration of Estate Laws of various states, the Administration of Estate Act, 1992 (AEA) for the FCT and the Wills, and Amendment Act, 1837 and 1853, respectively. Lagos has the Administration of Estate Law, 2015.[1188] There is also the Administration and Succession (Estates of Deceased Persons) Law.[1189] Typically, the Wills law of the States take the form of Lagos State Wills Law, except that section 2 of the latter law provides for dependent relatives. In addition, the Lagos State law recognises polygynous marriages.[1190]

1188. LSLN, 2015, V2.
1189. Cap 4, Laws of Anambra State of Nigeria, 1986.
1190. Section 2(1)(a) of the Lagos State Wills Law.

1245. The relevance and impact of the different regimes of laws is limited in most of the States because of steep customs and Sharia law. Statutory intervention was relevant with respect to the previous Marriage Act, 1958,[1191] and more so, when a Christian marriage was a legally recognised form of marriage, or where a foreigner is married to a Nigerian. In these relatively now, unusual cases, the common laws of England and some Statutes of general application would apply and some case law exist as to its application. A continuing relevant case is the rule in *Cole v. Cole.*[1192] Applicable legislation includes, the Statutes of Distribution, 1670 and 1685 and the Intestates Estate Act, 1890 (all Statutes of general application). However, a Christian marriage in itself, no longer confers the status of monogamy.

1246. There are other relevant and uniform statutory provisions such as the Statute of Frauds, 1677 (a Statute of general application) which by section IX, provides: 'And be it further enacted, That all Grants and Assignments of any Trust or Confidence shall likewise be in Writing, signed by the Party granting or assigning the same, or by such Last Will or Devise, or else shall likewise be utterly void and of none Effect.'[1193] This law applies generally with respect to Wills and trusts.

1247. The main regulations are the Supreme Court (Civil Procedure Rules, 1948) and the High Court Civil Procedure Rules of each States, which includes the Civil Procedure rules of the High Court of the FCT.

1248. In Lagos, Order 60 of the High Court of Lagos rules stipulates the procedure and processes for contentious probate and administration. By rule 1, suits in respect of Probate or Letters of Administration shall be instituted and carried on as nearly as possible in like manner and subject to the same rules of procedure as suits in respect of civil claims. Orders 57 makes general rules for administration, 58 for probate with Will annexed and 59 for intestacy.

1249. The Lagos State Administration of Estates Law defines 'administrator' as a person to whom administration is granted. The law also defines 'administration' as, with reference to the real and personal estate of a deceased person – letters of administration, whether general or limited, or with the Will annexed or otherwise. The law further defines 'personal representative' as the executor, original or by representation, or administrator for the time being of a deceased person and 'property' as including a thing in action and any interest in real or personal property. Thus, the term, 'personal representative' covers all who administer an estate. However, executors or executrix is function specific to Wills from where the executors, upon assenting to the role derive their authority. The Administrator is used in relation to all other forms of administering of the estate of a deceased person. The administrator's power is derived from the court. The executor takes full as opposed to bare title in the estate of the deceased upon the death of the deceased. The administrator does

1191. Cap 115, Laws of the Federation 1958. There are some disputes as to s. 36 of this Act which is now replicated as s. 49(5).
1192. [1898] 1 NLR 15.
1193. 1677 (29 Cha. 2) C A P. III.

so, after a grant by the court. The executor can thus be personally liable for any damages occasioned to the estate in this period. Once the executor assents to being executor and takes out probate he acts in a fiduciary capacity. The executor has a general power to sell but with respect to personality, the assent of the executor is important as the Will becomes operative with respect to the personalty of the deceased, only when that assent is made. The assent could be formal or informal but it could also be inferred from his conduct.

1250. The duties of both offices are fiduciary in nature. The personal representatives are to preserve the assets of the deceased, deal properly with them according to law and apply them in due course of administration for those entitled, according to the terms of the Will. Until the estate is distributed and the administration wound up, the personal representatives are to pay all ongoing bills and debts. Personal representatives ought to open a new Bank account for administration to keep an unimpeachable accounting. The primary duty of the executor is to distribute the estate according to the Will but the first duty is to pay established debts of the testator. This payment will usually be taken, if not provided for, from the personal estate of the deceased. Thus, the legatee has no right of property in the legacy until the executor determines that there is no need for such and assents to distribution. The assent vests the legacy in the specific legatee. Where the executor does not assent, the legatee's remedy is an action to have the estate administered. An executor who has assented to a gift, devise or legacy becomes a trustee of that gift for the person entitled. The duties are the same for the executor and administrator.

1251. Theoretically, there could be a lone executor, but it is more desirable that they are at least, two. One of two executors has authority to act for both and can bound the other, so it is important to be vigilant when there is more than one executor. Trustees must be minimally two in order to transfer an interest in land. The role of a trustee in a Will commences after the administration and it is important to streamline the roles, where the same persons are playing the role of executor and trusteeship. The line however is very thin as executors could become trustees by operation of law and from the whole circumstances of the case.[1194] A good case on the point is *Attenborough* v. *Solomon*.[1195] In that case, the House of Lords made a distinctive pronouncement an executor is vested with the title to the personalty of the deceased, by operation of law. However, once there is an assent to disposition, which can be formal, informal, or inferred from the conduct of the executors, the title to the property is transferred to those entitled, by operation of the terms of the Will. The executors are thereafter, left with the option of action to recover from those entitled if there remained any administration requiring funding. As Lord Haldane stated:

> The general principles of law which govern this case are not doubtful. The position of an executor is a peculiar one. He is appointed by the will, but then, by virtue of his office, by the operation of law and not under the bequest in the

1194. Arthur Dean, *When Does an Executor Become a Trustee?*, 1 Res Judicatae 92–97 (1935–1938).
1195. [1913] AC 76, [1912] UKHL 4; *see also Kirk v. Gregory* [1876] 1 Ex. D. 55.

will, he takes a title to the personal property of the testator, which vests him with the plenum dominium over the testator's chattels. He takes that, I say, by virtue of his office. The will becomes operative so far as its dispositions of personalty are concerned only if and when the executor assents to those dispositions. It is true that by virtue of his office he has a general power to sell or pledge for the purpose of paying debts and getting in the money value of the estate. He is executor and he remains executor for an indefinite time.

1252. This principle underlies the provision of Administration of Estates Act, 1991, which by Part 1, section 1(2), specifies that: 'an interest in land shall not be administered unless the administrator shows to the satisfaction of the court that other assets of the estate are insufficient to pay the intestate's debts and expenses of his funeral and of taking out administration'.

1253. Thus, from the moment assent to disposition is established, the executor's power to deal with property ends and the property can no longer be validly transferred in the capacity of executor and the executor, in fact, deals with the property henceforth in trust. The same principles apply to administrators so that in place of the Will is the Letters of Administration.

1254. A person who intermeddles with the estate of the deceased may be made an *executor de son tort.* Order 58, rule 28(3) of the Lagos High Court Civil Procedure rules makes it possible for such a person to be cited to take a grant of the probate for the estate. Such a citation should be entered only after six months of the passing of the testator.

§1. Background of Succession

1255. Succession means the actions and processes involved in receiving in one's legal ownership, the interests of another person in property upon the death of that other. Property means realty and personalty. It extends to the legal arrangements by which heirs may inherit from a deceased person.

1256. Succession could take two forms – testate or intestate. Testate succession occurs where the property encompassing real and personal is transmitted by a testamentary disposition in a document known as a Will which may also comprise some stated trusts. Terms relating to such dispositions are, 'devise', 'legacy' or 'bequest'. Until more recently, the term, 'devise' was used exclusively, to refer to real property succession while legacy and bequest were used to refer to succession of personal property. A legacy could be specific, such as an identifiable real property or personal item or 'general' which may refer to a sum of money or a number of items identified generically. There are also some other legally effective forms of death bed testamentary dispositions, usually oral but evidenced extraneously.[1196]

1196. *Sen v. Hedley* [1991] Ch. 425; [1991] EWCA Civ 13.

Nuncupative and death bed dispositions are recognised under customary law. A nuncupative Will is one in which a man makes his Will orally but in the presence of witnesses who would usually be male members of the family.

1257. Intestate succession occurs where a person dies without leaving a Will. The property of the deceased, in these circumstances, transmits according to the general law on administration of estates of persons who have died. Intestacy could also occur in partial, where a person's Will does not dispose of some property and fails to indicate how those properties should be distributed. There are also instances where the estate of a person is treated as intestate because the Will did not comply with stated conditions of a valid Will. These include: where the testator did not appoint executors in his Will; the executors died without proving the Will or the executors are incapacitated in mind or bodily physiology.[1197]

1258. A trust created in a Will must comply with the procedure for transfer and the validity of a trust unless such falls within known exceptions.

1259. With respect to intestate succession, the judiciary has been very active and much of the law, despite the enactments available in some states such as Lagos State, have turned on the interpretation and application of fundamental human rights provisions, as particularly contained in the Constitution of the Federation.

1260. The Supreme Court decisions have subjugated key aspects of discriminatory expressions of customary law, to the non-discriminatory and non-deprivation provisions of the Constitution whether by birth, or sex. Rhodes Vivour JSC who delivered the unanimous judgment in *Ukeje v. Ukeje*[1198] reiterated that this is the only policy that should be engaged on succession. The Supreme Court held in *Anekwe v. Nweke*[1199] contrary to the long lists of authority which were to the contrary, that a married woman cannot be ejected from her matrimonial home on the demise of the husband. Previously, the jurisprudence was hinged on the good conduct of the widow. Aside from *Ukeje v. Ukeje*,[1200] other key decisions from the apex court are *Salubi v. Nwariaku*,[1201] and *Obusez v. Obusez*.[1202] The provisions of section 48(l) of the Administration of Estates Act are supportive of the reasoning of the Supreme Court but the Act applies only to the FCT and covers only recognised monogamous form of marriage. The Lagos Law does not have an equivalent provision although it provides for election where the surviving spouse has a life interest in a dwelling-house. This implies that the surviving spouse must establish the evidence of the interest. The AEA provides for election in section 49.

1261. The said, section 48 of the AEA provides:

1197. Section 53, Administration of Estate Law, Lagos State.
1198. [2014] 11 NWLR (part 1418) 384; *See* s. 42(2) of the Constitution. Rhodes Vivour JSC on his valedictory on retirement from the service of the Supreme Court on the 22 March 2021.
1199. [2014] 9 NWLR (part 1412) 393; [2014] LPELR-22697 (SC).
1200. [2014] 11 NWLR (part 1418) 384.
1201. [2003] 7 NWLR (part 819) 426.
1202. [2007] NGSC 21; [2007] 2 All N.L.R. 458.

(1) In any case where it is shown that the residuary estate of the intestate comprises an interest in a dwelling-house in which the surviving spouse was resident at the time of the intestate's death and that the eviction of that spouse would entail or has entailed serious hardship, the court may, on the application made to it within twelve months of the taking out of representation order that the surviving spouse be allowed to remain in residence in the dwelling-house; subject to any limitation which the court may impose, having regard to the rights of all the parties ...

...

(3) Any order made under this section shall be revoked:
   (a) On the remarriage or death of the surviving spouse, whichever occurs first; or
   (b) on the application of any beneficiary of the intestate where it is shown that the financial position of the surviving spouse is such that no hardship would be suffered by the said spouse if the order is revoked.
(4) Upon the revocation of any order made in pursuance of subsection (3) of this section the interest, if any in the dwelling-house shall be distributed as part of the residuary estate of the intestate in accordance with the provisions of section 46 of this Law.
(5) In this section 'dwelling-house' shall include any building or part thereof which is occupied as a dwelling, and any yard, garden or sub-house occupied therewith.

1262. Death, is the thrust of the law on succession. On the one hand, it is a state of comprehension of and reasonable preparation for death with particular focus on what happens to one's existential acquisitions. Existence, in this sense includes the physiological remains of a person and then, the acquisitions. On the other hand, is failure to comprehend death and therefore, ill-preparedness for death and the dire consequences on one's self, one's acquisitions and society. These issues call into question different ambits of law, in particular family, socio-legal relations religion and other areas of studies in humanities.

1263. The views a society takes of death impacts the succession patterns embraced. Societies that embrace death as the inevitable and ultimate end of earthly, human life are more likely to be modelled on a pre-determined legal regime of testate succession with intestacy, operating in limited circumstances. Societies, on the other hand, which are less intuitive and thus less organised, are more likely to be superstitious about death, and intestacy is a default succession model. There could also be a preference based on another categorisation, that of structured and yet, to be fully structured societies and therefore developed and developing. Developed societies tend to have organised civil registration framework and registry.

1264. Development thrives when there is efficiency in land use and thus alienation and redistribution. These factors drive a testate succession framework and developed societies are ordered on these deliverables. Developing societies, on the other hand, are more likely than not, to have default succession framework – a hybrid of testate and intestate succession, falling to be defined as intestate, where the deceased property is distributed among sons according to customs. Most customary laws would limit property alienation thereby also, limiting land use and *a fortiori*, development. Intestacy is the rule rather than exception in this latter category. Only a limited body of very wealthy people will execute a Will, since an elite-middle class Will be torn between the customs and testacy with the result that intestacy will be frequently applied to this class as well. Succession and the policy bent a society adopts, drive a society in more ways than are readily comprehensible.

1265. An important feature of all the Law on Wills and administration is the place of customary norms, and although not mentioned specifically, on primogeniture. The States have respective internal laws which limit the extent to which a person can legitimately make a Will disposing of property. Usually, the customary law of the areas holds sway with respect to the personal home of a family or deceased patriarch where primogeniture obtains, or the variant of the custom, by which, the totality of the estate of the deceased transmits to an eldest surviving son who holds same in some form of trusts for the other sons of the family.[1203]

1266. A typical example is section 1(3) of the Lagos State Administration of Estate Laws (LSAELs)[1204] which provides: Nothing in this law affects the administration of the estates of deceased persons by or under the authority of any customary court nor unless otherwise expressly provided the distribution, inheritance or succession of any estate, where such distribution, inheritance or succession is governed by customary law whether such estate is administered under this law or by or under the authority of a customary court. In addition, section 49(5)(b) provides; any real property the succession to which cannot by customary law be affected by testamentary disposition shall descend in accordance with customary law anything herein to the contrary notwithstanding. Thus, intestacy necessitating resort to legislation occurs, not too often, in Nigeria.

1267. Understanding succession in Nigeria is to bear three things in mind. The laws in the South of Nigeria aim at preserving primogeniture in their customary variants and excluding monogamy-related, forms of intestacy. Intestacy laws and rules on them therefore are contemplated to apply only with respect to property outside these customary expressions. Thus, an intestacy, which engages primogeniture, entails that an administrator is dealing mainly with the personal effects, incorporeal property, choses in action and chattels of the intestate or, the estate of very rich individuals. The second pattern is with respect to application of the Sharia, *Ajibaye v. Ajibaye* discussed below has placed intestacy on the same stand as when customary law is engaged, that is, the ousting of statutory intestacy or indeed, testacy; the latter standing only, if it conforms with the Islamic method of distribution.

1203. *Olowu v. Olowu* [1985] LPELR 2604; [1985] 3 NWLR (part 13) 372; *Idehen v. Idehen* [1991] LPELR-SC.271/1989; [1991] 7 SC (part 111) 104[1991] 6 NWLR (part 198) 382; *Lawal Osula v. Lawal Osula* [1995] 10 SCNJ, 84; [1995] 9 NWLR (part 419) 259.

1204. Cap A3, Laws of Lagos State, 1994; A5, Laws of Lagos State, 2015.

1268. The third pattern is the approach of the judiciary. The judiciary is inclined to enforcing the Constitutional provisions on fundamental human rights on non-discrimination and deprivation. The judiciary can, however, only go so far. The reason is because aside from, the legislation on intestacy, testacy and the rules thereon, the Land Use Act (LUA), 1978 is a Constitutionally entrenched legislation which also aims at preserving customary laws of inheritance with respect to landed property. Efforts at a balance have, however, yielded a lean fruit with the position that the *lex situs* of the real estate property of the deceased is determined not by his personal law, but by the location of the property. This implies that strict regimes of inheritance by first sons can only apply to properties directly located in areas where custom in relation thereto, prevails.

Chapter 1. Intestate Succession

§1. The Opening of the Succession

1269. On the death of a person there is a duty placed on the executors, if there is a Will, or an applicant who is interested in the estate of the deceased to take steps to secure the estate and notify the Registrar of the probate registry. However, it must be noted that the only real formality accorded death is customary or if a Muslim, Islamic traditions.

1270. The apex Court has taken the position that succession is in States' legislative competence, making the State legislation of more relevance. The discussions will draw from the most referred succession framework, which is the Lagos State laws and also to the AEA which is applicable only in the FCT, Abuja.

1271. Section 20 of LSAEL provides that an application for the grant or revocation of probate or administration shall be made through the Probate Registry of the court.[1205] The Probate Division or registry is usually located within the High Court of the State or that of the FCT.

1272. The 'personal representatives' of the dead person are heirs and assigns for the time being with respect to real property. Thus, section 3 of the (LSAEL)[1206] provides:

> Real estate to which a deceased person was entitled for an interest not ceasing on his death shall on his death, and notwithstanding any testamentary disposition thereof, devolve from time to time on the personal representative of the deceased, in like manner as before the commencement of this Law chattels real devolved on the personal representative from time to time of a deceased person.
> The personal representatives for the time being of a deceased person are deemed in law his heirs and assigns within the meaning of all trusts and powers.
> The personal representatives shall be the representative of the deceased in regard to his real estate to which he was entitled for an interest not ceasing on his death as well as in regard to his personal estate.

1273. The rules of court also have relevant directives. The Court has very wide discretionary powers and it is always a counsel of prudence to align the laws on succession with the rules of court.[1207] For intestate succession, Orders 57, 59 and 60

1205. The same rule appears in the High Court of Lagos State (Civil Procedure) Rules 2012, by rule 1, Order 57.
1206. Similar provisions are in the Administration of Estate Act from ss 1–4.
1207. *See* s. 59 of the Lagos State Administration of Estates Law, Cap A3, Laws of Lagos State, 2004.

are of direct relevance. In Lagos, the processes for the grant of administration where no Will is available or annexed to an application for administration are contained in Order 59.

1274. Order 57, rule 1 stipulates that when any person subject to the jurisdiction of the Court dies, all Petitions for the granting of any Letters of Administration of the estate of the deceased person, with or without a Will attached, and all applications on other matters connected therewith shall be made to the Probate Registrar of the Court. Order 57, rule 3(1) stipulates that unless there is need for probate proceedings to be determined at a hearing before a court, an applicant for a grant of probate or administration in general may apply in person and need not apply through an agent, whether paid or unpaid, and may not be represented by any person acting or appearing to act as his adviser. A personal applicant excludes a Trust corporation.

1275. The judge, must ascertain from all applications, the time and place of the deceased's death and the value of the property to be covered by the Administration, thus all applications are required to contain a certificate of death of the deceased as well as enumerate and describe all properties. The application for administration requires a sworn affidavit of the accuracy of the content of the application to accompany its submission.

1276. The judge could also initiate the securing of the estate of the deceased. This can occur when the circumstances of the case appear so to require. On the death of a person or so soon after as may be the case, the judge may exercise a discretion to appoint and authorise an officer of the Court, or some other fit person, to take possession of the property of the deceased within its jurisdiction, or put it under seal and so keep it until it can be dealt with according to law.[1208] On such occasion, the judge may refuse to entertain any application if it is considered that there has been unreasonable delay by the applicant in making the application.

1277. An additional important actor on succession, aside from the Chief Judge of the State or the registrar, is the Public Trustee who can apply or be called upon to administer the estate of a deceased person or an infant or a mentally inefficient person.[1209]

1278. The judge of the Probate Division has wide powers and by Order 59, rule 6, all inquiries a judge sees fit to make shall be answered to his satisfaction before the issuance of Letters of Administration. The judge shall afford as great a facility for the obtaining of Letters of Administration as is consistent with due regard to the prevention of error and fraud.

1279. The Court has wide discretions to grant administration to a creditor, or next-of-kin under the conditions of bond and sureties. The court can also grant

1208. Order 57, rule 2(1 & 2).

1209. *See* for instance, the Public Trustee Law, Laws of Lagos State, Cap P. 27, 1994; Cap P. 19, 2015.

administration to a Trust corporation or the Public Trustee, both do not require bonds, sureties or guarantors. Unless the Registrar, not the judge, otherwise directs, and a guarantee is required, the sureties, if the gross value of the estate exceeds NGN 250,000, shall be at least, two persons. Where a Corporation is a proposed surety then there is no need for an additional surety. Other requirements are that a surety must be resident within the State; must not be in service as an officer of the Judiciary. Every surety other than a Corporation, shall justify his eligibility.[1210]

1280. The limit of the liability of the surety or sureties under a guarantee is the valued amount of the estate for administration.

1281. The grant when the judge so determines, in the case of administration with the Will annexed, shall not, issue within fourteen days of the death of the deceased, and no grant of administration, without the Will annexed, shall issue within twenty-one days of such death.

1282. In addition, where the special circumstances of the case require, the judge may, if he deems fit on the application of any person having interest in the estate of the deceased, grant Letters of Administration to an officer of the Court, Consular Officer or to a person in the service of the Government.[1211] The officer or person so appointed shall act under the direction of the judge, and shall be indemnified thereby. The judge is empowered to require and compel such an officer to file in Court the accounts of administration at intervals not exceeding twelve months.

1283. The LSAEL by section 10 makes vesting of property in intestacy between death and grant of administration to be in the Chief Judge in the same manner and to the same extent as it vests in the probate judge of Her Majesty's High Court of Justice in England. Section 7 of the AEA has the same provision. This makes the personal representative accountable to the court for the intervening period. The power to grant administration lies in the Chief Judge of the State. It is important to note the duties of the registrar of the Probate Division which includes that the registrar is to sign a grant of letter of Administration.[1212] Section 13 equates the right of an administrator of an intestacy with that of a testate executor or executrix.

I. Death

1284. As in all other aspects of society, customs, Islamic law and Statutes govern death and its management in Nigeria. Many people will prefer, upon death, to comply with customary procedures and formalities of death, burial of remains and funeral. There are customary forms of certifying death. This also applies to Islamic law. The veracity of such customary forms of death certification in the light of modernity and science may be difficult to account for. It is unclear for instance, how

1210. Order 59, rule 4(5), Lagos Civil Procedure Rules, 2012.
1211. Order 59, rule 8(1-3), Lagos Civil Procedure Rules.
1212. Order 59, rule 19, Lagos Civil Procedure Rules.

customs and other non-technological means of ascertaining human death treat coma and sundry near-death experiences. The custom of forty-eight hours and commencement of human decomposition may not bear close scrutiny in modern sciences.

1285. Persons who die in hospitals are more likely to be accorded modern scientific death certification. Hospitalisation in itself is as popular as may be expected. Some hospitals may not want to gain a reputation of persons dying within their premises or in care.

1286. All deaths are supposed to be compulsorily registered, but that is not what happens in fact. Customs do not require registration, neither do Islamic injunctions on death, so the toggle on this point is insurmountable. Although, the custodians of customs, etc., must have all the answers, there remain concerns on the certainty of non-hospital deaths and burials in Nigeria.

II. Death under Customs

1287. Under customs, when a person is suspected to have departed, elders are summoned according to the family guidelines on such issues. The elders ascertain death, presumably by pulse indications. When death is ascertained, it is announced by the town crier and information is disseminated to relevant relations who are to mourn the deceased. In the South East, this is an intensive process. The remains of the deceased are dressed by age grades of the person and family members. If the family chooses, the remains will be taken to hospital where a medical personnel should issue certificate of death and then the remains deposited in the mortuary until burial and funeral arrangements are concluded. In other instances, the remains are managed until the necessary ceremonies and rites are conducted for the burial. In the South Eastern States, this takes a few days and the ceremonies are geared towards aiding the ascension of the Soul of the departed person. The process is usually concluded within seven days but on the third day, it is expected that the silver cord would have been severed and the Soul ascended. It is considered that if this does not happen or the proper ceremonies are not conducted, the departed person's Soul may haunt the family members and environment.

1288. It is at the conclusion of the ceremonies that distribution of estate is conducted. The distribution pattern is well known and although, not individualistic as to be termed testate succession, is ascertainable. In the South West, every child of the deceased person gets a share of the estate. In the South East, the matter is gendered. Sons, distribute the property and assets of the father with the first son keeping the personal house of the departed father. Daughters distribute that of a mother who usually has only items of clothing and very unlikely, at the age of death, kitchen wares. In some other parts, such as the Middle of the South West, the first son takes all that a father has and distributes at his pleasure, having personally conducted the final burial rites of a father.

III. Hospital Death, Medical Certification and Registration of Deaths

1289. The structure and provisions for registration of deaths and returns are contained mainly in Parts III and IV of the Births, Deaths (Compulsory Registration) Act. Hospitals are required to ascertain and issue medical certificate of death. **Forms D1–D5** all indicate the format death certificate, registration and notification should take.

1290. Registration covers deaths that occur in Nigeria, from stillbirths, to other deaths on land. Deaths of Nigerians at sea, in foreign diplomatic offices, the highways, mass deaths, and death of those who are mentally inefficient are all required to be registered.

1291. Section 17B, D Act, makes it compulsory to register the death of every Nigerian or foreigner resident in Nigeria who has experienced it in Nigeria. It also provides that where a dead body is found and no information as to the place of death is available, the death shall be registered by the registrar of Births and Deaths for the area in which the body is found. Lagos State has a Coroner System Law, 2007, which appoints magistrates as coroners to hold inquests. The level of its relevance and effectiveness remains to be seen. Section 20 of the B, D Act, makes provisions for the registration of certificates of death from a coroner's inquest which should be registered without alteration. It also absolves other persons from any obligations concerning reporting where a coroner is engaged.

1292. Section 18 of the B, D Act stipulates the categories of persons who mandatorily are to provide information on any occurrence of death to the registrar. The Act also states the position of the medical practitioners on certification of death prior to registration. Section 19 provides that 'every qualified medical practitioner who has attended a person during his last illness shall without charge deliver to the person required to register the death a certificate in the prescribed form and such person shall deliver such certificate to the registrar and the cause of death as stated in the certificate shall be entered in the death registration form and such registers as may be prescribed'.

1293. Registration information includes the cause of death. Registration is free of charge where the registrar personally receives the information from any qualified informant, at any time before the expiration of seven days from the date of death or finding of the dead body of any person, if the death has not previously been registered. The Act does not define 'qualified informant' but this presumably refers to designated informant in line with section 18. In addition, subject to any other conditions concerning fees which the Registrar General may indicate, a death may after the expiration of thirty days but within twelve months be registered by the registrar or Deputy Chief Registrar in whose custody the relevant register of deaths may be at the time the report of death is received. However, after the expiration of twelve months from the date of death or finding of the dead body of any person, any registration of death shall only by permission, in this case, the written authority of the Deputy Chief Registrar. The Act does not exempt any person from penalties that may have become due or any action that may be taken against a person for failure on his part to register any death within the time specified but, any such death may be registered during the pendency of any such action.

IV. Forms

1294. The Forms of Registration and Certification are contained in the First Schedule to The Births, Deaths, Compulsory (Registration) Regulations S.1.6.
FEDERAL REPUBLIC OF NIGERIA
NATIONAL POPULATION COMMISSION
BIRTHS, DEATHS, ETC. (COMPULSORY REGULATION) ACT
(Cap B9 L.F.N.)
[Form **D.1A** (Regulation 24(1)).]
Medical certificate for cause of death
I, of do hereby certify that I have medically attended … .. to … .
who was (a) apparently, or stated to be … years,
that I last saw on the … 20 … was suffering from … .
that died as I am aware, or
(b) informed, on the day of, … 20 … , at
(c) and that the cause of death was to the best of my knowledge or belief as herein stated— Primary cause --Secondary cause ---
(d) and that the disease had continued
Witness my hand this … day of … 20 … Signature
Medical qualification address
* State address
[Form D.1 (Regulation 25(2)).]
Information required for registration of death
Registration centre … ..
Death Register Volume … .
Town/village …
Entry number …
LGA …
Date of registration …
Date …
Particulars of Deceased …
FOR PURPOSES OF RECORD ONLY
Name of deceased (surname first)
Sex male/female
Occupation
Date of death:
Day Month Year
Place of death: home/hospital, maternity home/traditional doctor's place/others
Name of village/town: (in Registration Area)
(a) Age at death … years;
(b) if under one year … months … days
Address of usual place of residence

Nationality: Nigerian/non-Nigerian
Nigerian (a) State of origin (b) Origin
Marital status: married/never married/widow/divorced/separated
(a) Literate/illiterate (b) If literate, level of education
(b) Is Death certified by a Medical Doctor? Yes/No
(c) Cause of Death
Particulars of informant-
Relationship of deceased-
Full name (surname first) –
Address of usual place of residence …
Signature of left thumb mark of informant Signature of registrar
FEDERAL REPUBLIC OF NIGERIA
NATIONAL POPULATION COMMISSION
BIRTHS, DEATHS, ETC. (COMPULSORY REGULATION) ACT
(Cap B9. L.F.N.)
[Form D. 5 (Regulation 30).]
Registrar's summons to appear and testify
I, … of … hereby required to appear before me, the undersigned Registrar of Births and Deaths, at … on the day of … 20 … at … o'clock in the … in the … noon, then and there testify of your knowledge concerning the death of …
If you fail to appear, you will be liable to a penalty of NGN 50,00.
Signature of Registrar …
Registration centre …
Address …

V. Missing Persons and Absentees

1295. The Administration of Estate Act and other Laws on Administration of Estate in Nigeria specifically provide for missing persons or persons who may be absent, but not missing, in the course of administration of estate.

1296. The personal representatives of an estate may appropriate any part of the estate of the deceased, including things in action, in their actual condition or state of investment, in or towards satisfaction of any legacy bequeathed by the deceased, or of any other interest or share in property, whether settled or not. To this end, it may be that the consent of certain persons may be required for such appropriation. The personal representatives, in making the appropriation, must however have regard to the rights of any person who may thereafter come into existence, or who cannot be found or ascertained at the time of appropriation, and of any other person whose consent is not required by the section.[1213] The Administration of Estates Act, 1992 and the Lagos State Administration of Estates Law provide for absentees or missing persons in sections 41 and 44 respectively. Section 41 of the AEA empowers personal representatives to dispense with the consent required of certain persons

1213. Section 41(8) of the AEA, 1992.

who are missing or cannot be traced. However, in making appropriation, the personal representatives shall make provision for missing persons and have regard for them although their consent to the appropriation is dispensed with.

1297. The personal representatives are expected to exercise such a discretion in a just and reasonable manner, taking cognisance of the respective rights of the persons interested in the property of the deceased. Although, the consent of a person who may come into existence after the time of appropriation, or who cannot be found or ascertained at that time may be dispensed with, the personal representative must always act in trust.[1214]

1298. Section 44 of the AEL makes more elaborate provisions extending to trusts, power of appointments and appropriation. By section 44(1)(C), no consent, except in relation to trusts created for specific consents of distribution of the estate, shall be required on behalf of a person who may come into existence after the time of appropriation, or who cannot be found or ascertained at that time. Once the personal representatives make the relevant appropriation, under the powers conferred by the section such appropriation is thereafter treated as an authorised investment,[1215] and may be retained or dealt with accordingly. Furthermore, an appropriation made in accordance with the section binds all persons interested in the property of the deceased whose consent had been dispensed with.[1216]

§2. The Heir

I. Capacity to Succeed

1299. Under customary law, the customs of different societies guide inheritance and who the heir is. Usually, it is the first son. *Idehen v. Idehen*[1217]typifies this position and is discussed more fully below. Another case in this light is *Ajibaye v. Ajibaye.*[1218] This latter contextualises Islamic inheritance regime within a succession regime. Both cases affirm that customary law regime of inheritance can supersede a Will no matter how well written, the Will, under certain circumstances.

1300. Under the general law, a preference is given in practice to the next of kin where this is indicated. Usually, this is the spouse or a first child. The Administration of Estates Laws, however, provides a graduated list detailed below. The list would usually apply where the deceased conducted a marriage under the Marriage Act or a recognised monogamous marriage from other jurisdictions.

1214. Section 41(4)(a) of AEA, 1992.
1215. Section 44(2)(2).
1216. Section 44(4) AEL.
1217. [1991] 6 NWLR (part 198) 382; [1991] 7 SCNJ 196; [1991] 7 SC (part 111) 104.
1218. [2007] All FWLR (part 359) 1321; [2007] 18 (8) LRLR 911.

1301. The term 'Next of Kin' as used in Nigeria is in effect a species of Will writing for persons in public or civil service and in some cases, the private sector. It is a declaration that is treated with care and, submissions of names in that category taken very seriously. Section 54(1) of the Lagos State Administration of Estates Law stipulates for instance, '... and references in such an instrument or will to statutory next of kin shall be construed, unless the context otherwise requires, as referring to the persons who would take beneficially on an intestacy under the foregoing provisions of this Part of this Law'. Furthermore, it is important to note section 54 of the LSAEL, which provides that references to any Statutes of Distribution or Trusts declared, in an instrument *inter vivos* made or in a Will coming into operation after the commencement of the Law, shall be construed as references to this part of the Law. The section further provides that in a Will made *inter vivos* or in a Will coming into operation after the commencement of the Law, references to statutory next of kin shall be construed, unless the context otherwise requires, as referring to the persons who would take beneficially on an intestacy under the foregoing provisions of the Part of the Law.

1302. In *Joseph* v. *Fajemilehin O. O & Anor,*[1219] the Court of Appeal defined the term, as 'the person declared to be the nearest of kindred to the declarant'.[1220] The court went on to note that such a person succeeds to the property in respect of which the declaration is made should the owner of the property die intestate.[1221] In Nigeria, the term is also used to refer to a person who can be contacted or notified in cases of emergencies or eventualities. For instance, one of the forms that is usually filled in interstate commuting, requires the information on next of kin. This is needed in case of any accident. In other words, where there is an accident involving that person, his next-of-kin shall be notified or informed. The term is also constantly put into use in hospitals where it connotes a person who can make medical decisions for a person who is incapacitated or unable to make such decisions, during emergencies. Another point of use is in financial documents by banks and other financial institutions. In this instance, next of kin means a person who can ensure that the proper steps are taken towards the recovery of the money held at the bank, at the demise of the owner. It is doubtful whether a Will can supersede a 'next of kin' record for a person in public or civil service in Nigeria. At any rate, public or civil servants rarely leave a Will.

1303. When a person who is in public or civil service, dies, without leaving a Will or indicating a next of kin, in order for such an estate to be administered, there is need for a Letter of Administration to be issued on such an estate. This scenario presents itself because of pension scheme, gratuity and succession to other entitlements of such a person.

1219. [2012] LPELR-9849(CA).
1220. [2012] LPELR-9849(CA) *per* Ejembi Eko, JCA 34 paras A–B.
1221. *Ibid.*

1304. *Obusez & Anor. v. Obusez & Anor*[1222] a Supreme Court decision addresses capacity to succeed and classes of heirs under a monogamous marriage and is discussed below under classes of heirs.

A. *Commorientes*

1305. The literal meaning of *commorientes* is 'simultaneous deaths'. The rule around this meaning in law, arises with regards to questions of entitlement in succession to property of deceased persons who die simultaneously, in the same circumstance, such that it is impossible relying on ordinary human permutations, to determine who died first. The very purpose of the principle is to avoid any doubt as to what should happen to an inheritance if it is not possible to determine who died first.

1306. The rule is usually subjected to any court order in place or that may override it, and runs like this: if two or more people die in circumstances where it is not possible to tell who died first, the deaths are presumed to have occurred in order of seniority, so the younger is deemed to survive the elder.

1307. Section 23 of the Lagos State Wills Law is on Presumption of survivorship in the circumstances of death at the same time. It takes effect to make seniority the order of death where two people die in circumstances which makes it uncertain who of the two died first. It provides: 'For the purposes of this Law, where two or more persons have died in circumstances rendering it uncertain which of them survived the other or others, such death (subject to any order of the court), shall be presumed to have occurred in order of seniority, and accordingly the younger shall be deemed to have survived the elder.'

1308. Section 184 of the United Kingdom Law of Property Act, 1925 is to the same effect. Titled 'Presumption of survivorship in regard to claims to property', it provides that: 'In all cases where, after the commencement of this Act, two or more persons have died in circumstances rendering it uncertain which of them survived the other or others, such deaths shall (subject to any order of the court), for all purposes affecting the title to property, be presumed to have occurred in order of seniority, and accordingly the younger shall be deemed to have survived the elder.'

1309. The best way to avoid the impact of the rule is to ensure that a Will is made and executed. More importantly, it appears that joint tenancy between husband and wife should no longer be encouraged in modern conditions. Tenancy in common is more sensible for spouses.

1310. With regards to survivorship under the same circumstances where spouses are involved, the LSAEL by section 49(3) provides: 'where the intestate and the intestate's husband or wife have died in circumstances rendering it uncertain which

1222. [2007] NGSC 21; [2007] 2 All N.L.R. 458.

of them survived the other, this section shall have effect as respects the intestate, as if the husband or wife had not survived the intestate'. This would make the property of the husband and wife devolve on intestacy and none of them will inherit the other.

1311. However, where there is a Will, it would mean that any property already given to the other would stand and fall into the estate of the other to be distributed according to that other's Will if there is one. However, all properties not already gifted by Will shall then fall to be distributed as part of an intestate estate or the residuary estate thereof. In the latter case to be distributed in the order of the next-of-kin.

1312. The Administration of Estates Act, 1992 makes similar provision by section 46(3): 'Where the intestate and the intestate's husband or wife have died in circumstances rendering it uncertain which of them survived the other, this section and the schedule thereto shall have effect as respects the intestate as if the husband or wife had not survived the intestate'

1313. It may be that the time has come to discourage joint tenancy for married persons because of the hazards accompanying it both in marriage and succession. A replacement for the interest of mortgage institutions in joint tenancy can be found in active direct policy strategies.

II. Intestacy of Non-Citizens

1314. The Lagos State High Court Civil Procedure Rules on probate has some rules for non-citizens who die without leaving a Will. By Order 59, rule 11, where a citizen of any foreign country dies within the jurisdiction of Lagos without leaving, within jurisdiction, a widower, widow or next of kin, the Probate Registrar shall collect and secure all moneys and other property belonging to the deceased, and shall then inform the nearest Consular Officer of such country of the death, transmitting to the Consular Officer a list containing inventory of monies and property of the deceased. Application may be made to the Court by any such Consular Officer or by any person authorised by him in writing and under Consular seal, for leave to administer the estate of the deceased, and the judge may make such order as to the security for payment of debts and the method of administration as the judge shall deem fit, and vary such order when and so often, as it is expedient.

1315. For foreigners who die in the FCT, rules 39 and 40 of Order 48 of the Civil Procedure Rules of the High Court of the FCT apply. Rule 39(1) stipulates that where a foreign citizen dies within the jurisdiction without leaving within the jurisdiction a widow or next of kin, or, if such person dies within a Government institution or had his usual place of residence there, the Magistrate having jurisdiction within that institution, or if he does not die within a Government station or his usual place of residence was not there, then the Secretary of the Local Government in charge of the institution in which he died, shall collect and secure all moneys and other property belonging to the deceased and shall then request the Secretary to the Government to inform the nearest consular officer of that country of the death of the deceased and transmit to him a list of the money and property of the deceased. Sub-rule (2) stipulates that where sub-rule (1) above, applies, the Local Government Secretary may appoint any Administrative Officer attached to the Local Government or with the consent of a magistrate, such a magistrate. Any Administrative officer attached to any other Local Government may also act in the place of the Local Government Secretary.

1316. An application may be made to a Court by a consular officer or by any person authorised by him in writing and under the consular seal, for leave to administer the estate of the deceased and the Court may make or vary such Order as to security for payment of debts and the method of administration as the Court shall think fit.[1223]

III. The Colonial Probate Act, 1892 and Its Application in Nigeria

1317. The Colonial Probate Order 1965, No. 1530 has an effective commencement date of 10 August 1965. It lists Nigeria in the Schedule at page 3 as one of the countries to which the Colonial Probates Act, 1892[1224] applies. It has to be noted that the Act refers to countries listed as possession. Nigeria gained her independence on the first day of October, 1960. There is no evidence that the Act has been repealed. The Act provides for reciprocity of probate and administration between countries listed and the United Kingdom.[1225]

1318. By section 2, where a country listed, has granted probate and administration it can be resealed in the United Kingdom by her Court of Probate and such administration or probate shall then have the same force and effect as if it were originally sealed in the United Kingdom, provided that any relevant duty with respect to an estate in the United Kingdom is paid and in the case of administration, that security has been given in a sum sufficient in amount to which the Letters of Administration relate. The Act also provides that where necessary an enquiry as to the domicile of the deceased person as at the time of death may be made.[1226]

1319. It may be worthy of note that Order 60, rule 3 stipulates that in probate or administration actions, service of a Writ of Summon may, by leave of a judge be allowed outside of Nigeria.

1320. Resealing may also be possible where the rules are complied with. The rules are discussed below.

1223. Rule 40(1), Order 48 of the Civil Procedure Rules of High Court of the Federal Capital Territory.
1224. 55 Vic. C. 6.
1225. Section 1.
1226. Section 2(2).

§3. THE SYSTEM OF DESCENT

I. The System of Descent

1321. An heir is the person legally entitled to the property or title or rank of another on that person's death. There are over three hundred tribes comprising the nation and as many monarchs or more with their titles and cabinets. The system of entitlement to their offices differs from one to the other. Thus, the heirship discussed below is in relation to property, comprising realty and personalty.

II. Classes of Heirs under Customs

1322. The classes of heirs for distribution of estate under Nigerian customs depend on the region and is identifiable in the system of distribution. It is essentially by bloodline. In the eastern parts of Nigeria, real property and the chattels of the father are inherited by the male children of a father while daughters inherit their mother's personalty. Where a mother owns real property, it is inherited by her last son. Where a father does not have sons, then his brothers are the next line of heirs.

1323. In the South West of the country, the custom recognised from a reasonable time immemorial is inheritance by all children of the deceased through the blood-line of a wife, commonly known as *idi-igi*. The customary system of inheritance also adopts a generational approach and is more akin to 'per stirpes' inheritance model. Where a child predeceases the testator, the share due would go to the issues of that child. The best-known case on the subject is *Dawodu v. Bankole.*[1227] In this case, the Federal Supreme Court heard evidence on the Yoruba custom and acknowledged it. This position was followed in *Administrator General v. Marian Amoke Olubamiwo & Ano.*,[1228] where it was canvassed that the per capita model of inheritance commonly known as *ori-ojori* should be adopted. The Court found that this system of heirship is a more recent development which can only be called into operation by the head of the family where per stirpes fails because of apparent inequity. The spouse in this custom if, a wife has no rights of inheritance or right to administration since she is a subject of inheritance.[1229]

1324. These are the classes of heirs with slight variation all through the South and Middle Belt of Nigeria. In the core North where Islam is the religion and heirs are in accordance with Sharia Law.

1227. [1962] All NLR 702.
1228. [1971] Suit No. M/153/1969 (decided 29 Mar. 1971).
1229. *Akinnubi v. Akinnubi* [1997] 2 NWLR (part 486) 144; *Ajayi v. Sunmonu* [1957] SCNLR 45; [1957] 2 FSC 33.

III. Classes of Heirs under Islamic Law

1325. Islamic law has a different perspective. Inheritance under Islamic law is briefly surmised as follows.

1326. The pattern of heirship discussed below conforms with the *Maliki* school predominantly practised in Nigeria.[1230]

1327. The general deducible principle is that unlike under some customary laws, a wife, and issues – both males and females can inherit a deceased man's estate. The shares are pre-determined and limit the power of the deceased to make a Will. A wife has clear inheritance rights even to the home of the deceased depending on the circumstances. Since the shares, are, however, reasonably pre-determinable and fairly, easily ascertainable, the classification of Islamic inheritance into testate or intestate may not be quite appropriate. In most of the Northern States with large Muslim population, *Ajibaye v. Ajibaye*[1231] decided that the pattern of inheritance for a Muslim, cannot be ousted by a Will.

1328. The general principle applicable to sharing is: 'men shall have a portion of what the parents and the near relatives leave, and woman shall have a portion of what the parents and near relatives leave, whether there is little or much of it'.[1232]

1329. Male children are reserved a right of a higher share nevertheless. However, females are guaranteed a share. As a daughter**,** where the deceased is survived by sons and daughters, each daughter gets equal to half of the share of each son. If the deceased leaves only one daughter and no son, the daughter is entitled to half of the inheritance. In case of two or more daughters but no son, the daughter would get two-thirds of inheritance and share this equally among themselves.

1330. Where the female is a mother and the deceased is a grandfather, survived by a child and the parents of the child, each of the parents, mother and father, would inherit one-sixth share of the net estate. If the deceased leaves no children and no brothers or sisters and his parents are the only heirs, the mother would get one-third and father, the remaining two-thirds of the estate. In case where the deceased leaves no child but leaves a mother, brothers and sisters, the mother would get one-sixth of the estate.

1331. Where the female is a wife, and the husband dies leaving no child but his wife, the wife would get one-fourth of his estate. If he leaves a child or children

---

1230. Vanessa Emery, *Women's Inheritance Rights in Nigeria: Transformative Practices*, available at: http://www.nigerianlawguru.com/articles/customary%20law%20and%20procedure/WOMEN%20INHERITANCE%20RIGHTS%20IN%20NIGERIA,TRANSFORMATIVE%20PRACTICES.pdf Accessed 25 Nov. 2020.

1231. [2007] All FWLR (part 359) 1321; [2007] 18 (8) LRLR 911.

1232. *See also*, *Yanusa v. Adesubokun* [1968] N.N.L.R. 97. *See also* Yahaya Mahmood, *[1961–1968] Sharia Law Reports of Nigeria* 15, 16(Spectrum Books Limited 1993).

along with a wife, the wife would get one-eighth. Where there is more than one wife, the wives would share equally from one-eighth.

1332. Where the female is a sister and the deceased is not survived by parents and children but leaves behind brother and sister, of the whole blood, each would get one-sixth and if there are more of such brother and sisters, they would share from one-third.

IV. Classes of Heirs under Legislation

1333. These classifications apply by virtue of section 47 of the AEA or for a State, typically, the Lagos State, section 47 of the Administration of Estates Law of Lagos State.

1334. This part thus focuses on the legislative framework. With respect to adoption, it has been stated in earlier parts, that in legislative framework, an adopted child is a biological child.

1335. Provisions are made in different State and Federal Legislation for classes of heirs and their respective entitlement in the intestacy of a person:

(A) Surviving Spouse.
(B) Descendants.
(C) Ascendants.
(D) Collaterals.
(E) Adoption.

1336. The provisions of the law in Nigeria confer the right of inheritance when a person dies intestate. The primary successor to the estate of the deceased is the surviving spouse, where the intestate conducted a statutory marriage, followed by the children of the marriage and then the parents of the intestate, where they are alive. The laws also make provisions for the issues of the intestate who include adopted children. The Lagos State Law makes reference to issue also with respect to that issue who might be *en ventre sa mere* (in the womb) at the death of the intestate. Thus, section 2(2) of the LSAEL provides: 'References to a child or issue living at the death of any person include a child or issue *en ventre sa mere* at the death.' By section 21 the Law provides that in any disposition of property, the words 'die without issue' or 'die without leaving issue' or 'have no issue' or any other words which may import either a want or failure of his issue, shall be construed to mean a want or failure of issue in the lifetime or at the time of the death of such person and not an indefinite failure of the issue, unless a contrary intention shall appear by the Will. This would ensure that children who are not born in marriage are able to receive the testator's bounties.

1337. Ascendants are parents of the intestate and collaterals include siblings, nephews and nieces of the whole blood. There are no provisions for grandparents.

The AEA on the other hand refers specifically to only persons who contract a valid monogamous marriage and are survived by a spouse or issue of that marriage.[1233]

1338. Section 47 of the AEA, 1992 provides for the distribution of residuary estate of an intestate,[1234] in this sense, residuary is used to denote the whole estate and not a portion or unappropriated part. Similar provisions are contained in section 49 of the LSAEL. The order is as follows:

(1) If the intestate leaves a spouse but does not leave children, or siblings whether of whole or half blood, or parents, then the residuary estate shall be held in trust for the surviving spouse absolutely.
(2) If the intestate leaves a spouse a child or children, but no parent, or siblings of the whole blood or nephews or nieces from siblings of the whole blood surviving, the personal effects of the intestate goes absolutely to the surviving spouse. A charge of a net sum of one-third of the estate exclusive of the personal effect with interest of 5% payable from the date of death until paid goes to the surviving spouse. The remaining shall be held as to the other two-thirds, on statutory trusts for the child or children of the intestate.
(3) If the intestate leaves a spouse and children and parents and it is not relevant whether the intestate had siblings or nephews and nieces surviving, then the surviving spouse takes the personal effects absolutely and one-quarter of the estate in monetary value, net of expenses on the estate with 5% as interest until paid or appropriated while the rest of the estate is divided into four, with one-quarter to the parents of the intestate on trusts as life interests and subsequently on trust for the children of the deceased while the remaining three quarters go to the children of the deceased.
(4) If the intestate leaves a spouse but no children and has surviving parents, siblings not being relevant, then the surviving spouse takes all the personal effects absolutely and, in addition, a charge of two-thirds of the estate with interest at 5% until paid or appropriated goes to the spouse then the remainder of one-third goes to the parent or parents in equal shares absolutely. If, this part fails, then the one-third is held on statutory trusts for the brothers and sisters of the whole blood of the intestate.
(5) If the intestate leaves children but no surviving spouse, the residuary estate of the intestate goes as to one-third to the parents of the intestate for life and subject to such life interest, on statutory trusts for the issue of the intestate and the remaining two-thirds are held on statutory trusts for the issue of the intestate.

1339. A leading case on the subject and how it relates to marriage is O*busez & Anor. v. Obusez & Anor.*[1235] The appeal before the Supreme Court centred on three questions:

1233. Section 57(2).
1234. This is contained in the second Schedule of the Act made pursuant to s. 47.
1235. [2007] NGSC 21; [2007] 2 All N.L.R. 458.

The extent to which State Laws (specifically, Lagos State)[1236] on the intestate administration of the estate of a deceased who was married under the Marriage Act conflicted with Constitutional provisions on legislative competence.
The extent to which State Law in relation to parties who married under the Act conflicts with the Constitutional competence of the National Assembly for, administration of estates and succession in respect of such parties are ancillary and supplemental to the valid legislative competence of the National Assembly on marital Annulment, Formation and Causes.[1237]
The validity or legal standing of the decision of the Court below which were based on the State laws and upon which the appellant was excluded from the administration of the estate of the deceased.

1340. The plaintiffs are the respondents at the Supreme Court while the defendants are the appellants. The action was brought before the Ikeja Judicial Division of the High Court of Lagos State of Nigeria on or about the 24 May 1991. The plaintiffs sought the reliefs of the court for a declaration that the only persons entitled to the estate of late Cornelius Paul Obusez are her children and herself and that the Letters of Administration be granted in solemn form to an Ademola Giwa (a lawyer) and herself.

1341. The first defendant-appellant by counter-claim sought a declaration that the defendants are the only persons entitled to administer the Estate of the late Cornelius Paul Obusez as well the grant of Letters of Administration in solemn form.

1342. The intestate, Mr Cornelius Obusez was from Ute-Ukpo near Agbor in Delta State of Nigeria. His wife and now, widow, Mrs. Sylvia Teckla Obusez is from Koko, also in Delta State. They got married on 8 July 1972 and the marriage was celebrated under the Marriage Act. There are five children of the marriage. The first child was born on 30 August 1973 and the last on 6 June 1982. Mr Cornelius Obusez died on 29 May 1988. At the time of his death, his first child was 15 years old and the last 6 years. The evidence shows that although, they lived together, the relationship between the couple was, sometime before and up to 29 May 1988, not quite smooth sailing. Among those who survived the intestate was the first defendant-appellant, his twin brother. The deceased in 1977, had taken out a Life Insurance Policy with American International Insurance Company Limited. The first respondent and the only two children of the couple at that time were named the beneficiaries.

1236. It is to be noted that all States have respective Administration of Estate Laws.

1237. These formulations came under s. 36 of the then Marriage Act, 1990 a section, which has since been expunged from the laws of the Federation. It further referred to items 60 and 67 of the Exclusive Legislative competence under the 1979 Constitution which are now items 61 and 68 of the 1999 Constitution. It further referred to s. 4(3) and (5) of the 1979 Constitution now s. 4(2) and (5) of the 1999 Constitution. The subsections delineate the powers of the National Assembly making laws by State which are inconsistent void to their extent of inconsistency.

1343. After a hearing in which the first plaintiff-respondent testified in her own behalf and the first defendant/appellant in his own behalf with additional two witnesses, the trial court held for the plaintiffs stating:

> Under Nigeria's Law of succession touching on Succession to the estate of Nigerians who contract marriages under the Marriage Act, the first plaintiff and her children are the only persons entitled to the estate of their husband and father. The first plaintiff is certainly not a chattel under that law. Further, as beneficiaries of that estate, the first plaintiff and children are entitled to a grant of Letters of Administration to administer the estate but because all the children are minor, it is lawful and proper that the second plaintiff be appointed a Co-Administrator with the first plaintiff. Accordingly, I make a Declaration that the first plaintiff and her five children are the only persons entitled to the estate of the late Cornelius Obusez … I further order that a Grant of Letters of Administration in solemn form for the administration of the said estate be issued to the first and second plaintiffs, Mrs Sylvia Teckla Obusez and Ademola Giwa Esq.[1238]

1344. The defendant-appellant was dissatisfied with this ruling and proceeded to the Court of Appeal. At the Court of Appeal, the justices examined the available evidence, noting that the court did not, but ought to have, examined the allegation of the defendant-appellant that the first appellant had been immoral and did not care for the deceased prior to his death. The Court of Appeal then examined this evidence. Oguntade JCA, noted:

> It is not the law that the surviving widow of a deceased person is automatically entitled to the grant of Letters of Administration in respect of the estate of the intestate. (*see Okon v. Administrator Cross River State* (1992) NWLR (Part 248) 473). The Court has a discretion in the matter. It is a correct statement of the law that a widow who has been guilty of moral misconduct may be passed over. A widow who since her husband's death has led an immoral life may also be passed over.[1239] Although there was evidence from the first defendant that the first plaintiff had conducted herself in a manner considered unacceptable, the trial court did not consider the unchallenged evidence. I have considered the evidence. At the highest, it shows the first plaintiff as insensitive and may be unwilling to conceded to the rival claims of the larger family of the intestate to share in the intestate's properties. But I do not see that the conduct or misconduct ascribed to her was sufficiently grave to lead to the conclusion that she was unfit to administer the estate of the intestate. The lower court however, should have considered the evidence and make a finding of fact thereon.[1240]

1238. [2007] NGSC 21-2. According to the court's records, the second plaintiff was a friend to the deceased.
1239. [2007] NGSC 21, 22.
1240. *Ibid.*

1345. The argument of the appellant is very critical. It remains so, despite the conclusions of the Supreme Court at that time, which continues to be the law. Tabai JSC who delivered the lead judgment of the Supreme Court restated the position of the law:

> Firstly, learned Counsel for the appellant invited this Court to depart from the principle in *Salubi v. Nwariaku* (2003) 20 WRN SC 53, submitting that the incidence of marriage under the Marriage Act on a surviving spouse upon which the decision was based is a matter which falls within Items 60 and 67 of the Exclusive Legislative List in the 1979 Constitution of the Federal Republic of Nigeria and in respect of which a State House of Assembly had no legislative competence. He contended that the legislative competence of the State House of Assembly was limited to matters in respect of Islamic and Customary Law marriages. According to counsel, the call for departure from *Salubi v. Nwariaku* is necessitated by the fact that the point being raised here was not canvassed before this Court in that case. It was further argued that section 49(5) of the Administration of Estates Law of Lagos State which is the equivalent of section 36 of the Marriage Act, is by virtue of the aforesaid Constitutional provisions, null and void. It was contended therefore, that only the customary law of Agbor applies in the administration of the deceased's estate and that by virtue thereof, the appellants who are the brothers of the deceased ought to have priority for appointment as administrators of the estate.[1241]

1346. The Counsel for the respondents on the other hand opposed the invitation for a departure from *Salubi v. Nwariaku*, submitting that the issue as to the incidence of marriage under the Marriage Act falling within the Exclusive Legislative List, by virtue of the Constitutional competences of the legislative houses did not arise. On her view, the applicable law is section 49(5) of the Administration of Estate Law of Lagos State. Furthermore, that it is not sustainable to argue that the stated section was a nullity as its purport is not to legislate in a matter beyond the legislative competence of the Lagos State House of Assembly. To the argument that the customary law of the deceased was applicable, counsel submitted that there was no basis for the application of Agbor customary law in the administration of the estate of the intestate since, at all times material to this case, the deceased was married under the Marriage Act and resident in Lagos State. Thus, on her view, the administration of the deceased's property fell squarely within section 49(5) of the Administration of Estates Law of Lagos State. The counsel concluded that since Letters of Administration were granted to the respondents under this law and in accordance with the non-contentions Probate Rules, they were legitimate, urging that the appeal be dismissed and the judgment of the Lower Courts affirmed.

1347. The Supreme Court in a unanimous judgment took the position that succession and questions pertaining to it were clearly different from matrimony and matrimonial causes, the latter matters, being under the exclusive legislative competence of the National Assembly. The Supreme Court emphasised that the omnibus

1241. [2007] NGSC 21,23. The items are now 61 and 68 of the Constitution of Nigeria.

item of incidentals could not be stretched to cover succession. According to one such denial which was presented by Justice Tabai, and restated by all the Supreme Court justices:[1242]

> The Constitutional provisions in Item 60 of the Exclusive List,[1243] in my view, pertains and is limited to the formation, annulment and dissolution of marriages and cannot be expanded to cover cases of succession to, distribution and administration of the estate of an intestate. Similarly, I do not think that Item 67 of the Exclusive Legislative List of the 1979[1244] Constitution can be construed to include matters beyond those specifically mentioned in Item 60. These specific, clear and unambiguous provisions both of the Constitution and the Administration of Estate Law of Lagos must be accorded their ordinary grammatical meaning which alone speaks and discloses the intention of the law makers. (*See Udoh v. O.H.M.B.* (1993)7 NWLR (part 304) 139; *7 Up Bottling Co Ltd v. Abiola & Sons (Nigeria) Ltd* (1995) 3 NWLR (Part 383) 257. In my view the construction of the Constitutional and Statutory provisions does not affect the decision on *Salubi v. Nwariaku* and there is therefore no basis for any departure there from).[1245]

1348. Based on the reasoning, the Supreme Court reaffirmed the decisions of the two lower courts which granted Letters of Administration to the widow of the deceased and the second plaintiff. The second plaintiff was as a matter of fact, not part of the family of the deceased.

1349. It is to be noted that section 36 of the Marriage Act referred to, no longer appears in the current Marriage Act as compiled in the Laws of the Federation. However, the same provision aside from being section 49 in the Lagos law, appears as sections 46 and 47 of the Administration of Estates Act, 1992.[1246]

1350. Significantly, section 57 of the 1992 Act provides that the provisions of the law do not apply to persons who died before the enactment of the Act and section 57(2) provides that the Act applies only to the administration of the estate of a person who died intestate or the undisposed part of the estate of a testator shall apply only to persons who contract a valid monogamous marriage and are survived by a spouse or issue of that marriage. Other relevant aspects are section 57(1)(b) which excludes the operation of the law with respect to administration of estate of those whose personal law is Islamic law. Section 57(3) restates the provisions in existing State laws on the subject – that any property the succession of which cannot according to customary law be affected by testamentary disposition shall

1242. Katsina-Alu; Niki Tobi; Mukhtar; Mohammed; Onnoghen; JJSC.
1243. Now item 61 of the 1999 Constitution.
1244. Now item 68 of the 1999 Constitution.
1245. [2007] NGSC 21, 24.
1246. As second Schedule. The same provision appears in States Administration of Estate laws and in Lagos as s. 49. *See also* ss 50, 51 and 52.

descend in accordance with such customary law, anything in the law to the contrary notwithstanding. The same provision appears in the LUA, 1978 by its sections 24 and 25.

1351. Section 58(1) defines monogamy as monogamous marriage and which has the meaning assigned to it under the Interpretation law.[1247] It can also be noted that this law is tidier than for instance, the provisions of the Lagos Law.

1352. The Supreme Court overruling the Courts below arrived at the same conclusion in *Salubi v. Nwariaku* that the State law guides questions of intestacy. Ayoola, JSC delivered the lead Judgment with which all the justices agreed. The deceased, Chief T.E.A. Salubi died intestate on 19 September 1982 survived by his widow whom he married under the then Marriage Ordinance.[1248] His wife was of Irish descent. Together they had two children. There were two other children born to Chief Salubi out of wedlock but whose paternity he acknowledged and who were in his lifetime raised in the matrimonial home with the consent of his lawful wife who accepted them as children of the family. The deceased had a successful career in the civil service and was a Minister in the then Midwest State. He died leaving a rather substantial estate comprising, *inter alia*, of landed property in Ovu, his hometown, Lagos, Sapele, Warri and Benin. Thus his property was mainly outside his native Urhobo land and the then Bendel State.[1249]

1353. Letters of Administration were on 14 June 1985 granted to his widow and the first defendant. The first defendant, Dr T.E.A Salubi is the first son of the deceased. However, the widow declined to be an administrator of the estate, leaving the first defendant as the sole administrator. The plaintiff, Mrs Benedicta Nwariaku, the eldest surviving child of the deceased, dissatisfied with the manner in which the first defendant had been managing the estate of the deceased, for herself as beneficiary of the estate of the deceased, sued the first defendant claiming an order setting aside the letter of administration granted to him and that the estate of the deceased be distributed to all the beneficiaries of the deceased's estate 'in accordance with Administration of Estate Law and the Marriage Ordinance Law which governs the estate of person whose marriage is governed by the Ordinance Law; and other relevant applicable laws. In addition, an order to compel the Probate Registrar (the second defendant) "to effect the distribution of the estate of the late Chief T.E.A Salubi to all beneficiaries under his estate as ordered by court"'.

1247. The Interpretation law by s. 18 defines monogamy as the voluntary marriage of one man to one woman and to the exclusion of all others. CAP. 192 LFN 1990 ACT CAP I23 L.F.N. 2004.

1248. The Marriage Ordinance was enacted in 1914 and by its long title was an Act to make provisions for the celebration of marriages. It was one of the statutes included in the Laws of Nigeria 1948 where it was Ch. 128 and the Laws of the Federation and Lagos 1958 where it was Ch. 115. Between 1914 and 1958 Nigeria passed through several constitutional phases, progressing from a unitary to a federal system of government with consequential apportionment of legislative powers between the Federal Legislature and State Legislatures.

1249. Bendel State now comprises two states, Edo and Delta. Benin is the capital of Edo while Asaba is the capital of Delta State.

1354. The plaintiff's argued that the deceased, having contracted a marriage under the Marriage Ordinance, was not a person to whom Native Law and custom applied, and that the consequence of this was that his widow was entitled to a two-thirds share of his estate. The first defendant's case, on the other hand, was that the deceased being and having lived as an Urhobo Chief and having died intestate as a matter of deliberate choice as an Urhobo chief, his estate devolved to be distributed in accordance with Urhobo Native Law and custom under which the first defendant as the deceased's eldest son inherited the deceased's estate which he could, in line with customs distribute at his discretion and as desired.

1355. At the trial, the honourable judge found that the estate was not to be administered in accordance with either the Administration of Estate Law of Bendel State, or Native Law and custom but as provided for in section 36(1) of the Marriage Ordinance. He preferred the enactment to Native Law and custom because the deceased and his widow had married in 1932 under the Marriage Ordinance and the deceased was thereby 'no longer a person to whom Native Law and custom is applicable, because by his conscious volition, he has Anglicised himself and obviously opted out of Native Law and custom of the Ovu people'. The judge stated further that section 36(1) of the Marriage Act (Ordinance) was to be preferred to the Administration of Estate Law because, as he put it, 'the Marriage Act as Federal Law is superior and overrides the State law dealing with Administration of Estate of persons dying intestate'. Applying section 36(1) of the Marriage Act, he found that the deceased's widow was entitled to one-third of the estate and his children to the remaining two-thirds. The first defendant appealed to the Court of Appeal while the widow of the deceased, after duly obtaining leave of the court, cross-appealed. Akintan, JCA, who delivered the lead judgment of the Court of Appeal held that the applicable law for the administration of the deceased's estate was 'English Law as stated in Section 36(1) of the Marriage Act, Cap. 115'. He reasoned that:

> since there was no express provision repealing the provisions of Section 36 of the Marriage Act in the Administration of Estate Law of Bendel State 1976 and the fact that the principle of law set out in the aforementioned Section 36 of the Marriage Act has long been in force in Nigeria for many years as already shown by decided cases on the subject matter, it is improbable that the legislature had the intention of replacing the age long principle of law set out in the said Section 36 of the Marriage Act without express and unequivocal provision to the effect in the Administration of Estate Law of Bendel State 1976.

1356. Applying section 39(2) of the 1979 Constitution (now section 42(2)), he held that the two issues of the deceased born out of wedlock during the subsistence of the marriage, were entitled to share in the estate of the deceased equally with the two issues of the lawful marriage. Some of the other issues pronounced upon by the court below were that the jurisdiction of the High Court of Bendel State (as it then was) was properly exercised in trying the case, notwithstanding that the letter of administration was in respect of properties within the State while the estate included landed properties outside the State and, that the action was properly constituted even though some of the beneficiaries were not made parties.

1357. At the Supreme Court, the main point of disagreement was whether the estate was to be distributed in accordance with English law or Urhobo Native Law and custom, both parties having accepted a common alternative position, that, if neither English law nor customary law was applicable, the estate fell to be distributed in accordance with the Administration of Estate Law of the Bendel State of Nigeria.

1358. The Supreme Court held that the Courts below should have confined themselves to the claim made which was for the declaration of the applicable law which in this case is not the Marriage Act but the Administration of Estates law by which the children and wife were all entitled to a share in the estate of the intestate.

1359. Ayoola, JSC stated:

> I am of the opinion that the court below was in error when it held that the applicable law governing the distribution of the estate is as prescribed in Section 36 of the Marriage Act even though that error was not of significant consequence to the method of distribution of the estate. The applicable enactment is Section 49(1) of the Administration of Estate Law, Laws of Bendel State. The court below should have made an order in terms that the estate of the deceased stood to be distributed to all the beneficiaries of the estate in accordance with that law.
> The court below should have confined itself to the terms of the relief sought. The letter of administration granted to the first defendant has been set aside and there has been no appeal from that decision. The applicable law for the distribution of the estate having been ascertained and stated, that should have been the end of the matter having regard to the plaintiff's claim. The orders made by the court below that the Probate Registrar should supervise the valuation of the assets of the estate and take charge of the estate were not claimed and cannot be consequential to a declaration of the applicable law.

1360. The Supreme Court having made the declaration ordered that the children of the intestate born in and out of marriage were to share equally in the estate of their father.

1361. The Marriage Act, retained as Cap 218 of the 1990 Laws of the Federation of Nigeria ('LFN') did not contain the provisions quoted, referred to as section 36(1) of the Marriage Act in the judgments of the trial court and of the Court of Appeal because that volume of LFN contained only federal statutes that were in consonance with the legislative list in the Constitution. The Constitution lists for the exclusive legislative competence, matters which only the Federal Legislature can legislate upon and in the Concurrent Legislative List were matters within the legislative competence of both the Federal and State Legislature. The residual matters are not listed. While the formation, annulment and dissolution of marriages other than marriages under Islamic law and customary law including matrimonial causes relating thereto were within the Exclusive Legislative List to be dealt with in Federal laws, by item 23 of the Schedule to the 1960 Constitution, item 60 of the Second Schedule to the 1979 Constitution and now item 61 of the Second Schedule to the 1999, Constitution, succession was neither in the exclusive nor in the Concurrent Legislative List in the Schedules but was and remains a residual matter.

1362. Section 49(1) of the Administration of Estate Law (Cap 2, Laws of the Bendel State of Nigeria), as its predecessor of the same title (Cap 1, Laws of the Western Region of Nigeria, 1959), provides regarding distribution of the estate of an intestate who died leaving a husband or wife and issue as follows:

> The surviving husband or wife shall take the personal chattels absolutely and, in addition, the residuary estate of the intestate (other than the personal chattels) shall stand charged with the payment of a net sum of money equivalent to the value of one-third of the residuary estate, free of death duties and costs, to the surviving husband or wife with interest thereon from the date of the death at the rate of two and a half pounds per cent per annum until paid or appropriated, and, subject to providing for that sum and the interest thereon, the residuary estate (other than the personal chattels) shall be held:
>
> a) as to one-third upon trust for the surviving husband or wife during his or her life, and, subject to such life interest, on the statutory trusts for the issue of the intestate, and
> b) as to the other two thirds for the issue of the intestate.

1363. A few points may be noted from the case. It is difficult to agree with the reasoning of the Supreme Court that matters of succession can be removed from marriage. It is true that because of the plural nature of Nigerian legal framework and the questions of different forms of marriage conducted simultaneously in one ceremony, the overall Nigerian framework on marriage and succession is chaotic. Statutory marriage formation and dissolution are contained in the exclusive legislative competence of the National Legislature. Succession is not mentioned, it is true. This is because succession has been dealt with by the Marriage Act itself and was all along section 36 of that Act. As the Supreme Court noted in *Salubi v. Nwariaku*[1250] without repeal from an appropriate authority, the compilers of the current Laws of the Federation, removed the said section 36 from the Marriage Act. Conceding that by so doing the law ceases to exist, succession with respect to statutory marriage remains within the province of the legislative competence of the National Assembly by the joint import of items 61, 67, 68 and Part II (2)(b) of the Second Schedule to the Constitution. Second, the courts in modern times are more inclined to alleviating the effect of patriarchy and supporting wives to achieve a contractual framework and autonomy in marriage relations. This is also the direction of Ghanaian [1251] and South Africa[1252] Laws. However, it is important that this is achieved through a principled legal route. It is thus not surprising to find in existence, laws

1250. [2003] 2 S.C. 161; [2003] 7 NWLR (part 819) 426; [2003] LPELR-SC.120/1997.
1251. *Gladys Mensah v. Stephen Mensah* [2012] JELR 68553 (SC); CIVIL APPEAL NO. J4/20/2011 • 22 Feb 2012.
1252. L.A. Forster, *Women's Rights in South Africa to Advance*, available at: https://www.brandsouthafrica.com/governance/developmentnews/cedaw-190111 (last accessed 3 Sep. 2020).

such as the Administration of Estates Act, 1991[1253] referred to above and Administration (Real Estate) Act.[1254] One thing common to all the laws is an attempt to enforce by fiat the operation of customary and Sharia modes of succession despite the existence of a marriage under the Act. Thus the Administration (Real Estate) Act provides as is usual with all laws relating to succession in Nigeria by section 2(a): When a person dies intestate after the commencement of this Act leaving any real property of whatsoever nature of which the intestate might have disposed by Will, the real property shall, for the purposes of administration, be deemed to be part of the personal estate of the intestate and shall be administered accordingly, so however that:

> (a) the real property the succession to which cannot by customary law or Islamic law be affected by testamentary disposition shall, notwithstanding anything to the contrary in this Act, descend in accordance with the provisions of such customary law.

1364. The LUA, 1978 has similar provisions by sections 24 and 25.

1365. The Lagos State Law clearly only deals with situations where a person having married under customary law then conducts a marriage under the Marriage Act, and by the provisions of the law the estate still falls to be administered under the Lagos State Laws, in spite of the monogamous marriage. The Lagos law recognises polygyny and the claim is therefore not surprising. However, the question raised has been a subject of contention. The Supreme Court has held that the subsequent marriage subsumes the first marriage making the marriage between the parties a monogamous one.

1366. The questions have now gone past the province of the judiciary and require clear articulation by the National Legislature. If monogamous marriage is under the exclusive legislative competence of the national assembly, then the only applicable law to monogamous marriages should be a Federal one, and in this case, the Administration of Estates Act, 1991. The Administration of Estates Laws of the various States can only apply to intestate succession where the intestate is neither subject to customary or Islamic law. It is of course suspected that by this, the State laws become moribund. In *Lawal v. Younan & Ors*,[1255] the Federal Supreme Court showed much concern about the place of customary laws and how powers related thereto affects persons who had prior to death, handled their affairs differently.[1256]

1367. These questions may also be finding vent in the jurisdiction of courts to handle formation and incidental matters concerning monogamous marriages. It is not clear why State High Courts have jurisdiction rather than the Federal High

1253. Cap 2.
1254. Cap 472 Laws of the Federal Capital Territory. It is to be noted that the Act has the Date 17 May 1917.
1255. [1961] All N.L.R. 257.
1256. [1961] All N.L.R. 257,265.

Court. It may be an accident of history due to development by which the Federal High Court which should have been conferred with the jurisdiction for matrimonial matters was not in existence until 1973 and even until date its spread is still not all over the Federation.[1257] What is clear is that the confusion requires resolution and a Constitutional one.

§4. The Rights of the State on *Bona Vacantia*

1368. There are two major ways by which bona *vacantia* can arise in private law in Nigeria, but, in fact, only one practical way. The one way is by virtue of the principles of company Law. Section 693 of the Companies and Allied Matter Act, 2020, provides that upon dissolution of a company, all property and rights whatsoever vested in or held on trust for the company immediately before its dissolution, including leasehold property (but not including property held by the company on trust for any other person) shall, subject and without prejudice to any order which may at any time be made by the court under section 691 or 692 of the Act, be deemed to be vested in the State without further assurance, as *bona vacantia*.

1369. Section 691 is on powers of the court to declare an existing order on dissolution of a company void, while section 692 is on the power of the Corporate Affairs Commission to strike off a defunct company from its Register.

1370. The other way to engage *bona vacantia* is abandonment of wealth or abandonment of property by a deceased person. This has near to impossible way to occur. First, where a person does not leave a Will upon demise, the process of administration entails a collation of all his estate in *personalty* and realty and a certificate issued. The certificate must be attested to by all Banks. It covers the estate's funds and stock. Realty is easier and can be quickly traced since only perhaps less than half the population may have real property aside, from family ancestral houses. With this position, all the laws on administration of estates provide for dependents, parents, brothers, sisters, uncles and then, customs. Under this last head and with villages of thousands of people relating to one ancestor, it is difficult to see any case of *bona vacantia*. This makes some of the rules, clearly taken from the English positions at the time of colonisation very obscure.

1371. Thus, the Administration of Estate Act states by section 47(5) that where any class of relatives or dependents of the intestate do not have a property or trust vested absolutely, then the gift fails regarding that class. The Act then goes on to provide in the Second Schedule item 6, to the same section 47 that 'in default of any person taking an absolute interest under the foregoing provisions, the residuary estate of the intestate shall be distributed in accordance with the customary law that would apply to the deceased person's estate as if this Law had not been passed'.[1258]

1257. Federal High Court Act Cap 134 L.F.N. 1990; Cap F12 L.F.N. 2004. The Matrimonial Causes Act came into force in 1970.

1258. Administration of Estates Act, Cap 2 1991.

1372. The Administration of Estates Act provides significantly by section 57:

(1) This Law shall not apply:
   (a) to deaths occurring before the commencement unless otherwise provided; or
   (b) to the estates of deceased persons, the administration of which is governed by Islamic law.
(2) The provisions of this Law relating to the administration of the estate of a person who died intestate or the undisposed part of the estate of a testator shall apply only to persons who contract a valid monogamous marriage and are survived by a spouse or issue of that marriage.
(3) Any property the succession of which cannot according to customary law be affected by testamentary disposition shall descend in accordance with such customary law, anything herein to the contrary notwithstanding.

1373. The Second Schedule to the Act made pursuant to section 47 then stipulates: 'In default of any person taking an absolute interest under the foregoing provisions, the residuary estate of the intestate shall be distributed in accordance with the customary law that would apply to the deceased person's estate as if this Law had not been passed.'

1374. The Lagos State Law makes provisions in close terms on property not vesting absolutely as in section 47(5) of the AEA.[1259] It then provides by section 49(1)(3)(f); in default of any person taking an absolute interest under the foregoing provisions, the residuary estate of the intestate shall belong to the State as *bona vacantia*, and in lieu of any right to escheat. By section 48(1)(d), escheat to the State for want of heirs is abolished. There is a proviso to section 49(1)(3)(f) – the State may, out of the whole or any part of the property devolving on it, provide, in accordance with the existing practice, for dependents, whether kindred or not, of the intestate, and other persons for whom the intestate might reasonably have been expected to make provision.

1375. Section 49(5) provides that where any person who is subject to customary law contracts a marriage in accordance with the provisions of the Marriage Act and such person dies intestate after the commencement of this Law leaving a widow or husband or any issue of such marriage, any property of which the said intestate might have disposed by Will shall be distributed in accordance with the provisions of this Law, any customary law to the contrary notwithstanding. There is then a further proviso:

(a) where by virtue of paragraph (f) of subsection (1) of this section the residuary estate would belong to the State as *bona vacantia* such residuary estate shall be distributed in accordance with customary law and shall not belong to the State; and

---

1259. Section 50(5) Lagos State Administration of Estates Law.

(b) any real property the succession to which cannot by customary law be affected by testamentary disposition shall descend in accordance with customary law anything herein to the contrary notwithstanding.

1376. The sum total of the provisions is that *bona vacantia* is practically impossible outside of commercial transactions, and financial frauds related thereto. The other basis for application of *bona vacantia* is when public officers hold and illegitimately profit from a public office.

1377. The nearest a State may legitimately have an interest in the estate of a deceased is by Order 57, rule 15 of the Lagos State Civil Procedure Rules, 2012. It stipulates that 'in any case in which it appears that the State is, or may be beneficially interested in the estate of a deceased person, notice of intended application for a grant shall be given by the applicant to the Lagos State Attorney-General and the Judge may direct that no grant shall issue within a specified time after the notice has been given'. This provision although not explicit may well relate to largesse from the estate or charity bestowed properly upon the State.

1378. Despite the current absence of a springboard for *Bona vacantia*, the law in this area can be driven in principle as an organising idea, so that in cases such as *Okelola v. Boyle*,[1260] where the Wills that were disputed appeared curious, intestacy should have been ordered in the whole circumstances of the case and the estate in line with section 49(1)(3)(f), vested in the State. The distribution of such estates would then be for viable and identifiable relations of the testator or to a charity with related objectives.

1260. [1998] 2 NWLR (part 539) 533. SC.

Chapter 2. Testamentary Succession

1379. A testamentary succession involves the last expression of Will by which, a person voluntarily disposes of own property. It could happen at any time within a person's testamentary capacity. The testament represents the record of that last Will, of which the best-known form in legal theory, is a Will.

1380. A Will speaks from death.[1261] This statement underlies two principles in the construction of Wills – the dispositions, and validity of the Will. In *Okelola v. Boyle*,[1262] the Supreme Court considered section 17 of the Wills law of Lagos State and stated that the Will being disputed should have been interpreted in the light of that section which provides that a Will shall be construed, with reference to the property comprised in it, to speak and take effect as if it had been executed immediately before the death of the testator unless, a contrary intention appears in the Will. The Supreme Court stated that a Will speaks from the death of the testator and therefore, the validity of the bequest is dependent upon whether the property belonged to the testator at the time of his death – not at the time he made the Will. However, the appellant did not appeal against the trial court's finding that the Will disputed was void because it purported to bequeath an undivided share in a jointly held property, the property had fallen into the hands of the testator who survived the other joint owners.

1381. Succession, as has been noted, is treated as a residuary competence not exclusive to the Nation's bicameral Assembly nor in its concurrent competence. The Courts have since legitimised the competence to legislate on residuary matters, at least with respect to Succession, as inhering in the State's Houses of Assembly. Each State, therefore, has its own testate succession regime. Some States have enacted own Wills Laws while others apply the Wills Act, 1837 and the Wills Amendment Act, 1882. The Wills Act is applicable in Nigeria as a Statute of general application and also usually incorporated by reference. In the Eastern States there are no specific local legislation. Lagos has a Wills Law. The discussion on Wills will be based on the Lagos law with comparisons where relevant, with the Wills Act.

1382. Wills Laws of different States, where they are applicable do not have significantly different provisions.[1263] In testate Succession, the legal framework in Nigeria is still largely based on English Law on the subject, that is, case law and pre-1900 legislation, despite enactments on the subject by some States. This position which was brought before the Court in *Osoba v. Osoba* (*In Re*)[1264] but was discountenanced, the Court of Appeal taking the position that it was not proved. According to Goff, LJ 'Some evidence was given of Nigerian law, from which it

1261. *Okelola v. Boyle* [1998] 2 NWLR (part 539) 533; *Amu v. Amu* [2000] 7 NWLR (part 663) 164, 170.
1262. [1998] 2 NWLR (part 539) 533. SC.
1263. English authorities are persuasive and may be referred to occasionally.
1264. [1978] EWCA Civ 3; [1979] 2 All ER 393; [1979] WLR 247; [1979] 1 WLR 247.

appears, for all relevant purposes, to be the same as English, but I am not satisfied that this was properly or sufficiently proved. However, it matters not for the moment … .'[1265]

1383. The Lagos State Wills Law provides that a Will includes 'a testament, a codicil and an appointment by Will or by writing in the nature of a Will in exercise of a power'.[1266]

1384. A State's Law on Will would usually enact a section that limits the extent to which a testator can deviate from customary rules and norms of inheritance.[1267] Another significant limitation is an exception to the general rule that a Will is revoked by the subsequent marriage of the testator, but not customary marriages, which are excluded from having such effect. A customary marriage as has been noted, in Nigeria, is potentially polygamous at the pleasure of the husband.

1385. Section 26 of the Wills Law of Lagos States, further, interprets a 'child' to include a child whose paternity has been acknowledged in accordance with the customary law applicable in the State, a child adopted whether before or after the commencement of the law and a child legitimated under the Legitimacy Law Cap L65, Laws of Lagos State. Section 21 of the law also makes provision for children of a testator who may be identified subsequent to death. Third, some of the State Wills laws may, in line with the English Inheritance (Provisions for Family and Dependants) Act, 1975 provide for dependent relations in a scheme akin to *Legitim.*[1268]

1386. The Lagos Wills Law which by section 1(1) provides that it shall be lawful for every person to bequeath or dispose of, property can be taken not to re-enact section 8 of the Wills Act, 1837 on *femme covert.* Section 8 provides that no Will made by any married woman shall be valid, except such a Will as might have been made by a married woman before the passing of the Act. Coverture (sometimes spelled couverture) was a legal doctrine whereby, upon marriage, a woman's legal rights and obligations were subsumed by those of her husband, in accordance with the wife's legal status of *feme covert.* An unmarried woman, a *feme sole*, had the right to own property and make contracts in her own name. Coverture arises from the legal fiction that a husband and wife are one person.[1269]

1265. [1978] EWCA Civ 3, 1, 4.
1266. Section 26. Although Order 60, rule 23(2) only states, that 'Will' includes a Codicil and any testamentary document or copy or reconstruction of it and s. 2 of the Administration of Estates Law states: 'will' includes codicil. *See* further Wills Law Cap 133 Laws of Western Nigeria and Wills Law of Lagos State 1990. *See Black v. Jobling* [1869] LR 1 P & D. 165 and *In re Savage* [1870] LR 2 P & D 78; Charles Harpum, *Megarry & Wade: The Law of Real Property* 11-012 (Sweet and Maxwell 6th ed. 2000); 14-012 (Charles Harpum, S. Bridge & M. Dixon, Sweet and Maxwell 7th ed. 2008).
1267. Section 1(1) Wills Law of Lagos State.
1268. More fully discussed below.
1269. The position of the married woman has since 1837 greatly improved by first, s. 1, of the Married Women's Property Act, 1882; later s. 3 of 1893; s. 37 of the Law of Property Act, 1925; s. 194 of the Supreme Court of Judicature (Consolidation) Act, 1925, etc. Today, a married woman in

1387. Section 1 of the Lagos Wills Law provides:

(1) It shall be lawful for every person to bequeath or dispose of, by his will executed in accordance with the provision of this law, all property to which he is entitled, either in law or in equity, or at the time of his death:

Provided that the provisions of this Law shall not apply to any property which the testator had no power to dispose of by will or otherwise under Customary Law to which he was subject.

The power given under this section shall extend to:

(a) all contingent, executory or other future interests in any property, whether the testator may or may not be ascertained as the person or one of the persons in whom the same respectively may become vested and whether he may be entitled thereto under the instrument by which the same respectively were created or under any disposition thereof by deed or will;
(b) all rights of entry for conditions broken and other rights of entry; and
(c) such property to which the testator may be entitled at the time of his death, notwithstanding that he may become entitled to the same subsequently to the execution of his will.

1388. It is worthy of note that Lagos State law contemplates polygynous marital relations. Immediately after section 1(1) of the Lagos Law is section 2 which indicates the beneficiaries of a Will to include; wife, or wives and children. Section 24 of the Lagos State Wills Law is on gift to a child who dies before the testator but who has living issue or children. The section mandates that the gift is valid subject to any obvious contradiction of that position from the Will itself by providing that testator's beneficiary is presumed to have died just after the testator's death. Section 24 states:

Where any person being a child or other issue of the testator for whose benefit a disposition shall be made for any interest not terminable at or before the death of such person, shall die in the lifetime of the testator leaving issue and any such issue of such person shall be living at the time immediately after the death of the testator, the disposition shall not lapse but take effect as if the death of such person had happened immediately after the death of the testator, unless a contrary intention shall appear by the Will.

---

the United Kingdom has the full capacity to make a will whether in respect of realty or *personalty* in accordance with acceptable rules on principles which includes rules as to survivorship on joint tenancy, tenancy in common or life interests. A life interest (or life rent in Scotland) has variations from jurisdiction to jurisdiction but is best described as a form of right, usually under a trust, that lasts only for the lifetime of the person benefiting from that right. A person with a life interest is known as a life tenant. A life interest ends when the life tenant dies.

1389. Unfortunately, the devise in *Idehen v. Idehen*[1270] were in these contemplated circumstances but failed on account of the custom of *igiogbe*, a custom which equates to primogeniture. It is also noteworthy, that customary law in some circumstances allows for testacy as regards certain properties not within the rules of primogeniture or its variations.[1271]

1390. Under customary law, a person who may have made a voluntary oral declaration, in the presence of witnesses, who testify on oath, could have such deposition admitted into customary probate as a customary Law Will in a customary court. Such a Will if it pertains to land in urban areas of Nigeria may fail, for not being in writing and the requirement that a Will must comply with both the Statute of Frauds and the Wills Act, or Law, and even more importantly, the LUA, 1978.

1391. It should also be noted that by virtue of received English Law and the principle of *Donatio Mortis Causa* a dying declaration, where the indicia of the title to the property is transferred may be validated by the court, if the Governor gives consent as required by section 22 of the LUA.[1272] *Donatio Mortis Causa* is a situation where a gift is made in a circumstance of immediate contemplation, rather, than expectation, of death. The essential requirements are that, the intention to give must be clear, the gift was made subject to an immediate contemplation of death, but where death does not occur, stands revoked. The dominion over the property must have passed either by direct transfer of property or by indicia of title. It applies to personalty as well as realty.[1273]

1392. Of relevance, although the impact on succession remains to be seen, is *AshakaCem Plc. v. Mubashsguru*[1274] in which the Nigerian Supreme Court held that an unsigned document could be admissible in evidence where oral evidence clarifying the document and its authorship is not in dispute.

§1. The Will

1393. A Will is a written document, that takes its internal validity from the testator's Will but must comply with the relevant legislation from which it takes its external validity. When a Will is written, the person deposing to the Will must have it signed or signed for at his direction, in the presence of, and attested to, by at least

1270. [1991] 6 NWLR (part 198) 382. The facts of *Idehen* is more fully discussed below. It is not clear whether the Lagos provision is in response to that case. The Lagos Law in any case, re-enacts the customary principles of devolution of property.
1271. In a sense, the practice of primogeniture and its variants may be described as testate succession of some form, albeit unwritten. The practice is but, retrograde in many respects as already noted.
1272. *See also* s. 24, Land Use Act Cap 202 L.F.N. 1990; Cap L5 L.F.N. 2004.
1273. *Sen v. Headley* [1991] 2 All ER 636; *see* further *Cain v. Moon* [1896] 2 Q.B. 283; *In re Wasserberg* [1915] 1 Ch. 195; *Dillion Re* [1890] L.R. 44 Ch. D. 76.
1274. [2018] 77 NSCQR 109.

two witnesses.[1275] The position of the signature of the testator remains significant as it must be a mirror of the absence of irregularities or worse, fraud.

1394. In *Ize-Iyamu v. Alonge,*[1276] the court held that for a Will to be valid in form, it must comply with the provision and requirements as set out in the different enabling legislation. Provisions on requirements of writing and validity are enacted in sections 4 of the Wills Law of Lagos State and 9 of the Wills Act.[1277] Section 9 of the Wills Act states: 'No will is valid unless: It is in writing, and signed by the testator, or by some other person in his presence and by his direction. It appears that the testator intended by his signature to give effect to the will.'

1395. Section 4 states: (1) No Will shall be valid unless:

(a) it is in writing.
(b) it is signed by the testator or signed in his name by some other person in his presence and by his direction, in such place on the will so that it is apparent on the face of the will that the testator intended to give effect by the signature to the writing signed as his will.
(c) the testator makes or acknowledges the signature in the presence of at least two witnesses present at the same time.
(d) the witnesses attest and subscribe the will in the presence of the testator but no form of attestation or publication shall be necessary.

1396. (2) No signature under this section or under any other provision of this Law shall be operative to give effect to any disposition or direction which is underneath or follows it nor shall it give effect to any disposition or direction inserted after the signature shall be made.[1278]

1397. When the requirement for writing is met, the Will it ought to then be delivered to the Probate Registry prior to or upon the testator's death. Order 58 of the High Court Rules guides the procedure and processes for the grant of probate with Will attached. The Rules provide that any person may deposit his Will for safe custody in the Probate Registry, sealed under his own seal and the seal of the Court. When there is an assignment of the whole interests under a Will, and the assignee applies for Probate, a copy of the instrument of assignment must be lodged in the Registry.

1275. In most parts of Eastern Nigeria, this is the Wills Act, 1837 and in Lagos, it is the Wills Law of Lagos State, Cap W2, 1990 (Laws of Lagos State 2004) and other States in Southern Nigeria. Legislation in equivalent form exist in other States of Southern Nigeria. Both the Wills Act by s. 9, and the Lagos State Law by s. 4(1)(b) have a provision by which someone else may sign the Will on behalf of the testator.

1276. [2007] ALL FWLR (part 371) 1570, 1587.

1277. Section 4 of the Wills Law, Lagos State and 6 of the Laws of Western Region of Nigeria, Cap 133, 1958.

1278. The last portion in the 1852 Wills Amendment Act is no attestation shall be necessary.

1398. Order 58, rule 2, requires that every original Will, of which probate or administration with Will annexed is granted, must be filed and kept in the Probate Registry in such manner as to secure at once its due preservation and convenient inspection. A copy of every such Will and of the probate or administration shall be preserved in the Registry. The rules also require that any person having in his possession or under his control any paper or writing of any deceased person, being or purporting to be testamentary, must deliver the original to the Probate Registrar of the Court within three months of having had knowledge of the death of the deceased.[1279]

1399. There is always an interplay between the Will and trust in Commonwealth jurisdictions. It is therefore important for a lawyer drafting a Will to be abreast of trust law and related developments.[1280] In *Osoba v. Osoba & Anor.*,[1281] the English Court of Appeal stated of a trust in a Will: 'The will, which is dated 24th June 1960, was executed in Nigeria. It appears to have been drawn by someone having a certain amount of legal knowledge but, whilst possessing the merit of brevity, it is not a very well-drawn instrument and is by no means free from ambiguity.' Ambiguities should as much as possible be avoided and the intentions of the testator made noticeably clear.

1400. Whether a document is a Will, or a Trust depends on astute compliance with the formalities of the laws relating to Wills. A Will may, of course, encompass a trust and some trusts have been upheld despite requirement of strict compliance to Wills Laws, to prevent failure of the trust, particularly with respect to the classes of trust known as secret trusts.

1401. The Will and the process of its making is a collective acknowledgement of the eventuality of death by the individual and society – the evidence that a person who is dying, can depart, trusting that the living will be worthy of that trust. It is important that this is so, otherwise, death becomes a foreclosure that can result in the living viewing death nihilistically. Not surprisingly, the judiciary has played a validating role for this approach and in Nigeria as well as most Commonwealth jurisdictions, works to validate a Will valid unless it becomes unworkable.

1402. In the making or the process of making a Will, a lawyer stands in the position of a medical doctor or a priest to a testator. Carelessness and ineptitude may be very costly both to the proposed beneficiaries, society and the lawyer.[1282] The upholding of a Will after a court case may be a pyrrhic victory as its gifts may have been rendered irrelevant by legal and extensive emotional costs, so the lawyer must

1279. Order 58, rule 15.
1280. *In re Osoba* [1979] 1 W.L.R. 247; [1978] EWCA Civ 3; [1979] 2 All ER 393.
1281. [1979] 1 W.L.R. 247; [1978] EWCA Civ 3; [1979] 2 All ER 393.
1282. *Ross v. Caunters* [1979] 3 All ER 580; *White v. Jones* [1993] 3 All ER 481. Here, a solicitor was held liable for delay in changing the Will of a testator who having falling out with his relations changed his Will to exclude them but on reconciling with them instructed his solicitors to change the Will yet again to include them but the solicitors delayed and the testator died without the Will having been changed.

be vigilant to the present responsibility. A solicitor can be held liable for breach of contract to a client as well as negligence in tort to a client, and even a proposed beneficiary under a Will.[1283] As Leach notes, '... It's the ships that go down that get the publicity ... It's the bad Wills a lawyer draws that turn up in case-books.'[1284]

1403. In *Osoba v. Osoba & Anor.*, the Appeal is from an order declaring upon the true construction of the Will of Patrick Jacob Osoba deceased. If the trust which appeared in the Will failed, the property being disputed would fall to be distributed as residuary estate of the deceased. The Will itself was valid.

1404. The Will, which is dated 24 June 1960, was executed in Nigeria. The testator a Nigerian, had lived considerably in the United Kingdom. The testator died on 21 April 1965 in Nigeria, where he was domiciled. His Will was duly proved in the High Court there on 19 September 1966 by the widow, Irene, and the first defendant. The Nigerian probate was sealed in the Principal Probate Registry of the High Court in United Kingdom on 25 August 1967, the estate in England being sworn at GBP 5,500. The estate now disputed and situate in England was valued at GBP 20,000 as at the time of proceedings. The other properties in Nigeria were assumed to be fully distributed, although, allowance was made for any other residue arising from the Nigerian administration at a future date.

1405. The testator was married twice. By his first marriage he had the three children named in his Will, of whom one is the plaintiff, who is the claimant for a partial intestacy as to the residuary estate. This marriage was dissolved by an order of the High Court of Lagos made on 16 December 1955. The testator subsequently married Irene, by whom he had one child and no more, the defendant Abiola. As it happened, Irene survived the testator, but she died on 7 February 1970, some years before the commencement of these proceedings, and so the first defendant is the surviving Nigerian and English personal representative of the testator. The second and third defendants are the executors of the widow's Will. The testator's mother predeceased him.

1406. It appears from a letter dated 8 September 1963, from the testator to his three elder children, that Abiola would be 9 years old on 6 November then next, so that she was a little over 5½ years old when the Will was made. In that letter the testator said that she was then in Standard 3, which was an elementary class, and the plaintiff stated in his affidavit in support of the originating summons, sworn on 16 June 1975, that Abiola was currently at the time of the proceedings, studying pharmacy at Ahmadu Bello University, Zaria, Nigeria. Her course being due to finish in June 1975. Service of the originating summons was effected on the first three defendants, but it proved impossible to serve Abiola and none of the defendants entered an appearance. In the circumstances an order was made on 15 March 1977 that the further proceedings in this action be carried on by the plaintiff against the four defendants and the Official Solicitor as defendants.

1283. *Ross v. Caunters* [1979] 3 All ER 580.

1284. Ruth Deech, *The Rule Against Perpetuities Abolished*, 4 O.J.L.S. 454, 455 (1984).

1407. By the order under appeal, though not from this part of it, the Official Solicitor was appointed to represent the interests of the defendant Abiola and of all other persons except the widow's executors, the defendants Nora Majekodunmi and P. Aduba, who are interested in the estate of the testator.

1408. The Vice-Chancellor Megarry had declared that upon the true construction of the Will of Patrick Jacob Osoba deceased, and in the events which have happened, that the residue of the estate of the testator, situate in England, is held upon trust for the persons other than the testator's mother, named in clause 3 of the said Will in equal shares absolutely. Those other persons were the testator's widow, and his daughter, the fourth defendant Abiola Osoba. So far as material, the Will runs as follows.

1409. By clause 1, the testator appointed the first defendant, his brother Luke Amiolemen Osoba, and his wife, Irene Osoba, to be his executors and executrix. By clause 2 he bequeathed to his wife all his personal chattels provided she is resident in Nigeria so long as she continues to be Mrs. Osoba. By clause 3, the testator indicated:

> I bequeath to my wife all rents from my leasehold property known as Nos. 7, 9 and 11, Custom Street, Lagos, for her maintenance and for the training of my daughter Abiola up to University grade and for the maintenance of my aged mother provided my wife is resident in Nigeria.

1410. By clause 4 the testator devised to his daughter Abiola the title, right and interest in his house and landed property known as No. 22 Macarthy Street, Lagos.

1411. By clause 5 the testator indicated:

> I bequeath and devise the residue of my personal and real property whatsoever and wheresoever to my wife upon trust to be used as in paragraph three above.

1412. Finally, by clause 6, the testator directed his wife to take care of his children by his first wife, each of whom he named, provided they are resident in Nigeria.

1413. At the Court of Appeal, it was noted that in construing a Will, the objective must turn on endeavouring to ascertain the testator's intention from the words he has used, in the light of such knowledge of relevant facts as may be available that he must have had.

1414. As Goff LJ, noted; 'the initial question of construction is, then, whether the words in the residuary clause do indicate an intention to make a gift with a superadded expression of purpose. He concluded that it was, and, that where there is but one beneficiary and the purpose is that of maintenance or education, that is tantamount to a gift to the beneficiary and the purpose is accordingly disregarded'.[1285]

1415. He noted further, analysing *Re Andrew's Trust*[1286] that there are two classes of cases between which the general distinction is sufficiently clear, although the precise line of demarcation is occasionally somewhat difficult to ascertain. Thus, if a gross sum be given, or if the whole income of the property be given, and a special purpose be assigned for that gift, the gift would be regarded as absolute, and the purpose merely as the motive of the gift, and therefore, the gift takes effect as to the whole sum or the whole income as the case may be.[1287]

1416. The court held that there is a general rule that when one sees a gift of income without any gift over to a particular named person for a particular purpose, that ordinarily, the purpose is a mere indication of motive and does not cut down the out and out gift. The Order of Vice-Chancellor Megarry was varied in accordance with the terms of judgment; the junior counsel was to agree and sign a Minute as to an inquiry into the questions of severance and marshalling. It was further ordered that taxation on common fund basis for purposes of legal Aid Act, be paid out of residue.

1417. In spite of the laws discussed, there is very little interest in Will making in Nigeria from the civil society. Very few people consider it worthwhile making Wills. In Nigeria, superstition has a huge role in the apathy towards Wills. Many Nigerians are wont to see the Will as an omen of death.[1288] In addition, Customary and Islamic laws pose a real challenge to a Will culture in Nigeria, since these are presented as default schemes.

1418. It is also worthy of note that a Will made by a minor in national service, particularly in war times may also be admitted as a Will even if made orally. In this category, perhaps may also be considered other testamentary devices such as *Donatio Mortis Causa* and Secret Trusts both of which are potentially recognisable in Nigeria based on received English law and jurisprudence.[1289]

§2. The Capacity to Make a Will

1419. A Will must be made when the mind is efficient and is possessed of the capacity to make or give instructions on dispositions that meets the requirement of the law. It must have within its tenor, comprehension of death as the impetus of the testament of Will.

1285. [1978] EWCA Civ 3, 1, 6.
1286. [1905] 2 Chancery, 48.
1287. *Osoba v. Osoba & Ors.* [1978] EWCA Civ 3, 1, 5.
1288. Kole Abayomi, *Wills: Law and Practice* 36–43 (Mbeyi & Associates (Nig.) Ltd. 2004); L. Okafor, *Leo on Living Trust* 60 ff (Prestige Books 2009).
1289. These are more fully discussed below in Part IV, Ch. 3.

1420. The first requirement of law in making a Will is capacity to do so, known as testamentary capacity. The two aspects of this that are of vital importance are, age and mental appreciation of the act and process of Will making. However, capacity also extends to entitlement to the estate and the capacity to deal with it or parts of it by Will.

1421. Aside from capacity based on age, the testator or testatrix must have the mental presence to know the nature of the act taken, an understanding of the beneficiaries as natural objects of benefaction and the extent of the properties involved where relevant. The latter, that is, extent of property, may be differently evaluated where an extraordinary rich person is involved.

1422. In the States where the Wills Act, 1837 applies, section 7 provides that the age of capacity to make a Will is 21; however, exemptions are made for certain category of persons such as soldiers in active service and other military personnel.[1290] Thus, persons in the armed forces who may not have attained this age, can, if at sea, make their Will.

1423. For States that have their Wills Law, the average age of capacity is 18 years.[1291] Thus, section 3 of the Wills Law of Lagos States provides that the Will of a person under age is invalid, and that subject to section 6 of the Law no Will made by any person under the age of 18 years shall be valid. Section 6 provides:

(1) Notwithstanding, the foregoing provisions of this Law any seaman, or mariner (not being a member of the Nigeria Navy) or crew of commercial airline being at sea or in the air may dispose of his estate though under the age of 18 years.
(2) A testamentary disposition made by a person to whom the preceding subsection applies shall, notwithstanding that such disposition has not been made in compliance with the formalities prescribed under the provisions of this Law, be valid if the court is satisfied that the instrument expresses the testamentary intention of the testator.

§3. Mental Capacity to Make a Will

1424. A person making a Will must be possessed of an efficient faculty of the mind not only, to understand the process of and the content of his Will, but to be seen to be so possessed. The Testator or testatrix must not be acting impulsively from any momentary pressure. Mental capacity runs through the underlying policy and law on wills. Thus, to validly revoke a Will, mental capacity must exist and continues to be relevant.[1292]

1290. Sections 7 and 11 Wills Act, 1837.
1291. Section 3, Wills Law of Lagos State and s. 5, Wills Law of Oyo State. Similar laws as to men of the armed forces exist and for Lagos, s. 6.
1292. *Lowthorpe-Lutwidge v. Lowthorpe-Lutwidge* [1935] All ER 338.

1425. The test to evaluate the condition of the will-maker is not that of medical science but legal science. In legal science, the question is one of fact to be determined by the court from the whole circumstances of the case. Thus, even a person who is mentally inefficient and in hospital can make a valid Will in a moment of mental efficiency. A person will qualify for both medical and legal definition of mental inefficiency, if the state of mind which is expressed is one which; no rational person could hold and which reasoning cannot eradicate from the expressions of the mind; and this state has the potential of influencing the provisions and processes of the Will revealed, when evaluated by a person on reason.

1426. Where a question arises as to the mental efficiency of a testator, the burden of proof of testamentary capacity lies on the person propounding the Will.[1293] This, in itself, calls for the objective assessment of the propounder which is why, it then falls on a court to resolve. The court has the competence and capacity of calling in all avenues of assessment, in order to reach a decision on the validity of a Will.

1427. In *Adebajo v. Adebajo*[1294] the Nigerian Supreme Court held that there is a presumption by the court that the testator is mentally competent if the Will is rational on the face of it falling back on the maxim, *omnia praeumuntur rite esse acta*, which is Latin for 'all things are presumed to have been done correctly and solemnly'. It is a presumption that forms part of the law of evidence which in succession is used in the sense that where the Will is regular on its face value it will be presumed until the contrary is proved that the Will complied with any necessary formalities. If the Will is duly executed and is established as a Will then it is a Will. In that case, despite the allegation of lack of mental capacity, the Supreme Court held that the contested Will was the last Will of a free and capable testator.

1428. In *Okelola v. Boyle*[1295] the testamentary capacity of the testator was also in question and if so, who bore the burden of proof. The appellant at the Supreme Court sought a determination of whether it is the propounder of the Will or its challenger who bears the burden to establish the due execution of a Will when the testamentary capacity of the testator is called into question.

1429. In *Okelola v. Boyle* under Yoruba customary law, three sons had inherited from their late father, a family property in Lagos. Two of the sons died childless and intestate. The surviving brother, Abiodun Otemuyiwa, had drawn up a Will in December 1972, while both his brothers were yet alive, in which he left his share in the property inherited from their father to Madam Olufunso Okelola, the appellant in this case.

1293. *Adebajo v. Adebajo* [1971] All NLR 599.
1294. [1971] All NLR 599.
1295. [1998] 2 NWLR (part 539) 533. SC.

1430. Abiodun died in 1977, following a stroke he had suffered two years earlier and which had left him paralysed. Like his deceased brothers, Abiodun had no offspring.

1431. After Abiodun's death, the Probate Registrar invited the appellant to the reading of a Will, apparently made by Abiodun in February 1976 and in terms of which all his property was to be inherited by A. Idowu George. The respondent, Miss Adebisi Boyle, was named an executrix in the 1976-Will. Upon hearing this, the appellant immediately filed a caveat to the grant of probate and initiated action against the respondent.

1432. The appellant claimed that the 1976-Will be set aside, that the devise of the property to George be declared null and void that the court would grant probate in respect of the 1972-Will and queried the testamentary capacity of the testator in making the 1976 Will.

1433. The respondent, in turn, counterclaimed that the 1972-Will, having been made while Abiodun's brothers were still alive, be declared null and void, a declaration that the 1976-Will was valid, probate should be granted to her in respect of the 1976-Will. She also sought an injunction restraining the appellant from trespassing on the property and damages for any trespass occasioned.

1434. The trial court found both Wills invalid on the grounds that since the 1972-Will was made while Abiodun's brothers were still alive, all the brothers held an undivided share in the property and the bequeathing of an undivided share derived by descent under Yoruba customary law was void. On the reasoning of the court, there was nothing for Abiodun to divide, and his purported Will in that regard, was void. So, the reasoning is that Yoruba custom was the same as the English position on joint tenancy.

1435. On the 1976-Will, the trial court found, that it had not been properly translated to Abiodun, who was an illiterate, and that showed that he could not have known and understood its contents. Furthermore, the fact that a non-existing person – whose name closely resembled that of the respondent – was named an executor showed once more that Abiodun could not have been fully aware of the making of the Will. Thus, the 1976-Will was not entitled to probate, the appellant succeeded in her main claim, failed in the other two, and the respondent's counter-claim was dismissed in its entirety.

1436. The Court of Appeal set aside the judgment of the trial court and declared the 1976-Will valid. It is against this decision that the appellant is before the Supreme Court. Sadly, the respondent passed away before this appeal was heard. By Order of Court, she was substituted by Mrs Joke Kiki. The Supreme Court held, unanimously allowing the appeal, that where the execution of a Will is challenged it is the propounder who is saddled with the burden to show, prima facie, that the testator not only duly executed the Will, but also possessed the testamentary capacity to do so. Only after that burden has been discharged, will it shift to the challenger to prove the allegations made against the making of the Will.

1437. Aside from his illness and paralysis of the right hand side of his body, the testator was also illiterate. Although the Will contained a jurat to verify that the contents of the Will were translated and explained to the testator in the Yoruba language (the Will was in English) the jurat was left unsigned. This fact, alongside others such as the mystery surrounding the execution, makes it impossible to find that the Will had been properly executed.

1438. The appeal therefore succeeded, and the judgment of the High Court was restored. The Supreme Court, however, stated that the 1972 Will did not appear void since as the time of death of the testator, the property had become fully owned by him. It is not clear what subsequently transpired in the case, whether the deceased property devolved on intestacy or the appellant following the nod of the Supreme Court applied for the probate of the Will or still more in line with Nigerian affairs, the matter was settled by family (in this case, extended), out of court. The report did not indicate whether there was a revocation clause but the courts did not refer to this, so it must be taken that there was no revocation clause. This raises another issue, if there was no revocation clause in the 1976 Will, it is a possibility that the testator did not recall that Will, seeing that the circumstances of his passing became torturous. The second Will had an executor, but the first had none, at least from the report. In the circumstances, the decision at the High Court would seem a preferred position. More will be said of this in the section on *Bona Vacantia.*

1439. There are factors that may Vitiate Sound Disposing Mind. These include; mistake, undue influence, lack of knowledge and approval of the Will or its making.

I. Mistake

1440. This would vitiate a Will depending on the nature. If the testator did not know and approve of a part of the Will, then that part may be omitted. If he was mistaken as to the whole document, then that may be an indication of lack of testamentary capacity and thus it would be taken that he has not made a Will at all.

II. Undue Influence

1441. This involves a finding of some condemnation of what the other party has done.

III. Lack of Knowledge and Approval

1442. This is one possible basis for bringing down a Will and is preferable to the claim based on undue influence unless it can be clearly shown that the other party's conduct was clearly condemnable.

1443. The English position on the subject remains relevant in Nigerian evaluation of the subject of mental capacity. In *Boughton v. Knight,*[1296] Sir J. Hannen explained that '… *sound mind* covers the whole subject, but emphasis is laid upon two particular functions of the mind, which must be sound in order to create a capacity for making a Will; there must be a memory to recall the several persons who may be fitting objects of the testator's bounty, and an understanding to comprehend their relationship to himself and their claims upon him'. The other presumption is that any serious mental inefficiency which affected the testator prior to execution of the Will was continuing at the time of execution and negated the testator's testamentary capacity. This is a rebuttable presumption. The essential test was stated by Cockburn CJ in *Banks v. Goodfellow*:[1297]

> it is essential … that a testator shall understand the extent of the property of which he is disposing; shall be able to comprehend and appreciate the claims to which he ought to give effect; and with a view to the latter object, that no disorder of the mind shall poison his affections, pervert his sense of right, or prevent the exercise of his natural faculties – that no insane delusion shall influence his will in disposing of his property and bring about a disposal of it which, if the mind had been sound, would not have been made.[1298]

1444. In *Parker v. Felgate*[1299] the testatrix gave instructions for a new Will and then went into a coma. When the Will came to be executed, the testatrix realised that she was signing her Will, but no longer had any real recollection of what it contained. It was held that the Will was valid and could be admitted to probate.

1445. The presumption, *omnia praeumuntur rite esse acta* was rebutted in *Cartwright v. Cartwright*[1300] and *Harwood v. Baker.*[1301] The rule will not avail to save a Will where the testator had not given his instructions to the solicitor directly but had done so through an intermediary.

§4. Different Types of Wills

1446. There are four main types of Wills; Simple; Testamentary Trust; Joint Will and Living Will.

1296. [1873] LR 3 P & D 64.
1297. [1870] L.R. 5 Q.B. 549.
1298. [1870] L.R. 5 Q.B. 549.
1299. [1883] 8 P&D 171.
1300. [1793] 1 Phill 90, 161 ER 923.
1301. [1840] 3 Moo PC 282.

1447. A simple Will is the better known and most in use in the current times. A simple Will meets with the simple standards for the validity of a Will. It effectively expresses the Will of the maker and disposes of his property, caters to funeral needs and any existing obligations or liabilities. It provides a person with needed rest of mind that one's affairs are closed in an orderly manner, decision on, and expressed Will on who is to receive bounties, funeral expenditures, provision for children and naming of a guardian for minor children.

1448. Testamentary Trust does some of the above but also places some assets in a trust for the benefit of some prospective beneficiaries. It also names the trustees and may provide specific duties.

§5. The Joint Will

1449. A joint Will is one in which two or more persons sign a Will as a separate and independent Will for the each and the other. This is sometimes preferred by spouses but has a major disadvantage in that the terms cannot be changed even after the death of one. It, however, obviates disputes on survivorship and may make execution easier.

1450. A living Will is one which makes provision for contingency or vicissitudes of life while one is still alive. This can stand with a Simple Will if both are properly drafted and executed.

I. Codicils

1451. A testamentary document is usually called a codicil if it is supplementary to a Will and adds to, varies, or revokes provisions in an existing Will. A codicil may be relevant where only minor changes to the Will are contemplated such as change of executor.

1452. Although sometimes indorsed on a Will, a codicil may be a separate document, and can stand by itself even if the Will to which it is supplementary is revoked. It means that although, simpler, much of the formalities (signing and witnessing) in relation to Will making remain important. It is important that the codicil recognises the primary Will. The document should state that it is a codicil related to a particular Will, by for instance, referring to the date of, and maker's signature in, the primary Will. The codicil, should very importantly, state the exact action the codicil takes. A codicil may be relevant where only minor changes to the Will are contemplated such as change of executor.

1453. Codicils are construed in such a way as not to disturb the provisions of a Will, no more than, is absolutely necessary to give effect to the codicil.

§6. Revocation of a Will

1454. A Will is ambulatory in nature. Death is the factual seal of a valid Will. A Will therefore, stands revocable, until the death of the maker, so long as, the mental related testamentary capacity exists prior to death.[1302] The fact of its ambulatory nature is the basis of the principled position associated with Will – that a person has ample opportunity for amendment or revocation of earlier Wills, as circumstances change and prevail upon a person.[1303] Thus, the laws provide room for dealing with alteration, an amendment by memorandum, codicil and wide, but principled, judicial exercise of discretion for admitting Wills to probate.

1455. The need to ensure that one's Will prevails may necessitate a revocation of all previous Wills and associated documents. The capacity required is the same as for a simple Will. The revocation of a Will cancels it, making it void and stripping it of a binding effect. When the intention is to revoke a Will, it is important to understand that it must be properly destroyed or cancelled or if only a part is intended to be removed and there is no immediate way to effect it, other than deletion, then the deletion must approximate to obliteration, in order that all words become illegible even by a magnifying lens. If a part of the Will is found when destruction was intended, it could imply that the seeming destruction was accidental. The burden of proving that a Will is invalid is with the person alleging the invalidity; the burden of proving that a valid Will has been revoked is with the person alleging revocation.[1304]

1456. There are three principal ways to revoke a Will; express revocation in a new Will or by a codicil, revocation by operation of law on account of marriage and revocation by destruction. Express revocation is the simplest method of revoking a Will and this can be achieved by validly executing a further Will with a revocation clause or a codicil drawn up for the purpose of revoking some clauses or parts of a Will. A writing or memorandum may also be used to revoke an earlier Will. Sections 13 of the Wills Law of Lagos and 20 of the Wills Act, 1837 state that a Will may be revoked by 'some writing declaring an intention to revoke the same'. The writing must, however, be duly executed, in the same way a Will is executed. A codicil can also be revoked by a new codicil clearly revoking the earlier one.

1457. Revocation may also be conditional. Revocation of a Will may be conditional and dependent on the fulfilment of some condition such as making another Will. In such cases, until that condition is fulfilled, revocation is ineffective. The doctrine of the Dependent Relative Revocation may, however, be raised to keep the conditionally revoked Will alive where no further Will was executed by the testator.

1458. In revoking a Will, the testator should declare in writing that he or she revokes all previous Wills and codicils. This is important because a Will cannot be

1302. [1870] L.R. 5 Q.B. 549.
1303. *Okelola v. Boyle* [1998] 2 NWLR (part 539) 533. SC.; *see also* Kole Abayomi, *supra* n. 1288.
1304. Sections 13 of the wills Law of Lagos State, 20 of the Wills Act, 1837.

revoked by presumptions. Section 12 of the Wills Law of Lagos provides that there can be no revocation by presumption from altered circumstance or revoked by any presumption of an intention, on the ground of changed circumstances.[1305]

1459. Section 13 of the Wills Law of Lagos provides for the circumstances under which revocation is valid.[1306] A Will or codicil, or any part thereof, is revoked as provided by section 11 [marriage], or by another Will or codicil executed in an appropriate manner or by some writing declaring an intention to revoke the same. These must be executed in the manner in which a Will is executed, or by the burning, tearing or otherwise destroying the rejected Will by the testator or some person but at the direction of the testator and in his presence, with the intention of revoking the same. The provision thus amplifies the intent and the act, not one without the other. Thus, where a person wishes to revoke a Will, he must take an equivocal step such as executing a document to that effect or making a new Will altogether.

1460. The Lagos Civil Procedure Rules by Order 58, rule 8 stipulates that any appearance of attempted revocation of a Will by burning, tearing or otherwise and every other circumstance leading to a presumption of revocation by the Testator, must be fully accounted for to the judge. There is a wide exercise of discretion in the probate court to facilitate the determination of the intent of the testator. This may prove useful sometimes, but it may also create a problem. It is thus in one's best interest to ensure that the principles associated with a valid Will are adhered to.

I. The Revocation Clause

1461. The Revocation Clause in a Will is important. as the clause makes it clear that the Testator is mindful of what he or she is doing and regards the Will revoking the previous as the only document to control distribution of one's estate. Where this is not done, a subsequent Will revokes earlier Wills and codicils only to the extent to which they are inconsistent. However, if a subsequent Will is established as completely inconsistent with an earlier one, the earlier Will is considered completely revoked.

1462. In *Beverley Lamothe v. Ronald Lamothe & 8 Ors*,[1307] the testatrix had made a will in 1993 which was purportedly revoked by a latter 1995 Will. In the first Will she had mainly disposed of her property in England. By the 1995 Will she disposed all her property in the Caribbean country of Dominica and appeared to dispose everything else in a residual clause. The earlier Will had benefitted a daughter in law who was not in the 1995. The judge thought this was not very relevant to the question of which of the two Wills ought to be admitted to probate. It was a difficult decision because of the circumstances of the case. The judge in assessment of the evidence of the parties noted:

1305. Section 19 of the Wills Act, 1837.
1306. Section 20 of the Wills Act.
1307. [2006] EWHC 1387 (Ch).

> I found all the witnesses to be honest and they all attempted to help the court to discover the relevant facts. The events about which they were giving evidence occurred some ten years or more ago and their recollections about them differ, particularly as to the dates when various events happened. I find nothing sinister in that and believe it to be an inevitable result of the passage of time. It was apparent that Ronald Lamothe was very upset at the death of his mother. He was acknowledged by his sister to be his mother's favourite and her death was a big blow to him. As a result, he clearly had a confused recollection of events that followed her death and, indeed some that preceded it. Albert Augustine was the only witness who had no financial interest in the outcome of this application.[1308]

1463. The Revocation clause which in all the circumstances of the case, the judge ruled was valid and intended to revoke the 1993 Will is: 'I revoke all former wills and codicils made by me and declare this to be my last will.'

1464. There was a second clause which dealt with her residuary estate: 'I devise all my real and personal property whatsoever and wheresoever situated not hereby or by any codicil specifically disposed of, including any property over which I may have a general power of appointment or disposition by will to my above mentioned children absolutely.'

1465. The judge held that the 1993 Will was revoked and that aside from the revocation clause, that he found support for the intention of the testatrix, in the disposal of the residuary estate, although the particular property in England which was the subject of dispute was not specifically mentioned or devised in the 1995 Will. The court referred to *Lowthorpe-Lutwidge v. Lowthorpe-Lutwidge*[1309] particularly, the statement which placed a heavy burden of proof 'upon a plaintiff who agrees that the testator was in every way fit to make a will, and that the will is perfectly clear and unambiguous in its terms, containing a revocatory clause in simple words, nevertheless the testator could not really intend to revoke the earlier bequests in earlier wills'. The court noted that in spite of this statement, the simple duty of a court and powers vested in a court to admit Wills of persons to probate are not whittled by this burden.

1466. In *Lowthorpe-Lutwidge v. Lowthorpe-Lutwidge* the question was whether the testator had successfully revoked a former Will. The testator had stated: 'I revoke all former wills this being my last will and testament.'

1467. The court held that the opening words in this clause were essential in determining the testator's intent. Should the opening words have simply stated 'This is my last will and testament' it would have failed to be sufficient for an express

1308. Paragraph 37.
1309. [1935] All ER 338.

revocation. The use of the word 'revoke' within the express clause within the Will was considered helpful in reaching a determination that the testator intended to revoke the previous Will.

1468. It may be that a clause such as: 'I revoke all earlier Wills to the extent that they relate to any part of my estate in any part of the world other than … '. may have saved the original English devise as it would or should where a person has specific properties in different jurisdictions.

II. Modes of Revocation

1469. A Will may be revoked in the following clear manner by law expressly or by operation of law.

A. Marriage

1470. A marriage can revoke a Will by operation of Law. The presumption associated with this principle is that a person who marries must wish to provide for a spouse and new family if there was an existing Will, then such a Will should stand automatically revoked.[1310] Section 11 of the Lagos Wills Law provides for revocation of Wills by marriage.[1311]

1471. Thus, every Will made by a man or a woman shall be revoked by his or her marriage (other than a marriage in accordance with customary law) except where such a Will made in exercise of a power of appointment which the property thereby appointed would not in default of such appointment pass to his or her heir, executor or administrator or the person entitled as his or her next-of-kin under any written law relating to the distribution of the estate of person dying intestate; or a Will expressed to be made in contemplation of the celebrating of that marriage.

1472. In the case of the latter, the names of the parties to the marriage contemplated must be clearly stated. Amendments to the Wills Act, 1837 have altered the perspectives and a Will which exists prior to the marriage depending on the intentions of the spouse may still take effect although, the name of the spouse is not stated in the Will.

1473. Section 18 of the Wills Act, 1837 has been varied and provides helpful language for the construction of section 11:

1310. *See* ss 11 and 13 of the Wills Law of Lagos State, and 18 of the Wills Act 1837.

1311. Section 18 of the Wills Act, now substituted by s. 18 of the Administration of Justice Act, 1982. The section which has some amendment subject to the Same Sex Marriage Registration Act, (Scotland) 2013 and other Orders, for 2014.

(1) A disposition in a will in exercise of a power of appointment shall take effect notwithstanding the testator's subsequent marriage unless the property so appointed would in default of appointment pass to his personal representatives.
(2) where it appears from a will that at the time it was made the testator was expecting to be married to a particular person and that he intended that the will should not be revoked by the marriage, the will shall not be revoked by his marriage to that person.
(3) Where it appears from a will that at the time it was made the testator was expecting to be married to a particular person and that he intended that a disposition in the will should not be revoked by his marriage to that person-
    (a) that disposition shall take effect notwithstanding the marriage; and
    (b) any other disposition in the will shall take effect also, unless it appears from the will that the testator intended the disposition to be revoked by the marriage.

1474. Where a person makes a Will prior to a marriage then the marriage revokes the Will unless it is clearly shown that the Will is in furtherance of a marriage to the same person whom the maker of the Will has married. The Will should state, so explicitly in Nigeria.[1312] The principle running through this requirement is, spouses are entitled to begin a life on a positive note of mutual respect, commitment, and trust. They are therefore, entitled to share in one another's life, fully, which encompasses financial and property provisions. An existing Will, that excludes a present spouse without justification, thus interferes with the optimal realisation of the objectives of marriage. A plausible justification in modern times will include the entering of a pre-nuptial contract with a spouse who is also informed of the existence of the Will. An exception within Nigerian jurisprudence is, customary marriages.

1475. Jadesimi v. Okotie-Eboh[1313] considered the effect of marriage to a particular person an existing Will contemplates. The case also brings to bear the theoretical implications of the double tier marriage of customary and monogamous.

1476. The deceased got married to his wife under Itsekiri native law and custom in 1941. The deceased made a Will in 1947. The couple decided to have a marriage ceremony under the Marriage Act in 1961. The deceased died in 1966.

1477. The court had to determine whether the Will made in 1947 had been revoked by the marriage ceremony of 1961 since the customary marriage was not recognised under the Marriage Act. The court held that a Will duly executed by the

1312. There is a twixt on this provision with the Wills Act, 1837 which is noted below. *See* s. 177 of the Law of Property Act 1925; s. 18 of the Administration of Justice Act 1982 provides an equivalent provision amending the Wills Act.
1313. [1996] 2 NWLR (part 429) 128.

testator in 1947 before his marriage in 1961 was not revoked because the Will was made in contemplation of his statutory marriage, which he solemnised by marrying the same woman.

1478. There are two other crucial related issues, one is where the marriage is voidable, that is the marriage was valid at the time it was contracted but later became subject to annulment for any reason and second is where the marriage is void *ab initio*.

1479. When the marriage is voidable, it does revoke the Will automatically as it was recognised by the law at the time it took place. Once the Will has been revoked by a valid marriage, the ending of that marriage, whether by annulment or divorce, does not alter the position that the voidable marriage was valid when contracted and revoked the Will at that time.

1480. On the other hand, a void marriage, does not revoke a Will. A void marriage makes no difference to the parties' testamentary position, whereas a valid or voidable one does.

B. Destruction with Intention to Revoke

1481. A Will is revoked by destruction with the intention of revoking the Will.

1482. The principle underlying putting an end to a Will by destruction is an assurance that the Will was indeed obliterated. The court in determining that a Will was indeed destroyed requires the establishment of the facts from which it can distil an intention manifesting a rejection of the Will. In other words, all the destroying in the world without intention will not revoke a Will, nor all the intention in the world without destroying-, the two must be present, intent and action.[1314]

1483. A Will can be revoked by 'burning, tearing or otherwise destroying the same by the testator or by some person in his presence with the intention of revoking same'.[1315] The destruction may be carried out by someone other than the testator, but for the revocation to be valid, the act of destruction must be carried out at the testator's direction and in his presence.

1484. If a Will is destroyed accidentally, without the intention to revoke it, a copy of that Will or a reconstructed one, can be submitted for probate and may be admitted.

1314. *Cheese v. Lovejoy* [1877] 2 PD 251.

1315. *See* s. 13 of the Lagos Wills Law and s. 20 of the Wills Act, 1837. *See* for fuller discussion Kole Abayomi, *supra* n. 1288, Ch. 9.

1485. Where a Will is found to be mutilated at the death of the testator, the propounder of the Will must first, rebut the presumption that the testator destroyed the Will, with the intent of revoking it.

1486. A Will or codicil revoked by destruction cannot be revived.

C. Duly Executed Writing Declaring Intention to Revoke

1487. A Will may be revoked expressly or if the Court so determines, impliedly by another Will or codicil. It could also be revoked by another writing, but such writing must comply with all the formal requirements in relation to Wills.[1316]

D. Codicil

1488. A codicil may revoke some parts of a Will. A codicil may revoke a Will altogether, if its contents are vastly different and fundamentally affects the provisions of the Will to which it relates or it fails to refer to the existing Will. A codicil itself, can also be revoked by a new codicil.

1489. These are all sensible rules to secure the testator's Will – rules which are in place through experiences to look out for the living and the living to keep a watchful guard on the Will of a former member of the human family. As Friedman writes quite accurately:

> in the history of the law of Wills, the magical and the economic natures of the document reinforced each other at least in one regard: they both tended toward standardisation and uniformity of text and toward formality in execution and procedures. Undoubtedly, too, the sense of the supernatural in the law of Wills reinforced the popularity of the document. ... Perhaps too, the economic-formal and the magic-religious side of the Will joined hands in yet another regard. So solemn a piece of paper encourages the belief that the document itself is sacred, apart from and in addition to what it says. Though the document can be created only formally, it can be revoked by destruction, by killing it – burning, tearing, or obliterating its texts. The Will is the sole, authentic voice of a man who is dead. Its vitality begins when his life ceases, and it is an almost mystical extension of his personality after death.[1317]

1316. This problem has however been obviated or qualified in England by s. 177 of the Law of Property Act, 1925 and in some States in Nigeria, such as Lagos and Oyo. In Lagos by s. 11 of the Wills Edict 1990 and s. 13 of the Wills Edict of Oyo State with identical provisions which provide for the validity of Wills made in contemplation of the particular marriage and that a customary law marriage does not revoke a Will.

1317. L.M. Friedman, *The Law of the Living, The Law of the Dead: Property, Succession and Society*, Wis. L. Rev. 340 (1966).

III. Presumptions

1490. There are two rebuttable presumptions that apply if a Will is missing at death, or if a Will is found mutilated at death. This could be a presumption that the testator has destroyed the Will with the intention of revoking it, where evidence demonstrates that the testator was previously in possession of the Will. The presumption is rebuttable where it can be shown that this was not the case, and that the testator could not have intended a revocation. It may not be impossible in line with Order 58, rules 14 and 20 that if the Will cannot be found and the presumption that it has been revoked is rebutted, for a draft or a copy of the missing Will to be substituted particularly if there is a sworn affidavit supporting the application to admit the Will to probate and the Will is being admitted in common form.

1491. Where a Will is found to be mutilated at the death of the testator the propounder of the Will must first rebut the presumption that the testator destroyed the Will with the intention of revoking it.

1492. As has been earlier noted, a Will revoked by destruction stands permanently revoked and cannot be revived. Other contemplable forms of revocation of a Will maybe may be undone by revival, re-execution and compliance with all formalities showing an intention to revive same.[1318]

1493. Section 15 of the Lagos Wills Law provides for revival. Thus, no Will or codicil, or any part thereof, which shall be in any manner revoked, shall be revived otherwise than by the re-execution thereof, or by a codicil executed in a manner hereinbefore required, and showing an intention to revive the same. Furthermore, when any Will or codicil which shall be partly revoked and afterwards wholly revoked, shall be revived such revival shall not extend so much thereof as shall have been revoked before the revocation of the whole thereof, unless an intention to the contrary be shown.[1319]

1494. The whole documents regarding a Will are read together where doubts arise.

§7. Provisions in a Will

1495. While some Wills may be invalid because of non-compliance with formalities, yet the law on formalities for Will is embedded in sound policy. In applying and construing these formalities, the courts have been more inclined to validating rather than invalidating Wills. In the Nigerian case of *Igboidu v. Igboidu*[1320] the Court of Appeal held that the testator's Will must be given priority.

1318. Section 15 of Wills Law. *See* s. 22 Wills Act, 1837.
1319. Section 22 of the Wills Act, 1837.
1320. [1999] 1 NWLR (part. 585) 27.

1496. The role of lawyers in providing the windows for formalities is accentuated by human experiences and changing circumstances to which the law responds in its ordinary place as the 'ruler' for orderliness in society. The main purpose of prescribing and adhering to formalities in Wills is to provide a safeguard for the testator as benefactor and the beneficiaries. The law aims at cushioning the testator from forgery, undue influence, dispositions and revocations in the 'heat of the moment'.

1497. There is also an additional crucial function of formalities which in themselves provide solemnity for the process – a process which on all accounts should command honesty, temperance and sombreness for all who are involved. Lodging and admittance to probate also ensure standardisation.[1321]

1498. The basic parts of the structure of a Will are:

(1) Testator's name and address.
(2) Recitation of the nature of the document.
(3) Revocation of previous Wills.
(4) Appointment of executors (and trustees).
(5) Dispositions.
(6) Administrative powers for executors and trustees in addition to their powers under applicable legislation.
(7) Execution.
   - Testimonium (recitation that the testator signs to validate his Will).
   - Attestation clause (reciting the presence of the testator and witnesses on signature by the testator).
   - Signature of testator and witnesses.

I. The Testator

1499. The Will must be in writing and dated. Order 58, rule 7(2) of the Lagos Probate Rules requires though, that where there is doubt as to the date on which a Will was executed, the judge may require such evidence as may be necessary to establish the date.

1500. The testator's clause must identify the maker of the Will. If the testamentary document is more than one, since all documents must be treated as one, then it is crucial that the lawyer puts them together for the testator at the time of execution. It is not necessary, although it may be prudent to execute each page of the Will. Thus, if only the last page of the Will is executed, any other pages ought to be attached to it at the time of execution (or incorporated by reference). Although case

1321. L.M. Friedman, *supra* n. 1317; R.A. Onuoha, *The Will Option in Property Settlement: Whose will?*, 22 JPPL 136 (2003); Megarry & Wade, *The Law of Real Property* 14–01 (Sweet & Maxwell- Thompson Reuters (Legal) Limited, 7th ed. 2008); Caroline Sawyer, *Succession, Wills & Probate* Introduction (Cavendish Publishing Limited, 1995).

law demonstrates that securing of the pages has been liberally considered. The testator must sign and date the Will, in the presence of at least two disinterested witnesses present at the same time.[1322] The stage for this provision was set in *Ellis v. Smith*[1323] in a related case under the Statute of Frauds requiring three witnesses for a Will of freehold realty but not at the same time. Delivering the judgment of the court in which the Will was reluctantly validated, Willes CJ said, 'I think the cases admitting the attestation at three different times have gone too far ... I have known one man swear that he did not see the testator sign and the other two swear that he signed it before the three ... an inlet is made for great frauds and impositions. But when they attest it *simul et semel* they are a check on each other and prevent frauds.'

1501. A person signing on the behalf of the testator may sign his own name but in the presence of the testator and by his direction. A testator may also validly acknowledge a signature on his behalf subsequently. However, such an acknowledgement will be valid if it can be established that the Will was signed before the acknowledgement; the signature is visible at the time of the acknowledgement and the signature acknowledged by words or conduct of the testator.

1502. Section 4(1)(b) of the Wills Law of Lagos State provides that no Will shall be valid unless, 'it is signed by the testator or signed in his name by some other person in his presence and by his direction, in such place on the Will so that it is apparent on the face of the Will that the testator intended to give effect by the signature to the writing signed as his Will'. Section 4(2) further provides that 'no signature under this section or under any other provisions of this law shall be operative to give effect to any disposition or direction which is underneath or follows it nor shall it give effect to any disposition or direction inserted after the signature shall be made'. Thus, the testator's signature must be placed at the end of the Will. If this is not observed, any text following the signature will be ignored, or the entire Will may be invalidated if what comes after the signature is so material that ignoring it would defeat the testator's intentions.

1503. The Wills Act provides that the testator must sign it at the foot or at its end to prevent the addition of further clauses and forgeries.[1324] The Amendment Act of 1852 provides for the signature to be somewhere about the end. In the states of the former Western Region,[1325] section 7 of the Wills Law 1958, generally re-enacted as individual State law, provides that a Will is deemed to be valid if the signature is placed at or after, or following, or under, or beside or opposite to the end of the Will.

1504. The intendment of these provisions is simply to ensure that the Will is real and not vitiated by forgeries or any form of bad motive and to keep testators on their

---

1322. Sections 4(1) of the Wills Law of Lagos and, 9 of the Wills Act.
1323. [1754] 30 ER 205.
1324. Section 9 of the Wills Act, 1837.
1325. These are: Ondo, Oyo, Ekiti and Osun States of Nigeria.

toes. The position of the signature is a vital aspect of disputations on Wills. One crucial aspect of all the laws on the position of the testator's signature is that it must be so positioned to make it apparent that the maker of the Will intended by his signature, to give effect to the Will.

1505. There is a difference between the testator intending to give effect to the Will by the signature and having testamentary intention; the latter means that the testator intended the document to operate as his Will, whereas the former means that he intended that the document should, by his signature on it and the other necessary formalities being completed, be executed so as to comply with the rules as to validity of Wills.

1506. The usual signature of the testator must be available in cases where the issue for determination surrounds the signature of the testator.

1507. It has been canvassed that for the Nigerian jurisdiction, a written Will that does not fully comply with the requirements of the Wills legislation, should be admitted to probate as a customary one. However, the better view is that a Will must be an antithesis of customary inheritance, and must comply fully with the Statutory requirements, even more so.

II. Signature or Acknowledgement in the Presence of Witnesses

1508. The witnesses as, the testator, must also be persons who possess minimal competence, enough maturity of body and mind to understand the nature of the act they are witnesses to. The testator must sign the Will or acknowledge a signature on his behalf, in the presence of two witnesses.

1509. It must be noted that there is an amendment of the Wills Act 1837 by which section 9 is adapted for the impact of the corona Virus pandemic but, in a time specific framework. Thus, presence can now be electronically by virtual meeting. The amendment reads: … 'For the purposes of paragraphs(c) and (d) of subsection (1), in relation to wills made on or after 31 January 2020 and on or before 31 January 2022, "presence" includes presence by means of video conference or other visual transmission.'[1326]

1510. Where the Will is witnessed by potential beneficiaries the Will may yet be admitted to probate but the beneficiary and potential heirs, will be denied the gift.[1327] Thus, a witness or his spouse cannot take under the Will beneficially although if there is such a gift, their attestation remains valid.[1328] At common law, probate was denied altogether. If witnesses are designated to receive property under

1326. The Wills Act, 1837(Electronic Communications) (Amendment) (Coronavirus) Order, 2020.
1327. This is the provision of s. 8 of the Wills Law.
1328. Section 15 of the Wills Act, 1837.

the Will, this has the effect, in many jurisdictions, of either (i) disallowing them to receive under the Will, or (ii) invalidating their status as a witness.

1511. Section 9 of the Lagos State Law is noteworthy as it provides that a creditor whose fund has been charged to the property or estate of a Will or whose spouse attests the execution of such Will remains capable of being a witness to prove the validity or invalidity of the Will, in spite of such charge. Section 10 enables an executor to also be a witness to proving the Will.[1329] In addition, where a gift to any person fails by reason of the fact that he is an attesting witness or the spouse of an attesting witness, such person shall not have any right to a grant as a beneficiary named in the Will, although, this is, without prejudice to a right to a grant in any other capacity.[1330]

III. Attesting the Will by the Witnesses

1512. The Will must have an attestation Clause. An attestation clause strengthens the presumption that the Will is regular and has met all requirements.

1513. The Witnesses need not sign in the presence of each other, but they must sign or acknowledge in the presence of the testator. It has been held that a visually impaired person cannot be a witness as he cannot see the testator's signature but the courts have left open the question of a Will prepared in Braille if the testator acknowledged his signature to the witness. However, a visually impaired person can make a Will with or without a Braille.

IV. Executors

1514. Executors are appointed by the Will of the executor and are to be preferred. Failure to appoint though may not be fatal to the validity of a Will as the court can exercise a discretion to appoint executors.

1515. Generally, executors should not be less than two or more than four. The executor has the duty of gathering up the estate, paying debts, taxes and funeral expenses, and ultimately of distributing the estate to those entitled. It is therefore important that the consent of the executors should be sought and obtained before appointment or so soon thereafter. The Court has a duty to inform the executors and obtain formal response.

1516. The executors are to process and obtain probate in respect of a Will. The executor's power is derived from the Will and he is obliged to prove the Will by obtaining a grant of probate from the High Court, though he may carry out preliminary duties on the death of the testator as the property vests in him immediately. If

1329. These provisions are replicated from ss 16 and 17 of the Wills Act, 1837.
1330. Order 58, rule 21 of the Lagos Civil Procedure Rules.

a sole or only surviving executor who has obtained probate dies having himself appointed an executor, the latter, on proving the original executor's Will, becomes executor of the original also. This chain of representation may be continued indefinitely until broken by failure to appoint an executor, or failure of an executor to obtain a grant of probate.[1331] An Executor can also be a Witness.[1332]

V. Alteration

1517. It is best to avoid alterations in Wills. Where this cannot be avoided, then the alteration must be so thoroughly done, that the provision intended to be altered is completely obliterated and not visible to the naked eye or magnifying tools. In *Adams* (Deceased), *Re*,[1333] the court took the position that the scoring so thoroughly, through a part of a Will so that it was impossible to see by the naked eye whether it had been signed or executed at all was to be treated as the destruction and revocation of the Will. The testator crossed out clauses in his Will that he intended to revoke so efficiently that the clauses could no longer be read and were completely illegible. As both the attesting witnesses and testator's signatures had been obliterated the Will was held to have been validly revoked.

1518. Where the deletion cannot be so properly done, then the witnesses as well as the testator must sign against the alterations, a process that is re– execution of the Will. Section 14 of the Lagos State Law provides for the testator to sign the alteration and the witnesses to subscribe the alteration on the margin of the Will or some other part of the Will. Section 14 provides:

> No obliteration, interlineation, or alteration made in any Will after the execution thereof shall be valid or have any effect except in so far as the words or effect, of the Will before such alteration shall not be apparent, unless such alteration shall be executed in the like manner as is hereinbefore required for the execution of the Will:
>
> Provided that the will, with such alteration as part thereof, shall be deemed to be duly executed if the signature of the testator and the subscription of the witness be made in the margin or on some other part of the will opposite or near to such alteration or at the foot or end of or opposite to a memorandum referring to such alteration and written at the end or some other part of the will.

1519. The section makes it possible for the original Will to be admitted to probate where there is an alteration but the alteration has not destroyed the original provisions. Thus, any alteration must be done such the words or effect, of the Will before such alteration shall not be apparent.

1331. The term 'personal representatives' includes both executors and administrators although it is better to use executors with respect to Wills as this is usual.
1332. Section 10 Wills Law of Lagos State and s. 17 Wills Act.
1333. [1990] 2 ALL ER 97; [1990] Ch. 601.

1520. A similar provision appears in section 21 of the Wills Act, 1837. The rules are designed to ensure that only alterations made by the testator or with the testator's knowledge and approval are given effect. It is clearly best to ensure that all alterations, whenever made, are signed or initialled by the testator and witnessed, to make clear what his true intentions are.

1521. The Civil Procedure rules by Order 58, rule 11(4) of the Lagos Probate Rules states that, where no satisfactory evidence is adduced respecting the time when an erasure or obliteration was made and the words erased or obliterated are not entirely effaced, and can, on inspection of the Will, be ascertained, they shall form part of the Probate. Where any words have been erased which might have been of importance, an affidavit shall be required to verify the position.

1522. In *Cheese v. Lovejoy*[1334] the testator wrote across the Will stating 'all these are revoked' and then crossed parts of the Will out and went on to throw the Will away. A housemaid later found the document, preserved it and it was produced on the testator's death. The Will was held to be valid. The court held that though, the testator had crossed out the gifts and expressed a desire to cancel the gifts, the words expressing gifts were still legible and therefore the gifts in the Will remained valid in the form in which it was.

1523. Section 14 as 21, envisages two ways in which alterations to a Will can be made and the Will retains its validity. Alterations can be made but executed as a Will. Second, the Will remains valid if, the alteration is deemed to be duly executed. Both the testator and the witnesses must sign and follow the process for signature and attestation in acknowledging the alterations. If a memorandum is added to the documentation, the process is the same.

1524. The Probate rules provide additional guidance by Order 58, rules 7, 11 and 20. The admission of the Will to probate shall not be affected by any alteration on the face of the Will which appears to the judge to be of no practical importance.[1335] However, where in a Will, there is any obliteration, interlineations or other alteration which is not authenticated in the manner prescribed by law or by the re-execution of the Will or by the execution of a Codicil, the judge shall require evidence to show whether the alteration was present at the time the Will was executed and shall give directions as to the form in which the Will is to be proved.

1525. Significantly, where the judge considers that in any particular case, a photocopy of the original Will would not be satisfactory for purposes of record, he may require that an engrossment suitable for photo reproduction be lodged. Where a Will contains traces of alterations which are not admissible to proof, there shall be lodged an engrossment of the Will in the form in which it is to be proved. Any engrossment lodged in this respect, must reproduce the punctuation, spacing and division into paragraphs of the Will and may be required to be made 'bookwise' on durable

1334. [1877] 2 PD 251.
1335. Order 58, rule 7(1) of the Lagos Civil Procedure Rules.

paper in a continuing format, flowing from page to page. Where any pencil writing appears on a Will, then it is required that a copy of the Will is lodged or of the pages or sheets containing the pencil writing and those portions which appear in pencil in the original are underlined in red ink.[1336]

1526. A codicil confirming a Will gives effect to any alterations of the Will existing at the date of the codicil unless the codicil shows that the testator was treating the Will as being unaltered.

§8. Restrictions

I. The *Legitim*

1527. Originating in Roman Law, *Legitim* is part of Civil and Scots law. The *Legitim* is the legal rights in a person's moveable estate that cannot be disposed of, by Will. It is that part of an estate that children or other close relatives can claim against the descendant's testament.

1528. The fund amounts to one-third where a spouse is still living and one-half, if not. The children of deceased children can represent their ancestor.

1529. The extent to which a person can transfer real property in Nigeria by testate succession is limited by customary and Islamic law and in particular, the LUA, 1978.[1337] *Idehen v. Idehen*[1338] and that line of case law make writing of Will in the light of customs an uphill task. The various laws already referred to under intestacy having similar impact.

1530. The extent to which the State can legitimately interfere with one's Will with regards to acquisition in the light of the common human experience of departure from the earth by reason of death, has been a constant basis of enquiry and discourse in law and philosophy in particular.

1531. A typical provision of the State qualification of the power of a testator would follow the language of the Lagos State Wills Law which by section 1(1) provides:

> 'Power to dispose property by will'. It shall be lawful for every person to bequeath or dispose of, by his will executed in accordance with the provision of this law, all property to which he is entitled, either in law or in equity, or at the time of his death— Provided that the provisions of this Law shall not apply to any property which the testator had no power to dispose of by will or otherwise under Customary Law to which he was subject.

1336. Rule 20, Order 58.
1337. Cap 202 L.F.N. 1990; Cap L5 L.F.N. 2004 – ss 24 and 25.
1338. [1991] 6 NWLR (part 198) 382.

1532. In *Idehen v. Idehen*[1339] the testator, a wealthy gentleman of Bini origin in Edo State of Nigeria, left a Will. He died on 18 September 1979 leaving a number of devises and bequests by his Will to several of his descendants. The customary law in practice in Benin is primogeniture, a variant in which the first son of a deceased patriarch, acquires his living houses in consideration, so to speak of performing first and second funeral rights for the deceased father. By this custom, the houses where a person lived and died constitute what is classified as the 'Igiogbe'. The first son predeceased his father and by his Will, he devised the relevant properties to his son, that is the father's grandson. There were three houses involved. However, there was a second son who, thought that he stepped into the shoes of a first son by the death of his elder brother. The second son sought from the court a declaration vindicating this position and that therefore he was entitled to inherit the properties that comprised the *igiogbe* despite the Will of his late father. At the Supreme Court, he was the first Respondent. At the trial court, he was the plaintiff in an action against the executors of the testator challenging the validity of the Will and a declaration that he was entitled to the *igiogbe* and in line with customary law, also entitled to a disproportionately larger share of the remaining part of the deceased estate as against the other children of the testator. The executors are the appellants in the action at the Supreme Court and defendants at the trial. The trial court after hearing the parties concluded that the case comprised questions of fact and law. On the question of fact, which was whether the Will was valid or was forged, the Court held that it was satisfied that the Will was not forged but was duly prepared for the Testator and lodged at the Probate in the usual manner. On the question of law, which was compliance with section 6 of the Wills Law of Edo State[1340] on the signature of the testator at requisite attestation, the court took the position that on assessment of the available evidence, the Will was duly subscribed and that therefore, the testator died testate. The trial court consequently held, that the testator having taken into cognisance the provisions of the Wills law, specifically, sections 3(1) and 28 to devise the *igiogbe* to his first son and since the second son stepped into his shoes, the second son, became the lawful beneficiary of the *igiogbe* by the Will of the Testator. [1341] Although, the Will did not state this, the court stated that it took effect impliedly and by operation of law.

1533. The appellant's counsels took the position that the subsection did not go to testamentary capacity to dispose of property by Will but to the subject matter, that is the property. The position was that any other interpretation would lead to the 'absurd' result that every disposition by Will would be avoided by the customary

---

1339. [1991] 6 NWLR (part 198) 382; [1991] 7 SCNJ 196; [1991] 7 SC (part 111) 104; *see also John Imade v. Odemwingie Otabor* [1998] 4 NWLR (part 544) 20.

1340. Cap 172, Laws of Bendel State, 1976 (Edo State was a part of the then Bendel State which was subsequently divided into two States – Delta and Edo).

1341. Section 3(1), Wills Law, Cap 172, Laws of Bendel State, 1976 provides: 'subject to any customary law relating thereto, it shall be lawful for every person to devise, bequeath or dispose of, by his will executed in the manner hereinafter required, all real estate and all personal estate which he shall be entitled to, either at law or in equity, at the time of his death and which if not so devised, bequeathed and disposed of would devolve upon the heir at law of him, or if he became entitled by descent, of his ancestor or upon his executor or administrator'.

law relating to succession on intestacy. The counsel to the respondents, on the other hand, took the position that the subsection constituted a complete restriction on testamentary capacity. The Supreme Court reviewing all earlier authorities, reiterated the position it took in *Oke v. Oke*[1342] and *Olowu v. Olowu*[1343] and stated that 'the expression subject to customary law relating thereto could not have been intended to qualify the testamentary capacity so unambiguously conferred on every Bini citizen by section 3(1) of the Wills Law. It is only subject to any customary law affecting the property to be disposed'.[1344]

1534. The Supreme Court allowed the appeal and declared the Will invalid in part, and that the *Igiogbe* falls to be inherited by the first respondent. However, while arriving at the same conclusion Karibi-Whyte JSC stated that he would consider the proper process to be that the Will is valid with respect to a portion of the devise and the failed devices fell into intestacy, so that applying intestacy, the first respondent inherits the properties in customary law.

1535. The decision established the precedent which accords with others, in restricting testamentary capacity relative to primogeniture and other core customary inheritance patterns. It may be that the customary pattern serves the interest of the living. In *Idehen*, the larger issues of the impact of the law interfering not just with the Will of a person, but also in family life requires more enquiries and findings on the extent to which outcomes such as occurred in *Idehen* can drive family cohesion and perhaps, sibling rivalry.

1536. A good case for restriction of testamentary capacity based on the Sharia is *Ajibaye v. Ajibaye.*[1345] Here the Court of Appeal held in spite of the testator's written Will that his estate must be administered in line with the Sharia. Although, a Muslim, the testator had lived mainly as a non-practicing Muslim. The testator had lived in Lagos although, he is a native of Kwara State. The Kwara State Wills Law[1346] by section 4 states: 'it shall be lawful for every person to bequeath or dispose of by his will executed in accordance with the provisions of this law, all property to which he is entitled, either in law or in equity, at the time of his death. Provided that the provisions of this law shall not apply to the will of a person who immediately before his death was subject to Islamic Law'.

1537. The testator, Alhaji Disu Ajibaye had made a Will dated 30 September 2002. The testator died on 29 January 2004. His Will indicated: 'I also direct and want my estate to be shared in accordance with the English Law and as contained in this Will having chosen English Law to guide my transactions and affairs in my life time notwithstanding the fact that I am a Muslim.' The available evidence showed that only the last and youngest wife of the deceased, the Appellant, had

1342. [1974] 3 SC 1; [1974] 1 All N.L.R. (part 1) 443.
1343. [1985] LPELR 2604; [1985] 3 NWLR (part 13) 372.
1344. [1991] LPELR-SC. 271/1989, pp. 13–14.
1345. [2007] All FWLR (part 359) 1321.
1346. Cap 168 Laws of Kwara State 1991.

knowledge of the making and existence of the Will. The appellant claimed enforcement of the disposition in accordance with the terms of Will of the testator, but the respondents objected to this, claiming that the applicable law was the Wills Law of Lagos State particularly as the testator had indicated that his burial should be conducted in accordance with Islamic (Muslim) rites without drinking of alcohol either on the date of his death, burial or the prayer of the eighth day.[1347] The Lagos Wills Law recognises polygyny and provides for variation of a Will to accommodate financial provision for dependants.

1538. At the High Court, it was agreed that the testator was a Muslim and could only have his estate distributed in accordance with the Wills laws of Kwara State and neither the Wills Law of Lagos State or the Wills Act, 1837 could save the Will. The High Court found that the Will dated 30 September 2002 purporting to be the Will of a Muslim, Alhaji Disu Ajibaiye, governed by Muslim personal law, disposing by Will all his property in accordance with the Wills Act, 1837 of England, is invalid, null and void having regards to section 4(1) of the Wills Law of Kwara State.

1539. At the Court of Appeal, affirming the judgment of the High Court, the court noted the misconception of the testator that he had a choice in the matter of a Will. Furthermore, despite the allegation of the appellants on how the testator had conducted his affairs prior to his death, had children out of wedlock, sold and consumed alcohol, the testator was a Muslim and had not renounced his faith. According to the Court of Appeal, to state otherwise, is 'merely splitting hairs' and making a 'distinction without a difference' and that if ' … the deceased … committed any wrong when he was alive … he can only be sanctioned by the law of his faith. It is not for the appellant or anyone to judge.'[1348]

1540. This decision changed the earlier position represented by *Apatira v. Akanke*[1349] on the place of the intention of the testator in determining choice of applicable law to a Will. In *Apatira*, a Muslim, male, made a Will in English form but the Will did not comply with all the requirements of the Wills Act 1837, although it appeared to have satisfied that of Islamic law, the court held that the testator made the Will with a clear intention that the Wills Act, 1837 should govern it and its validity therefore, fell to be determined under the Wills Act.

1541. It may also be worth noting that despite the customary norm that a married woman is the 'property' of her husband, and in spite of a marriage under that

1347. This is a special rite of burial by Muslims done on the 8th day after a person dies.
1348. [2007] All FWLR (part 359) 1321.
1349. [1994] 17 NLR 149; *see also Lawal Osula v. Lawal Osula* [1995] 10 SCNJ, 84; [1995] 9 NWLR (part 419) 259.

norm, a married woman in Nigeria by virtue of the fundamental human rights provisions of the Constitution can write a Will. In *Oke v. Oke*,[1350] a husband was held incapable of devising a house built on a family land given to his wife by her own family.

1542. If the customary norm were to be taken to a theoretical conclusion, then once the property became *seised* of the wife, then the husband would be in a position to dispose of it, but this was not the case. The land was taken to remain the property of the wife's maiden family and by the principle of *quicquid plantatur solo cedit*, the land and the development thereon remained the property of the wife's maiden family.

1543. The customary law regime presents a discouragement to families in giving the best, for instance, valuable education, to female children.

1544. Wills making and their validity should be more contemporaneous by reappraising the subordination of one's Will to customary laws and other extraneous considerations. It is important to promote the culture of Will making. Aside from improving on the law, forms and procedural trajectories, it may be desirable to limit the appellate jurisdiction for probate matters to the Court of Appeal.

1545. Intestacy, drives a *dead hand society* which impacts such society in more ways than succession. Inevitably, the wealth generated remain in a few hands – the hands ruling the living from the grave. It is also riddled with strife, intrigues and rancour, leaving the deceased with very minimal or 'no say'. The prospects of such eventuality may also force some to fritter away their wealth in their lifetime in order to make it impossible for those whom they may not wish to benefit from their wealth, from doing so. Some other people may resort to the instrument of trust as a way of protecting prospective children 'wealth-fritterers' or 'meddling relations'. The disadvantage of trust is that it keeps the *settlor* on the edge.

1546. Testacy, on the other hand, obviates these outcomes by enhancing the capacity of a person to speak from death and have a say in what happens to one's wealth and indeed, physical remains. In so doing, the concept of Will impacts on the general consciousness and moral competence of the populace; promotes wealth redistribution and also ultimately, no matter how indirectly, impacts positively on the attitude of the living to acquisition and accumulation of things. In some other cases, individuals have used Wills to re-order their personal lives by making the contents known in their lifetime. This encouraged would be freeloaders and loafers to find and pursue meaningful pathways and some beneficiaries became carers if some happenstance rendered the potential testator incapacitated. It is thus important to stretch the elasticity of testamentary capacity without losing its vital synergy in a solemn act as Will making.

1350. [1974] 3 SC 1.

1547. In *Okelola v. Boyle* the Supreme Court giving a nod of validity to the 1972 Will undermines the testate succession principle that quite aside from the Will taking effect only on the death of the testator for the validity of the gifts, it is also the case to enable the testator to continue to adjust his Will to the changed circumstances of life. Such changed circumstances make it worthwhile knowing where the appellant was in the course of the two years when the testator had become paralysed and the circumstances that led to the making of a new Will. In addition, it would be interesting to know whether those circumstances ameliorated the formalities which ought to have been complied with. When this is addressed, then the question of the limits of compliance within the circumstances would be reached judiciously.

1548. *Idehen v. Idehen* presents a further compelling need to encourage, rather than discourage testate succession in Nigeria. In that case, the death of the first son of the deceased before his, was a tragedy. The testator's Will was a state of continuing assent to the place of the departed first son in his Will, expressed by vesting his *igiogbe* on his issues. It cannot be that the testator did not, being an influential Chief of the Kingdom, did not know of the customs. The emotional and factual rational that resulted in his action ought not to have been undermined and discountenanced.

1549. In *Occlestone v. Fullalove*,[1351] Sir James LJ states in a near regime:

> I must say that to me it appears a shocking and a perverse thing to say that religion, morality, or public policy compels the law to throw difficulties in the way of a man who is desirous of not committing posthumously a great crime, and who is desirous of making for his misconduct the best reparation he can both to society and to the unfortunate beings of whose existence he is the author. What would be the natural – I would almost say the illegitimate – feelings of a wretched being towards that law by which, and towards that religion and morality in the name of which, he finds himself deprived of the provision which his sire had carefully tried to make for him, and in consequence made, it may be, the inmate of a union workhouse, or a pariah outcast infesting in the public streets?

1550. This approach may have informed the provision of section 21 of the LSAEL which provides that in any disposition of property, the words 'die without issue' or 'die without leaving issue' or 'have no issue' or any other words which may import either a want or failure of his issue, shall be construed to mean a want or failure of issue in the lifetime or at the time of the death of such person and not an indefinite failure of the issue, unless a contrary intention shall appear by the Will.

1351. [1873] 9 Ch. 147.

II. Maintenance Provisions

1551. Some of the State Wills laws may, in line with the English Inheritance (Provisions for Family and Dependants) Act, 1975 provide for dependent relations. Section 2 of the Wills Law of Lagos and section 4 of Oyo States now contained such provisions by which spouses and children could apply for financial provision, if excluded from a Will of the Testator. Thus, a testator that makes a Will which leaves the surviving spouse (or other entitled dependent) without 'reasonable financial provision' falls into this category and provisions are made to protect such persons. The persons included are, the wife or wives or husband of the deceased; former wife or husband who has not remarried and a child or children of the deceased.

1552. The same principles that guide application of the English provisions are envisaged. The English Act confers wide powers on the Probate Court aimed at improving provision for a surviving spouse and extends to all children of the deceased, together with non-relatives who were treated as part of the family or else were dependent on the deceased. It also covers the powers of the courts to make orders. The Court, nevertheless, must act sensibly in making provisions for applicants who had some sort of moral claim or some other reason to be maintained by the deceased beyond the mere fact of a blood relationship, and for whom, the deceased had failed to provide.

§9. Interpretation of a Will

1553. The first duty of a Court of probate is to determine what Will or even what clauses of a Will are to be admitted to probate. Once that has been determined the Court is then concerned with the interpretation of a Will that has become contentious.

1554. In construing a Will, the objective must turn on endeavouring to ascertain the testator's intention from the words he has used, in the light of such knowledge of relevant facts as may be available that he must have had.[1352] The Will must have been executed with testamentary intent and capacity. Absence of fraud, duress, undue influence, or mistake must be established.

1555. In *Okelola v. Boyle* the Supreme Court considered section 17 of the Wills law of Lagos State and stated that the 1972 Will should have been interpreted in the light of that section which provides that a Will shall be construed, with reference to the property comprised in it, to speak and take effect as if it had been executed immediately before the death of the testator unless a contrary intention appears in the Will.

1352. *Osoba v. Osoba & Ors* [1978] EWCA Civ 3, 1,4; [1979] 2 All ER 393; [1979] WLR 247; [1979] 1 WLR 247.

§10. Admitting a Will to Probate

1556. Probate is the judicial process by which a Will is considered for validity and general administration of a deceased person's estate determined. The process and procedure for admitting a Will to probate are drawn from the Civil Procedure Rules of the High Courts of the States and that of the FCT. They are all similarly premised. Lagos State High Court Civil Procedure Rules, 2012 is a typical form and is adopted in the following analysis on the rules of court as they apply to Will. This part of the discussion deals with the principles as applicable to probate of Wills, while the practice is dealt with under acquisition and administration of the estate.

1557. Section 59 of the Lagos State Administration of Estates Law, confers power to make rules in relation to administration of estates on the Chief Judge. Thus, Rules of Court made under the High Court Law, with respect to the grant of probate or administration and the administration of estates, to the extent they are not inconsistent with the Law, have effect as if made under the Law.

1558. Probate also means to prove. It provides the avenue for a court to consider and determine that the Will of a testator is authentic in common or solemn form. Where the Will is duly executed, and without issues, the court grants probate in common form. A probate in common form, will usually be the case where the testator's Will is on a monogamous family. This is known as non-contentious probate. The commencement of a Probate action whether or not any caveat has been entered, operates to prevent the sealing of a grant until application for a grant is made by the person shown to be entitled thereto by the decision of the judge in such action.

1559. The Rules provide guidance on how a Probate judge should proceed in Orders 57, 58 and 60. Order 58 is the specific order for grant of probate or administration, with Will attached. When a testator fully disposes of the estate by Will and the Will is dully executed, the executors apply for probate, a grant of which, legitimises and facilitates the distribution of the estate according to the Will. However, when a testator's Will does not provide for executors, or when the executors appointed by the Will cannot act or renounces executorship, then the court appoints administrators who acts as executors appointed under the Will. Administration could also arise where there is a Will in the custody of a corporation sole which applies and is granted administration of the estate of the deceased.

1560. By Order 58, rules 4–12, the judge has wide powers in relation to whether or not to uphold a Will and admit or not admit it to probate. Once doubts on the authenticity of the Will are found, then the judge must invite the executors or, the executors on their own initiative (who wish to be cautious) to prove the Will in solemn form. This procedure must be done in open court with all interested persons summoned to be present. The probate is then granted at the end of the proceedings, if favourable, in solemn form. This is known as contentious probate, granted in solemn form. Some of the issues that could lead to a contentious probate are the Will is contested and a caveat is entered or the executors renounce probate.

1561. A Will may be contested as to form or substance. Where the form is contested the issues will arise as to due execution, attestation, dating etc. but when the substance of the Will is contested, the issues that arise may relate to testamentary capacity, undue influence, and limitation by law.

I. Guidelines for the Judge

1562. The Court has power to require information on all persons closely related to the probate. Thus, where it has information upon an ex parte application, that any paper of the deceased, being or purporting to be testamentary is in the possession or under the control of any person, the Court may order that the paper be produced and brought before the court. This exercise of discretion may be prior to, or in, the course of proceeding in respect of probate or administration. In this connection, it is to be noted that there is a provision in the Criminal Law of Lagos State related to Wills. Section 289 of the Lagos State Criminal Code Law provides penalty for concealing of Wills. Any person who with intent to defraud, conceals any testamentary document, whether the testator is living or dead commits a felony and is liable on conviction to imprisonment for fourteen years.

1563. Further exercises of discretion avail the probate judge. To provide assurance on validity, terms, condition or date of execution of the Will, every Will in respect of which an application for a grant is made must be submitted to probate, along with an affidavit. The affidavit must be marked by the signatures of the applicant and the person before whom the oath in relation to the application is sworn. The judge may exercise a discretion on the attachment of the Will to the affidavit, so where the attachment of a Will to the affidavit for probate, might result in the loss of the Will, the judge may allow a photocopy to be marked or exhibited in lieu of the original document.

1564. On receiving an application for Administration with Will attached, a judge is required to inspect the Will, and determine the validity of the Will. The judge is to assess whether the requirements of signature by the testator and subscribing by two witnesses are met. If the judge determines that the Will does not appear to be so signed and subscribed, then the admission of the Will to probate or administration, ceases at this point. However, if the judge determines otherwise, and that the Will appears to be so signed and subscribed, the judge then proceeds to the next stage – the attestation clause to determine whether the wording of the attestation does indicate that the Will has in fact, been executed in accordance with the relevant enactments, in this case, the Wills Law of Lagos State. The attestation clause does not need to be in any special words but must be an aspect of the Will, by which witnesses attest to the signature of the testator, in their presence, as the maker of the content of the Will.

1565. Order 58, rule 5(1), stipulates exceptions to what could otherwise lead to the invalidity of the Will. Thus, where a Will contains no attestation clause or the attestation clause is insufficient or where it appears to the judge that there is some doubt about the due execution of the Will, the court can exercise a discretion requiring an Affidavit to be sworn to the due execution of the Will. This should be from one or more of the attesting witnesses or, if no attesting witness is conveniently available, from any other person who was present at the time the Will was executed. Where this is satisfactorily done, then the Will may be considered for admission to probate. In furtherance of the general principle that it is in the interest of law that a Will is validated than it fails, rule 5(2) provides a further window. The judge is empowered to accept evidence on affidavit from any person who may satisfactorily show that the signature on the Will is the handwriting of the deceased, or of any other matter which may raise a presumption in favour of the due execution of the Will. Thus, suppose that both subscribing witnesses are dead or, from other circumstances, an affidavit cannot be obtained from either of them, resort is then to be had to an affidavit sworn to, by other persons present at the execution of the Will. Furthermore, if no such affidavit can be obtained, proof shall be required of the fact of these prevailing circumstances – the handwriting of the deceased, the subscribing witnesses, and also of any circumstances raising a presumption in favour of the due execution of the Will.

1566. Where the Testator was blind or illiterate, the judge shall not grant administration with the Will attached, unless the judge is first satisfied, by proof or by what appears on the face of the Will, that the Will was read over to the deceased before its execution or that he had at that time knowledge of its contents.

II. Order of Priority to Grant of Probate and Administration with Will Attached

1567. The order of priority for the grant of probate is as follows:

(i) the Executor;
(ii) any residuary legatee or devisee holding in trust for any other person;
(iii) any residuary legatee or devisee for life;
(iv) the ultimate residuary legatee or devisee, including one entitled on the happening of any contingency or where the residue is not wholly disposed of by the Will, any person entitled to share in the residue not so disposed of, or the personal representative of any such person.

1568. However, the residuary legatee or devisee whose legacy or devise is vested in interest shall be preferred to one entitled on the happening of a contingency, and where the residue is not in terms wholly disposed of, the judge may, if he is satisfied that the testator has nevertheless disposed of the whole or substantially the whole of the estate as ascertained at the time of the application for the grant, allow a grant to be made (subject to Order 57, rule 15[1353] of the Rules), to any legatee or devisee entitled to, or to a share in the estate so disposed of, without regard to the persons entitled to share in any residue not disposed of by the Will.

1569. The next order of priority is as follows:

(i) any specific legatee or devisee or any creditor or, subject to Order 59, rule 14 sub-rule (3),[1354] the personal representative of any such person or where the estate is not wholly disposed of by Will, any person who, notwithstanding that the amount of the estate is such that he has no immediate beneficial interest therein, may have a beneficial interest in the event of an accretion or increase to it;
(ii) any specific legatee or devisee entitled on the happening of any contingency, or any person having no interest under the Will who would have been entitled to a grant, if the deceased had died wholly intestate;
(iii) when the beneficial interest in the whole estate of the deceased is vested absolutely in a person who has renounced his right to a grant of administration with the Will attached and has consented to such administration being granted to the person or persons who would be entitled to his own estate if he himself had died intestate, administration may be granted to such person or one or more but not exceeding four of such persons.

1570. On iii, a surviving spouse is not regarded as a person in whom the estate has vested absolutely unless he or she would be entitled to the whole of the estate, whatever its value may be.

III. Executorship

1571. The executors appointed in the Will are to apply for probate or renounce executorship. The judge may on the application of any person claiming an interest under a Will, give notice to the Executors therein named, to come in and prove the Will, or to renounce Probate, and they, or some or one of them, shall within twenty-one days after notice, come in and prove or renounce accordingly.[1355] An executor can renounce a Will by signing a renunciation witnessed by a disinterested person in the Will.

1572. Persons entitled to the estate of the deceased under a Will may have assigned their whole interest in the estate to one or more persons. The Rules stipulate that in the absence of a proving Executor, the assignee or assignees shall

1353. Order 57, rule 15 requires that where the State is or may be beneficially interested in the estate of a deceased person, notice of intended application for a grant shall be given by the Applicant to the Lagos State Attorney General and the Judge may direct that no grant shall issue within a specified time after the notice has been given.
1354. Order 59, sub-rule 14 (c)exempts a Trust Corporation from having to seek the leave of court or to be joined by application, with a person entitled to grant of administration.
1355. Order 58, rule 18.

replace, in order of priority for a grant of probate, the assignor or, in the case of more than one assignor, the assignor with the highest priority. Furthermore, on proof of the Will, probate may be granted, where there is more than one assignee, on the consent of the other or others, to any one or more of the assignees, but not exceeding four. Furthermore, where a minor who is sole Executor has no interest in the residuary estate of the deceased, administration with the Will attached for the use and benefit of the minor until he attains the age of 18 years shall, unless the judge otherwise directs, be granted to the person entitled to the residuary estate. A minor's right to administration may be renounced only by a person assigned as a Guardian as stipulated and authorised to renounce by the judge.

1573. The office of executors derives from the testator's Will. The grant of probate confirms their authority to act and the estate vests in them from the death of the testator. Nevertheless, executors act as officers of the court, deriving their ultimate authority from court and not necessarily from the Will appointing them. They act in a fiduciary capacity for the testator as well as the estate beneficiaries. Thus by Order 57, rule 16, 'every person to whom a grant of Probate or Letters of Administration shall have been made and every Administrator appointed by the judge shall, file in Court the accounts of his Administration every twelve (12) months from the date of the grant or the appointment until the completion of the administration'.

1574. Where a person appointed as an executor in a Will, survives the testator but either dies having appeared to prove the Will but not having taken out probate or, fails to appear, having been called on by the Court to take Probate, the right of the person in respect of the executorship wholly ceases making renunciation of executorship unnecessary. The estate in these circumstances will be administered as if, that executor had not been appointed executor.[1356]

1575. The court is empowered to hold an executor liable for contempt of court, to pay a fine, as well as, other discretionary penalties for taking possession and administering or otherwise dealing in any part of the property of the deceased, without applying for Probate within three months of the testator's death. The same consequence arises where there has been a dispute and after the termination of a suit in respect of such dispute for probate or administration, the executor deals in the estate without applying for and obtaining a grant of probate.

1576. An executor can renounce probate but by rule 25, renunciation of probate by an executor does not operate as renunciation of any right which he may have to a grant of administration in some other capacity unless he expressly renounces that right as well. To obtain a grant in that other capacity, however, requires the direction of the judge, since, unless the judge otherwise directs, no person who has renounced a grant in one capacity may obtain a grant in some other capacity. It is also noteworthy, that a renunciation of probate or administration may be retracted at any time on the order of the judge in so far as, probate has not been granted to another person entitled in a lower capacity. It is only in exceptional circumstances

1356. Order 58, rule 13, High Court of Lagos Civil Procedure Rules.

that leave may be given to an executor to retract a renunciation of Probate after a grant has been made to another person entitled in a lower degree.

1577. By Order 57, rule 13, where one of several Executors is a minor, probate may be granted to the adult executors, with power reserved for making the like grant to the minor on his attaining the age of 18 years. Whereas, administration for the use and benefit of the minor until he attains the age of 18 years may be granted to parents or guardians only if the adult Executors renounce or, on being cited to accept or refuse a grant, fail to make an effective application. Furthermore, a minor Executor's right to probate on attaining the age of 18 years shall not be renounced by any person on his behalf.

IV. Citation

1578. A citation is a writ commonly used in probate courts for the purpose of commanding the cite to appear at a specified time and to do the act named or show cause why he should not do so. The process is analogous to a summons. It is issued under the seal of the Probate Court. In such application, the person making the citation is the citor while the person being required to take steps to apply for a grant is the citee. A citation is used in non-contentious probate matters and may be to make a person accept or refuse a grant; take probate or propound a Will. A caveat must be entered by the Citor before a citation is issued. Order 58, rule 27 covers the steps to be taken.

1579. The Registrar is to settle every citation before one is issued. Every averment in a citation and such other information as the Registrar may require shall be verified by an affidavit sworn to by the person issuing the citation. The Registrar may in special circumstances accept an affidavit sworn to by the citor's legal practitioner.

1580. A citation to take a grant cannot be issued while proceedings as to the validity of the Will are pending. A citation calling on an Executor who has intermeddled in the estate of the deceased to show cause why he should not be ordered to take a grant may be issued at the instance of any person interested in the estate at any time after the expiration of six months from the death of the deceased.

1581. Under the rules, there are two instances where citation can be issued with regards to the conduct of executors or to propound the Will. It is provided that citation should be made where there is a Will and the executor either renounces or delays to take the necessary grant or probate. The nearest person entitled to the estate may then apply for a citation. Another instance involving the executor is where power is reserved to an executor, a citation can be issued at the instance of the remaining executors or the executors of the last surviving person to the deceased.[1357] Order 58, rule 28 covers the instances and steps required. A citation to propound a Will is directed to the executors named in the Will and to all persons who have an interest under the Will. To qualify as citor, in this instance a person must have an interest contrary to that of the Executors and such other persons that may have had interests under the Will. Order 58, rule 29 covers the instances and steps to be taken in this regard.

1582. The judge has wide discretion. Thus, notices in the nature of citation shall be given in such manner as the judge directs. The citation shall be served personally on the person cited unless a judge, on cause shown by affidavit, directs some other mode of service which may include notice by advertisement. The Will referred to in a citation must be lodged in the Registry before the citation is issued, except where the Will is not in the Citor's possession and the judge is satisfied that it is not practicable to require it to be lodged.

1583. In general, a person who has been cited to appear may, within eight days of service of the citation upon him or at any time thereafter, if no application has been made by the Citor, for the grant to be made to him instead, enter an appearance in the Registry by filing Probate Form 6 on caveat and making an entry in the appropriate book, and shall thereafter serve on the Citor a copy of Form 5 – (a notice of Warning to caveator) sealed with the seal of the Registry.[1358]

1584. Under Order 28 that is with respect of a citation to accept or refuse a grant, a person cited who is willing to accept or take a grant may apply ex parte to the judge for an Order for a grant on filing an affidavit showing that he has entered an appearance and that he has not been served by the citor with notice of any application for a grant to himself.

1585. Where the citee fails to take the steps, on propounding the Will, the door opens for the citor to apply for the grant, instead. When the time limited for appearance has expired, the citor may, apply to be granted the probate in two scenarios. Where no person cited has entered an appearance, the citor may apply to the judge for an Order to be granted the probate as if the Will were invalid. Such an application must be supported by an affidavit showing that the citation was duly served on all persons interested in the estate. Second, in the case where a person who has not entered an appearance proceeds with reasonable diligence to propound the Will, the citor may apply to a judge by summons to be granted the probate instead. The citation in this case must be served on every person earlier cited who had entered an appearance.

1586. In the case of a citation calling on an Executor who has intermeddled in the estate of the deceased, a citor can apply to the judge by summons for an Order

1357. Order 28, rule 2. Power reserved occurs where there is more than one executor, if one of the executors does not want to act, such an executor can have power reserved such that he needs not take an active role in the administration of the estate.

1358. Order 27, rule 7.

served on the person cited, requiring such person to take a grant within a specified time; or for a grant to be made to the citor or some other person so specified in the Summons. However, any application along these lines must be supported by an affidavit showing that the citation was duly served and that the person cited has not entered an appearance. In addition, in the case of a citation in relation to power reserved, the remaining executors can apply to the judge for an order that a note be made on the grant, that the Executor in respect of whom power was reserved has been duly cited, did not appear and that all rights or interest in respect thereof have ceased.

V. Probate Caveat

1587. A probate caveat is a document seeking to prevent a grant of probate or administration to executors or named persons. It must be completed in the proper format and filed in the probate court registry. Section 21 of the LSAEL provides for caveats to be lodged where necessary.[1359]

1588. Order 59, rule 18 provides for caveat and its processes. The purpose of a caveat is to ensure that no grant, whether with Will annexed or not, is sealed, without notice to, and actively engaging the person who placed the caveat referred to as the caveator. There are four notable formats in relation to caveat, the notice by a caveator – this is to be done in Probate Form 3. The second format is in Probate Form 4, when a caveat is entered by a legal practitioner on behalf of a caveator. The third is Probate Form 5 which is completed by someone who has an interest in the estate of the deceased different from that of the caveator as a warning to a caveator. Finally, there is Probate Form 6, when attendance of a caveator or citor is required in response to a warning.

1589. A notice in the form of a caveat is filed at the Probate registry when necessary, to prohibit a grant of probate or issue of Letters of Administration. It could also be done by posting but at the risk of the caveator or a person warning. There is no specific time for a caveat to be entered, but bearing in mind that the rules provide that no caveat shall operate to prevent the sealing of a grant on the day on which the caveat is entered, the prospective caveator must be vigilant. The minimum time frame for the grant of administration provides a guide; with Will, is after fourteen days of application, and without a Will, twenty-one days. The caveat should therefore be entered soon enough, following the reading of the Will, or the advertisement of the court in a National Newspaper for administration.

1590. The process of entering a caveat is initiated by completing Probate Form 3 in the appropriate book at the Registry and obtaining an acknowledgement. A legal practitioner may enter a caveat on behalf of the caveator but the name of the caveator must be indicated with other particulars as in Probate Form 4. A caveat has a

1359. Section 17, Administration of Estates Act, 1991.

time frame of three months from the date it is entered but this is without prejudice to further or other caveats and whether there is a warning.

1591. The Registrar is to maintain a record of index of caveats and on receiving an application for a grant, the registrar has to search and cause a search to be made of this register and if a caveat exists notify the applicant. The Registrar must reject an application if a caveat exists.

1592. A person with a contrary interest in the estate referred to as 'the person warning', can notify the registry in the proper form of interests in the estate. A warning in Probate Form 5 may then issue from the Registry to the caveator. The warning or its copy, must then be served on the caveator. The person warning may be claiming under a Will, in which case the notice must state the interest in, and date of the Will. The warning requires the caveator to provide in Probate Form 6, particulars of any contrary interest which the caveator may have in the estate of the deceased. In cases where the caveator does have an interest contrary to that of the person warning, then he or she, has eight days from proof of service to enter an appearance in the Registry by filing the duly completed Probate Form 6, sealed with the seal of the Registry and making an entry in the appropriate book.[1360] When there is notice of warning, the caveator is required to enter an appearance at the probate. Once a caveator has entered an appearance to a warning, such caveat shall remain in force until the commencement of a probate action.

1593. However, where the caveator fails to respond, the person warning is expected to file an affidavit in the Registry showing that the warning was duly served and that the caveator did not respond. Where the person warning files such affidavit and it is accepted, then the caveat ceases to be operative. Except with the leave of the judge, no further caveat may be entered by or on behalf of any caveator whose caveat has ceased to have effect.

1594. The caveator who has not entered an appearance to a warning may at any time withdraw the caveat. This is done by giving notice at the Registry whereupon, the caveat ceases to have effect. However, if a warning notice exists, then the caveator has a duty to also immediately notify the person warning of the withdrawal of the caveat.

1595. A caveator may not have an interest contrary to that of the person warning, but objects to the sealing of a grant to that person. In such a case, the caveator may issue and serve a notice before the Registrar stating such objections within eight days of service of the warning, or in the extended time, where an affidavit of 'no response' by the person warning has not been filed.

1596. If a claimant other than the caveator, proceeds to court in the matter of the estate, the Probate Registrar must, give notice of the commencement of the action

1360. The time frame for filing of Form 6, is extended where the person warning has yet to file the above affidavit indicating that the caveator has failed to respond to the warning.

to the caveator. Such duty remains upon the registrar with respect to any subsequent entry of a caveat at any time as long as the action is pending.

1597. All caveats and citations remain in force until the determination of the rightful person to apply for a grant by the court. The judge has a discretion which must be exercised judiciously.

VI. The Grant

1598. On the reading of the Will, it is mandatory for the judge to provide assurances that the seal was unbroken and only broken in the presence of the executors, beneficiary and named interested parties.

1599. The judge if, after these preliminary assessments and considering of the evidence, determines that the Will was not duly executed, Probate shall be refused and the Will marked as Probate refused. Where this is not the case, then the judge shall grant the probate with the Will annexed.

1600. No original Will shall be given out for any purpose without the direction in writing of a judge. On payment of the prescribed fee, a certified transcript under the seal of the Court of the probate or administration with the Will annexed may be obtained from the Court.

1601. Where the person to whom, a grant would otherwise be made is a minor, the Court has the power to issue a grant to a different person for his use and benefit until he attains the age of 18.[1361] The grant may be made to both parents of the minor jointly. It could also be made to any guardian appointed by a judge; in the absence of a guardian able and willing to act, and the minor has attained the age of 16 years, to some kin nominated by the minor. Where the minor is a married woman, the grant may be made to any next-of-kin or to her spouse if nominated by her.

1602. However, it is to be noted that section 29 of the LSAEL prescribes infancy as under 21. Thus, section 29, on administration during minority of executor, requires that where an infant is sole executor of a Will, administration with the Will annexed shall be granted to his guardian, or to such other person as the court thinks fit, until the infant attains the age of 21 years, and on his attaining that age and not before, probate of the Will may be granted to him. Furthermore, where a testator by his Will appoints an infant to be an executor the appointment shall not operate to transfer any interest in the property of the deceased to the infant, or to constitute him a personal representative for any purpose unless and until probate is granted to him under this section.

1361. Order 57, rule 12 of the Lagos Civil Procedure Rules.

1603. It must be taken that the law prevails over the rules where there is a conflict, thus, the age of 21 must be the age of majority for this purpose until the conflict is formally resolved.

VII. Resealing

1604. Order 28, rule 26 authorises resealing. The Registrar of the court to which the application for resealing is made must send notice of the resealing to the Court which made the grant.

1605. An application for the resealing of probate or administration with Will attached, which was granted by a court outside Lagos State is required to be made by the person to whom the probate or administration was originally granted or by any person authorised in writing to apply on behalf of such a person. A limited or temporary grant can only be resealed by leave of the court. Every grant lodged for resealing must have attached, a copy of any Will to which the grant relates or its Certified True Copy by the authority of the Court that originally made the grant was made.

1606. Unless the court grants leave, a grant shall not be resealed unless it was made to such a person as is mentioned in paragraph (a) or (b) of Order 57, rule 10 sub-rule (1) or to a person to whom a grant could be made under Order 57, rule 10 sub-rule (2).[1362]

1607. Where the Registry receives notice from outside the State of the resealing of a grant that was made in the State, then the resealing court must be notified of any amendment or revocation in respect of the grant.

1608. The requirements for the application of resealing are:

(i) Tax Clearance Certificate.
(ii) Advertisement of the application as directed by the judge, supported by an oath.
(iii) Bonds, sureties are required except where it appears that the grant does not necessitate urgency as mentioned in paragraphs (a) to (f) of Order 59, rule 4 sub-rule (1), such as to a creditor or the personal representative of a creditor or to a person who has no immediate beneficial interest in the estate of the deceased but may have such an interest in the event of an accretion or increase to the estate.

1362. By Order 59, sub-rule 10(2) (2) where no Order has been made as stated specifically with respect to the above, then to the Executor named in the Will if the Will is written in English or in an indigenous language; and where the Will describes the duties of a named person in terms sufficient to constitute him, an Executor according to the tenor of the Will, to that person or, where the whole of the estate in the State consists of immovable property, then a grant limited to those immovable property may be made in accordance with the law that would have been applicable, if, the deceased had died domiciled in the State.

1609. Bonds and sureties may also be excepted where the applicant is the Administrator-General or a Trust Corporation.

Chapter 3. Acts *Inter Vivos* Related to the Estate

§1. Estate Planning

1610. Estate planning is the process of handling and managing one's affairs in life with death or possible incapacitation in mind. It is a prudent competence that determines how one's assets will be preserved, managed, and distributed after death or in the event of one's incapacitation. It is usually, a comprehensive plan that covers management of assets with documents that are effective during one's lifetime as well as other documents that are not in effect until death. Individuals have various reasons for planning an estate, such as preserving family wealth, providing for a surviving spouse and children, funding children's or grandchildren's education, or leaving their legacy behind to a charitable cause. Planning covers the devise and bequest of assets or funds to heirs and the settlement of estate taxes. Professionalism is necessary for estate planning if one must avoid pyrrhic polemics.

1611. The ultimate general goal of estate planning is to provide an orderly transition from life on earth to passing from earth. This general goal implicates a specific goal of ensuring that beneficiaries receive assets in dignity and one's life is a memorial of elegance. A further goal is to minimise estate tax, gift tax, income tax and other taxes. Various strategies can be used to limit taxes on an estate, from creating trusts to making charitable donations.

1612. The most basic step in estate planning involves writing a Will. A Will is a legal document that provides instructions on how an individual's property and custody of minor children, if any, should be handled after death. There are other identifiable estate planning tasks which extend to: appropriate ways of limiting estate taxes by setting up trust accounts; establishing a guardian for living dependents; creating or updating beneficiaries on plans such as life insurance and setting up funeral arrangements. Estate planning tasks may also involve establishing annual gifting to qualified charitable and non-profit organisations which may help reduce the taxable part of an estate.

1613. Assets that could make up an individual's estate include landed property such as houses. Other assets include cars, stocks, artwork, life insurance, pensions, and debt.

1614. In Nigeria, estate planning is unpopular because of customs and Sharia law. However, a few persons engage estate planning by executing Wills and, a limited number through Trusts.

§2. Donations

1615. A donation is a gift for charity, humanitarian aid, or to benefit a cause. Donations are usually given by people who really want to help someone in need. Usually, it comes in forms of cash, services, and goods like clothing, food, toys, and even vehicles. A donation may satisfy medical needs such as blood or organs for transplant. When the donation is from a Charity, it is sometimes referred to as gifts in kind. It differs from a grant in that a grant would usually proceed from organised bodies who have set criteria for approving the grants. A grant is also usually purpose specific while donations may be used in exercise of discretion. It differs from a trust essentially in that a trust allows a settlor reasonable control of use and beneficiary while a donation is more ambulatory and allows the done reasonable exercise of discretion.

1616. The person or institution giving a gift is called the donor, and the person or institution getting the gift is called the done. A variant of donation is the donation *mortis causa* sometimes also classified as a Trust rather than donation.

1617. Donations are legally structured that their perfection is not dependent on consideration but must be accepted by the donee. Thus, it is only when the donation is made in fact, that it acquires legal status as a transfer or property. At common law, an agreement to donate is treated as an imperfect contract void for want of consideration which neither a court of law nor equity can enforce.

1618. With respect to donations for political objectives, the law of some countries may prohibit or restrict the extent to which politicians may accept gifts or donations of large sums of money, especially from business or lobby groups. No such law exists in Nigeria. Donations, when made to a qualified non-profit charitable, religious, educational, or public service organisation may be deductible as a contribution in the calculation of income tax. In such cases, the state's tax revenue is affected, requiring that the state (and the public in general) pay attention where possible, in ensuring that the taxable funds are judiciously used.

§3. Trusts

1619. Trusts are created to preserve or generate wealth or both, whether they are family trusts providing alternatives to the law of succession, or commercial trusts, furthering financial interests and options in the financial world.[1363] As has been overly noted: 'of all the exploits of equity, the largest and most important is the invention and development of the Trust. It is an "institute" of great elasticity and generality; as elastic, as general as contract. This perhaps forms the most distinctive achievement of English lawyers. It seems to us almost essential to civilization, and yet there is nothing quite like it in foreign law'.[1364]

1620. Trust developed with a distinctive feature of the beneficial interest under the concept being imbued with incidents of property rights, which, continue to engage the attention of scholars and practitioners. Emerging to cater for the social

1363. Elizabeth Cooke & Hayton David, *Land Law and Trusts*, in *Laws Futures* Ch. 22 (David Hayton ed. Oxford 2000).
1364. F.W. Maitland, *Lectures on Equity* Ch. III, 22.

exigencies of the thirteenth century England, on family and personal property affairs in a solo sense, the unique success of the trust concept since its maiden debut has given natural vent to its enormous potentials in the world of commerce both at municipal and international levels.

1621. The basic advantage and attraction of the trust is the office of the trustee.[1365] In the development of the trust institution, extreme care has been paid to this office. The trustee is separate from the trust property and is virtually independent of the settlor and beneficiary although responsible and accountable to the office and in effect, to both beneficiary and settlor. As a result of this separateness, scrutiny and monitoring is possible and effective. The trustee has the legal estate of the property while the beneficiary has the equitable estate. Once constituted the settlor cannot reverse the trust unless there is clear provision in the trust instrument to that end.

1622. The further versatility of trust is that the settlor while he is unable to benefit as of right from a trust arrangement can do so if, he has expressly provided for it or the law draws a presumption or an implication as in resulting and constructive trusts respectively. A trustee could also be a beneficiary of a trust subject to the general rules on the fiduciary nature of the trustee's duties.

1623. The legal term 'trust' draws from its ordinary connotation. It is a relationship of trust created either expressly or by necessary presumptions or implications whereby a party known as the settlor divests or is by law divested of control over a particular item of property. The property then legally vests in another party known as the trustee, who holds same in trust for a beneficiary. It thereby creates the triangular magic by which neither the settlor, nor the trustee benefits as of right from the property which is the subject matter of the trust but the property stands for the use of the beneficiary.

1624. The most common tool of *inter vivos* transfer of property in Nigeria is trusts or donations. If these two forms of disposition are used, then the documents must be perfected in one's lifetime using transfers in the manner appropriate to the gift or donation. Many Trust companies usually, subsidiary of banks have sprung up for administration and management of private trusts. The use of Special Purpose Vehicles is also emerging for the purpose of estate planning. Charitable Trusts are also important and operate in Nigeria, usually as incorporated trusts. There is also Office of the Public Trustee which is invariably always a part of the Ministry of Justice of each State of the Federation. The trust from its humble beginnings in *uses* and the Statute of Charitable Uses 1601, has gained considerable global relevance.[1366] As a result of her relationship with English jurisprudence, it may be worth mentioning The Hague Convention on Trust.

1365. David Hayton, *The Irreducible Core Content of Trusteeship*, in *Trends in Contemporary Trust Law* 47 (A.J. Oakley ed., Clarendon Press 1996).

1366. David Hayton, *Developing the Law of Trusts for the Twenty-First Century*, 106 L.Q.R. 87 (1990); F.W. Maitland, supra n. 1364.

1625. The Hague Convention on the Law Applicable to Trusts and on their Recognition, or Hague Trust Convention[1367] is a multilateral treaty that applies to trusts with the main objective of harmonising the understanding and recognition of trust. It applies to only countries that are signatories to the Convention. The Convention applies to only express trust with a view to resolving conflict of law issues that may arise from cross-border trusts.

1626. A private trust, once properly created or constituted, is stamped at the relevant Ministry of Internal Revenue Services, usually at nominal value. Where the trust is connected with an incorporated Company, then it requires registration at the Federal Corporate Affairs Commission with head office in Abuja, the FCT. There are also offices of the Commission in the capital of each State of the Federation.

I. Testamentary Trusts

1627. A Will may create a trust; the trust could be express or secret. Implied trusts could also arise testamentary, because of unwilled residue of the estate of the deceased or the conduct of the personal representatives. In intestate administration, the residue of the proceeds of sale of items of the estate, any investments for the time being representing the same, including any part of the estate of the deceased which may be retained unsold and is not required for the administration, is in Law referred to as 'the residuary estate of the intestate'.

1628. Testamentary trusts that are express are usually created by the testator-settlor for the better management of the estate or to cater for children who are minor or physically challenged individuals. A personal representative may be a trustee where the Will states so specifically, but the personal representative is always a trustee for sale, with conversion of real and personal property where the person died intestate but subject to the provisions contained in the Will, if there is one.[1368]

II. Charitable Trust

1629. Laws in relation to trusts in Nigeria are based mainly on the pre-1900 received English Laws on the subject.[1369] Charitable Trusts require incorporation as an Incorporated Trust with the Corporate Affairs Commission. This is required by the Companies and Allied Matters Act, 2020. The nature of investments which Trustees can make include Securities issued by or on behalf of the Federal Government; regional governments (now State Governments) or Statutory Companies, as listed in the First Schedule to the Government and other Securities (Local Trustees'

1367. Signed 1 Jul. 1985, entered into force 1 Jan. 1992, and as of September 2017 ratified by fourteen countries available at: https://en.wikipedia.org/wiki/Hague_Trust_Convention (last retrieved 3 Sep. 2020).
1368. Section 37 LSAESL and 33 AEA.
1369. The Trustee Act, 1893 is applicable by virtue of the pre 1900 received English Laws.

Powers) Act, 1957. This position has been improved and now trustees can invest in equities and debentures of public Companies in line with the supplementary Statute, the Trustee Investments Act, 1962.[1370]

1630. In *Income Tax Special Commissioners v. Pemsel,*[1371] the House was asked whether, in a taxing statute applying to the whole of the United Kingdom and allowing for deductions from and allowances against the income of land vested in trustees for charitable purposes, the words 'charitable purposes' should be understood according to their meaning in English law, or whether they should be given a meaning which was common to the law of England, Scotland and Ireland. The House held, providing the impetus for order in the relationship between charities and the State, that the deduction should be allowed. Lord Macnaghten made his now famous statement:

> Charity in its legal sense comprises four principal divisions: trusts for the relief of poverty; trusts for the advancement of education; trusts for the advancement of religion; and trusts for other purposes beneficial to the community, not falling under any of the preceding heads. The trusts last referred to are not the less charitable in the eye of the law, because incidentally they benefit the rich as well as the poor, as indeed, every charity that deserves the name must do either directly or indirectly.

1631. The list of what qualifies as charitable is endless and coherence was and remains somewhat difficult. In principle, trusts cannot be set up to benefit a purpose. The fundamental reason for this, is, there is no person with legal standing to enforce the trust. A purpose is not a person; only a person can get the ear of the court. The maxim, equity does not act in vain is apposite. In *Re Astor's Settlement Trusts,*[1372] the testator, Waldorf Astor, had set up a trust in his Will for 'the maintenance ... of good understanding between nations' and 'the preservation of the independence and integrity of newspapers' with money from the shares he owned in his newspaper *The Observer*. On challenge of the trust as one for an abstract purpose, it was held; the trust failed for lack of beneficiaries. In the judgment the court stated:

> But if the purposes are not charitable, great difficulties arise both in theory and in practice. In theory, because having regard to the historical origins of equity it is difficult to visualise the growth of equitable obligations which nobody can enforce, and in practice, because it is not possible to contemplate with equanimity the creation of large funds devoted to non-charitable purposes which no court and no department of state can control, or in the case of maladministration reform ... A court of equity does not recognize as valid a trust which it cannot both enforce and control ....[1373]

1370. The two Acts are now in the 2004 Compilation of the Laws of the Federation as Cap T22
1371. [1891] AC 531; [1891] HL 20. *See also In re Macduff, Macduff v. Macduff* [1896] 2 Ch. 451.
1372. [1952] Ch. 534.
1373. [1952] Chs 534, 541–542; 549.

1632. In *James Egubson v. Joseph Ikechukwu*[1374] the second main issue before the Supreme Court of Nigeria is the power of the court to remove a trustee of an incorporated association and appoint a new one by virtue of the Land (Perpetual Succession) Act. The Supreme Court referring to *Jubril Martins v. Saka Tinubu & Ors*,[1375] noted that only the body issuing the certificate therewith could exercise … such powers.[1376] Also referring to *Glover v. Giles*[1377] with approval the Court stated:

> As a general proposition of law the court has no power to declare void a certificate of incorporation issued by a Minister of State or Commissioner or Registrar as duly incorporating an institution under the provisions of a statute. That was the view long ago expressed by the Court in England in *Glover v. Giles.*[1378] Therefore, the question which the court had to determine is whether the incorporating can be declared void on the ground of irregularity. The Court said it had no such powers conferred upon it.[1379]
>
> On examination of the relevant sections 2(3) and section (1) of the Land (Perpetual Succession) Act and the two judicial authorities (referred to above) the Supreme Court concluded that had the High Court appointed the plaintiffs, as trustees in place of the defendant, it would have been an incompetent exercise of jurisdiction in the matter, especially as the corporation itself is not a party to the proceedings.

1374. [1977] ALL NLR 194; [1976] 6 SC 1; [1977] LPELR-SC. 183/1975.
1375. 13 N.L.R 124.
1376. The plaintiffs had applied for a new certificate to have the plaintiffs replace the defendant as trustees of the Church on ground that the original certificate was lost. However, the High Court found that the original certificate was not lost. The Commissioner for the Land (Perpetual Succession), of the Ministry of Internal Affairs had issued a new certificate but on receipt of better particulars and information withdrew the certificate as having been obtained by misrepresentation. The defendants had then applied to the court to reinstate them as the recognised trustees, which the Court declined.
1377. [1881] 18 Ch. 173; 50 L.J. Ch. 568; 45 L.T. 344.
1378. [1881] 18 Ch. D. 173.
1379. [1881] 18 Ch. D.173, 179. The court stated: 'It appears to me clear that before the certificate was granted by the Registrar it was his duty to satisfy himself whether the application was made by authority of a general meeting of the society specially called for the purpose, and he was at liberty to require the person making the application to verify that authority by a statutory declaration, and upon this being done, and the certificate being granted according to the terms of the Act, the society became incorporated. Now, it is said, I can declare that incorporation to be void, on the ground that no proper meeting was held, and it is said that the meeting which was held on the 10th of April, 1879, was not a proper meeting within the meaning of the Act because it was not summoned in compliance with certain rules of the society with regard to the summoning of general meetings. In my view I have no power, to inquire into that at all, and I cannot declare the incorporation to be void. The incorporation of persons into bodies corporate is a prerogative of the Crown and, although in this case the prerogative is exercised under certain statutory provisions, the incorporation is none the less an exercise of the prerogative. There is a perfectly well-known method by which an incorporation may be recalled or made void.'

III. Private Trusts

1633. There are three types of private trusts known to English jurisprudence, the express, constructive and resulting. Express trust is more commonly used for formal transactions, with relations or Wills. Resulting trust is implied because it requires a distilling or deduction of an objective intention of the settlor.[1380] Constructive trusts are a construct from the circumstances surrounding the parties and the subject of the trust. Both resulting and constructive trusts usually arise in family and succession settings.

1634. Where the settlor acts intentionally, the trust could be express or resulting and the consequences matter. Where the trust takes effect by operation of law alone, and is constructive, it is important as it may not be validated as remedial. A court cannot declare a trust lightly. A court does not create a trust neither does it make an imperfect gift or donation of a trust. The leading case is *Milroy v.* Lord.[1381] The more recent case of *T. Choithram International SA v. Pagarani*[1382] is discussed below.

1635. When a trust is express, the terms of the trust are distillable from the trust itself; the instrument creating it if written or from the words if created orally.

1636. Resulting trusts are implied where property which ought to be is not properly disposed of. It means 'to spring back'. It arises in two ways: an automatic resulting trusts and presumed resulting trusts. The first is implied where there is a gap in the equitable title of property triggering the maxim 'equity abhors a vacuum'. A piece of property should have an owner. There are three clear instances where an automatic resulting trust can be implied. These are; upon the failure of an express trust; surplus property; or upon the dissolution of an unincorporated association. An example of the first is where a purported express trust fails for lack of objects and the subject matter of the trust results back to the estate of the deceased. An example of a presumed resulting trust is where a party advances money for the purchase of a property which was not a loan, and a resulting trust is said to arise for the party who provided the funds in the property purchased. *Kotoye v. Saraki*[1383] demonstrates a typical resulting trust.[1384] The circumstances in which property will become subject to a resulting trust were recently examined by the House of Lords in *Westdeutsche Landesbank Girozentrale v. Islington London Borough Council.*[1385]

1380. *Dyer v. Dyer* [1788] 2 Cox Eq Cas 92; [1788] EWHC Exch J8; 30 ER 42.

1381. [1862] 4 De GF and J 264, [1862] EWHC Ch J78, [1862] EngR 951, [1862] 45 ER 1185; *Re Rose* [1952] Ch. 499; M*ascall v. Mascall* [1984] 50 P and CR 119, [1984] EWCA Civ 10; *T. Choithram International SA v. Pagarani* [2000] UKPC 46, 1 WLR 1, 2 All ER 492.

1382. [2000] UKPC 46, 1 WLR 1, 2 All ER 492.

1383. [1994] 7 NWLR (Part 357) 414.

1384. [1994] JELR 18873 (SC); Other useful cases are: *Re Vandervell's Trust* (No. 2) [1974] Ch. 269; *Goodman v. Gallant* [1986] Fam. 106; *Gissing v. Gissing* [1971] 1 A.C 886; *Twinsectra Ltd v. Yardley and Others* [2002] UKHL 12; [2002] 2 A.C. 164.

1385. [1996] AC 669.

The House identified two sets of circumstances. The first is where A makes a voluntary payment to B or pays (wholly or in part) for the purchase of property which is vested either in B alone or in the joint names of A and B, there is a presumption that A did not intend to make a gift to B; the money or property is held on trust for A (if he is the sole provider of the money) or in the case of a joint purchase by A and B in shares proportionate to their contributions. It is important to stress that this is only a presumption, which presumption is easily rebutted either by the counter presumption of advancement or by direct evidence of A's intention to make an outright transfer. The other instance is where A, transfers property to B on express trusts, but the trusts declared do not exhaust the whole beneficial interest. It is clear too that gifts which fail in Will have the same result.

1637. An example of constructive trust is where a trustee makes a profit for himself from his position as trustee. The most popular case on this point is *Keech v. Sandford.*[1386] In that case, the trustee was totally honest but the Court held, nevertheless, that receiving a profit from a trust relationship is not in line with principle. Lord Browne –Wilkinson restated the basis for constructive trust in *Westdeutsche Landesbank v. Islington*:[1387] 'Equity operates on the conscience of the owner of the legal interest. In the case of a trust, the conscience of the legal owner requires him to carry out the purposes for which the property was vested in him (express or implied trust) or which the law imposes on him by reason of his unconscionable conduct (constructive trust).' Other highlights of the judgment are:

(i) Since the equitable jurisdiction to enforce trusts depends upon the conscience of the holder of the legal interest being affected, he cannot be a trustee of the property if and so long as he is ignorant of the facts alleged to affect his conscience.
(ii) In order to establish a trust, there must be identifiable trust property.
(iii) Once a trust is established, as from the date of its establishment the beneficiary has, in equity, a proprietary interest in the trust property, which proprietary interest will be enforceable in equity against any subsequent holder of the property (whether the original property or substituted property into which it can be traced) other than a purchaser for value of the legal interest without notice.

1638. A trustee is in a fiduciary relationship not only to the beneficiaries of the trust but also owes duties of a fiduciary nature in relation to the trust property. A trust property survives the insolvency or bankruptcy of the trustee, carrying with it a 'mark' of identification. Thus, any one meddling with it must do so with great care or else at his peril, for the trust property can be traced into the hands of any one and

1386. [1726] Sel Cas t King 61; 25 ER 223; *see* further *Soar v. Ashwell* [1893] 2 Q.B 390; *Attorney General for Hong Kong v. Charles Reid* [1994] 1 A.C. 324; *Royal Brunei Airline SDN. BHD. v. Pillip Tan Kok Ming* [1995] 2 A.C. 378; *See also* the Canadian case of *Rathwell v. Rathwell* [1978] 2 SCR 436; *Sorochan v. Sorochan* [1986] 2 SCR 38; [1986] 29 D.L.R. (4th) 1.

1387. [1996] 2 All ER 961, 988.

into whatever it has transmuted into unless it falls into the hands of a bona fide purchaser for value of the legal estate without notice of its trust character or content.[1388] The rights of a beneficiary if established, enables the tracing of property and this has significant effect on the existence of the property that is subject of a trust. This perspective has driven the emerging role of the trust in diverse aspects of commerce, particularly securitisation and structured finance.

1639. The Lagos State Limitation of Action Law, provides by section 32 that six years is the limitation of rights of action against trustees.[1389]

IV. Secret Trust

1640. A Will may be structured such that it could embody both the terms of a Will, express or secret trusts. A person could also provide for errors of his lifetime or prejudice of society through a secret trust in the Will, if he feels inclined to secrecy or privacy although it must be borne in mind that once admitted to probate, a Will is a public document.[1390] A secret trust could also be abused by lawyers but not in a country such as Nigeria with extensive family networking.

1641. A secret trust is a disposition of property the terms of which are kept private by the '*disponor*'. The 'trust' is either declared *inter vivos*[1391] and oral evidence admissible to show its existence or it is declared in a testamentary disposition[1392] and parole evidence admissible to show its terms. In the most cases, it arises either in informal dispositions on intestacy[1393] or written testamentary dispositions.[1394] As is usual in most of the cases, the disponor is unwilling to reveal the terms of the trust for reasons of undesirable publicity that might follow the revelation of his identity or that of the object of his bounty. It may also be that a testator is undecided as to the terms of his Will. Such intentions may then be fully disclosed to another person usually, a trusted friend or a Solicitor who may appear to be the beneficiary of the gift or a trustee of such gift for another. Whatever the reasons may be for creating such a trust, as Lord Cairns said of the doctrine in *Jones v. Badley*[1395] 'it is a … case of trust'. The essential elements of a valid secret

1388. *See* the case of *Foskett v. Mckeown* [2001] 1 A.C. 102; [2002] 2 W.L.R. 129.
1389. Cap L.84, Laws of Lagos State.
1390. Diana Kincald, *The Tangled Web: The Relationship Between a Secret Trust and the Will* 420 (Conveyancer and Property Lawyer 2000).
1391. *Sellack v. Harris* [1708] 2 Eq. Ca. Ab. 46; *Strickland v. Altridge* [1804] 9 Ves. Jr. 516.
1392. *Thynn v. Thynn* 1 Vern. 296; *See also*, *Halsbury's Laws of England* Vol. 38 3rd ed. 823; *Words & Phrases Legally Defined* Vol. 5, 1970 (Butterworth London), 229. As we shall *see* below, this trust is very much like the '*Donatio Mortis Causa*' in nature and development.
1393. *Sellack v. Harris* [1708] 2 Eq. Ca. Ab. 46.
1394. *Thynn v. Thynn* 1 Vern. 296; *Halsbury's Laws of England ibid* 823; *Words & Phrases Legally Defined* 229. As we shall *see* below, this trust is very much like the '*Donatio Mortis Causa*' in its origin, nature and development.
1395. [1868] 3 Ch. App. 362, 364; *See also* David Kincaid, *The Tangled Web: The Relationship Between a Secret Trust and the Will*, Conv. & P.L. 420 (2000).

trust, were, restated in the more recent case of, *Ottaway v. Norman*[1396]by Brightman J, after an extensive review of previous authorities:

(i) the intention of the testator to subject the primary *done* to an obligation in favour of the secondary *donee*;
(ii) communication of that intention to the primary *donee*;
(iii) and acceptance of that obligation by the primary *done* either expressly or by acquiescence.

1642. A Secret Trust is classified into two:

(1) Where there is no trust declared in respect of a gift on the face of a Will and in intestacy situations.[1397]
(2) Where a trust is written on the face of the Will and the details are declared outside the Will.

1643. The former is referred to as the fully secret trust while the latter is generally referred to as the

1644. Half secret trust.[1398] In *Re Maddock, Llewelyn v. Washington*[1399] Collins M.R, stated that it is a well-established principle:

> where a person, knowing that a testator, in making a disposition in his favour, intends it to be applied for purposes other than for his own benefit, either expressly promises or by silence implies, that he will carry the testator's intention into effect, and the property is left to him upon the faith of that promise or undertaking, it is in effect a trust, and in such a case the Court will not allow the devisee to set up the Statute of Frauds, or, rather the Statute of Wills, by which the Statute of Frauds is now in this respect superseded, and for this reason: The devisee, by his conduct, has induced the testator to leave him the property, and as the Lord Justice Turner says in *Russell v. Jackson* [(1855) 2 K. & J. 313; 25 L.J. Ch. 241.], no one can doubt that, if the devisee had stated that he would not carry into effect the intentions of the testator, the disposition in his favour would not have been found in the Will.

1645. The Secret trust appears to exist in contravention of the Wills Act 1837, section 9 and the equivalent provisions in States with their own Laws on the subject. This section which applies to all testamentary gifts including trusts is the crux of the controversy over the secret trust. The testator either in a bid to deliberately avoid the provisions of the Act, in ignorance of its provisions and its effect, would often make testamentary dispositions in the form of trusts, which do not comply

---

1396. [1971] 3 All ER 1325.
1397. *McCormick v. Grogan* [1869] L.R. 4 H.L. 82.
1398. *Blackwell v. Blackwell* [1929] All E.R 71.
1399. [1902] 2 Ch. 220.

with the Act, necessitating the intervention of the court, as a final arbiter on whether such a trust is valid in spite of the provisions of the Act or it should simply fail as being in contravention of the Statute.

1646. It is then argued that these trusts are *inter vivos* ones, valid '*dehors*' the Will.[1400] There appears to be several dicta by the Courts to support this view. *In re Maddock,* 'dehors' was used a few times by the court, 'so it seems to me to be wholly consistent with the admission that nothing *dehors* the Will can be treated as part of the Will that the Court should intervene to prevent a legatee from committing fraud by insisting on his rights under the Will to the prejudice of his *cestui que trust*'.[1401]

1647. In re Young[1402] was more emphatic and Danckwerts J. expressed the view that the whole theory of the formation of a secret trust is that the Wills Act has nothing to do with the matter because the forms required by the Wills Act are entirely disregarded, since the persons do not take by virtue of the gift in the Will, but by virtue of the secret trusts imposed upon the beneficiary, who does in fact take under Will.

1648. Consequently, a beneficiary who witnesses the Will is not estopped by the provisions of the Wills Act from taking under the Will since the gift is *dehors* the Will. On this view, the half secret trust is actually an express trust and that the only question left for answer is the status of the beneficiary. Is the hunt for the beneficiary taking place within the Will or is it outside the Will? If the hunt for the beneficiary is within the Will then, the nomination of the beneficiary becomes a testamentary disposition in which case the formalities governing testamentary dispositions would have to govern it. If the hunt is outside the Will, then the formalities of the Wills Act would not govern it.

1649. In *Re Maddock,* Cozens-Hardy LJ was not at all sure what the basis of enforcement of the secret trust was, but as he said 'whether the true principle be trust, or contract, or estoppel, it seems to me that, as between the devisee or legatee and the persons interested under the memorandum, all the same consequences must follow as would follow if the memorandum had in fact, formed part of the Will'.[1403] Maudsley, noted that, 'there are indeed difficulties in any theory, and it may be that more than one theory has been relied on, on different occasions and that the cases are not reconcilable on any single theory'.[1404] In reality, however, the courts have simply been more inclined to be lenient on the Will of the departed and

1400. Jill E. Martin, *Hanbury & Martin's Modern Equity* 154 (Sweet & Maxwell 15th ed. 1997); *see also* another variant of the argument of *dehors* based on incorporation by reference practice by Bryn Perrins 'Secret Trusts: the Key to Dehors' [1985] Conv. 360.

1401. *In re Maddock* [1902] 2 Ch. 220.

1402. [1951] Ch. 344, [1950] 2 All E.R. P. 1245.

1403. [1902] 2 Ch. 220.

1404. R.H. Maudsley [1955] 18 M.L.R. 524; E. Wyndham White, *Secret Trusts: Admissibility of Evidence*, 2(4) Mod. L. Rev. (notes) 319 (1939).

a witness to a secret trust in a Will in which he is a beneficiary will take his benefit free of the Will and formalities thereto. The decline of cases on secret trust, however, may be telling its own story.

V. Gifts and the Case of *T Choithram International SA v. Pagarani*[1405]

1650. The case arose out of the death of Thakurdas Choithram Pagarani. Shortly before his death he had tried to transfer various assets to the Choithram International Foundation, a philanthropic body he had created. Throughout his life Mr Pagarani was outstandingly generous in his charitable giving. His gifts amounted to many millions in United States of America currency.

1651. Mr Pagarani was born in 1914 in India. He was a devout Hindu. In 1928 he married Lalibai Thakurdas Pagarani, his first wife, by whom he had six daughters. In about 1937 Mr Pagarani left India and eventually established a supermarket business in Sierra Leone. Lalibai and their children remained in India. In Sierra Leone he met and in 1944, married Virginia Harding who bore him eight children including three sons. Mr Pagarani remained in Sierra Leone until the 1980s but used to return to India to visit his Indian family and those members of his Sierra Leone family whom he had taken to India to be brought up according to Indian ways and customs.

1652. In the legal proceedings, the claimants had alleged that the marriage to Virginia Harding was void for non-compliance with the *lex loci celebrationis*, but that claim was rejected and not appealed.[1406] The Court at first instance also found:

> having made generous provision for his first wife and each of his children, [he] intended to leave much of the remainder of his wealth to charity, to the exclusion of his children. This he hoped to achieve by setting up a foundation to serve as an umbrella organisation for those charities which he had already established and which would in due course be the vehicle to receive most of his assets when he died. This was from all accounts, a longstanding intention of the deceased.

1653. The businesses carried on by TCP were outstandingly successful and spread widely throughout the world. They were usually named 'T. Choithram and Sons' and were often known simply as 'Choithrams'. In 1989 Mr Pagarani brought most of his business under the umbrella of the first various offshore companies (including T Choithram International SA), in effect, holding companies. He was not the sole owner of the shares in those companies, but he held a majority share.

1405. [2000] UKPC 46, 1 WLR 1, 2 All ER 492.

1406. Suit No 184 of 1992 of the High Court of Justice of the British Virgin Islands (Civil) page 4 of the judgment of Georges J at first instance.

1654. At the end of 1991, Mr Pagarani was diagnosed as suffering from cancer. He left his home in Dubai, where he had primarily established himself after he left Sierra Leone in the 1980s, and came to London to stay with his son. Preparations were made for an elaborate ceremony at which he was to establish the Choithram International Foundation and make the contested gift to the Foundation. As Mr Pagarani's condition worsened various family members were summoned to his bedside. In an upstairs bedroom in his son's house on 17 February 1992 Mr Pagarani executed the Foundation's trust deed in the presence of various persons. Immediately after signing the Foundation trust deed Mr Pagarani said certain words of which recollection by witnesses varied. In substance, he was thought to have said: 'I now give all my wealth to the Trust' or 'I have given everything to the Trust'. Mr Pagarani then said to the group's accountant, Mr Param (who was in attendance) that he, knew what to do and that he should transfer all his balances and shares with the companies to the Foundation. On the same day, 17 February 1992, the other trustees present in London signed the trust deed. The remaining Trustees of the Foundation who were not in London signed the Foundation trust deed shortly thereafter.

1655. Later that same day meetings of the board of directors of each of the companies were held acknowledging the earlier gifts. The Articles of Association contained certain pre-emption rights, which the other shareholders duly waived.

1656. Mr Pagarani had also prepared a Will, which gave all his wealth to the Foundation. However, at the time the Will was drafted, the Foundation had not been constituted. The Will was never signed. It was also found that Mr Pagarani had asked a new Will to be prepared and for arrangements to be made to transfer his assets *inter vivos.*

1657. In the event, no transfer documents were ever signed. Shortly afterwards Mr Pagarani was admitted to intensive care where he died. His relatives, who stood to benefit from an intestacy, claimed the assets had never been transferred to the Foundation and fell to be distributed with his estate. The relatives who were trustees of the Foundation claimed that the gift to the Foundation was valid, and that the shares in the companies had not been transferred properly in the manner specified by law in the International Business Companies Act.

1658. The Court of first instance and Appeal held that a trust was not duly constituted. On appeal to the Privy Council, Lord Browne-Wilkinson summed up the point: The central and most important question was this: on the basis that Mr Pagarani intended to make an immediate absolute gift 'to the Foundation', but had not vested the gifted property in all the trustees of the Foundation, are the trusts of the Foundation trust deed enforceable against the deposits and the shares, or was it (as the judge at first instance and the Court of Appeal had held) a case where there has been an imperfect gift which cannot be enforced against Mr Pagarani's estate whatever his intentions might have been. The judge and the Court of Appeal had taken the view that a perfected gift could only be made in one of two ways: a transfer of the gifted asset to the donee, accompanied by an intention in the donor to make a gift; or by the donor declaring himself to be a trustee of the gifted property for the donee.

1659. For the first case, the donor must have done everything necessary to be done which is within his own power to do in order to transfer the gifted asset to the donee. If the donor has not done so, the gift is incomplete since neither the Court nor the donee had an equity to perfect an imperfect gift, for which there is a long line of authority. Moreover, the court will not give a benevolent construction to treat ineffective words of outright gift as taking effect as if the donor had declared himself a trustee for the done.

1660. The Privy Council opined that the facts of the case were novel and raised a new point not previously judicially considered. The Council held that equity meant that since the trust property was vested in one trustee, Mr Pagarani, at the time the gift was intended this was sufficient to make the conveyance to the foundation valid. The Council distinguished *Bridge v. Bridge*[1407] which had established that the vesting of the trust property in one trustee, the donor, out of many was not sufficient to constitute the trust.

§4. Insurance Contracts

1661. An insurance contract is a document representing the agreement between an insurance company and the insured. Central to any insurance contract is the insuring agreement, which specifies the risks that are covered, the limits of the policy, and the term of the policy. The most common type of optional insurance contract in Nigeria is life insurance contract.

1662. The Administration of Estate Act, by section 53 provides for insurance and superannuation benefits.

1663. Section 53 (I) requires that where the intestate during his lifetime takes out life insurance policy or contributes to any social security scheme or superannuation fund or provident fund, the right in the benefit of such insurance policy or social security scheme or superannuation or provident fund shall devolve on the personal representatives as part of the estate of the intestate.The other subsections of section 53 are 2 to 5 which are discussed below.

> (2) The provision of this section shall not apply to: (a) trust policies; or (b) policies taken out for the purpose of securing loans. (3) Where the estate of the intestate is not sufficient to provide adequate financial provision for the child or children of the intestate such child or children, as the case may be, may apply to the court for an Order directing the personal representatives to make such payments out of the benefit accruing from such insurance policy or social

1407. [1852] 16 Beav. 315.

security scheme or superannuation or provident fund as may be reasonably necessary for the maintenance of such child or children. (4) An application under the provisions of this section shall be made within six months of the taking out of the Letters of Administration. (5) In any case where: (a) an application is not made within the time limit prescribed under subsection (4) of this section; or (b) an order is not granted by the court; then, the personal representatives shall transfer the right in the benefit of such insurance policy or social security scheme or superannuation or provident fund to the person to whom or for whose benefit any nomination was made in the scheme.

Chapter 4. Acquisition and Administration of the Estate

§1. The Seisin

1664. The property of the deceased may comprise of landed property and personalty. The passing or transfer of land is subject to both customary and Islamic law as well as legislation.

1665. In Nigeria, theoretically, the highest title a person can have to land is a leasehold. The principal legislation governing landed property in Nigeria is the LUA.[1408] The LUA is incorporated as part of the Constitution of the Federation, and by section 315(5)(d), nothing in the Constitution shall invalidate it. A review of the Act shall have to pass through the nation's bicameral Assembly.

1666. The LUA vests all land in the State in the Governor of the State or the President, in the case of the FCT (with the Minister of the territory as delegate).[1409] Section 1 of the Act provides that all land comprised in the territory of each State of the Federation is vested in the Governor of that State, to be held in trust, and administered for the use and common benefit of all Nigerians.

1667. The Governor is empowered to designate land into urban areas in respect of which a certificate of occupancy is issued on terms and usually for a tenor of ninety-nine years. The Governor is also empowered to lawfully grant statutory rights of occupancy to any person for all purposes whether or not the land is in an urban area or not. By section 6, land in non-urban areas have complex administrative policies relating to holding, use, and designation for agricultural and grazing purposes which could be granted by the local government area as customary rights of occupancy.[1410] All dealings in land, involving alienation – by assignment, mortgage, transfer of possession, sublease etc., require the consent of the Governor in the case of statutory rights occupancy or local government council for customary rights of occupancy.[1411] The Act provides for transitional provisions on land for urban and non-urban areas such that holders prior to the Act are deemed to hold for urban, statutory rights and for the latter customary rights.[1412]

1668. By section 46(1) the National Council of States may make regulations for the purpose of carrying the Act into effect and particularly with regard to some matters such as the transfer by assignment or otherwise howsoever, of any rights of occupancy, whether statutory or customary, including the conditions applicable to the transfer of such rights to persons who are not Nigerians.

1408. Land Use Act, Cap 202, L.F.N. 1990; Cap L5, L.F.N. 2004.
1409. Section 51(2) of the LUA.
1410. Sections 6, 10, 34, 36 etc. of the Land Use Act.
1411. Sections 21 and 22 of the Land Use Act.
1412. Sections 34 for urban areas and 36 for non-urban areas.

1669. More importantly by section 24, which is captioned, 'Devolution of rights of occupancy on death', the Act provides for the devolution of the rights of an occupier upon death. Accordingly:

(i) in the case of a customary right of occupancy, unless non-customary law or any other customary law applies, be regulated by the customary law existing in the locality in which the land is situated; and
(ii) in the case of a statutory right of occupancy (unless any non-customary law or other customary law applies) be regulated by the customary law of the deceased occupier at the time of his death relating to the distribution of property of like nature to a right of occupancy:
So, however, that—
(iii) no customary law prohibiting, restricting or regulating the devolution on death to any particular class of persons or the right to occupy any land shall operate to deprive any person of any beneficial interest in such land (other than the right to occupy the same) or in the proceeds of sale thereof to which he may be entitled under the rules of inheritance of any other customary law;
(iv) a statutory right of occupancy shall not be divided into two or more parts on devolution by the death of the occupier, except with the consent of the Governor.

1670. In addition, section 25 provides for the effect of deed or Will where non-customary law applies. Thus, in the case of the devolution or transfer of rights to which any non-customary law applies, no deed or Will shall operate to create any proprietary right over land except that of a plain transfer of the totality of the rights of occupation over the whole of the land.

1671. Other relevant enactments, reinforce the position of the LUA on customary tenors and system of inheritance of land and real property.[1413] In *Umeadi v. Chibunze*[1414] the Supreme Court affirmed as binding a contract of sale of land entered into on customary oaths to a deity. Thus, devolution by testacy is meant to be, in fact, unworkable in Nigeria.

§2. The System of Acquisition

I. Vesting of the Estate

1672. The personal representatives for the time being of a deceased person are deemed in law as the heirs and assigns within the meaning of all trusts and powers.[1415] Furthermore, the real estate to which a deceased person was entitled for an

1413. Sections 1(3), 49(5) etc. of the LSAEL and 57(3) & 47(6) of the Administration of Estates Act.
1414. [2020] 10 NWLR (part 1733) 405.
1415. Section 1, AEA; 3 LSAEL.

interest not ceasing on his death, and in spite of any testamentary disposition in relation to the real estate, devolves from time to time on the personal representative of the deceased who are also, the representatives of the deceased in regard to the personal estate.

1673. The real estate of a deceased person devolves on the personal representatives of the deceased who may be appointed by Will, the court or operate by virtue of the laws on intestacy as administrators. The two principal legislations considered in this part are the Administration of Estate Act, applicable in the FCT and the LSAEL. As has been noted above, both, as indeed, all other such laws in Nigeria are similarly premised. The Rules are also similar and the Lagos Rules will be used as a model.

1674. When a person dies, the executors, where there is a Will are required to gather in the estate, obtain a death certificate with which in addition to other requirements, they are to apply for grant of probate to the Probate Registry to administer the estate. The executors are appointed by the Will and derive their base authority from it, so are able to begin administration but by Lagos law, cannot act for more than three months and an intermeddling executor, not more than six months. There is penalty for executors who continue to act after three months of the death of the testator without applying for grant of probate.[1416]

1675. It is also worth noting that section 15 of the LSAEL provides that all causes of action subsisting against or vested in a person at death survives him whether against or, as the case may be, for the benefit of his estate, with exceptions for some regimes of tortious liabilities, such as defamation, some contractual such as breach of promise to marry or statutory such as damages for adultery.[1417]

1676. The proposed administrators where there is no Will are to apply for administration and obtain a grant to gather in the property of the deceased into their control, but cannot transfer title like executors until administration is issued.

1677. The Court can summon any person named as executor in a Will to prove or renounce probate of the Will and perform any other directions of the court as may aid the ascertainment of administration.[1418]

1416. Order 58, rule 19.
1417. Interestingly, subs. (5) provides that the rights conferred are in addition to and not in derogation of any rights conferred on the dependants of deceased persons by the Fatal Accidents Law, or the Carriage by Air Act, 1932 of the United Kingdom and so much of this Law as relates to causes of action against the estates of deceased persons shall apply in relation to causes of action under the said Law and the said Act as it applies in relation to other causes of action not expressly excepted from the operation of subs. (1) of this section.
1418. Section 23 of the LSAEL; 18, Administration of Estates Act, 1991.

1678. Section 2 of the Administration of Estates Act, 1992, provides that an interest in land shall not be administered unless the administrator shows to the satisfaction of the court that other assets of the estate are insufficient to pay the intestate's debts and expenses of his funeral and of taking out administration. On the provision of devolution, there is a slight variation in the Administration of Estates Act, that is not exactly replicated in the Lagos Law in section 2(2): 'an interest in land shall not be administered unless the administrator shows to the satisfaction of the court that other assets of the estate are insufficient to pay the intestate's debts and expenses of his funeral and of taking out administration'. The Lagos law, however, makes the provision that the real and personal estate of deceased are assets for payment of debts, funeral expenses and expenses in relation to probate such as filing fees, advertisement fees, etc.

1679. The Lagos Law by section 1(3) provides that: nothing in the Law affects the administration of the estates of deceased persons by or under the authority of any customary court nor unless otherwise expressly provided the distribution, inheritance or succession of any estate where such distribution, inheritance or succession is governed by customary law whether such estate is administered under this Law or by or under the authority of a customary court.

1680. It may be that the two related provisions are addressing the same subject – non-alienation of land under customary prisms because of the intestacy or indeed testacy of the deceased person. Since the executors of a deceased person can act within three months before the possibility of penalty for so acting, it implies that the Lagos Act may have preferred funeral expenditure and debts to the safeguard of the land.

II. Procedure

1681. When a person subject to the jurisdiction of the Court dies, all petitions for the granting of any probate or Letters of Administration of the estate of the deceased person, with or without a Will annexed, and all applications in relation to the grant is made to the Probate Registrar of the Court. Although a Will may be held by the Testator, his lawyer or be lodged with the probate Registry of the State, it is best lodged with the Probate Registry. The various rules of the High Court do not make lodgement with the registry compulsory but in practice it is and it is also prudent to do so. Order 58, rule 2 of Lagos rules, requires that every original Will, of which probate or administration with Will annexed is granted, must be filed and kept in the Probate Registry in such manner as to secure at once its due preservation and convenient inspection.

1682. A copy of every such Will and of the probate or administration shall be preserved in the Registry.

1683. Order 57 of the Lagos Rules deals with the general rules on administration. Usually the practice procedure involves, in the case of proving of the Will, an application by the executors where the Will was not deposited with the probate registry, but where it was so deposited, then the registry notifies and invites the solicitor, if known, such other persons interested in the Will or the estate of the deceased. In the case of an intestate, an application is made by the solicitor or persons interested in the estate. The application includes attachment of the death Certificate of the Testator, payment of prescribed fees which includes estate duties and other government taxes.

1684. By Order 57, rule 3, a person may apply personally for grant of probate. An application can be made without an intermediary, unless the application proceeds by motion or by action, in which case, a legal practitioner must be engaged. Where an application had been made by a legal practitioner on behalf of the applicant which has not been withdrawn, then a personal application cannot be made successfully without the direction of the judge. When a Will has been deposited in the Registry by a personal applicant, the personal applicant is no longer at liberty to withdraw it, nor can it be delivered to the applicant or to any other person unless, in special circumstances, the judge so directs. Where a legal practitioner applies on behalf of a personal applicant, the legal practitioner provides the court with telephone number, e-mail address and address of place of business within the jurisdiction of the Court.

1685. The applicant is required to furnish the probate registry with all information necessary to enable the papers leading to the grant to be prepared in the Registry or the personal applicant may prepare such papers and lodge them unsworn.[1419]

1686. Every application for a grant must be supported by a sworn affidavit applicable to the circumstances of the case. The affidavit should contain details on domicile of the deceased as at the time of death. Where it is necessary to describe the deceased in a grant by some name in addition to his true name, the applicant shall state in the oath the true name of the deceased and shall depose that some specified part of the estate, was held in that other name; or as to any other reason that demands the inclusion of the other name in the grant. The sworn oath and its requirements apply to guarantors all the deponents or sureties unless this is waived by the judge in special circumstances.

1687. Other documents that are also required include the passport sized photographs of the applicant.

1688. The judge may require a proof of identity of the deceased or of the applicant for the grant beyond those contained in the oath.[1420]

1689. For administration without Will, the judge shall require evidence, in addition to that offered by the applicant, where necessary, in relation to the identity of

1419. Order 57, rule 3(6).
1420. Order 57, rule 5(2).

the deceased or of the applicant; the relationship of the applicant to the deceased; any person or persons in existence with a right equal or prior to that of the applicant to the grant of probate or administration sought; any other matter which may be considered by the judge relevant to the question whether the applicant is the proper person to whom the grant should be made. The judge has wide discretion to ascertain all information provided.

1690. Order 59, rule 1, makes exceptions on aspects of an estate in respect of which fees may not be charged or paid for an intestacy. These include gratuity where a person was in employment of a State or the Federal Government as well as pension from a pension or provident fund established by law. Exceptions are also made in computations related to funeral expenses as for instance with respect to cause of action that survives the dead person.

1691. Where there is no action from any of the parties named, executors, administrators and any of the category of persons claiming to be a creditor or legatee or the next-of-kin or one of the next of kin of a deceased may apply for and obtain a Summons from the Court requiring the Executor or Administrator, as the case may be, to attend Court and show cause why an Order for the administration of the property of the deceased should not be made.

1692. In some other instances, when the circumstances of the case require it, the action for administering an estate may spring from the judge. The judge, on the death of a person or as so soon after, may appoint and authorise an officer of the Court, or some other fit person, to take possession of the deceased person's property within its jurisdiction, or put it under seal and so keep it until it can be dealt with according to law.[1421]

1693. Once the procedure is carried through, and there are no caveats and citations, probate is granted in a common form authorising dealing in the estate and distribution of the estate. Where personalty is a part of the estate of the deceased, a separate fee is attracted. Other actions are ascertainment of the estate, and reading of the Will. Obtaining a Letter of administration is procedurally more complicated as the appropriate administrator must be identified; publication in National Daily News Media, usually print, is a necessity, and needs to be done. This is a precautionary measure for possible entry of caveat. Sureties are needed and bonds entered. All these have to be done prior to an enrolment application for a Letter of Administration for the estate of an intestate.

1694. Section 24 of the LSAEL provides for the number of persons who can be granted probate as maximum of four persons.[1422] The Law does not appear to provide a minimum but in practice the minimum is two persons. That the minimum number of persons who can be granted administration is two is deducible from

1421. Order 57, rule 2(1) of the Lagos State Civil Procedure Rules, 2012.
1422. Section 19 of the Administration of Estates Act, 1991.

Obusez v. Obusez.[1423] With respect to administration, without Will, by Order 59, rule 12 where it is necessary to have additional personal representatives, application can be made to the registry. Furthermore, section 26 of the LSAEL provides for the power of the court to exercise its discretion on who to grant administration of the estate of a deceased person and in so doing to take account of all interested persons.[1424]Thus, if after the grant, there is need for additional personal representative, an application is made to the judge supported by an affidavit by the personal applicant, the consent of the person proposed to be added as personal representative and such other evidence as the judge may require and the judge may then direct that a note shall be made on the original grant of the addition of a further personal representative, or the original grant may be impounded or revoked and such orders made as the circumstances of the case may require.

1695. Where the beneficiary is an infant or a life interest arises from the Will, probate may be granted to a Trust corporation which could be the Public Trustee.[1425]

1696. In a case of intestacy, and where the special circumstances of the case require, the judge on the application of any person having interest in the estate of the deceased may, exercise a discretion, to grant Letters of Administration to an officer of the Court, Consular Officer or to a person in the service of the Government. In such a case, the officer or person so appointed shall act under the direction of the judge, and shall be indemnified. Such an officer will be compelled to file in Court the accounts of his administration at intervals not exceeding twelve months.[1426] When the machinery of the court is put in motion to secure the estate of a deceased person, on an account of delayed application, the judge may refuse to entertain such application.

1697. Where the Court grants administration to persons other than the executors appointed by the testator, then they are not to act while administration as granted is in force. Thus, by section 11 of the LSAEL, where administration has been granted in respect of any real or personal estate of a deceased person, no person shall have power to bring any action or otherwise act as executor of the deceased person in respect of the estate comprised in or effected by the grant until the grant has been recalled or revoked.

1698. Where administration involves a minor, a person of inefficient mind, or if a life interest arises under the Will or intestacy, administration is granted either to a trust corporation, with or without an individual, or to not less than two individuals.[1427]

1423. [2007] 2 ALL N.L.R. 458; [2007] 10 NWLR (part 1043) 430.
1424. *See* s. 21 of the Administration of Estates Act, 1991.
1425. Sections 24(1) Lagos State Law and 19(1) of It is to be noted that by s. 25(2) probate cannot be granted to a syndic or nominee on behalf of a trust corporation.
1426. Order 59, rule 8(1-3) Lagos State Civil Procedure Rules, 2012.
1427. Section 19, AEA; 24 LSAEL.

1699. It takes a minimum of fourteen days of the death of the deceased, for an application for grant of administration with the Will annexed and twenty-one days without the Will annexed, to be determined. No grant of probate or administration is valid if obtained before those specified days. The Court does not have a discretion on this, although the judge may trigger acquisition of the estate of the deceased.[1428]

1700. Where a Will is the basis of administration, the Will is a public document and is usually available for inspection once proved and admitted for probate and distribution.

§3. Administration of the Estate

1701. Administration of Estate is a subject matter that falls into residuary competence for the peace, order and good government of the State or the Federation.[1429] The Federal Laws are saved by virtue of section 315(1) and (4) of the Constitution. For Testate Succession, there is the Wills Act, 1837, a Statute of general application and the Wills Amendment Act, 1853. States are entitled to make separate laws and some have done so. A State law on the subject is called the Wills Law of the State. The laws are in principle all the same and aim at preserving the customary inheritance pattern of the indigenes regarding primogeniture and preservation of male lineage and interests such as proper burial of the testator. However, those States which have no separate law apply the Wills Act as a default law. This should also apply in the FCT. The same goes for intestate succession. There is the Administration of Estates Act, 1992.[1430] Various States have separate Administration of Estates Law. In principle they are all the same, making provision for the persons who dies without a Will and preserving order as to whether the testator died as a public or civil servant, whereby the record of service would indicate a next of kin; was in a monogamous marriage in which case the surviving spouse has the prior right of administration the estate or the testator died polygynous, in which case all the gates must be represented where each dutifully has a bloodline. It is also noteworthy that all references are to testator, it is not conceptualised that a wife has any property and at any rate, the usual trend is that husbands predecease wives. It may also be that the use of the masculine gender has become all too familiar.

1702. Upon the grant of administration, the interval between the death of the deceased and the grant of administration, where there is no Will, the estate is vested in the Chief Judge of the State, and where there is a Will, the estate vests on the executors.

1428. Order 57, rule 2(1), Lagos State Civil Procedure Rules, 2012.
1429. Section 4 of the Constitution of the Federal Republic of Nigeria, Cap C23, Laws of the Federation.
1430. Cap 64, signed into law 31 Dec. 1991. This Act came into force as a Military Decree but is saved by virtue of s. 315(1) and (4) of the Constitution.

1703. The Law interprets 'Administration'. It means, with reference to the estate of a deceased person; Letters of Administration –whether general or limited, or, with the Will annexed or otherwise. On the other hand, 'Administrator' means a person to whom administration is granted.[1431]

1704. Section 22 of the AEA provides for administration pending litigation titled administration *pendente lite*. This is administration pending completion of litigation where the Will is disputed. It empowers the Court to appoint an administrator and if necessary, pay remuneration from the 'deceased' estate.[1432]

1705. In an intestacy, where the estate is insolvent, pursuant to section 34(1) of AEA, funeral, testamentary, and administration expenses are prioritised outgoings in administration.[1433] Next is taxes and the following is wages and like obligations.[1434]

1706. Where the deceased estate is solvent, then the order of payments in administration is contained in section 34(2) and the order of priority of payments appears in Part 2 of First Schedule.

1707. The ordering is made subject to any contrary intention distillable from, where there is a, Will.

1708. Items 1 and 2 of Part 2 of First Schedule are properties treated as residuary estates to which the Will maker has not specifically attached some obligations. Items 3 and 4 are specifically charged by the Will maker for payments of debts. Items 5–7 are the last to be drawn on for payments of debts since they are specifically appointed as gifts. They are as follows:

(1) The first prior payment in administration is property of the deceased undisputed of by Will, subject to the retention there out of a fund sufficient to meet any pecuniary legacies.
(2) Property of the deceased not specifically disposed of by Will but included (either by a specific or general description) in a residuary gift, subject to the retention out of such property of a fund sufficient to meet any pecuniary legacies, so far as not provided for as aforesaid.
(3) Property of the deceased specifically appropriated or disposed of by Will (either by a specific or general description) for the payment of debts.
(4) Property of the deceased charged with, or disposed of by Will (either by a specific or general description) subject to a charge for the payment of debts.

1431. Section 2 of the LSAEA. Presentation means the probate of a will and administration, and the expression 'taking out representation' refers to the obtaining of the probate of a will or of the grant of administration; 58(1) AEA.
1432. Similar provision appears in s. 27 of the Lagos Law.
1433. *See* Sch. 1, Administration of Estate Act, 1992. For Lagos State, *see* s. 38(1) and Part 1 of the Schedule.
1434. The list is contained in the First Schedule, Part 1. Similar provisions appear for Lagos State in s. 38(1) and Part 1 of the Schedule to the Law.

(5) The fund, if any retained to meet pecuniary legacies.
(6) Property specifically disposed of by Will, rateably according to value.
(7) Property appointed by Will under a general power, rateably according to value.[1435]

1709. It is to be noted that while the Act by section 35 abolishes retainer preference,[1436] and payment of debts by personal representatives subject, however, to section 35(2), which makes good such payments where they are made in good faith prior to the personal representative discovering that the estate of the deceased person is insolvent, the Lagos Law sustains retainer preference. Thus, the Lagos State Law by section 38(2) provides that the right of retainer of a personal representative and his right to prefer creditors may be exercised in respect of all assets of the deceased, but the right of retainer shall only apply to debts owing to the personal representative in his own right whether solely or jointly with another person. However, the provision does not affect the right of retainer of a personal representative, or his right to prefer creditors.

1710. Section 50 declares a statutory trust for sale for issues of an intestate in respect of the intestate's residuary estate. The trust is based on equality for children of the deceased who have attained the age of 21 or are married and are living as at the date of death of the deceased. The other class of children protected is those who are living in the same circumstances but their parents predeceased the testator.

I. Rights of Spouses

1711. A spouse has a right of election on any life interest in the estate of the deceased intestate. Section 51 provides specifically for right of surviving spouse to have own life interest redeemed in the case of intestacy, which the personal representatives can allow and then subsequently, distribute the estate as residuary free of the redeemed interest.

1712. An election under the section is exercisable only, if, at the time of the election, the whole of the residuary estate consists of property in possession. It is noteworthy though, that for the purpose of this section, a life interest in property partly in possession and partly not in possession may be treated as consisting of two separate life interests in those respective parts of the property.

1435. Similar provision exists in the Lagos State Law. Section 38(3) and Part 2 to the Schedule of the Lagos State Administration of Estates Law, Lagos State.

1436. A right to retainer refers to the authority by which the executor or administrator of the estate of a deceased person reserves out of the assets an amount sufficient to pay any debt due to him from the deceased in priority to the other creditors whose debts are of equal degree.

1713. The right extends to the period of twelve months from the date on which representation on estate of the intestate is first taken out.[1437] If the right is not exercised within the twelve months, then it is foreclosed, unless, in requesting for an extension of time, the surviving husband or wife satisfies the court that the limitation to the said period of twelve months will operate unfairly. Some specific ground on which the spouse can rely are that in consequence of the representation first taken out being probate of a Will subsequently revoked on the ground that the Will was invalid; or in consequence of a question whether a person had an interest in the estate, or as to the nature of an interest in the estate, not having been determined at the time when representation was first taken out; or in consequence of some other circumstances affecting the administration or distribution of the estate. In considering for the purposes of the section, the question when representation was first taken out, a grant limited to trust property shall be left out of account and a grant limited to real estate or to personal estate shall be left out of account unless a grant limited to the remainder of the estate has previously been made or is made at the same time.

1714. The exercise of election is done by notifying the personal representative (or, where there are two or more personal representatives of whom one is the tenant for life all of them except the tenant for life) in writing; and a notification in writing under the subsection is not revocable except with the consent of the personal representative. The procedure is different where the tenant for life is the sole personal representative. In this case, such an exercise of right can only be done by the person giving a notice to the probate registrar within the requisite twelve-month period. The grounds of extension of time should be the same.

1715. An infant can elect as tenant for life and such election is as valid and binding as it would be if the tenant for life were of age, but the personal representatives are bound to deal with the interest in the same manner as with any other part of the residuary estate to which the infant, tenant for life, is absolutely entitled.

1716. The powers of personal representatives in respect of interests of surviving spouse extends to raising money on the security of the estate to the net sum of money equivalent to the value of one-third or two-thirds of the residuary estate, as the case may be, or any part thereof.[1438] The rule then requires that such a surviving spouse who is a sole personal representative of the deceased and entitled to a life interest in part of the residuary estate but who has elected to have the life interest redeemed may give written notice of the election to the Registrar by filing a notice in Probate Form 7 with such variations as circumstances may require. A notice so filed shall be noted on the grant and the record open to inspection.[1439] The Chief Judge is enjoined to make probate rules for keeping a record of such notices and

1437. 'Presentation' means the probate of a will and administration, and the expression 'taking out representation' refers to the obtaining of the probate of a will or of the grant of administration – *see* s. 2 of the LSAEA.

1438. Section 52 of the LSAEL.

1439. Order 59, rules 17 & 1, Lagos State Civil Procedure Rules, 2012.

making that record available to the public. It is not clear how a spouse could be a sole personal representative, since as has been noted the cases indicate that although the law does not provide a minimum number of personal representatives, they are to be a minimum of two persons.[1440]

II. Personal Representatives

1717. The term 'Personal representative' from the interpretation of the law means the executor, original, or by representation; or administrator for the time being of a deceased person.[1441]

1718. It has been noted above that the number of personal representatives should be a maximum of four persons. The personal representative is not bound to distribute the estate of the deceased before the expiration of one year from the death.[1442]

1719. The personal representatives of a deceased person hold the real and personal estate as trustees for the persons who are beneficially entitled with power, so far as may be required for purposes of administration, to sell the real estate. They can also call in part of the personal estate, sell and convert it into money. Usually, any reversionary interests are not to be sold until they fall into possession, unless the personal representatives see special reason for sale. Personal chattels are also not to be sold, unless required for purposes of administration, and there are no other viable options.

1720. Personal representatives are required to pay all funeral, testamentary and administration expenses, debts and other liabilities as are properly payable from the net money raised from any sale or conversion of real and personal estate, excluding any overheads, and outstanding cash to the account of the estate. In the latter case, where it is not disposed of by Will, if any. Only after this, having regard to the rules of administration can the personal representatives out of the residue of the fund, set aside a fund sufficient to provide for any pecuniary legacies bequeathed by the Will (if any) of the deceased.

1721. During the subsistence of any life interest and pending the distribution of the whole or any part of the estate of the deceased, the personal representatives may invest the residue of the fund, not distributed, in any investments for the time being authorised by statute for the investment of trust money, with power, at the discretion of the personal representatives, to change such investments for others of a like nature.

1722. Furthermore, when required to do so by the court, the personal representatives must exhibit on oath in court, a full inventory of the estate and when so

1440. *Obusez v. Obusez* [2007] 47 LRLR (vol. 187) 112.
1441. Section 58, Administration of Estates Act, 1991; s. 2 LSAEL.
1442. Sections 44, AEA and 47 LSAEL.

required, render an account of the administration of the estate to the court. They may also be required, when necessary, to deliver up the grant of probate or administration to that court.[1443]

1723. It is therefore not in the place of other persons, not so authorised to act as if they are personal representatives. Where this occurs, besides the other liabilities such an intermeddling person may incur, there is liability to a fine of not less than NGN 50,000 as the judge, having regard to the condition of the person so interfering and the other circumstances of the case, may deem fit to impose.[1444]

1724. The Law specifies rights of actions that could lie against personal representatives. Section 15 of the LSAEL confers rights of action on interested persons, against personal representative and vice versa on all causes of action subsisting against or vested in the deceased which shall survive against or, as the case may be, for the benefit of his estate. Causes of action that are exempt are; defamation or seduction or for inducing one spouse to leave or remain apart from the other or to claims for damages on the ground of adultery. Where liability is established against the personal representatives, by section 15(6), payment of judgment debt is provable in the administration of the estate, notwithstanding that it is a demand in the nature of unliquidated damages arising otherwise than by a contract, promise or breach of trust.

1725. Where a cause of action survives for the benefit of the estate of a deceased person, the damages recoverable for the benefit of the estate of that person, shall not include any exemplary damages; in the case of a breach of promise to marry shall be limited to such damage, if any, to the estate of that person as flows from the breach of promise to marry.

1726. In addition, where the death of that person has been caused by the act or omission which gives rise to the cause of action, the damage shall be calculated without reference to any loss or gain to 'deceased' estate consequent on that death. Funeral expenses may be included in the computation of damages. However, no proceedings in respect of a cause of action in tort which by virtue of the section survived against the estate of a deceased person are maintainable, unless either, proceedings against the deceased in respect of that cause of action were pending at the date of death; or the cause of action arose not earlier than three years before the death. The proceedings to be maintainable must have commenced not later than six months after the personal representative took out representation.

1727. Furthermore, where damage has been suffered by reason of any act or omission in respect of which a cause of action would have subsisted against any person if that person had not died before or at the same time as the damage was suffered, then it is deemed, to have been subsisting against the deceased before death

1443. Sections 11 of the AEA; 3 and 14, LSAEL.
1444. Order 57, rule 17.

such cause of action in respect of, that act or omission, as would have subsisted, if, he had died after the damage was suffered.

1728. The rights so conferred, for the benefit of the estate of the deceased, and maintainable by the personal representatives are in addition to, and not in derogation of any rights conferred on the dependents of deceased persons by the Fatal Accidents Law, or the Carriage by Air Act, 1932 of the United Kingdom and so much of the Law as relates to causes of action against the estates of deceased persons 'shall apply in relation to causes of action under the said Law and the said Act as it applies in relation to other causes of action not expressly excepted'.[1445]

§4. Limitation Period for Probate Actions

1729. The Limitation Law of Lagos State[1446] provides for limitation of probate actions as twelve years from when the right to receive the property or gift arose, six years for arrears of interest in funds. The FCT, Abuja, has the same provisions as section 32 of its Limitation Act.[1447]

1730. The Limitation Law of Lagos State, by section 33, on actions to recover the personal estate of deceased persons, requires that no action in respect of any claim to the personal estate of a deceased person or to any share or interest in such estate, whether under a Will or on intestacy, Will be brought after the expiration of twelve years from the date when the right to receive the share or interest accrued. In addition, no action to recover arrears of interest in respect of any legacy or damages in respect of such arrears will be brought after the expiration of six years from the date on which the interest became due.

1731. The period of limitation fixed, does not apply to an action against a personal representative or any person claiming, where the claim is founded on any fraud to which the personal representative was party or privy.[1448]

1732. It must be noted though, that Order 60, rule 1, of the Lagos Civil Procedure Rules stipulates that suits in respect of Probate or Letters of Administration shall be instituted and carried on as nearly as possible in like manner and subject to the same rules of procedure as suits in respect of civil claims. It is not clear how the Court will interpret the two provisions in relation to a suit for the revocation of a grant to the Personal representatives or administrators rather than interests. It may be that the ordinary limitation time of six years for contracts will apply where the estate comprises of property other than real property and twelve years where the estate consists of real property by the provisions of section 16 of the Limitation Law.

1445. Section 15(5) LSAEL.
1446. Cap L84, 2015.
1447. Limitation Act Ch. 522 Laws of the Federal Capital Territory.
1448. *See also* s. 32(4)(a) of the Limitation Law of Lagos State, Cap L, 84, 2015.

1733. Where the estate consists of real property, accrual of rights of action on death of owner in possession, the time of twelve years begins to count from the death of the testator and not when representation was taken out. Thus, section 18 of the Limitation Law provides that where a person brings an action to recover any land of a deceased person, whether under a c or an intestacy; and the deceased person, was on the date of the death in possession of the land and was the last person entitled to the land, in the case of a rent – charge created by Will or taking effect on the death, was in possession of the land charged, the right of action will be deemed to have accrued on the date of death.

Concluding Remarks

1734. Family Law and Succession in Nigeria form a socio-historical account of the people of Nigeria. It is impossible to understand Nigeria without an in-depth account of this perspective. It is also accurate to state that contemporary legal understanding is an important aspect of not only an account of the social and historical life of the people but also their political and developmental aspiration. Law is the engine room of human life and interaction, without its continuing servicing as an engine, and in this case, intermittent refreshment to conform to aspirations gleaned from the intelligence and rationality of humans for the holistic advancement of human experiences from generation to generation, the engine fails, as all engines.

1735. Formation of family and its incidents is a toggle between the customs of the people and modernity reflected in the character of the law with which it is in collision, and in this case, Federal law. The federal laws aim at modernising the custom and face so much obstacle that success has become illusory. The idea is to promote monogamy propped up by its incidents. However, the effect has been a hybrid of monogamy and polygamy – a formal, compact statutory marriage with other amphibious marriages. The rules to formalise monogamous marriage are stringent providing for void and voidable marriages. The question which family law must resolve is the boundaries of the State in making rules on this aspect of family, especially in the light of modern exigencies on human rights and the impact of these rules on societal cohesion and children's wellbeing.

1736. The provisions of the Child's Rights Act, requiring all births and adoptions to be registered with the Chief Registrar of the National Population Commission under the Births, Deaths, Etc., (Compulsory) Registration Act, 1992, Laws of the Federation, 2004 demonstrates that there can be no legitimate argument to sustain any position that the itemisation of births, marriages and deaths as functions of local government in the Constitution excludes the function of the National Population Commission as the registrar of Status in Nigeria for births, marriages and deaths. Any contrary argument is foreclosed by the fact that the Child's Rights Act was enacted well into the democratic dispensation in Nigeria. The Birth, Deaths Act and Regulation as many other enactments have gaps but the intendment of the Act and its objectives are clear. It is for the Federal Government to put its house in order and drum the law and its intendment home – it is also about time.

1737. An adversarial system provides fair play in matrilineal societies but not in patrilineal. Although Nigerian civil system is adversarial, and the courts, in principle, have often stated that matrimonial causes are based on the adversarial system, the practical approach of the courts and the provisions of the MCA are inspired by and evince an inquisitorial system. This latter approach is to be preferred and any future review of the relevant legislation must take account of this gap to fill it. An adversarial system provides fair play in matrilinies but not in patrilinies. An inquisitorial system of matrimonial causes gives women and children a fairer space and fairer chance at flourishing in a patrilineal culture.

1738. An inquisitorial system of matrimonial causes gives women and children a fair space in a patrilineal culture. Although Nigerian civil system is adversarial, and the courts, in principle, have often stated that matrimonial causes are based on the same system, the practical approach of the courts and the provisions of the MCA are inspired by and evince an inquisitorial system. This latter approach is to be preferred and any future review of the relevant legislation must make this appear in policy.

1739. Family is very important in Nigeria and so the ancestry. Ancestry is prized and is traced through primogeniture and its incidental socio-customary machinery – paternalism. Marriage continues to be a supportive platform to these systems and is taken very seriously. The introduction of monogamy to the Nigerian society has been very positive and beneficial. Its permeation into the fabrics of society is slow but steady. Thus, the present laws in relation to annulment, formation and dissolution are quite in consonance with the development of monogamy in a long-held tradition of polygyny. The concepts of judicial separation, restitution of conjugal rights are very influential supportive mechanisms for the preservation of marriage and should therefore continue to be part of Nigerian law of family.

1740. So many Nigerians admire and are proud of customs. Customs are worthy immemorial with continuing relevance when subjected to contemporary human experiences. One such customary notion noted above is the relationship between science and custom in the perception of human, gorillas and chimpanzees, by which some customary norms contemplate gorillas and chimpanzees as unfortunate human beings foisted with wildlife, while science has since gleaned a perspective that the duo are the closest to human species. However, as the framework of norms and societal contracts evolve in time, customs require re-examination in the light of the nature of the human society and its propensity for change, adaptation and growth. Absent a continuing means of internal and external validity, the reduction of society into a state of nature is a certainty as those members of society who outgrow the customs and way of doing things will be unable to cope. Unable to cope, they would be forced out of the society overtime, leaving it to a base nature. This is a major impetus of the general economic and emigration crisis in Africa. The repugnancy doctrine has achieved minimal success in engaging customs, so has education also impacted minimally.

1741. It has been noted that family is very important in Nigeria and in the present times is reliant on primogeniture and patriarchy for sustainability. The Supreme Court in *Oduche v. Oduche* reaffirmed that Nigeria is a patrilineal society. This reaffirmation is important and buttresses the fact of society being patriarchal as well. The main objection to patriarchy, paternalism and primogeniture in modern societies, however, is their propensity to arrogating authority by fiat, rather than by merit, to one segment of society, thereby, driving uncompromising inequality, and *a fortiori*, tension in society. The systems have inherent attributes of divisiveness, creating aggrieved classes, unnegotiable subservience and discouragement of dialogue. Modern society thrives in equality as a means of driving the most important and potent attributes of the human race: reason and, liberty, that is based on reason. Reason assures society of the capacity of constituent members to embrace analytical reasoning and dialogue in conflict resolution.

1742. Reason aims at improving the human condition in a viable, sustainable manner. It is from this framework that a workable democracy emerges. Democracy is a replacement for patriarchy, as it viably and sustainably, operates in institutionalised power distribution unlike patriarchy. A pure democracy may still drive patriarchy but it would be in an informed free choice and *a fortiori*, sustainable framework. In addition, a well-ordered civil data registration system may be a viable alternative to the positive aspects of primogeniture. More than the impact of bigamy on population and the synergy of family life is its overall impact on societal cohesion and advancement of human evolution. The idea of bigamy and the impact of its unenforceability in Nigeria are devastating. Its unenforceability detracts from the finer essence and aspiration of persons and permeates the society in circular motions undermining human ideals of trust and honesty. It advances and undermines emotional health and stability for adults and children, reinforcing the baser human propensities and thereby, forestalling constructive deployment of the mind for so many.

1743. Adoption is a veritable tool for bridging not only any gap that may exist in marriages without children and marriages for altruistic modern notions of marriage but also integrating children and societies with one another especially in a diverse country such as Nigeria. The law should be more harmonised and the processes for adoption, simplified and transparent. Wardship should follow the same path to indicate that indeed, the State is interested in children not just as creation and *a fortiori*, pro-life tool of argument, but as valuable human beings. The prohibition of international adoption ought to be reviewed.

1744. As was noted earlier, Nigeria is a pro-life nation, but the fallout of gender-related preferences and sundry practices as paternal acknowledgement leave in their trail many orphanages, orphanages better known and more commonly referred to as 'motherless babies homes'. Underlying the description is the need to return to the drawing table on the content and quality of life not only for children, but for all, and address the socio-legal context that leaves children belonging to mothers when they are homeless and orphans. The quality of life and evolution of the individual should be a stronger policy drive for life considerations than the theoretical pro-life regime in operation at the moment.

1745. Nigeria is a pro-life country. To move this classification from theory to policy, filiation and relevant orders have to gain a place in policy as a commitment to parental responsibility.

1746. Although population control and family planning are gaining ascendency in global family policies, they remain an autonomous realm in Nigeria and women in Southern Nigeria are increasingly choosing small families. Any positive impact of this choice, however, remains to be seen in the face of unchecked bigamy and impact of patriarchy. It is important that population control is given teeth in policy and practice. Human evolution demands this in a natural evolutionary manner but aided by policy implementations.

1747. Are there perhaps lessons to take from succession? Lagos State has since abolished bigamy from its laws for being in disuse. Yet, it neither abolished nor recognised polygamy, although it does recognise multiplicity of wives in its Wills Law.

1748. In a bid to sustain primogeniture, the rules on inheritance in Nigeria has all but, been gulped up by the customary form of succession, leaving off the benefits of human development, always guided by experiences, by which, the progressive effect of testate succession on the individual and society are in the back wheel of the experience of a typical Nigerian. This state of affairs should receive a revision that places more importance on the inherent aspect of human self-actualisation.

1749. Intestacy, drives a *dead hand society* which impacts such society in more ways than succession. Inevitably the wealth generated remain in a few hands – the hands ruling the living from the grave. It is also riddled with strife, intrigues and rancour, leaving the deceased with very minimal or 'no say'. The prospects of such eventuality may also force some to fritter away their wealth in their lifetime in order to make it impossible for those whom they may not wish to benefit from their wealth, from doing so.

1750. Testacy, on the other hand, obviates these outcomes by enhancing the capacity of a person to speak from death and have a say in what happens to one's wealth and indeed, physical remains. In so doing, the concept of Will impacts the general consciousness and moral competence of the populace; promotes wealth redistribution and also ultimately, no matter how indirectly, impacts positively on the attitude of the living to acquisition and accumulation of things. In some other cases, individuals have used Wills to re-order their personal lives by making the contents known in their lifetime. This strategy encouraged would be freeloaders and loafers to find and pursue meaningful pathways and some beneficiaries became carers if some happenstance rendered the potential testator incapacitated. It is, thus, important to stretch the elasticity of testamentary capacity without losing its vital synergy in a solemn act as Will making.

1751. There is, therefore, a need to make Wills more contemporaneous by changing the position of its subservience to customary laws. *Idehen v. Idehen* demonstrates this compelling need. The death of the first son of the deceased before his was a tragedy. The testator's Will was an effort to comfort the departed by vesting his *igiogbe* on the children of his first son. The emotional and factual rationale that resulted in this action of the testator ought not to have been dismissed.

Selected Bibliography

Abayomi, K. *Wills: Law and Practice* (Mbeyi & Associates (Nig.) Ltd. Lagos, 2004).

Diala, A.C. 'Reform of the Customary Law of Inheritance in Nigeria: Lessons from South Africa', *African Human Rights Law Journal* (AHRLJ) 14 (2014): 633–654.

Agbede, O.I. *Legal Pluralism* (Shaneson C.I. Limited, Ibadan, 1991).

Aguda, Akinola. *Select Law Lectures and Papers* (Associated Publishers Nigeria Ltd., 1971).

AjaNwachukwu, M.A. 'A legal Analysis of the nebulous Concept of Childhood in Nigeria', Beijing Law Review 7 (2016): 122–126.

Akpamgbo, C. '"Woman to Woman" Marriage and the Repugnancy Clause' *Africa Law Studies* 14 (1977): 87.

Amadiume, I.E. *Male Daughters, Female Husbands: Gender and Sex in an African Society* (London: Zed Books, 1998).

Ambali, M.A. *The Practice of Muslim Family Law in Nigeria* (Zaria: Tamaza Publishing, 2003).

Attah, M. 'Divorcing Marriage from Marital Assets: Why Equity and Women Fail in Property Readjustment Actions in Nigeria'. *Journal of African Law* 62(3) (2018): 427–446.

Aristotle. *Metaphysics* (Claremont, California: Pomona Press, 2008).

Becker, L.C. *Property Rights*: *Philosophic Foundation* (London: Routledge & Kegan Paul, 1977).

Bentham, J. *Of Laws in General* Ed., by Hart, H.L.A. (OLG, London: Athlone Press, 1970).

Berry, C.J. 'Property and Possession: Two Replies To Locke – Hume and Hegel' in edited by R.J. Pennock & W.J. Chapman, *Property*, Nomos vol. XXII (1970): 89.

Boparai, H. 'The Customary and Statutory Law of Marriage in Nigeria', *Rabel Journal of Comparative and International Private Law* 46(3) (1982): 530–557.

Cadigan, J. 'Woman-to-Woman Marriage: Practices and Benefits in Sub-Saharan Africa'. *Journal of Comparative Family Studies* 29(1) (1998): 89.

Carter, J.C. 'The Ideal and the Actual in the Law'. Am. L. Rev. 24 (1890): 752–771.

Cathrein, V. (1911). 'Property'. Vol. XII *The Catholic Encyclopaedia* 5.

Chinwuba, N. 'Ending Inequality in Nigeria: Refreshing Approach from the Nation's Judiciary'. *International Journal of Law, Policy and the Family* 29(3) (2015): 341–350.

Chinwuba, N. Human Identity: Child Rights and the Legal Framework for Marriage in Nigeria'. Marriage and Family Review 51(4) (2015): 305–336.

Chinwuba, N. 'Interaction of Customs and Colonial Heritage: Their Impact on Marriage and Children in Nigeria'. Anthropos 10(1) (2016): 1–20.

Chinwuba, N. 'Daughter/Widow Retention in Nigeria: Survey and Analysis from Case Law'. Journal of Comparative Law in Africa 2(1) (2016): 82–99.

Chinwuba, N. 'Filling the Gaps Between Colonial Legal Heritage and Prevailing Local Customs in Family Relations: The Place of Secret Trust'. *African Journal of International and Comparative Law* 24(1) (2016): 45–63.

Chinwuba, N. 'Development in Nigeria and the Imperative of redefining customs in Law'. *Uniuyo Journal of Commercial and Property Law* 4 (2020) 142–163.

Chinwuba, N. 'Requirement of Publicity in Marriage Framework: When Should We Construct Bridges or Build Walls?'. *Ahmadu Bello University Journal of Contemporary Issues in Sharia and Comparative Law* 1(1) (2020): 1.

Chinwuba, N.N. 'Human Rights and Child's Wellbeing as Impetus for Sustainable Development in Nigeria: Why Accountability in Adult Relationships Is Crucial'. Madonna University Law Journal (2013–2014): 62–81.

Chinwuba Obi, S.N. *Customary Law Manual: A manual of customary laws obtaining In Anambra and Imo States of Nigeria* (Government Printer: Enugu, 1977).

Cohen, G.A. *If You're an Egalitarian How Come You're So Rich* (Cambridge, Massachusetts, London: Harvard University Press, 2000).

Cholbi, M. 'Paternalism and Our Rational Powers'. Mind 126 (2017): 501.

Cross, R. 'The Absolute Bars to Divorce'. Modern Law Review 9 (1946): 75.

Descartes. *Philosophical Works of* Ed., by Haldane, E. S. & Ross, G. R. T. (Two Volumes, Cambridge, 1931).

Dadem, Y.Y. *Property Law and Practice* (Jos: University of Jos Press, 1995).

Dada, J.A. 'Judicial Remedies for Human Rights Violations in Nigeria: A Critical Appraisal'. Journal of Law, Policy and Globalization 10(1) (2013): 1–18 also available at www.iiste. (last accessed 10 August 2010).

Dagan, H. 'Property's Structural Pluralism: On Autonomy, the Rule of Law, and the Role of Blackstonian Ownership'. Brigham-Kanner Prop. RTS. Conf. J. 3 (2014); *Tel Aviv University Law Faculty Papers.* Working Paper 181.

Doma-Kutigi, H. 'Certification of Islamic Marriages in Nigeria: Realities, Challenges, and Solutions'. *Electronic Journal of Islamic and Middle Eastern Law* 7 (2019): 22–36.

Durojaye, E.'Woman, But not Human: Widowhood Practices and Human Rights Violations in Nigeria'. *International Journal of Law, Policy and the Family* 27(2) (2013): 176–196.

Dworkin, R. *Sovereign Virtue- The Theory and Practice of Equality* (Cambridge, Massachusetts, London: Harvard University Press,, 2001).

Efe, C.J. 'The Need for the Statutory Introduction of the Concept of "Matrimonial Property" in Nigeria'. Journal of African Law 63(1) (2019).

Eekelaar, J. *Family Law and Personal Life* (Oxford, United Kingdom: Oxford University Press, 2006).

Epstein, R.A. 'Why Restrain Alienation'. Columb. L. Rev. 85 (1985): 970.

Ezejiofor, G. 'Sources of Nigerian Law' in C.O. Okonkwo (Ed.), *Introduction to Nigerian Law* (London: Sweet & Maxwell, 1980).

Greene, B. 'The Institution of Woman-Marriage in Africa: A Cross Cultural Analysis'. Ethnology 37(4) (1998): 395–412.

Hamilton, W.H. 'Property – According to Locke'. Yale L. J. 41 (1931): 864.

Halsbury's Laws of England. Words & Phrases Legally Defined Vol. 38 (London: Butterworth, 1970).

Hanbury & Martin. *Modern Equity* Ed., by Jill Martin, 19th ed. (Sweet & Maxwell, 2012).

Harris-Short, S. & J. Miles *Family Law*, 2nd ed. (New York, United States of America: Oxford University Press Inc, 2011).

Hayton, D. 'Developing the Law of Trusts for the Twenty- First Century'. Law Quarterly Review 106 (1990): 87.

Hayton, D. 'The Irreducible Core Content of Trusteeship'. In *Trends in Contemporary Trust Law*, edited by A.J. Oakley (Oxford: Clarendon Press, 1996), 47.

Hegel, G.W.F. *Philosophy of Right*, translated by T.M. Knox (Oxford: Clarendon Press, 1942).

Hegel, G.W.F. *Lectures on the Philosophy of Religion*, vol. 1 (Oxford, United Kingdom: Oxford University Press, 2006).

Held, V. 'Locke on Nozick'. Social Research (1986): 169.

Henaghan, M. 'The Normal Order of Family Law'. Oxford Journal of Legal Studies (2008): 165.

Hill-Smith, A. 'Rights of Parking and the Ouster Principle after *Batchelor* v. *Marlow*'. Conveyancer (2007): 223.

Hobbes, T. *Leviathan* (Penguin Books, 1985-Reprint).

Honoré, A.M. 'Ownership'. In *Oxford Essays in Jurisprudence*, edited by A.G. Guest (Oxford, United Kingdom: Oxford University Press, 1961), 107.

Htun, M. & S. Weldon. 'State Power, Religion, and Women's Rights: A Comparative Analysis of Family Law'. *Indiana Journal of Global Legal Studies* 18(1) (2011): 146.

Ihonvbere, J.O. 'How to Make an Undemocratic Constitution: The Nigerian Example'. Third World Quarterly 21(2) (2000): 343–366.

Jenkinson, S. 'The Co-Respondent's Role in Divorce Reform after 1923'. In *Fifty Years in Family Law-Essays for Stephen Cretney*, edited by Rebecca Probert & Chris Barton (Intersentia, 2012), 201–215.

Kamaldeen, M. 'A Doctrinal Review of Literature on Multi-tiered Marriage in Nigerian Family Law'. Being paper presented at the Postgraduate Colloquium on Innovation in Postgraduate Research (Organised by Goal Centre, Islamic Science University Malaysia, USIM) on 10 June, 2015.

Kasunmu, A. 'The Principle of Acknowledgement or Recognition of Paternity Under Customary Law in Nigeria'. International and Comparative Law Quarterly 13(3) (1964): 1093–1103.

Kelsen, H. 'Pure Theory of Law'. Tul. L. Rev. 34 (1950–1960): 269.

Kincaid, D. 'The Tangled Web: The Relationship Between a Secret Trust and the Will'. [2000] Conv. & P. L. 420.

Locke, J. *Two Treatises of Government*, 2nd edn, by P. Laslett (Cambridge University Press, 1967).

Lopata, B.B. 'Property Theory in Hobbes'. *Political Theory* 1(ii) (1973): 203.

Lowe, N. 'Grounds for Divorce and Maintenance between Former Spouses/ England and Wales'. Available at ceflonline.net ›wp-content › uploads › England-Divorce (2020) (Last accessed 27/02/2020).

MacDougall, P.R. 'The Right of Women to Name Their Children'. Law & Inequality 3 (1985): 91.
McHugh, J.T. 'What Is the Difference Between a "Person" and a "Human Being" Within the Law'. Special Issue on Public Law 54(3) (1992): 445.
McLean, J. 'Property as Power and Resistance'. In *Property and the Constitution*, edited by Jean McLean (Oxford-Portland Oregon: Hart Publishing, 1999).
Mujuzi, J.D. 'Bride Wealth (Price) and Women's Marriage-Related Rights in Uganda: A Historical Constitutional Perspective and Current Developments'. *International Journal of Law, Policy and the Family* 24(3) (2010): 414–430.
Mwenda, K.K., F.N.M. Mumba & J. Mvula-Mwenda. 'Property-Grabbing under African Customary Law: Repugnant to Natural Justice, Equity, and Good Conscience, Yet a Troubling Reality'. *Geo Wash. Intl. Rev.* 37 (2005): 949.
Nagel, T. 'Hobbes Concept of Obligation'. *The Philosophical Review* LXVIII (1959): 68.
Nairn, R. *Tranquil Mind – An Introduction to Buddhism & Meditation* (Kairon Press CC:Cape Town, 2004).
Nozick, R. *Anarchy, State and Utopia* (New Jersey: Blackwell Publishing, 2006).
Nwogugu, E.I. *Family Law in Nigeria* (Ibadan: HEBN Studies in Nigerian Law, 1990).
Nwogugu, E.I. 'What Next in Nigerian Family Law?' [2006] 7 NIALS Founders' Day Lecture (Lagos: Nigerian Institute of Advanced Legal Studies, 2006).
Oba, A.A. 'Can a Person Subject to Islamic Law Make a Will in Nigeria? *Ajibaye* v. *Ajibaye* & Mr. Dadem's Wild Goose Chase'. CALS Review of Nigerian Law & Practice (2008).
Oboler, R. 'Is the Female Husband a Man? Woman/Woman Marriage among the Nandi of Kenya'. 19(1) *Ethnology* (1980): 69–88.
Plato. *The Republic* (Wordsworth Classics, 1927), Vol. X, 323.
Pollock, F. 'The Lawyer as a Citizen of the World'. LQR 48 (1932): 37.
Okoro, N. *The Customary Laws of Succession in Eastern Nigeria and The Statutory and Judicial Rules Governing Their Application* (London,: Sweet and Maxwell, 1966).
Olaniyan, H.A. 'A Review of Judicial and Legislative Approach of Nigeria to Discretionary Jurisdiction over Foreign Causes'. *International Journal of Business and Social Science* 3(12) (2012): 204–218.
Omotola, J.E. 'Primogeniture and Illegitimacy in African Customary Law: The Battle for Survival of Culture'. Indiana Int'l & Comparative Law Review 15(1) (2004): 115.
Oyebanji, B. 'Proposals for Reform of Marriage Law in Nigeria', In *The Marriage Laws of Nigeria*, edited by T.O. Aguda (Being Papers Presented at a National Workshop – Nigerian Institute of Advanced Legal Studies, Lagos, 1981), 147.
Pateman, C. 'The Shame of the Marriage Contract'. In *Women's Views of the Political World of Men*, edited by J.H. Stiehm (Transnational Publishers, INC New York, 1984), 67–97.
Peters, D. 'Feminism and the Institution of Polygamy: A Forward-Looking Approach'. Nigerian Current Legal Problems 4&5 (1996–1998): 1–27.
Perrins, B. 'Secret Trusts: The Key to Dehors'. Conveyancer (1985): 360.

Radin, M.J. 'The Liberal Conception of Property: Cross Currents in the Jurisprudence of Takings'. Colum. L. R. 88 (1988): 1667.
Rahmatian, A. 'Termination of Marriage in Nigerian Family Laws: The Need for Reform and the Relevance of the Tanzanian Experience'. *International Journal of Law, Policy and the Family* 10 (1996): 281.
Rawls, J.A. *Theory of Justice* (Cambridge: Belknap Press, 1971).
Rawls, J.A. *Justice as Fairness* (A Restatement) edited by Erin Kelly (Cambridge: The Belknap Press, 2001).
Rose-Ackerman, S. 'Inalienability and the Theory of Property Rights'. Columb. L. Rev. 85 (1985): 931.
Rousseau, J.J. *Discourse on the Origin of Inequality* (Mineola, New York: Dover Books, 2004).
Sagay, I.E. 'Legitimacy, Legitimation and Rights of Inheritance in Nigerian Contemporary Law'. JPPL 16, 17 & 18 (1992/1993): 1.
Sagay, I.E. 'The Judiciary in a Modern Democracy'. In *Nigeria- Issues in the 1999 Constitution*, edited by I.A. Ayua, D.A. Guobadia & A.O. Adekunle (Lagos: Nigerian Institute of Advanced Legal Studies, 2000), 76–112.
Stone, O.M. 'Matrimonial Causes Rules'. Modern Law Review 20(4) (1957): 415–417.
Suleiman, D.E. 'Mental Health Disorders in Nigeria: A Highly Neglected Disease'. Journal of Annals of Nigerian Medicine 10(2) (2016): 47–48.
Tait, A.A. 'The Return of Coverture'. Michigan Law Review 114 (2016): 99.
Tamblyn, N. 'The Duty to Help the World's Poor'. King's Law Journal 23(3) (2012): 312–328.
Taylor, A.E. 'The Ethical Doctrine of Hobbes'. Philosophy 13 (1938): 407.
Tessy, N.S. 'Is a Discretion Statement Necessary?'. *Modern Law Review* 21 (1958): 48.
Thompson, M.P. 'Domicile of Dependence: The Last Remnant of a Relic'. *The International and Comparative Law Quarterly* 32(1) (1983): 237–240.
Ude, P.U. 'Policy Analysis on Nigerian Lunacy Act (1958): The Need for a New Legislation'. *Journal of Psychiatry* 19(1) (2015): 1–6.
Udosen, J.I. 'The Judiciary and The Role of Customary Courts in Nigeria'. *Global Journal of Politics and Law Research* 5(6) (2017): 39.
Uzodike, E.N.U. 'A Decade of the Matrimonial Causes Act, 1970'. *Nigerian Current Law Review* (1983): 55.
Uzodike, E.N.U. 'Nigeria: Defining the Ambit of Custom'. *Fam. L.* 29 (1990–1991): 399.
Uzodike, E.N.U. 'Maintenance – Sixteen Years after the Matrimonial Causes Act'. *Journal of Private & Property Law* 8 & 9 (1987 & 1988): 21.
Wacke, A. 'Freedom of Contract and Restraint of Trade Clauses in Roman and Modern Law'. Law and History Review 11 (1993): 1.
Waldron, J. 'Property Law'. In *A Companion to Philosophy of Law and Legal Theory*, edited by D. Paterson (New Jersey: Blackwell Publishers, 1996).
Waldron, J. *The Right to Private Property* (Oxford: Clarendon Press, 1988).
Westbrook, A.H. 'Mental Health Legislation and Involuntary Commitment in Nigeria: A Call for Reform'. *Washington University Global Studies* 10(2) (2011): 396–418.

Selected Bibliography

Williams, S. 'Nigeria, Its Women and International Law: Beyond Rhetoric'. *Human Rights Law Review* 4(2) (2004): 229.

White, E.W. 'Secret Trusts: Admissibility of Evidence'. M.L.R. (notes) (1993): 319.

Yekini, A. 'Proof of Nigerian Marriages in Foreign Courts: Any Lessons from *Kareem* v. *Secretary of State for Home Department?*. In *Reflections on Dynamics of the Law- Essays in Honour of O. A. Adigun Fagbohun*, edited by Funminiyi Adeleke (Ojo, Lagos: Faculty of Law, Lagos State University, 2019), 460–478.

Yusuff, A.O.A. 'The Rights of the Mentally Ill and the Nigerian Society: Enhancing Dignity in Mental Health through Legislation'. *Journal of Law, Policy and Globalization* 52 (2016): 172–184.

Workshop Papers

Dafe, C.I. 'Probate and Administration of Estate: The Role of the Probate Registry' Text of a paper Presented at the National Workshop Organised by the National Judicial Institute from 5 to 9 September 2016 available at: https://www.practice+and+procedure+of+probate+in+nigeria&oq= (last accessed 7 July 2020).

1998: Handbook on Civil Registration and Vital Statistics Systems Computerisation, United Nations New York, available at: http://unstats.un.org/UNSD/demographic/sources/civilreg/default.htmUnstats.un.org. accessed 18 August 2020.

Table of Cases

Table of Statutes

Table of Statutory Instruments

Working Papers

Table of Conventions and International Instruments – with the Status of Nigeria

NOTED

Index

The numbers here refer to paragraph numbers.

www.ingramcontent.com/pod-product-compliance
Ingram Content Group UK Ltd.
Pitfield, Milton Keynes, MK11 3LW, UK
UKHW020130290926
15471UKWH00003B/387

9 789403 539607